MICROECONOMIC THEORY
A Mathematical Approach

Economics Handbook Series

MICROECONOMIC THEORY
A Mathematical Approach

Third Edition

James M. Henderson

Professor of Economics
University of Minnesota

Richard E. Quandt

Professor of Economics
Princeton University

McGraw-Hill Book Company

New York   St. Louis   San Francisco   Auckland   Bogotá   Hamburg
Johannesburg   London   Madrid   Mexico   Montreal   New Delhi
Panama   Paris   São Paulo   Singapore   Sydney   Tokyo   Toronto

MICROECONOMIC THEORY
A Mathematical Approach

1 2 3 4 5 6 7 8 9 0 FGFG 8 9 8 7 6 5 4 3 2 1 0

This book was set in Times Roman. The editors were Bonnie E. Lieberman
and Frances A. Neal; the production supervisor was Leroy A. Young.
New drawings were done by J & R Services, Inc.
Fairfield Graphics was printer and binder.

Library of Congress Cataloging in Publication Data

Henderson, James Mitchell, date
    Microeconomic theory.

    Includes index.
    1. Microeconomics   2. Economics, Mathematical.
I. Quandt, Richard E., joint author.   II.   Title.
HB171.5.H424   1980   330′.01′51   79-22064
ISBN 0-07-028101-7.

CONTENTS

Appendix: Mathematical Review

PREFACE
TO THE THIRD EDITION

The rapid growth of knowledge in microeconomics has made it desirable to revise *Microeconomic Theory* a second time. This has also provided an opportunity for making a number of improvements that were suggested by colleagues and students over the years.

The level of mathematics remains basically unchanged. An attempt has been made to improve the exposition of optimization in the Appendix, and to make the mathematical treatment of various topics conform more closely to modern practice. This has led, for example, to more emphasis on the concept of quasi-concavity in the treatment of utility functions, and to less emphasis on difference equations in the treatment of dynamic problems. As before, calculus is the basic mathematical tool. Readers are urged to refresh their memories about the mathematics by reading the Appendix and working its exercises before beginning Chapter 2.

The changed importance of some topics has led to a reorganization of chapters. The theory of the consumer, the theory of the firm, and the analysis of multimarket equilibrium each now occupies two chapters. Chapters 2 and 4 deal with the basic theories of the consumer and the firm, respectively, and Chapters 3 and 5 are devoted to extensions of each. The elements of multimarket equilibrium are covered in Chapter 9, with questions of existence and stability of equilibrium the subject of Chapter 10. The second edition's chapter on linear models has been eliminated and some of its material introduced into other chapters on the basis of its logical relation to the topics of those chapters. Thus, linear-programming approaches to the theory of the firm are now covered in Chapter 5, the theory of games in Chapter 8, and input-output analysis in Chapter 10. A number of new exercises have been added, and solutions for even-numbered exercises are now provided at the end of the volume.

Among the new topics for the third edition are the duality theory of the consumer (Chapter 3) and producer (Chapter 5), the concept of risk aversion (Chapter 3), production under uncertainty (Chapter 5), futures markets (Chapter 6), cooperative games and the Nash bargaining solution (Chapter 8), the introduction of money into the utility function (Chapter 9), Lindahl equilibrium and equity (Chapter 11), and exhaustible resources and human capital (Chapter 12). A number of other extensions are included where appropriate.

Suggestions for improvements have been made by many colleagues and students who have often helped us to a better understanding of difficult points in microeconomic theory. In particular we remember the suggestions or assistance of Harvey S. Rosen, Hugo Sonnenschein, and Michael Spence; Meir Barnea read through the entire manuscript and offered many valuable suggestions. To them and many others whom we have not explicitly mentioned we express our deep thanks.

We hope that few new errors have been introduced in this edition. As before, our work is thoroughly intermingled and we take equal responsibility for the final result.

James M. Henderson
Richard E. Quandt

PREFACE
TO THE SECOND EDITION

The experience of using *Microeconomic Theory* in graduate and advanced undergraduate courses over a number of years, the many helpful suggestions of colleagues and students, and recent developments in economics have all provided incentives for a major revision. The second (enlarged) edition differs from the first in three major respects. There have also been some minor changes in the mathematical tools used in the text.

First, an attempt has been made to include a fair amount of new material that either appeared in the economic literature since the publication of the first edition or was considered too new or difficult for inclusion at the earlier time. Examples are the constant-elasticity-of-substitution production function (Chapter 3), a proof for the existence of equilibrium in a competitive economy (Chapter 5), the case of the revenue-maximizing monopolist (Chapter 6), and the theory of second best (Chapter 7). Many other extensions are included in the appropriate chapters.

A second change of major significance is the addition of a new chapter on linear models. It replaces the fragmentary treatments of linear programming, input-output analysis, and game theory which are in three different chapters of the first edition. These topics are now covered in an extended and unified manner in Chapter 9. Unlike the first eight chapters, this new chapter is method oriented rather than subject oriented.

The inclusion of exercises at the end of each chapter is the third major change. Their inclusion was the most frequent recommendation for change received from users of the first edition. The exercises contain both concrete illustrations and extensions of the materials in the text. The ability to work the exercises is an important aspect of gaining a working knowledge of microeconomic theory.

The level of mathematics has remained substantially unchanged. The emphasis remains upon methods and applications rather than detailed proofs. The calculus is the basic mathematical tool. A treatment of simple differential equations has been added. The concepts of convex and concave functions, which have gained increased importance in the economic literature, are introduced. Elementary convex-set theory is employed in Chapters 5 and 9. In only one instance is significantly more advanced mathematics, namely Brouwer's fixed-point theorem, employed. It is used to prove the existence of competitive equilibrium in Chapter 5. As before, readers are urged to refresh their memories about the mathematics and fill whatever gaps may exist by reading the Appendix (and working its exercises) before beginning Chapter 2.

Suggestions for improvements in the first edition have been made by many colleagues and students to whom profound thanks are hereby expressed. It is hoped that few new errors have been introduced. As before, the authors' work is thoroughly intermingled and they take equal responsibility for the final result.

James M. Henderson
Richard E. Quandt

PREFACE
TO THE FIRST EDITION

The last two decades have witnessed an increasing application of mathematical methods to nearly every branch of economics. The theories of individual optimizing units and market equilibrium which are included within the microeconomics branch are no exception. Traditional theory has been formulated in mathematical terms, and the classical results proved or disproved. The use of mathematics has also allowed the derivation of many new results. Mathematical methods are particularly useful in this field since the underlying premises of utility and profit maximization are basically mathematical in character.

In the early stages of this development economists were rather sharply divided into two groups: the mathematical economists and the literary, or nonmathematical, economists. Fortunately, this sharp division is breaking down with the passage of time. More and more economists and students of economics are becoming acquainted with at least elementary mathematics and are learning to appreciate the advantages of its use in economics. On the other side, many mathematically inclined economists are becoming more aware of the limitations of mathematics. It seems a safe prediction that before too many more years have passed the question of the use of mathematics in microeconomic theory will be only a matter of degree.

As the number of economists and students of economics with mathematical training increases, the basic problem shifts from that of teaching mathematics to economists to that of teaching them economics in mathematical terms. The present volume is intended for economists and students of economics who have some mathematical training but do not possess a high degree of mathematical sophistication. It is not intended as a textbook on mathematics for economists. The basic concepts of microeconomic theory are developed with the aid of intermediate mathematics. The selection of topics and the order of presentation are indicated by economic, rather than mathematical, content.

This volume is intended for readers who possess some knowledge, though not necessarily a great deal, of both economics and mathematics. The audience at which it is aimed includes advanced undergraduate and graduate students in economics and professional economists who desire to see how intermediate mathematics contributes to the understanding of some familiar concepts. Advanced knowledge in one of these fields can partially compensate for a lack of training in the other. The reader with a weak background in microeconomics will not fully appreciate its problems or the limitations of the mathematical methods unless he consults some of the purely literary works in this area. A limited number of these are contained in the lists of selected references at the end of each chapter.

A one-year college course in calculus, or its equivalent, is sufficient mathematical preparation for the present volume.[1] A review of the mathematical concepts employed in the text is contained in the Appendix. The Appendix is not adequate for a reader who has never been exposed to calculus, but it should serve the dual purpose of refreshing the reader's memory on topics with which he has some familiarity and of introducing him to the few concepts that are employed in the text but are not usually covered in a first course in calculus—specifically, Cramer's rule, Lagrange multipliers, and simple difference equations. The reader interested in extending his knowledge of specific mathematical concepts will find a list of references at the end of the Appendix.

In order to simplify the reader's introduction to the use of mathematical methods in microeconomic theory, two- and three-variable cases are emphasized in Chapters 2 and 3. The more general cases are emphasized in the later chapters. The analysis is frequently accompanied by diagrams, in order to provide a geometric interpretation of the formal results. The formal analysis is also illustrated with specific numerical examples. The reader may test his comprehension by working through the examples and working out the proofs and extensions of the analysis that are occasionally left as exercises.

The authors have both served as senior partners in the preparation of this volume, with each contributing approximately one-half of the material. Henderson is primarily responsible for Chapters 3, 5, 6, and 8, and Quandt is primarily responsible for Chapters 2, 4, 7, and the Appendix. However, the manuscript was prepared in very close collaboration, and each author helped plan, review, and revise the work of the other. Therefore, all errors and defects are the responsibility of both.

The authors are indebted to many of their teachers, colleagues, and students for direct and indirect aid in the production of this volume. Their

---

[1] The reader without this background is referred to the first fifteen chapters of R. G. D. Allen, *Mathematical Analysis for Economists* (London: Macmillan, 1938).

greatest debt is to their former teacher, Wassily W. Leontief. His general outlook is in evidence throughout the volume, and he is responsible for much of the authors' affection for microeconomic theory. The authors gratefully acknowledge the advice and criticism of William J. Baumol, who read the entire manuscript in an intermediate stage and offered numerous suggestions for its improvement. Others who deserve specific mention are Robert Dorfman, W. Eric Gustafson, Franklin M. Fisher, Carl Kaysen, and Seymour E. Harris. The marginal productivities of the inputs of the authors' above-mentioned friends are strictly positive in all cases.

The authors also owe a very significant debt to the economists who pioneered the application of mathematical methods to microeconomic theory. Their written works provide the framework for this book. The outstanding pioneers are J. R. Hicks and Paul A. Samuelson, but there are many others. The names and works of many of the pioneers can be found in the lists of selected references at the end of each chapter.

James M. Henderson
Richard E. Quandt

MICROECONOMIC THEORY
A Mathematical Approach

ONE

INTRODUCTION

Economics is not a clearly defined discipline. Its frontiers are constantly changing, and their definition is frequently a subject of controversy. A commonly used definition characterizes economics as the study of the use of limited resources for the achievement of alternative ends. This definition is adequate if interpreted broadly enough to include the study of unemployed resources and to cover situations in which the ends are selected by economists themselves. More specifically, economics may be defined as a social science which covers the actions of individuals and groups of individuals in the processes of producing, exchanging, and consuming goods and services.

1-1 THE ROLE OF THEORY

Explanation and prediction are the goals of economics as well as most other sciences. Both theoretical analyses and empirical investigations are necessary for the achievement of these goals. The two are usually inextricably intertwined in concrete examples of research; yet there is a real distinction between them. Theories employ abstract deductive reasoning whereby conclusions are drawn from sets of initial assumptions. Purely empirical studies are inductive in nature. The two approaches are complementary, since theories provide guides for empirical studies and empirical studies provide tests of the assumptions and conclusions of theories.

Basically, a theory contains three sets of elements: (1) data which play the role of parameters and are assumed to be given from outside the analytical framework; (2) variables, the magnitudes of which are determined within the theory; and (3) behavior assumptions or postulates which define the set of operations by which the values of the variables are determined. The conclusions of a theoretical argument are always of a *what would happen if* nature. They state what the results of economic processes would be if the initial assumptions were satisfied, i.e., if the data were in fact given and the behavior assumptions justified.

Empirical investigations allow comparisons of the assumptions and conclusions of theories with observed facts. However, the requirement of a strict conformity between theory and fact would defeat the very purpose of theory. Theories represent simplifications and generalizations of reality and therefore do not completely describe particular situations. The data-variable distinctions and behavior assumptions of the theories presented in subsequent chapters are satisfied by few, if any, actual market situations. A stricter conformity to facts would require a separate, highly detailed theory for each individual market situation, since each possesses its own distinctive characteristics. Applied theories of this nature, however valuable for specific research projects, are of little general value. The more general theories are fruitful because they contain statements which abstract from particulars and find elements which many situations have in common. Increased understanding is realized at the cost of the sacrificed detail. It is then possible to go from the general to the specific. The cases described by pure theories provide insight into economic processes and serve as a background and starting point for applied theories and specific empirical studies.

1-2 MICROECONOMICS

Like most other disciplines, economics is divided into branches and subbranches. The major branches are *microeconomics*, which is the study of the economic actions of individuals and well-defined groups of individuals, and *macroeconomics*, which is the study of broad aggregates such as total employment and national income.

Both branches deal with the determination of prices and incomes and the use of resources. However, microeconomics concentrates on the analysis of individual prices and markets, and the allocation of specific resources to particular uses. In micro theories the determination of the incomes of individuals is encompassed within the general pricing process: Individuals earn their incomes by selling factors of production, the prices of which are determined in the same manner as all other prices. On the other hand, the goals of macroeconomic theories generally are the determination of national income, aggregate resource employment, and aggregate price indices, with only secondary emphasis placed upon the interrelations among the components of the various aggregates.

Since the problems of individual price determination are assumed away in macro theory, the relationship between individual units and the aggregates is not clear. If it were, the analysis would be classified as micro theory. The simplifications introduced by aggregation are not without reward, since they make it possible to describe the position and progress of the economy as a whole in terms of a few simple aggregates. This would be impossible if the micro emphasis on individual behavior and relative prices were maintained.

Following this established separation of subject matter, the present volume is limited to a systematic exposition of microeconomic theory. The theories of individual behavior in a perfectly competitive economy are developed in Chaps. 2 through 5. The behavior of individual consumers is treated in Chaps. 2 and 3, and that of individual producers in Chaps. 4 and 5. In this analysis the prices of goods bought or sold are considered as given parameters, the magnitudes of which the individual cannot influence. The quantities of goods bought and sold are the variables determined in these theories. The perfectly competitive market for a single commodity is introduced in Chap. 6. The prices of all other commodities are assumed to be given parameters, and the price of the commodity in question, as well as the volume of its purchases and sales, is shown to be determined by the independent actions of all its buyers and sellers.

Microeconomic theories are sufficiently flexible to permit many variations in their underlying assumptions. For example, the assumption that no single individual is able to influence prices or the actions of other individuals is modified in Chaps. 7 and 8. Despite the variation of this basic premise, there are some easily recognizable similarities between the analyses of Chap. 7 and 8 and those of earlier chapters. Up to this point the analysis deals with individual consumers and producers and with markets for a single commodity (except for the brief treatement of differentiated oligopoly). The relationship among all markets is largely ignored. This omission is remedied in Chaps. 9 and 10, which deal with multimarket equilibrium in which all prices are determined simultaneously.

The final chapters cover two other important aspects of microeconomics. An important use of theory is to serve as a guide to *what ought to be*. The branch of microeconomics which covers these problems is known as welfare economics and is the subject of Chap. 11. The degree of conformity between theory and fact is of great importance in welfare economics. If one were interested in pure description, a divergence between theory and fact would suggest that the theory is faulty for that particular purpose. When the theory becomes a welfare ideal, such a divergence leads to the conclusion that the actual situation is faulty and should be remedied. Finally, the assumption of a static world in which consumers and producers do not plan for the future is relaxed in Chap. 12. The logical connection of these last two chapters with the earlier ones is easily discernible, and the possibility of relaxing the various assumptions of the basic theories increases their flexibility and generality.

1-3 THE ROLE OF MATHEMATICS

The theories of the present volume are cast in mathematical terms. The mathematics is not an end in itself, but rather a set of tools which facilitates the derivation and exposition of the economic theories. Mathematics is useful for translating verbal arguments into concise and consistent forms. However, it does more than this. Mathematics provides the economist with a set of tools often more powerful than ordinary speech; mathematics possesses concepts and allows operations for which no manageable verbal equivalents exist. The use of mathematics enlarges the economist's tool kit and widens the range of possible inferences from initial assumptions.

Purely verbal analysis was the first stage in the historical development of economic theory. However, as quantitative relationships were formulated in increasing numbers and as theories became increasingly complex, purely verbal analyses became more tedious and more difficult to formulate consistently. Mathematical relations underlay most of these early theories, though they were seldom made explicit. The recognition that more rigorous formulations were often necessary led to the acceptance of plane geometry as an important tool of analysis. Plane geometry was and is highly useful, but it possesses many limitations. One of the most serious of these is the limitation of theoretical arguments to two, or at most three, variables. The increasing use of other mathematical tools reflects the belief that plane geometry is not adequate for rigorous economic reasoning in many cases.

The calculus and some simple concepts of simultaneous-equation systems are the major mathematical tools used in the present volume. Some notions of convex sets and a fixed-point theorem are used in particular discussions. Some general results are illustrated by two-dimensional geometry. The explicit use of mathematics does not mean that the authors believe that all verbal analyses should be discarded. Verbal analyses are preferable to mathematical analyses for some purposes. They serve to fill in many details, state important qualifications, and suggest new topics for rigorous investigation.

The mathematical concepts used in the text are reviewed in the Appendix. All except mathematically sophisticated readers should read, or at least skim, the Appendix *before* beginning Chap. 2.

TWO

THE THEORY OF CONSUMER BEHAVIOR

The postulate of rationality is the customary point of departure in the theory of the consumer's behavior. The consumer is assumed to choose among the available alternatives in such a manner that the satisfaction derived from consuming commodities (in the broadest sense) is as large as possible. This implies that he is aware of the alternatives facing him and is capable of evaluating them. All information pertaining to the satisfaction that the consumer derives from various quantities of commodities is contained in his *utility function.*

The concepts of utility and its maximization are void of any sensuous connotation. The assertion that a consumer derives more satisfaction or utility from an automobile than from a suit of clothes means that if he were presented with the alternatives of receiving as a gift either an automobile or a suit of clothes, he would choose the former. Things that are necessary for survival—such as vaccine when a smallpox epidemic threatens—may give the consumer the most utility, although the act of consuming such a commodity has no pleasurable sensations connected with it.

The nineteenth-century economists W. Stanley Jevons, Léon Walras, and Alfred Marshall considered utility measurable, just as the weight of objects is measurable. The consumer was assumed to possess a *cardinal* measure of utility, i.e., he was assumed to be capable of assigning to every commodity or combination of commodities a number representing the amount or degree of utility associated with it. The numbers representing amounts of utility could be manipulated in the same fashion as weights. Assume, for example, that the utility of A is 15 units and the utility of B 45 units. The consumer would "like" B three times as strongly as A. The differences between utility numbers could be compared, and the comparison could lead to a statement such as "A is preferred to B twice as much as C is preferred to D." It was also assumed by the nineteenth-century economists that the additions to a consumer's total utility resulting from consuming additional units of a commodity decrease as he consumes more of it. The consumer's behavior can be deduced from the above assumptions. Imagine that a certain price, say 2 dollars, is charged for coconuts. The consumer, confronted with coconuts, will not buy any if the amount of utility he surrenders by paying the price of a coconut (i.e., by parting with purchasing power) is greater than the utility he gains by consuming it. Assume that the utility of a dollar is 5 utils and remains approximately constant for small variations in income, and that the consumer derives the following increments of utility by consuming an additional coconut:

Unit	Additional utility
Coconut 1	20
Coconut 2	9
Coconut 3	7

The consumer will buy at least one coconut, because he surrenders 10 utils in exchange for 20 utils and thus increases his total utility.[1] He will not buy a second coconut, because the utility loss exceeds the gain. In general, the consumer will not add to his consumption of a commodity if an additional unit involves a net utility loss. He will increase his consumption only if he realizes a net gain of utility from it. For example, assume that the price of coconuts falls to 1.6 dollars. Two coconuts will now be bought. A fall in the price has increased the quantity bought. This is the sense in which the theory predicts the consumer's behavior.

The assumptions on which the theory of cardinal utility is built are very restrictive. Equivalent conclusions can be deduced from much weaker assumptions. Therefore it will *not* be assumed in the remainder of this chapter that the consumer possesses a cardinal measure of utility or that the additional utility derived from increasing his consumption of a commodity diminishes.

If the consumer derives more utility from alternative A than from alternative B, he is said to prefer A to B.[2] The postulate of rationality is equivalent to the following statements: (1) for all possible pairs of alternatives A and B the consumer knows whether he prefers A to B or B to A, or

---

[1] The price is 2 dollars; the consumer loses 5 utils per dollar surrendered. Therefore the gross loss is 10 utils, and the gross gain is 20 utils.

[2] A chain of definitions must eventually come to an end. The word "prefer" can be defined to mean "would rather have than," but then this expression must be left undefined. The term "prefer" is also void of any connotation of sensuous pleasure.

whether he is indifferent between them; (2) only one of the three possibilities is true for any pair of alternatives; (3) if the consumer prefers A to B and B to C, he will prefer A to C. The last statement ensures that the consumer's preferences are consistent or *transitive*: if he prefers an automobile to a suit of clothes and a suit of clothes to a bowl of soup, he must prefer an automobile to a bowl of soup.

The postulate of rationality, as stated above, merely requires that the consumer be able to rank commodities in order of preference. The consumer possesses an *ordinal* utility measure; i.e., he need not be able to assign numbers that represent (in arbitrary units) the degree or amount of utility that he derives from commodities. His ranking of commodities is expressed mathematically by his utility function. It associates certain numbers with various quantities of commodities consumed, but these numbers provide only a ranking or ordering of preferences. If the utility of alternative A is 15 and the utility of B is 45 (i.e., if the utility function associates the number 15 with alternative or commodity A and the number 45 with alternative B), one can only say that B is preferred to A, but it is meaningless to say that B is liked three times as strongly as A. This reformulation of the postulates of the theory of consumer behavior was effected only around the turn of the last century. It is remarkable that the consumer's behavior can be explained just as well in terms of an ordinal utility function as in terms of a cardinal one. Intuitively one can see that the consumer's choices are completely determinate if he possesses a ranking (and only a ranking) of commodity bundles according to his preferences. One could visualize the consumer as possessing a rank-ordered list of all conceivable alternative commodity bundles that can be purchased for a sum of money equal to his income; when the consumer receives his income, he simply purchases the bundle at the top of the list.[1] Therefore it is not necessary to assume that he possesses a cardinal measure of utility. The much weaker assumption that he possesses a consistent ranking of preferences is sufficient.

The basic tools of analysis and the nature of the utility function are discussed in Sec. 2-1. The individual consumer's optimum consumption levels are determined in Sec. 2-2, and it is shown that the solution of the consumer's maximum problem is invariant with respect to positive monotonic transformations of his utility function. Demand functions are derived in Sec. 2-3, and the analysis is extended to the problem of choice between income and leisure in Sec. 2-4. The effect of price and income variations on consumption levels is examined in Sec. 2-5. The theory is finally generalized to an arbitrary number of commodities in Sec. 2-6.

---

[1] How much a particular bundle on the list is liked is irrelevant; only the bundle at the top of the list will be purchased.

2-1 BASIC CONCEPTS

The Nature of the Utility Function

Consider the simple case in which the consumer's purchases are limited to two commodities. His ordinal utility function is

$$U = f(q_1, q_2) \tag{2-1}$$

where q_1 and q_2 are the quantities of the two commodities Q_1 and Q_2 which he consumes. It is assumed that $f(q_1, q_2)$ is continuous, has continuous first- and second-order partial derivatives, and is a regular strictly quasi-concave function.[1] Furthermore, it is assumed that the partial derivatives of (2-1) are strictly positive. This means that the consumer will always desire more of both commodities. These assumptions are sometimes modified to cover special cases. Nonnegative consumption levels normally constitute the domain for the utility function, though in some cases the domain is limited to positive levels.

The consumer's utility function is not unique (see Sec. 2-2). In general, any single-valued increasing function of q_1 and q_2 can serve as a utility function. The utility number U^0 assigned to any particular commodity combination indicates that it is preferable or superior to all combinations with lower numbers and inferior to those with higher numbers.

The utility function is defined with reference to consumption during a specified period of time. The level of satisfaction that the consumer derives from a particular commodity combination depends upon the length of the period during which he consumes it. Different levels of satisfaction are derived from consuming ten portions of ice cream within one hour and within one month. There is no unique time period for which the utility function *should* be defined. However, there are restrictions upon the possible length of the period. The consumer usually derives utility from variety in his diet and diversification among the commodities he consumes. Therefore, the utility function must not be defined for a period so short that the desire for variety cannot be satisfied. On the other hand, tastes (the shape of the function) may change if it is defined for too long a period. Any intermediate period is satisfactory for the static theory of consumer behavior.[2] The present theory is static in the sense that the utility function is defined with reference to a single time period, and the consumer's optimal expenditure pattern is analyzed only

---

[1] A strictly quasi-concave function for which $2f_{12}f_1f_2 - f_{11}f_2^2 - f_{22}f_1^2 > 0$. The positiveness of the expression makes certain derivations easier, and the assumption of regularity is made for convenience, since strict quasi-concavity alone guarantees only the weak inequality $\geq$. See Sec. A-3.

[2] The theory would break down if it were impossible to define a period that is neither too short from the first point of view nor too long from the second.

with respect to this period. No account is taken of the possibility of transferring consumption expenditures from one period to another.[1]

Indifference Curves

A particular level of utility or satisfaction can be derived from many different combinations of Q_1 and Q_2.[†] For a given level of utility U^0, Eq. (2-1) becomes

$$U^0 = f(q_1, q_2) \tag{2-2}$$

where U^0 is a constant. Since the utility function is continuous, (2-2) is satisfied by an infinite number of combinations of Q_1 and Q_2. Imagine that the consumer derives a given level of satisfaction U^0 from 5 units of Q_1 and 3 units of Q_2. If his consumption of Q_1 were decreased from 5 to 4 without an increase in his consumption of Q_2, his satisfaction would certainly decrease. In general, it is possible to compensate him for the loss of 1 unit of Q_1 by allowing an increase in his consumption of Q_2. Imagine that an increase of 3 units in his consumption of Q_2 makes him indifferent between the two alternative combinations. Other commodity combinations which yield the consumer the same level of satisfaction can be discovered in a similar manner. The locus of all commodity combinations from which the consumer derives the same level of satisfaction forms an *indifference curve*. An *indifference map* is a collection of indifference curves corresponding to different levels of satisfaction. The quantities q_1 and q_2 are measured along the axes of Fig. 2-1. One indifference curve passes through every point in the positive quadrant of the $q_1 q_2$ plane. Indifference curves correspond to higher and higher levels of satisfaction as one moves in a northeasterly direction in Fig. 2-1. A movement from point A to point B would increase the consumption of both Q_1 and Q_2. Therefore B must correspond to a higher level of satisfaction than A.

Indifference curves cannot intersect as shown in Fig. 2-2. Consider the points A_1, A_2, and A_3. Let the consumer derive the satisfaction U_1 from the batch of commodities represented by A_1 and similarly U_2 and U_3 from A_2 and A_3. The consumer has more of both commodities at A_3 than at A_1, and therefore $U_3 > U_1$. Since A_1 and A_2 are on the same indifference curve,

---

[1] The present analysis is static in that it does not consider what happens after the current income period. The consumer makes his calculations for only one such period at a time. At the end of the period he repeats his calculations for the next one. If the consumer were capable of borrowing, one would consider his total liquid resources available in any time period instead of his income proper. Conversely, he may save, i.e., not spend all his income on consumption goods. Provision can be made for both possibilities without changing the essential points of the analysis (see Sec. 12-2).

[†] By definition, a commodity is an item of which the consumer would rather have more than less. Otherwise he is dealing with a discommodity. In reality a commodity may become a discommodity if its quantity is sufficiently large. For example, if the consumer partakes of too many portions of ice cream, it may become a discommodity for him. It is assumed in the remainder of the chapter that such a point of saturation has not been reached.

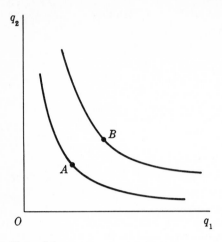

Figure 2-1

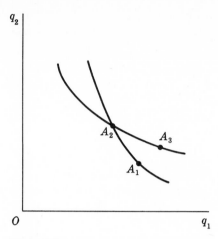

Figure 2-2

$U_1 = U_2$. The points A_2 and A_3 are also on the same indifference curve, and therefore $U_2 = U_3$. This implies $U_1 = U_3$. Therefore, A_1 and A_3 are on the same indifference curve, contrary to assumption.

The assumption that the utility function is strictly quasi-concave restricts the shape of the indifference curves. Consider two distinct points on a given indifference curve where $U^0 = f(q_1^0, q_2^0) = f(q_1^{(1)}, q_2^{(1)})$. Strict quasi-concavity (see Sec. A-2) ensures that

$$U[\lambda q_1^0 + (1 - \lambda)q_1^{(1)}, \lambda q_2^0 + (1 - \lambda)q_2^{(1)}] > U^0$$

for all $0 < \lambda < 1$. Thus, all interior points on a line segment connecting two points on an indifference curve lie on higher indifference curves. This means that an indifference curve expresses q_2 as a strictly convex function of q_1, sometimes expressed by saying that indifference curves are "convex to the origin."

The Rate of Commodity Substitution

The total differential of the utility function is

$$dU = f_1 \, dq_1 + f_2 \, dq_2 \qquad (2\text{-}3)$$

where f_1 and f_2 are the partial derivatives of U with respect to q_1 and q_2. The total change in utility (compared to an initial situation) caused by variations in q_1 and q_2 is approximately the change in q_1 multiplied by the change in utility resulting from a unit change of q_1 plus the change in q_2 multiplied by the change in utility resulting from a unit change in q_2. Let the consumer move along one of his indifference curves by giving up some Q_1 in exchange for Q_2. If his consumption of Q_1 decreases by dq_1 (therefore, $dq_1 < 0$), the resulting loss of utility is approximately $f_1 \, dq_1$. The gain of utility caused by acquiring some Q_2 is approximately $f_2\,dq_2$ for similar reasons. Taking arbitrarily small increments, the sum of these two terms must equal zero in the limit, since the total change in utility along an indifference curve is zero by definition.[1] Since the analysis runs in terms of ordinal utility functions, the magnitudes of $f_1\,dq_1$ and $f_2\,dq_2$ are not known. However, it must still be true that the sum of these terms is zero. Setting $dU = 0$,

$$f_1\,dq_1 + f_2\,dq_2 = 0$$

yields
$$-\frac{dq_2}{dq_1} = \frac{f_1}{f_2} \tag{2-4}$$

The slope of an indifference curve, dq_2/dq_1, is the rate at which a consumer would be willing to substitute Q_1 for Q_2 per unit of Q_1 in order to maintain a given level of utility. The negative of the slope, $-dq_2/dq_1$, is the *rate of commodity substitution* (RCS) of Q_1 for Q_2, and it equals the ratio of the partial derivatives of the utility function.[2] The reciprocal of the RCS is the rate at which the consumer would be willing to substitute Q_2 for Q_1 per unit of Q_2.

In a cardinal analysis the partial derivatives f_1 and f_2 are defined as the *marginal utilities* of the commodities Q_1 and Q_2.[†] This definition is retained in the present ordinal analysis. However, the partial derivative of an ordinal utility function cannot be given a cardinal interpretation. Therefore, the numerical magnitudes of individual marginal utilities are without meaning. The consumer is not assumed to be aware of the existence of marginal utilities, and only the economist need know that the consumer's RCS equals the ratio of marginal utilities. The signs as well as the ratios of marginal utilities are meaningful in an ordinal analysis. A positive value for f_1 signifies that an increase in q_1 will increase the consumer's satisfaction level and move him to a higher indifference curve.

Since the utility function is a regular strictly quasi-concave function, the strict inequality

$$2f_{12}f_1f_2 - f_{11}f_2^2 - f_{22}f_1^2 > 0 \tag{2-5}$$

is satisfied at each point within its domain (see Sec. A-3). By further differentiation of (2-4) the rate of change of the slope of the indifference curve is[3]

$$\frac{d^2q_2}{dq_1^2} = -\frac{1}{f_2^3}(f_{11}f_2^2 - 2f_{12}f_1f_2 + f_{22}f_1^2) \tag{2-6}$$

---

[1] Imagine the utility function as a surface in three-dimensional space. Then the total differential (2-3) is the equation of the tangent plane to this surface at some point. This justifies the use of the word "approximate" in the above argument (see Sec. A-2).

[2] The rate of commodity substitution is frequently referred to in the literature of economics as the *marginal* rate of substitution. Cf. J. R. Hicks, *Value and Capital* (2d ed., Oxford: Clarendon Press, 1946), pt. I.

[†] The marginal utility of a commodity is often loosely defined as the increase in utility resulting from a unit increase in its consumption.

[3] Note that (2-6) is obtained by taking the total derivative of the slope of the indifference curve instead of the partial derivative.

Inequality (2-5) ensures that the parenthesized term on the right-hand side of (2-6) is negative. Since $f_2 > 0$, regular strict quasi-concavity dictates that the negative slope of the indifference curve becomes larger algebraically and smaller in absolute value as Q_1 is substituted for Q_2. The indifference curve becomes flatter, and the RCS, which is the absolute value of its slope, decreases. As the consumer moves along an indifference curve, he acquires more Q_1 and less Q_2, and the rate at which he is willing to sacrifice Q_2 to acquire yet more Q_1 declines. The increasing relative scarcity of Q_2 increases its relative value to the consumer, and the increasing relative abundance of Q_1 decreases its relative value.

Existence of the Utility Function

It is not intuitively obvious that real-valued functions that can serve as utility functions exist for all consumers. A consumer's preferences must satisfy certain conditions in order to be representable by a utility function. A set of sufficient conditions for the existence of a utility function is expressed in the following assumptions:

1. The various commodity combinations available to the consumer stand in a relation to each other, denoted by R. The meaning of R is "is at least as well liked as." The relation R is complete: For any pair of commodity combinations A_1 and A_2 either $A_1 R A_2$, $A_2 R A_1$, or both. Furthermore, R is reflexive: $A_1 R A_1$, whatever A_1 may be. Finally, R is transitive: If $A_1 R A_2$ and $A_2 R A_3$, then $A_1 R A_3$.
2. The set of all commodity combinations available to the consumer is connected. If A_1 and A_2 are available to the consumer, one can find a continuous path of available combinations connecting A_1 and A_2.
3. Given some commodity combination A_1, one may consider the set of all combinations at least as well liked as A_1 and the set of all combinations not more liked than A_1. These two sets are closed. This means that if one selected for consideration an infinite sequence of commodity combinations which converged to some limiting combination A_0, and if each member of the sequence were at least as well liked as A_1, then the limiting combination would also be at least as well liked as A_1. This condition ensures the continuity of the consumer's preferences and rules out "jumps." It ensures, for example, that if two commodity combinations differ from each other only slightly and if one of these is preferred to some given combination A_1, then the other will be at least as well liked as A_1.

It might seem that these conditions are so unrestrictive as to be almost always satisfied. It is easy, however, to cite preference structures that do not satisfy them. Consider the following case. Let there be two commodities Q_1 and Q_2, and consider two commodity combinations $A_1 = (q_1^{(1)}, q_2^{(1)})$ and $A_2 = (q_1^{(2)}, q_2^{(2)})$. Imagine that the preference structure of the consumer is given by the following rule: A_1 is preferred to A_2 if either $q_1^{(1)} > q_1^{(2)}$ or $q_1^{(1)} = q_1^{(2)}$ and $q_2^{(1)} > q_2^{(2)}$. In this situation the preference ordering is said to be *lexicographic* and no utility function exists.

The lexicographic ordering violates the third of the above assumptions. Consider the combination $A = (q_1^0, q_2^0)$, and let Δq_1 and Δq_2 denote positive increments from A. The combination $(q_1^0 + \Delta q_1, q_2^0 - \Delta q_2)$ is preferred to A by virtue of the lexicographic ordering. Select particular positive values for the increments, and consider the infinite sequence of commodity combinations the ith member of which is

$$A_i = (q_1^0 + (\tfrac{1}{2})^i \Delta q_1, q_2^0 - \Delta q_2)$$

A_i is clearly preferred to A for any i, but the limit of the sequence

$$\lim_{i \to \infty} A_i = (q_1^0, q_2^0 - \Delta q_2)$$

is inferior to A in violation of the third assumption.

2-2 THE MAXIMIZATION OF UTILITY

The rational consumer desires to purchase a combination of Q_1 and Q_2 from which he derives the highest level of satisfaction. His problem is one of maximization. However, his income is limited, and he is not able to purchase unlimited amounts of the commodities. The consumer's budget constraint can be written as

$$y^0 = p_1 q_1 + p_2 q_2 \qquad (2\text{-}7)$$

where y^0 is his (fixed) income and p_1 and p_2 are the prices of Q_1 and Q_2 respectively. The amount he spends on the first commodity $(p_1 q_1)$ plus the amount he spends on the second $(p_2 q_2)$ equals his income (y^0).

The First- and Second-Order Conditions

The consumer desires to maximize (2-1) subject to (2-7). Form the Lagrange function

$$V = f(q_1, q_2) + \lambda (y^0 - p_1 q_1 - p_2 q_2) \qquad (2\text{-}8)$$

where λ is an as yet undetermined multiplier (see Sec. A-3). The first-order conditions are obtained by setting the first partial derivatives of (2-8) with respect to q_1, q_2, and λ equal to zero:

$$\frac{\partial V}{\partial q_1} = f_1 - \lambda p_1 = 0$$

$$\frac{\partial V}{\partial q_2} = f_2 - \lambda p_2 = 0 \qquad (2\text{-}9)$$

$$\frac{\partial V}{\partial \lambda} = y^0 - p_1 q_1 - p_2 q_2 = 0$$

Transposing the second terms in the first two equations of (2-9) to the right and dividing the first by the second yields

$$\frac{f_1}{f_2} = \frac{p_1}{p_2} \tag{2-10}$$

The ratio of the marginal utilities must equal the ratio of prices for a maximum. Since f_1/f_2 is the RCS, the first-order condition for a maximum is expressed by the equality of the RCS and the price ratio.

The first two equations of (2-9) may also be written as

$$\frac{f_1}{p_1} = \frac{f_2}{p_2} = \lambda \tag{2-11}$$

Marginal utility divided by price must be the same for all commodities. This ratio gives the rate at which satisfaction would increase if an additional dollar were spent on a particular commodity. If more satisfaction could be gained by spending an additional dollar on Q_1 rather than Q_2, the consumer would not be maximizing utility. He could increase his satisfaction by shifting some of his expenditure from Q_2 to Q_1.

The Lagrange multiplier λ can be interpreted as the marginal utility of income. Since the marginal utilities of commodities are assumed to be positive, the marginal utility of income is positive.

The second-order condition as well as the first-order condition must be satisfied to ensure that a maximum is actually reached. Denoting the second direct partial derivatives of the utility function by f_{11} and f_{22} and the second cross partial derivatives by f_{12} and f_{21}, the second-order condition for a constrained maximum requires that the relevant bordered Hessian determinant be positive:

$$\begin{vmatrix} f_{11} & f_{12} & -p_1 \\ f_{21} & f_{22} & -p_2 \\ -p_1 & -p_2 & 0 \end{vmatrix} > 0 \tag{2-12}$$

Expanding (2-12)

$$2f_{12}p_1p_2 - f_{11}p_2^2 - f_{22}p_1^2 > 0 \tag{2-13}$$

Substituting $p_1 = f_1/\lambda$ and $p_2 = f_2/\lambda$ from (2-9) and multiplying through by $\lambda^2 > 0$

$$2f_{12}f_1f_2 - f_{11}f_2^2 - f_{22}f_1^2 > 0 \tag{2-14}$$

Inequality (2-14), which is the same as (2-5), is satisfied by the assumption of regular strict quasi-concavity. This assumption ensures that the second-order condition is satisfied at any point at which the first-order condition is satisfied. Inequality (2-14) is also the condition for the global univalence of solutions for Eqs. (2-9) (see Sec. A-2). Thus, regular strict quasi-concavity also ensures that constrained-utility-maximization solutions are unique.

Assume that the utility function is $U = q_1 q_2$, that $p_1 = 2$ dollars, $p_2 = 5$ dollars, and that the consumer's income for the period is 100 dollars. The budget constraint is

$$100 - 2q_1 - 5q_2 = 0$$

Form the function

$$V = q_1 q_2 + \lambda(100 - 2q_1 - 5q_2)$$

and set its partial derivatives equal to zero

$$q_2 - 2\lambda = 0$$

$$q_1 - 5\lambda = 0$$

$$100 - 2q_1 - 5q_2 = 0$$

Solving the three linear equations gives $q_1 = 25$, $q_2 = 10$, and $\lambda = 5$. The second-order condition holds, as the reader may verify by performing the necessary differentiation. The consumer maximizes utility by consuming this combination.

Figure 2-3 contains a graphic presentation of this example. The price line AB is the geometric counterpart of the budget constraint and shows all possible combinations of Q_1 and Q_2 that the consumer *can* purchase. Its equation is $100 - 2q_1 - 5q_2 = 0$. The consumer can purchase 50 units of Q_1 if he buys no Q_2, 20 units of Q_2 if he buys no Q_1, etc. A different price line corresponds to each possible level of income; if the consumer's income were 60 dollars, the relevant price line would be CD. The indifference curves in this example are a family of rectangular hyperbolas.[1] The consumer desires to

[1] Hyperbolas the asymptotes of which coincide with the coordinate axes.

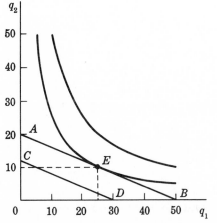

Figure 2-3

reach the highest indifference curve that has at least one point in common with AB. His equilibrium is at point E, at which AB is tangent to an indifference curve. Movements in either direction from point E result in a diminished level of utility. The constant slope of the price line, $-p_1/p_2$ or $-\frac{2}{3}$ in the present example, must equal the slope of the indifference curve. Forming the ratio of the partial derivatives of the utility function, the slope of the indifference curves in the present example is $-q_2/q_1$, and hence the RCS equals $q_2/q_1 = \frac{10}{25}$, which equals the ratio of prices as required. The second-order condition is satisfied. The indifference curves are convex, and the RCS is decreasing at the equilibrium point: $-d^2q_2/dq_1^2 = -2q_2/q_1^2 < 0$.

The Choice of a Utility Index

The numbers which the utility function assigns to the alternative commodity combinations need not have cardinal significance; they need only serve as an *index* of the consumer's satisfaction. Imagine that one wishes to compare the satisfaction a consumer derives from one hat and two shirts and from two hats and five shirts. The consumer is known to prefer the latter to the former combination. The numbers that are assigned to these combinations for the purpose of showing the strength of his preferences are arbitrary in the sense that the difference between them has no meaning. Since the second batch is preferred to the first batch, the number 3 could be assigned to the first and the number 4 to the second. However, any other set of numbers would serve as well, as long as the number assigned to the second batch exceeded that assigned to the first. Thus 3 for the first batch and 400 for the second would provide an equally satisfactory utility index. If a particular set of numbers associated with various combinations of Q_1 and Q_2 is a utility index, any positive monotonic transformation of it is also a utility index.[1] Assume that the original utility function is $U = f(q_1, q_2)$. Now form a new utility index $W = F(U) = F[f(q_1, q_2)]$ by applying a positive monotonic transformation to the original utility index. The function $F(U)$ is an increasing function of U.[†] It can be demonstrated that maximizing W subject to the budget constraint is equivalent to maximizing U subject to the budget constraint.

   Imagine that (q_1^0, q_2^0) is the commodity bundle that uniquely maximizes $f(q_1, q_2)$ subject to the budget constraint. Let $(q_1^{(1)}, q_2^{(1)})$ be any other bundle also satisfying the budget constraint. Then by assumption $f(q_1^0, q_2^0) > f(q_1^{(1)}, q_2^{(1)})$ for any choice of $(q_1^{(1)}, q_2^{(1)})$. But by the definition of monotonicity $W(q_1^0, q_2^0) = F[f(q_1^0, q_2^0)] > F[f(q_1^{(1)}, q_2^{(1)})] = W(q_1^{(1)}, q_2^{(1)})$, which proves that the utility function $W(q_1, q_2)$ is maximized by the commodity bundle (q_1^0, q_2^0).

---

[1] A function $F(U)$ is a positive monotonic transformation of U if $F(U_1) > F(U_0)$ whenever $U_1 > U_0$.

[†] Examples are provided by the transformations $W = aU + b$, provided that a is positive, and by $W = U^2$, provided that all utility numbers are nonnegative.

Two Special Cases

The first-order conditions (2-9) are not always necessary for a maximum. Two exceptions are pictured in Fig. 2-4. In the first case (see Fig. 2-4a) the indifference curves are concave rather than convex; i.e., the assumption that the utility function is quasi-concave is violated. The indifference curves are bowed away from the origin, and the RCS is increasing throughout. The first-order condition for a maximum is satisfied at the point of tangency between the price line and an indifference curve, but the second-order condition is not. Therefore this point represents a local utility mini-mum, and the consumer can increase his utility by moving from the point of tangency toward either axis. He consumes only one commodity at the optimum. If he spends all his income on one commodity, he can buy y^0/p_1 units of Q_1 or y^0/p_2 units of Q_2. Therefore he will buy only Q_1 or only Q_2, depending upon whether $f(y^0/p_1, 0) \gtrless f(0, y^0/p_2)$. In the example shown in Fig. 2-4a he will buy only Q_2. In the second case (see Fig. 2-4b) the indifference curves have the appropriate shape, but they are everywhere less steep than the price line. Tangency is not possible; the first-order condition cannot be fulfilled because of the restrictions $q_1 \geqq 0$, $q_2 \geqq 0$. The consumer's optimum position is again given by a corner solution, and he purchases only Q_2 at the optimum.

Assume that the utility function of Fig. 2-4b is either strictly concave or has a positive monotonic transformation that is. The Kuhn-Tucker conditions (see Sec. A-3) are applicable. The consumer desires to maximize utility subject to the following inequality constraints:

$$y^0 - p_1 q_1 - p_2 q_2 \geqq 0 \qquad q_1 \geqq 0 \qquad q_2 \geqq 0$$

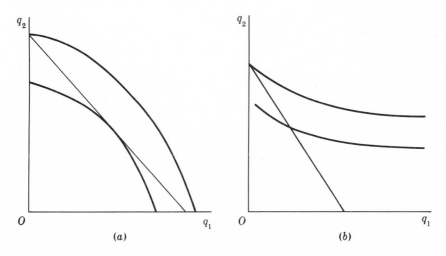

(a) (b)

Figure 2-4

The consumer is allowed to spend less than his income, and the nonnegative consumption requirements are made explicit. The Lagrange function is again given by (2-8). The Kuhn-Tucker conditions[1] for a utility maximum require that

$$V_1 = f_1 - \lambda p_1 \leqq 0 \qquad\qquad q_1 V_1 = 0$$

$$V_2 = f_2 - \lambda p_2 \leqq 0 \qquad\qquad q_2 V_2 = 0$$

$$V_3 = y^0 - p_1 q_1 - p_2 q_2 \geqq 0 \qquad \lambda V_3 = 0$$

where the V_i are the partial derivatives of (2-8). If $f_1 > \lambda p_1$, the consumer could increase utility by increasing q_1. If $f_1 < \lambda p_1$, he could increase utility by decreasing q_1 unless q_1 already equaled zero. In the example shown in Fig. 2-4b, $V_1 < 0$ and $V_2 = 0$. Hence, $f_1/f_2 < p_1/p_2$.

The last pair of the Kuhn-Tucker conditions state that λ, the marginal utility of income, would equal zero if the consumer were to spend less than his income in equilibrium. However, this will not happen as long as positive marginal utilities are assumed.

2-3 DEMAND FUNCTIONS

Ordinary Demand Functions

A consumer's ordinary demand function (sometimes called a Marshallian demand function) gives the quantity of a commodity that he will buy as a function of commodity prices and his income. Ordinary demand functions are called simply demand functions unless it is necessary to distinguish them from another type of demand function. They can be derived from the analysis of utility maximization. The first-order conditions for maximization (2-9) consist of three equations in the three unknowns: q_1, q_2, and λ.† The demand functions are obtained by solving this system for the unknowns. The solutions for q_1 and q_2 are in terms of the parameters p_1, p_2, and y^0. The quantity of Q_1 (or Q_2) that the consumer purchases in the general case depends upon the prices of all commodities and his income.

As above, assume that the utility function is $U = q_1 q_2$ and the budget constraint $y^0 - p_1 q_1 - p_2 q_2 = 0$. Form the expression

$$V = q_1 q_2 + \lambda(y^0 - p_1 q_1 - p_2 q_2)$$

and set its partial derivatives equal to zero:

$$\frac{\partial V}{\partial q_1} = q_2 - p_1 \lambda = 0$$

[1] The Kuhn-Tucker conditions are necessary and sufficient given concave functions if a constraint qualification is satisfied (see Sec. A-3). This constraint qualification is assumed to be satisfied for all examples used in the text.

† Assume that the second-order conditions are fulfilled.

$$\frac{\partial V}{\partial q_2} = q_1 - p_2\lambda = 0$$

$$\frac{\partial V}{\partial \lambda} = y^0 - p_1 q_1 - p_2 q_2 = 0$$

Solving for q_1 and q_2 gives the demand functions:[1]

$$q_1 = \frac{y^0}{2p_1} \qquad q_2 = \frac{y^0}{2p_2}$$

The demand functions derived in this fashion are contingent on continued optimizing behavior by the consumer. Given the consumer's income and prices of commodities, the quantities demanded by him can be determined from his demand functions. Of course, these quantities are the same as those obtained directly from the utility function. Substituting $y^0 = 100$, $p_1 = 2$, $p_2 = 5$ in the demand functions gives $q_1 = 25$ and $q_2 = 10$, as in Sec. 2-2.

Two important properties of demand functions can be deduced: (1) the demand for any commodity is a single-valued function of prices and income, and (2) demand functions are homogeneous of degree zero in prices and income; i.e., if all prices and income change in the same proportion, the quantities demanded remain unchanged.

The first property follows from the strict quasi-concavity of the utility function; a single maximum, and therefore a single commodity combination, corresponds to a given set of prices and income.[2] To prove the second property assume that all prices and income change in the same proportion. The budget constraint becomes

$$ky^0 - kp_1 q_1 - kp_2 q_2 = 0$$

where k is the factor of proportionality. Expression (2-8) becomes

$$V = f(q_1, q_2) + \lambda(ky^0 - kp_1 q_1 - kp_2 q_2)$$

and the first-order conditions are

$$f_1 - \lambda k p_1 = 0$$

$$f_2 - \lambda k p_2 = 0 \qquad\qquad (2\text{-}15)$$

$$ky^0 - kp_1 q_1 - kp_2 q_2 = 0$$

The last equation of (2-15) is the partial derivative of V with respect to the Lagrange multiplier and can be written as

$$k(y^0 - p_1 q_1 - p_2 q_2) = 0$$

---

[1] Notice that these demand functions are a special case in which the demand for each commodity depends only upon its own price and income.

[2] If the utility function were quasi-concave but not *strictly* quasi-concave, the indifference curves would possess straight-line portions, and maxima would not need to be unique. In this case more than one value of the quantity demanded may correspond to a given price, and the demand relationship is called a *demand correspondence* rather than a demand function.

Since $k \neq 0$,

$$y^0 - p_1 q_1 - p_2 q_2 = 0$$

Eliminating k from the first two equations of (2-15) by moving the second terms to the right-hand side and dividing the first equation by the second,

$$\frac{f_1}{f_2} = \frac{p_1}{p_2}$$

The last two equations are the same as (2-7) and (2-10). Therefore the demand function for the price-income set (kp_1, kp_2, ky^0) is derived from the same equations as for the price-income set (p_1, p_2, y^0). It is also easy to demonstrate that the second-order conditions are unaffected. This proves that the demand functions are homogeneous of degree zero in prices and income. If all prices and the consumer's income are increased in the same proportion, the quantities demanded by the consumer do not change. This implies a relevant and empirically testable restriction upon the consumer's behavior; it means that he will not behave as if he were richer (or poorer) in terms of real income if his income and prices rise in the same proportion. A rise in money income is desirable for the consumer, *ceteris paribus*, but its benefits are illusory if prices change proportionately. If such proportionate changes leave his behavior unaltered, there is an absence of "money illusion."

Compensated Demand Functions

Imagine a situation in which some public authority taxes or subsidizes a consumer in such a way as to leave his utility unchanged after a price change. Assume that this is done by providing a lump-sum payment that will give the consumer the minimum income necessary to achieve his initial utility level. The consumer's compensated demand functions give the quantities of the commodities that he will buy as functions of commodity prices under these conditions. They are obtained by minimizing the consumer's expenditures subject to the constraint that his utility is at the fixed level U^0.

Assume again that the utility function is $U = q_1 q_2$. Form the expression

$$Z = p_1 q_1 + p_2 q_2 + \mu(U^0 - q_1 q_2)$$

and set its partial derivatives equal to zero:

$$\frac{\partial Z}{\partial q_1} = p_1 - \mu q_2 = 0$$

$$\frac{\partial Z}{\partial q_2} = p_2 - \mu q_1 = 0$$

$$\frac{\partial Z}{\partial \mu} = U^0 - q_1 q_2 = 0$$

Solving for q_1 and q_2 gives the compensated demand functions:

$$q_1 = \sqrt{\frac{U^0 p_2}{p_1}} \qquad q_2 = \sqrt{\frac{U^0 p_1}{p_2}}$$

The reader can easily verify that these functions are homogeneous of degree zero in prices.

Demand Curves

In general, the consumer's ordinary demand function for Q_1 is written as

$$q_1 = \phi(p_1, p_2, y^0)$$

or, assuming that p_2 and y^0 are given parameters,

$$q_1 = D(p_1)$$

It is often assumed that the demand function possesses an inverse such that price may be expressed as a unique function of quantity. An *inverse* demand function $p_1 = D^{-1}(q_1)$ is a function such that $D[D^{-1}(q_1)] = q_1$.

The shape of the demand function depends upon the properties of the consumer's utility function. It is generally assumed that demand curves are negatively sloped: the lower the price, the greater the quantity demanded. In exceptional cases the opposite relationship may hold. An example is provided by ostentatious consumption: If the consumer derives utility from a high price, the demand function may have a positive slope. The nature of price-induced changes in the quantity demanded is analyzed in detail in Sec. 2-5. Elsewhere in this volume it is assumed that demand functions are negatively sloped.

The consumer's compensated demand curve for Q_1 is constructed in a similar fashion with p_2 and U^0 as given parameters. In Sec. 2-5 it is shown that the convexity of the indifference curves ensures that compensated demand curves are always downward sloping.

Possible shapes for ordinary and compensated demand curves are shown in Fig. 2-5. The ordinary demand curve is labeled DD and the compensated demand curve is labeled $D'D'$. The values at their point of intersection, p_1^0 and q_1^0, satisfy both functions. At this point the utility level achieved for the ordinary demand curve equals the level prescribed for the compensated demand curve, and the minimum income for the compensated demand curve equals the fixed income for the ordinary demand curve. At prices greater than p_1^0 income compensation will be positive, and the compensated demand curve will yield higher quantities for each price. At prices less than p_1^0 income compensation will be negative, and the compensated demand curve will yield lower quantities for each price.

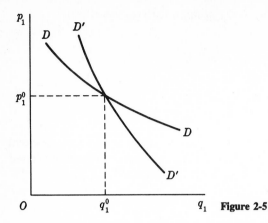

Figure 2-5

Price and Income Elasticities of Demand

The own elasticity of demand for $Q_1(\varepsilon_{11})$ is defined as the proportionate rate of change of q_1 divided by the proportionate rate of change of its own price with p_2 and y^0 constant:

$$\varepsilon_{11} = \frac{\partial(\ln q_1)}{\partial(\ln p_1)} = \frac{p_1}{q_1} \frac{\partial q_1}{\partial p_1} \tag{2-16}$$

A numerically large value for an elasticity implies that quantity is proportionately very responsive to price changes. Commodities which have numerically high elasticities ($\varepsilon_{11} < -1$) are often called luxuries, whereas those with numerically small elasticities ($\varepsilon_{11} > -1$) are called necessities. Price elasticities of demand are pure numbers independent of the units in which prices and outputs are measured. The elasticity ε_{11} is negative if the corresponding demand curve is downward sloping.

The consumer's expenditure on Q_1 is $p_1 q_1$, and

$$\frac{\partial(p_1 q_1)}{\partial p_1} = q_1 + p_1 \frac{\partial q_1}{\partial p_1} = q_1 \left(1 + \frac{p_1}{q_1} \frac{\partial q_1}{\partial p_1} \right) = q_1(1 + \varepsilon_{11})$$

The consumer's expenditures on Q_1 will increase with p_1 if $\varepsilon_{11} > -1$, remain unchanged if $\varepsilon_{11} = -1$, and decrease if $\varepsilon_{11} < -1$.

A cross-price elasticity of demand for the ordinary demand function relates the proportionate change in one quantity to the proportionate change in the other price. For example,

$$\varepsilon_{21} = \frac{\partial(\ln q_2)}{\partial(\ln p_1)} = \frac{p_1}{q_2} \frac{\partial q_2}{\partial p_1} \tag{2-17}$$

Cross-price elasticities may be either positive or negative.

Taking the total differential of the budget constraint (2-7) and letting $dy^0 = dp_2 = 0$,

$$p_1 \, dq_1 + q_1 \, dp_1 + p_2 \, dq_2 = 0$$

Multiplying through by $p_1 q_1 q_2 / y^0 q_1 q_2 \, dp_1$, and rearranging terms,

$$\alpha_1 \varepsilon_{11} + \alpha_2 \varepsilon_{21} = -\alpha_1 \qquad (2\text{-}18)$$

where $\alpha_1 = p_1 q_1 / y^0$ and $\alpha_2 = p_2 q_2 / y^0$ are the proportions of total expenditures for the two goods. Equation (2-18) is called the Counnot aggregation condition. If the own-price elasticity of demand for Q_1 is known, (2-18) can be used to evaluate the cross-price elasticity of demand for Q_2. If $\varepsilon_{11} = -1$, $\varepsilon_{21} = 0$. If $\varepsilon_{11} < -1$, $\varepsilon_{21} > 0$, and if $\varepsilon_{11} > -1$, $\varepsilon_{21} < 0$.

Own- and cross-price elasticities of demand for compensated demand functions can be defined in an analogous manner by inserting compensated rather than ordinary demand functions in (2-15) and (2-17). Equation (2-18) does not hold for compensated demand functions. Taking the total differential of the utility function (2-1) and letting $dU = 0$,

$$f_1 \, dq_1 + f_2 \, dq_2 = 0$$

Using the first-order condition $p_1 / p_2 = f_1 / f_2$, multiplying through by $p_1 q_1 q_2 / y^0 q_1 q_2 \, dp_1$, and rearranging terms,

$$\alpha_1 \xi_{11} + \alpha_2 \xi_{21} = 0 \qquad (2\text{-}19)$$

where the compensated price elasticities are denoted by ξ_{11} and ξ_{21}. Since $\xi_{11} < 0$, it follows from (2-19) that $\xi_{21} > 0$.

Returning to the example $U = q_1 q_2$, the own- and cross-price elasticities for the ordinary demand function are

$$\varepsilon_{11} = -\frac{p_1}{q_1} \frac{y^0}{2 p_1^2} = -\frac{p_1}{y^0 / 2 p_1} \frac{y^0}{2 p_1^2} = -1$$

$$\varepsilon_{21} = \frac{p_1}{q_2} 0 = 0$$

This is a special case. Not all demand functions have unit own and zero cross elasticities or even constant elasticities. In general, elasticities are a function of p_1, p_2, and y^0. The reader can verify that the compensated elasticities for this example are $\xi_{11} = -\frac{1}{2}$ and $\xi_{21} = \frac{1}{2}$.

An income elasticity of demand for an ordinary demand function is defined as the proportionate change in the purchases of a commodity relative to the proportionate change in income with prices constant:

$$\eta_1 = \frac{\partial (\ln q_1)}{\partial (\ln y)} = \frac{y}{q_1} \frac{\partial \phi (p_1, p_2, y)}{\partial y} \qquad (2\text{-}20)$$

where η_1 denotes the income elasticity of demand for q_1. Income elasticities can be positive, negative, or zero, but are normally assumed to be positive.

Taking the total differential of the budget constraint (2-7),

$$p_1 \, dq_1 + p_2 \, dq_2 = dy$$

Multiplying through by y/y, multiplying the first term on the left by q_1/q_1, the second by q_2/q_2, and dividing through by dy,

$$\alpha_1\eta_1 + \alpha_2\eta_2 = 1 \tag{2-21}$$

which is called the Engel aggregation condition. The sum of the income elasticities weighted by total expenditure proportions equals unity. Income elasticities cannot be derived for compensated demand functions since income is not an argument of these functions.

2-4 INCOME AND LEISURE

If the consumer's income is payment for work performed by him, the optimum amount of work that he performs can be derived from the analysis of utility maximization. One can also derive the consumer's demand curve for income from this analysis. Assume that the consumer's satisfaction depends on income and leisure. His utility function is

$$U = g(L, y) \tag{2-22}$$

where L denotes leisure. Both income and leisure are desirable. In the preceding sections it is assumed that the consumer derives utility from the commodities he purchases with his income. In the construction of (2-22) it is assumed that he buys the various commodities at constant prices, and income is thereby treated as generalized purchasing power (see Sec. 3-6).

The rate of substitution of income for leisure is

$$-\frac{dy}{dL} = \frac{g_1}{g_2}$$

Denote the amount of work performed by the consumer by W and the wage rate by r. By definition,

$$L = T - W \tag{2-23}$$

where T is the total amount of available time.[1] The budget constraint is

$$y = rW \tag{2-24}$$

Substituting (2-23) and (2-24) into (2-22),

$$U = g(T - W, rW) \tag{2-25}$$

To maximize utility set the derivative of (2-25) with respect to W equal to zero:[2]

$$\frac{dU}{dW} = -g_1 + g_2 r = 0$$

---

[1] For example, if the period for which the utility function is defined is one day, $T = 24$ hours.
[2] The composite-function rule is employed.

and therefore
$$-\frac{dy}{dL} = \frac{g_1}{g_2} = r \qquad (2\text{-}26)$$

which states that the rate of substitution of income for leisure equals the wage rate. The second-order condition states

$$\frac{d^2U}{dW^2} = g_{11} - 2g_{12}r + g_{22}r^2 < 0$$

Equation (2-26) is a relation in terms of W and r and is based on the individual consumer's optimizing behavior. It is therefore the consumer's supply curve for work and states how much he will work at various wage rates. Since the supply of work is equivalent to the demand for income, (2-26) indirectly provides the consumer's demand curve for income.

Assume that the utility function, defined for a time period of one day, is given by $U = 48L + Ly - L^2$. Then

$$U = 48(T - W) + (T - W)Wr - (T - W)^2$$

and setting the derivative equal to zero,

$$\frac{dU}{dW} = -48 - Wr + r(T - W) + 2(T - W) = 0$$

Therefore
$$W = \frac{T(r + 2) - 48}{2(r + 1)}$$

and y may be obtained by substituting in (2-24). The second-order condition is fulfilled, since

$$\frac{d^2U}{dW^2} = -2(r + 1) < 0$$

for any positive wage. In the present case the individual's supply function has the following characteristics:

1. Since T, the total available time, is 24 (hours), at a zero wage the individual will not work at all.
2. Since dW/dr is positive, hours worked will increase with the wage.
3. Irrespective of how high the wage becomes, the individual will never work more than 12 hours per day, since $\lim_{r \to \infty} W = 12$.

2-5 SUBSTITUTION AND INCOME EFFECTS

The Slutsky Equation

Comparative statics analysis examines the effect of perturbations in exogenous variables (such as prices and incomes in the present case) on the solution values for the endogenous variables (namely, quantities). Changes in prices and income will normally alter the consumer's expenditure pattern, but the new quantities (and prices and income) will always satisfy the first-order conditions (2-9). In order to find the magnitude of the effect of price and income changes on the consumer's purchases, allow all variables to vary simultaneously. This is accomplished by total differentiation of Eqs. (2-9):

$$f_{11}\,dq_1 + f_{12}\,dq_2 - p_1\,d\lambda = \lambda\,dp_1$$

$$f_{21}\,dq_1 + f_{22}\,dq_2 - p_2\,d\lambda = \lambda\,dp_2 \qquad (2\text{-}27)$$

$$-p_1\,dq_1 - p_2\,dq_2 \qquad\quad = -dy + q_1\,dp_1 + q_2\,dp_2$$

In order to solve this system of three equations for the three unknowns, dq_1, dq_2, and $d\lambda$, the terms on the right must be regarded as constants. The array of coefficients formed by (2-27) is the same as the bordered Hessian determinant (2-12). Denoting this determinant by $\mathscr{D}$ and the cofactor of the element in the first row and the first column by $\mathscr{D}_{11}$, the cofactor of the element in the first row and second column by $\mathscr{D}_{12}$, etc., the solution of (2-27) by Cramer's rule (see Sec. A-1) is

$$dq_1 = \frac{\lambda\mathscr{D}_{11}\,dp_1 + \lambda\mathscr{D}_{21}\,dp_2 + \mathscr{D}_{31}(-dy + q_1\,dp_1 + q_2\,dp_2)}{\mathscr{D}} \qquad (2\text{-}28)$$

$$dq_2 = \frac{\lambda\mathscr{D}_{12}\,dp_1 + \lambda\mathscr{D}_{22}\,dp_2 + \mathscr{D}_{32}(-dy + q_1\,dp_1 + q_2\,dp_2)}{\mathscr{D}} \qquad (2\text{-}29)$$

Dividing both sides of (2-28) by dp_1 and assuming that p_2 and y do not change ($dp_2 = dy = 0$),

$$\frac{\partial q_1}{\partial p_1} = \frac{\mathscr{D}_{11}\lambda}{\mathscr{D}} + q_1\frac{\mathscr{D}_{31}}{\mathscr{D}} \qquad (2\text{-}30)$$

The partial derivative on the left-hand side of (2-30) is the rate of change of the consumer's purchases of Q_1 with respect to changes in p_1, all other things being equal. *Ceteris paribus*, the rate of change with respect to income is

$$\frac{\partial q_1}{\partial y} = -\frac{\mathscr{D}_{31}}{\mathscr{D}} \qquad (2\text{-}31)$$

Changes in commodity prices change the consumer's level of satisfaction, since a new equilibrium is established which lies on a different indifference curve.

Consider a price change that is compensated by an income change that leaves the consumer on his initial indifference curve. An increase in the price of a commodity is accompanied by a corresponding increase in his income such that $dU = 0$ and $f_1\,dq_1 + f_2\,dq_2 = 0$ by (2-3). Since $f_1/f_2 = p_1/p_2$, it is also true that $p_1\,dq_1 + p_2\,dq_2 = 0$. Hence, from the last equation of (2-27), $-dy + q_1\,dp_1 + q_2\,dp_2 = 0$, and

$$\left(\frac{\partial q_1}{\partial p_1}\right)_{U=\text{const}} = \frac{\mathscr{D}_{11}\lambda}{\mathscr{D}} \qquad (2\text{-}32)$$

Equation (2-30) can now be rewritten as

$$\frac{\partial q_1}{\partial p_1} = \left(\frac{\partial q_1}{\partial p_1}\right)_{U=\text{const}} - q_1 \left(\frac{\partial q_1}{\partial y}\right)_{\text{prices}=\text{const}} \tag{2-33}$$

Equation (2-33) is known as the *Slutsky equation*. The quantity $\partial q_1/\partial p_1$ is the slope of the ordinary demand curve for Q_1, and the first term on the right is the slope of the compensated demand curve for Q_1.

An alternative compensation criterion is that the consumer is provided enough income to purchase his former consumption bundle so that $dy = q_1\,dp_1 + q_2\,dp_2$. This is the equation that led to (2-32). Here

$$\left(\frac{\partial q_1}{\partial p_1}\right)_{q_1, q_2=\text{const}} = \frac{\mathscr{D}_{11}\lambda}{\mathscr{D}}$$

which can be substituted for the first term on the right of (2-33). At first glance it might appear remarkable that two rather different compensation schemes led to the same result. However, they only define the same derivative, and may lead to quite different results for any finite move. A consumer can be induced to stay on the same indifference curve in the finite case, but he cannot be induced to purchase the same bundle if relative prices change. All subsequent analysis here is based upon (2-33).

The Slutsky equation may be expressed in terms of the price and income elasticities described in Sec. 2-3. Multiplying (2-33) through by p_1/q_1 and multiplying the last term on the right by y/y,

$$\varepsilon_{11} = \xi_{11} - \alpha_1\eta_1 \tag{2-34}$$

The price elasticity of the ordinary demand curve equals the price elasticity of the compensated demand curve less the corresponding income elasticity multiplied by the proportion of total expenditures spent on Q_1. Hence, the ordinary demand curve will have a greater demand elasticity than the compensated demand curve; that is, ε_{11} will be more negative than ξ_{11} if the income elasticity of demand is positive.

Direct Effects

The first term on the right-hand side of (2-33) is the *substitution effect*, or the rate at which the consumer substitutes Q_1 for other commodities when the price of Q_1 changes and he moves along a given indifference curve.[1] The second term on the right is the *income effect*, which states the rate at which the consumer's purchases of Q_1 would change with changes in his income, prices remaining constant. The sum of the two rates gives the total rate of change for Q_1 as p_1 changes.

In the present case the multiplier λ is the derivative of utility with respect to income with prices constant and quantities variable. From the utility

---

[1] Slutsky called this the *residual variability* of the commodity in question.

function (2-1) it follows that $\partial U/\partial y = f_1(\partial q_1/\partial y) + f_2(\partial q_2/\partial y)$. Substituting $f_1 = \lambda p_1$ and $f_2 = \lambda p_2$,

$$\frac{\partial U}{\partial y} = \lambda \left(p_1 \frac{\partial q_1}{\partial y} + p_2 \frac{\partial q_2}{\partial y} \right) = \lambda$$

which follows from the partial derivative of the budget constraint (2-7) with respect to y: $1 = p_1(\partial q_1/\partial y) + p_2(\partial q_2/\partial y)$. This confirms the result inferred from (2-11) at an earlier stage.

Solving (2-27) for $d\lambda$,

$$d\lambda = \frac{\lambda \mathscr{D}_{13}\, dp_1 + \lambda \mathscr{D}_{23}\, dp_2 + \mathscr{D}_{33}(-dy + q_1\, dp_1 + q_2\, dp_2)}{\mathscr{D}} \tag{2-35}$$

Assume now that only income changes, i.e., that $dp_1 = dp_2 = 0$. Then (2-35) becomes

$$\frac{\partial \lambda}{\partial y} = -\frac{\mathscr{D}_{33}}{\mathscr{D}} = -\frac{f_{11}f_{22} - f_{12}^2}{\mathscr{D}} \tag{2-36}$$

Since $\mathscr{D}$ is positive, the rate of change of the marginal utility of income will have the same sign as $-(f_{11}f_{22} - f_{12}^2)$. This would be negative if the utility function were strictly concave. However, for ordinal utility functions only strict quasi-concavity is assumed, and the theory does not predict whether the marginal utility of income is increasing or decreasing with income.

By (2-32) the substitution effect is $\mathscr{D}_{11}\lambda/\mathscr{D}$. The determinant $\mathscr{D}$, which is the same as (2-12), is positive. Expanding $\mathscr{D}_{11}$,

$$\mathscr{D}_{11} = -p_2^2$$

which is clearly negative. This proves that the sign of the substitution effect is always negative and that the compensated demand curve is always downward sloping.

A change in real income may cause a reallocation of the consumer's resources even if prices do not change or if they change in the same proportion. The income effect is $-q_1(\partial q_1/\partial y)_{\text{prices=const}}$ and may be of either sign. The final effect of a price change on the purchases of the commodity is thus unknown. However, an important conclusion can still be derived: The smaller the quantity of Q_1, the less significant is the income effect. A commodity Q_1 is called an *inferior good* if the consumer's purchases decrease as income rises and increase as income falls; i.e., if $\partial q_1/\partial y$ is negative, which makes the income effect positive. A *Giffen good* is an inferior good with an income effect large enough to offset the negative substitution effect and make $\partial q_1/\partial p_1$ positive. This means that as the price of Q_1 falls, the consumer's purchases of Q_1 will also fall. This may occur if a consumer is sufficiently poor so that a considerable portion of his income is spent on a commodity such as potatoes which he needs for his subsistence. Assume now that the price of potatoes falls. The consumer who is not very fond of potatoes may suddenly discover that his real income has increased as a result of the price fall. He will then buy fewer potatoes and purchase a more palatable diet with the remainder of his income.

The Slutsky equation can be derived for the specific utility function assumed in the previous examples. State the budget constraint in the general implicit form $y - p_1q_1 - p_2q_2 = 0$, and form the function

$$V = q_1q_2 + \lambda(y - p_1q_1 - p_2q_2)$$

Setting the partial derivatives equal to zero,

$$q_2 - \lambda p_1 = 0$$

$$q_1 - \lambda p_2 = 0$$

$$y - p_1q_1 - p_2q_2 = 0$$

The total differentials of these equations are

$$dq_2 - p_1\,d\lambda = \lambda\,dp_1$$

$$dq_1 - p_2\,d\lambda = \lambda\,dp_2$$

$$-p_1\,dq_1 - p_2\,dq_2 = -dy + q_1\,dp_1 + q_2\,dp_2$$

Denote the determinant of the coefficients of these equations by $\mathcal{D}$ and the cofactor of the element in the ith row and jth column by $\mathcal{D}_{ij}$. Simple calculations show that

$$\mathcal{D} = 2p_1p_2$$

$$\mathcal{D}_{11} = -p_2^2$$

$$\mathcal{D}_{21} = p_1p_2$$

$$\mathcal{D}_{31} = -p_2$$

Solving for dq_1 by Cramer's rule gives

$$dq_1 = \frac{-p_2^2\lambda\,dp_1 + p_1p_2\lambda\,dp_2 - p_2(-dy + q_1\,dp_1 + q_2\,dp_2)}{2p_1p_2}$$

Assuming that only the price of the first commodity varies,

$$\frac{\partial q_1}{\partial p_1} = -\frac{p_2\lambda}{2p_1} - \frac{q_1}{2p_1}$$

The value of λ is obtained by substituting the values of q_1 and q_2 from the first two equations of the first-order conditions into the third and solving for λ in terms of the parameters p_1, p_2, and y. Thus $\lambda = y/2p_1p_2$. Substituting this value into the above equation and then introducing into it the values of the parameters ($y = 100$, $p_1 = 2$, $p_2 = 5$) and also the equilibrium value of q_1 (25), a numerical answer is obtained:

$$\frac{\partial q_1}{\partial p_1} = -12.5$$

The meaning of this answer is the following: If, starting from the initial equilibrium situation, p_1 were to change, *ceteris paribus*, the consumer's purchases would change at the rate of 12.5 units of Q_1 per dollar of change in the price of Q_1; furthermore the direction of the change in the consumer's purchases is opposite to the direction of the price change. The expression $-p_2\lambda/2p_1$ is the substitution effect, and its value in the present example is -6.25. The expression $-q_1/2p_1$ is the income effect, also with a value of -6.25.

Cross Effects

The Slutsky equation (2-33) and its elasticity representation (2-34) can be extended to account for changes in the demand for one commodity resulting from changes in the price of the other. The generalized forms are

$$\frac{\partial q_i}{\partial p_j} = \frac{\mathscr{D}_{ji}\lambda}{\mathscr{D}} + q_j \frac{\mathscr{D}_{3i}}{\mathscr{D}} = \left(\frac{\partial q_i}{\partial p_j}\right)_{U=\text{const}} - q_j \left(\frac{\partial q_i}{\partial y}\right)_{\text{prices}=\text{const}} \tag{2-37}$$

and
$$\varepsilon_{ij} = \xi_{ij} - \alpha_j \eta_i \tag{2-38}$$

for $i, j = 1, 2$. The signs of the cross-substitution effects ($i \neq j$) are not known in general. Let $S_{ij} = \mathscr{D}_{ji}\lambda/\mathscr{D}$ denote the substitution effect when the quantity of the ith commodity is adjusted as a result of a variation in the jth price. Since $\mathscr{D}$ is a symmetric determinant,[1] $\mathscr{D}_{12} = \mathscr{D}_{21}$, and it follows that $S_{ij} = S_{ji}$. The substitution effect on the ith commodity resulting from a change in the jth price is the same as the substitution effect on the jth commodity resulting from a change in the ith price.

This is a remarkable conclusion. Imagine that the consumer's demand for tea increases at the rate of 2 cups of tea per 1-cent increase in the price of coffee. One can infer from this that his purchases of coffee would increase at the rate of 2 cups of coffee per 1-cent increase in the price of tea.

Sum the compensated demand elasticities for Q_1 as a result of changes in p_1 and p_2:

$$\xi_{11} + \xi_{12} = \frac{p_1 \mathscr{D}_{11}\lambda}{q_1 \mathscr{D}} + \frac{p_2 \mathscr{D}_{21}\lambda}{q_1 \mathscr{D}} = \frac{\lambda(p_1 \mathscr{D}_{11} + p_2 \mathscr{D}_{21})}{q_1 \mathscr{D}} = 0 \tag{2-39}$$

The term in parentheses equals zero since it is an expansion of the determinant of (2-27) in terms of alien cofactors; i.e., the cofactors of the elements of the first column are multiplied by the negative of the elements in the last column. Thus, the negative compensated elasticity for Q_1 with respect to p_1 equals in absolute value the positive compensated elasticity for Q_1 with respect to p_2.

Sum the negative of the ordinary demand elasticities for Q_1 as a result of

---

[1] A determinant is symmetric if its array is symmetric around the principal diagonal.

changes in p_1 and p_2 as given by (2-38):

$$-(\varepsilon_{11} + \varepsilon_{12}) = -(\xi_{11} + \xi_{12}) + (\alpha_1 + \alpha_2)\eta_1 = \eta_1 \qquad (2\text{-}40)$$

from (2-39) and $\alpha_1 + \alpha_2 = 1$. The income elasticity of demand for a commodity equals the negative of the sum of ordinary price elasticities of demand for that commodity with respect to its own and the other price.

Substitutes and Complements

Two commodities are substitutes if both can satisfy the same need of the consumer; they are complements if they are consumed jointly in order to satisfy some particular need. These are loose definitions, but everyday experience may suggest some plausible examples. Coffee and tea are most likely substitutes, whereas coffee and sugar are most likely complements. A more rigorous definition of substitutability and complementarity is provided by the cross-substitution term of the Slutsky equation (2-37). Accordingly, Q_1 and Q_2 are substitutes if the substitution effect $\mathcal{D}_{21}\lambda/\mathcal{D}$ is positive; they are complements if it is negative. If Q_1 and Q_2 are substitutes (in the everyday sense) and if compensating variations in income keep the consumer on the same indifference curve, an increase in the price of Q_1 will induce the consumer to substitute Q_2 for Q_1. Then $(\partial q_2/\partial p_1)_{U=\text{const}} > 0$. For analogous reasons, $(\partial q_2/\partial p_1)_{U=\text{const}} < 0$ in the case of complements.[1]

All commodities cannot be complements for each other. Hence only substitutability can occur in the present two-variable case. This theorem is easily proved. Multiply (2-30) by p_1, (2-31) by y, and (2-37) for $i = 1$ and $j = 2$ by p_2, and add:

$$\frac{\mathcal{D}_{11}\lambda}{\mathcal{D}} p_1 + q_1 \frac{\mathcal{D}_{31}}{\mathcal{D}} p_1 + \frac{\mathcal{D}_{21}\lambda}{\mathcal{D}} p_2 + q_2 \frac{\mathcal{D}_{31}}{\mathcal{D}} p_2 - \frac{\mathcal{D}_{31}}{\mathcal{D}} y$$

$$= \frac{1}{\mathcal{D}} [\mathcal{D}_{11}\lambda p_1 + \mathcal{D}_{21}\lambda p_2 - \mathcal{D}_{31}(y - p_1 q_1 - p_2 q_2)]$$

$$= \frac{1}{\mathcal{D}} [\mathcal{D}_{11}\lambda p_1 + \mathcal{D}_{21}\lambda p_2 - \mathcal{D}_{31}(0)] = 0$$

The final bracketed term equals zero since it is an expansion in terms of alien cofactors as in (2-39). Substituting $S_{ij} = \mathcal{D}_{ji}\lambda/\mathcal{D}$,

$$S_{11}p_1 + S_{12}p_2 = 0 \qquad (2\text{-}41)$$

The substitution effect for Q_1 resulting from changes in p_1, S_{11}, is known to be negative. Hence (2-41) implies that S_{12} must be positive, and in terms of the definitions of substitutability and complementarity this means that Q_1 and Q_2 are necessarily substitutes.

---

[1] This provides a rationale for the definitions. When $(\partial q_2/\partial p_1)_{U=\text{const}} = 0$, Q_1 and Q_2 are independent.

Commodities i and j are *gross substitutes* or *gross complements* according to whether the total effect $\partial q_i / \partial p_j$ is positive or negative. In the two-good case it is possible for a pair of goods to be substitutes in terms of S_{ij}, and at the same time to be gross complements. In the n-good case it is also possible for them to be complements in terms of the S_{ij}, and at the same time be gross substitutes. A two-good example is provided by the utility function $U = q_1 q_2 - q_2$ with the domain $q_1 > 1, q_2 > 0$. Maximizing subject to the budget constraint yields the demand function $q_2 = (y - p_1)/2p_2$, which is valid for the domain $p_1 < y$. Here $\partial q_2 / \partial p_1 < 0$ to make the commodities gross complements even though they are substitutes in terms of S_{12}.

2-6 GENERALIZATION TO n VARIABLES

The foregoing analysis of the consumer is now generalized to the case of n commodities. The generalization is not carried out in detail, but the first few steps are indicated. If there are n commodities, the utility function is

$$U = f(q_1, q_2, \ldots, q_n)$$

and the budget constraint is given by

$$y - \sum_{i=1}^{n} p_i q_i = 0$$

Forming the Lagrange function as above,

$$V = f(q_1, q_2, \ldots, q_n) + \lambda \left(y - \sum_{i=1}^{n} p_i q_i \right)$$

Setting the partial derivatives equal to zero,

$$\frac{\partial V}{\partial q_i} = f_i - \lambda p_i = 0 \qquad i = 1, \ldots, n \tag{2-42}$$

Conditions (2-42) can be modified to state the equality for all commodities of marginal utility divided by price. The partial derivative of V with respect to λ is again the budget constraint. There are a total of $(n + 1)$ equations in $(n + 1)$ variables (n q's and λ). The demand curves for the n commodities can be obtained by solving for the q's. Conditions (2-42) can be stated alternatively as

$$-\frac{\partial q_i}{\partial q_j} = \frac{p_j}{p_i}$$

for all i and j; i.e., the rate of commodity substitution of commodity i for commodity j must equal the price ratio p_j / p_i. Second-order conditions must be fulfilled in order to ensure that a batch of commodities that satisfies (2-42) is optimal. The bordered Hessian determinants must alternate in sign:

$$
\begin{vmatrix} f_{11} & f_{12} & -p_1 \\ f_{21} & f_{22} & -p_2 \\ -p_1 & -p_2 & 0 \end{vmatrix} > 0, \qquad \begin{vmatrix} f_{11} & f_{12} & f_{13} & -p_1 \\ f_{21} & f_{22} & f_{23} & -p_2 \\ f_{31} & f_{32} & f_{33} & -p_3 \\ -p_1 & -p_2 & -p_3 & 0 \end{vmatrix} < 0,
$$

$$
\ldots, (-1)^n \begin{vmatrix} f_{11} & f_{12} & \cdots & f_{1n} & -p_1 \\ f_{21} & f_{22} & \cdots & f_{2n} & -p_2 \\ \cdots\cdots\cdots\cdots\cdots\cdots\cdots\cdots\cdots \\ f_{n1} & f_{n2} & \cdots & f_{nn} & -p_n \\ -p_1 & -p_2 & \cdots & -p_n & 0 \end{vmatrix} > 0
$$

which is a generalization of condition (2-12).

The assumption of convexity for indifference curves in two dimensions may also be extended to indifference hypersurfaces in n dimensions. The first of the second-order conditions for the n-dimensional case is the same as the second-order condition for the two-dimensional case, which was demonstrated to result in a decreasing RCS between the commodities. In n dimensions the second-order conditions result in decreasing RCSs between every pair of commodities. The satisfaction of the second-order conditions is ensured by the regular strict quasi-concavity of the utility function.

Other theorems can also be generalized in straightforward fashion. The Slutsky equations (2-37) and (2-38) hold for $i, j = 1, \ldots, n$. The generalization of (2-41) is

$$
\sum_{j=1}^{n} S_{ij}p_j = 0 \qquad i = 1, \ldots, n \tag{2-43}
$$

It still follows that all commodities cannot be complements for each other. However, some pairs of commodities can be complements; i.e., some $S_{ij} < 0$ for $i \neq j$. Gross substitutes and complements may also be defined.

All the elasticity relations generalize. The n-commodity forms for (2-18), (2-19), and (2-21) respectively are

$$
\sum_{i=1}^{n} \alpha_i \varepsilon_{ij} = -\alpha_j \qquad j = 1, \ldots, n
$$

$$
\sum_{i=1}^{n} \alpha_i \xi_{ij} = 0 \qquad j = 1, \ldots, n
$$

$$
\sum_{j=1}^{n} \alpha_j \eta_j = 1
$$

and the general forms for (2-39) and (2-40) respectively are

$$
\sum_{j=1}^{n} \xi_{ij} = 0 \qquad i = 1, \ldots, n
$$

$$
-\sum_{j=1}^{n} \varepsilon_{ij} = \eta_i \qquad i = 1, \ldots, n
$$

2-7 SUMMARY

Nineteenth-century economic theorists explained the consumer's behavior on the assumption that utility is measurable. This restrictive assumption was abandoned around the turn of the last century, and the consumer was assumed to be capable only of ranking commodity combinations consistently in order of preference. This ranking is described mathematically by the consumer's ordinal utility function, which always assigns a higher number to a more desirable combination of commodities. The consumer is normally assumed to have a regular strictly quasi-concave utility function which implies a decreasing rate of commodity substitution (RCS).

The basic postulate of the theory of consumer behavior is that the consumer maximizes utility. Since his income is limited, he maximizes utility subject to a budget constraint, which expresses his income limitation in mathematical form. The consumer's RCS must equal the price ratio for a maximum. In diagrammatic terms, the optimum commodity combination is given by the point at which his income line is tangent to an indifference curve. The second-order condition for a maximum is guaranteed by the convexity assumption.

The consumer's utility function is not unique. If a particular function describes appropriately the consumer's preferences, so does any other function which is a positive monotonic transformation of the first. Other kinds of transformations do not preserve the correct ranking, and the utility function is unique up to a positive monotonic transformation.

The consumer's ordinary demand functions for commodities can be derived from his first-order conditions for utility maximization. These state quantities demanded as functions of all prices and the consumer's income. Ordinary demand functions are single-valued and homogeneous of degree zero in prices and income: a proportionate change in all prices and the consumer's income leaves the quantity demanded unchanged. The consumer's compensated demand functions for commodities are constructed on the assumption that his income is increased or decreased following a price change in order to leave him at his initial utility level. The compensated demand functions state quantities demanded as functions of all prices. They are single-valued and homogeneous of degree zero in prices. A demand curve is obtained by stating quantity demanded as a function of own price on the assumption that the other arguments of the demand function are given parameters. Price elasticities are defined for both types of demand functions, and income elasticities are defined for ordinary demand functions.

In general, the amount of labor performed by a consumer affects his level of utility. The amount of labor performed by the consumer can be determined on the basis of the rational-decision criterion of utility maximization. The equilibrium conditions are similar to those which hold for the selection of an optimal commodity combination.

The consumer's reaction to price and income changes can be analyzed in terms of substitution and income effects. The effect of a given price change can be analytically decomposed into a substitution effect, which measures the rate at which he would substitute commodities for each other by moving along the same indifference curve, and an income effect as a residual category. If the price of a commodity changes, the quantity demanded changes in the opposite direction if the consumer is forced to move along the same indifference curve: the substitution effect is negative. If the income effect is positive, the commodity is an inferior good. If the total effect is positive, it is also a Giffen good. Substitutes and complements are defined in terms of the sign of the substitution effect for one commodity when the price of another changes: a positive cross-substitution effect means substitutability, and a negative one, complementarity. Gross substitutes and complements are defined in terms of the full effect of price changes on quantity. In conclusion, the generalization of the theory to n commodities is indicated.

EXERCISES

2-1 Determine whether the following utility functions are regular strictly quasi-concave for the domain $q_1 > 0$, $q_2 > 0$: $U = q_1 q_2$; $U = q_1^\gamma q_2$; $U = q_1^2 + q_2^2$; $U = q_1 + q_2 + 2q_1 q_2$; $U = q_1 q_2 - 0.01(q_1^2 + q_2^2)$; and $U = q_1 q_2 + q_1 q_3 + q_2 q_3$.

2-2 Let $f(q_1, q_2)$ be a strictly concave utility function, and let $q_j^{(2)} = (q_j^0 + q_j^{(1)})/2$, $j = 1, 2$, where superscripts denote particular values for the variables. Prove that

$$f(q_1^{(2)}, q_2^{(2)}) - f(q_1^0, q_2^0) > f(q_1^{(1)}, q_2^{(1)}) - f(q_1^{(2)}, q_2^{(2)})$$

2-3 Find the optimum commodity purchases for a consumer whose utility function and budget constraint are $U = q_1^{1.5} q_2$ and $3q_1 + 4q_2 = 100$ respectively.

2-4 The locus of points of tangency between income lines and indifference curves for given prices p_1, p_2 and a changing value of income is called an income expansion line or Engel curve. Show that the Engel curve is a straight line if the utility function is given by $U = q_1^\gamma q_2$, $\gamma > 0$.

2-5 Show that the utility functions $U = Aq_1^\alpha q_2^\beta$ and $W = q_1^{\alpha/\beta} q_2$ are monotonic transformations of each other where A, α, and β are positive.

2-6 Let a consumer's utility function be $U = q_1^6 q_2^4 + 1.5 \ln q_1 + \ln q_2$ and his budget constraint $3q_1 + 4q_2 = 100$. Show that his optimum commodity bundle is the same as in Exercise 2-3. Why is this the case?

2-7 Construct ordinary and compensated demand functions for Q_1 for the utility function $U = 2q_1 q_2 + q_2$. Construct expressions for ε_{11}, ξ_{12}, and η_1.

2-8 Derive the elasticity of supply of work with respect to the wage rate for the supply curve for work given by the example in Sec. 2-4.

2-9 Prove that Q_1 and Q_2 cannot both be inferior goods.

2-10 Verify that $S_{11} p_1 + S_{12} p_2 = 0$ for the utility function $U = q_1^\gamma q_2$.

2-11 Let $U = f(q, H)$ be a utility function the arguments of which are the quantity of a commodity (q) and the time taken to consume it (H). The marginal utilities of both arguments are positive. Let W be the amount of work performed, $W + H = 24$ (hours), r be the wage, and p be the price of q. Formulate the appropriate constrained utility maximization problem. Find an expression for dH/dr. Is its sign determined unambiguously?

2-12 Imagine that coupon rationing is in effect so that each commodity has two prices: a dollar price and a ration-coupon price. Assume that there are three commodities and that the consumer has a dollar income y and a ration-coupon allotment z. Also assume that this allotment is not so liberal that any commodity combination that he can afford to purchase with his dollar income can also be purchased with his coupons. Formulate his constrained-utility-maximization problem assuming a strictly concave utility function. Derive conditions for a maximum. Interpret the conditions from an economic point of view. Find a sufficient condition which guarantees that the imposition of rationing does not alter the consumer's purchases.

SELECTED REFERENCES

Debreu, Gerard: *Theory of Value* (New York: Wiley, 1959). The theory of the consumer is discussed in chap. 4 from an advanced and modern mathematical point of view.

Friedman, M.: *Essays in Positive Economics* (Chicago: University of Chicago Press, 1953), "The Marshallian Demand Curve," pp. 47–99. An analysis of the various types of demand functions and demand curves.

Georgescu-Roegen, N.: "The Pure Theory of Consumer Behavior," *Quarterly Journal of Economics*, vol. 50 (August, 1936), pp. 545–593. A mathematical analysis of ordinal utility theory.

Hicks, J. R.: *Value and Capital* (2d ed., Oxford: Clarendon Press, 1946). Chaps. I–III contain an exposition of ordinal utility theory. The mathematical analysis is in an appendix.

Linder, S. B.: *The Harried Leisure Class* (New York: Columbia University Press, 1970). An analysis of the effect on consumption of the time required for consumption activities. The mathematical analysis is in an appendix.

Marshall, Alfred: *Principles of Economics* (8th ed., London: Macmillan, 1920). Chaps. I–IV, book III, contain a nonmathematical discussion of wants, utility, marginal utility, and demand from the cardinalist viewpoint.

Samuelson, P. A.: *Foundations of Economic Analysis* (Cambridge, Mass.: Harvard University Press, 1948). Chaps. V and VII contain a comprehensive analysis of utility theory using fairly advanced mathematics.

Slutsky, E. E.: "On the Theory of the Budget of the Consumer," *Giornale degli Economisti*, vol. 51 (July, 1915), pp. 1–26. Also reprinted in American Economic Association, *Readings in Price Theory* (Homewood, Ill.: Irwin, 1952), pp. 27–56. The article upon which the modern mathematical theory of consumer behavior is based. Fairly difficult mathematics.

Theil, H.: *Theory and Measurement of Consumer Demand* (Amsterdam: North-Holland, 1975). The mathematics of demand theory is developed in the first three chapters, using calculus and matrix algebra.

THREE

TOPICS IN CONSUMER BEHAVIOR

The basic theory of consumer behavior developed in Chap. 2 has been extended in many directions, and has been applied to cover optimal behavior for a variety of specific types of utility functions. Some of these extensions and special applications are discussed in this chapter.

A utility function that generates estimable linear expenditure functions is discussed in Sec. 3-1. Separable and additive utility functions are defined and their special properties considered in Sec. 3-2. The properties of homogeneous and homothetic utility functions are the subject of Sec. 3-3. Utility functions are defined in terms of prices and income in Sec. 3-4, and further relations between utility and demand functions are established. The theory of revealed preference whereby important theorems follow from observable consumer behavior is summarized in Sec. 3-5.

In Sec. 3-6 it is proved that a group of commodities may be treated as a single composite commodity if their prices always change in the same proportion. Measures for the "consumer's surplus" that is gained from the consumption of a commodity are discussed in Sec. 3-7. The theory of consumer behavior is extended to cover choice under uncertainty in Sec. 3-8. This analysis is applied to problems of insurance in Sec. 3-9.

3-1 A LINEAR EXPENDITURE SYSTEM

For many years economic theorists analyzed the optimal behavior of consumers and econometricians estimated consumer demand and expenditure relations, with little communication between the two. Theorists would provide examples that were of little aid for empirical work, and econometricians would estimate relations that had little connection with utility maximization. Fortunately, the gap between theory and empirical work has narrowed, and a number of theoretically sound examples that allow empirical estimation have been developed. An example is presented in this section.

Consider the utility function[1]

$$U = \alpha_1 \ln (q_1 - \gamma_1) + \alpha_2 \ln (q_2 - \gamma_2)$$

with the domain $q_1 > \gamma_1$, $q_2 > \gamma_2$. The γ's may be interpreted as minimum subsistence quantities and are positive. The α's are also positive. Apply the positive monotonic transformation $U' = U/(\alpha_1 + \alpha_2)$ to obtain

$$U' = \beta_1 \ln (q_1 - \gamma_1) + \beta_2 \ln (q_2 - \gamma_2)$$

The coefficients β_1 and β_2 ($\beta_1 + \beta_2 = 1$) are called "share" parameters.

Form the function

$$Z = \beta_1 \ln (q_1 - \gamma_1) + \beta_2 \ln (q_2 - \gamma_2) + \lambda (y - p_1 q_1 - p_2 q_2)$$

and set its first partial derivatives equal to zero:

$$\frac{\partial Z}{\partial q_1} = \frac{\beta_1}{q_1 - \gamma_1} - \lambda p_1 = 0$$

$$\frac{\partial Z}{\partial q_2} = \frac{\beta_2}{q_2 - \gamma_2} - \lambda p_2 = 0 \tag{3-1}$$

$$\frac{\partial Z}{\partial \lambda} = y - p_1 q_1 - p_2 q_2 = 0$$

The reader can verify that the second-order condition is satisfied. By evaluating (2-36) the reader can also establish that the marginal utility of income is decreasing in this example.

Solving (3-1) for optimal quantities gives the demand functions

$$q_1 = \gamma_1 + \frac{\beta_1}{p_1} (y - p_1 \gamma_1 - p_2 \gamma_2)$$

$$q_2 = \gamma_2 + \frac{\beta_2}{p_2} (y - p_1 \gamma_1 - p_2 \gamma_2) \tag{3-2}$$

Multiplying the first equation of (3-2) by p_1 and the second by p_2 gives the

[1] The function is known as the Klein-Rubin or Stone-Geary utility function. See L. R. Klein and H. Rubin, "A Constant-Utility Index of the Cost of Living," *Review of Economics Studies*, vol. 15 (1947–48), pp. 84–87; R. C. Geary, "A Note on a Constant Utility Index of the Cost of Living," *Review of Economic Studies*, vol. 18 (1949–50), pp. 65–66; R. Stone, "Linear Expenditure Systems and Demand Analysis: An Application to the Pattern of British Demand," *Economic Journal*, vol. 64 (1954), pp. 511–527.

expenditure functions

$$p_1q_1 = p_1\gamma_1 + \beta_1(y - p_1\gamma_1 - p_2\gamma_2)$$
$$p_2q_2 = p_2\gamma_2 + \beta_2(y - p_1\gamma_1 - p_2\gamma_2)$$

(3-3)

which are linear in income and prices, and thus suitable for linear regression analysis.

3-2 SEPARABLE AND ADDITIVE UTILITY FUNCTIONS

Utility functions have been assumed to be regular strictly quasi-concave, differentiable, and increasing. A few specific examples are considered in Chap. 2 and Sec. 3-1. The properties of utility functions that satisfy some additional general assumptions are considered here and in Sec. 3-3. Separability is the first assumption to be considered. A utility function is *strongly separable* in all of its arguments if it can be written as

$$U = F\left[\sum_{i=1}^{n} f_i(q_i)\right]$$

(3-4)

where F and the f_i are increasing functions. An example is provided by $U = \ln(q_1^\alpha + q_2^\beta + q_3^\gamma)$. A utility function is *strongly additive* if it can be written as

$$U = \sum_{i=1}^{n} f_i(q_i)$$

(3-5)

where the f_i are increasing. Additivity is a special case of separability. An example is provided by $U = q_1^\alpha + q_2^\beta + q_3^\gamma$. Any utility function that has a monotonic transformation which is additive may be treated as being additive for all theorems applicable to additive functions. The function $U = q_1^\alpha q_2$ is separable but does not appear to be additive. However, its log transformation $F(U) = \alpha \ln q_1 + \ln q_2$ is additive. Similarly, the antilog of $U = \ln(q_1^\alpha + q_2^\beta + q_3^\gamma)$ is strongly additive.

Differentiating (3-4) with respect to q_i and q_j and dividing one derivative by the other

$$\text{RCS} = \frac{F'f_i'}{F'f_j'} = \frac{f_i'}{f_j'}$$

(3-6)

It follows from (3-4) that in general the marginal utility of each commodity depends upon the quantities of all commodities. However, (3-6) shows that the RCS between Q_i and Q_j depends only upon the quantities q_i and q_j. Consequently, the assumption of strong separability allows pair-wise analyses that are not possible in the general case.

An additive utility function also has the property that all cross partials equal zero, i.e., $\partial^2 U/\partial q_i \partial q_j = 0$ for all $i \neq j$, and the regular strict quasi-concavity condition is $f_{11}f_2^2 + f_{22}f_1^2 < 0$ in the two-variable case.

A utility function is *weakly separable* if the variables can be partitioned in two (or more) groups $(q_1, \ldots, q_k)$ and $(q_{k+1}, \ldots, q_n)$ such that

$$U = F[f_1(q_1, \ldots, q_k) + f_2(q_{k+1}, \ldots, q_n)]$$

and *weakly additive* if

$$U = f_1(q_1, \ldots, q_k) + f_2(q_{k+1}, \ldots, q_n)$$

Here separability means that the RCSs for pairs of variables within the same group are unaffected by quantities for variables outside the group. Additivity means that cross partials for pairs of commodities in different groups are identically zero.

3-3 HOMOGENEOUS AND HOMOTHETIC UTILITY FUNCTIONS

A utility function is homogeneous of degree k if

$$f(tq_1, \ldots, tq_n) = t^k f(q_1, \ldots, q_n) \tag{3-7}$$

where k is a constant and t is any positive real number such that $(tq_1, \ldots, tq_n)$ is within the domain of the function. The partial derivatives of a function homogeneous of degree k are homogeneous of degree $k-1$. Differentiating (3-7) partially with respect to q_i using the function of a function rule (see Sec. A-2) on the left:

$$t f_i(tq_1, \ldots, tq_n) = t^k f_i(q_1, \ldots, q_n)$$

Thus, the RCS for Q_i and Q_j:

$$\frac{t f_i(tq_1, \ldots, tq_n)}{t f_j(tq_1, \ldots, tq_n)} = \frac{t^{k-1} f_i(q_1, \ldots, q_n)}{t^{k-1} f_j(q_1, \ldots, q_n)} = \frac{f_i(q_1, \ldots, q_n)}{f_j(q_1, \ldots, q_n)}$$

is invariant with respect to proportionate changes in consumption levels. It also follows that if a consumer is indifferent between two consumption bundles, she will also be indifferent between any other two bundles that use the same multiple of the first pair (see Exercise 3-2).

The indifference curves corresponding to two different utility functions are identical if one function is a monotonic increasing function of the other. Consequently, the properties exhibited by homogeneous functions are exhibited by all functions that are monotonic increasing functions of homogeneous functions. Utility functions within this broad class, which includes homogeneous functions, are called *homothetic*. If a utility function is homothetic, rates of commodity substitution will depend upon relative rather than absolute commodity quantities. Examination of RCS equations can indicate whether or not a specific utility function is homothetic. For example, $U = a - 1/q_1^a q_2$ is not a homogeneous function; however, it is homothetic since $f_1/f_2 = \alpha q_2/q_1$.

3-4 INDIRECT UTILITY FUNCTIONS AND DUALITY IN CONSUMPTION

Indirect Utility Functions

Let $v_i = p_i/y$. The budget constraint now may be written as

$$1 = \sum_{i=1}^{n} v_i q_i \tag{3-8}$$

Since optimal solutions are homogeneous of degree zero in income and prices, nothing essential is lost by this transformation to "normalized" prices. The utility function $U = f(q_1, \ldots, q_n)$ together with (3-8) gives the following first-order conditions for utility maximization:

$$f_i - \lambda v_i = 0 \quad i = 1, \ldots, n$$
$$1 - \sum_{i=1}^{n} v_i q_i = 0 \tag{3-9}$$

Ordinary demand functions are obtained by solving (3-9):

$$q_i = D_i(v_1, \ldots, v_n) \tag{3-10}$$

The *indirect utility function* $g(v_1, \ldots, v_n)$ is defined by

$$U = f[D_1(v_1, \ldots, v_n), \ldots, D_n(v_1, \ldots, v_n)] = g(v_1, \ldots, v_n) \tag{3-11}$$

It gives maximum utility as a function of normalized prices. The direct utility function describes preferences independent of market phenomena. The indirect utility function reflects a degree of optimization and market prices.

Applying the composite-function rule (Sec. A-2) to (3-11)

$$g_j = \sum_{i=1}^{n} f_i \frac{\partial q_i}{\partial v_j} = \lambda \sum_{i=1}^{n} v_i \frac{\partial q_i}{\partial v_j} \quad j = 1, \ldots, n \tag{3-12}$$

where the second equalities are based on (3-9). Partial differentiation of (3-8) with respect to v_j yields

$$\sum_{i=1}^{n} v_i \frac{\partial q_i}{\partial v_j} = -q_j \quad j = 1, \ldots, n$$

Thus, (3-12) implies

$$q_j = -\frac{g_j}{\lambda} \quad j = 1, \ldots, n \tag{3-13}$$

which is called *Roy's identity*. Optimal commodity demands are related to the derivatives of the indirect utility function and the optimal value of the Lagrange multiplier (i.e., the marginal utility of income). Substituting (3-13) into the last equation of (3-9) gives $\lambda = -\sum_{i=1}^{n} v_i g_i$ and

$$q_j = \frac{g_j}{\sum_{i=1}^{n} v_i g_i} \qquad j = 1, \ldots, n$$

to provide an alternative form for Roy's identity.

Now consider an optimization problem in which (3-11) is minimized subject to (3-8) with normalized prices as variables and quantities as parameters. Form the function[1]

$$Z = g(v_1, \ldots, v_n) + \mu \left(\sum_{i=1}^{n} v_i q_i - 1 \right)$$

and set its partials equal to zero:

$$\frac{\partial Z}{\partial v_i} = g_i - \mu q_i = 0 \qquad i = 1, \ldots, n$$

$$\frac{\partial Z}{\partial \mu} = \sum_{i=1}^{n} v_i q_i - 1 = 0$$

(3-14)

"Inverse demand functions" are obtained by solving (3-14) for the prices as functions of quantities:

$$v_i = V_i(q_1, \ldots, q_n) \tag{3-15}$$

Finally, let a direct utility function $h(q_1, \ldots, q_n)$ be defined by

$$U = g[V_1(q_1, \ldots, q_n), \ldots, V_n(q_1, \ldots, q_n)] = h(q_1, \ldots, q_n) \tag{3-16}$$

This provides a parallel to the direct problem in which quantities are variables and prices are parameters.

Duality Theorems

The relationships between the direct and indirect utility functions may be described by a set of duality theorems. The following illustrative theorems are provided without proof.

Theorem 1 Let f be a finite regular strictly quasi-concave increasing function which obeys the interior assumption.[2] The g determined by (3-11) is a finite regular strictly quasi-convex[3] decreasing function for positive prices.

---

[1] The reader may verify that the Lagrange multiplier is positive for this form of the function.

[2] The utility for a commodity combination in which one or more quantities is zero is lower than the utility for any combination in which all quantities are positive.

[3] A function $g(\mathbf{v})$ where $\mathbf{v}$ is an n-component vector is strictly quasi-convex if

$$g[\lambda \mathbf{v}^{(1)} + (1 - \lambda)\mathbf{v}^{(2)}] < \max [g(\mathbf{v}^{(1)}), g(\mathbf{v}^{(2)})]$$

for $0 < \lambda < 1$ for all pairs of distinct points $\mathbf{v}^{(1)}$ and $\mathbf{v}^{(2)}$ within its domain.

Theorem 2 Let g be a finite regular strictly quasi-convex decreasing function in positive prices. The h determined by (3-16) is a finite regular strictly quasi-concave increasing function.

Theorem 3 Under the above assumptions

$$h(q_1, \ldots, q_n) = g[V_1(q_1, \ldots, q_n), \ldots, V_n(q_1, \ldots, q_n)]$$

and $\quad g(v_1, \ldots, v_n) = h[D_1(v_1, \ldots, v_n), \ldots, D_n(v_1, \ldots, v_n)]$

The direct utility function determined by the indirect is the same as the direct utility function that determined the indirect.

Duality in consumption forges a much closer link between demand and utility functions for the purposes of empirical demand studies. It is sometimes possible to go from demand functions to the indirect utility function by using Roy's identity, and then to the corresponding direct utility function. Duality is also useful in comparative statics analysis. Homotheticity, separability, and additivity each have counterparts for the indirect utility function. Consequently, many theoretical analyses can be conducted in terms of either the direct or indirect utility function, whichever is more convenient.

An Example

Consider the example provided by the indirect utility function $g = a - v_1^2 v_2$. The quasi-convex indifference curves are shown in Fig. 3-1. These look very much like the quasi-concave indifference curves in commodity-space given in Fig. 2-1. Indifference curves are convex in both cases. There is a major difference, however, because in Fig. 3-1 utility increases as the consumer moves toward the origin. All points on the interior of the line segment AC yield lower utility levels than yielded by points A and C. The difference between quasi-concave and quasi-convex is reflected in the direc-

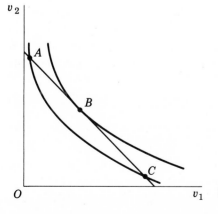

Figure 3-1

tion in which utility increases, not in the shape of the indifference curves. The point of tangency B gives minimum utility for the budget constraint pictured in Fig. 3-1.

Demand curves for the example may be derived using (3-13)

$$q_1 = \frac{2}{3v_1} \qquad q_2 = \frac{1}{3v_2} \tag{3-17}$$

By minimizing the appropriate function the reader may verify that the inverse demand functions are

$$v_1 = \frac{2}{3q_1} \qquad v_2 = \frac{1}{3q_2}$$

and that the corresponding direct utility function is

$$U = a - \left(\frac{2}{3q_1}\right)^2 \frac{1}{3q_2} = a - \frac{4}{27q_1^2 q_2} \tag{3-18}$$

which is a strictly quasi-concave increasing function.

It was noted in past examples that the utility function $U^* = q_1^2 q_2$ generates the demand functions (3-17). Consequently, (3-18) must be a monotonic transformation of this function. The transformation in this case is

$$U = a + \frac{4}{27}\left(-\frac{1}{U^*}\right)$$

Finally, note that

$$U = a - \frac{4}{27(2/3v_1)^2(1/3v_2)} = a - v_1^2 v_2$$

which establishes duality.

Utility-Expenditure Duality

Consider the minimization of the expenditures necessary to achieve a specified utility level. The solution for q_i yields the compensated demand functions (see Sec. 2-3). If the solutions for q_i are substituted in $\sum_{i=1}^{n} p_i q_i$ one obtains the expenditure function $E(p_1, \ldots, p_n, U^0)$, which gives the minimum expenditure necessary to achieve a given utility level. It is easy to show that E is homogeneous of degree one in prices and monotone increasing in U^0. It can also be shown that the expenditure function corresponding to a regular strictly quasi-concave utility function admitting no satiation is concave in prices. Finally, Shephard's lemma states that the partial derivative of E with respect to the ith price is the ith compensated demand function. This can be shown as follows. Denote the ith compensated demand function by $q_i = q_i(p_1, \ldots, p_n, U^0)$. Then

$$E(p_1, \ldots, p_n, U^0) = \sum_{i=1}^{n} p_i q_i(p_1, \ldots, p_n, U^0)$$

and
$$\frac{\partial E}{\partial p_i} = q_i(p_1, \ldots, p_n, U^0) + \sum_{j=1}^{n} p_j \frac{\partial q_j(p_1, \ldots, p_n, U^0)}{\partial p_i}$$

But the compensated demands are obtained by minimizing expenditures for a given utility level U^0; hence the change in total expenditures that is due to a small change in a price is zero. It follows that the second term above is zero and $\partial E/\partial p_i = q_i(p_1, \ldots, p_n, U^0)$.

For the example that generated (3-17) and (3-18) the compensated demand functions are

$$q_1 = \frac{2^{1/3} p_2^{1/3} (U^0)^{1/3}}{p_1^{1/3}} \qquad q_2 = \frac{p_1^{2/3} (U^0)^{1/3}}{2^{2/3} p_2^{2/3}}$$

The expenditure function is

$$E = p_1^{2/3} p_2^{1/3} (U^0)^{1/3} (2^{1/3} + 2^{-2/3})$$

and Shepherd's lemma is easily verified by differentiating E partially with respect to p_1 and p_2 respectively.

The duality between utility and expenditure functions is formally identical to the duality between production and cost functions. A more complete explanation is contained in Sec. 5-4.

3-5 THE THEORY OF REVEALED PREFERENCE

It is assumed in previous sections that the consumer possesses a utility function. The theory of revealed preference allows prediction of the consumer's behavior without specification of an explicit utility function, provided that she conforms to some simple axioms. In addition, the existence and nature of her utility function can be deduced from her observed choices among commodity bundles.

Assume that there are n commodities. A particular set of prices $p_1^0, p_2^0, \ldots, p_n^0$ is denoted by $\mathbf{p}^0$, and the corresponding quantities bought by the consumer by $\mathbf{q}^0$. The consumer's total expenditures are given by $\mathbf{p}^0\mathbf{q}^0$ which is defined as the sum $\sum_{i=1}^{n} p_i^0 q_i^0$.

Consider an alternative batch of commodities $\mathbf{q}^1$ that could have been purchased by the consumer but was not. The total cost of $\mathbf{q}^1$ at prices $\mathbf{p}^0$ must be no greater than the total cost of $\mathbf{q}^0$:

$$\mathbf{p}^0\mathbf{q}^1 \leqq \mathbf{p}^0\mathbf{q}^0 \tag{3-19}$$

Since $\mathbf{q}^0$ is at least as expensive a combination of commodities as $\mathbf{q}^1$, and since the consumer refused to choose combination $\mathbf{q}^1, \mathbf{q}^0$ is "revealed" to be preferred to $\mathbf{q}^1$.

Weak Axiom of Revealed Preference

If $\mathbf{q}^0$ is revealed to be preferred to $\mathbf{q}^1$, the latter must never be revealed to be preferred to $\mathbf{q}^0$.

The only way in which q^1 can be revealed to be preferred to q^0 is to have the consumer purchase the combination q^1 in some price situation in which he could also afford to buy q^0. In other words, q^1 is revealed to be preferred if

$$p^1 q^0 \leqq p^1 q^1 \qquad (3\text{-}20)$$

The axiom states that (3-20) can never hold if (3-19) does. Consequently (3-19) implies the opposite of (3-20) or

$$p^0 q^1 \leqq p^0 q^0 \quad \text{implies that} \quad p^1 q^0 > p^1 q^1 \qquad (3\text{-}21)$$

Strong Axiom of Revealed Preference

If q^0 is revealed to be preferred to q^1, which is revealed to be preferred to $q^2, \ldots,$ which is revealed to be preferred to q^k, q^k must never be revealed to be preferred to q^0. This axiom ensures the transitivity of revealed preferences, but is stronger than the usual transitivity condition.

At the beginning of this chapter the cardinal approach to utility theory was rejected on the grounds that there is no reason to assume that the consumer possesses a cardinal measure of utility. By the same token one could question whether she even possesses an indifference map. It can fortunately be proved that a consumer who always conforms to the above axioms must possess an indifference map. Her indifference map could be constructed with a high degree of accuracy (the "true" indifference map could be approximated as closely as is desired) by confronting her with various appropriately chosen price sets and observing her purchases.[1] If the consumer does not conform to the axioms, she is said to be "irrational." Her inconsistent actions mean that she does not possess an indifference map, and the shape of her utility function cannot be determined by observing her behavior.

The meaning of the Weak axiom is illustrated in Fig. 3-2 for the two-commodity case. Assume that when prices were given by the lines designated by p^0 the consumer purchased commodity combination q^0, and when prices were given by p^1 she purchased q^1. In both of the cases shown in Fig. 3-2 she could have purchased q^1 at the p^0 prices since q^1 lies below the line p^0. Given this choice, the Weak axiom states that q^0 must be unobtainable when she purchases q^1; that is, q^0 must lie above the line p^1. The Weak axiom is satisfied by the behavior shown in Fig. 3-2a. It is violated by the behavior shown in Fig. 3-2b. In this case it is not possible to find convex indifference curves with the property that one curve is tangent to p^0 at q^0 and another is tangent to p^1 at q^1.

---

[1] The proof of this theorem is somewhat difficult and is not reproduced here. See H. S. Houthakker, "Revealed Preference and the Utility Function," *Economica*, n.s., vol. 17 (May, 1950), pp. 159–174.

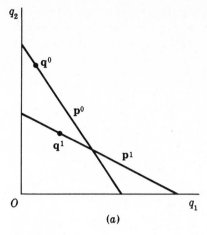

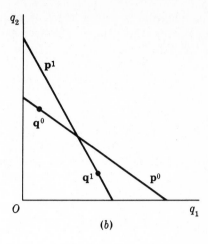

Figure 3-2

The Substitution Effect

It can be proved from revealed-preference theory that the substitution effect is negative.[1] Assume that the consumer is forced to move along a given indifference hypersurface in n dimensions. When prices are given by $\mathbf{p}^0$, she purchases the batch $\mathbf{q}^0$ rather than the batch $\mathbf{q}^1$ which lies on the same indifference hypersurface. Since she is indifferent between $\mathbf{q}^0$ and $\mathbf{q}^1$ and yet purchases $\mathbf{q}^0$, the latter combination must not be more expensive than the former:

$$\mathbf{p}^0\mathbf{q}^0 \leqq \mathbf{p}^0\mathbf{q}^1 \tag{3-22}$$

The combination $\mathbf{q}^1$ is purchased at prices $\mathbf{p}^1$. This implies that $\mathbf{q}^0$ must not be cheaper at the $\mathbf{p}^1$ prices than $\mathbf{q}^1$:

$$\mathbf{p}^1\mathbf{q}^1 \leqq \mathbf{p}^1\mathbf{q}^0 \tag{3-23}$$

Moving the right-hand terms in (3-22) and (3-23) to the left,[2]

$$\mathbf{p}^0\mathbf{q}^0 - \mathbf{p}^0\mathbf{q}^1 = \mathbf{p}^0(\mathbf{q}^0 - \mathbf{q}^1) = -\mathbf{p}^0(\mathbf{q}^1 - \mathbf{q}^0) \leqq 0 \tag{3-24}$$

$$\mathbf{p}^1\mathbf{q}^1 - \mathbf{p}^1\mathbf{q}^0 = \mathbf{p}^1(\mathbf{q}^1 - \mathbf{q}^0) \leqq 0 \tag{3-25}$$

Adding together (3-24) and (3-25),

$$-\mathbf{p}^0(\mathbf{q}^1 - \mathbf{q}^0) + \mathbf{p}^1(\mathbf{q}^1 - \mathbf{q}^0) = (\mathbf{p}^1 - \mathbf{p}^0)(\mathbf{q}^1 - \mathbf{q}^0) \leqq 0 \tag{3-26}$$

---

[1] This is only one of several theorems that can be deduced from the theory. Others are (1) the homogeneity of the demand functions of zero degree in prices and incomes (Sec. 2-3), and (2) the equality of the cross-substitution effects (Sec. 2-5). See P. A. Samuelson, *Foundations of Economic Analysis* (Cambridge, Mass.: Harvard University Press, 1948), pp. 111–112; and J. R. Hicks, *A Revision of Demand Theory* (Oxford: Clarendon Press, 1956), p. 127.

[2] The term $\mathbf{q}^0 - \mathbf{q}^1$ denotes the n differences $q_1^0 - q_1^1, q_2^0 - q_2^1, \ldots, q_n^0 - q_n^1$.

This inequality asserts that the sum of all quantity changes multiplied by the corresponding price changes is nonpositive if the consumer moves along a given indifference curve. Assume now that only the price of the first commodity changes, all other prices remaining constant. Then (3-26) reduces to

$$(p_1^1 - p_1^0)(q_1^1 - q_1^0) < 0 \tag{3-27}$$

The strict inequality must hold in (3-27) by the assumption that the price change is nonzero and that q_1^1 and q_1^0 are distinct, i.e., that price is a single-valued function of demand. If the price increases, the quantity bought must decrease and vice versa. This proves that the substitution effect is negative.

3-6 COMPOSITE COMMODITIES

The *composite commodity theorem* states that if the prices for a group of m ($< n$) commodities always change in the same proportion in n-commodity-space, the aggregate demand for the m commodities behaves as if they were a single commodity.[1] The theorem allows a substantial simplification in many analyses through a reduction in the number of goods considered. For example, a two-commodity analysis in which the price of only one good changes is representative of an n-commodity analysis in which the price of only one good changes.

An alternative form for the Slutsky equation (2-37) is obtained by multiplying both sides by $p_i p_j$:

$$p_i p_j \frac{\partial q_i}{\partial p_j} = p_i p_j S_{ij} - p_i p_j q_j \left(\frac{\partial q_i}{\partial y}\right)_{\text{prices=const}} \tag{3-28}$$

Since
$$p_i p_j \frac{\partial q_i}{\partial p_j} = p_i q_i \left(\frac{p_j}{q_i} \frac{\partial q_i}{\partial p_j}\right) = p_i q_i \varepsilon_{ij}$$

where ε_{ij} is the elasticity of demand for Q_i with respect to p_j, the left-hand side of (3-28) expresses the value of the change in demand for commodity i from a given proportionate change in p_j.

Assume that the prices of all commodities in the composite group rise in the same proportion. The value of the demand increment is obtained by summing (3-28):

$$\sum_{i=1}^{m} \sum_{j=1}^{m} p_i p_j \frac{\partial q_i}{\partial p_j} = \sum_{i=1}^{m} \sum_{j=1}^{m} p_i p_j S_{ij} - \sum_{j=1}^{m} p_j q_j \sum_{i=1}^{m} p_i \left(\frac{\partial q_i}{\partial y}\right)_{\text{prices=const}} \tag{3-29}$$

This has the same form as (3-28), and it can be established that the substitution term of (3-29) is negative. From the determinantal conditions cor-

[1] This discussion follows J. R. Hicks, *Value and Capital* (2d ed., Oxford: Clarendon Press, 1946), pp. 312–313.

responding to strict quasi-concavity given in Sec. A-3 it follows that[1]

$$\sum_{j=1}^{m} \sum_{i=1}^{m} k_i k_j \frac{\mathcal{D}_{ij}}{\mathcal{D}} < 0$$

for all k_i and k_j not all zero where $\mathcal{D}$ is the relevant bordered Hessian and the $\mathcal{D}_{ij}$ are its cofactors. Remember that $S_{ij} = \mathcal{D}_{ji}\lambda/\mathcal{D}$. Let $k_i = p_i$ and $k_j = \lambda p_j$ so that

$$\sum_{j=1}^{m} \sum_{i=1}^{m} p_i p_j S_{ij} < 0$$

which establishes that the substitution term of (3-29) is negative.

From (2-43) $\sum_{i=1}^{n} p_j S_{ij} = 0$, and it follows that

$$\sum_{j=1}^{m} \sum_{i=m+1}^{n} p_j p_i S_{ij} > 0$$

The aggregate of the commodities (there may only be one) outside the composite group behaves as a substitute, given proportionate changes for the prices of the composite commodity.

3-7 CONSUMER'S SURPLUS

A consumer normally pays less for a commodity than the maximum amount that she would pay rather than forego its consumption. Several measures of such consumer's surplus have been proposed. Three are considered here. Attention is limited to a consideration of the good under investigation and a composite commodity called "money," with consumption quantities of q and M respectively. Let the distance OA in Fig. 3-3a represent the consumer's income. She achieves a tangency solution at point D on indifference curve I_2. If she were unable to consume Q, she would be at A on the lower indifference curve I_1. She would have to be given an income increment of AB dollars to restore her to indifference curve I_2. This increment, called *compensating income variation*, is denoted by c, and provides a measure of consumer's surplus.

At the given prices the consumer would be willing to forego AC dollars of income rather than lose her opportunity to consume good Q. With income OC her consumption is at E, which is on the same indifference curve as A. The amount corresponding to AC is called *equivalent income variation*, is denoted by e, and provides an alternative measure of consumer's surplus. A third measure is provided by the demand curve in Fig. 3-4 for the price-quantity combination $p_0 q_0$. It equals the area ABp_0, which is the difference between the area lying under the demand curve ($OABq_0$) and the consumer's expenditure ($Op_0 Bq_0$), and is denoted by s.

---

[1] See Hicks, *loc. cit.*

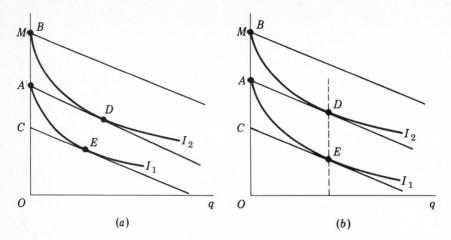

Figure 3-3

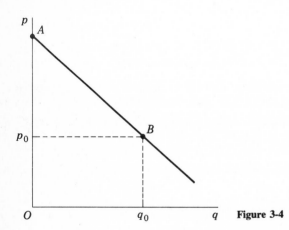

Figure 3-4

It can be shown that $c \geqq s \geqq e$.[†] The strict inequalities hold for the case pictured in Fig. 3-3a as a consequence of the income effect (Sec. 2-5). If the consumer were to pay more to consume the good, her demand would decline because of her lower effective income, and the area under the demand curve would exceed the amount that she would pay rather than forego consumption of the good.[1] Figure 3-3b depicts a case in which the income effect is zero throughout. A perpendicular such as the line through D and E connects points with the same RCS. The indifference curves are "parallel" with a

---

[†] See R. C. Willig, "Consumer's Surplus without Apology," *American Economic Review*, vol. 66 (September, 1976), pp. 589–597.

[1] Inferior goods (Sec. 2-5) are ignored in this discussion.

constant vertical distance between a pair of indifference curves. In this case $AB = AC$, and the three measures of consumer's surplus are the same.

Duality theory (see Sec. 3-4) can be used to determine incremental consumer's surplus when the price of a commodity changes. Let the initial prices of n commodities be $p_1^0, \ldots, p_n^0$ and let the consumer's income be y^0. Her indirect utility function is $g(v_1^0, \ldots, v_n^0) \equiv U^0$ where $v_i^0 = p_i^0/y_i^0$ $i = 1, \ldots, n$, and her expenditure function is $E(p_1^0, \ldots, p_n^0, U^0) = y^0$. If p_1^0 changes to p_1, $E(p_1, p_2^0, \ldots, p_n^0, U^0) = y^0 + c$ where c is compensating variation and

$$c = E(p_1, p_2^0, \ldots, p_n^0, U^0) - E(p_1^0, \ldots, p_n^0, U^0)$$

Defining $p_1 = p_1^0 + \Delta p_1$ and using the definition of a partial derivative,

$$c = \frac{\partial E(p_1^0 + \theta \Delta p_1, p_2^0, \ldots, p_n^0, U^0)}{\partial p_1} \Delta p_1$$

for some $0 < \theta < 1$. By Shephard's lemma the partial derivative $\partial E/\partial p_1$ is the compensated demand function $q_1(p_1^0 + \theta \Delta p_1, p_2^0, \ldots, p_n^0, U^0)$. It follows from the mean value theorem for integrals (see Sec. A-4) that

$$c = \int_{p_1^0}^{p_1} q_1(p_1^0, \ldots, p_n^0, U^0) \, dp_1 \tag{3-30}$$

Incremental consumer surplus can thus be approximated by the area between the two prices to the left of the compensated demand function. In practice, the distinction between the ordinary and compensated demand functions is often neglected. The corresponding area in Fig. 3-4 would then be p_0pCB. If p is the price at which demand equals zero, the incremental surplus (3-30) coincides with the triangle ABp_0, which may also be written as

$$c = \int_0^{q_0} \psi(q) \, dq - p_0 q_0$$

where $\psi(q)$ is the inverse demand function and q_0 the quantity demanded at p_0.

Consider an example in which the utility function is $U = q^{0.5} + 2M$. The reader may verify that the demand curve is given by $q = 1/(16p)^2$, and the inverse demand curve by $p = 1/(4\sqrt{q})$. If $p = 0.05$, $q = 25$, and consumer's surplus is

$$s = \int_0^{25} \frac{1}{4\sqrt{q}} \, dq - pq = 2.50 - 1.25 = 1.25$$

Evaluating the income effect from (2-31),

$$\frac{\partial q}{\partial y} = \frac{f_{12} - pf_{22}}{\mathscr{D}}$$

where the subscript 1 denotes Q, the subscript 2 denotes money, and p is the price of Q. Since the second derivatives of the utility function are independent of p, a zero income effect throughout requires that $f_{12} = f_{22} = 0$

throughout. Since the utility function also satisfies the strict quasi-concavity condition (2-5), it follows that $f_{11} < 0$. The marginal utility of Q is declining.

It follows that the utility function must be strongly additive with the form

$$U = f(q) + kM$$

where k is a constant marginal utility of money. The Marshallian concept of the constant marginal utility of money is equivalent to the more modern concept of a zero-income effect. The first-order conditions for utility maximization reveal that the corresponding inverse demand curve for Q is $p = f'(q)/k$.

Consumer's surplus need not be applied on an all-or-none basis. Incremental analyses are common. In fact, they are essential for inverse demand functions such as $p = q^{-a}$ which are undefined at $q = 0$. For illustration, consider the gain of consumer's surplus that would occur if price were decreased from p_0 to p_1 with a corresponding quantity increment from q_0 to q_1. The change of consumer's surplus is

$$\Delta s = \int_{q_0}^{q_1} \psi(q) \, dq - (p_1 q_1 - p_0 q_0)$$

Let $\psi(q) = q^{-0.5}$ with $p_0 = 0.25$, $p_1 = 0.20$. The reader may verify that $\Delta s = 1$.

3-8 THE PROBLEM OF CHOICE IN SITUATIONS INVOLVING RISK

The traditional theory of consumer behavior does not include an analysis of uncertain situations. Von Neumann and Morgenstern showed that under some circumstances it is possible to construct a set of numbers for a particular consumer that can be used to predict her choices in uncertain situations. Great controversy has centered around the question of whether the resulting utility index is ordinal or cardinal. It will be shown that von Neumann–Morgenstern utilities possess at least some cardinal properties.

The previous analysis is unrealistic in the sense that it assumes that particular actions on the part of the consumer are followed by particular, determinate consequences which are knowable in advance. All automobiles of the same model and produced in the same factory do not always have the same performance characteristics. As a result of random accidents in the production process some substandard automobiles are occasionally produced and sold. The consumer has no way of knowing ahead of time whether the particular automobile which she purchases is of standard quality or not. Let A represent the situation in which the consumer possesses a satisfactory automobile, B a situation in which she possesses no automobile, and C one in which she possesses a substandard automobile. Assume that the consumer prefers A to B and B to C.† Present her with a choice between two alternatives: (1) She can maintain the status quo and have no car at all. This is a choice with certain outcome; i.e., the probability of the outcome equals unity. (2) She can obtain a lottery ticket with a chance of winning either a satisfactory automobile (alternative A) or an unsatisfactory one (alternative C). The consumer may prefer to retain her income (or money) with certainty, or she may prefer the lottery ticket with dubious outcome, or she may be indifferent between them. Her decision will depend upon the chances of winning or losing in this particular lottery. If the probability of C is very high, she might prefer to retain her money with certainty; if the probability of A is very high, she might prefer the lottery ticket. The triplet of numbers (P, A, B) is used to denote a lottery offering outcome A with probability $0 < P < 1$, and outcome B with probability $1 - P$.

The Axioms

It is possible to construct a utility index which can be used to predict choice in uncertain situations if the consumer conforms to the following five axioms:

Complete-ordering axiom For the two alternatives A and B one of the following must be true: the consumer prefers A to B, she prefers B to A, or she is indifferent between them. The consumer's evaluation of alternatives is transitive: if she prefers A to B and B to C, she prefers A to C.

Continuity axiom Assume that A is preferred to B and B to C. The axiom asserts that there exists some probability P, $0 < P < 1$, such that the consumer is indifferent between outcome B with certainty and a lottery ticket (P, A, C).

Independence axiom Assume that the consumer is indifferent between A and B and that C is any outcome whatever. If one lottery ticket L_1 offers outcomes A and C with probabilities P and $1 - P$ respectively and another L_2 the outcomes B and C with the same probabilities P and $1 - P$, the consumer is indifferent between the two lottery tickets. Similarly, if she prefers A to B, she will prefer L_1 to L_2.

Unequal-probability axiom Assume that the consumer prefers A to B. Let $L_1 = (P_1, A, B)$ and $L_2 = (P_2, A, B)$. The consumer will prefer L_2 to L_1 if and only if $P_2 > P_1$.

Compound-lottery axiom Let $L_1 = (P_1, A, B)$, and $L_2 = (P_2, L_3, L_4)$, where $L_3 = (P_3, A, B)$ and $L_4 = (P_4, A, B)$, be a compound lottery in which the prizes are

---

† Not having a car is assumed preferable to owning a substandard one because of the nuisance and expense involved in its upkeep.

lottery tickets. L_2 is equivalent to L_1 if $P_1 = P_2 P_3 + (1 - P_2) P_4$. Given L_2 the probability of obtaining L_3 is P_2. Consequently, the probability of obtaining A through L_2 is $P_2 P_3$. Similarly, the probability of obtaining L_4 is $(1 - P_2)$, and the probability of obtaining A through L_4 is $(1 - P_2) P_4$. The probability of obtaining A with L_2 is the sum of the two probabilities. The consumer evaluates lottery tickets only in terms of the probabilities of obtaining the prizes, and not in terms of how many times she is exposed to a chance mechanism.

These axioms are very general, and it may be difficult to object to them on the grounds that they place unreasonable restrictions upon the consumer's behavior. However, they rule out some types of plausible behavior. Consider a person who derives satisfaction from the sheer act of gambling. It is conceivable that there exists no P other than $P = 1$ or $P = 0$ for such a person, so that she is indifferent between outcome B with certainty and the uncertain prospect consisting of A and C: she will always prefer the gamble. If she has a fear of gambling, she may always prefer the "sure thing" to the dubious prospect. This type of behavior is ruled out by the continuity axiom and the compound lottery axiom.

The axioms have been developed for situations in which there are only two outcomes. Assuming that the pair-wise axioms hold, analysis is easily extended to cases with any number of outcomes. Let

$$L = (P_1, \ldots, P_n, A_1, \ldots, A_n)$$

denote a lottery with n outcomes where $0 < P_i < 1$ is the probability of outcome A_i and $\sum_{i=1}^{n} P_i = 1$.

Expected Utility

Assume that a utility index exists which conforms to the five axioms. The *expected utility* for the two-outcome lottery $L = (P, A, B)$ is

$$E[U(L)] = PU(A) + (1 - P)U(B) \tag{3-31}$$

Consider the lotteries $L_1 = (P_1, A_1, A_2)$ and $L_2 = (P_2, A_3, A_4)$. An expected utility theorem states that if L_1 is prefered to L_2, $E[U(L_1)] > E[U(L_2)]$. The significance of this theorem is that uncertain situations can be analyzed in terms of the maximization of expected utility.

The proof of the theorem is straightforward. Select outcomes such that B, the best, is preferred to all other outcomes under consideration, and W, the worst, is inferior to all other outcomes under consideration. By the continuity axiom Q_i's exist such that A_i is indifferent to (Q_i, B, W) $(i = 1, \ldots, 4)$. Thus L_1 and L_2 are equivalent to, i.e., have the same expected utilities as, the lotteries (Z_1, B, W) and (Z_2, B, W) respectively where $Z_1 = P_1 Q_1 + (1 - P_1) Q_2$ and $Z_2 = P_2 Q_3 + (1 - P_2) Q_4$. By assumption L_1 is preferred to L_2, and it follows from the unequal probability axiom that $Z_1 > Z_2$. Since origin and unit of measure are arbitrary for utility indexes, let $U(B) = 1$ and $U(W) = 0$. Now, $E[U(L_1)] = Z_1$ and $E[U(L_2)] = Z_2$, establishing the theorem.

In Sec. 2-2 it is established that any positive monotonic transformation of the utility function leaves the ranking of certain outcomes unchanged. This result does not hold for the ranking of uncertain outcomes in terms of expected utility. As an example consider the utility numbers

$$U(A_1) = 25 \qquad U(A_2) = 64 \qquad U(A_3) = 36 \qquad U(A_4) = 49$$

The lottery $L_1 = (0.5, A_1, A_2)$ is preferred to $L_2 = (0.4, A_3, A_4)$ since $E[U(L_1)] = 44.5 > E[U(L_2)] = 43.8$. Perform the monotonic transformation $V = U^{0.5}$. Now, L_2 is preferred to L_1 since $E[V(L_1)] = 6.5 < E[V(L_2)] = 6.6$.

Expected utility rankings are invariant under increasing linear transformations. Assume that $L_1 = (P_1, A_1, B_1)$ is preferred to $L_2 = (P_2, A_2, B_2)$ so that

$$E[U(L_1)] = P_1 U(A_1) + (1 - P_1)U(B_1) > P_2 U(A_2) + (1 - P_2)U(B_2) = E[U(L_2)]$$

Now let $V = a + bU$ where a and b are constants with $b > 0$. The expected utility of L_1 for the index V is simply a linear transformation of the expected utility for the index U:

$$P_1[a + bU(A_1)] + (1 - P_1)[a + bU(B_1)] = a + bE[U(L_1)]$$

and clearly,

$$a + bE[U(L_1)] > a + bE[U(L_2)]$$

establishing invariance under a linear transformation.

The expected utility formula may be used to construct utility numbers for a person who conforms to the von Neumann–Morgenstern axioms. Arbitrarily assign utility numbers to two certain outcomes A_1 and A_2. For example, if A_2 is preferred to A_1, let $U(A_1) = 20$ and $U(A_2) = 1000$. Now consider the outcome A_3. If A_3 lies between A_1 and A_2 in the preference ranking, ask the consumer for a value of P such that she is indifferent between A_3 and (P, A_1, A_2). If $P = 0.8$, solve

$$U(A_3) = 0.8U(A_1) + 0.2U(A_2) = 216$$

If A_4 is preferred to all three alternatives, its utility can be obtained by asking the consumer for a value of P such that she is indifferent between A_2 and (P, A_1, A_4). If $P = 0.6$, solve

$$1000 = (0.6)(20) + 0.4U(A_4)$$

for $U(A_4) = 2470$. The process can be continued indefinitely, and will not lead to contradictory results as long as the five axioms are obeyed.

The utilities in the von Neumann–Morgenstern analysis are cardinal in a restricted sense. They are derived from the consumer's risk behavior and are valid for predicting her choices as long as she maximizes expected utility. They are derived by presenting her with mutually exclusive choices; therefore, it is meaningless to attempt to infer from the utility of event A and the utility of event B the utility of the joint event A and B. Von Neumann–Morgenstern utilities possess some, but not all, the properties of cardinal measures. If $U(A) = kU(B)$, it is not meaningful to assert that the consumer prefers A k times as much as B. Utility ratios are not invariant under linear transformations. In general,

$$\frac{U(A)}{U(B)} \neq \frac{a + bU(A)}{a + bU(B)}$$

However, the utility numbers provide an *interval* scale, and differences between them are meaningful. This follows from the fact that the relative magnitudes of differences between utility numbers are invariant with respect to linear transformations:

$$V(A) - V(B) = b[U(A) - U(B)]$$

In contrast to the traditional theory of the consumer, the sign of the rate of change of marginal utility (the second derivative of the utility function) is relevant, since it is invariant with respect to linear transformations. This is particularly important in Sec. 3-9. Such comparisons do not imply, however, that the consumer would prefer to have C over B to B over A, since the chosen alternative must have the highest utility number.

Interpersonal comparisons of utility are still impossible. However, the construction of von Neumann–Morgenstern utilities does permit: (1) the complete ranking of alternatives in situations characterized by certainty, (2) the comparison of utility differences by virtue of the above cardinal property, and (3) the calculation of expected utilities, thus making it possible to deal with the consumer's behavior under conditions of uncertainty.

3-9 BEHAVIOR UNDER UNCERTAINTY

The utility function is treated in very general terms in Sec. 3-8. It is now assumed that the utility function: (1) has the single argument "wealth" measured in monetary units, (2) is strictly increasing, and (3) is continuous with continuous first- and second-order derivatives.

Attitudes toward Risk

The expected value of the lottery (P, W_1, W_2), where the W_i are different wealth levels, is the sum of the outcomes, each multiplied by its probability of occurrence

$$E[W] = PW_1 + (1 - P)W_2$$

A person is *risk neutral* relative to a lottery if the utility of the expected value of the lottery equals the expected utility of the lottery, i.e., if

$$U[PW_1 + (1 - P)W_2] = PU(W_1) + (1 - P)U(W_2) \tag{3-32}$$

Such a person is only interested in expected values and is totally oblivious to risk. She is indifferent between the lotteries (0.5; 1; 1,000,000) and (0.5; 500,000; 500,001). If she is risk neutral toward all lotteries, (3-32) implies that she has a linear utility function of the form $U = \alpha + \beta W$ with $\beta > 0$. The utility analysis developed for certain situations is applicable for risk-neutral persons facing uncertainty. All that is necessary is to replace certain values with expected values.

A person is a *risk averter* relative to a lottery if the utility of its expected value is greater than the expected value of its utility:

$$U[PW_1 + (1 - P)W_2] > PU(W_1) + (1 - P)U(W_2) \tag{3-33}$$

Such a person prefers a certain outcome to an uncertain one with the same expected value. If (3-33) holds for all $0 < P < 1$ and all W_1 and W_2 within the domain of the utility function, the utility function is strictly concave over its domain since (3-33) is identical to the definition of strict concavity given in Sec. A-2. If $d^2U/dW^2 < 0$, the utility function is strictly concave and the consumer is a risk averter.

Introspection and observed behavior suggest that most people are risk averse in most of their dealings. Nonetheless, the analysis can cover equally well a person who prefers uncertain outcomes. A person is a *risk lover* relative to a lottery if the utility of its expected value is less than its expected utility. In this case the inequality of (3-33) is reversed. A risk lover will always take a fair bet (i.e., one in which the expected value of the gain equals the expected value of the loss). Following the argument used for a risk averter, if $d^2U/dW^2 > 0$, the utility function is strictly convex and the consumer is a risk lover.

It is possible for a person to be a risk averter in some situations and a risk lover in others. Consider, for example, a low-income person who is risk averse in almost all of her dealings except that she will pay a dollar for a lottery ticket with an expected value of 50 cents—for example, one chance in a million to win 500,000 dollars. Her behavior might appear inconsistent, but it would be consistent if her utility function had the shape depicted in Fig. 3-5. W_1 is her wealth position if she loses the lottery, and W_2 is her position if she wins. Her utility function is strictly concave for $0 \le W \le W_0$ and strictly convex for $W > W_0$. Consequently, she is risk averse for all uncertain situations in which the best outcome is no greater than W_0. Nearly all of her observed behavior is in this range. She is willing to pay a premium for a small chance to leave her low-income situation behind.

The sign of the second derivative of the utility function provides an indication of the consumer's attitude, but since its magnitude is not invariant under a linear transformation, it cannot be used to indicate the level of risk

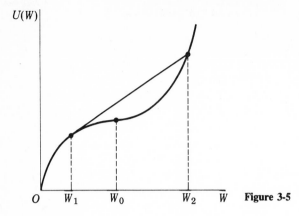

Figure 3-5

aversion or preference. A measure of *absolute risk aversion,*[1] r, is provided by the ratio of the second and first derivatives.

$$r = -\frac{U''(W)}{U'(W)} = -\frac{d \ln U'(W)}{dW} \tag{3-34}$$

This measure is positive, negative, or zero as the consumer averts, prefers, or is neutral toward risk. Let $V = a + bU$ with $b > 0$:

$$r = -\frac{V''(W)}{V'(W)} = -\frac{bU''(W)}{bU'(W)} = -\frac{U''(W)}{U'(W)}$$

which establishes the desired invariance.

Consider a quadratic utility function, $U = W - \alpha W^2$ with $\alpha > 0$ and the domain $0 < W < 1/(2\alpha)$. It describes risk-averse behavior since $U'' = -2\alpha < 0$. Evaluating (3-34)

$$r = \frac{2\alpha}{1 - 2\alpha W}$$

with $dr/dW = 4\alpha^2/(1 - 2\alpha W)^2 > 0$. Here risk aversion increases with wealth. Most often one would assume that the opposite is the case. The utility function $U = \ln(W + \alpha)$ with $\alpha > 0$ exhibits decreasing risk aversion.

Consider the class of utility functions that exhibit constant risk aversion. Let $r = c$, and rewrite (3-34) as

$$\frac{d \ln U'(W)}{dW} = -c$$

Integrating with respect to W

$$\ln U'(W) = -cW + k_1$$

---

[1] The product rW provides a measure of *relative risk aversion.*

where k_1 is the constant of integration. Take the antilog,

$$U'(W) = e^{k_1} e^{-cW}$$

and integrate again

$$U(W) = e^{k_1} \int e^{-cW} dW = -\frac{e^{k_1}}{c} e^{-cW} + k_2$$

where k_2 is another constant of integration. Finally, perform a linear transformation with $a = -(k_2 c)/e^{-k_1}$ and $b = c/e^{k_1}$ so that

$$V(W) = -e^{-cW}$$

is a general form for a utility function with constant absolute risk aversion.

Risk and Insurance

Assume that the consumer faces the risk that she will suffer a loss of A dollars with probability P if there is a fire. This is equivalent to the lottery $(P, W_0 - A, W_0)$ where W_0 is her initial wealth position. If she pays an insurance company R dollars, they will give her A dollars if the fire takes place. Thus, she is assured of a wealth of $W_0 - R$ whether or not there is a fire. The maximum amount that she is willing to pay for insurance can be obtained by solving

$$U(W_0 - R) = PU(W_0 - A) + (1 - P)U(W_0)$$

for R. The expected value of the loss from fire is PA. If the consumer is risk averse, the solution value R is greater than PA, and she will buy insurance if its price is no greater than R. If the price is greater than R, she will not buy insurance despite her risk aversion. Since insurance companies desire to meet expenses and earn a profit, they will try to keep the price of insurance greater than PA. In a perfect market all risk lovers, all risk neutrals, and some risk averters will not buy insurance.

Let the consumer's utility function be $U = W^{0.5}$. Let $W = 90,000$, $A = 80,000$, and $P = 0.05$. The relevant equation is

$$(90,000 - R)^{0.5} = 0.95(90,000)^{0.5} + 0.05(10,000)^{0.5}$$

with the solution $R = 5900$. The expected value of the loss is $PA = 4000$. The risk-averse consumer is willing to pay an extra 1900 to avoid the risk of fire.

Insurance policies may differ from one another in a number of regards. Some have a deductible feature whereby the first D dollars of loss is not reimbursed. Others have a coinsurance feature whereby the insured must pay a fraction $0 < \alpha < 1$ of any loss. Imagine that a consumer with an automobile faces the risk of a minor accident with probability P_1 and a major accident with probability P_2, but cannot have both. The resultant losses are A and B dollars respectively where $A < B$. Assume that she is risk averse and must choose between a deductible and a coinsurance policy. Furthermore let D and

α be selected so that the expected value of the loss is equal for both policies and is equal to the premium, R, for each:

$$R = P_1(A - D) + P_2(B - D) = P_1(1 - \alpha)A + P_2(1 - \alpha)B \tag{3-35}$$

Under these circumstances the consumer will always purchase the deductible policy because it yields a higher expected utility. This is proved by establishing the inequality

$$P_1U(W_0 - D - R) + P_2U(W_0 - D - R) + (1 - P_1 - P_2)U(W_0 - R)$$
$$> P_1U(W_0 - \alpha A - R) + P_2U(W_0 - \alpha B - R) + (1 - P_1 - P_2)U(W_0 - R)$$

Subtract $(1 - P_1 - P_2)U(W_0 - R)$ from both sides, divide through by $(P_1 + P_2)$, and collect like terms:

$$U(W_0 - D - R) > Q_1U(W_0 - \alpha A - R) + Q_2U(W_0 - \alpha B - R) \tag{3-36}$$

where $Q_1 = P_1/(P_1 + P_2)$ and $Q_2 = P_2/(P_1 + P_2)$. Since $D = Q_1\alpha A + Q_2\alpha B$ from (3-35), the inequality (3-36) must hold for a risk-averse consumer for it may be interpreted as a special case of (3-33) whereby the utility of expected value exceeds the expected value of utility.

3-10 SUMMARY

Extensions of the basic theory of consumer behavior and the properties of particular utility functions are considered. A log linear utility function with minimum consumption requirements generates linear expenditure functions which are amenable to statistical parameter estimation.

A utility function is strongly separable if it can be written as a function of functions of individual consumption levels. Its RCS for a pair of commodities depends only upon the consumption levels for those commodities. A utility function is strongly additive if it can be written as the sum of functions of individual consumption levels. Additivity is a special case of separability. Additivity means that the marginal utility of each commodity is independent of the consumption levels of all other commodities. A utility function is homothetic if it can be written as a positive monotonic transformation of a homogeneous function. Homothetic functions have the important property that RCSs depend only upon the proportions in which commodities are consumed.

Indirect utility functions give optimal utility levels as functions of prices and income. They are obtained by substituting demand functions into the direct utility function. Roy's identity relates commodity demands to the derivatives of the indirect utility function. Duality theorems further relate the direct and indirect utility functions. These help provide a theoretical basis for empirical work, and allow many theoretical analyses to be conducted in terms of indirect utility functions.

The basic theory of consumer behavior can be restated in terms of the theory of revealed preference, which makes no use of differential calculus and arrives at essentially the same conclusions as the preceding analysis. The results are obtained by presenting the consumer with hypothetical price-income situations and observing her choices. Her indifference curves can be derived, and future choices can be predicted on the basis of past choices if the consumer's behavior satisfies the fundamental axioms of revealed preference.

If prices for a group of commodities always change in the same proportion, the demand for the group will behave in the same manner as the demand for a single commodity. This composite-commodity theorem means that several commodities may be aggregated and treated as a single commodity for many theoretical analyses. A consumer normally gains a surplus from the consumption of a commodity in the sense that she pays less than the maximum amount she would pay rather than forego consumption of the commodity. Several different monetary measures of this surplus have been proposed. In general these are not equal. If the income effect for a commodity is identically equal to zero: (1) the principal measures of consumer's surplus are equal, (2) consumer's surplus equals the area under the demand curve less expenditure, (3) the marginal utility of a composite commodity comprising all other commodities is constant, and (4) the marginal utility of the commodity under investigation is decreasing.

The approach of von Neumann and Morgenstern is concerned with the consumer's behavior in situations characterized by uncertainty. If the consumer's behavior satisfies some crucial axioms, her utility function can be derived by presenting her with a series of choices between a certain outcome on the one hand and a probabilistic combination of two uncertain outcomes on the other. The utility function thus derived is unique up to a linear transformation, and provides a ranking of alternatives in situations that do not involve risk. Consumers maximize expected utility, and von Neumann–Morgenstern utilities are cardinal in the sense that they can be combined to calculate expected utilities and can be used to compare differences in utilities. The expected utility calculation can be used to determine the consumer's choices in situations involving risk.

With wealth as the single argument of the utility function, the utility of the expected value of the outcome of an uncertain situation exceeds the expected utility of the outcome for a risk-averse consumer; i.e., her utility function is strictly concave. Similarly, risk lovers and risk neutrals have strictly convex and linear utility functions respectively. The index of absolute risk aversion is defined as the ratio of the second and first derivatives of the utility function. Risk-averse consumers will pay a premium for insurance to convert an uncertain outcome into a certain one.

EXERCISES

3-1 Which of the following utility functions are (*a*) strongly separable, or (*b*) additive with respect to all variables: $U = (q_1^{1/4} + q_2^{1/2})^{1/2}$; $U = q_1 q_2 + q_3 q_4$; $U = \beta_1 \ln(q_1 - \gamma_1) + \beta_2 \ln(q_2 - \gamma_2)$;

$U = (q_1 + 2q_2 + 3q_3)^{1/4}$. Show for each strongly separable or additive function what the F and f_i functions are.

3-2 Prove that if the consumer is indifferent between commodity bundles $(q_1^0, \ldots, q_n^0)$ and $(q_1^{(1)}, \ldots, q_n^{(1)})$ and has a homothetic utility function, she will also be indifferent between the bundles $(tq_1^0, \ldots, tq_n^0)$ and $(tq_1^{(1)}, \ldots, tq_n^{(1)})$.

3-3 Prove that an additive, strictly quasi-concave utility function is concave.

3-4 Construct an indirect utility function that corresponds to the direct function $U = \alpha \ln q_1 + q_2$. Use Roy's identity to construct demand functions for the two goods. Are these the same as the demand functions derived from the direct utility function?

3-5 A consumer is observed to purchase $q_1 = 20$, $q_2 = 10$ at prices $p_1 = 2$, $p_2 = 6$. She is also observed to purchase $q_1 = 18$, $q_2 = 4$ at the prices $p_1 = 3$, $p_2 = 5$. Is her behavior consistent with the axioms of the theory of revealed preference?

3-6 Let the consumer's utility function be $f(q_1, q_2, q_3) = q_1 q_2 q_3$, and her budget constraint $y = p_1 q_1 + p_2 q_2 + p_3 q_3$. Consider $q_1 + (p_2/p_1)q_2 = q_c$ as a composite good. Formulate the consumer's optimization problem in terms of q_c and find the demand function for q_c.

3-7 Let the consumer's inverse demand curve be $p = a - bq$ with $a, b > 0$, and assume that a sales tax of $100t$ percent is imposed so that the unit price she pays is increased to $p(1 + t)$. Prove that her loss of consumer's surplus will always exceed the revenue raised by the government through the imposition of the tax.

3-8 A consumer who conforms to the von Neumann–Morgenstern axioms is faced with four situations A, B, C, and D. She prefers A to B, B to C, and C to D. Experimentation reveals that the consumer is indifferent between B and a lottery ticket with probabilities of 0.4 and 0.6 for A and D respectively, and that she is indifferent between C and a lottery ticket with probabilities of 0.2 and 0.8 for B and D respectively. Construct a set of von Neumann–Morgenstern utility numbers for the four situations.

3-9 Show which of the following utility functions exhibit decreasing risk aversion: $U(W) = (W + \alpha)^\beta$, $\alpha \geq 0$, $0 < \beta < 1$; $U(W) = W$; $U(W) = \ln(W + \alpha)$, $\alpha \geq 0$; $U(W) = W^3$.

3-10 A consumer who obeys the von Neumann–Morgenstern axioms and has an initial wealth of 160,000 is subject to a fire risk. There is a 5 percent probability of a major fire with a loss of 70,000 and a 5 percent probability of a disastrous fire with a loss of 120,000. Her utility function is $U = W^{0.5}$. She is offered an insurance policy with the deductibility provision that she bear the first 7620 of any fire loss. What is the maximum premium that she is willing to pay for this policy?

3-11 Let a consumer's strictly quasi-concave utility function be $U = f(q) + 3M$ where M is the quantity of a composite commodity with unit price. Assume that her demand function for Q is $q = p^{-\alpha}$ where $\alpha > 0$. Determine $f(q)$ by solving a differential equation formed from the first-order condition for utility maximization.

SELECTED REFERENCES

Arrow, K. J.: *Aspects of the Theory of Risk-Bearing* (Helsinki: Academic Bookstore, 1965). Contains excellent discussions of expected utility maximization, risk aversion, and insurance.

Currie, J. M., J. A. Murphy, and A. Schmitz: "The Concept of Economic Surplus and Its Use in Economic Analysis," *Economic Journal*, vol. 81 (December, 1971), pp. 741–799. A detailed and nonmathematical survey with an extensive bibliography.

Friedman, M., and L. J. Savage: "The Utility Analysis of Choices Involving Risk," *Journal of Political Economy*, vol. 56 (August, 1948), pp. 279–304. Also reprinted in American Economic Association, *Readings in Price Theory* (Homewood, Ill.: Irwin, 1952), pp. 57–96. An analysis of situations with uncertain outcomes leading to a hypothesis concerning utility as a function of income. Simple mathematics.

Hicks, J. R.: *Value and Capital* (2d ed., Oxford: Clarendon Press, 1946). An analysis of composite commodities is contained in the appendix.

——: *A Revision of Demand Theory* (Oxford: Clarendon Press, 1956). A discussion of consumer theory relying on the theory of revealed preference and employing little mathematics.

Houthakker, H. S.: "Revealed Preference and the Utility Function," *Economica*, n.s., vol. 17 (May, 1950), pp. 159–174. Contains a proof of the existence of indifference curves for consumers who satisfy the axioms of revealed-preference theory.

Katzner, D. W.: *Static Demand Theory* (New York: Macmillan, 1970). A modern and abstract treatment; illuminating but not easy.

Lau, L. J.: "Duality and the Structure of Utility Functions," *Journal of Economic Theory*, vol. 1 (December, 1969), pp. 374–396. An extensive treatment of the relations between direct and indirect utility functions employing the calculus.

Pratt, J. W.: "Risk Aversion in the Small and in the Large," *Econometrica*, vol. 32 (January–April, 1964), pp. 122–136. Introduces the concepts of relative and absolute risk aversion in mathematical terms.

Richter, M. K.: "Revealed Preference Theory," *Econometrica*, vol. 34 (July, 1966), pp. 635–645. A modern approach using advanced mathematics.

Samuelson, Paul A.: *Foundations of Economic Analysis* (Cambridge, Mass.: Harvard, 1948). Composite commodities, revealed preference theory, and consumer surplus are treated in chaps. VI and VII.

von Neumann, J., and O. Morgenstern: *Theory of Games and Economic Behavior* (2d ed., Princeton, N. J.: Princeton University Press, 1947). Chap. 1 and an appendix contain the original statement of the von Neumann–Morgenstern approach.

Willig, R. D.: "Consumer's Surplus without Apology," *American Economic Review*, vol. 66 (September, 1976), pp. 589–597. A sophisticated justification of using the concept of consumer's surplus in practical situations.

FOUR

THE THEORY OF THE FIRM

A firm is a technical unit in which commodities are produced. Its entrepreneur (owner and manager) decides how much of and how one or more commodities will be produced, and gains the profit or bears the loss which results from his decision. An entrepreneur transforms inputs into outputs, subject to the technical rules specified by his production function. The difference between his revenue from the sale of outputs and the cost of his inputs is his profit, if positive, or his loss, if negative.

The entrepreneur's production function gives mathematical expression to the relationship between the quantities of inputs he employs and the quantities of outputs he produces. The concept is perfectly general. A specific production function may be given by a single point, a single continuous or discontinuous function, or a system of equations. This chapter is limited to production functions given by a single continuous function with continuous first- and second-order partial derivatives. The analysis is first developed for the relatively simple case in which two inputs are combined for the production of a single output, and then extended to more general cases.

An input is any good or service which contributes to the production of an output. An entrepreneur normally will use many different inputs for the production of an output. Some of his inputs may be the outputs of other firms. For example, steel is an input for an automobile producer and an output for a steel producer. Other inputs—such as labor, land, and mineral resources—are not produced. For a specified period of time, inputs are classified as either fixed or variable. A fixed input is necessary for production, but its quantity is invariant with respect to the quantity of output produced. Its costs are incurred by the entrepreneur regardless of his *short-run* maximizing decisions. The necessary quantity of a variable input depends upon the quantity of output produced. The distinction between fixed and variable inputs is temporal. Inputs which are fixed for one period of time are variable for a longer period. The entrepreneur of a machine shop may require a period of three months in order to buy new machinery or dispose of existing machinery. He will consider machinery as a fixed input in planning production for a one-month period, and as a variable input in planning production for a one-year period. All inputs are variable, given a sufficiently long period of time.

The formal analysis of the firm is similar to the formal analysis of the consumer in a number of respects. The consumer purchases commodities with which he "produces" satisfaction; the entrepreneur purchases inputs with which he produces commodities. The consumer possesses a utility function; the firm, a production function. The consumer's budget equation is a linear function of the amounts of commodities he purchases; the competitive firm's cost equation is a linear function of the amounts of inputs it purchases.

The differences between the analyses of the consumer and firm are not quite as obvious as the similarities. A utility function is subjective, and utility does not possess an unambiguous cardinal measure; a production function is objective, and the output of a firm is easily measured. A single firm may produce more than one output. The maximization process of the entrepreneur may go beyond that of the consumer. The rational consumer maximizes utility for a given income. The analogous action for the entrepreneur is to maximize the quantity of his output for a given cost level, but often he may consider his cost variable. He may desire to minimize the cost of producing a given output level, or maximize the profit he obtains from the production and sale of a commodity.

The problems of an entrepreneur who uses two inputs for the production of a single output are discussed in the first three sections of this chapter. The first covers the nature of his production function and the derivation of productivity curves and isoquants, the second covers alternative modes of optimizing behavior, and the third covers factor demands derived from optimizing behavior. In Sec. 4.4 cost functions are derived from production relations. The problems of an entrepreneur who uses one input for the production of two outputs are covered in Sec. 4-5, and the analysis is generalized for arbitrary numbers of inputs and outputs in Sec. 4-6.

4-1 BASIC CONCEPTS

The Production Function

Consider a simple production process in which an entrepreneur utilizes two variable inputs (X_1 and X_2) and one or more fixed inputs in order to produce a single output (Q). His production function states the quantity of his output (q)

as a function of the quantities of his variable inputs (x_1 and x_2):

$$q = f(x_1, x_2) \tag{4-1}$$

where (4-1) is assumed to be a single-valued continuous function with continuous first- and second-order partial derivatives. The production function is defined only for nonnegative values of the input and output levels. Negative values are meaningless within the present context. The domain of the production function may not include all of the nonnegative quadrant, and may differ from case to case. The production function normally is assumed to be increasing, i.e., the $f_i > 0$, within its domain. It is assumed to be a regular strictly quasi-concave function when output is maximized or cost minimized, and a strictly concave function when profit is maximized.

The entrepreneur is able to use many different combinations of X_1 and X_2 for the production of a given level of output. In fact, since (4-1) is continuous, the number of possible combinations is infinite. The entrepreneur's technology is all the technical information about the combination of inputs necessary for the production of his output. It includes all physical possibilities. The technology may state that a single combination of X_1 and X_2 can be utilized in a number of different ways and therefore can yield a number of different output levels. The production function differs from the technology in that it presupposes technical efficiency and states the *maximum* output obtainable from every possible input combination. The best utilization of any particular input combination is a technical, not an economic, problem. The selection of the best input combination for the production of a particular output level depends upon input and output prices and is the subject of economic analysis.

Input and output levels are rates of flow per unit of time. The period of time for which these flows, and hence the short-run production function, are defined is subject to three general restrictions: it must be (1) sufficiently short so that the entrepreneur is unable to alter the levels of his fixed inputs, (2) sufficiently short so that the shape of the production function is not altered through technological improvements, and (3) sufficiently long to allow the completion of the necessary technical processes. The selection of a particular time period within the specified limits is arbitrary. The analysis can be shifted to a long-run basis by relaxing condition (1) and defining the production function for a period long enough to allow variation of the heretofore fixed inputs. The major difference between a short-run and long-run analysis is the number of variable inputs. Nearly all the results for a short-run period will follow in a slightly altered form for a long-run period.

Product Curves

The total product of X_1 in the production of Q is defined as the quantity of Q that can be secured from the input of X_1 if X_2 is assigned the fixed value x_2^0:

$$q = f(x_1, x_2^0) \tag{4-2}$$

The input level x_2^0 is treated as a parameter, and q becomes a function of x_1 alone. The relation between q and x_1 may be altered by changing x_2^0. A representative family of total product curves is presented in Fig. 4-1. Each curve gives the relationship between q and x_1 for a different value of x_2^0. Normally, an increase of x_2^0 will result in a reduction of the quantity of X_1 necessary to produce each output level within the feasible range. If one total product curve lies to the left of another, it corresponds to a higher value for x_2^0: $x_2^{(1)} > x_2^{(2)} > x_2^{(3)}$.

Average and marginal products for X_1 are defined in an analogous manner for particular values of x_2^0. The *average product* (AP) of X_1 is its total product divided by its quantity:

$$AP = \frac{q}{x_1} = \frac{f(x_1, x_2^0)}{x_1}$$

The *marginal product* (MP) of X_1 is the rate of change of its total product with respect to variations of its quantity, i.e., the partial derivative of (4-1) with respect to x_1:

$$MP = \frac{\partial q}{\partial x_1} = f_1(x_1, x_2^0) \tag{4-3}$$

Families of AP and MP curves can be constructed by assigning different values to x_2^0.

The AP and MP curves corresponding to the leftmost of the total product curves in Fig. 4-1 are presented in Fig. 4-2. The AP for a point on a total product curve equals the slope of a line segment connecting that point with the origin. *OK* and *OJ* in Fig. 4-1 are examples. AP increases for movements along the total product curve from the origin to point *J*, and decreases thereafter. Point *J* corresponds to the maximum point on the AP curve in Fig. 4-2.

The MP for a point on a total product curve equals the slope of the

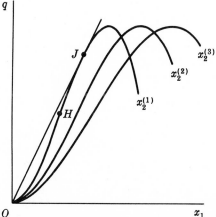

Figure 4-1

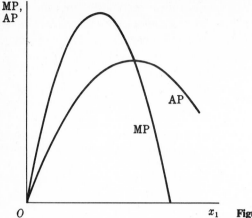

O x_1 **Figure 4-2**

tangent to the curve at that point. In Fig. 4-1 MP increases from the origin to the point of inflexion H where the slope of the tangent is at a maximum, and decreases thereafter. MP and AP are equal at the maximum AP at point J where the slope of the tangent equals the slope of the line segment.[1]

The product curves given in Figs. 4-1 and 4-2 satisfy the almost universal *law of diminishing marginal product*. The MP of X_1 will eventually decline as x_1 is increased with x_2^0 remaining unchanged.[2] This law does not rule out the initial phase of increasing MP exhibited in the present example. Consider a production process in which labor and land are combined for the production of wheat and compute the quantity of wheat produced as more and more labor is applied to a fixed amount of land. Initially an increase in the number of laborers employed may allow specialization and result in an increasing MP of labor. However, after these initial economies have been realized, increasing applications of labor will result in smaller and smaller increases in the output of wheat. The quantity of labor becomes greater and

---

[1] To determine the maximum value of AP, set its partial derivative with respect to x_1 equal to zero:

$$\frac{\partial \text{AP}}{\partial x_1} = \frac{x_1 f_1(x_1, x_2^0) - f(x_1 x_2^0)}{x_1^2} = 0$$

If a fraction equals zero, its numerator must equal zero:

$$x_1 f_1(x_1, x_2^0) - f(x_1 x_2^0) = 0$$

Moving the second term to the right, and dividing through by x_1,

$$f_1(x_1, x_2^0) = \frac{f(x_1, x_2^0)}{x_1}$$

MP and AP are equal at the point of maximum AP if such a point exists.

[2] This law has been stated in a number of alternative forms. See K. Menger, "The Laws of Return," in O. Morgenstern (ed.), *Economic Activity Analysis* (New York: Wiley, 1954), pp. 419–482.

greater relative to the fixed quantity of land. The law of diminishing marginal product concerns the relative quantities of the inputs and is not applicable if both inputs are increased.

The output elasticity of X_1, denoted by ω_1, is defined as the proportionate rate of change of Q with respect to X_1:

$$\omega_1 = \frac{\partial(\ln q)}{\partial(\ln x_1)} = \frac{x_1}{q}\frac{\partial q}{\partial x_1} = \frac{\text{MP}}{\text{AP}} \tag{4-4}$$

Output elasticities may be expressed as ratios of marginal and average products, and are positive if MP and AP are positive. The output elasticity of an input will be greater than, equal to, or less than unity as its MP is respectively greater than, equal to, or less than its AP. The entire product analysis may be applied to variations of x_2 with x_1 as a parameter.

For a specific example, consider the production function given by the sixth-degree equation

$$q = Ax_1^2 x_2^2 - Bx_1^3 x_2^3 \tag{4-5}$$

where $A, B > 0$. The corresponding productivity curves are depicted in Figs. 4-1 and 4-2.† Letting $Ax_2^2 = k_1$ and $Bx_2^3 = k_2$, the family of total product curves for X_1 is given by the cubic equation

$$q = k_1 x_1^2 - k_2 x_1^3$$

where k_1 and k_2 depend upon the fixed value assigned to x_2. The AP and MP curves are given by the quadratic equations

$$\text{AP} = k_1 x_1 - k_2 x_1^2 \qquad \text{MP} = 2k_1 x_1 - 3k_2 x_1^2$$

AP reaches a maximum at $x_1 = k_1/2k_2$, and MP reaches a maximum at $x_1 = k_1/3k_2$. Since $x_1, k_1, k_2 > 0$, MP reaches its maximum at a smaller input of X_1 than AP. The reader may verify that AP $=$ MP at $x_1 = k_1/2k_2$. The output elasticity for X_1 is

$$\omega_1 = \frac{2k_1 - 3k_2 x_1}{k_1 - k_2 x_1}$$

The reader may verify that ω_1 declines as x_1 increases.

Another and somewhat different example is provided by the production function $q = x_1^\alpha x_2^{1-\alpha}$ with $0 < \alpha < 1$. The MP and AP for X_1 decline continuously and are not equal for any value of x_1:

$$\text{AP} = \frac{q}{x_1} \qquad \text{MP} = \alpha\frac{q}{x_1}$$

The output elasticity for X_1 equals the constant α.

---

† The values $A = 0.09$ and $B = 0.0001$ were used for the construction of the curves in Figs. 4-1 and 4-2.

Isoquants

An isoquant is the firm's counterpart of the consumer's indifference curve. It is the locus of all combinations of x_1 and x_2 which yield a specified output level. For a given output level, (4-1) becomes

$$q^0 = f(x_1, x_2) \tag{4-6}$$

where q^0 is a parameter. The locus of all the combinations of x_1 and x_2 which satisfy (4-6) forms an isoquant. Since the production function is continuous, an infinite number of input combinations lie on each isoquant. Three curves from a family of isoquants are shown in Fig. 4-3. All the input combinations which lie on an isoquant will result in the output indicated for that curve. Within the relevant range of operation an increase of both inputs will result in an increased output. The further an isoquant lies from the origin, the greater the output level which it represents: $q^{(3)} > q^{(2)} > q^{(1)}$.

The slope of the tangent to a point on an isoquant is the rate at which X_1 must be substituted for X_2 (or X_2 for X_1) in order to maintain the corresponding output level. The negative of the slope is defined as the *rate of technical substitution* (RTS):

$$\text{RTS} = -\frac{dx_2}{dx_1}$$

The RTS for the firm is analogous to the RCS for the consumer. The RTS at any point is the same for movements in either direction.

The total differential of the production function is

$$dq = f_1\,dx_1 + f_2\,dx_2 \tag{4-7}$$

where f_1 and f_2 are the partial derivatives of q with respect to x_1 and x_2 (the MPs of X_1 and X_2). Since $dq = 0$ for movements along an isoquant,

$$0 = f_1\,dx_1 + f_2\,dx_2$$

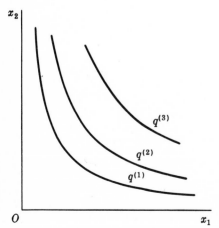

$$x_2$$

$$q^{(3)}$$

$$q^{(2)}$$

$$q^{(1)}$$

$$O \qquad\qquad x_1 \qquad \textbf{Figure 4-3}$$

and
$$\text{RTS} = -\frac{dx_2}{dx_1} = \frac{f_1}{f_2} \qquad (4\text{-}8)$$

The RTS at a point equals the ratio of the MP of X_1 to the MP of X_2 at that point.

Isoquants of the shape presented in Fig. 4-3 (rectangular hyperbolas which are negatively sloped throughout) can be derived for the production function given by (4-5). Let $z = x_1 x_2$, and rewrite (4-5) as

$$q^0 = Az^2 - Bz^3$$

Form the cubic equation

$$Bz^3 - Az^2 + q^0 = 0$$

which can be solved for z. Treat the smallest positive real root as the solution for z. The value of z depends upon the parameter q^0:

$$z = \psi(q^0) \qquad \text{or} \qquad x_1 x_2 = \psi(q^0)$$

which defines the isoquants as a family of rectangular hyperbolas, since $\psi(q^0)$ is constant for any fixed value of q^0.

The MP of X_1 may become negative if the application of X_1 is sufficiently large. One can imagine a situation in which the quantity of labor employed relative to the quantities of the other inputs is so large that an increase of labor would result in congestion and inefficiency. The definition of the production function as giving the maximum output for every possible input combination does not rule out this possibility. If the MP of X_1 is negative and the MP of X_2 positive,[1] the RTS is negative, as at point A in Fig. 4-4. A movement along the isoquant from A to B would result in a reduction of both x_1 and x_2. Clearly, point B is preferable to A if the entrepreneur must pay

---

[1] This situation will never arise for the production function given by (4-5). If the MP of one of its inputs is negative, the MP of the other must also be negative.

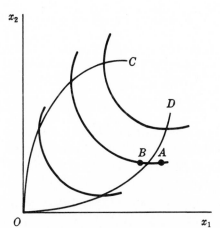

O x_1 **Figure 4-4**

positive prices for the inputs. A rational entrepreneur will never operate on a positively sloped section of an isoquant; i.e., he will never use a factor combination which results in a negative MP for one of the inputs. The *ridge lines OC and OD* enclose the area of rational operation.

Shape of the Production Function

Production functions are normally assumed to possess convex isoquants, bowed toward the origin with a decreasing RTS as X_1 is substituted for X_2 along an isoquant. The isoquants in Fig. 4-3 are of this shape, and those in Fig. 4-4 are of this shape within the area defined by the ridge lines.

Consider an appropriate domain for the production function given by (4-5), $q = Ax_1^2 x_2^2 - Bx_1^3 x_2^3$. Output is positive for $0 < x_1 x_2 < A/B$. It is an increasing function (has positive MPs) for $0 < x_1 x_2 < 2A/3B$. The inequality for a regular strictly quasi-concave function as given by (2-5) is also satisfied for $0 < x_1 x_2 < 2A/3B$. Thus, (4-5) is a positively valued, increasing, regular strictly quasi-concave function over this domain.

In the two-dimensional case a production function is a strictly concave function (see Sec. A-3) if

$$f_{11} < 0 \qquad f_{22} < 0$$

and

$$\begin{vmatrix} f_{11} & f_{12} \\ f_{21} & f_{22} \end{vmatrix} = f_{11}f_{22} - f_{12}^2 > 0 \tag{4-9}$$

The second direct partials of (4-5) are negative for $x_1 x_2 > A/3B$. The Hessian (4-9) is positive only for the domain

$$\frac{2A}{5B} < x_1 x_2 < \frac{2A}{3B} \tag{4-10}$$

Thus, (4-5) is a positively valued, increasing, strictly concave function over this domain.

Domains are more easily determined for the class of production functions given by $q = Ax_1^\alpha x_2^\beta$ with $\alpha, \beta > 0$. Output and both MPs are positive for $x_1, x_2 > 0$. The convexity of isoquants for positive input values is easily verified

$$x_2 = \left(\frac{q^0}{A}\right)^{1/\beta} x_1^{-\alpha/\beta}$$

$$\frac{d^2 x_2}{dx_1^2} = \frac{\alpha(\alpha + \beta)}{\beta^2} \left(\frac{q^0}{A}\right)^{1/\beta} x_1^{-(\alpha+2\beta)/\beta} > 0$$

The isoquants will be of the desired shape for any positive values of α and β.

Now consider conditions under which functions of the above class will be strictly concave. The second direct partials of the production function will be negative as required for its concavity if α and β are each less than one:

$$f_{11} = \alpha(\alpha - 1)\frac{q}{x_1^2} \qquad f_{22} = \beta(\beta - 1)\frac{q}{x_2^2}$$

An evaluation of (4-9) yields

$$\alpha(\alpha - 1)\frac{q}{x_1^2}\beta(\beta - 1)\frac{q}{x_2^2} - \left(\frac{\alpha\beta q}{x_1 x_2}\right)^2 = (1 - \alpha - \beta)\frac{\alpha\beta q^2}{x_1^2 x_2^2}$$

which can be positive, negative, or zero depending upon the values of α and β. If $\alpha + \beta < 1$, it is positive and the production function is strictly concave for all positive values of x_1 and x_2. If $\alpha + \beta = 1$, it is zero and the production function is concave but not strictly concave. If $\alpha + \beta > 1$, it is negative and the production function is neither concave nor convex.

Elasticity of Substitution

If a production function has convex isoquants, the RTS of X_1 for X_2 and the input ratio x_2/x_1 will both decline as X_1 is substituted for X_2 along an isoquant. The elasticity of substitution (σ) is a pure number that measures the rate at which substitution takes place. It is defined as the proportionate rate of change of the input ratio divided by the proportionate rate of change of the RTS:

$$\sigma = \frac{d \ln (x_2/x_1)}{d \ln (f_1/f_2)} = \frac{f_1/f_2}{x_2/x_1}\frac{d(x_2/x_1)}{d(f_1/f_2)}$$

Substituting $d(x_2/x_1) = (x_1 dx_2 - x_2 dx_1)/x_1^2$

$$d(f_1/f_2) = \frac{\partial(f_1/f_2)}{\partial x_1}dx_1 + \frac{\partial(f_1/f_2)}{\partial x_2}dx_2 \quad \text{and} \quad dx_2 = -(f_1/f_2)dx_1$$

from (4-8),

$$\sigma = \frac{f_1(f_1 x_1 + f_2 x_2)}{f_2 x_1 x_2\left[f_1\frac{\partial(f_1/f_2)}{\partial x_2} - f_2\frac{\partial(f_1/f_2)}{\partial x_1}\right]}$$

and evaluating the bracketed term in the denominator from (4-8)

$$\sigma = \frac{f_1 f_2(f_1 x_1 + f_2 x_2)}{x_1 x_2 \mathcal{D}} \tag{4-11}$$

where $\mathcal{D} = 2f_{12}f_1 f_2 - f_1^2 f_{22} - f_2^2 f_{11}$ is positive by the assumption of strict quasi-concavity. Since all of the terms in (4-11) are positive, the elasticity of substitution will be positive. Some production functions have constant elasticities of substitution, but in general σ will vary from point to point on the production function. The value of $\mathcal{D}$ reflects the rate of change of the slope of an isoquant. As $\mathcal{D}$ becomes larger the isoquant becomes more highly curved.

Consider the class of production functions given by $q = Ax_1^\alpha x_2^\beta$ with $\alpha, \beta > 0$. Evaluating (4-11),

$$\sigma = \frac{\alpha q}{x_1}\frac{\beta q}{x_2}\frac{(\alpha q + \beta q)}{x_1 x_2}\frac{x_1^2 x_2^2}{q^3 \alpha\beta(\alpha + \beta)} = 1$$

Production functions of this class have unit elasticity of substitution throughout.

4-2 OPTIMIZING BEHAVIOR

The present analysis is limited to the case in which the entrepreneur purchases X_1 and X_2 in perfectly competitive markets at constant unit prices. His total cost of production (C) is given by the linear equation

$$C = r_1x_1 + r_2x_2 + b \tag{4-12}$$

where r_1 and r_2 are the respective prices of X_1 and X_2, and b is the cost of any fixed inputs. An isocost line is defined as the locus of input combinations that may be purchased for a specified total cost:

$$C^0 = r_1x_1 + r_2x_2 + b \tag{4-13}$$

where C^0 is a parameter.

Solving (4-12) for x_1,

$$x_1 = \frac{C^0 - b}{r_1} - \frac{r_2}{r_1}x_2$$

The slopes of the isocost lines equal the negative of the input price ratio. The intercept of an isocost line on the x_1 axis $[(C^0 - b)/r_1]$ is the amount of X_1 that could be purchased if the entire outlay, exclusive of the cost of the fixed inputs, were expended upon X_1 and the intercept on the x_2 axis $[(C^0 - b)/r_2]$ is the amount of X_2 that could be purchased if this amount were expended upon X_2. Three of a family of isocost lines are given in Fig. 4-5. The greater the total outlay to which an isocost line corresponds, the greater the intercepts on the x_1 and x_2 axes, and therefore the further it lies from the origin: $C^{(3)} > C^{(2)} > C^{(1)}$. The family of isocost lines completely fills the nonnegative quadrant of the x_1x_2 plane.

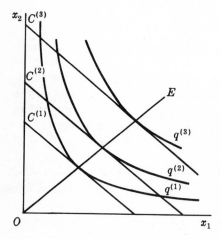

Figure 4-5

Constrained Output Maximization

The consumer maximizes utility subject to his budget constraint. The analogous problem for the firm is the maximization of output (4-1) subject to a cost constraint (4-13). The entrepreneur would desire to obtain the greatest possible output for a given cost outlay. Form the function

$$V = f(x_1, x_2) + \mu(C^0 - r_1 x_1 - r_2 x_2 - b)$$

where $\mu \neq 0$ is an undetermined Lagrange multiplier, and set the partial derivatives of V with respect to x_1, x_2, and μ equal to zero:

$$\frac{\partial V}{\partial x_1} = f_1 - \mu r_1 = 0$$

$$\frac{\partial V}{\partial x_2} = f_2 - \mu r_2 = 0$$

$$\frac{\partial V}{\partial \mu} = C^0 - r_1 x_1 - r_2 x_2 - b = 0$$

Moving the price terms to the right of the first two equations and dividing the first by the second,

$$\frac{f_1}{f_2} = \frac{r_1}{r_2} \tag{4-14}$$

First-order conditions state that the ratio of the MPs of X_1 and X_2 must be equated with the ratio of their prices.

The first-order conditions may be stated in a number of equivalent forms. Solving the first two equations for μ,

$$\mu = \frac{f_1}{r_1} = \frac{f_2}{r_2} \tag{4-15}$$

The contribution to output of the last dollar expended upon each input must equal μ. The multiplier μ is the derivative of output with respect to cost with prices constant and quantities variable.[1]

---

[1] Assuming that cost is variable, the differential of the cost equation (4-12) is

$$dC = r_1 \, dx_1 + r_2 \, dx_2$$

Substituting $r_1 = f_1/\mu$ and $r_2 = f_2/\mu$ from the first-order conditions,

$$dC = \frac{1}{\mu}(f_1 \, dx_1 + f_2 \, dx_2)$$

Dividing this expression into the differential of the production function (4-7), the derivative of output with respect to cost with prices constant is

$$\frac{dq}{dC} = \mu \frac{f_1 \, dx_1 + f_2 \, dx_2}{f_1 \, dx_1 + f_2 \, dx_2} = \mu$$

Finally, substituting RTS $= f_1/f_2$ from (4-8) into (4-14),

$$RTS = \frac{r_1}{r_2} \tag{4-16}$$

The first-order conditions may also be expressed as the equality of the RTS and the input price ratio. The three formulations of the first-order conditions given by (4-14), (4-15), and (4-16) are equivalent alternatives. If one is satisfied, all three are satisfied.

The formulation given by (4-16) has a clear geometric interpretation. The optimum input combination is given by the point of tangency between an isoquant and the relevant isocost line. If $C^{(3)}$ (see Fig. 4-5) is the predetermined level of cost, the maximum output is $q^{(3)}$. The outputs corresponding to all other isoquants which have points in common with the given isocost line, such as $q^{(1)}$ and $q^{(2)}$, are less than $q^{(3)}$.

Second-order conditions require that the relevant bordered Hessian determinant be positive:

$$\begin{vmatrix} f_{11} & f_{12} & -r_1 \\ f_{21} & f_{22} & -r_2 \\ -r_1 & -r_2 & 0 \end{vmatrix} > 0$$

The second-order conditions may be utilized to demonstrate that the rate of change of the slope of the tangent to an isoquant must be positive $(d^2x_2/dx_1^2 > 0)$ at the point of tangency with an isocost line.[1] The assumption that the production function is regular strictly quasi-concave will ensure that the second-order condition is satisfied whenever the first-order conditions are. The argument is the same as that used to derive (2-14) from (2-12).

Constrained Cost Minimization

The entrepreneur may desire to minimize the cost of producing a prescribed level of output. In this case (4-12) is minimized subject to (4-6). Form the function

$$Z = r_1x_1 + r_2x_2 + b + \lambda[q^0 - f(x_1, x_2)]$$

and set the partial derivatives of Z with respect to x_1, x_2, and λ equal to zero:

$$\frac{\partial Z}{\partial x_1} = r_1 - \lambda f_1 = 0$$

$$\frac{\partial Z}{\partial x_2} = r_2 - \lambda f_2 = 0 \tag{4-17}$$

$$\frac{\partial Z}{\partial \lambda} = q^0 - f(x_1, x_2) = 0$$

---

[1] The formal derivation is identical with that used to demonstrate that the rate of change of the slope of the indifference curve must be positive at the point of maximum utility (see Sec. 2-2).

Since r_1 and f_1 are both positive, λ is also positive. Moving the price terms of the first two equations to the right, and dividing the first by the second,

$$\frac{f_1}{f_2} = \frac{r_1}{r_2} \quad \text{or} \quad \frac{1}{\lambda} = \frac{f_1}{r_1} = \frac{f_2}{r_2} \quad \text{or} \quad RTS = \frac{r_1}{r_2}$$

The first-order conditions for the minimization of cost subject to an output constraint are similar to those for the maximization of output subject to a cost constraint. The multiplier λ is the reciprocal of the multiplier μ, or the derivative of cost with respect to output level (defined as marginal cost in Sec. 4-4). In the present case, the entrepreneur finds the lowest isocost line which has at least one point in common with a selected isoquant. He could produce $q^{(1)}$ (see Fig. 4-5) at a cost of $C^{(3)}$ or $C^{(2)}$, but $C^{(1)}$ is lower than either of these. His minimum cost is given by the isocost line which is tangent to the selected isoquant.

The second-order condition requires that the relevant bordered Hessian determinant be negative:

$$\begin{vmatrix} -\lambda f_{11} & -\lambda f_{12} & -f_1 \\ -\lambda f_{21} & -\lambda f_{22} & -f_2 \\ -f_1 & -f_2 & 0 \end{vmatrix} < 0$$

Substituting $-f_1 = -r_1/\lambda$ and $-f_2 = -r_2/\lambda$, multiplying the first two columns of the array by $-1/\lambda$, and then multiplying the third row by $-\lambda^2$ and the third column by λ,[†]

$$\begin{vmatrix} -\lambda f_{11} & -\lambda f_{12} & -\dfrac{r_1}{\lambda} \\ -\lambda f_{21} & -\lambda f_{22} & -\dfrac{r_2}{\lambda} \\ -\dfrac{r_1}{\lambda} & -\dfrac{r_2}{\lambda} & 0 \end{vmatrix} = \lambda^2 \begin{vmatrix} f_{11} & f_{12} & -\dfrac{r_1}{\lambda} \\ f_{21} & f_{22} & -\dfrac{r_2}{\lambda} \\ \dfrac{r_1}{\lambda^2} & \dfrac{r_2}{\lambda^2} & 0 \end{vmatrix} = -\frac{1}{\lambda} \begin{vmatrix} f_{11} & f_{12} & -r_1 \\ f_{21} & f_{22} & -r_2 \\ -r_1 & -r_2 & 0 \end{vmatrix} < 0$$

Since $\lambda > 0$,

$$\begin{vmatrix} f_{11} & f_{12} & -r_1 \\ f_{21} & f_{22} & -r_2 \\ -r_1 & -r_2 & 0 \end{vmatrix} > 0$$

the second-order condition is the same as that for the constrained-output-maximization case.

If the production function is regular strictly quasi-concave, every point of tangency between an isoquant and an isocost line is the solution of both a constrained-maximum and a constrained-minimum problem. If $q^{(1)}$ (see Fig.

† The multiplication of the first column by $-1/\lambda$ increases the value of the determinant by the same multiple. The multiplication of both the first and second columns by $-1/\lambda$ increases the value of the determinant by $1/\lambda^2$. Its value is left unchanged if the entire array is now multiplied by λ^2 (see Sec. A-1).

4-5) is the maximum output which can be obtained from an outlay of $C^{(1)}$ dollars, $C^{(1)}$ dollars is the minimum cost for which the output $q^{(1)}$ can be produced. The locus of tangency points (OE in Fig. 4-5) gives the *expansion path* of the firm. The rational entrepreneur will select only input combinations which lie on his expansion path. Formally, the expansion path is an implicit function of x_1 and x_2:

$$g(x_1, x_2) = 0 \qquad (4\text{-}18)$$

for which the first- and second-order conditions for constrained maxima and minima are fulfilled.

Consider the production function given by (4-5) as an example. Compute the ratio of the MPs of X_1 and X_2:

$$\frac{f_1}{f_2} = \frac{2Ax_1x_2^2 - 3Bx_1^2x_2^3}{2Ax_1^2x_2 - 3Bx_1^3x_2^2} = \frac{x_2(2Ax_1x_2 - 3Bx_1^2x_2^2)}{x_1(2Ax_1x_2 - 3Bx_1^2x_2^2)} = \frac{x_2}{x_1}$$

and set it equal to the ratio of the input prices

$$\frac{x_2}{x_1} = \frac{r_1}{r_2}$$

Putting this first-order condition in the form of an implicit function, the expansion path is given by the linear equation

$$r_1x_1 - r_2x_2 = 0$$

This corresponds to the expansion path OE in Fig. 4-5.

The production function $q = ax_1^\alpha x_2^\alpha$ also has isoquants with the slope $f_1/f_2 = x_2/x_1$. This production function appears quite different from (4-5). Nonetheless, it has the same family of isoquants. If we follow the analysis of Chap. 2, this indicates that the production functions are positive monotonic transformations of one another over the domain for which (4-5) is regular strictly quasi-concave: $0 < x_1x_2 < 2A/3B$. Again let $z = x_1x_2$ so that $q = az^\alpha$, and perform the positive monotonic transformation $q^* = (q/a)^{1/\alpha}$ so that $q^* = z$. Now differentiate (4-5) with respect to z:

$$\frac{dq}{dz} = 2Az - 3Bz^2$$

This derivative is positive for $0 < z < 2A/3B$, which establishes that (4-5) is a positive monotonic transformation of $q^* = z$, which in turn is a positive monotonic transformation of the exponential production function.

Profit Maximization

The entrepreneur is usually free to vary the levels of both cost and output, and his ultimate aim is the maximization of profit rather than the solution of constrained-maximum and -minimum problems. The total revenue of an entrepreneur who sells his output in a perfectly competitive market is given by the number of units he sells multiplied by the fixed unit price (p) he receives. His profit (π) is the difference between his total revenue and his total cost:

$$\pi = pq - C$$

or substituting $q = f(x_1, x_2)$ from (4-1) and $C = r_1x_1 + r_2x_2 + b$ from (4-12),

$$\pi = pf(x_1, x_2) - r_1x_1 - r_2x_2 - b$$

Profit is a function of x_1 and x_2 and is maximized with respect to these variables.

Setting the partial derivatives of π with respect to x_1 and x_2 equal to zero,

$$\frac{\partial \pi}{\partial x_1} = pf_1 - r_1 = 0 \qquad \frac{\partial \pi}{\partial x_2} = pf_2 - r_2 = 0$$

Moving the input-price terms to the right,

$$pf_1 = r_1 \qquad pf_2 = r_2 \tag{4-19}$$

The partial derivatives of the production function with respect to the inputs are the MPs of the inputs. The value of the MP of X_1 (pf_1) is the rate at which the entrepreneur's revenue would increase with further application of X_1. The first-order conditions for profit maximization (4-19) require that each input be utilized up to a point at which the value of its MP equals its price. The entrepreneur can increase his profit as long as the addition to his revenue from the employment of an additional unit of X_1 exceeds its cost. The maximum profit-input combination lies on the expansion path, since (4-19) is a special case of (4-14).

Second-order conditions require that the principal minors of the relevant Hessian determinant alternate in sign:

$$\frac{\partial^2 \pi}{\partial x_1^2} = pf_{11} < 0 \qquad \frac{\partial^2 \pi}{\partial x_2^2} = pf_{22} < 0 \tag{4-20}$$

and

$$\begin{vmatrix} \dfrac{\partial^2 \pi}{\partial x_1^2} & \dfrac{\partial^2 \pi}{\partial x_1 \partial x_2} \\ \dfrac{\partial^2 \pi}{\partial x_2 \partial x_1} & \dfrac{\partial^2 \pi}{\partial x_2^2} \end{vmatrix} = p^2 \begin{vmatrix} f_{11} & f_{12} \\ f_{21} & f_{22} \end{vmatrix} > 0 \tag{4-21}$$

Conditions (4-20) imply that profit must be decreasing with respect to further applications of *either* X_1 or X_2. Condition (4-21) ensures profit is decreasing with respect to further applications of *both* X_1 and X_2. Since $p > 0$, conditions (4-20) require that the MPs of both inputs be decreasing. If the MP of one of the inputs were increasing, a small movement from the point at which the first-order conditions are satisfied would result in an increase in the value of that MP. Since its price is constant, the entrepreneur could increase his profit by increasing its quantity.

Conditions (4-20) and (4-21) require that the production function be strictly concave in the neighborhood of a point at which the first-order conditions are satisfied with $x_1, x_2 \geq 0$ if such a point exists. Solutions are limited to strictly concave regions of the production function with non-negative input and output levels. If the production function possesses no such region, competitive profit-maximization solutions of the type described here cannot be achieved. If the production function is strictly concave, a point at which the first-order conditions are satisfied is a unique profit-maximizing solution.

4-3 INPUT DEMANDS

Input Demand Functions

The producer's input demands are derived from the underlying demand for the commodity which he produces. His input demand functions are obtained by solving his first-order conditions (4-19) for x_1 and x_2 as functions of r_1, r_2, and p. These are defined for strictly concave regions of his production function where his second-order conditions are satisfied. The producer's input demand functions are analogous to the consumer's ordinary demand functions in many regards. It is obvious from (4-19) that input demand functions are homogeneous of degree zero in the three prices (cf. Sec. 2-3). Elasticities may be defined for each of the inputs with respect to each of the prices. The input demand curve for X_1 is obtained by graphing the input demand function as a function of r_1 alone on the assumption that r_2 and p are given parameters.

Consider the class of production functions given by $q = Ax_1^\alpha x_2^\beta$ with $\alpha, \beta > 0$ and $\alpha + \beta < 1$ which were shown in Sec. 4-1 to be strictly concave for $x_1, x_2 > 0$. Form the profit function

$$\pi = pAx_1^\alpha x_2^\beta - r_1 x_1 - r_2 x_2$$

and set its partial derivatives equal to zero:

$$\frac{\partial \pi}{\partial x_1} = p\alpha Ax_1^{\alpha-1} x_2^\beta - r_1 = 0$$

$$\frac{\partial \pi}{\partial x_2} = p\beta Ax_1^\alpha x_2^{\beta-1} - r_2 = 0$$

Solving these equations for x_1 and x_2, the corresponding input demand functions are

$$x_1 = \left(\frac{\alpha}{r_1}\right)^{(1-\beta)/\gamma} \left(\frac{\beta}{r_2}\right)^{\beta/\gamma} (Ap)^{1/\gamma} = \phi_1(r_1, r_2, p)$$

$$x_2 = \left(\frac{\alpha}{r_1}\right)^{\alpha/\gamma} \left(\frac{\beta}{r_2}\right)^{(1-\alpha)/\gamma} (Ap)^{1/\gamma} = \phi_2(r_1, r_2, p)$$

(4-22)

where $\gamma = 1 - \alpha - \beta$. The demand for each input will decrease as r_1 or r_2 increases, and increase as p increases.

As prices change the producer will alter his input levels to satisfy his first-order conditions (4-19). Differentiating (4-19) totally and rearranging terms,

$$pf_{11}\,dx_1 + pf_{12}\,dx_2 = -f_1\,dp + dr_1$$
$$pf_{21}\,dx_1 + pf_{22}\,dx_2 = -f_2\,dp + dr_2$$

(4-23)

Solving (4-23) for dx_1 and dx_2 by Cramer's rule,

$$dx_1 = \frac{1}{p\mathcal{H}}\left[f_{22}\,dr_1 - f_{12}\,dr_2 + (f_{12}f_2 - f_{22}f_1)\,dp\right]$$

(4-24)

$$dx_2 = \frac{1}{p\mathcal{H}}\left[-f_{21}\,dr_1 + f_{11}\,dr_2 + (f_{21}f_1 - f_{11}f_2)\,dp\right]$$

where $\mathcal{H} = (f_{11}f_{22} - f_{12}^2) > 0$ by assumption of strict concavity.

Dividing both sides of the first equation of (4-24) by dr_1 and letting $dr_2 = dp = 0$,

$$\frac{\partial x_1}{\partial r_1} = \frac{f_{22}}{p\mathcal{H}} < 0$$

(4-25)

Since $p > 0$, and $f_{22} < 0$ by (4-20), the rate of change of the producer's purchases of X_1 with respect to changes in its price with all other prices constant is always negative, and the producer's input demand curves are always downward sloping. This is one of the few cases in economics in which the sign of a derivative is unambiguous. There is only a substitution effect. There is no counterpart for the income effect of the consumer in the theory of the profit-maximizing producer.[1]

Dividing both sides of the first equation of (4-24) by dr_2 and letting $dr_1 = dp = 0$,

$$\frac{\partial x_1}{\partial r_2} = -\frac{f_{12}}{p\mathcal{H}}$$

This derivative will have a sign the opposite of the second cross partial f_{12}. In most cases considered by economists, an increase in the quantity of one input will increase the marginal product of the other; that is, $f_{12} > 0$. Therefore, an increase in one input price normally will reduce the usage of the other input.

Dividing both sides of (4-23) by dp and letting $dr_1 = dr_2 = 0$,

$$\frac{\partial x_1}{\partial p} = \frac{(f_{12}f_2 - f_{22}f_1)}{p\mathcal{H}}$$

Normally an increase in output price will cause an increase in input demand, and this derivative is positive. For it to be negative it is necessary that $f_{12} < 0$, *and* that $f_{12}f_2$ be greater in absolute value than $f_{22}f_1$.

---

[1] A counterpart of the Slutsky equation, of course, may be obtained for the entrepreneur who maximizes output subject to a cost constraint. He will have a nonsymmetric "cost effect."

An Application of the Le Chatelier Principle

The profit function for the n-input case is

$$\pi = f(x_1, x_2, \ldots, x_n) - \sum_{i=1}^{n} r_i x_i \tag{4-26}$$

The Le Chatelier principle states that

$$\left(\frac{\partial x_i^*}{\partial r_i}\right)_0 \leq \left(\frac{\partial x_i^*}{\partial r_i}\right)_1 \leq \cdots \leq \left(\frac{\partial x_i^*}{\partial r_i}\right)_{n-1} \qquad i = 1, \ldots, n \tag{4-27}$$

where the subscript outside the parentheses designates the number of additional constraints that have been appended to the maximization of (4-26). The subscript 0 denotes unconstrained optimization, 1 denotes a case in which (4-26) is maximized subject to one constraint, 2 denotes a case in which it is maximized subject to the constraint of 1 and another constraint, and so on. The constraints are constructed so that the x_i^* are optimal regardless of the number of constraints.

In the unconstrained case, (4-25) shows that an increase in an input's price will result in a reduction in demand. This comes about through output reduction, and in most cases the substitution of other inputs for the input with the increased price. The introduction of new constraints cannot increase the opportunity to substitute other inputs, and may well decrease such opportunity. The Le Chatelier principle as given by (4-27) reflects this by stating that the absolute value of demand reduction following a price increase cannot be increased as additional constraints are introduced, and may be decreased. A general proof of the Le Chatelier principle is based upon the special properties of the Hessian of the strictly concave production function. An illustration of the principle for the two-input case is given here.

Let x_1 and x_2 be labor and capital respectively, and compare the effect of an increase in the wage rate, r_1, upon the firm's demand for labor in the long run when the quantity of capital is variable with the effect in the short run when the quantity of capital is fixed. The long-run effect is given by (4-25). For the short-run effect maximize

$$\pi = pf(x_1, x_2^*) - r_1 x_1 - r_2 x_2^*$$

by setting the labor derivative equal to zero,

$$\frac{\partial \pi}{\partial x_1} = pf_1 - r_1 = 0$$

It is clear that x_1^* is still optimal. Totally differentiate the first-order condition:

$$pf_{11} \, dx_1 - dr_1 = 0$$

and use this result together with (4-25) to evaluate (4-27):

$$\left(\frac{\partial x_1^*}{\partial r_1}\right)_0 = \frac{f_{22}}{p\mathcal{H}} \leq \frac{1}{pf_{11}} = \left(\frac{\partial x_1}{\partial r_1}\right)_1$$

Since f_{11} and f_{22} are both negative, $f_{11}f_{22} \geqq (f_{11}f_{22} - f_{12}^2)$, and the desired inequality follows. The long-run employment reduction will be greater than the short-run reduction unless $f_{12} = 0$, in which case they will be the same.

4-4 COST FUNCTIONS

The economist frequently assumes that the problem of optimum input combinations has been solved and conducts his analysis of the firm in terms of its revenues and costs expressed as functions of output. The problem of the entrepreneur is then to select an output at which his profit is maximized.

Short-Run Cost Functions

Cost functions can be derived from the information contained in Secs. 4-1 and 4-2.† Consider the system of equations consisting of the production function (4-1), the cost equation (4-12), and the expansion path function (4-18):

$$q = f(x_1, x_2)$$

$$C = r_1x_1 + r_2x_2 + b$$

$$0 = g(x_1, x_2)$$

Assume that this system of equations can be reduced to a single equation in which cost is stated as an explicit function of the level of output and input prices plus the cost of fixed inputs

$$C = \phi(q, r_1, r_2) + b \tag{4-28}$$

With regard to the input prices the cost function ϕ is (1) nondecreasing, (2) homogeneous of degree one, and (3) concave. Property (1) is clear from the indifference diagram. If one or more input prices increase and those inputs are used at positive levels, it is necessary to move to a higher isocost line to secure any specified output. Property (2) is obvious from the cost equation. For a specified output let $(r_1^0, r_2^0, x_1^0, x_2^0)$ and $(r_1^{(1)}, r_2^{(1)}, x_1^{(1)}, x_2^{(1)})$ denote two cost-minimizing solutions. Let $r_i^{(2)} = \lambda r_i^0 + (1 - \lambda)r_i^{(1)}$ $(i = 1, 2)$.

Now

$$\phi(q, r_1^{(2)}, r_2^{(2)}) = r_1^{(2)}x_1^{(2)} + r_2^{(2)}x_2^{(2)} = [\lambda r_1^0 + (1 - \lambda)r_1^{(1)}]x_1^{(2)} + [\lambda r_2^0 + (1 - \lambda)r_2^{(1)}]x_2^{(2)}$$

By cost minimization,

$$r_1^0 x_1^{(2)} + r_2^0 x_2^{(2)} \geqq \phi(q, r_1^0, r_2^0)$$

$$r_1^{(1)} x_1^{(2)} + r_2^{(1)} x_2^{(2)} \geqq \phi(q, r_1^{(1)}, r_2^{(1)})$$

† The term *cost function* is used to denote cost expressed as a function of output and input prices. The term *cost equation* is used to denote cost expressed in terms of input levels and input prices.

Consequently,

$$\phi(q, r_1^{(2)}, r_2^{(2)}) \geqq \lambda\phi(q, r_1^0, r_2^0) + (1 - \lambda)\phi(q, r_1^{(1)}, r_2^{(1)})$$

which establishes concavity. The general form of the cost function is considered further in Sec. 5-4. Here it is now assumed that input prices are invariant so that cost may be stated simply as a function of output level plus the cost of the fixed inputs.

$$C = \phi(q) + b \tag{4-29}$$

The cost of the fixed inputs, *the fixed cost*, must be paid regardless of how much the firm produces, or whether it produces at all. The cost function gives the minimum cost of producing each output and is derived on the assumption that the entrepreneur acts rationally. A cost-output combination for (4-29) can be obtained as follows: (1) select a point on the expansion path, (2) substitute the corresponding values of the input levels into the production function to obtain the corresponding output level, (3) multiply the input levels by the fixed input prices to obtain the total variable cost for this output level, and (4) add the fixed cost.

A number of special cost relations which are also functions of the level of output can be derived from (4-29). Average total (ATC), average variable (AVC), and average fixed (AFC) costs are defined as the respective total, variable, and fixed costs divided by the level of output:

$$\text{ATC} = \frac{\phi(q) + b}{q} \qquad \text{AVC} = \frac{\phi(q)}{q} \qquad \text{AFC} = \frac{b}{q}$$

ATC is the sum of AVC and AFC. Marginal cost (MC) is the derivative of total cost with respect to output:

$$\text{MC} = \frac{dC}{dq} = \phi'(q)$$

The derivatives of total and total variable cost are identical since the fixed-cost term vanishes upon differentiation.

Specific cost functions may assume many different shapes. One possibility which exhibits properties often assumed by economists is depicted in Figs. 4-6 and 4-7. Total cost is a cubic function of output. ATC, AVC, and MC are all second-degree curves which first decline and then increase as output is expanded. MC reaches its minimum before ATC and AVC, and AVC reaches its minimum before ATC. The reader may verify that the MC curve passes through the minimum points of both the AVC and ATC curves.[1] The AFC curve is a rectangular hyperbola regardless of the shapes of the other cost curves; the fixed cost is spread over a larger number of units as output is expanded, and therefore AFC declines monotonically. The vertical distance

[1] Set the derivative of ATC (or AVC) equal to zero, and put the equation in a form which states the equality between ATC (or AVC) and MC.

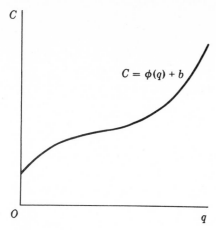

Figure 4-6

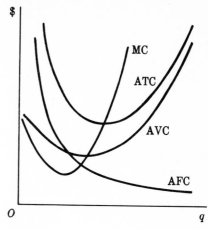

Figure 4-7

between the ATC and AVC curves equals AFC and hence decreases as output is increased.

The production function $q = Ax_1^\alpha x_2^\beta$ with $\alpha, \beta > 0$ yields the total cost function

$$C = \tilde{a}q^{1/(\alpha+\beta)} \tag{4-30}$$

where

$$a = (\alpha + \beta)\left(\frac{r_1^\alpha r_2^\beta}{A\alpha^\alpha \beta^\beta}\right)^{1/(\alpha+\beta)}$$

This cost function is convex, linear, or concave as $(\alpha + \beta)$ is respectively less than, equal to, or greater than one. AC and MC are

$$\text{AC} = aq^{(1-\alpha-\beta)/(\alpha+\beta)} \qquad \text{MC} = \frac{a}{(\alpha+\beta)}\,q^{(1-\alpha-\beta)/(\alpha+\beta)} = \frac{1}{(\alpha+\beta)}\,\text{AC}$$

Figure 4-8a gives AC and MC for a case with $\alpha + \beta < 1$. The production function is strictly concave, the total cost function is strictly convex, and AC and MC are strictly increasing with $\text{AC} < \text{MC}$ throughout. Figure 4-8b illustrates $\alpha + \beta = 1$. The total cost function is linear; AC and MC are constant and equal. Finally, Figure 4-8c illustrates $\alpha + \beta > 1$. The total cost function is strictly concave; AC and MC are strictly decreasing with $\text{AC} > \text{MC}$ throughout.

Figure 4-8a illustrates the general proposition that a strictly concave production function generates a strictly convex total cost function. Totally differentiating the first-order conditions for cost minimization given by (4-17) and rearranging terms,

$$\lambda f_{11}\,dx_1 + \lambda f_{12}\,dx_2 + f_1\,d\lambda = dr_1$$
$$\lambda f_{21}\,dx_1 + \lambda f_{22}\,dx_2 + f_2\,d\lambda = dr_2$$
$$f_1\,dx_1 + f_2\,dx_2 = dq$$

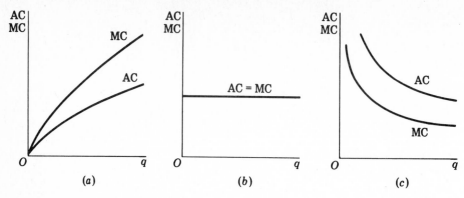

Figure 4-8

Using Cramer's rule to solve for $d\lambda$,

$$d\lambda = \frac{1}{\mathcal{D}} [(f_{21}f_2 - f_{22}f_1)\, dr_1 + (f_{12}f_1 - f_{11}f_2)\, dr_2 + \lambda \mathcal{H}\, dq] \tag{4-31}$$

where $\mathcal{H} = f_{11}f_{22} - f_{12}^2$ and $\mathcal{D} = 2f_{12}f_1f_2 - f_{11}f_2^2 - f_{22}f_1^2$. Letting $dr_1 = dr_2 = 0$,

$$\frac{\partial \lambda}{\partial q} = \frac{\lambda \mathcal{H}}{\mathcal{D}} > 0$$

Since $\lambda > 0$ is MC, this is the second derivative of the total cost function. It is strictly positive since the assumption of strict concavity dictates that both $\mathcal{H}$ and $\mathcal{D}$ be positive.

The revenue of an entrepreneur who sells his output at a fixed price is also a function of the level of his output. Therefore, his profit is a function of the level of his output:

$$\pi = pq - \phi(q) - b$$

To maximize profit, set its derivative with respect to q equal to zero:

$$\frac{d\pi}{dq} = p - \phi'(q) = 0$$

Moving the MC to the right,

$$p = \phi'(q) \tag{4-32}$$

The entrepreneur must equate his MC with the constant selling price of his output. He can increase his profit by expanding his output if the addition to his revenue (p) of selling another unit exceeds the addition to his cost (MC).

The second-order condition for profit maximization requires that

$$\frac{d^2\pi}{dq^2} = -\frac{d^2C}{dq^2} < 0$$

or multiplying by -1 and reversing the inequality,

$$\frac{d^2C}{dq^2} > 0$$

MC must be increasing at the profit-maximizing output. If MC were decreasing, the equality of price and MC would give a point of minimum profit. The second-order condition will be satisfied if the total cost function is strictly convex at a point at which the first-order condition is satisfied. This implies that the underlying production function is strictly concave. If the total cost function is strictly convex over a domain, an output at which the first-order condition is satisfied is a unique profit-maximizing output over that domain.

The level of the entrepreneur's fixed cost (b) generally has no effect upon his optimizing decisions during a short-run period. It must be paid regardless of the level of his output and merely adds a constant term to his profit equation. The fixed-cost term vanishes upon differentiation, and MC is independent of its level. Since the first- and second-order conditions for profit maximization are expressed in terms of MC, the equilibrium output level is unaffected by the level of fixed cost. The mathematical analyses of optimization in the present section and in Sec. 4-2 can generally be carried out on the basis of variable cost alone.

The level of fixed cost has significance for the analysis of short-run profit maximization in one special case. The entrepreneur has an option not recognized by the calculus. He can discontinue production and accept a loss equal to his fixed cost. This option is optimal if his maximum profit from the production of a positive output level is a negative amount (a loss) with a greater absolute value than the level of his fixed cost. The entrepreneur need never lose more than the amount of his fixed cost. He will produce at a loss in the short run if his loss is less than the amount of his fixed cost, i.e., if revenue exceeds total variable cost, and he is able to recover a portion of his outlay on the fixed inputs.

A geometric description of profit maximization is contained in Fig. 4-9. The optimum output (q^0) is given by the intersection of a horizontal line drawn at the level of the going price (p^0) and the rising portion of the MC curve. The entrepreneur's revenue is given by the area of the rectangle Op^0Bq^0, total cost by $OADq^0$, and profit by Ap^0BD.

As an example consider the cubic total cost function

$$C = 0.04q^3 - 0.9q^2 + 10q + 5 \qquad (4\text{-}33)$$

Assume that the price of q is 4 dollars per unit. Equating MC and price,

$$0.12q^2 - 1.8q + 10 = 4$$

which yields the quadratic equation

$$q^2 - 15q + 50 = 0$$

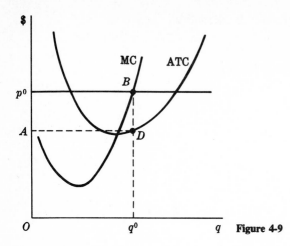

Figure 4-9

the roots of which are $q = 5$ and $q = 10$. Two different outputs satisfy the first-order condition for profit maximization, and the rate of change of MC must be calculated for both. The rate of change of MC:

$$\frac{d^2C}{dq^2} = 0.24q - 1.8$$

is negative for $q = 5$ and positive for $q = 10$. An output of 10 units yields a maximum profit, and an output of 5 a minimum. Profit at 10 units, however, is negative:

$$\pi = 4q - (0.04q^3 - 0.9q^2 + 10q + 5)$$
$$= 40 - 55 = -15$$

The entrepreneur's ATC curve lies above the price line for every output, and his maximum profit is a loss of 15 dollars. He should discontinue production, since his fixed cost (5 dollars) is less than the smallest loss which he can incur from a positive output level.

Long-Run Cost Functions

Let the levels of the entrepreneur's fixed inputs be represented by a parameter k, which gives the "size of his plant"—the greater the value of k, the greater the size of his plant. The entrepreneur's short-run problems concern the optimal utilization of a plant of given size. In the long run he is free to vary k and select a plant of optimum size. The shapes of the entrepreneur's production and cost functions depend upon his plant size. These are uniquely determined in the short run. In the long run he can choose between cost and production functions with different shapes. The number of his alternatives equals the number of different values which k may assume.

Once he has selected the shapes of these functions, i.e., selected a value for k, he is faced with the conventional short-run optimization problems.

As an illustration, consider the case of an entrepreneur operating a grocery store. The "size of his plant" is given by the number of square feet of selling space which he possesses. Assume that the only possible alternatives are 5000, 10,000, and 20,000 square feet and that he currently possesses 10,000. His present plant size is the result of a long-run decision made in the past. When the time comes for the replacement of his store, he will be able to select his plant size anew. If conditions have not changed since his last decision, he will again select 10,000 square feet. If the store has been crowded and he anticipates a long-run increase in sales, he will build 20,000 square feet. Under other conditions he may build a store with 5000 square feet. Once he has built a new store, his problems concern the optimal utilization of a selling area of given size.

Assume that k is continuously variable and introduce it explicitly into the production function, cost equation, and expansion path function:

$$q = f(x_1, x_2, k)$$

$$C = r_1 x_1 + r_2 x_2 + \psi(k)$$

$$0 = g(x_1, x_2, k)$$

Fixed cost is an increasing function of plant size: $\psi'(k) > 0$. The shapes of the families of isoquants and isocost lines and the shape of the expansion path depend upon the value assigned to the parameter k. Generally, two of the above relations may be utilized to eliminate x_1 and x_2, and total cost may be expressed as a function of output level and plant size:

$$C = \phi(q, k) + \psi(k) \qquad (4\text{-}34)$$

which describes a family of total cost curves generated by assigning different values to the parameter k. As soon as plant size is assigned a particular value $k = k^{(0)}$, (4-34) is equivalent to the particular total cost function given by (4-29), and the short-run analysis is applicable.

The entrepreneur's long-run total cost function gives the minimum cost of producing each output level if he is free to vary the size of his plant. For a given output level he computes the total cost for each possible plant size and selects the plant size for which total cost is a minimum. Figure 4-10 contains the total cost curves corresponding to three different plant sizes. The entrepreneur can produce the output OR in any of the plants. His total cost would be RS for plant size $k^{(1)}$, RT for $k^{(2)}$, and RU for $k^{(3)}$. The plant size $k^{(1)}$ gives the minimum production cost for the output OR. Therefore, the point S lies on the long-run total cost curve. This process is repeated for every output level, and the long-run total cost curve is defined as the locus of the minimum-cost points.

The long-run cost curve is the envelope of the short-run curves; it touches each and intersects none. Write the equation for the family of short-run cost

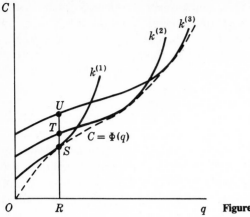

Figure 4-10

functions (4-34) in implicit form:

$$C - \phi(q, k) - \psi(k) = G(C, q, k) = 0 \tag{4-35}$$

and set the partial derivative of (4-35) with respect to k equal to zero:

$$G_k(C, q, k) = 0 \tag{4-36}$$

The equation of the envelope curve (the long-run cost curve) is obtained by eliminating k from (4-35) and (4-36) and solving for C as a function of q (see Sec. A-2):

$$C = \Phi(q)$$

Long-run total cost is a function of output level, given the condition that each output level is produced in a plant of optimum size. The long-run cost curve is not something apart from the short-run cost curves. It is constructed from points on the short-run curves. Since k is assumed continuously variable, the long-run cost curve (see Fig. 4-10) has one and only one point in common with each of the infinite number of short-run cost curves.

Since AC equals total cost divided by output level, the minimum AC of producing a particular output level is attained at the same plant size as the minimum total cost of producing that output level. The long-run AC curve can be derived by dividing long-run total cost by output level, or by constructing the envelope of the short-run AC curves. The two constructions are equivalent.

The long-run MC curve can be constructed by plotting the derivative of long-run total cost with respect to output level, or can be derived from the short-run MC curves. However, the long-run MC curve is not the envelope of the short-run MC curves. Short-run MC equals the rate of change of short-run variable cost with respect to output level; long-run MC is the rate of change of total cost assuming that all costs are variable. Therefore, portions of short-run MC curves may lie below the long-run MC curve. The long-run MC curve may be defined as the locus of those points on the short-run MC curves which correspond to the optimum plant size for each output.[1] The equivalence of the two methods of deriving the long-run MC curve is obvious in Fig. 4-10. The long-run total cost curve is tangent to each short-run curve at the output for which the short-run curve in question represents optimum plant size. Since the MCs are defined as the slopes of the tangents of these curves, the long-run and short-run MCs are equal at such points.

Assume that the entrepreneur desires to construct a plant for use during a number of short-run periods and that he expects to receive the same price for his product during each of the short-run periods. Since conditions remain unchanged from one period to the next, he will produce the same level of output in each period. His profit during one of the periods is the difference between his revenue and cost with plant size variable:

$$\pi = pq - \Phi(q)$$

Set the derivative of π equal to zero:

$$\frac{d\pi}{dq} = p - \Phi'(q) = 0$$

or
$$p = \Phi'(q)$$

Profits are maximized by equating long-run MC to price, if long-run MC is increasing (second-order condition). Once the optimum output is determined, the optimum value for k can be determined from (4-35) and (4-36).

Consider the family of short-run cost curves generated by

$$C = 0.04q^3 - 0.9q^2 + (11 - k)q + 5k^2 \tag{4-37}$$

For the plant size $k = 1$, the short-run cost curve is the one given by (4-33). Setting the partial derivative of the implicit form of (4-37) with respect to k equal to zero,

$$G_k(C, q, k) = q - 10k = 0$$

which has the solution $k = 0.1q$. Substituting into (4-37) gives the long-run cost function:

$$C = 0.04q^3 - 0.9q^2 + (11 - 0.1q)q + 5(0.1q)^2$$
$$= 0.04q^3 - 0.95q^2 + 11q$$

Long-run fixed cost equals zero.

---

[1] It *is not correct* to construct the long-run MC curve by selecting the points on the short-run MC curves which correspond to the optimum output (i.e., point of minimum AC) for each plant size.

Let the price of the entrepreneur's product be 4 dollars, as in the example for a short-run cost function. Setting price equal to long-run MC,

$$4 = 0.12q^2 - 1.9q + 11$$

which yields the quadratic equation

$$0.12q^2 - 1.9q + 7 = 0$$

with the roots $q \approx 5.83$ and $q = 10$. Profit is maximized at an output of 10 units. Utilizing the relation $k = 0.1q$, the optimum-size plant is given by $k = 1$. The entrepreneur's profit per short-run period is

$$\pi = pq - (0.04q^3 - 0.95q^2 + 11q) = 40 - 55 = -15$$

As in the last example, the maximum operating profit is a loss of 15 dollars. In the long run the entrepreneur is unable to earn a positive profit and will not construct a plant of any size.

The situation is quite different if price is increased to 6 dollars. Setting long-run MC equal to price yields the quadratic equation

$$0.12q^2 - 1.9q + 5 = 0$$

with the roots $q \approx 3.3$ and $q = 12.5$. Profit is maximized at an output of 12.5 units. Profit is positive for this plant size:

$$\pi = 75 - 67.1875 = 7.8125$$

and the entrepreneur will construct a plant of the optimum size ($k = 1.25$).

4-5 JOINT PRODUCTS

Some production processes will yield more than one output. Sheep raising is the classic example of such a process. Two outputs, wool and mutton, can be produced in varying proportions by a single production process.[1] The case of joint products is distinguished on technical rather than organizational grounds and exists whenever the quantities of two or more outputs are technically interdependent. Cases in which a single firm produces two or more technically independent products are excluded by this definition.

Basic Concepts

Consider the simplest case in which an entrepreneur uses a single input (X) for the production of two outputs (Q_1 and Q_2). In implicit form his production

---

[1] The production of joint products does not require an extended analysis unless they can be produced in varying proportions. If two products are always produced in a fixed proportion $q_1/q_2 = k$ where k is a constant, the analysis for a single output can be applied. Define a compound unit of output as k units of Q_1 and 1 unit of Q_2 with a price of $kp_1 + p_2$ and treat it as a single output.

function is

$$H(q_1, q_2, x) = 0 \qquad (4\text{-}38)$$

where q_1, q_2, and x are the respective quantities of Q_1, Q_2, and X. Assume that (4-38) can be solved explicitly for x:

$$x = h(q_1, q_2) \qquad (4\text{-}39)$$

The cost of production *in terms of* X is a function of the quantities of the two outputs. It is customary to assume that (4-39) is a positive-valued increasing function over a domain in which q_1 and q_2 are positive or nonnegative. In addition it is normally assumed that (4-39) is regular strictly quasi-convex for constrained optimization, and strictly convex for profit maximization.

A *product transformation curve* is defined as the locus of output combinations that can be secured from a given input of X:

$$x^0 = h(q_1, q_2)$$

Three of a family of product transformation curves are presented in Fig. 4-11. The further a curve lies from the origin, the greater the input of X to which it corresponds:

$$x^{(3)} > x^{(2)} > x^{(1)}$$

The slope of the tangent to a point on a product transformation curve is the rate at which Q_2 must be sacrificed to obtain more Q_1 without varying the input of X. The negative of the slope is defined as the *rate of product transformation* (RPT):

$$\text{RPT} = -\frac{dq_2}{dq_1}$$

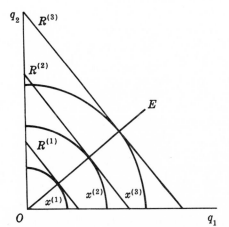

Figure 4-11

Taking the total differential of (4-39),

$$dx = h_1 \, dq_1 + h_2 \, dq_2$$

Since $dx = 0$ for movements along a product transformation curve,

$$\text{RPT} = -\frac{dq_2}{dq_1} = \frac{h_1}{h_2} \tag{4-40}$$

The RPT at a point on a product transformation curve equals the ratio of the marginal cost of Q_1 *in terms of* X to the marginal cost of Q_2 *in terms of* X at that point.

Alternatively, the RPT can be expressed in terms of the MPs. The inverse-function rule applies:

$$\frac{\partial q_1}{\partial x} = \frac{1}{h_1} \qquad \frac{\partial q_2}{\partial x} = \frac{1}{h_2} \tag{4-41}$$

Substituting into (4-40),

$$\text{RPT} = -\frac{dq_2}{dq_1} = \frac{\partial q_2/\partial x}{\partial q_1/\partial x} \tag{4-42}$$

The RPT equals the ratio of the MP of X in the production of Q_2 to the MP of X in the production of Q_1. An assumption that (4-39) is increasing ensures that both MPs are positive, as rational operation requires; the slopes of the product transformation curves are negative; and the RPT is positive.

Taking the total derivative of (4-42), the rate of change of the RPT is

$$-\frac{d^2 q_2}{dq_1^2} = \frac{1}{h_2^3}(h_{11}h_2^2 - 2h_{12}h_1h_2 + h_{22}h_1^2) \tag{4-43}$$

An assumption that (4-39) is regular strictly quasi-convex ensures that (4-43) is positive, i.e., that the RPT increases as a movement is made from left to right along a product transformation curve. As more Q_1 and less Q_2 is produced with a fixed input quantity, an increasing amount of Q_2 must be sacrificed per unit of Q_1. Since (4-43) is positive, a product transformation curve gives q_2 as a function of q_1 with negative second derivative, i.e., q_2 as a strictly concave function of q_1. Such product transformation curves are bowed away from the origin as pictured in Fig. 4-11.

The system of product transformation curves in Fig. 4-11 is generated by the implicit production function

$$q_1^2 + q_2^2 - x = 0$$

The product transformation curves are concentric circles:

$$x^0 = q_1^2 + q_2^2$$

with $\text{RPT} = q_1/q_2$. For $q_1, q_2 > 0$, the slopes of the product transformation curves are negative, and the RPT positive. The rate of change of the RPT as given by (4-43) equals $(q_1^2 + q_2^2)/q_2^3$ in this case.

Constrained Revenue Maximization

If the entrepreneur sells his outputs at fixed prices, his revenue is given by the linear equation

$$R = p_1 q_1 + p_2 q_2 \qquad (4\text{-}44)$$

where p_1 and p_2 are the prices of Q_1 and Q_2 respectively. An isorevenue line is the revenue counterpart of an isocost line and is defined as the locus of output combinations that will earn a specified revenue. Three of a system of isorevenue lines are presented in Fig. 4-11. They are parallel straight lines with slopes equal to the negative of the ratio of the output prices ($-p_1/p_2$).

 To solve the constrained-maximization problem of an entrepreneur who desires to maximize revenue for a specified input of X, form the function

$$W = p_1 q_1 + p_2 q_2 + \mu[x^0 - h(q_1, q_2)]$$

where μ is an undetermined Lagrange multiplier, and set its partial derivatives equal to zero:

$$\frac{\partial W}{\partial q_1} = p_1 - \mu h_1 = 0$$

$$\frac{\partial W}{\partial q_2} = p_2 - \mu h_2 = 0$$

$$\frac{\partial W}{\partial \mu} = x^0 - h(q_1, q_2) = 0$$

Moving the second terms of the first two equations to the right and dividing the first by the second,

$$\frac{p_1}{p_2} = \frac{h_1}{h_2} = \text{RPT}$$

or substituting from (4-41),

$$\frac{p_1}{p_2} = \frac{\partial q_2/\partial x}{\partial q_1/\partial x} = \text{RPT} \qquad (4\text{-}45)$$

The RPT must be equated with the fixed price ratio. In geometric terms, the specified product transformation curve must be tangent to an isorevenue line.

 The first-order conditions may also be stated as

$$\mu = \frac{p_1}{h_1} = \frac{p_2}{h_2}$$

or substituting from (4-41),

$$\mu = p_1 \frac{\partial q_1}{\partial x} = p_2 \frac{\partial q_2}{\partial x}$$

The value of the MP of X in the production of each output must equal μ, the derivative of R with respect to x with prices constant.[1]

The second-order condition requires that the relevant bordered Hessian determinant be positive:

$$\begin{vmatrix} -\mu h_{11} & -\mu h_{12} & -h_1 \\ -\mu h_{21} & -\mu h_{22} & -h_2 \\ -h_1 & -h_2 & 0 \end{vmatrix} > 0$$

Expanding,

$$\mu(h_{11}h_2^2 - 2h_{12}h_1h_2 + h_{22}h_1^2) > 0$$

Since $\mu > 0$,

$$(h_{11}h_2^2 - 2h_{12}h_1h_2 + h_{22}h_1^2) > 0$$

With $h_2 > 0$ as required by the first-order condition, it follows from (4-43) that the second-order condition requires that the product transformation curve have an increasing RPT at a point at which the first-order conditions are satisfied. If (4-39) is regular strictly quasi-convex over a domain, a point at which the first-order conditions are fulfilled is a unique constrained revenue maximum over that domain.

An entrepreneur might desire to minimize the amount of X necessary to obtain a specified revenue. In this case he would minimize (4-39) subject to a revenue constraint. Geometrically, he desires to reach the lowest product transformation curve that has a common point with a specified isorevenue line. For constrained revenue maximization he desires to reach the highest isorevenue line possessing a common point with a specified product transformation curve. If the product transformation curves are strictly concave, every point of tangency between an isorevenue line and a product transformation curve represents the solution of both a constrained-revenue-maximization and a constrained-input-minimization problem. The locus of all points of tangency (see OE in Fig. 4-11) is an *output expansion path* similar in interpretation to the input expansion path of the single-product firm.

---

[1] The total differential of (4-44) in this case is

$$dR = p_1\, dq_1 + p_2\, dq_2$$

or substituting $p_1 = \mu h_1$ and $p_2 = \mu h_2$,

$$dR = \mu(h_1\, dq_1 + h_2\, dq_2)$$

Dividing this by the differential of (4-44), the total derivative of R with respect to x with prices constant is

$$\frac{dR}{dx} = \frac{\mu(h_1\, dq_1 + h_2\, dq_2)}{h_1\, dq_1 + h_2\, dq_2} = \mu$$

and is called the marginal-revenue product of X.

Profit Maximization

Express profit as a function of q_1 and q_2:

$$\pi = p_1q_1 + p_2q_2 - rh(q_1, q_2)$$

and set its partial derivatives equal to zero:

$$\frac{\partial \pi}{\partial q_1} = p_1 - rh_1 = 0$$

$$\frac{\partial \pi}{\partial q_2} = p_2 - rh_2 = 0$$

Moving the price terms to the right and dividing by the marginal costs in terms of X,

$$r = \frac{p_1}{h_1} = \frac{p_2}{h_2}$$

or substituting from (4-41),

$$r = p_1 \frac{\partial q_1}{\partial x} = p_2 \frac{\partial q_2}{\partial x} \tag{4-46}$$

The value of the MP of X for the production of each output must be equated to the price of X.† The entrepreneur could increase profit by increasing his employment of X if its return in the production of either product exceeded its cost.

Second-order conditions require that

$$-rh_{11} < 0 \qquad \begin{vmatrix} -rh_{11} & -rh_{12} \\ -rh_{21} & -rh_{22} \end{vmatrix} > 0$$

Expanding the second determinant,

$$r^2(h_{11}h_{22} - h_{12}^2) > 0$$

Since $r > 0$, the second-order conditions can be stated as

$$h_{11} > 0 \qquad h_{11}h_{22} - h_{12}^2 > 0 \tag{4-47}$$

Both together imply that $h_{22} > 0$. The marginal cost of each output in terms of X must be increasing. Conditions (4-47) require that the production relation (4-39) be strictly convex in a neighborhood about a point at which the first-order conditions (4-46) are satisfied. If (4-39) is strictly convex throughout, any maximum that is achieved will be a global maximum.

Consider profit maximization by an entrepreneur whose product trans-

---

† Following the derivations of (4-45) and the note on page 96, it is not surprising to learn that profit maximization requires that $r = dR/dx$. The rate at which the application of an additional unit of X would increase the entrepreneur's revenue must equal its price.

formation curves are given by a system of concentric circles. His profit is

$$\pi = p_1 q_1 + p_2 q_2 - r(q_1^2 + q_2^2)$$

Setting the partial derivatives equal to zero

$$\frac{\partial \pi}{\partial q_1} = p_1 - 2rq_1 = 0 \qquad \frac{\partial \pi}{\partial q_2} = p_2 - 2rq_2 = 0$$

The first-order conditions can be stated as

$$r = \frac{p_1}{2q_1} = \frac{p_2}{2q_2}$$

Second-order conditions (4-47) are satisfied:

$$2 > 0 \qquad 4 - 0 = 4 > 0$$

4-6 GENERALIZATION TO m VARIABLES

The analysis of the firm is easily generalized to cover a production process with s outputs and n inputs. The production function is stated in implicit form as

$$F(q_1, \ldots, q_s, x_1, \ldots, x_n) = 0 \tag{4-48}$$

where (4-48) is assumed to possess continuous first- and second-order partial derivatives which are different from zero for all its nontrivial solutions. It is assumed that (4-48) is an increasing function of the q's and a decreasing function of the x's. Thus, in implicit form (4-1) is written as $q - f(x_1, x_2) = 0$, and (4-39) as $h(q_1, q_2) - x = 0$. Finally, it is assumed that (4-48) is regular strictly quasi-convex over a relevant domain.

Profit Maximization

Profit is the difference between the total revenue from the sale of all outputs and the expenditure upon all inputs.

$$\pi = \sum_{i=1}^{s} p_i q_i - \sum_{j=1}^{n} r_j x_j \tag{4-49}$$

The entrepreneur desires to maximize profit subject to the technical rules given by the production function. Form the function

$$J = \sum_{i=1}^{s} p_i q_i - \sum_{j=1}^{n} r_j x_j + \lambda F(q_1, \ldots, x_n)$$

and set each of its $(s + n + 1)$ partial derivatives equal to zero:

$$\frac{\partial J}{\partial q_i} = p_i + \lambda F_i = 0 \qquad i = 1, \ldots, s$$

$$\frac{\partial J}{\partial x_j} = -r_j + \lambda F_{s+j} = 0 \qquad j = 1, \ldots, n \qquad (4\text{-}50)$$

$$\frac{\partial J}{\partial \lambda} = F(q_1, \ldots, x_n) = 0$$

where $F_i(i = 1, \ldots, s + n = m)$ is the partial derivative of (4-48) with respect to its ith argument.

Select any two of the first s equations of (4-50), move the second terms to the right, and divide one by the other:[1]

$$\frac{p_j}{p_k} = \frac{F_j}{F_k} = -\frac{\partial q_k}{\partial q_j} \qquad j, k = 1, \ldots, s \qquad (4\text{-}51)$$

The RPT for every pair of outputs—holding the levels of all other outputs and all inputs constant—must equal the ratio of their prices. For the kth output and the jth input, (4-50) implies that

$$\frac{r_j}{p_k} = -\frac{F_{s+j}}{F_k} = \frac{\partial q_k}{\partial x_j} \quad \text{or} \quad r_j = p_k \frac{\partial q_k}{\partial x_j} \quad \begin{array}{l} k = 1, \ldots, s \\ j = 1, \ldots, n \end{array}$$

The value of the marginal product of each input with respect to each output is equated to the input price. Finally, consider two inputs. The first-order conditions become

$$\frac{r_j}{r_k} = -\frac{\partial x_k}{\partial x_j} \qquad j, k = 1, \ldots, n$$

The RTS for every pair of inputs—holding the levels of all outputs and all other inputs constant—must equal the ratio of their prices.

The second-order conditions for the maximization of profit require that the relevant bordered Hessian determinants alternate in sign:

$$\begin{vmatrix} \lambda F_{11} & \lambda F_{12} & F_1 \\ \lambda F_{21} & \lambda F_{22} & F_2 \\ F_1 & F_2 & 0 \end{vmatrix} > 0, \ldots, (-1)^m \begin{vmatrix} \lambda F_{11} & \cdots & \lambda F_{1m} & F_1 \\ \cdots\cdots\cdots\cdots\cdots \\ \lambda F_{m1} & \cdots & \lambda F_{mm} & F_m \\ F_1 & \cdots & F_m & 0 \end{vmatrix} > 0 \qquad (4\text{-}52)$$

Multiplying the first two columns of the first array and the first m of the last by $1/\lambda$, and multiplying the last row of both arrays by λ,

$$\lambda \begin{vmatrix} F_{11} & F_{12} & F_1 \\ F_{21} & F_{22} & F_2 \\ F_1 & F_2 & 0 \end{vmatrix} > 0, \ldots, (-1)^m \lambda^{m-1} \begin{vmatrix} F_{11} & \cdots & F_{1m} & F_1 \\ \cdots\cdots\cdots\cdots\cdots \\ F_{m1} & \cdots & F_{mm} & F_m \\ F_1 & \cdots & F_m & 0 \end{vmatrix} > 0$$

---

[1] The implicit-function rule, $F_i/F_j = -\partial q_j/\partial q_i$, is utilized in (4-51) (see Sec. A-2).

Since $\lambda < 0$ from (4-50), the second-order conditions require that

$$\begin{vmatrix} F_{11} & F_{12} & F_1 \\ F_{21} & F_{22} & F_2 \\ F_1 & F_2 & 0 \end{vmatrix} < 0, \ldots, \quad \begin{vmatrix} F_{11} & \cdots & F_{1m} & F_1 \\ \cdots\cdots\cdots\cdots\cdots \\ F_{m1} & \cdots & F_{mm} & F_m \\ F_1 & \cdots & F_m & 0 \end{vmatrix} < 0 \qquad (4\text{-}53)$$

Conditions (4-53) are satisfied by the assumption that (4-48) is regular strictly quasi-convex. This assumption encompasses the assumptions that (4-1) is strictly concave and that (4-39) is strictly convex as special cases. Consider the one-output–two-input case of (4-1). The implicit product function is $q - f(x_1, x_2) = 0$ with the partial derivatives $F_1 = 1$, $F_2 = -f_1$, and $F_3 = -f_2$. In this case, conditions (4-53) are

$$\begin{vmatrix} 0 & 0 & 1 \\ 0 & -f_{11} & -f_1 \\ 1 & -f_1 & 0 \end{vmatrix} < 0 \qquad \begin{vmatrix} 0 & 0 & 0 & 1 \\ 0 & -f_{11} & -f_{12} & -f_1 \\ 0 & -f_{21} & -f_{22} & -f_2 \\ 1 & -f_1 & -f_2 & 0 \end{vmatrix} < 0$$

Expand each determinant by the last element in its first row, then by the last element in its first column; multiply both columns of the second determinant by -1, and finally multiply the second determinant by -1:

$$f_{11} < 0 \qquad \begin{vmatrix} f_{11} & f_{12} \\ f_{21} & f_{22} \end{vmatrix} > 0$$

which imply the strict concavity of (4-1). This result is easily generalized to the one-output–n-input case. It also can be shown that conditions (4-53) for the implicit form of the s-output–one-input production relation is equivalent to strict convexity for the explicit form of this relation.

Substitution Effects

The profit-maximizing entrepreneur will respond to changes in input and output prices by varying his input and output levels in order to continue to satisfy the first-order conditions (4-50). By total differentiation of (4-50)

$$\lambda F_{11}\, dq_1 + \cdots + \lambda F_{1m}\, dx_n + F_1\, d\lambda = -dp_1$$
$$\cdots\cdots\cdots\cdots\cdots\cdots\cdots\cdots\cdots\cdots\cdots$$
$$\lambda F_{m1}\, dq_1 + \cdots + \lambda F_{mm}\, dx_n + F_m\, d\lambda = dr_n \qquad (4\text{-}54)$$
$$F_1\, dq_1 + \cdots + F_m\, dx_n = 0$$

Assume that the price changes are given and treat (4-54) as a system of $(m + 1)$ linear equations in $(m + 1)$ variables: dq_i ($i = 1, \ldots, s$), dx_j ($j = 1, \ldots, n$), and $d\lambda$. Using Cramer's rule (see Sec. A-1) to solve (4-54) for dq_j and dx_j,

$$dq_j = \frac{-\mathscr{D}_{1j}\,dp_1 - \cdots + \mathscr{D}_{mj}\,dr_n}{\mathscr{D}} \qquad j = 1, \ldots, s$$

$$dx_j = \frac{-\mathscr{D}_{1,s+j}\,dp_1 - \cdots + \mathscr{D}_{m,s+j}\,dr_n}{\mathscr{D}} \qquad j = 1, \ldots, n$$

$$(4\text{-}55)$$

where $\mathscr{D}$ is the determinant of the coefficients of (4-54) and $\mathscr{D}_{ij}$ is the cofactor of the element in the ith row and jth column of the array. The determinant $\mathscr{D}$ is the same as the highest-order determinant of (4-52).

The rate of change of quantity with respect to a price is determined by dividing both sides of (4-55) by the price differential and letting the remaining price differentials equal zero:

$$\frac{\partial q_j}{\partial p_k} = \frac{\partial q_k}{\partial p_j} = -\frac{\mathscr{D}_{kj}}{\mathscr{D}} \qquad j, k = 1, \ldots, s$$

$$\frac{\partial x_j}{\partial r_k} = \frac{\partial x_k}{\partial r_j} = \frac{\mathscr{D}_{s+k,s+j}}{\mathscr{D}} \qquad j, k = 1, \ldots, n$$

$$\frac{\partial q_j}{\partial r_k} = \frac{\partial x_k}{\partial p_j} = \frac{\mathscr{D}_{s+k,j}}{\mathscr{D}} \qquad \begin{matrix} j = 1, \ldots, s \\ k = 1, \ldots, n \end{matrix}$$

$$(4\text{-}56)$$

Since $\mathscr{D}$ is a symmetric determinant, the partial derivatives (4-56) are also symmetric. There is no counterpart of the consumer's nonsymmetric income effect in the theory of the profit-maximizing firm. The total effect for the firm is a symmetric substitution effect.

Most of the derivatives of (4-56) may be of either sign depending upon the particular form of the implicit production function. The signs of own-price effects, however, can be determined. It follows from (4-52) that $\mathscr{D}_{jj}$ and $\mathscr{D}$ must be of opposite sign for $j = 1, \ldots, m$. Therefore,

$$\frac{\partial q_j}{\partial p_j} > 0 \qquad j = 1, \ldots, s \qquad \frac{\partial x_k}{\partial r_k} < 0 \qquad k = 1, \ldots, n$$

An increase of the jth output price, with other prices constant, will always increase the production of the jth output. An increase of the kth input price, with other prices constant, will always decrease the use of the kth input.

4-7 SUMMARY

The production function for the one-output–two-variable-inputs case gives the maximum output level that can be secured from each possible input combination. It is assumed to be positive valued and increasing over a relevant domain. For some purposes it is assumed to be regular strictly quasi-concave, and for others to be strictly concave. Product curves are obtained by treating the quantity of one of the variable inputs as a parameter and expressing output as a function of the quantity of the other. An output elasticity for an input is the proportionate rate of change per 1 percent change of the input. An isoquant is the locus of all input combinations that yield a specified output level. A regular strictly quasi-concave production function generates convex isoquants. The elasticity of substitution relates proportionate changes in the input ratio to proportionate changes in the rate of technical substitution along an isoquant.

The entrepreneur may desire to maximize his output level for a given cost, or he may desire to minimize the cost of producing a given output level. The first-order conditions for both problems require that the rate of technical substitution between the inputs be equated to their price ratio. In diagrammatic terms, both require tangency between an isoquant and an isocost line. The locus of such tangency points is the expansion path of the firm. Second-order conditions require that the production function be regular strictly quasi-concave in the neighborhood of a point at which the first-order conditions are satisfied. The entrepreneur may allow both output level and cost to vary and maximize his profit. First-order conditions require that the value of the marginal physical product of each input be equated to its price. Second-order conditions require that the production function be strictly concave in the neighborhood of a point at which the first-order conditions are satisfied. This means that the marginal products of both inputs must be decreasing.

The producer's demand for an input is derived from the underlying demand for the commodity which he produces. His input demand functions are obtained by solving his first-order conditions for his input levels as functions of input and output prices. An input demand curve relates the demand for an input to its own price; these curves are always downward sloping. An application of the Le Chatelier principle establishes that the long-run reduction in the demand for an input following an increase of its price cannot be smaller than the short-run reduction.

Given the entrepreneur's production function, cost equation, and expansion path function, his total cost can be expressed as a function of his output level. In the short run, the cost of his fixed inputs must be paid, regardless of his output level. The first-order condition for profit maximization requires the entrepreneur to equate his marginal cost to the selling price of his output. The second-order condition requires that marginal cost be increasing. This strict convexity of the cost function will be achieved if the underlying production function is strictly concave. The entrepreneur is able to vary the levels of his fixed inputs in the long run and therefore is able to select a particular short-run cost function. His long-run total cost function is the envelope of his alternative short-run total cost functions. Long-run profit maximization requires that long-run marginal cost be equated to selling price and that long-run marginal cost be increasing.

Two or more outputs are often produced jointly in a single production process. In the simplest case the quantities of two outputs can be expressed as a function of the quantity of a single input. A product transformation curve is the locus of all output combinations that can be secured from a given input level. The production relation normally is assumed to be regular strictly quasi-convex and thus to have concave product transformation curves. The entrepreneur may desire to maximize the revenue he obtains from a given input level. First-order conditions require that he equate the rate of product transformation to the ratio of his output prices. In diagrammatic terms he will operate at a point at which an isorevenue line is tangent to a particular product transformation curve. Regular strict quasi-convexity of the production relation ensures satisfaction of the second-order condition. If he desires to maximize profit, he must equate the value of the marginal product of the input with respect to each output to its price. Second-order conditions require that the production relation be strictly convex in the neighborhood of a point at which the first-order conditions are satisfied.

In the general case n inputs are used for the production of s outputs, and the production function is stated in implicit form. It is assumed to be increasing with respect to output levels, decreasing with respect to input levels, and regular strictly quasi-convex over a relevant domain. The first-order conditions for profit maximization require that: (1) the rate of product transformation between every pair of outputs equal their price ratio, (2) the value of the marginal product of each input with respect to each output equal the input price, and (3) the rate of technical substitution between every pair of inputs equal their price ratio. Substitution effects with respect to price variations can be computed, but there is no counterpart for the consumer's nonsymmetric income effect.

EXERCISES

4-1 Construct the average and marginal product functions for X_1 which correspond to the production function $q = x_1x_2 - 0.2x_1^2 - 0.8x_2^2$. Let $x_2 = 10$. At what respective values of x_1 will the AP and MP of X_1 equal zero?

4-2 Determine the domain over which the production function $q = 100(x_1 + x_2) + 20x_1x_2 - 12.5(x_1^2 + x_2^2)$ is increasing and strictly concave.

4-3 Derive an input expansion path for the production function $q = A(x_1 + 1)^\alpha(x_2 + 1)^\beta$ where $\alpha, \beta > 0$.

4-4 Assume that an entrepreneur's short-run total cost function is $C = q^3 - 10q^2 + 17q + 66$. Determine the output level at which he maximizes profit if $p = 5$. Compute the output elasticity of cost at this output.

4-5 A family of short-run total cost curves is generated by $C = 0.04q^3 - 0.9q^2 + (10 - \ln k)q + 8k^2$ where $k > 1$ denotes plant size. Determine the firm's long-run total cost curve.

4-6 An entrepreneur uses one input to produce two outputs subject to the production relation $x = A(q_1^\alpha + q_2^\beta)$ where $\alpha, \beta > 1$. He buys the input and sells the outputs at fixed prices. Express his profit-maximizing outputs as functions of the prices. Prove that his production relation is strictly convex for $q_1, q_2 > 0$.

4-7 An entrepreneur produces one output with two inputs using the production function $q = Ax_1^\alpha x_2^{1-\alpha}$. He buys the inputs and sells the outputs at fixed prices. He is subject to a quota which allows him to purchase no more than x_1^0 units of X_1. He would have purchased more in the absence of the quota. Determine the entrepreneur's conditions for profit maximization. What is the optimal relation between the value of the marginal product of each input and its price? What is the optimal relation between the RTS and the input price ratio?

SELECTED REFERENCES

Allen, R. G. D.: *Mathematical Economics* (London: Macmillan, 1956). Chap. 18 contains a mathematical statement of the theory of the firm. The necessary algebra is developed in the text.

Carlson, Sune: *A Study on the Theory of Production* (New York: Kelley & Millman, 1956). An exposition of the theory of the firm in terms of simple mathematics.

Frisch, Ragnar: *Theory of Production* (Chicago: Rand McNally, 1965). Differential and integral calculus are used extensively in this treatise.

Hicks, J. R.: *Value and Capital* (2d ed., Oxford: Clarendon Press, 1946). The theory of the firm is developed in chaps. VI–VII. The mathematical analysis is contained in an appendix.

Menger, K.: "The Laws of Return," in O. Morgenstern (ed.), *Economic Activity Analysis* (New York: Wiley, 1954), pp. 419–482. A mathematical study of alternative formulations of the law of diminishing returns.

Samuelson, Paul A.: *Foundations of Economic Analysis* (Cambridge, Mass.: Harvard University Press, 1948). Chap. 4 contains a mathematical statement of the theory of the firm.

Silverberg, E.: "The Le Chatelier Principle as a Corollary to a Generalized Envelope Theorem," *Journal of Economic Theory*, vol. 3 (June, 1971), pp. 146–155. A general discussion with illustrations using the calculus and matrix algebra.

TOPICS IN THE THEORY OF THE FIRM

The basic theory of the firm, perhaps even more than the theory of the consumer, has been extended and applied to a very wide range of problems. Some of these extensions and applications are discussed in this chapter. The properties of homogeneous production functions are the subject of Sec. 5-1, and the properties of constant-elasticity-of-substitution (CES) production functions are the subject of Sec. 5-2. The Kuhn-Tucker analysis is illustrated for two different types of production discontinuities in Sec. 5-3. The duality between production and cost functions is discussed in Sec. 5-4. Shephard's lemma is also covered there. In Sec. 5-5 the theory of the firm is extended to cover uncertain price and output situations by introducing profit into the entrepreneur's utility function. Linear production functions are described in Sec. 5-6. The general concepts of linear programming are developed in Sec. 5-7 with examples drawn from linear production theory. Yet a different type of duality is established for pairs of linear-programming systems.

5-1 HOMOGENEOUS PRODUCTION FUNCTIONS

"Returns to scale" describes the output response to a proportionate increase of all inputs. If output increases by the same proportion, returns to scale are constant for the range of input combinations under consideration. They are increasing if output increases by a greater proportion and decreasing if it increases by a smaller proportion. A single production function may exhibit all three types of returns. Some economists assume that production functions exhibit increasing returns for small amounts of the inputs, then pass through a stage of constant returns, and finally exhibit decreasing returns to scale as the quantities of the inputs become greater and greater.

Properties

Returns to scale are easily defined for homogeneous production functions. A production function is homogeneous of degree k if

$$f(tx_1, tx_2) = t^k f(x_1, x_2) \qquad (5\text{-}1)$$

where k is a constant and t is any positive real number. If both inputs are increased by the factor t, output is increased by the factor t^k. Returns to scale are increasing if $k > 1$, constant if $k = 1$, and decreasing if $0 < k < 1$. Homogeneity of degree one is often assumed for production functions.[1]

Following the derivations of Sec. 3-3, the partial derivatives of a function homogeneous of degree k are homogeneous of degree $k - 1$. Homogeneity of degree one is of particular interest in this regard. If a production function is homogeneous of degree one, the marginal products of X_1 and X_2 are homogeneous of degree zero; i.e., they remain unchanged for proportionate changes of both inputs. In particular

$$f_1(x_1, x_2) = f_1\left(\frac{x_1}{x_2}, 1\right)$$

$$f_2(x_1, x_2) = f_2\left(\frac{x_1}{x_2}, 1\right)$$

where $t = 1/x_2$. The MPs depend only upon the proportion in which X_1 and X_2 are used.

The isoquants for a homogeneous production function possess the same properties as the indifference curves for a homogeneous utility function as described in Sec. 3-3. The RTS depends upon the ratios in which the inputs are used, not their absolute quantities. A straight line emanating from the origin in the positive quadrant connects input points with equal RTS. Consequently, the expansion path which is the locus of points with RTS equal to the fixed input price ratio is a straight line if the production function is homogeneous of any degree. Any production function that can be expressed as a monotonic increasing function of a homogeneous function is called homothetic, and has the same isoquants as its underlying homogeneous functions although the quantities corresponding to each isoquant are generally different. The production function given by (4-5) is homothetic, but not homogeneous.

One of the most widely used homogeneous production functions is the

---

[1] A function which is homogeneous of degree one is said to be linearly homogeneous. This, of course, does not imply that the production function is linear.

Cobb-Douglas function:

$$q = Ax_1^\alpha x_2^{1-\alpha} \tag{5-2}$$

where $0 < \alpha < 1$. Increasing the levels of both inputs by the factor t,

$$f(tx_1, tx_2) = A(tx_1)^\alpha (tx_2)^{1-\alpha} = tAx_1^\alpha x_2^{1-\alpha}$$

The Cobb-Douglas function is homogeneous of degree one. The MPs of both inputs are homogeneous of degree zero:

$$f_1(x_1, x_2) = \alpha Ax_1^{\alpha-1} x_2^{1-\alpha}$$
$$f_2(x_1, x_2) = (1 - \alpha)Ax_1^\alpha x_2^{-\alpha}$$
$$f_1(tx_1, tx_2) = \alpha At^{\alpha-1}x_1^{\alpha-1}t^{1-\alpha}x_2^{1-\alpha} = \alpha Ax_1^{\alpha-1}x_2^{1-\alpha}$$
$$f_2(tx_1, tx_2) = (1 - \alpha)At^\alpha x_1^\alpha t^{-\alpha}x_2^{-\alpha} = (1 - \alpha)Ax_1^\alpha x_2^{-\alpha}$$

In Sec. 4-1 it is shown that this production function is positively valued, increasing, and regular strictly quasi-concave over the domain $x_1, x_2 > 0$.

The expansion path generated by the Cobb-Douglas function is linear. The first-order conditions for a constrained optimum require that

$$\frac{r_1}{r_2} = \frac{f_1}{f_2} = \frac{\alpha Ax_1^{\alpha-1}x_2^{1-\alpha}}{(1 - \alpha)Ax_1^\alpha x_2^{-\alpha}} = \frac{\alpha x_2}{(1 - \alpha)x_1}$$

Therefore, the expansion path is given by the implicit function

$$(1 - \alpha)r_1 x_1 - \alpha r_2 x_2 = 0$$

which describes a straight line emanating from the origin in the isoquant plane.

Euler's Theorem and Distribution

Euler's theorem states that the following condition is satisfied by a homogeneous function:[1]

$$x_1 f_1 + x_2 f_2 = kf(x_1, x_2) \tag{5-3}$$

This theorem yields a number of results of interest in economics. For example, dividing (5-3) by q,

$$\omega_1 + \omega_2 = k$$

The sum of the output elasticities [see (4-4)] for X_1 and X_2 equals the degree of homogeneity.

---

[1] Differentiating (5-1) partially with respect to t using the composite-function rule on the left,

$$x_1 f_1(tx, tx_2) + x_2 f_2(tx_1, tx_2) = kt^{k-1}f(x_1, x_2)$$

Equation (5-3) is obtained by substituting $t = 1$.

Assuming that the production function is homogeneous of degree one, and substituting $q = f(x_1, x_2)$,

$$x_1 f_1 + x_2 f_2 = q \qquad (5\text{-}4)$$

Total output equals the MP of X_1 multiplied by its quantity plus the MP of X_2 multiplied by its quantity. If the firm were to pay the suppliers of each input its marginal physical product, total output would be just exhausted. Total payments would exceed output if the degree of homogeneity were greater than one and would be less than output if it were less than one.

Euler's theorem played a major rule in the development of the marginal-productivity theory of distribution. The basic postulates of this theory are: (1) each input is paid the value of its marginal product, and (2) total output is just exhausted. Since these conditions are satisfied by production functions homogeneous of degree one, it was mistakenly assumed that all production functions must be of this type.

The Cobb-Douglas function was utilized to attempt an empirical verification of the marginal-productivity theory of distribution. The variable q represented aggregate output, and x_1 and x_2 were aggregate inputs of labor and capital respectively. Euler's theorem is satisfied:

$$q = x_1(\alpha A x_1^{\alpha-1} x_2^{1-\alpha}) + x_2[(1-\alpha) A x_1^{\alpha} x_2^{-\alpha}]$$
$$= \alpha A x_1^{\alpha} x_2^{1-\alpha} + (1-\alpha) A x_1^{\alpha} x_2^{1-\alpha}$$

Substituting from (5-2),

$$q = \alpha q + (1-\alpha)q$$

If each factor is paid its marginal product, total output is distributed between labor and capital in the respective proportions α and $(1-\alpha)$. Paul Douglas estimated α from aggregate time-series data and compared his estimates with labor's share of total output.[1]

The condition of product exhaustion is equivalent to the condition that maximum long-run profit equal zero. Multiplying (5-4) through by the price of the product

$$x_1(pf_1) + x_2(pf_2) = pq$$

Substituting $r_1 = pf_1$ and $r_2 = pf_2$ from the first-order conditions for profit maximization,

$$r_1 x_1 + r_2 x_2 = pq \qquad (5\text{-}5)$$

Long-run total outlay equals long-run total revenue. Following the assumptions of the marginal-productivity theory, (5-5) leads to the startling conclusion that long-run profit equals zero regardless of the level of the product price.

---

[1] See the references listed at the end of this chapter.

The analysis of the marginal-productivity theory of distribution is misleading, if not erroneous. The conventional analysis of profit maximization breaks down if the entrepreneur sells her output at a constant price and possesses a production function which is homogeneous of degree one. The reader can verify that in this case her profit function is also homogeneous of degree one:

$$t\pi = pf(tx_1, tx_2) - r_1 t x_1 - r_2 t x_2$$

Three outcomes are possible. If the prices are such that some factor combination yields a positive profit, profit can be increased to any level by selecting a sufficiently large value for t. In this case the profit function has no finite maximum. If the prices are such that every factor combination yields a negative profit, the entrepreneur will go out of business.

The third possibility, to which the marginal-productivity theorists generally limited their analysis, is the most interesting. In this case there is no factor combination which will yield a positive profit, but the combination (x_1^0, x_2^0) yields a zero profit. From the homogeneity of the profit function it follows that the factor combination (tx_1^0, tx_2^0) will also yield a zero profit. Maximum long-run profit equals zero, but the size of the firm is indeterminate. If the entrepreneur can earn a zero profit for a particular factor combination, her profit remains unchanged if she doubles or halves her scale of operations. If an arbitrary scale of operations is imposed upon the entrepreneur, Euler's theorem holds, and her product is just exhausted.

The assumption of a homogeneous production function is not necessary for the fulfillment of the postulates of the marginal-productivity theory. The postulates are fulfilled if (1) the production function is not homogeneous, (2) the first- and second-order conditions for profit maximization are fulfilled, and (3) the entrepreneur's maximum profit equals zero. Conditions (1) and (2) have been assumed throughout the development of the theory of the firm in Secs. 4-1 and 4-2. In Chap. 6 it is demonstrated that the free entry and exit of competing firms will result in the satisfaction of condition (3). Condition (3) requires that

$$\pi = pq - r_1 x_1 - r_2 x_2 = 0$$

Substituting $r_1 = pf_1$ and $r_2 = pf_2$ (the first-order conditions), and solving for q,

$$q = x_1 f_1 + x_2 f_2$$

Here the result of (5-4) is attained without the use of Euler's theorem. Furthermore, since the production function is not homogeneous, the entrepreneur's optimum factor combination is generally determinate.

The indeterminacy problem can be viewed in terms of the inability of the entrepreneur to satisfy her second-order conditions for profit maximization. Differentiate (5-4) totally,

$$(f_1 + x_1 f_{11} + x_2 f_{21})\, dx_1 + (f_2 + x_1 f_{12} + x_2 f_{22})\, dx_2 = dq$$

Alternátely, let $dx_2 = 0$ and divide by dx_1, and let $dx_1 = 0$ and divide by dx_2:

$$f_1 + x_1 f_{11} + x_2 f_{21} = \frac{\partial q}{\partial x_1} = f_1$$

$$f_2 + x_1 f_{12} + x_2 f_{22} = \frac{\partial q}{\partial x_2} = f_2$$

Subtract f_1 from both sides of the first equation and solve for f_{11}, and subtract f_2 from both sides of the second and solve for f_{22}:

$$f_{11} = -\frac{x_2}{x_1} f_{21} \qquad f_{22} = -\frac{x_1}{x_2} f_{12} \tag{5-6}$$

Thus, $f_{12} = f_{21}$ is positive if f_{11} and f_{22} are negative as assumed. Evaluating the Hessian of the production function using (5-6),

$$f_{11} f_{22} - f_{12}^2 = \left(-\frac{x_2}{x_1} f_{12} \right) \left(-\frac{x_1}{x_2} f_{12} \right) - f_{12}^2 = 0$$

A production function homogeneous of degree one is concave, but it has linear subregions in which it is not strictly concave.

Production functions homogeneous of degree one are used often and meaningfully in economics despite the indeterminacy problems for the individual firm. A number of assumptions are invoked to cope with this problem. Two possible assumptions are: (1) Firm size and firm numbers are determined by some arbitrary mechanism subject to the condition that industry output satisfies industry demand. (2) An industry possesses a production function homogeneous of degree one even though the individual firms within the industry do not possess such production functions. In Chaps. 7 and 8 it is shown that firm size may be determinate if firms operate under conditions of imperfect competition.

Long-Run Cost Functions

It is possible to construct long-run cost functions with all inputs variable for homogeneous production functions with convex indifference curves. Let (x_1^0, x_2^0) be the optimum input combination for the production of one unit of Q. The corresponding production cost is $a = r_1 x_1^0 + r_2 x_2^0$. Since the expansion path for a homogeneous production function is linear, all optimum input combinations may be written as (tx_1^0, tx_2^0). Therefore, the production function and cost equation may be written as

$$q = f(tx_1^0, tx_2^0) = t^k$$

$$C = (r_1 x_1^0 + r_2 x_2^0)t = at$$

Solving the first equation for t and substituting into the second, the total cost function is

$$C = aq^{1/k}$$

with
$$\frac{dC}{dq} = \frac{a}{k} q^{(1-k)/k} \qquad \frac{d^2C}{dq^2} = \frac{a(1-k)}{k^2} q^{(1-2k)/k}$$

Functions homogeneous of degree one have constant MC and ATC and a linear long-run total cost function. MC is increasing throughout for $k < 1$ and decreasing throughout for $k > 1$. The second-order condition that MC be increasing can be satisfied only if the degree of homogeneity is less than one.

The production function $q = Ax_1^\alpha x_2^\beta$ with $\alpha, \beta > 0$ is homogeneous of degree $\alpha + \beta$:

$$q = A(tx_1)^\alpha (tx_2)^\beta = t^{\alpha+\beta} Ax_1^\alpha x_2^\beta$$

Equation (4-30) gives long-run cost functions for production functions of this class. The cost function for the Cobb-Douglas production function with $\alpha + \beta = 1$ is

$$C = aq$$

where
$$a = \frac{r_1^\alpha r_2^{1-\alpha}}{A\alpha^\alpha (1-\alpha)^{1-\alpha}}$$

5-2 CES PRODUCTION FUNCTIONS

A production function which belongs to the CES class has two major characteristics: (1) it is homogeneous of degree one, and (2) it has a constant elasticity of substitution (see Sec. 4-1). Production functions which lack one or both of these characteristics do not belong to the CES class. In Sec. 4-1 it was shown that the production functions $q = Ax_1^\alpha x_2^\beta$ have constant unit elasticities of substitution. Thus, all production functions in this class satisfy criterion (2). However, criterion (1) is satisfied only for $\alpha + \beta = 1$, that is, for the Cobb-Douglas function. The production function $q = Ax_1^\alpha x_2^{1-\alpha} + x_1$ is homogeneous of degree one, but does not have a constant elasticity of substitution and is not a member of the CES class.

Properties

By advanced methods it has been shown that the class of CES production functions may be expressed in the form[1]

$$q = A[\alpha x_1^{-\rho} + (1-\alpha)x_2^{-\rho}]^{-1/\rho} \tag{5-7}$$

where the parameters $A > 0$ and $0 < \alpha < 1$. It is easily verified that (5-7) is homogeneous of degree one:

$$A[\alpha(tx_1)^{-\rho} + (1-\alpha)(tx_2)^{-\rho}]^{-1/\rho} = tA[\alpha x_1^{-\rho} + (1-\alpha)x_2^{-\rho}]^{-1/\rho}$$

---

[1] See K. Arrow, H. B. Chenery, B. Minhas, and R. M. Solow, "Capital-Labor Substitution and Economic Efficiency," *Review of Economics and Statistics*, vol. 43 (August, 1961), pp. 228–232.

The marginal products of the inputs are

$$\frac{\partial q}{\partial x_1} = \frac{\alpha}{A^\rho}\left(\frac{q}{x_1}\right)^{\rho+1} \qquad \frac{\partial q}{\partial x_2} = \frac{1-\alpha}{A^\rho}\left(\frac{q}{x_2}\right)^{\rho+1}$$

which are positive for the domain $x_1, x_2 > 0$. The rate of technical substitution is

$$\text{RTS} = \frac{\alpha}{1-\alpha}\left(\frac{x_2}{x_1}\right)^{\rho+1} \tag{5-8}$$

The RTS is decreasing and the isoquants convex for $\rho > -1$. This also establishes that a CES production function is regular strictly quasi-concave for the domain $x_1, x_2 > 0$.

An expression for the elasticity of substitution for production functions homogeneous of degree one is obtained by substituting (5-6) into (4-11)

$$\sigma = \frac{f_1 f_2 (x_1 f_1 + x_2 f_2)}{f_{12}(x_1 f_1 + x_2 f_2)^2}$$

and invoking Euler's theorem (5-3),

$$\sigma = \frac{f_1 f_2}{f_{12} q} \tag{5-9}$$

For (5-7),

$$f_{12} = \frac{(1+\rho)\alpha(1-\alpha)q^{1+2\rho}}{A^{2\rho}(x_1 x_2)^{1+\rho}}$$

Evaluating (5-9) for (5-7),

$$\sigma = \frac{1}{1+\rho} \qquad \rho = \frac{1-\sigma}{\sigma} \tag{5-10}$$

Thus, the parameter ρ is closely related to the constant elasticity of substitution. The inequality $\rho > -1$ is equivalent to $\sigma > 0$.

Isoquants

The particular shape of the convex isoquants generated by a CES function depends upon the value of σ. Two limits and three intermediate cases describe the possible isoquant configurations.

Case 1 $\sigma \to 0$, $\rho \to +\infty$. The RTS (5-8) approaches zero if $x_1 > x_2$ or $+\infty$ if $x_1 < x_2$, and in the limit substitution is impossible. The curvature of the isoquants approaches a right angle.

Case 2 $0 < \sigma < 1$, $\rho > 0$. The isoquants for (5-7) can be written as

$$\alpha x_1^{-\rho} + (1-\alpha)x_2^{-\rho} = \left(\frac{q}{A}\right)^{-\rho} = K \tag{5-11}$$

where K is a positive constant for any selected positive value of q. Neither term on the left-hand side of (5-11) can be negative. Therefore, neither term can exceed K in value. As $x_1 \to 0$, $ax_1^{-\rho} \to +\infty$. Since there is an upper limit K on the value of $ax_1^{-\rho}$, x_1 cannot equal zero. By similar reasoning, x_2 cannot equal zero. Thus, an isoquant neither cuts nor approaches the axes. It is asymptotic to $x_1 = (K/\alpha)^{-1/\rho}$ and $x_2 = [K/(1-\alpha)]^{-1/\rho}$.

Case 3 $\sigma = 1, \rho = 0$. It has been observed that the CES production function becomes the Cobb-Douglas function for $\sigma = 1$. The interpretation of this case is not obvious from (5-7). When the parameter $\rho = 0$, (5-11) becomes an identity and is not helpful in establishing the properties of this case. These properties may be examined by making use of L'Hôpital's rule which states that[1] if

$$\lim_{z \to b} h(z) = 0 \qquad \text{and} \qquad \lim_{z \to b} g(z) = 0$$

and if

$$\lim_{z \to b} \frac{h'(z)}{g'(z)} = \alpha$$

then

$$\lim_{z \to b} \frac{h(z)}{g(z)} = \alpha$$

Write the natural logarithm of (5-7) as the quotient of two functions of ρ:

$$\ln q - \ln A = \frac{-\ln [\alpha x_1^{-\rho} + (1-\alpha)x_2^{-\rho}]}{\rho} = \frac{h(\rho)}{g(\rho)}$$

where $h(\rho) \to 0$ and $g(\rho) \to 0$ as $\rho \to 0$. Taking the derivative of the numerator,

$$h'(\rho) = \frac{\alpha x_1^{-\rho} \ln x_1 + (1-\alpha)x_2^{-\rho} \ln x_2}{\alpha x_1^{-\rho} + (1-\alpha)x_2^{-\rho}}$$

which converges to $\alpha \ln x_1 + (1-\alpha)\ln x_2$ as $\rho \to 0$. Finally, $g'(\rho) = 1$. By L'Hôpital's rule the limiting case is

$$\ln q - \ln A = \alpha \ln x_1 + (1-\alpha)\ln x_2$$

and $q = Ax_1^{\alpha}x_2^{1-\alpha}$ which is the Cobb-Douglas function.

Case 4 $\sigma > 1, -1 < \rho < 0$. The exponents of the terms on the left of (5-11) are positive. Isoquants will meet both axes. If $x_1 = 0$, $x_2 = [K/(1-\alpha)]^{-\rho}$, and if $x_2 = 0$, $x_1 = (K/\alpha)^{-\rho}$.

Case 5 $\sigma \to +\infty, \rho \to -1$. In the limit the exponents of both terms on the left of (5-11) are one, and the isoquants are straight lines. The inputs are perfect substitutes in this limiting case.

---

[1] See T. M. Apostol, *Calculus* (2d ed., New York: Wiley, 1967), vol. I, pp. 292–295.

The Equilibrium Condition

The CES production function (5-7) is cumbersome and difficult to manipulate. Its RTS, however, is quite simple, and this is one of the reasons for its popularity and wide use. Substituting for σ from (5-10), and letting the RTS (5-8) equal the input price ratio,

$$\frac{\alpha}{1-\alpha}\left(\frac{x_2}{x_1}\right)^{1/\sigma} = \frac{r_1}{r_2}$$

and
$$\frac{x_2}{x_1} = a\left(\frac{r_1}{r_2}\right)^{\sigma} \tag{5-12}$$

where $a = [(1-\alpha)/\alpha]^{\sigma}$. The reader can verify from (5-12) that the constant elasticity of substitution is also the constant elasticity of the input use ratio (x_2/x_1) with respect to the input price ratio.

Equation (5-12) states that the input use ratio is a simple power function of the input price ratio. Since this function is linear in the logarithms of the variables, the parameters a and σ are amenable to estimation by linear regression analysis from time-series data. If x_1 and x_2 are labor and capital respectively, (5-12) shows how the capital-labor ratio for a particular good changes with changes in the wage-capital rental ratio.

A Generalized CES Production Function

The CES production function is defined to be homogeneous of degree one. It is here generalized to cover any degree of homogeneity. Consider the production function

$$q = B[\alpha x_1^{-\rho} + (1-\alpha)x_2^{-\rho}]^{-k/\rho} \tag{5-13}$$

with the domain $x_1, x_2 > 0$ where B, α, and k are positive. This function is homogeneous of degree k:

$$B[\alpha(tx_1)^{-\rho} + (1-\alpha)(tx_2)^{-\rho}]^{-k/\rho} = t^k B[\alpha x_1^{-\rho} + (1-\alpha)x_2^{-\rho}]^{-k/\rho}$$

The MPs are

$$\frac{\partial q}{\partial x_1} = \frac{k\alpha q^{(k+\rho)/k}}{B^{\rho/k}x_1^{(\rho+1)}} \qquad \frac{\partial q}{\partial x_1} = \frac{k(1-\alpha)q^{(k+\rho)/k}}{B^{\rho/k}x_2^{(\rho+1)}}$$

The function (5-13) can be expressed as a positive monotonic transformation of (5-7). Isoquants are unaltered by such transformations. Consequently, the RTS for (5-13) is given by (5-8), the elasticity of substitution by (5-10), and the first-order condition for constrained cost minimization by (5-12). If $k < 1$, (5-13) is strictly concave, and the first-order conditions for profit maximization given by (4-19) are meaningful.

5-3 THE KUHN-TUCKER CONDITIONS

The Kuhn-Tucker conditions are useful for the analysis of a wide range of topics in the theory of the firm. Corner solutions such as those illustrated in Sec. 2-2 may occur for the firm as well as the consumer. Two examples are given here to suggest further situations that may be covered by Kuhn-Tucker. In the first the entrepreneur has the choice of either producing or purchasing an input. In the second she must determine how much, if any, overtime labor to purchase.

An Input Option

Assume that an entrepreneur has the following two-input production function:

$$q = f(x_{11} + x_{12}, x_2)$$

where x_{11} is the quantity of X_1 that the entrepreneur produces and x_{12} is the quantity that she purchases in the market at a constant price of r_1 dollars per unit. The entire quantity, x_2, of the second input is purchased at the fixed price r_2 dollars per unit. The entrepreneur's production function for the input is

$$x_{11} = g(x_3)$$

where x_3 is the quantity of a third input used for the production of X_1. Its constant price is r_3. It is assumed that $x_{11} = 0$ implies that $x_3 = 0$.

The appropriate Lagrange function for profit maximization is

$$Z = pf(x_{11} + x_{12}, x_2) - r_1 x_{12} - r_2 x_2 - r_3 x_3 + \lambda [g(x_3) - x_{11}]$$

Assuming that both production functions are concave, the Kuhn-Tucker conditions for profit maximization are

$$\frac{\partial Z}{\partial x_{11}} = pf_1 - \lambda \leq 0 \qquad\qquad x_{11} \frac{\partial Z}{\partial x_{11}} = 0$$

$$\frac{\partial Z}{\partial x_{12}} = pf_1 - r_1 \leq 0 \qquad\qquad x_{12} \frac{\partial Z}{\partial x_{12}} = 0$$

$$\frac{\partial Z}{\partial x_2} = pf_2 - r_2 \leq 0 \qquad\qquad x_2 \frac{\partial Z}{\partial x_2} = 0 \qquad (5\text{-}14)$$

$$\frac{\partial Z}{\partial x_3} = \lambda g' - r_3 \leq 0 \qquad\qquad x_3 \frac{\partial Z}{\partial x_3} = 0$$

$$\frac{\partial Z}{\partial \lambda} = g(x_3) - x_{11} \geq 0 \qquad\qquad \lambda \frac{\partial Z}{\partial \lambda} = 0$$

It is also required that the five variables be nonnegative.

Three general outcomes are possible: (1) the input is purchased but not produced; (2) it is produced but not purchased; and (3) it is both produced and purchased. The prevailing case is determined by comparing the marginal production cost of X_1 with the value of its marginal product. From the first and fourth inequalities of (5-14)

$$\text{MC}_{x_1} = \frac{r_3}{g'(x_3)} \geq \lambda \geq pf_1$$

The input will be produced as long as $\text{MC}_{x_1} \leq r_1$. If the input is purchased but not produced, $x_{11} = 0$, and $x_{12} > 0$, the equilibrium relations of (5-14) yield $pf_1 = r_1 \leq \lambda$. If it is produced but not purchased, $x_{11} > 0$ and $x_{12} = 0$, $pf_1 = \lambda \leq r_1$. Finally, if it is both produced and purchased, the equilibrium marginal-production cost equals the market price of the input.

A Discontinuous Labor Contract

Thus far, it has been assumed that an entrepreneur can purchase as much of an input as she desires at a constant price. One need not look far to find cases that violate this assumption. Assume that an entrepreneur has a labor contract whereby she may purchase up to $\bar{L}$ units of labor at the going wage rate w, but must pay an overtime premium to secure additional units of labor. Specifically, assume that she can obtain as much as $0.2\bar{L}$ additional units at a wage of $1.5w$—call this time-and-one-half labor— and get another $0.2\bar{L}$ units at a wage of $2w$—call this double-time labor. Let $L_1, L_2,$ and L_3 be purchased quantities of regular, time-and-one-half, and double-time labor respectively. Labor use is subject to the following inequality restrictions:

$$\bar{L} \geq L_1 \qquad 0.2\bar{L} \geq L_2 \qquad 0.2\bar{L} \geq L_3 \qquad (5\text{-}15)$$

Capital is the only other input, and production is governed by the concave production function $q = f(L_1 + L_2 + L_3, K)$.

The Lagrange function in this case is

$$V = pf(L_1 + L_2 + L_3, K) - wL_1 - 1.5wL_2 - 2wL_3 - rK + \mu_1(\bar{L} - L_1)$$
$$+ \mu_2(0.2\bar{L} - L_2) + \mu_3(0.2\bar{L} - L_3) \qquad (5\text{-}16)$$

where p and r are the fixed output and capital prices respectively. The Kuhn-Tucker conditions are:

$$\frac{\partial V}{\partial L_1} = pf_L - w - \mu_1 \leq 0 \qquad L_1 \frac{\partial V}{\partial L_1} = 0$$

$$\frac{\partial V}{\partial L_2} = pf_L - 1.5w - \mu_2 \leq 0 \qquad L_2 \frac{\partial V}{\partial L_2} = 0$$

$$\frac{\partial V}{\partial L_3} = pf_L - 2w - \mu_3 \leq 0 \qquad L_3 \frac{\partial V}{\partial L_3} = 0$$

$$\frac{\partial V}{\partial K} = pf_K - r \leq 0 \qquad K \frac{\partial V}{\partial K} = 0$$

$$\frac{\partial V}{\partial \mu_1} = \bar{L} - L_1 \geqq 0 \qquad \mu_1 \frac{\partial V}{\partial \mu_1} = 0$$

$$\frac{\partial V}{\partial \mu_2} = 0.2\bar{L} - L_2 \geqq 0 \qquad \mu_2 \frac{\partial V}{\partial \mu_2} = 0$$

$$\frac{\partial V}{\partial \mu_3} = 0.2\bar{L} - L_3 \geqq 0 \qquad \mu_3 \frac{\partial V}{\partial \mu_3} = 0$$

and the requirement that each of the seven variables be nonnegative.

Recalling that $\mu_i = \partial V^*/\partial L_i^*$ where the * indicate optimal values, these variables may be interpreted as shadow profits for each of the three classes of labor, i.e., the amount by which the value of the marginal product of labor exceeds the wage payment for each. The following seven general cases are possible depending upon parameter values:

Case

1. $L_1 = 0$	$L_2 = 0$	$L_3 = 0$	$pf_L \leqq w$
2. $0 < L_1 < \bar{L}$	$L_2 = 0$	$L_3 = 0$	$pf_L = w$
3. $L_1 = \bar{L}$	$L_2 = 0$	$L_3 = 0$	$w \leqq pf_L \leqq 1.5w$
4. $L_1 = \bar{L}$	$0 < L_2 < 0.2\bar{L}$	$L_3 = 0$	$pf_L = 1.5w$
5. $L_1 = \bar{L}$	$L_2 = 0.2\bar{L}$	$L_3 = 0$	$1.5w \leqq pf_L \leqq 2w$
6. $L_1 = \bar{L}$	$L_2 = 0.2\bar{L}$	$0 < L_3 < 0.2\bar{L}$	$pf_L = 2w$
7. $L_1 = \bar{L}$	$L_2 = 0.2\bar{L}$	$L_3 = 0.2\bar{L}$	$pf_L \geqq 2w$

The entrepreneur equates the value of the marginal product of labor to the appropriate wage rate insofar as she can. No production is desirable in case 1. One of the three wage rates prevails in cases 2, 4, and 6. In cases 3 and 5 the optimal value for the MP of labor lies between two wage rates; in case 7, where all available labor is being used, it may exceed the double-time wage.

5-4 DUALITY IN PRODUCTION

The analysis of duality given in Sec. 3-4 can be applied with little modification to cover maximization of output subject to a cost constraint for the firm. However, minimization of cost subject to an output constraint is a more interesting problem for the firm, and duality for the firm is focused upon this problem. An important duality for the firm exists between the production and cost functions. The derivation of the cost function from the production function is covered in Sec. 4-4. The derivation of the production function from the cost function is considered here.

Consider the firm's isoquant defined by $q^0 = f(x_1, x_2)$, and the first-order condition for cost minimization for this output: $-dx_2/dx_1 = r_1/r_2$. Solve these equations for the input functions

$$x_1 = \psi_1(r_1/r_2, q^0)$$
$$x_2 = \psi_2(r_1/r_2, q^0)$$

(5-17)

where x_1 and x_2 are cost-minimizing values expressed as functions of the ratio of the input prices and the prescribed output level.[1] Now differentiate the cost equation $C = r_1x_1 + r_2x_2$, given (5-17) and the first-order conditions $r_i = \lambda f_i$:

$$\frac{\partial C}{\partial r_i} = x_i + \lambda\left(f_1\frac{\partial\psi_1}{\partial r_i} + f_2\frac{\partial\psi_2}{\partial r_i}\right) = x_i > 0 \qquad i = 1, 2$$

(5-18)

where λ is the Lagrange multiplier in the constrained-cost-minimization problem. The bracketed term equals $\partial q^0/\partial r_i = 0$ along the isoquant. Equation (5-18) is known as *Shephard's lemma*. The partial derivatives of the cost function (4-28) with respect to the input prices equal the cost-minimizing values for the inputs.

$$\frac{\partial C(q, r_1, r_2)}{\partial r_1} = x_1 \qquad \frac{\partial C(q, r_1, r_2)}{\partial r_2} = x_2$$

(5-19)

Since the variable cost function is homogeneous of degree one in the input prices, its partial derivatives[2] are homogeneous of degree zero in the input prices, and depend upon the input price ratio rather than absolute input prices. Under appropriate conditions, the two equations (5-19) may be solved for the two variables q and r_2/r_1 with the solution for q providing the underlying production function. In practice (5-19) may be very difficult to solve.

Typical duality theorems state that (1) a concave production function yields a cost function homogeneous of degree one in input prices, given specified regularity conditions, (2) a cost function homogeneous of degree one in input prices yields a concave production function, given specified regularity conditions, and (3) the cost function derived from a particular production function will in turn yield that production function.

As an example, consider the cost function (4-30),

$$C = \gamma(r_1^\alpha r_2^\beta)^{1/(\alpha+\beta)}$$

where $\gamma = (\alpha + \beta)(A\alpha^\alpha\beta^\beta)^{-1/(\alpha+\beta)}$ which was derived for the production function $q = Ax_1^\alpha x_2^\beta$. Equations (5-19) are

$$\left(\frac{\alpha}{\alpha + \beta}\right)\gamma q^{1/(\alpha+\beta)}(r_2/r_1)^{\beta/(\alpha+\beta)} = x_1$$

$$\left(\frac{\beta}{\alpha + \beta}\right)\gamma q^{1/(\alpha+\beta)}(r_2/r_1)^{-\alpha/(\alpha+\beta)} = x_2$$

[1] These are not the same as the input demand functions (4-22) which are derived from profit maximization.

[2] Remember that the partial derivatives of the variable and total cost functions are the same.

in this case. These equations are most easily solved for q by raising both sides of the first equation to the power α, both sides of the second to the power β, and multiplying. This yields the production function $q = Ax_1^\alpha x_2^\beta$.

5-5 PRODUCTION UNDER UNCERTAINTY

The expected utility analysis developed in Secs. 3-8 and 3-9 may be applied when the firm is subject to uncertainty. It is assumed that the producer has a utility function for which profit is the argument, and that she obeys the von Neumann–Morgenstern axioms. Two examples are presented in this section. In the first, output is certain, and price is subject to uncertainty. In the second, price is certain, and output is subject to uncertainty.

Assume that output price can realize one of n distinct values $(p_1, \ldots, p_n)$ with the respective probabilities $(v_1, \ldots, v_n)$ where $\Sigma_{i=1}^n v_i = 1$. The firm's expected profit is

$$E[\pi] = \sum_{i=1}^n v_i[p_i q - C(q)]$$

Setting the derivative of output equal to zero,

$$\frac{dE[\pi]}{dq} = \sum_{i=1}^n v_i[p_i - C'(q)] = \bar{p} - C'(q) = 0 \tag{5-20}$$

where $\bar{p}$ is the expected value of price. To maximize expected profit the entrepreneur simply equates expected price to marginal cost, and the analysis is little altered by the introduction of uncertainty.

Now consider a situation in which the entrepreneur desires to maximize the expected utility of profit

$$E[U(\pi)] = \sum_{i=1}^n v_i U(\pi_i)$$

where $\pi_i = p_i q - C(q)$. Output level is again the decision variable.

$$\frac{dE[U(\pi)]}{dq} = \sum_{i=1}^n v_i U'(\pi_i)[p_i - C'(q)] = 0 \tag{5-21}$$

If $d^2U/d\pi^2 = 0$, the entrepreneur is risk neutral, $U'(\pi_i)$ is a constant, and she equates marginal cost to expected price as in (5-20).

The result is different, however, if the entrepreneur is assumed to be risk averse. In this case $d^2U/d\pi^2 < 0$, and

$$\sum_{i=1}^n v_i U'(\pi_i)[p_i - C'(q^*)] < 0 \tag{5-22}$$

where q^* is the output level that provides a solution for (5-20). Let the outcomes be numbered so that p_i and π_i increase with i. Then the square-bracketed terms increase from most negative to most positive, and the $U'(\pi_i)$ decrease with i. Consequently, (5-22) has a smaller value than (5-20).

Since MC is increasing, $\hat{q}$, the equilibrium value for output, must be lower than q^*. Thus, $\bar{p} > C'(\hat{q})$, and equilibrium MC is lower than expected price. Risk aversity leads to lower output levels than would be produced in its absence. An opposite conclusion is reached if the entrepreneur prefers risk, but this assumption is seldom made.

For an example, assume that the possible price vector is $(6, 7, 8, 9, 10)$ with the probability of each being 0.2. Let $U(\pi) = \ln \pi$ and $C = 0.05q^2$. The expected value for price is $\bar{p} = 8$ and solution of (5-20) provides $q^* = 80$. Equation (5-21) is

$$\frac{dE[U(\pi)]}{dq} = \sum_{i=1}^{5} \left(0.2 \frac{p_i - 0.1q}{p_i q - 0.05 q^2}\right) = 0$$

The reader may verify that $\hat{q} \approx 74.88$ provides an approximate solution.

Now consider the case of a farmer with a guaranteed price of p and a target output level of $\bar{q}$. Her actual output may differ from $\bar{q}$ as a result of weather. Assume that there are n possible output levels $(\delta_1 \bar{q}, \ldots, \delta_n \bar{q})$ with the respective probabilities $(v_1, \ldots, v_n)$ where the $v_i \delta_i$ as well as the v_i are nonnegative and sum to one. The farmer's target output level determines her costs and is the relevant decision variable. The expected utility of her profit is

$$E[U(\pi)] = \sum_{i=1}^{N} v_i U[p \delta_i \bar{q} - C(\bar{q})]$$

Setting its derivative equal to zero,

$$\frac{dE[U(\pi)]}{d\bar{q}} = \sum_{i=1}^{n} v_i U'(\pi_i)[\delta_i p - C'(\bar{q})] = 0 \tag{5-23}$$

Equation (5-23) may be treated as a special case of (5-21) with $p_i = \delta_i p$. Uncertainty with respect to output leads to the same general result as uncertainty with respect to price. Here, expected MC will be less than price.

For an example, let the δ_i be $(0.6, 0.8, 1.0, 1.2, 1.4)$ and the v_i be $(0.1, 0.2, 0.4, 0.2, 0.1)$. Let $p = 5$, $C = 0.04\bar{q}^2 + \bar{q}$, and $U(\pi) = -e^{-0.01\pi}$ which has constant absolute risk aversion (see Sec. 3-9). Equating expected MC to price, $\bar{q} = 50$. Expected utility is

$$E[U(\pi)] = -\sum_{i=1}^{5} v_i e^{-0.01(p\delta_i \bar{q} - 0.04\bar{q}^2 - \bar{q})}$$

and the first-order condition is

$$\frac{dE[U(\pi)]}{d\bar{q}} = 0.01 \sum_{i=1}^{5} v_i (p\delta_i - 0.08\bar{q} - 1)e^{-0.01(p\delta_i \bar{q} - 0.04\bar{q}^2 - \bar{q})} = 0$$

The reader may verify that $\bar{q} \approx 43.59$ provides an approximate solution.

5-6 LINEAR PRODUCTION FUNCTIONS

A linear production activity is a process by which one or more outputs are produced in fixed proportions by the application of one or more inputs in fixed proportions. It is homogeneous of degree one and thus yields constant returns to scale. If all inputs are increased (or decreased) proportionately, all outputs will be increased (or decreased) by the same proportion. A linear production function is formed from a collection of linear production activities that may be utilized simultaneously.

The One-Output Case

Consider a linear production activity by which a single output is produced from m inputs. The activity is completely described by a set of coefficients a_i ($i = 1, \ldots, m$) which give the quantities of the inputs necessary to produce one unit of the output. Requisite input levels are uniquely determined for any specified output level:

$$x_i = a_i q \qquad i = 1, \ldots, m \tag{5-24}$$

The maximum output that can be secured from a specified set of input quantities is

$$q = \min_i \left(\frac{x_i}{a_i} \right) \qquad a_i > 0 \tag{5-25}$$

Each input can become the factor that limits output. It follows from (5-24) that the quantity x_i will support an output of x_i/a_i units, but all other inputs must be available in the appropriate amounts to achieve this output level. Therefore, the smallest x_i/a_i determines the maximum producible output level. Portions of the quantities of some inputs may remain unused because of a relative dearth of a limiting input.

Let the coefficients for a two-input activity be $a_1 = 2$ and $a_2 = 5$. An output of 1 unit requires $x_1 = 2$ and $x_2 = 5$, an output of two units requires $x_1 = 4$ and $x_2 = 10$, and so on. If an entrepreneur possessed 4 units of the first input and 20 units of the second, she could produce 2 units of output:

$$q = \min \left(\tfrac{4}{2}, \tfrac{20}{5} \right) = 2$$

The first input is limiting, and the entrepreneur must leave 10 of her 20 units of the second unused. Figure 5-1 contains an isoquant diagram for this activity. The expansion path OE is the locus of points with x_1 and x_2 in the ratio $2:5$. Each isoquant makes a right angle at the expansion path. Starting from a point on the expansion path, an increment of one input without a proportionate increment of the other will not allow an increase of output. Point A with the coordinates $x_1 = 4$ and $x_2 = 20$ lies on the isoquant $q^0 = 2$.

Now assume that the entrepreneur has n distinct linear production activities that she can utilize individually or jointly for the production of her output. Let a_{ij} ($i = 1, \ldots, m; j = 1, \ldots, n$) be the quantity of the ith input required to produce one unit of output using the jth activity. The outcomes of the activities are additive. Total output is

$$q = \sum_{j=1}^{n} q_j$$

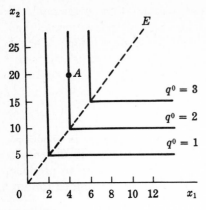

Figure 5-1

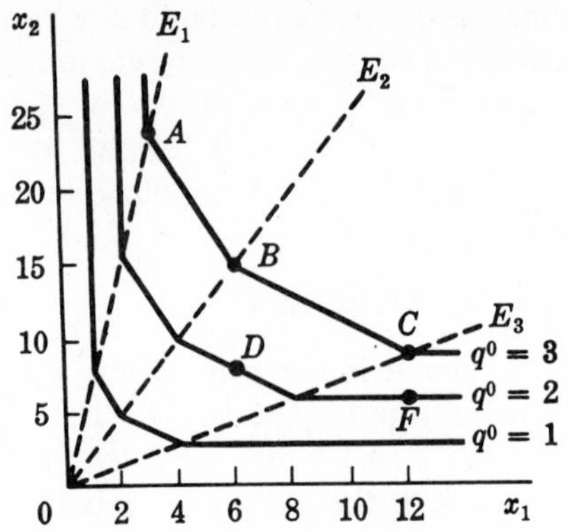

Figure 5-2

where q_j is the quantity produced using the jth activity, and total input requirements are

$$x_i = \sum_{j=1}^{n} a_{ij}q_j \qquad i = 1, \ldots, m \tag{5-26}$$

Composite input requirements per unit output, α_i $(i = 1, \ldots, m)$, are weighted averages of the coefficients for the individual activities:

$$\alpha_i = \sum_{j=1}^{n} \lambda_j a_{ij} \qquad i = 1, \ldots, m \tag{5-27}$$

with $0 \leq \lambda_j \leq 1$ and $\sum_{j=1}^{n} \lambda_j = 1$ where $\lambda_j = q_j/q$ is the proportion of total output produced by the jth activity. Composite activities allow substitution among inputs that substantially changes the form of (5-25). The maximum output that can be secured from a specified set of input quantities is

$$q = \min \left(\frac{x_i}{\alpha_i} \right) \qquad \alpha_i > 0 \tag{5-28}$$

The minimum ratio x_i/α_i is limiting, but the λ_j are selected to maximize the minimum ratio.

Assume that an entrepreneur can produce her output using two inputs and three activities with

$$a_{11} = 1 \qquad a_{12} = 2 \qquad a_{13} = 4$$

$$a_{21} = 8 \qquad a_{22} = 5 \qquad a_{23} = 3$$

Figure 5-2 is an isoquant diagram for this linear production function. The expansion paths for activities 1, 2, and 3 are OE_1, OE_2, and OE_3 respectively. Consider the isoquant for $q_1^0 = 3$. Points A, B, and C give input requirements if only one of the activities is used. The line segment AB gives the input requirements for all composite activities formed from activities 1 and 2 that can be used to produce 3 units. This is a special case of (5-27) with

$$x_1 = 3\alpha_1 = 3[\lambda + 2(1 - \lambda)]$$

$$x_2 = 3\alpha_2 = 3[8\lambda + 5(1 - \lambda)]$$

as λ varies from zero (point B) to one (point A). Similarly, the line segment BC gives input requirements for the composite activities formed from 2 and 3. Input substitution with composite activities is not possible to the left of OE_1, that is, for $x_2/x_1 > 8$. Only activity 1 will be employed, and some of X_2 will remain unused. To the right of OE_3, that is, for $x_2/x_1 < \frac{3}{4}$, only activity 3 will be employed, and some of X_1 will remain unused.

The isoquants derived in Chap. 4 give x_2 as strictly convex functions of x_1, and have RTSs that are continuous and decreasing. The isoquants in Fig. 5-2 give x_2 as convex (but not strictly convex) functions of x_1, and have RTSs that are discontinuous and nonincreasing. Linear production functions will always generate isoquants of this general form. The isoquants provide a graphic solution for (5-28); i.e., they give the maximum output levels that can be secured from each input combination. Inefficient activities are eliminated. A simple or composite activity is inefficient if some other simple or composite activity requires no more of any input and less of at least one input. It is evident from Fig. 5-2 that combinations of activities 1 and 3 are inefficient. Input requirements for $q^0 = 3$ are given by a line segment connecting A and C which lies above the line segments AB and BC.

Multiple-Output Cases

The concept of a linear production function is easily interpreted to accommodate more than one output. Assume that each of s outputs is produced by a linear production activity using m inputs. A particular output still may be produced by more than one activity. Let a_{ij} be the quantity of the ith input required for the production of one unit of the jth output. The input requirements for the production of a specified set of output levels is of the same form as (5-26):

$$x_i = \sum_{j=1}^{s} a_{ij}q_j \qquad i = 1, \ldots, m \tag{5-29}$$

where q_j is the specified quantity of the jth output. Now substitution among outputs as well as inputs is possible.

Linear production activities may yield more than one output in the most general case. Assume that each of n linear activities yields s outputs and uses m inputs. Let z_j $(j = 1, \ldots, n)$ denote the level of the jth activity. The selection of a unit level for the activity is arbitrary as long as the outputs and inputs are in the appropriate proportions. Let a_{ij} be the quantity of the ith output produced and b_{ij} be the quantity of the ith input required by one unit of the jth activity. The outputs and inputs generated by a specified set of activity levels are

$$q_i = \sum_{j=1}^{n} a_{ij} z_j \qquad i = 1, \ldots, s$$

$$x_i = \sum_{j=1}^{n} b_{ij} z_j \qquad i = 1, \ldots, m$$

(5-30)

Composite activities again are defined as weighted averages of simple activities.

5-7 LINEAR PROGRAMMING

Linear programming covers problems in which a linear function is maximized or minimized subject to a system of linear inequalities including the requirement that the values of all variables be nonnegative. Since linear functions are concave, linear programming provides a special case for which the Kuhn-Tucker analysis may be used (see Exercise 5-8). However, the special properties of linear systems allow the use of a different, though equivalent, approach.

A general format for linear programming is to find values for the variables q_j ($j = 1, \ldots, n$) that maximize

$$y = p_1 q_1 + p_2 q_2 + \cdots + p_n q_n \tag{5-31}$$

subject to $\qquad a_{i1} q_1 + a_{i2} q_2 + \cdots + a_{in} q_n \leq x_i^0 \qquad i = 1, \ldots, n$ (5-32)

and $\qquad\qquad\qquad q_j \geq 0 \qquad j = 1, \ldots, n$ (5-33)

The familiar notation p, q, and x is convenient for discussion of programs formed with linear production activities. However, the programming framework covers a much wider range of problems. In general, the parameters p_j, a_{im}, and x_i may be positive, negative, or zero with interpretations depending upon the problem under consideration. The format (5-31) to (5-33) is quite general. If a linear function is to be minimized, the problem may be written in the standard format by maximizing its negative. If a constraint is of the form $\geq$, the inequality may be reversed to conform to (5-32) by multiplying through by -1. If the ith constraint is a strict equality, it may be represented by two weak inequalities, $\leq$ and $\geq$. The second inequality may then be reversed by multiplying through by -1.

The particular linear-programming system considered here is one in which an entrepreneur selects n output levels, the q's, to maximize her revenue (5-31) with fixed output prices, the p's. She has fixed quantities, the x_i^0's, of m inputs.[1] The production technology is described by the input-output

---

[1] There are no purchased inputs in this example. This can be added without much difficulty.

coefficients, the a_{ij}, which give the fixed requirement of input i necessary to produce one unit of output j. The inequalities (5-32) state that the entrepreneur is limited by her input endowments. She can use less than her endowment of an input, but she cannot use more. Finally, (5-33) states that output levels cannot be negative.

The Feasible Point Set

Any set of real numbers that satisfies (5-32) and (5-33) is a feasible solution for the linear-programming system. The collection of all feasible points in n-dimensional space (R^n) forms the *feasible point set* for the system.

It is useful to review some of the general properties of point sets in R^n before deriving the specific properties of feasible point sets.[1] A *convex set* has the property that every point on a straight-line segment connecting any two points in the set is also in the set. A *boundary point* has adjacent points that are in the set and adjacent points that are not in the set. All points adjacent to an *interior point* are in the set. A set is *closed* if it contains all its boundary points, and *open* if it contains none. The *null set* with no points and a set with a single point are both defined to be convex and closed. The set of all points in R^n is closed; it has no boundary points and includes them all. A linear equation such as the equality form of the ith constraint of (5-32) defines a *hyperplane* in R^n. A hyperplane is a line in R^2, a plane in R^3, and an $(n-1)$-dimensional surface in R^n. If $a_{ij} = 0$, the hyperplane is parallel to the q_j axis. If $x_i^0 = 0$, it includes the origin for R^n. The hyperplane defined by the ith constraint separates R^n into a *closed half-space*

$$a_{i1}q_1 + a_{i2}q_2 + \cdots + a_{in}q_n \leq x_i^0$$

the points of which satisfy the ith constraint and an *open-half space*,

$$a_{i1}q_1 + a_{i2}q_2 + \cdots + a_{in}q_n > x_i^0$$

the points of which violate the ith constraint. Half-spaces are convex sets, and closed half-spaces are closed convex sets. The point set which satisfies the jth nonnegativity constraint of (5-33) is also a closed half-space and therefore is closed and convex.

The points that satisfy each of the constraints of (5-32) and (5-33) considered individually form a closed convex set. A feasible solution for the programming system must satisfy all $(m+n)$ of the constraints. The feasible point set contains points that are in each of the $(m+n)$ sets formed by the constraints; i.e., it is the *intersection* of the $(m+n)$ sets. A theorem in point-set theory states that the intersection of a finite number of closed convex sets is itself a closed convex set. The nonnegativity constraints, (5-33), place lower bounds on the values of the variables. It follows that the feasible point set for a linear-programming system is always closed, convex, and

---

[1] See also Sec. 10-1. The definitions of a closed set given here and in Sec. 10-1 are equivalent.

bounded from below.[1] This is important because the properties of such sets are well known.

For illustration, assume that an entrepreneur can produce two outputs using three inputs with input endowments of $x_1^0 = 18$, $x_2^0 = 8$, and $x_3^0 = 14$. The entrepreneur's production opportunities are described by the following constraints:

$$q_1 + 3q_2 \leqq 18$$

$$q_1 + q_2 \leqq 8$$

$$2q_1 + q_2 \leqq 14 \tag{5-34}$$

$$q_1, q_2 \geqq 0$$

Each of the constraints restricts solutions to a closed half-space. The nonnegativity constraints limit solutions to the nonnegative quadrant. It is convenient to limit consideration of the remaining constraints to this quadrant.

The relevant hyperplanes, lines in R^2, are plotted in Fig. 5-3. The first constraint of (5-34) limits solutions to points that lie on or below the line that contains points A and B, the second limits solutions to points that lie on or below the line that contains B and C, and the third limits solutions to points that lie on or below the line that contains C and D. The feasible point set is defined by the solid-line boundary $OABCD$. It is closed and convex, and in this example it is bounded from above as well as below. Every point in the set satisfies all the constraints given by (5-34), and every point not in the set violates one or more of the constraints. Point E ($q_1 = 5$, $q_2 = 4$) satisfies the first, third, and nonnegativity constraints of (5-34), but it is not feasible because it violates the second.

---

[1] This is not quite enough to establish that a programming system has a finite optimal solution. It also must be established that the feasible point set is not null. Then a sufficient condition for finiteness is that the feasible point set be bounded from above, i.e., that a vector $(u_1, \ldots, u_n)$ exists such that $u_j \geqq q_j$ for all $(q_1, \ldots, q_n)$ in the feasible point set.

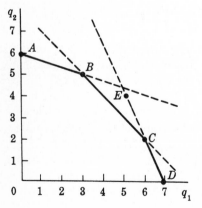

Figure 5-3

Optimal Solutions

Once the feasible point set has been defined, the next task is to find a point in the set that maximizes the value of the objective function (5-31). Two additional concepts in point-set theory are useful for this purpose. An *extreme point* of a closed convex set is a boundary point that does not lie on a line connecting any pair of points in the set. Points O, A, B, C, and D in Fig. 5-3 are extreme points. A hyperplane that contains a boundary point of a closed convex set is a *supporting hyperplane* for the set if the entire set is in one of the closed half-spaces defined by it.

Assume that an optimal solution exists for the programming system given by (5-31) to (5-33). Let $(q_1^0, q_2^0, \ldots, q_n^0)$ be any point in the feasible point set. Insert these values into (5-31) to obtain the corresponding value of the objective function y^0:

$$y^0 = p_1 q_1^0 + p_2 q_2^0 + \cdots + p_n q_n^0$$

Define a closed half-space which contains all points with objective function values no greater than y^0:

$$p_1 q_1 + p_2 q_2 + \cdots + p_n q_n \leqq y^0 \tag{5-35}$$

and an open half-space which contains all points with values greater than y^0:

$$p_1 q_1 + p_2 q_2 + \cdots + p_n q_n > y^0 \tag{5-36}$$

The selected point is optimal if (5-35) is a supporting hyperplane for the feasible point set, and the set defined by (5-36) is null. If (5-35) is not a supporting hyperplane, the selected point is not optimal. In this case the set defined by (5-36) contains at least one feasible point with a value of y greater than y^0. Since a supporting hyperplane does not contain interior points of the feasible set, it follows that optimal points are always on the boundary of the feasible set. A theorem of particular importance for linear programming states that *a closed convex set which is bounded from below has one or more extreme points in every supporting hyperplane.*[1] This means that if a programming system has an optimal solution, there will be at least one extreme point that is optimal. The search for an optimal solution may be limited to a finite number of points since the number of extreme points is finite. This means that at most m of the n q's need have positive values in an optimal solution.

Assume that the entrepreneur whose production opportunities are described by (5-34) and pictured in Fig. 5-3 sells her output at the fixed prices p_1 and p_2, and desires to maximize her total revenue. The case in which $p_1 = 1$, $p_2 = 2$, and

$$y = q_1 + 2q_2$$

is pictured in Fig. 5-4a. The hyperplane defined by $y^0 = 7$ is the lowest broken

---

[1] A proof is given by G. Hadley, *Linear Programming* (Reading, Mass.: Addison-Wesley, 1962), pp. 62–63.

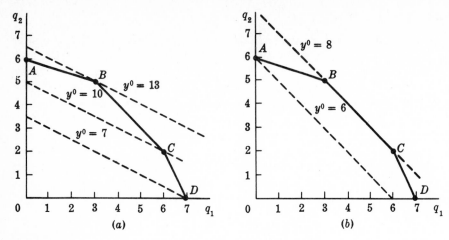

Figure 5-4

line. It contains the extreme point D ($q_1 = 7$, $q_2 = 0$). The corresponding open half-space defined by (5-36) contains feasible points, A, B, and C, for example. Therefore, D is not optimal. Extreme point C ($q_1 = 6$, $q_2 = 2$) is in the hyperplane defined by $y^0 = 10$. The corresponding open half-space contains feasible points, and C is not optimal. Extreme point B ($q_1 = 3$, $q_2 = 5$) is optimal. It is contained in the supporting hyperplane defined by $y^0 = 13$. The corresponding open half-space contains no feasible points. The optimal solution occurs at an extreme point and is unique.

Figure 5-4b depicts the same feasible point set with different output prices and a different objective function: $p_1 = p_2 = 1$, and

$$y = q_1 + q_2$$

Extreme point A ($q_1 = 0$, $q_2 = 6$) is in the hyperplane defined by $y^0 = 6$. This point is clearly not optimal. Extreme points B and C, and all points on the intervening edge of the feasible set are contained in the optimal supporting hyperplane defined by $y^0 = 8$. There is not a unique optimal solution in this case. There are optimal boundary points that are not extreme points. Nonetheless, there are extreme points that are optimal.

The boundary of the feasible point set in Fig. 5-4 is the linear-programming counterpart of the product transformation curve defined for the continuous case in Sec. 4-5. In the continuous case a product transformation curve gives x_2 as a strictly concave function of x_1 with a rate of product transformation (RPT) that is continuous and increasing. For the linear-programming counterpart, x_2 is a concave (but not strictly concave) function of x_1 with an RPT that is discontinuous and nondecreasing. An optimum point for revenue maximization depends upon the ratio of the output prices in both cases.

Duality

Consider the following linear-programming system. Find values for r_i ($i = 1, \ldots, m$) that maximize

$$C = r_1 x_1 + r_2 x_2 + \cdots + r_m x_m \qquad (5\text{-}37)$$

subject to

$$a_{11} r_1 + a_{21} r_2 + \cdots + a_{m1} r_m \geq p_1$$

$$a_{12} r_1 + a_{22} r_2 + \cdots + a_{m2} r_m \geq p_2$$

$$\cdots\cdots\cdots\cdots\cdots\cdots\cdots\cdots\cdots\cdots \qquad (5\text{-}38)$$

$$a_{1n} r_1 + a_{2n} r_2 + \cdots + a_{mn} r_m \geq p_n$$

and

$$r_i \geq 0 \qquad i = 1, \ldots, m \qquad (5\text{-}39)$$

Linear-programming systems always come in pairs. The system (5-37) to (5-39) is the *dual* of the system (5-31) to (5-33). The initial system has m constraints and n variables; its dual system has n constraints and m variables. The initial objective function is maximized, and the dual objective function is minimized. The objective function coefficients and constraint constants are interchanged in the two systems, and the direction of the inequalities is reversed. The coefficient a_{ij} is in the ith row and jth column of the array for (5-32) and in the jth row and ith column of the array for (5-38). Duality is a symmetric relation. The reader may verify that the initial system is the dual of its dual.[1]

A system and its dual are related in a number of ways. Some of the more important duality theorems are stated here. *If a finite optimal solution exists for one of the systems, a finite optimal solution exists for the other. If feasible solutions exist for both systems, finite optimal solutions exist for both.*

Assume that optimal solutions exist and have been found for both systems. Let these be denoted by $q_1^*, \ldots, q_n^*$ and $r_1^*, \ldots, r_m^*$. A major duality theorem states that *the optimal value of a variable in one system is zero if the corresponding constraint in the other system is satisfied as a strict inequality, and nonnegative if the corresponding constraint is satisfied as an equality*:

$$a_{i1} q_1^* + \cdots + a_{in} q_n^* < x_i^0 \qquad \text{implies} \qquad r_i^* = 0$$

$$a_{i1} q_1^* + \cdots + a_{in} q_n^* = x_i^0 \qquad \text{implies} \qquad r_i^* \geq 0 \qquad (5\text{-}40)$$

$$i = 1, \ldots, m$$

and

$$a_{1j} r_1^* + \cdots + a_{mj} r_m^* > p_j \qquad \text{implies} \qquad q_j^* = 0$$

$$a_{1j} w_1^* + \cdots + a_{mj} r_m^* = p_j \qquad \text{implies} \qquad q_j^* \geq 0 \qquad (5\text{-}41)$$

$$j = 1, \ldots, n$$

---

[1] Multiply (5-37) and (5-39) by -1 to put this system in the standard format, apply the rules given above to find its dual, and then multiply its dual objective function and constraints by -1. The resultant system is the same as that given by (5-31) and (5-32).

An allied theorem states that *if the optimal value of a variable in one system is positive, the optimal values of the variables for the other system satisfy the corresponding constraint as an equality*:

$$r_i^0 > 0 \quad \text{implies} \quad a_{i1}q_1^* + \cdots + a_{in}q_n^* = x_i^0 \tag{5-42}$$

$$i = 1, \ldots, m$$

$$q_j^* > 0 \quad \text{implies} \quad a_{1j}r_1^* + \cdots + a_{mj}r_m^* = p_j \tag{5-43}$$

$$j = 1, \ldots, n$$

Insert the optimal q_j^* into (5-31) and (5-32), multiply the ith constraint by r_i^* ($i = 1, \ldots, m$), and sum the resultant m constraints:

$$\sum_{i=1}^{m} r_i^* \sum_{j=1}^{n} a_{ij}q_j^* = \sum_{i=1}^{m} r_i^* x_i^0 \tag{5-44}$$

The equality follows from (5-42).† Insert the optimal r_i^* into (5-37) and (5-38), multiply the jth constraint by q_j^* ($j = 1, \ldots, n$), and sum the resultant n constraints:

$$\sum_{j=1}^{n} q_j^* \sum_{i=1}^{m} a_{ij}r_i^* = \sum_{j=1}^{n} q_j^* p_j \tag{5-45}$$

The equality follows from (5-43). The left-hand sides of (5-44) and (5-45) are the same. Substituting from (5-37) into (5-44) and from (5-31) into (5-45),

$$R = \sum_{j=1}^{n} p_j q_j^* = \sum_{i=1}^{m} x_i^0 r_i^* = C \tag{5-46}$$

The optimal values of the objective functions for the two programming systems are equal.

The optimal value of the dual variable, r_i^*, gives the rate at which the optimal value of (5-31) would increase per unit increase of x_i^0 with the other input endowments unchanged. Its interpretation is the same as that for a multiplier in a Kuhn-Tucker analysis (see Exercise 5-8). The dual variables are interpreted as imputed input prices for the system considered here. For some systems they may be interpreted as competitive market prices. The left-hand side of the jth constraint of (5-38) gives the unit production cost for the jth output in terms of the imputed input prices. The dual constraints state that unit cost equals or exceeds price (unit revenue) for each output. From (5-43) it follows that unit cost equals price for each output that is produced. The imputed input prices lead to efficiency in the sense that it is not possible for the entrepreneur to increase her profit by changing her output levels.

The dual objective function gives the value of the entrepreneur's input

---

† If $r_i^* > 0$, the corresponding constraint is an equality and remains an equality after multiplication. If $r_i^* = 0$, the corresponding constraint reduces to the trivial equality $0 = 0$ after multiplication. Thus, (5-44) is a sum of equalities.

stocks in terms of the imputed input prices. By (5-40) the optimal value of her input stock equals her maximum revenue. If the owners of the input stocks were paid the imputed input prices, total revenue would be exhausted, and total profit would equal zero. If the optimal outputs satisfy the ith input constraint as a strict inequality, the entrepreneur will have an unused quantity of the ith input, and (5-46) states that its imputed price will be zero. Only scarce, i.e., fully utilized, inputs can have positive prices.

The dual system for the case shown in Fig. 5-4a is: minimize

$$C = 18r_1 + 8r_2 + 14r_3$$

subject to

$$r_1 + r_2 + 2r_3 \geq 1$$

$$3r_1 + r_2 + r_3 \geq 2$$

$$r_1, r_2, r_3 \geq 0$$

The optimal solution for the initial system is $q_1^* = 3, q_2^* = 5, y^* = 13$. The equality holds for the first and second input constraints in the initial system, and the strict inequality holds for the third. An optimal solution for the dual system follows easily from (5-40) and (5-41). By (5-40), $r_3^* = 0$, and from (5-41)

$$r_1^* + r_2^* = 1$$

$$3r_1^* + r_2^* = 2$$

These equations have the solution $r_1^* = 0.5, r_2^* = 0.5$. An evaluation of the dual objective function confirms that $C^* = 13$ as stated by (5-46).

5-8 SUMMARY

Extensions of the basic theory of the firm, and the properties of particular production and cost functions are considered. A number of interesting results arise if the entrepreneur's production function is homogeneous of degree one. A proportionate variation of all input levels results in a proportionate change of output level and leaves the marginal products of the inputs unchanged. The sum of the output elasticities for the inputs equals one. Euler's theorem has been utilized to demonstrate that total output is just exhausted if each input is paid its marginal physical product. However, the assumptions of competitive profit maximization break down if the entrepreneur's long-run production function is homogeneous of degree one.

A CES production function is homogeneous of degree one and has a constant elasticity of substitution throughout. The isoquants for CES functions range from right angles to straight lines as the elasticity of substitution ranges from its limits of zero to $+\infty$. The Cobb-Douglas production function has a constant elasticity of substitution of unity and is a member of the CES class. The first-order conditions for a CES function state the input use ratio as a function, linear in logarithms, of the input price ratio.

The Kuhn-Tucker analysis is useful for a wide range of problems in the theory of the firm. Two problems involving major discontinuities are considered here. Duality between production and cost functions allows the derivation of production functions from cost functions as well as the converse. Shephard's lemma states that the derivative of the cost function with respect to an input price equals the cost-minimizing use level for that input.

Uncertainty is introduced into the theory of the firm by assuming that the entrepreneur's utility is a function of the profit that she earns from production. If the entrepreneur is risk averse, under the usual assumptions she will select an output at which expected price exceeds expected MC. A risk-neutral entrepreneur will produce more to equate the two, and a risk lover will produce even more.

A linear production activity is characterized by fixed proportions for input and output levels. A linear production function is formed from a number of linear activities that may be used simultaneously. Input substitution is possible if two or more linear activities are available for an output.

Linear programming covers the maximization of a linear function of n nonnegative variables subject to m linear inequality constraints. The nonnegative points in n-dimensional space that satisfy the constraints of a linear-programming system form its feasible point set. The set is closed, convex, and bounded from below. If a finite maximum value for the objective function exists, it will occur at one or more extreme points of the feasible point set. A linear-programming system with n variables and m constraints has a dual system with m variables and n constraints. The variables of one system give the marginal values of the constraints of the other. The optimal values of the objective functions of the two systems are equal.

EXERCISES

5-1 Each of the following production functions is homogeneous of degree one. In each case, derive the marginal products for X_1 and X_2 and demonstrate that they are homogeneous of degree zero:

$$(a) \quad q = (ax_1 x_2 - bx_1^2 - cx_2^2)/(\alpha x_1 + \beta x_2)$$

$$(b) \quad q = Ax_1^\alpha x_2^{1-\alpha} + bx_1 + cx_2$$

5-2 An entrepreneur uses two distinct production processes to produce two distinct goods, Q_1 and Q_2. The production function for each good is CES, and the entrepreneur obeys the equilibrium condition for each. Assume that Q_1 has a higher elasticity of substitution and a lower value for the parameter a than Q_2 [see (5-12)]. Determine the input price ratio at which the input use ratio would be the same for both goods. Which good would have the higher input use ratio if the input price ratio were lower? Which would have the higher use ratio if the price ratio were higher?

5-3 An entrepreneur has the production function $q = Ax_1^\alpha x_2^{1-\alpha}$. She buys inputs and sells the output at fixed prices, but is subject to a quota which allows her to purchase no more than x_1^0

units of X_1. She would have purchased more in the absence of the quota. Use the Kuhn-Tucker analysis to determine the entrepreneur's conditions for profit maximization. What is the optimal relation between the value of the marginal product of each input and its price? What is the optimal relation between the RTS and the input price ratio?

5-4 Use Shephard's lemma to find the production function that corresponds to the cost function $C = (r_1 + 2\sqrt{r_1 r_2} + r_2)q$, and demonstrate that it is CES.

5-5 A farmer, who sells at a fixed price of 5 dollars per unit and has the cost function $C = 3.5 + 0.5q^2$, plants to maximize profit under certainty. After planting she discovers that she can have a fertilizer applied that will increase her yield 40 percent with a probability of 0.25, 60 percent with a probability of 0.5, and 88 percent with a probability of 0.25. Her utility function is $U = \sqrt{\pi}$. Determine the maximum amount that she is willing to pay for the fertilizer application. Contrast this amount with the expected value of the increase in her profit as a result of fertilizer application.

5-6 A linear production function contains four activities for the production of one output using two inputs. The input requirements per unit output are

$$a_{11} = 1 \qquad a_{12} = 2 \qquad a_{13} = 3 \qquad a_{14} = 5$$

$$a_{21} = 6 \qquad a_{22} = 5 \qquad a_{23} = 3 \qquad a_{24} = 2$$

Are any of the activities inefficient in the sense that there is no input price ratio at which they would be used?

5-7 Each of n linear activities yields s outputs and uses m inputs as described by (5-30). An entrepreneur possesses fixed quantities of each of the inputs. She desires to maximize her total revenue from the sale of the outputs at constant market prices. Formulate her optimization problem as a linear-programming system, and derive its dual programming system.

5-8 Consider the basic linear-programming problem given in (5-31) to (5-33). Use the Kuhn-Tucker conditions to establish that the dual system constraints (5-39) and the equilibrium conditions (5-40) to (5-43) are satisfied.

SELECTED REFERENCES

Arrow, K., H. B. Chenery, B. Minhas, and R. M. Solow: "Capital-Labor Substitution and Economic Efficiency," *Review of Economics and Statistics*, vol. 43 (August, 1961), pp. 228–232. The original statement of the properties of the CES production function.

Baumol, W. J.: *Economic Theory and Operations Analysis* (4th ed., Englewood Cliffs, N.J.: Prentice-Hall, 1977). Chaps. 8 and 12 cover Kuhn-Tucker analysis and linear programming respectively. The mathematics is fairly elementary.

Dorfman, R., P. A. Samuelson, and R. Solow: *Linear Programming and Economic Analysis* (New York: McGraw-Hill, 1958). An elementary presentation of linear programming and the input-output model.

Gale, David: *The Theory of Linear Economic Models* (New York: McGraw-Hill, 1960). An original approach to linear programming, games, and input-output. The necessary advanced mathematics is summarized in chap. 2.

Hadley, G.: *Linear Programming* (Reading, Mass.: Addison-Wesley, 1962). A text with economic applications. Matrix algebra and point-set theory are used.

Jorgenson, D. W., and L. J. Lau: "The Duality of Technology and Economic Behavior," *Review of Economic Studies*, vol. 41 (April, 1974), pp. 181–200. An advanced discussion of duality for the firm.

McCall, J. J.: "Probabilistic Microeconomics," *Bell Journal of Economics and Management Science*, vol. 2 (Autumn, 1971), pp. 403–433. A summary of analysis of the firm under uncertainty. Some knowledge of continuous probability theory is required.

McFadden, Daniel: "Constant Elasticity of Substitution Production Functions," *Review of Economic Studies*, vol. 30 (June, 1963), pp. 73–83. Fairly advanced mathematics is employed.

Shephard, R. W.: *Theory of Cost and Production Functions* (Princeton, N.J.: Princeton University Press, 1970). Fundamental discussions of duality in production. Advanced mathematics is used.

Varian, H. R.: *Microeconomic Analysis* (New York: W. W. Norton, 1978). Chap. 1 contains an advanced modern mathematical statement of the theory of the firm.

MARKET EQUILIBRIUM

The behavior of consumers and entrepreneurs has been analyzed on the assumption that they are unable to affect the prices at which they buy and sell. The isolated consumer is confronted with given prices, and he purchases the commodity combination that maximizes his utility. The entrepreneur faces given output and input prices and decides to produce an output level for which his profit is maximized. Each must solve a maximum problem. The individual actions of all consumers and entrepreneurs together determine the prices which are considered parameters by each one alone. Prices are determined in the market where consumers and entrepreneurs meet and exchange commodities. The consumer is the buyer and the entrepreneur the seller in the market for a final good. Their roles are reversed in a market for a primary input such as labor. Some inputs are outputs of other firms. Wheat is an input for the milling industry, but an output of agriculture. Both buyers and sellers are entrepreneurs in the markets for such intermediate goods. The analysis of market equilibrium seeks to describe the determination of the market price and the quantity bought and sold. The present chapter is focused upon behavior in individual markets.

The basic assumptions and characteristics of a perfectly competitive market are outlined in Sec. 6-1. Market demand functions are derived in Sec. 6-2. Market supply functions are derived for short-run and long-run periods in Sec. 6-3, which also contains a discussion of external economies and diseconomies. Demand and supply functions are used for the determination of commodity-market equilibria in Sec. 6-4. The analysis is applied to a problem in taxation in Sec. 6.5. The market equilibrium analysis is extended to factor markets in Sec. 6-6. The existence and uniqueness of market equilibrium are discussed in Sec. 6-7; stability is discussed in Sec. 6-8. The properties of equilibrium in markets with lagged supply reactions are the subject of Sec. 6-9. A simple futures market is considered in Sec. 6-10.

6-1 THE ASSUMPTIONS OF PERFECT COMPETITION

A perfectly competitive commodity market satisfies the following conditions: (1) firms produce a homogeneous commodity, and consumers are identical from the sellers' point of view in that there are no advantages or disadvantages associated with selling to a particular consumer; (2) both firms and consumers are numerous, and the sales or purchases of each individual unit are small in relation to the aggregate volume of transactions; (3) both firms and consumers possess perfect information about the prevailing price and current bids, and they take advantage of every opportunity to increase profits and utility respectively; (4) entry into and exit from the market is free for firms and consumers in the long run.

Condition (1) ensures the anonymity of firms and consumers. With regard to the firm, it is equivalent to the statement that the product of the firm is indistinguishable from products of others: trademarks, patents, special brand labels, etc., do not exist. Consumers have no reason to prefer the product of one firm to that of another. The uniformity of consumers ensures that an entrepreneur will sell to the highest bidder. Custom and other institutional rules of thumb (such as the "first-come–first-served" rule) for distributing output among consumers are nonexistent.

Condition (2) ensures that many sellers face many buyers. If firms are numerous, an individual entrepreneur can increase or reduce his output level without noticeably altering the market price. An individual consumer may raise or lower his demand for the commodity without any perceptible influence on the price. The individual buyer or seller acts as if he had no influence on price and merely adjusts to what he considers a given market situation. Thus, buyers are "price takers" in that they adjust the quantities purchased so that these quantities are optimal for them given the prevailing price, without ever considering that their purchases may, in turn, further affect the price. Sellers observe a market price and adjust quantities sold so that these quantities are optimal from their point of view without considering that their sales may affect the price.

Condition (3) guarantees perfect information on both sides of the market. Buyers and sellers possess complete information with respect to the quality and nature of the product and the prevailing price. Since there are no uninformed buyers, entrepreneurs cannot attempt to charge more than the prevailing price. Consumers cannot buy from some entrepreneurs at less than the prevailing price for analogous reasons. Since the product is homogeneous and everybody possesses perfect information, a single price must prevail in a perfectly competitive market. This can be proved by assuming on the contrary that the commodity is sold at two different prices. By hypothesis, consumers are aware of the facts that (1) the commodity can be bought at two different prices, (2) one unit of the commodity is exactly the same as any other. Since consumers are utility maximizers, they will not buy the commodity at the higher price. Therefore a single price must prevail.

The last condition ensures the unimpeded flow of resources between alternative occupations in the long run. It assumes that resources are mobile and always move into occupations from which they derive the greatest advantage. Firms move into markets in which they can make profits and leave those in which they incur losses. Resources such as labor tend to be attracted to industries the products of which are in great demand. Inefficient firms are eliminated from the market and are replaced by efficient ones.

Perfect competition among sellers prevails if an individual seller has only an imperceptible influence on the market price and on the actions of others. Each seller acts as if he had no influence. Analogous conditions must hold for perfect competition among buyers. A market is perfectly competitive if perfect competition prevails on both the sellers' and the buyers' sides of the market. The market price which was considered a parameter in previous chapters is now a variable, and its magnitude is determined jointly by the actions of buyers and sellers.

6-2 DEMAND FUNCTIONS

The market demand function for a commodity is obtained by summing the demand functions of individual consumers. An individual producer, however, because of his small size relative to the market does not face the market demand function. His demand function reflects his assumption that he can sell all that he desires at a going market price.

Market Demand

Following the derivation of Sec. 2-3 as generalized in Sec. 2-6, the ith consumer's demand for Q_j depends upon the price of Q_j, the prices of all other commodities, and his income:

$$D_{ij} = D_{ij}(p_1, p_2, \ldots, p_m, y_i)$$

The consumer's demand functions are obtained from his first-order conditions for utility maximization, assuming that his second-order conditions are fulfilled. He will react to price and income changes by changing his commodity demands so as to maintain the equality of his RCS and the price ratio for every pair of commodities and, at the same time, to satisfy his budget constraint.

The consumer's demand for Q_j may vary as a result of a change in p_k ($k \neq j$), even though p_j remains unchanged, or in response to changes in his income, all prices remaining constant. All other prices and the consumer's income are assumed constant in order to isolate behavior in the jth market. His demand for Q_j is then a function of p_j alone:

$$D_{ij} = D_{ij}(p_j) \tag{6-1}$$

The quantity demanded still depends upon the prices of other commodities and the consumer's income, but these variables are now treated as parameters. To satisfy his first-order conditions the consumer will vary his demands for commodities other than Q_j as p_j changes. These variations generally are ignored in an analysis centered upon the market for Q_j.

Omitting the commodity subscript j in (6-1),

$$D_i = D_i(p) \qquad i = 1, 2, \ldots, n$$

The aggregate demand for Q at any price is the sum of the quantities demanded by the n individual consumers at that price:

$$D = \sum_{i=1}^{n} D_i(p) = D(p) \tag{6-2}$$

where D is the aggregate demand. The form of (6-2) is the result of the assumptions that all other prices and the incomes of all n consumers are constant. The demands of individual consumers normally are assumed to be monotonically decreasing functions of price, but the possibility of an increasing function of price exists for a Giffen good (see Sec. 2-5). Clearly, if the individual demand functions are monotonically decreasing, the aggregate demand function is also monotonically decreasing. If some individual demand functions are decreasing and others increasing, the net effect upon the aggregate demand function is ambiguous in general.

The aggregate demand curve for a commodity is obtained by plotting (6-2). The shape and position of the aggregate demand curve may change as the parameters of (6-2) change, i.e., as the prices of other commodities and consumers' incomes change. In fact, the aggregate demand curve may shift with changes in the distribution of income without any variation in aggregate income. If one consumer's income is reduced and another's increased by exactly the same amount, the corresponding individual demand curves are likely to shift, and the aggregate demand curve will be affected unless the shifts exactly compensate each other.

In terms of the conventional diagrams the aggregate demand curve is the horizontal sum of the individual demand curves. Parts (a) and (b) of Fig. 6-1 represent the demand curves of the only two consumers in a hypothetical competitive market.[1] Part (c) is their aggregate demand curve which is constructed by letting the distance OL equal the sum of the distances ON and OM.

---

[1] Two consumers do not constitute the large number necessary for perfect competition. They are simply used to illustrate the behavior of a large number.

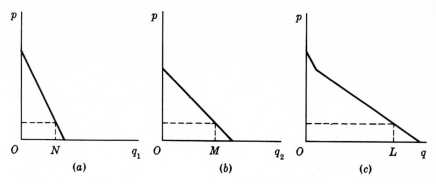

Figure 6-1

Producer Demand

The aggregate or market demand function confronts the aggregate of all sellers. The individual entrepreneur considers himself incapable of influencing market price. A change in his output results in an imperceptible movement along the market demand curve, and he believes that he can sell any quantity that he is able to produce at the prevailing price. The demand curve for the output of an individual entrepreneur appears to him as a horizontal line given by

$$p = \text{constant}$$

The market demand curve is not the horizontal sum of the demand curves faced by individual firms.

The firm's total revenue is

$$R = pq$$

Marginal revenue is the rate at which total revenue increases as a result of a small increase in sales. In mathematical terms,

$$\frac{dR}{dq} = p$$

since p is a constant. The marginal revenue curve faced by the individual firm is identical with its demand curve.

6-3 SUPPLY FUNCTIONS

The supply functions of individual firms can be defined for (1) a very short period during which output level cannot vary, (2) a short run during which output level can be varied but plant size cannot, and (3) a long run in which all inputs are variable.

The Very Short Period

Assume that the entrepreneur decides every morning how much to produce that day. His output decision is instantly implemented, and he spends the rest of the day trying to sell his output at the highest possible price. He cannot increase his output during the day and sells a given stock of the commodity.[1] Since an output q^0 has already been produced, the marginal cost of any output less than q^0 is zero. Output cannot be increased beyond this point in the very short period, and the marginal cost of higher outputs may be considered infinite. The marginal cost curve is represented by a vertical line at this point.

The firm maximizes profit by selling a quantity for which $MC = p$. Since the MC of any output less than q^0 is zero and the MC of any output greater than q^0 is infinite, the equality $MC = p$ cannot be satisfied, and the firm will expand sales to the point at which price ceases to exceed MC. Therefore, it will sell its entire output (i.e., its entire stock of the commodity) at the prevailing price.[2] This maximizes profit, because the prevailing price is the highest price at which the output can be sold. Quantity sold does not respond to price changes. In general, the aggregate supply function states the quantity that will be supplied by all producers as a function of the price. Since the output of each firm is fixed, the aggregate supply of the commodity is also given and does not depend upon the price. The supply curve is a vertical line, and its distance from the price axis is equal to the sum of the outputs of the individual firms.

The Short Run

The supply function of a perfectly competitive firm states the quantity that it will produce as a function of market price and can be derived from the first-order condition for profit maximization. The horizontal coordinate of a point on the rising portion of the MC curve corresponding to a given price measures the quantity that the firm would supply at that price. The firm's short-run supply curve is identical with that portion of its short-run MC curve which lies above its AVC curve. Its supply function is not defined for outputs less than the abscissa of the intersection of its MC and AVC curves. Quantity supplied would be zero at all prices less than the ordinate of this point. The firm's supply curve consists of the segments OA and BC in Fig. 6-2.

The ith firm's short-run MC is a function of its output:

$$MC_i = \Phi_i'(q_i) \tag{6-3}$$

---

[1] The present analysis is simplified by assuming that production and all other adjustments occur instantaneously. It may be more realistic to assume that output is produced as a continuous and steady stream. If production is a time-consuming process, a change in the level of output cannot be realized immediately. The very short period is then any length of time shorter than the period which elapses between the change in the level of inputs and the corresponding change in the output level.

[2] Since the present analysis is static, it is not possible to hold the commodity for sale at a later date.

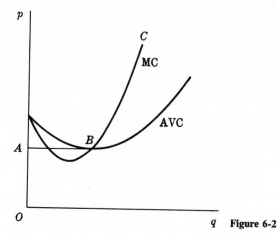

q **Figure 6-2**

The supply function of the ith firm is obtained from its first-order condition for profit maximization by letting $p = \mathrm{MC}$ and solving (6-3) for $q_i = S_i$:

$$S_i = S_i(p) \qquad \text{for } p \geqq \min \mathrm{AVC}$$
$$S_i = 0 \qquad \text{for } p < \min \mathrm{AVC}$$

The aggregate supply function for Q is obtained by summing the n individual supply functions. The aggregate supply is

$$S = \sum_{i=1}^{n} S_i(p) = S(p)$$

The aggregate supply curve is the horizontal sum of the individual supply curves.

The second-order condition for maximum profit requires the MC curve to be rising. The firm's supply function is therefore monotonically increasing for prices at or above minimum AVC. The horizontal sum of monotonically increasing functions is itself monotonically increasing, and thus the short-run aggregate supply function has positive slope.[1]

Let the total cost curve be

$$C_i = 0.1q_i^3 - 2q_i^2 + 15q_i + 10$$

Then

$$\mathrm{MC}_i = 0.3q_i^2 - 4q_i + 15$$

---

[1] The aggregate supply curve will coincide with the price axis for prices below the minimum AVC of all firms. For this segment supply is a nondecreasing function of price; i.e., no output is produced as price increases. It is possible that the MC curves of individual firms may have negatively sloped portions in the relevant range where $\mathrm{MC} > \mathrm{AVC}$. The individual firm's supply curve will then be discontinuous. In an exceptional case the aggregate supply curve could be discontinuous.

Setting $MC_i = p$ and solving for q_i,[†]

$$q_i = S_i = \frac{4 + \sqrt{1.2p - 2}}{0.6} \qquad (6\text{-}4)$$

The individual supply function is relevant for all prices greater than, or equal to, minimum AVC. The AVC function is

$$AVC_i = 0.1q_i^2 - 2q_i + 15$$

The minimum point on the AVC function is located by setting the derivative with respect to q_i equal to zero and solving for q_i:[‡]

$$\frac{d(AVC_i)}{dq_i} = 0.2q_i - 2 = 0 \qquad q_i = 10$$

Substituting $q_i = 10$ in the AVC function gives the value 5. When the price is less than 5 dollars, the firm will find it most profitable to produce no output. The firm's supply function is

$$S_i = \frac{4 + \sqrt{1.2p - 2}}{0.6} \qquad \text{if } p \geqq 5$$

$$S_i = 0 \qquad \text{if } p < 5$$

Assuming that the industry consists of 100 identical firms, the aggregate supply function is

$$S = 100 \frac{4 + \sqrt{1.2p - 2}}{0.6} \qquad \text{if } p \geqq 5$$

$$S = 0 \qquad \text{if } p < 5$$

At a price of 22.50 dollars the aggregate supply will be 1500 units.

The Long Run

The firm's long-run optimal output is determined by the equality of price and long-run MC. Zero output is produced at prices less than AC, and the firm's long-run supply function consists of that portion of its long-run MC function for which MC exceeds AC. The mathematical derivation of the long-run aggregate supply function is similar to the derivation of the short-run supply function. The MC function of the ith firm is

$$MC_i = \Phi_i'(q_i) \qquad i = 1, \ldots, n$$

Setting $p = MC_i$ and solving for $q_i = S_i$

$$S_i = S_i(p) \qquad i = 1, \ldots, n \qquad (6\text{-}5)$$

[†] The mathematical solution (6-4) describes a curve with two branches corresponding to the $+$ and $-$ signs before the square root. The branch corresponding to the $-$ sign has a negative slope and can be disregarded, since the second-order condition requires MC to be rising.

[‡] The reader may verify that the second-order condition for a minimum is satisfied.

The aggregate supply function is then obtained by adding the n individual supply functions in (6-5). In the absence of external effects the long-run supply function is positively sloped for the same reason as the short-run supply function.

External Economies and Diseconomies

The individual firm's total costs have been assumed to be a function of only its output level. However, the firm's total costs may frequently depend upon the output level of the industry as a whole. External economies are realized if an expansion of industry output lowers the total cost curve of each firm in the industry. External diseconomies are realized if an expansion of industry output raises the total cost curve of each firm.[1] External economies or diseconomies may be caused by many factors. An expansion of the industry's output may lead to a better trained and more efficient labor force, with a consequent reduction in the costs of the ith firm without any diminution of its own output; a reduction of the industry's output may lead to less training and a consequent increase in the costs of the ith firm. External diseconomies could occur if an increase in the industry's output drove up the prices of raw materials and thus increased the total costs of the ith firm.

Assume in general that the long-run costs of the ith firm depend upon the industry output level as well as its own output level.[2]

$$C_i = \Phi_i(q_i, q) \qquad i = 1, 2, \ldots, n$$

where q_i is the output of the ith firm and $q = \sum_{i=1}^{n} q_i$. Each entrepreneur provides a small part of industry output and maximizes profit with respect to his own output on the assumption that this output level does not affect the industry output level The profit functions are

$$\pi_i = R_i - C_i \qquad i = 1, 2, \ldots, n$$

where $R_i = pq_i$. Differentiate π_1 with respect to q_1 (considering q constant), π_2 with respect to q_2, etc., and set the resulting partial derivatives equal to zero:

$$\frac{\partial \pi_i}{\partial q_i} = p - \frac{\partial \Phi_i(q_i, q)}{\partial q_i} = 0 \qquad i = 1, 2, \ldots, n \qquad (6\text{-}6)$$

The second-order conditions require that $\partial^2 \Phi_i(q_i, q)/\partial q_i^2 > 0$ for all $i = 1, 2, \ldots, n$. Substituting $q = \sum_{i=1}^{n} q_i$, solving the system of n equations given by

---

[1] External effects need not be unambiguously economies or diseconomies. It is possible that an increase in industry output will raise the total cost curves of some firms and lower the total cost curves of others.

[2] An even more general formulation would make the cost function an explicit function of the individual output levels: $C_i = \Phi_i(q_1, q_2, \ldots, q_n)$.

(6-6) for the q_i, and writing $S_i = q_i$,

$$S_1 = S_1(p)$$
$$S_2 = S_2(p)$$
$$\cdots \cdots \cdots$$
$$S_n = S_n(p)$$

(6-7)

Each entrepreneur bases his behavior on his own MC function. Each obser-ves or anticipates industry output and selects his output to equate price and marginal cost. If all entrepreneurs anticipate the same industry output and if this industry output is consistent with their individual output levels, no further adjustment is necessary. Otherwise some or all individual MC curves will shift from their anticipated positions, and entrepreneurs will adjust their output levels correspondingly. This sequence will continue until no further adjustments are necessary. The supply functions (6-7) state each firm's optimal supply as a function of the price after all these adjustments have taken place. The aggregate supply function is obtained as before by adding the individual supply functions (6-7):

$$S = \sum_{i=1}^{n} S_i(p) = S(p)$$

The aggregate supply function may have negative slope in the presence of external economies. The second-order conditions require that the individual MC curves be rising when the output of the industry is assumed to be a given parameter.

Consider a simplified example in which the industry is represented by two competitive firms with the total cost functions

$$C_1 = \alpha q_1^2 + (\alpha + \beta)^2 q_1 + \beta q_1 q \qquad C_2 = \alpha q_2^2 + (\alpha + \beta)^2 q_2 + \beta q_2 q$$

where $q = q_1 + q_2$. The coefficient α must be positive; otherwise, marginal cost would become negative for sufficiently high values of q_1 or q_2. The coefficient β may have either sign. If $\beta < 0$ there are external economies, and if $\beta > 0$ there are external diseconomies. The first-order conditions cor-responding to (6-6) are

$$p - 2\alpha q_1 - (\alpha + \beta)^2 - \beta q = 0 \qquad p - 2\alpha q_2 - (\alpha + \beta)^2 - \beta q = 0$$

Solving these equations for $q_1 = S_1$ and $q_2 = S_2$,

$$S_1 = S_2 = \frac{p}{2(\alpha + \beta)} - \frac{(\alpha + \beta)}{2}$$

Therefore, the aggregate supply function is linear in this case:

$$S = S_1 + S_2 = \frac{p}{(\alpha + \beta)} - (\alpha + \beta)$$

Irrespective of the sign of $(\alpha + \beta)$, the intercept of the supply curve is $p = (\alpha + \beta)^2 > 0$. If there are external diseconomies ($\beta > 0$), the supply curve will have a positive slope, and the supply will increase less rapidly with price than in the absence of such diseconomies. If there are external economies ($\beta < 0$), the supply curve will have positive or negative slope as the denominator ($\alpha + \beta$) is positive or negative.[1] The long-run supply curve will be negatively sloped only if the cost reductions due to expanding industry output are sufficiently large to offset the cost increases due to expanding firm outputs.

6-4 COMMODITY-MARKET EQUILIBRIUM

Short-Run Equilibrium

The market forces which determine the price and the quantity sold can be regarded as manifesting themselves through the aggregate demand and supply functions. The slope of the demand function $[D'(p)]$ is normally negative. The slope of the supply function $[S'(p)]$ is positive in the absence of external economies. $S'(p)$ will be assumed to be positive, unless otherwise specified.

Imagine that buyers and sellers arrive in the market without any fore-knowledge as to what will become the going price. Since the commodity is homogeneous, a single price must prevail. The quantity demanded must equal the quantity supplied at the equilibrium price:

$$D(p) - S(p) = 0 \qquad (6\text{-}8)$$

If the equality does not hold for some $p = p_e$, buyers' and sellers' desires are inconsistent: either buyers want to purchase more than sellers are supplying, or sellers are supplying more than buyers wish to purchase. The equality in (6-8) ensures that the buyers' and sellers' desires are consistent.

Assume that production is instantaneous and producers arrive in the market without any actual output. Buyers and sellers attempt to enter into contracts that are favorable to them. Whenever a buyer and seller enter into a contract, they both reserve the right to *recontract* with any person who makes a more favorable offer. Assume that some consumer makes an initial bid and offers a price of p^0 dollars for the commodity. This price is recorded and made public by an auctioneer who is an impartial observer of the trading process. Buyers and sellers will attempt to enter into contracts with each other at the price p^0. If p^0 is lower than the equilibrium price p_e, consumers who are willing to buy at this price find that the quantity offered is not sufficient to satisfy their desires. Some of the consumers who have not been able to satisfy their demand will be induced to raise their bids in the hope of tempting sellers away from other consumers. As soon as this higher price $p^{(1)}$ is recorded and made public by the auctioneer, sellers break their old contracts and recontract at the higher price. As higher prices are offered, the

---

[1] The supply function is not defined if $(\alpha + \beta) = 0$. However, as $(\alpha + \beta) \to 0$, $S \to \infty$ for any positive price.

quantity demanded declines, since marginal consumers are driven out of the market and each consumer demands less. Simultaneously the quantity offered by sellers increases. The process of recontracting continues as long as the price announced by the auctioneer is below the equilibrium price, i.e., as long as the quantity demanded exceeds the quantity supplied. When the equilibrium price is reached, neither consumers nor producers have an incentive to recontract any further. Recontracting is discontinued, entrepreneurs instantaneously produce and deliver the output for which they have contracted, and the exchange is completed. If the arbitrary initial price p^0 happens to exceed p_e, some producers will be unable to sell the quantity which is the optimal quantity for them at that price. They cannot find consumers who want to enter into contracts with them. In order to avoid such an outcome, the sellers who have been unable to find buyers at the initial price will reduce the price. Consumers who have contracted at the higher price will find it advantageous to recontract. The process of recontracting continues until the equilibrium price is reached. When p_e is established, both buyers' and sellers' desires are satisfied, and no one can benefit from further recontracting.

An equilibrium price-quantity combination must satisfy both the demand and supply functions. It is a price-quantity combination for which the desires of buyers and sellers are consistent with each other. An equilibrium price is determined by solving the *equilibrium condition* (6-8) for p. An equilibrium quantity is determined by substituting an equilibrium price in either the demand or the supply function. Since an equilibrium price-quantity combination satisfies both the demand curve and the supply curve, the above operation is equivalent to finding the coordinates of an intersection point of the demand and supply curves.

Assume that the demand and supply curves are

$$D = -50p + 250 \qquad S = \tfrac{100}{3}p$$

Setting $D - S = 0$,

$$-50p + 250 - \tfrac{100}{3}p = 0$$

and therefore

$$p = 3 \qquad D = S = 100$$

These functions are illustrated in Fig. 6-3.

Long-Run Equilibrium

If the plant size is variable, the equilibrium of the *existing* firms in the market is given by the intersection of the long-run supply curve with the corresponding demand curve. The long-run cost and supply curves include "normal profit," i.e., the minimum remuneration necessary for the firm to remain in existence. It is the profit that accrues to the entrepreneur as payment for managerial services, for providing organization, for risk-bearing, etc. If the

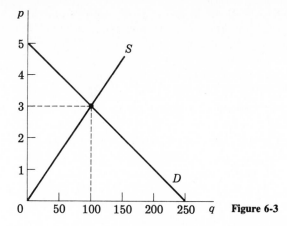

Figure 6-3

intersection of the demand curve and the long-run supply curve occurs at a price at which firms in the industry earn more than normal profit, new entrepreneurs may be induced to enter. The assumption of free entry guarantees that they are able to enter the industry, produce the same homogeneous product, and possess the same complete information as the old firms. The new producers will add their supplies to the already existing supply, and as a result the long-run supply curve will shift to the right. New producers will continue to enter as long as they can make positive profits, and the supply curve will continue to shift to the right until its intersection with the demand curve determines a price at which new entrants would earn zero profits.

The converse argument can be made for the case in which existing firms make losses. Some firms will withdraw from the industry, and the aggregate supply will diminish; the supply curve will shift to the left. Firms will continue to leave the industry until the intersection of the demand curve with the supply curve determines a price for which losses (and therefore profits) are zero for the highest cost firm in the industry.

Demand must equal supply, and the potential profits of new entrants must equal zero for long-run equilibrium. The supply function of the ith firm is $S_i = S_i(p)$. Let n be the number of firms in the industry. Assuming that all firms are identical with respect to their cost functions, the aggregate supply function is

$$S(p) = nS_i(p) \tag{6-9}$$

As before, the aggregate demand function is

$$D = D(p) \tag{6-10}$$

In addition to the equality of demand and supply, long-run equilibrium requires that profit equal zero for each firm:

$$\pi_i = pS_i - \Phi(S_i) = 0 \tag{6-11}$$

where $\Phi(S_i)$ is the long-run total cost of the ith firm for an output $q_i = S_i = S/n$. Equation (6-11) requires the equality of price and AC: $p = \Phi(S_i)/S_i$. Equations (6-8) to (6-11) can generally be solved for the variables (D, S_i, p, n). In the long run the forces of perfect competition determine not only the price and the quantity, but the number of firms within the industry as well.

The argument is illustrated in Fig. 6-4. The left-hand side of the diagram shows the cost curves of a typical or "representative" firm. The right-hand side shows the market demand and supply curves with the horizontal scale compressed. The final equilibrium from the industry's point of view is at the intersection of the demand and supply curves, provided that profits are zero. From the entrepreneur's point of view, equilibrium is attained when price equals MC and AC. Optimality is ensured by $p = $ MC, and zero profits by $p = $ AC. Every firm operates at the minimum point of its AC curve in long-run equilibrium, since MC = AC at the minimum point of the AC curve.

The long-run supply curve S is defined to include the supplies offered by firms already in the market, but not the supplies of potential producers. Firms are making positive profits in the situation characterized by the supply curve S (Fig. 6-4b). New firms enter, and the supply curve shifts to S'. If the supply curve had been defined to include all supplies (by actual and potential producers, as in S^*), the intersection of the demand and supply curves would have determined the final equilibrium without any shifting. The supply curve S is given for fixed n in (6-9). S^* is obtained from (6-11) by letting p equal minimum AC. The horizontal long-run industry supply curve S^* is also the industry's long-run AC curve and its long-run MC curve in the present case. In Sec. 5-1 it was shown that production functions homogeneous of degree one generate constant AC = MC for fixed factor prices and generate zero profit levels by Euler's theorem if inputs are paid the values of their marginal

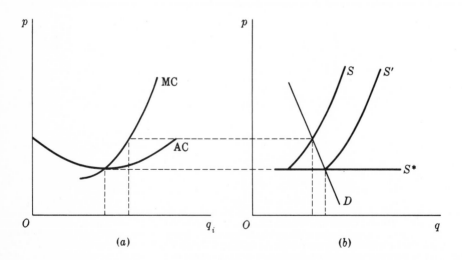

Figure 6-4

products. These conditions are the same as those for the industry as a whole in the situation pictured in Fig. 6-4. Therefore, it is often assumed that the industry has a long-run production function homogeneous of degree one even though the firms within the industry do not.

Long-run supply curves are not always horizontal. The supply curve will be upward sloping if firms do not have identical cost functions and there are no offsetting external economies. External economies (diseconomies) can generate downward (upward) sloping long-run supply curves in the identical-cost-function case.

Differential Cost Conditions and Rent

The symmetry assumption is convenient for purposes of exposition, but is not necessary for the attainment of equilibrium. Firms may choose their own technology, entrepreneurs may differ with respect to organizing ability, and they may have built plants of different size as a result of divergent price expectations. Some entrepreneurs may possess scarce factors such as fertile land that are not available to others. Under any of these conditions the cost functions of all firms may not be identical.

Assume that there are two distinct types of firms. Their long-run AC and MC curves are shown in parts (*a*) and (*b*) of Fig. 6-5. Part (*c*) shows the industry supply curve and five hypothetical demand curves. The supply curve is based on the assumption that there are fifty firms in each category. Assume that the number of firms in each category cannot be increased. For example, the number of low-cost producers (category I) may be unalterably given by the quantity of some scarce resource such as fertile land. New firms are unable to enter category I even though the firms in this category are making profits.

Consider the demand curve D_4. Each low-cost firm produces an output of 16 units, and each of the other firms produces an output of 10 units. The latter operate at the minimum point of their AC curves and earn normal profits.

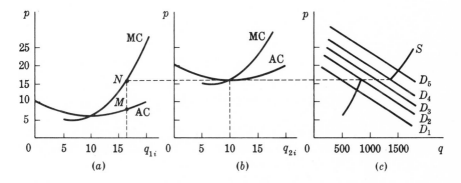

Figure 6-5

Each low-cost firm earns a unit of profit NM above normal. If the demand curve shifted to D_2, all high-cost firms (category II) would leave the industry, but each low-cost firm would still earn the same positive profit. They would earn positive profits even if the demand curve were D_1. With D_3 some, but not all, of the high-cost firms would leave the industry. Those remaining would earn a normal profit. If the demand curve were D_5, all firms in the industry would earn profits in excess of normal, and a third group of firms (not shown in Fig. 6-5) might find it profitable to enter the industry. The low-cost firms would still be in the most favorable position.

Assume that the total cost functions of representative firms in the two categories are

$$C_{1i} = 0.04q_{1i}^3 - 0.8q_{1i}^2 + 10q_{1i} \qquad C_{2i} = 0.04q_{2i}^3 - 0.8q_{2i}^2 + 20q_{2i}$$

The corresponding average and marginal cost functions are

$$MC_{1i} = 0.12q_{1i}^2 - 1.6q_{1i} + 10 \qquad MC_{2i} = 0.12q_{2i}^2 - 1.6q_{2i} + 20$$
$$AC_{1i} = 0.04q_{1i}^2 - 0.8q_{1i} + 10 \qquad AC_{2i} = 0.04q_{2i}^2 - 0.8q_{2i} + 20$$

The minimum points of the respective average cost curves are at the points $q_{1i} = 10$, $p = 6$, and $q_{2i} = 10$, $p = 16$. The supply curve of an individual low-cost firm is derived by setting $MC_{1i} = p$:

$$p = 0.12q_{1i}^2 - 1.6q_{1i} + 10$$

Solving this quadratic equation for q_{1i},

$$q_{1i} = \frac{1.6 \pm \sqrt{2.56 - 0.48(10 - p)}}{0.24}$$

The minus sign preceding the square root must be disregarded because it corresponds to the situation in which the individual firm's second-order condition for maximization is not fulfilled. Substituting S_{1i} for q_{1i}, the supply curve is

$$S_{1i} = 0 \qquad \text{if } p < 6$$
$$S_{1i} = \frac{1.6 + \sqrt{2.56 - 0.48(10 - p)}}{0.24} \qquad \text{if } p \geq 6$$

By analogous reasoning the supply curve of the representative high-cost firm is

$$S_{2i} = 0 \qquad \text{if } p < 16$$
$$S_{2i} = \frac{1.6 + \sqrt{2.56 - 0.48(20 - p)}}{0.24} \qquad \text{if } p \geq 16$$

Maintaining the assumption that there are fifty firms in each category, the aggregate supply function is described by the following set of three equations:

$$S = 0 \qquad\qquad\qquad\qquad\qquad \text{if } 0 \le p < 6$$

$$S = 50 \frac{1.6 + \sqrt{2.56 - 0.48(10 - p)}}{0.24} \qquad\qquad \text{if } 6 \le p < 16$$

$$S = \frac{160}{0.24} + \frac{50}{0.24} [\sqrt{2.56 - 0.48(10 - p)} + \sqrt{2.56 - 0.48(20 - p)}] \qquad \text{if } p \ge 16$$

Assume that the relevant demand curve is D which has the equation

$$D = -100p + 2050$$

The relevant segment of the supply curve is given by

$$S = 50 \frac{1.6 + \sqrt{2.56 - 0.48(10 - p)}}{0.24}$$

Setting $D = S$ and solving for p and S gives $p = 13$, $S = 750$.† If $p = 13$, each low-cost firm will produce 15 units at an average cost of 7 dollars. The high-cost firms produce nothing. The total quantity is, as determined by solving the demand and supply relations, $(50)(15) = 750$ units. Each low-cost firm earns a 90-dollar profit.

Low-cost firms can produce at a lower AC than the others because they possess some scarce factor, such as fertile land, which is not available to the latter. If the demand curve intersects the supply curve at a point at which some firms earn more than normal profit, a considerable profit advantage is enjoyed by those who possess the scarce resource. Some (potential) producers, seeing the large profits made by the low-cost firms, would want to persuade the owners of the fertile land (landlords) to hire it out to them rather than to the firms currently employing it. They would try to accomplish this by offering to pay more for the use of the land than existing firms are paying. The present users would match these offers until competition drove up the amount paid for the use of fertile land to the point where no differential profit advantage could be derived from employing it. The owners will thus be able to exact from the firms using the scarce resource their entire profit in excess of normal. The sums thus exacted are the *rent* paid by the entrepreneur for the use of the scarce resource. One may conclude that no advantage can be derived from being a more efficient (low-cost) producer: the differential profit advantage is wiped out by the extra rent that the low-cost producer must pay. In the present example, the scarce resources employed by each low-cost firm earn a rent of 90 dollars. If an entrepreneur happened to own the scarce resource himself, no actual payment would take place, and the rent would accrue to him. Rent is thus defined to be that part of a person's or firm's

---

† If it is not obvious by inspection which supply-curve segment is the relevant one, let $D = S$ for each of the three supply-curve segments separately and solve for the price. Only one of the three prices calculated will be in the range that is appropriate for the particular supply-curve segment used. This segment is the relevant one.

income which is above the minimum amount necessary to keep that person or firm in its given occupation. Whether it is actually paid to the owner of the scarce resource is immaterial. Distributive shares are distinguished by function, and not by the individual to whom they accrue.

6-5 AN APPLICATION TO TAXATION

A sales tax generally changes the individual entrepreneur's optimum output level. It shifts the individual supply curves and therefore also the aggregate supply curve. This alters the equilibrium price-quantity combination. Sales taxes are either *specific* or *ad valorem*. A specific tax is stated in terms of the number of dollars which the entrepreneur has to pay per unit sold. An ad valorem tax is stated in terms of a percentage of the sales price.

Assume that the sales tax is a specific tax of t dollars per unit. The total costs of the representative entrepreneur are

$$C_i = \phi(q_i) + b_i + tq_i$$

The first-order condition for profit maximization requires him to produce the output level for which $MC = p$:

$$\phi'(q_i) + t = p$$

or
$$\phi'(q_i) = p - t \tag{6-12}$$

The entrepreneur equates the marginal cost of production plus the unit tax to the price. The second-order condition requires that the MC curve be rising. The entrepreneur's supply function is obtained by solving (6-12) for q_i and setting $q_i = S_i$ for all prices greater than, or equal to, minimum AVC:

$$S_i = S_i(p - t)$$

The aggregate supply function is obtained by summing the individual supply functions:

$$S = \sum_{i=1}^{n} S_i(p - t) = S(p - t)$$

The aggregate supply is a function of the net price $(p - t)$ received by sellers. If, in the absence of a sales tax, aggregate supply is S^0 units at the price of p^0 dollars, entrepreneurs will supply the same quantity S^0 with a sales tax of 1 dollar if the price paid by consumers is $p^0 + 1$ dollars. This is equivalent to a vertical upward shift of the supply curve by 1 dollar. Entrepreneurs are willing to supply less than before at every price. In order to determine the equilibrium price-quantity combination, set demand equal to supply,

$$D(p) - S(p - t) = 0$$

and solve for p.

Let an ad valorem tax rate be $100v$ percent of the sales price. Total costs are

$$C_i = \phi(q_i) + b + vpq_i$$

Setting MC plus unit tax equal to price,

$$\phi'(q_i) + vp = p$$

or
$$\phi'(q_i) = p(1 - v)$$

Therefore the individual supply function is

$$S_i = S_i[p(1 - v)]$$

and the aggregate supply function is

$$S = \sum_{i=1}^{n} S_i[p(1 - v)] = S[p(1 - v)]$$

Aggregate supply is a function of the net price, and the sales tax involves an upward shift of the supply curve which is proportional to the height of the original supply curve above the quantity axis. The equilibrium price-quantity combination is again determined by setting demand equal to supply.

Let the industry consist of 100 firms with identical cost functions

$$C_i = 0.1q_i^2 + q_i + 10$$

Setting MC equal to price, solving for q_i, and setting $q_i = S_i$,

$$S_i = 0 \qquad \text{if } p < 1$$
$$S_i = 5p - 5 \qquad \text{if } p \geq 1$$

The aggregate supply function is

$$S = 0 \qquad \text{if } p < 1$$
$$S = 500p - 500 \qquad \text{if } p \geq 1$$

Assume that the demand function is

$$D = -400p + 4000$$

Setting demand equal to supply, the equilibrium price-quantity combination is

$$p = 5 \qquad D = S = 2000$$

Assume now that a specific tax of t dollars is imposed. The representative total cost function becomes

$$C_i = 0.1q_i^2 + (1 + t)q_i + 10$$

Setting MC equal to price and solving for $q_i = S_i$,

$$S_i = 0 \qquad \text{if } p < 1 + t$$
$$S_i = 5(p - t) - 5 \qquad \text{if } p \geq 1 + t$$

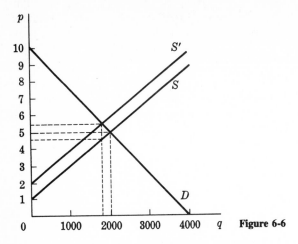

Figure 6-6

Hence the aggregate supply function is

$$S = 0 \qquad\qquad \text{if } p < 1 + t$$
$$S = 500(p - t) - 500 \qquad \text{if } p \geq 1 + t$$

Setting demand equal to supply and solving for p,

$$p = 5 + \tfrac{5}{9}t$$

If the tax rate is 90 cents per unit of sales, the equilibrium price-quantity combination is

$$p = 5.50 \qquad D = S = 1800$$

The price rises and the quantity sold diminishes as a result of the tax. The price rise is less than the amount of the unit tax. The 50-cent increase in the price represents that portion of the unit tax that is passed on to the consumer; the remainder of 40 cents is the burden on the entrepreneur. The example is pictured in Fig. 6-6. The supply curve is S before and S' after the tax is imposed. The tax is 90 cents, the vertical distance between S and S'. The price paid rises from 5 dollars to 5.50, and the price received by entrepreneurs falls to 4.60. The reader may verify that the proportion of the unit tax passed on to the consumer is the greater, the smaller are the slopes (algebraically) of the demand and supply curves. *Ceteris paribus*, the price varies directly, and the quantity inversely with the tax rate.[1]

6-6 FACTOR-MARKET EQUILIBRIUM

The foregoing sections are limited to perfectly competitive commodity mar-kets. Analogous conclusions can be reached with respect to markets for

[1] The analysis can be used to show the effects of subsidies by treating a subsidy as a negative tax.

inputs which are nonproduced factors of production. A factor market is perfectly competitive if (1) the factor is homogeneous and different buyers are indistinguishable from the sellers' point of view, (2) buyers and sellers are numerous, (3) both buyers and sellers possess perfect information, and (4) buyers and sellers are free to enter or leave in the long run. Consumers purchase commodities because they derive satisfaction from them. Inputs are purchased for the sake of the contribution they make to production. The demand curves for final products are derived from the consumers' utility functions on the assumption of utility maximization. The demand curves for inputs are derived from production functions on the assumption of profit maximization.

Demand Functions

A rational entrepreneur's optimum input combination satisfies the condition that the price of each input equals the value of its MP. The first-order conditions for profit maximization were solved in Sec. 4-3 to obtain the firm's input demands as functions of input prices and the product price. For the one-output–two-input case:

$$D_{i1} = D_{i1}(r_1, r_2, p)$$
$$D_{i2} = D_{i2}(r_1, r_2, p)$$

where D_{ij} is the ith firm's demand for the jth input. Assuming that all other prices are constant, and neglecting the input subscripts, the ith firm's demand function for a particular input is

$$D_i = D_i(r)$$

where r is the price of the input. The aggregate demand function is obtained by summing the individual demand functions. If there are m firms demanding the input,

$$D = \sum_{i=1}^{m} D_i(r) = D(r)$$

In Sec. 4-3 it was shown that individual input demand curves are always negatively sloped. Therefore, aggregate input demand curves also are always negatively sloped; that is, $\partial D / \partial r < 0$.

Supply Functions

Inputs are either primary or produced. Produced inputs are the outputs of some other firms. The supply function of a produced input is the aggregate supply function of the firms that produce it. Such functions are derived in Sec. 4-3. Different procedures are employed for nonproduced factors such as labor, which normally are assumed to be in the possession of consumers who sell them to producers in order to obtain income to purchase commodities. Sometimes it is assumed that the consumers will sell their entire stock at whatever market price may prevail. In this circumstance the factor supply function is a vertical straight line with abscissa equal to the aggregate factor stock. A more interesting case is one in which consumers gain utility from retaining some of or all their factor stocks.

For the case of labor it was assumed in Sec. 2-4 that utility is a function of leisure and income:

$$U = g(T - W, y)$$

where T is the total amount of available time (the length of the period for which the utility function is defined) and W the amount of work performed in terms of hours. It was shown that the utility-maximizing individual allocates his time between work and leisure in such fashion that

$$\frac{g_1}{g_2} = r \qquad (6\text{-}13)$$

where r is the wage rate and g_i is the partial derivative of the utility function with respect to its ith argument. The g_i's depend upon income and the amount of work performed. Since $y = rW$, (6-13) contains only the variables r and W. Solving (6-13) for W and setting $W = S_i$, the labor supply function of the ith individual is

$$S_i = S_i(r)$$

The supply function states the amounts of work that the individual is willing to perform as a function of the wage rate. The aggregate supply function is obtained by summing the individual supply functions. If there are n individuals who are willing to supply labor at some wage rate, the aggregate supply function is

$$S = \sum_{i=1}^{n} S_i(r) = S(r)$$

The supply curve may have negative slope, positive slope, or both. If individuals value leisure highly and are more concerned with increasing their time for leisure than raising their incomes, the supply curve of labor may be negatively sloped: the higher the wage, the less work is performed.

Market Equilibrium

Given the demand and supply functions for an input the equilibrium price-quantity combination is determined by invoking the equilibrium condition $D = S$. Market forces similar to those discussed in Sec. 6-4 will change the existing situation whenever the actual price differs from the equilibrium price. Equilibrium is reached only when the quantity demanded equals the quantity supplied. As in product markets, no participant can improve his position by recontracting after equilibrium has been reached.

Since the equilibrium price-quantity combination must lie on both the demand and supply curves, it must also satisfy the producer's equilibrium conditions from which the demand curve is derived. The equilibrium price of an input is always equal to the value of its marginal product; i.e., the value of the marginal dollar spent on inputs is the same in every use.[1] This equality is a necessary condition for profit maximization, and every entrepreneur can reach his optimum point in a perfectly competitive market if his second-order conditions for maximization are fulfilled.

6-7 THE EXISTENCE AND UNIQUENESS OF EQUILIBRIUM

Thus far, the analysis of market equilibrium has been based upon the assumption that a unique price-quantity equilibrium exists for each isolated market under investigation. It is not difficult to construct examples for which this existence assumption is violated: supply and demand are not equal at any nonnegative price-quantity combination. Likewise, examples exist for which the assumption of uniqueness is violated: supply and demand are equal at more than one nonnegative price-quantity combination. This section is limited to general observations and the discussion of some specific cases. The problems of existence and uniqueness are considered more deeply within a multimarket framework in Chap. 10.

Existence

A competitive market equilibrium will exist if there is one or more non-negative prices at which demand and supply are equal and nonnegative. In terms of the conventional diagram, equilibrium will exist if the demand and supply curves have at least one point in common in the nonnegative quadrant.

Three situations in which the supply and demand curves have no point in common are pictured in Fig. 6-7. Supply exceeds demand at every non-negative price for the case pictured in Fig. 6-7a. No equilibrium exists according to the definition given above. The definition of equilibrium is easily broadened to cover this case. Let $p = 0$ if $S(0) > D(0)$. A *free good* has a price of zero and is characterized by an excess of supply over demand. Consumers can get all they want for nothing. Air and water may be considered free goods. Up to some critical point water may be there for the taking. Beyond this point purification and transportation may become necessary and lead to a positive supply price.

Fig. 6-7b covers a case in which the demand price is less than the supply price at each nonnegative output. The amounts that consumers are willing to

---

[1] This has an analog in the theory of consumer behavior. Recall that $f_1 = \lambda p_1$ is one of the equilibrium conditions for the consumer, where f_1 is the marginal utility of the first good and λ is the marginal utility of money. Then $f_1(1/\lambda) = p_1$, or the price of the commodity must equal its marginal utility multiplied by the additional amount of money that has to be paid per unit of additional utility $(1/\lambda)$.

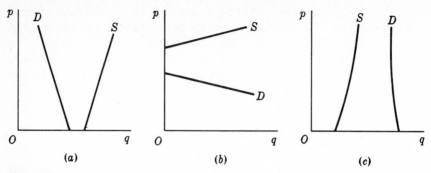

Figure 6-7

pay are inadequate to compensate producers. Market equilibrium does not exist by the definitions thus far given. Again it is possible to broaden the definitions to cover such cases. An equilibrium exists with zero output if supply price exceeds demand price for all nonnegative outputs. It is technologically possible to produce solid-gold school-lunch boxes, but none are produced because parents are not willing to pay enough to allow producers to cover their costs.

The free-good and zero-production cases are meaningful. They are covered by the general methods described in Chap. 10. Many other cases in which equilibrium cannot be achieved are the result of poor model specification. If such cases are encountered, the assumptions of their underlying producer and consumer models must be altered in order to provide a meaningful framework for analysis. Figure 6-7c provides an example. Demand exceeds supply for every price, and there is no meaningful interpretation that can be placed upon this situation.

Uniqueness

It is possible that more than one equilibrium exists, i.e., that demand and supply are equal at more than one nonnegative price-quantity combination. Points A and B in Fig. 6-8a are both equilibria. The demand curve is downward sloping in the normal fashion, but the supply curve bends back as price increases. Quantity is a single-valued function of price, but price is not a single-valued function of quantity. Some economists have found evidence that a "backward-bending" supply curve exists for labor markets in some developing countries. The supply curve is positively sloped at relatively low wage rates, and an increase in the wage rate brings forth an increased supply of labor. However, as the wage rate continues to increase and the income of each worker increases, a point is reached at which the workers prefer leisure to yet more income.

Let δ be the difference in the slopes of the demand and supply curves: $\delta = D'(p) - S'(p)$. If the demand curve is negatively sloped throughout and

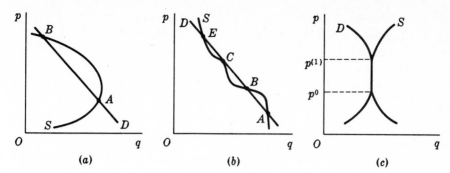

Figure 6-8

the supply curve is positively sloped throughout, $\delta < 0$ for all prices and there cannot be more than one equilibrium point. If $\delta < 0$ at an equilibrium price p^0, demand will be less than supply at a price slightly higher than p^0 and will be greater than supply at a price slightly lower than p^0. As long as $\delta < 0$ the demand curve will remain to the left of the supply curve at prices above p^0 and to the right at prices below p^0. Hence, there cannot be a second equilibrium point. A similar argument can be utilized to prove that there cannot be more than one equilibrium point if $\delta > 0$ throughout.

In Fig. 6-8a $\delta < 0$ for equilibrium point A. At B the demand and supply curves are both negatively sloped. The demand curve is more steeply sloped than the supply curve and $\delta > 0$ at B.† Four equilibrium points are shown in Fig. 6-8b. The supply curve has negative slope throughout, reflecting external economies. The values of δ are negative at equilibrium point A, positive at B, zero at C, and negative at E. In general, ignoring equilibrium points at which $\delta = 0$, δ must alternate in sign at adjacent equilibrium points. Equilibrium points with $\delta = 0$ may lie between or on either side of the points with alternating sign.

There will be a range of equilibrium points with $\delta = 0$ if the demand and supply curves are coincident for all or a portion of their lengths. Such a case is shown in Fig. 6-8c. Here, the equilibrium quantity is unique, but any price from p^0 through $p^{(1)}$ is an equilibrium price.

6-8 THE STABILITY OF EQUILIBRIUM

Equilibrium price and quantity are determined by the equality of demand and supply. Equilibrium is characterized by the acquiescence of buyers and sellers in the *status quo*: no participant in the market has an incentive to modify his behavior. However, the existence of an equilibrium point does not guarantee

---

† The derivatives $D'(p)$ and $S'(p)$ are functions of price. Hence, a steeper downward slope for the demand curve means that $D'(p) > S'(p)$.

that it will be attained. There is no guarantee that the equilibrium price will be established if the market is not in equilibrium when the contracting begins. There is also no reason to assume that the initial price will happen to be the equilibrium price. Moreover, changes in consumer preferences will generally shift the demand curve, and innovations will shift the supply curve. Both factors tend to disturb an established equilibrium situation. The change defines a new equilibrium, but there is again no guarantee that it will be attained.

In general, a disturbance denotes a situation in which the actual price is different from the equilibrium price. An equilibrium is *stable* if a disturbance results in a return to equilibrium and *unstable* if it does not.[1] It was implicitly assumed in the discussion of equilibrium in Sec. 6-4 that the market equilibrium was stable.

Static Stability

A disturbance usually creates an adjustment process in the market. For example, if the actual price is less than the equilibrium price, the adjustment may consist of some buyers raising their bids for the commodity. Static analysis abstracts from the time path of the adjustment process and considers only the nature of the change, i.e., whether it is toward, or away from, equilibrium.

Define

$$E(p) = D(p) - S(p)$$

as the excess demand at price p. In Fig. 6-9 excess demand is positive at the price p^0, negative at the price $p^{(1)}$. Stability conditions are derived from assumptions about the market behavior of buyers and sellers. The *Walrasian stability condition* is based on the assumption that buyers tend to raise their bids if excess demand is positive and sellers tend to lower their prices if it is negative. If this behavior assumption is correct, a market is stable if a price rise diminishes excess demand,[2] i.e., if

$$\frac{dE(p)}{dp} = E'(p) = D'(p) - S'(p) < 0 \qquad (6\text{-}14)$$

---

[1] This is not a rigorous definition of stability and is only one of several alternative definitions. See P. A. Samuelson, *Foundations of Economic Analysis* (Cambridge, Mass.: Harvard University Press, 1948, pp. 260–262.

[2] Rewrite the demand and supply functions in inverse form $P_d = D^{-1}(q)$, $p_s = S^{-1}(q)$, and define excess demand price $F(q) = p_d - p_s = D^{-1}(q) - S^{-1}(q)$. The *Marshallian stability condition* states that producers will raise their output when $F(q) > 0$ and lower it when $F(q) < 0$. Thus equilibrium is stable in the Marshallian sense if $dF(q)/dq = F'(q) = D^{-1'}(q) - S^{-1'}(q) < 0$. If the demand curve has negative slope and the supply curve positive slope, an equilibrium is stable according to both definitions. If the demand and supply curves have slopes of the same sign, an equilibrium will be stable according to one definition and unstable according to the other.

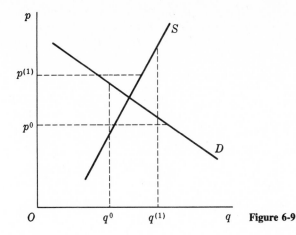

Figure 6-9

This condition is satisfied automatically if the demand curve has negative slope and the supply curve has positive slope. If both are positively sloped, the supply curve must be flatter than the demand curve $[S^{-1'}(q) < D^{-1'}(q)]$ to satisfy (6-14). If both are negatively sloped, the supply curve must be steeper than the demand curve.

The negatively sloped supply curve depicted in Fig. 6-8b yields four equilibrium points. The successive equilibrium points A, B, and E are alternately stable and unstable by the Walrasian behavior assumption (6-14). The supply curve is steeper than the demand curve at A, and the equilibrium is stable at this point. Another intersection B can exist only if the supply curve becomes less steep than the demand curve; B is therefore unstable. By similar reasoning, D is again stable. The stability condition (6-14) is not sufficient to cover equilibrium point C. Excess demand is positive at prices less than p_e and also at prices higher than p_e. The price will tend to rise for downward or upward deviations from equilibrium. Point C is classed as *semistable*.

Dynamic Stability: Lagged Adjustment

The static stability condition (6-14) is stated in terms of the rate of change of excess demand with respect to price. Nothing is said about the time path of adjustment. One might not expect instantaneous adjustments in the present model. If the initial price is not equal to the equilibrium price, it changes, and recontracting takes place. If the new price is still different from the equilibrium price, it is again forced to change. The dynamic nature of the recontracting may be formalized in a model in which recontracting takes place during periods of fixed length, say, one hour, with the auctioneer announcing the new price at the beginning of each period. The analysis of dynamic stability investigates the course of price over time, i.e., from period to period.[1] Equilibrium is stable in the dynamic sense if the price converges to (or approaches) the equilibrium price over time; it is unstable if the price change is away from equilibrium.

The assumption that a positive excess demand tends to raise price can be modeled in many different ways. A commonly used mathematical model is

$$p_t - p_{t-1} = kE(p_{t-1}) \tag{6-15}$$

where p_t is the price in period t and k is a positive constant. Equation (6-15) expresses one possible type of behavior for buyers and sellers. Assuming that there is a positive excess demand $E(p_{t-1})$ in period $(t-1)$, it expresses the assumption that an excess demand of $E(p_{t-1})$ induces buyers to bid a price $p_t = p_{t-1} + kE(p_{t-1}) > p_{t-1}$ in the following period. Assume that the demand and supply functions are

$$D_t = ap_t + b \tag{6-16}$$

$$S_t = Ap_t + B \tag{6-17}$$

Excess demand in period $(t-1)$ is

$$E(p_{t-1}) = (a - A)p_{t-1} + b - B$$

Substituting this into (6-15),

$$p_t - p_{t-1} = k[(a - A)p_{t-1} + b - B]$$

and
$$p_t = [1 + k(a - A)]p_{t-1} + k(b - B) \tag{6-18}$$

The first-order difference equation (6-18) describes the time path of price on the basis of the behavior assumption contained in (6-15). Given the initial condition $p = p_0$ when $t = 0$, its solution is

$$p_t = (p_0 - p_e)[1 + k(a - A)]^t + p_e \tag{6-19}$$

where
$$p_e = \frac{b - B}{A - a}$$

is the equilibrium price determined from (6-16) and (6-17) by setting $D_t - S_t = 0$ and solving for $p_e = p_t$. The equilibrium is stable if the actual price level approaches the equilibrium level as t increases. The price level converges to p_e without oscillations if $0 < 1 + k(a - A) < 1$. The right-hand side of this inequality holds if

$$a < A \tag{6-20}$$

The left-hand side holds if

$$k < \frac{1}{A - a}$$

---

[1] The prices which are recorded from period to period are potential, rather than realized, until equilibrium is reached. As long as $D \neq S$, none of the contracts is executed, and recontracting continues.

Condition (6-20) is automatically fulfilled if the supply curve has positive slope $(A > 0)$. The price level moves upward over time if the initial price is less than the equilibrium price and downward if it is greater. If the slope of the supply curve is negative, stability requires that the slope of the demand curve $(1/a)$ be algebraically greater than the slope of the supply curve $(1/A)$; i.e., the supply curve must cut the demand curve from above. Equilibrium is unstable if the supply curve cuts the demand curve from below, and any deviation from equilibrium is followed by increasing deviations from it. If k is sufficiently large and $a - A$ is negative, $1 + k(a - A)$ is also negative, and the price level must oscillate over time.[1]

Both static and dynamic stability depend upon the slopes of the demand and supply curves. Dynamic stability depends in addition on the magnitude of the parameter k which indicates the extent to which the market adjusts to a discrepancy between the quantities demanded and supplied per unit of time. A large k indicates that buyers and sellers tend to "overadjust": if excess demand is positive, bidding by buyers is sufficiently active to raise the price above the equilibrium level. Each adjustment is in the right direction, but is exaggerated in magnitude. Dynamic analysis thus takes into account the strength of reactions to disturbances.

The dynamic stability of equilibrium can be analyzed diagrammatically in the following fashion. Plotting price along the horizontal axis, the dotted line in Fig. 6-10a represents the excess demand function. Assuming that $k < 1$, the solid line represents $kE(p_{t-1})$. The 45-degree line in Fig. 6-10b represents the locus of points defined by $p_t = p_{t-1}$. The function

$$p_t = p_{t-1} + kE(p_{t-1}) = f(p_{t-1})$$

is obtained by adding the ordinates (corresponding to the same abscissa) of

---

[1] If $1 + k(a - A)$ is greater than -1 (but less than zero), the amplitude of the oscillations decreases over time, and the time path approaches the equilibrium level. If it is less than -1, the market is subject to increasing price fluctuations.

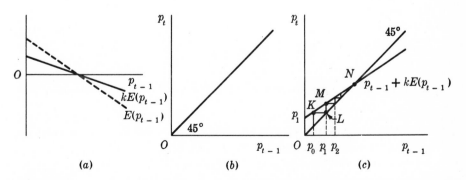

Figure 6-10

the solid lines in Figs. 6-10a and 6-10b. The result is shown in Fig. 6-10c. Assume that the initial price is p_0. The price in the following period, p_1, is given by the ordinate of the point on $f(p_{t-1})$ directly above p_0. In order to calculate the price in the following period, p_1 is transferred to the horizontal axis by drawing a horizontal line from K to L. L lies on a 45-degree line, and the abscissa of each point on it equals its ordinate. The price p_2 is found by moving vertically to M on $f(p_{t-1})$. All subsequent prices are found in this manner. The price level converges in the present example to the equilibrium price given by the intersection of $f(p_{t-1})$ and the 45-degree line.[1] The stability of equilibrium depends upon the slope of the excess demand function and the magnitude of k. If the excess demand function in Fig. 6-10a were positively sloped, the function $f(p_{t-1})$ would cut the 45-degree line from below, and the equilibrium would be unstable. If the excess demand function had negative slope, as in Fig. 6-10a, but k were very large, $f(p_{t-1})$ would have negative slope, and the price level would oscillate.

The static and dynamic approaches to stability are fundamentally different. Static stability need not imply dynamic stability, but dynamic stability implies static stability. The reason for this discrepancy is that dynamic analysis is a more inclusive tool for investigating the properties of equilibrium. Static analysis concerns itself only with the direction of the adjustment and neglects the magnitude of the adjustment from period to period.

Let

$$D_t = -0.5p_t + 100$$

$$S_t = -0.1p_t + 50$$

and let $k = 6$. The equilibrium is stable in the static Walrasian sense if $D'(p) - S'(p) < 0$. Substituting from the demand and supply functions, $-0.5 - (-0.1) = -0.4 < 0$. Dynamic stability requires $-1 < 1 + k(a - A) < 1$. Substituting the appropriate values gives

$$1 + k(a - A) = -1.4$$

and the required left-hand inequality does not hold. The market will exhibit explosive oscillations.

Dynamic Stability: Continuous Adjustment

Equation (6-15) describes a price adjustment process that occurs over discrete intervals of time. An alternative approach is based on the assumption that

---

[1] It can be easily verified that point N is the equilibrium point. At N, $p_t = p_{t-1}$ (for the 45-degree line) and $p_t = p_{t-1} + kE(p_{t-1})$. Substituting p_{t-1} for p_t,

$$p_{t-1} = p_{t-1} + kE(p_{t-1})$$

or $kE(p_{t-1}) = 0$. Excess demand equals zero at point N.

adjustment takes place continuously. Equation (6-15) is then replaced by

$$\frac{dp}{dt} = kE(p) \tag{6-21}$$

where k and $E(p)$ have the same meaning as before.[1] Substituting the demand and supply functions (6-16) and (6-17), (6-21) becomes

$$\frac{dp}{dt} = k(a - A)p + k(b - B) \tag{6-22}$$

which is a first-order differential equation. Its solution (see Sec. A-6) is

$$p = (p_0 - p_e)e^{k(a-A)t} + p_e$$

where p_0 is the initial price at $t = 0$ and $e = 2.71828\ldots$ is the base of the system of natural logarithms.

The equilibrium price p_e is dynamically stable, that is, $p \to p_e$ as $t \to \infty$, if $(a - A) < 0$, which will be the case if the demand function is negatively and the supply function positively sloped. The magnitude of the adjustment coefficient influences the speed with which convergence or divergence takes place, but in contrast to the lagged adjustment model it plays no role in determining whether an equilibrium is stable or not. The static and dynamic stability conditions are identical in this case.

An equilibrium point is *locally* stable if the system returns to it, given a small initial deviation from equilibrium. It is *globally* stable if the system returns to it for any initial deviation from equilibrium. Linear models such as (6-22) have unique equilibrium points in general, and if they are locally stable, they are also globally stable. Nonlinear models may have several equilibrium points, and, in any event, the local stability of an equilibrium point does not guarantee its global stability.

A linear approximation is useful in determining the local stability of nonlinear models. Assume that the excess demand function $E(p)$ is some complicated function of p so that the differential equation (6-21) is difficult or impossible to solve directly. The approximate equality

$$\frac{E(p) - E(p_e)}{p - p_e} \approx E'(p_e) \tag{6-23}$$

where p_e is an equilibrium price, follows from the definition of a derivative. In the limit, as $p \to p_e$, (6-23) holds exactly, and for small deviations of p from p_e the approximation may be expected to be good. Substituting $E(p_e) = 0$, solving (6-23) for $E(p)$, and substituting the result on the right-hand side of (6-21),

$$\frac{dp}{dt} = kE'(p_e)(p - p_e)$$

---

[1] The value of p is defined for all values of t. It is customary in this case to omit the subscript t. The dependence of p on t may be indicated explicitly by writing $p(t)$.

which is a linear equation since $E'(p_e)$, the derivative of excess demand evaluated at p_e, is a constant. The root of the characteristic equation (valid in the neighborhood of p_e) is $kE'(p_e)$. Thus, if the excess demand function is negatively sloped in the neighborhood of p_e, the equilibrium is locally stable. The static and dynamic conditions again are identical.

The existence of global stability can often be ascertained by a technique known as *Liapunov's direct method*. First find a Liapunov function, $V(p)$, such that $V(p) > 0$ if $p \neq p_e$ and $V(p_e) = 0$. If dV/dt is negative whenever $p \neq p_e$, the equilibrium solution is globally stable.[1] An appropriate Liapunov function is often provided by

$$V(p) = (p - p_e)^2$$

the squared distance of the actual point p at time t from the equilibrium point.

For illustration, consider the nonlinear excess demand function $E = b/p - a$ where $p_e = b/a$ with a, $b > 0$, and

$$\frac{dp}{dt} = k\left(\frac{b}{p} - a\right)$$

Differentiating $V(p)$,

$$\frac{dV}{dt} = 2(p - p_e)\frac{dp}{dt}$$

Substituting for p_e and dp/dt,

$$\frac{dV}{dt} = -\frac{2k(ap - b)^2}{ap}$$

which is negative for all $p \neq p_e$ since k, a, and p are positive. Thus, an equilibrium for this model is globally stable.

6-9 DYNAMIC EQUILIBRIUM WITH LAGGED ADJUSTMENT

Producers' supply functions show how they adjust their outputs to the prevailing price. Since production takes time, the adjustment may not be instantaneous, but may become perceptible in the market only after a period of time. Agricultural commodities often provide good examples of lagged supply. Production plans are made after the harvest. The output corresponding to these production plans appears on the market a year later. Assume that the demand and supply functions are

$$D_t = ap_t + b \tag{6-24}$$

$$S_t = Ap_{t-1} + B \tag{6-25}$$

---

[1] More advanced treatises distinguish between *stability* and *asymptotic stability*. See J. La Salle and S. Lefschetz, *Stability by Liapunov's Direct Method* (New York: Academic, 1961), pp. 31–32.

The market is in dynamic equilibrium if the price remains unchanged from period to period, i.e., if $p_t = p_{t-1}$. Equating (6-24) and (6-25) yields the unique equilibrium price $p_e = (B - b)/(a - A)$. The quantity demanded in any period depends upon the price in that period, but the quantity supplied depends upon the price in the previous period. It is assumed that the quantity supplied in period t is always equal to the quantity demanded in that period; that is, p_t adjusts to bring about the equality of D_t and S_t as soon as S_t appears on the market. This implies that no producer is left with unsold stocks and no consumer with an unsatisfied demand. Therefore

$$D_t - S_t = 0$$

Substituting from (6-24) and (6-25),

$$ap_t + b - Ap_{t-1} - B = 0$$

Solving for p_t,

$$p_t = \frac{A}{a} p_{t-1} + \frac{B - b}{a} \tag{6-26}$$

Assuming that the initial condition is given by $p = p_0$ when $t = 0$, the solution of the first-order difference equation (6-26) is

$$p_t = (p_0 - p_e)\left(\frac{A}{a}\right)^t + p_e \tag{6-27}$$

The solution (6-27) describes the path of the price as a function of time. Some of the possible time paths are illustrated in Figs. 6-11a and 6-11b.

Assume that the initial supply does not equal the equilibrium amount as a result of a disturbance such as a drought. Let the initial supply equal q_0 in Fig.

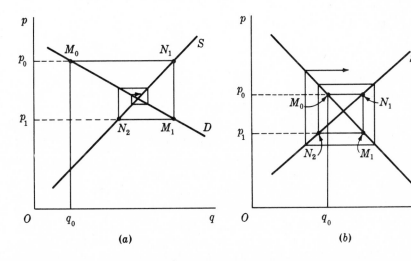

(a)   (b)

Figure 6-11

6-11a. The corresponding initial price is p_0. Consumers demand p_0M_0, and this quantity equals the initial supply. The price p_0 induces entrepreneurs to supply the quantity p_0N_1 in the next period. The price falls instantaneously to p_1. The quantity demanded is then p_1M_1 (which equals p_0N_1, the quantity supplied in that period). In the following period the price p_1 induces a supply of p_1N_2. This process continues indefinitely, producing a cobweb pattern. The price level fluctuates, but converges to the equilibrium level indicated by the intersection of the demand and supply curves. The same mechanism operates in Fig. 6-11b, but the price fluctuations tend to become larger and larger: the market is subject to explosive oscillations.

The market is dynamically stable if $p_t \to p_e$ as $t \to \infty$. If the absolute value of the quotient (A/a) is less than one, the first term on the right of (6-27) will vanish as $t \to \infty$, and the market will be dynamically stable. If the slopes of the demand $(1/a)$ and supply curves $(1/A)$ have opposite sign, price will oscillate about the equilibrium price level. If the slope of the demand curve has smaller absolute value than the slope of the supply curve, $1/|a| < 1/|A|$, the oscillations will decrease in amplitude, and the market is dynamically stable as shown in Fig. 6-11a. If the slope of the demand curve has greater absolute value than the slope of the supply curve, $1/|a| > 1/|A|$, the oscillations will increase in amplitude, and the market is dynamically unstable as shown in Fig. 6-11b. Finally, if the slopes of the demand and supply curves are equal in absolute value, $1/|a| = 1/|A|$, the oscillations will have constant amplitude, and the market is dynamically unstable.

If the demand and supply curves slope in the same direction, A/a is positive, and the price level will not oscillate, but will either increase or decrease continually.[1] The same conditions hold as above: price will converge

---

[1] The price may remain constant if the demand and supply curves coincide. No unique equilibrium is defined in this case. See Sec. 6-7.

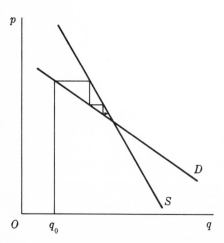

$O \qquad q_0 \qquad\qquad\qquad\qquad q$ **Figure 6-12**

to its equilibrium value if the demand curve has smaller absolute slope than the supply curve (Fig. 6-12), and will diverge in either an upward or downward direction if the demand curve has greater absolute slope.

The conditions for dynamic stability are not the same as in the simple dynamic case. Buyers and sellers react to excess demand in the simple dynamic case. Excess demand is zero in cobweb situations. Buyers react to given supplies in terms of the prices they offer. Sellers respond to given supplies in terms of the prices they offer. Sellers respond to given prices in terms of the quantities they supply in the following period.

6-10 A FUTURES MARKET

Futures markets have been instituted for some commodities with uncertain future prices. Buyers and sellers agree to transact at a specified price at a future date. Thereby, the future price for such transactions is known with certainty. Futures markets are common for agricultural commodities. A risk-averse farmer who sells for future delivery can avoid price uncertainty. A processor of agricultural products who buys for future delivery can contract for sale of his output, given a certain input cost. People who buy and sell for these reasons are said to *hedge* against price uncertainty. Others who have no direct interest in the commodity may also buy and sell in a futures market. A buyer (seller) can sell (buy) at the actual market price at the future date in order to cover his contract. Such a person will participate in a futures market if he can increase his expected utility by buying or selling the lottery offered by the market.

Differing expectations as to future price can lead to futures-market transactions. It is assumed here that expectations are identical in the sense that everyone expects that future price will be one of the n values $(p_1, \ldots, p_n)$ with the respective probabilities $(v_1, \ldots, v_n)$. In order to emphasize that a futures market does not require some participants who prefer risk, an example is given for which all buyers and sellers are risk averse, though not to the same degree, and all obey the von Neumann–Morgenstern axioms (see Sec. 3-8).

Hedging

Consider a farmer who produces the commodity under investigation. Let his cost function $C(q)$ be strictly convex, and his utility function $U(\pi)$ be strictly concave. If the farmer sells in the futures market at the going price p^*, he maximizes utility by equating this price to his MC. If he does not sell in the futures market, his first-order condition for expected utility maximization [see (5-21)] is

$$\frac{dE[U(\pi)]}{dq} = \sum_{i=1}^{n} v_i U'(\pi_i)[p_i - C'(q)] = 0 \qquad (6\text{-}28)$$

Let U_0 be the maximum utility value determined from (6-28). The utility level from futures-market participation is

$$U^* = U[p^*q^* - C(q^*)] = V(p^*)$$

where q^* is a solution for $p^* = C'(q^*)$. Clearly, $dU^*/dp^* > 0$. Let p_0^* be the solution of $U_0 = V(p^*)$. For $p^* < p_0^*$ the farmer will not sell in the futures market; he prefers price uncertainty to the certainty provided by the futures market. For $p^* > p_0^*$ he will sell his entire output as determined by his MC function; he then prefers the certainty of the futures market.

For illustration let $U = \ln(\pi + 10)$ and $C = 0.5q^2$ with $p_1 = 4$, $p_2 = 8$, and $v_1 = v_2 = 0.5$. An approximate solution for (6-28) is $q_0 \approx 5.246$ and $U^0 \approx 3.245$. Also,

$$V(p_0^*) = \ln(0.5p_0^{*2} + 10) \approx 3.245$$

has the solution $p_0^* \approx 5.598$. The farmer's futures-market supply function[1] is

$$S = 0 \qquad \text{if} \qquad p^* < 5.598$$
$$S = p^* \qquad \text{if} \qquad p^* > 5.598$$

The construction of a futures-market demand function for a processor of agricultural output is left for the reader (see Exercise 6-13).

Risk Assumption

A person without a direct interest in a commodity may buy or sell in its futures market if he can increase his utility. He avoids taking delivery of or having to provide the commodity through an offsetting transaction at the prescribed future date. Let his utility be a function of his asset position $U = U(A)$ with an initial position of $U_0 = U(A_0)$. Let D denote his excess demand in the futures market such that $D > 0$ means that he is buying for future delivery at p^*, and $D < 0$ means that he is selling. His expected utility is

$$E[U(A)] = \sum_{i=1}^{n} v_i U[A_0 + (p_i - p^*)D] \qquad (6\text{-}29)$$

The first-order condition for his expected utility maximization is

$$\frac{dE[U(A)]}{dD} = \sum_{i=1}^{n} v_i U'(A_i)(p_i - p^*) = 0 \qquad (6\text{-}30)$$

The participant's excess demand function is obtained by solving (6-30) for $D = D(p^*)$. Let p_0^* be a solution for $D(p_0^*) = 0$. If $p^* > p_0^*$, the participant will sell in the futures market, and if $p^* < p_0^*$, he will buy.

---

[1] Each farmer's overall supply function has a discontinuity since output jumps from 5.246 to 5.598 at p_0^*.

For example, let $U(A) = \ln(A)$. Substituting into (6-30) gives

$$D = \frac{6 - p^*}{(8 - p^*)(p^* - 4)} A_0$$

For any given $4 < p^* < 8$, futures-market purchases will equal a fixed proportion of the participant's assets. Assume that this proportion cannot exceed 1, which occurs at $p \approx 4.44$. Assume that there are 10,000 identical participants each with $A_0 = 9056.25$ who serve as buyers in the futures market, and 1000 identical farmers as described above who serve as sellers. Equating aggregate demand to aggregate supply

$$\frac{(6 - p^*)}{(8 - p^*)(p^* - 4)} 90{,}562.5 = 1000p^*$$

which has the solution $p^* = 5.75$ and $q = 5750$.

6-11 SUMMARY

The theory of perfect competition analyzes the factors that determine price and quantity in markets in which (1) the product is homogeneous and buyers are uniform, (2) buyers and sellers are numerous, (3) buyers and sellers possess perfect information, (4) there are free entry and exit for both buyers and sellers in the long run. The participants in the market act as if they had no influence on the price, and each individual regards it as a given parameter.

The price and the quantity bought and sold are determined by supply and demand. The aggregate demand function is derived from the demand functions of individual consumers, which, in turn, are derived from the individual consumers' first-order conditions for utility maximization. The aggregate supply function is derived from individual supply functions which are based on the individual firms' first-order conditions for profit maximization. Equilibrium is attained when demand equals supply. The equality of demand and supply guarantees that buyers' and sellers' desires are consistent. The analysis of a perfectly competitive market is extended to specific and ad valorem sales taxes.

The analysis of perfectly competitive factor markets is similar to the analysis of commodity markets. The equilibrium price-quantity combination is determined by demand and supply, and the equality of demand and supply ensures the consistency of buyers' and sellers' desires. The demand function for a factor is derived from the individual firms' first-order conditions for profit maximization. The supply function for a primary input such as labor is derived from the individual laborers' first-order conditions for utility maximization. Equilibrium in a factor market ensures that the price of a factor equals the value of its marginal product.

The existence of demand and supply functions does not necessarily imply that demand and supply are equal at one or more nonnegative price-quantity combinations. The concept of market equilibrium is extended to cover two situations in which demand and supply are not equal. A *free-good* equilibrium is characterized by an excess of supply over demand at a zero price. A *zero-production* equilibrium is characterized by supply price exceeding demand price for all nonnegative outputs. It is possible that more than one price-quantity equilibrium may exist for a market. Multiple equilibria cannot occur if the difference in the slopes of the demand and supply curves is negative for all prices, or if the difference is positive for all prices.

The existence of an equilibrium point does not guarantee its attainment. The analysis of the stability of equilibrium is concerned with the effects of disturbances. Equilibrium is stable if a disturbance is followed by a return to equilibrium and unstable if it is not. The static analysis of stability considers merely the direction of the adjustment which follows the disturbance; dynamic analysis considers the time sequence of the adjustment process as well. A dynamic model with lagged adjustment demonstrates that a market which is stable according to the static analysis may be dynamically unstable. A dynamic model with continuous adjustment enriches the static model by describing the path of price over time following a disturbance. Both static and dynamic analyses contain assumptions about the behavior of buyers and sellers. According to the assumption of the Walrasian stability condition, buyers and sellers react to excess demand.

Special dynamic problems arise in markets in which supply reactions are lagged. In markets of this type both buyers and sellers are assumed to react to price. The time path of the market price oscillates and produces a cobweb-like path pattern if the demand and supply curves have slopes of opposite sign; an equilibrium is stable if the absolute value of the slope of the demand curve is less than the absolute value of the slope of the supply curve.

Competitive-market analysis is extended to cover contracts for the future purchase and sale of a commodity at a fixed price that may differ from the market price at that date. Each participant buys or sells a quantity that maximizes his expected utility. People who *hedge* use a futures market to convert an uncertain price prospect into a certain one. Others use futures markets to purchase lotteries that increase their expected utility.

EXERCISES

6-1 Two hundred consumers derive utility from the consumption of two goods. Each has the utility function $U = 10q_1 + 5q_2 + q_1q_2$. Each has a fixed income of 100 dollars. Assume that the price of Q_2 is 4 dollars per unit. Express the aggregate demand for Q_1 as a function of p_1. Is the aggregate demand curve downward sloping?

6-2 Construct a short-run supply function for an entrepreneur whose short-run cost function is $C = 0.04q^3 - 0.8q^2 + 10q + 5$.

6-3 A good Q is produced using only one input X. The market for Q is supplied by 100 identical competitive firms each of which has the production function $q = x^\beta$ where $0 < \beta < 1$. Each firm behaves as if the price of X were constant. However, the industry as a whole faces an upward sloping supply curve for $X : r = b(100x)$ where $b > 0$. Derive the industry's long-run supply curve.

6-4 The long-run cost function for each firm that supplies Q is $C = q^3 - 4q^2 + 8q$. Firms will enter the industry if profits are positive and leave the industry if profits are negative. Describe the industry's long-run supply function. Assume that the corresponding demand function is $D = 2000 - 100p$. Determine equilibrium price, aggregate quantity, and number of firms.

6-5 Consider an industry with n identical firms in which the ith firm's total cost function is $C_i = aq_i^2 + bq_iq$ $(i = 1, \ldots, n)$, where $q = q_1 + q_2 + \cdots + q_n$. Derive the industry's supply function.

6-6 Construct an effective supply curve for an industry which has two sources of supply: domestic production with the supply curve $S = 20 + 8p$, and (2) an unlimited supply of imports at a fixed price of 20.

6-7 Determine equilibrium price and quantity for a market with the following demand and supply functions: $D = 20 - 2p$ and $S = 40 - 6p$. Assume that a specific tax of 1 dollar per unit is imposed. Compute the changes in equilibrium price and quantity.

6-8 Assume fifty firms supply commodity Q at location I and fifty at location II. The cost of producing output q_i for the ith firm (in either location) is $0.5q_i^2$. The cost of transporting the commodity to the market from location I is 6 dollars per unit and from location II, 10 dollars per unit. Determine the aggregate supply function.

6-9 A consumer allocates a fixed amount of time to labor and leisure. He derives satisfaction from the time he retains as leisure, L, and the income, y, that he secures by selling his labor at a fixed wage rate. His utility function is $U = Ly + aL$ where a is a positive parameter. Derive the consumer's supply function for labor. Is his labor supply curve upward sloping?

6-10 Assume that aggregate demand and supply functions are given by $D = 25/p$ and $S = \sqrt{5p}$. Is the dynamic process defined by (6-21) locally stable?

6-11 Determine whether equilibrium solutions exist for markets with the following demand and supply functions:

(*a*) $D = 12 - 3p$; $S = -10 + 2p$.
(*b*) $D = 16 - 2p$; $S = 20 - 2p$.
(*c*) $D = 50 - 4p$; $S = 10 + 10p - p^2$.
(*d*) $D = 50 - 4p$; $S = 2 + 10p - p^2$.

6-12 Consider the following markets which are characterized by lagged supply response:

(*a*) $D_t = 40 - 10p_t$; $S_t = 2 + 9p_{t-1}$.
(*b*) $D_t = 30 - 5p_t$; $S_t = 20 - p_{t-1}$.

Determine equilibrium price and quantity for each market. Assume an initial price 20 percent below the equilibrium price for each market, and determine the number of periods necessary for each price to adjust to within 1 percent of equilibrium.

6-13 A sugar refiner has a strictly concave production function for which labor and raw sugar cane are the only inputs. His production of refined sugar and purchase of inputs will take place next spring, but he must determine his future production level today. The future prices of refined sugar and labor are known with certainty, but the price of raw sugar will assume one of the values $(r_1, \ldots, r_n)$ with the respective probabilities $(v_1, \ldots, v_n)$. Show how you would determine his futures-market raw sugar demand.

SELECTED REFERENCES

Baumol, W. J.: *Economic Dynamics* (2d ed., New York: Macmillan, 1959). Chap. 7 contains a nonmathematical discussion of comparative statics, dynamics, and the cobweb theorem.

Boulding, K. W.: *Economic Analysis: Microeconomics* (4th ed., New York: Harper & Row, 1966), vol. I. The model of a perfectly competitive economy is developed in nonmathematical terms in pt. I.

Buchanan, N. S.: "A Reconsideration of the Cobweb Theorem," *Journal of Political Economy*, vol. 47 (February, 1939), pp. 67–81. An extension of the cobweb theorem with the use of geometry.

Ellis, H. S., and William Fellner: "External Economies and Diseconomies," *American Economic Review*, vol. 33 (September, 1943), pp. 493–511. Also reprinted in American Economic Association, *Readings in Price Theory* (Chicago: Irwin, 1952), pp. 242–263. A geometric elucidation of these concepts.

Knight, F. H.: *Risk, Uncertainty and Profit* (Boston: Houghton Mifflin, 1921). Also reprinted by the London School of Economics in 1937. A nonmathematical analysis of a perfectly competitive economy with emphasis on the effect of uncertainty on profits.

Marshall, Alfred: *Principles of Economics* (8th ed., London: Macmillan, 1920). Book V contains a nonmathematical analysis of supply and demand and the determination of market equilibrium.

Samuelson, Paul A.: *Foundations of Economic Analysis* (Cambridge, Mass.: Harvard University Press, 1948). Chap. IX contains a discussion of market stability. A knowledge of advanced calculus is necessary.

Schneider, Erich: *Pricing and Equilibrium* (London: William Hodge, 1952). Chap. 4 contains a discussion of equilibrium in a single perfectly competitive market in geometric terms.

Stigler, George J.: *The Theory of Price* (3d ed., New York: Macmillan, 1966). Theories of perfect competition are developed in chap. 10 without the use of mathematics.

SEVEN

MONOPOLY, MONOPSONY, AND MONOPOLISTIC COMPETITION

Thus far, conditions of perfect competition have been assumed to prevail in all markets. A perfectly competitive industry contains a large number of firms selling a homogeneous product. Each firm faces a horizontal demand curve and maximizes profit by selecting an output level at which marginal cost equals market price.

Now attention is turned to markets in which firms have noticeable influence upon price. *Monopoly* is a situation in which a market contains a single seller. A monopolist's demand curve is the same as the corresponding market demand curve. She cannot assume that price is unaffected by her actions. She recognizes that (except for the rare case of a Giffen good) the price she receives declines as her output expands. She is a price setter rather than a price taker.

Buyers as well as sellers may have influence upon price. *Monopsony* describes a market with a single buyer. A monopsonist is not a price taker. She recognizes that the price she pays generally will increase as she increases her purchases.

The theory of *monopolistic competition* blends elements of both monopoly and perfect competition. It covers an industry with a large number of firms selling closely related, but differentiated, products. Each firm, though small in relation to the market as a whole, possesses some control over the price at which it sells.

The traditional theory of monopoly is developed in Sec. 7-1, extended to cover price discrimination in Sec. 7-2, and applied to special situations in Sec. 7-3. Monopsony is the subject of Sec. 7-4. Monopolistic competition is described in Sec. 7-5.

7-1 MONOPOLY: BASIC THEORY

There is no distinction between the industry and the firm in a monopolistic market. The monopolistic firm is the industry; it has no competitors.[1] A monopolist's individual demand curve possesses the same general properties as the industry demand curve for a perfectly competitive market. It is an aggregate of the demand curves of individual consumers and is assumed to be negatively sloped. The quantity of her sales is a single-valued function of the price which she charges:

$$q = f(p) \tag{7-1}$$

where $dq/dp < 0$. The demand curve is assumed to have a unique inverse, and price may be expressed as a single-valued function of quantity:

$$p = F(q) \tag{7-2}$$

where $dp/dq < 0$. A major difference between a monopolist and a perfect competitor is that the monopolist's price decreases as she increases her sales. A perfect competitor accepts price as a parameter and maximizes profit with respect to variations of her output level; a monopolist may maximize profit with respect to variations of either output or price. Of course, she cannot set both independently since her price (output level) is uniquely determined by her demand curve once she has selected her output level (price). The price-quantity combination which maximizes profit is invariant with respect to her choice of the independent variable.

Average and Marginal Revenue

The monopolist's total revenue (R) is price multiplied by quantity sold:

$$R = pq \tag{7-3}$$

Her marginal revenue (MR) is the derivative of her total revenue with respect to her output level. Differentiating (7-3) with respect to q,

$$\text{MR} = \frac{dR}{dq} = p + q\frac{dp}{dq} \tag{7-4}$$

Since $dp/dq < 0$, MR is less than price. The MR of a perfect competitor is also defined by (7-4). Her MR equals price since $dp/dq = 0$. The monopolist's MR equals price less the rate of change of price with respect to quantity multiplied by quantity. If the perfect competitor expands her sales by 1 unit, her

---

[1] In a broad sense all products compete for the limited incomes of consumers. The term monopoly defines a situation in which a single firm produces a commodity for which there are no *close* substitutes. The prices of all other commodities are assumed constant, as is always the case for the analysis of a single market, and the competition of other commodities for the consumer's income is reflected in the position and shape of the monopolist's demand curve.

revenue will increase by the market value of the additional unit. The monopolist must decrease the price she receives for every unit in order to sell an additional unit.

Linear demand and MR curves are pictured in Fig. 7-1. Demand is monotonically decreasing, and MR is less than price for every output greater than zero. The rate of decline of MR is twice the rate of decline of price:

$$p = a - bq \qquad R = aq - bq^2 \qquad MR = \frac{dR}{dq} = a - 2bq$$

Since $dp/dq = -b$ is a constant, the distance between the two curves $[q(dp/dq) = bq]$ is a linear function of output. Total revenue for the price-quantity combination (p^0, q^0) equals the area of the rectangle Op^0Tq^0. The area $OASq^0$ which lies under the MR curve also equals total revenue:

$$\int_0^q (a - 2bq)\, dq = aq - bq^2 = R$$

This result is applicable to demand curves which are not linear. In general

$$\int_0^q \left(p + q\, \frac{dp}{dq} \right) dq = pq = R$$

since the integration constant equals zero. Total revenue is given by the area lying under the MR curve.

The elasticity of demand (e) at a point on a demand curve is defined as the absolute value of the rate of proportionate change of output divided by the rate of proportionate change of price:[1]

$$e = -\frac{d(\ln q)}{d(\ln p)} = -\frac{p}{q}\frac{dq}{dp} \qquad (7\text{-}5)$$

[1] Since attention is limited to negatively sloped demand curves, it is convenient to define the elasticity of demand as a positive number. This is in contrast to Sec. 2-3 where elasticities of demand take the signs of the slopes of the demand curves to which they refer.

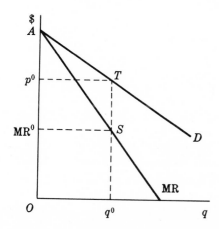

Figure 7-1

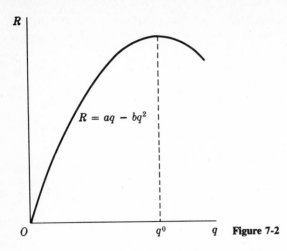

$R = aq - bq^2$

Figure 7-2

MR as given by (7-4) can be expressed in terms of price and demand elasticity:

$$\text{MR} = p\left(1 + \frac{q}{p}\frac{dp}{dq}\right) = p\left(1 - \frac{1}{e}\right) \tag{7-6}$$

MR is positive if $e > 1$, zero if $e = 1$, and negative if $e < 1$. The difference between MR and price decreases as demand elasticity increases, and MR approaches price as demand elasticity approaches infinity.

A parabolic total revenue curve which corresponds to the linear demand curve of Fig. 7-1 is presented in Fig. 7-2. The first derivative of total revenue (MR) is monotonically decreasing and reaches zero at the output level q^0. Total revenue is increasing and $e > 1$ for $q < q^0$, is at a maximum and $e = 1$ for $q = q^0$, and is declining and $e < 1$ for $q > q^0$.

Profit Maximization: Cost Function

The monopolist's total revenue and total cost can both be expressed as functions of output:

$$R = R(q) \qquad C = C(q)$$

Her profit is the difference between her total revenue and total cost:

$$\pi = R(q) - C(q) \tag{7-7}$$

To maximize profit set the derivative of (7-7) with respect to q equal to zero:

$$\frac{d\pi}{dq} = R'(q) - C'(q) = 0$$

or

$$R'(q) = C'(q) \tag{7-8}$$

MR must equal MC for profit maximization. The monopolist can increase her profit by expanding (or contracting) her output, as long as the addition to her revenue (MR) exceeds (or is less than) the addition to her cost (MC). Since MR is positive for a profit-maximizing output, it follows from (7-6) that the monopolist will always select an elastic point on her demand curve, i.e., a point at which $e > 1$. There is no similar restriction upon the equilibrium value of e for a competitive market.

The second-order condition for profit maximization requires that

$$\frac{d^2\pi}{dq^2} = R''(q) - C''(q) < 0$$

or adding $C''(q)$ to both sides of the inequality,

$$R''(q) < C''(q) \qquad (7\text{-}9)$$

The rate of increase of MR must be less than the rate of increase of MC. The second-order condition is *a fortiori* satisfied if MR is decreasing and MC increasing, as is generally assumed. If MC is decreasing, (7-9) requires that MR be decreasing at a more rapid rate. If both conditions for profit maximization are satisfied for more than one output level, the one which yields the greatest profit can be selected by inspection.

The first-order condition can be satisfied in each of the three cases presented in Fig. 7-3. The equalization of MR and MC for (*a*) determines a quantity of q^0 and a price of p^0. The monopolist can set the price p^0 and allow the consumers to purchase q^0, or she can offer q^0 for sale and allow the consumers to determine a price of p^0. The second-order condition requires that the algebraic value of the slope of the MC curve exceed that of the MR curve, i.e., the MC curve must cut the MR curve from below. This condition is satisfied at the intersection points in (*a*) and (*b*). MR = MC does not yield a point of maximum profit in (*c*) since the MC curve cuts the MR curve from above at their only point of intersection. The first-order condition can be satisfied, but the second-order condition cannot.

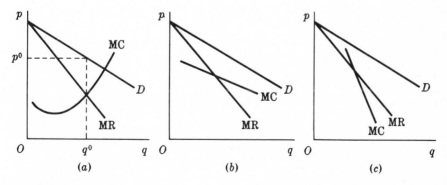

Figure 7-3

If a monopolist followed the rule of a perfect competitor and equated MC to price, she would produce a greater output and charge a lower price. This is obvious by Fig. 7-3a. The coordinates of the intersection point of the MC and demand curves give a price less than p^0 and a quantity greater than q^0.

Consider a monopolist who faces a linear demand curve:

$$p = 100 - 4q \qquad R = pq = 100q - 4q^2 \qquad (7\text{-}10)$$

and produces at a constant MC of 20 dollars. Her total cost is a linear function of her output level:

$$C = 50 + 20q \qquad (7\text{-}11)$$

Her profit is

$$\pi = (100q - 4q^2) - (50 + 20q)$$

Setting MR equal to MC,

$$100 - 8q = 20$$
$$q = 10 \qquad p = 60 \qquad \pi = 350$$

The second-order condition is satisfied: the rate of change of MC (zero) exceeds the rate of change of MR (-8). If the monopolist were to follow the rule of the perfect competitor and set price equal to MC:

$$100 - 4q = 20$$
$$q = 20 \qquad p = 20 \qquad \pi = -50$$

she would sell a larger quantity at a lower price and earn a smaller profit. In this example the monopolist's 350 dollar profit would be reduced to a 50 dollar loss.

Profit Maximization: Production Function

The analysis of monopoly is usually conducted in terms of cost functions. There are situations, however, in which it is desirable to consider a monopolist's production function and input purchases explicitly. Assume that a monopolist uses two inputs which she purchases in competitive markets to produce her output. Her profit is

$$\pi = R(q) - r_1 x_1 - r_2 x_2$$

Setting the partial derivatives of profit with respect to inputs equal to zero,

$$\frac{\partial \pi}{\partial x_i} = R'(q)h_i - r_i = 0 \qquad i = 1, 2 \qquad (7\text{-}12)$$

where $q = h(x_1, x_2)$ and $h_i = \partial q / \partial x_i$. Rearranging terms,

$$R'(q)h_i = r_i \qquad i = 1, 2$$

Profit maximization requires that the monopolist set the value of the *marginal-revenue product* of each input equal to its price. In monopoly marginal revenue times marginal product equals input price; in perfect competition output price times marginal product equals input price.

The second-order conditions for profit maximization require that

$$\pi_{11} < 0 \qquad \pi_{22} < 0 \qquad \pi_{11}\pi_{22} - \pi_{12}^2 > 0 \qquad (7\text{-}13)$$

where $\pi_{ij} = \partial^2 \pi / \partial x_i \partial x_j$. By further differentiation of (7-12),

$$\pi_{ii} = R'(q)h_{ii} + R''(q)h_i^2 < 0 \qquad i = 1, 2$$

or by rearranging terms and substituting from (7-12),[1]

$$R''(q) < -\frac{R'(q)h_{ii}}{h_i^2} = -\frac{r_i h_{ii}}{h_i^3} = C''(q) \qquad i = 1, 2 \qquad (7\text{-}14)$$

The rate of increase of MC attributable to varying either of the inputs must exceed the rate of increase of MR. The third inequality of (7-13) requires that the rate of increase of MC obtained by varying both of the inputs must exceed the rate of increase of MR.

Since $R''(q) = 0$ for a perfect competitor, $C''(q)$ must be positive, or equivalently, her production function must be strictly concave in the neighborhood of an equilibrium point. Since $R''(q)$ is normally negative for a monopolist, her $C''(q)$ may also be negative and still satisfy (7-14). Thus, it is possible to have a monopoly equilibrium at a point at which the production function is not strictly concave, i.e., a point at which $h_{ii} > 0$. Strict concavity of the production function at a point at which (7-12) is satisfied is sufficient for monopoly equilibrium, but not necessary.

7-2 MONOPOLY: PRICE DISCRIMINATION

The monopolist need not always sell her entire output in a single market for a uniform price. In some cases she can increase her profit by selling at more than one price. Two such cases are presented here. In the first she is able to

---

[1] Let $F(q, x_1, x_2) = q - h(x_1, x_2)$, and

$$\frac{\partial x_i}{\partial q} = -\frac{F_q}{F_{x_i}} = -\frac{1}{h_i}$$

and by further differentiation,

$$\frac{\partial^2 x_i}{\partial q^2} = \frac{h_{ii}(\partial x_i / \partial q)}{h_i^2} = -\frac{h_{ii}}{h_i^3}$$

The last equality of (7-14) is derived using the composite-function rule:

$$C''(q) = \frac{\partial^2 C}{\partial x_i^2}\left(\frac{\partial x_i}{\partial q}\right)^2 + \frac{\partial C}{\partial x_i}\frac{\partial^2 x_i}{\partial q^2} = -\frac{r_i h_{ii}}{h_i^3}$$

set a different price in each of two distinct markets. In the second she is able to set a continuum of prices.

Market Discrimination

Consider a situation in which a monopolist sells in two markets and ask whether she will charge the same price in both. Price discrimination is feasible only if buyers are unable to purchase the product in one market and resell it in another. Otherwise, arbitrageurs would buy in a low-price market and resell in a high-price market at a profit, and thereby equalize price in all markets. Personal services are seldom transferable, and their sale frequently provides an opportunity for price discrimination. The resale of such commodities as electricity, gas, and water, which require physical connections between the facilities of the producer and consumer, is extremely difficult, and price discrimination is widely followed in setting utility rates. Price discrimination is often possible in spatially separated markets such as the "home" and "foreign" markets of a monopolist who sells abroad; resale can be prevented by a sufficiently high tariff.

If a monopolist practices price discrimination in two distinct markets, her profit is the difference between her total revenue from both markets and her total cost of production:

$$\pi = R_1(q_1) + R_2(q_2) - C(q_1 + q_2) \tag{7-15}$$

where q_1 and q_2 are the quantities which she sells in the two markets, $R_1(q_1)$ and $R_2(q_2)$ are her revenue functions, and $C(q_1 + q_2)$ is her cost function. Setting the partial derivatives of (7-15) equal to zero,

$$\frac{\partial \pi}{\partial q_1} = R_1'(q_1) - C'(q_1 + q_2) = 0$$

$$\frac{\partial \pi}{\partial q_2} = R_2'(q_2) - C'(q_1 + q_2) = 0$$

or

$$R_1'(q_1) = R_2'(q_2) = C'(q_1 + q_2)$$

The MR in each market must equal the MC of the output as a whole. If the MRs were not equal, the monopolist could increase total revenue without affecting total cost by shifting sales from the low MR market to the high one. The equality of the MRs does not necessarily imply the equality of prices in the two markets. Denoting the prices and the demand elasticities in the two markets by $p_1, p_2, e_1,$ and e_2 and utilizing (7-6), the equality of the MRs implies

$$p_1\left(1 - \frac{1}{e_1}\right) = p_2\left(1 - \frac{1}{e_2}\right)$$

and

$$\frac{p_1}{p_2} = \frac{1 - 1/e_2}{1 - 1/e_1}$$

Price will be lower in the market with the greater demand elasticity. The prices will be equal if and only if the demand elasticities are equal.

Second-order conditions require that the principal minors of the relevant Hessian determinant

$$\begin{vmatrix} R_1'' - C'' & -C'' \\ -C'' & R_2'' - C'' \end{vmatrix}$$

alternate in sign beginning with the negative sign. Expanding the principal minors,

$$R_1'' - C'' < 0 \qquad (R_1'' - C'')(R_2'' - C'') - (C'')^2 > 0$$

These imply that $R_2'' - C'' < 0$. The MR in each market must be increasing less rapidly than the MC for the output as a whole.

Assume that the monopolist whose demand and cost functions are given by (7-10) and (7-11) is able to separate her consumers into two distinct markets:[1]

$$p_1 = 80 - 5q_1 \qquad\qquad R_1 = 80q_1 - 5q_1^2$$
$$p_2 = 180 - 20q_2 \qquad\qquad R_2 = 180q_2 - 20q_2^2$$
$$C = 50 + 20(q_1 + q_2)$$

Setting the MR in each market equal to the MC of the output as a whole,

$$80 - 10q_1 = 20 \qquad 180 - 40q_2 = 20$$

Solving for q_1 and q_2 and substituting into the demand, profit, and elasticity equations,

$$q_1 = 6 \qquad p_1 = 50 \qquad e_1 = 1.67$$
$$q_2 = 4 \qquad p_2 = 100 \qquad e_2 = 1.25$$
$$\pi = 450$$

Second-order conditions are satisfied:

$$-10 < 0 \qquad \begin{vmatrix} -10 & 0 \\ 0 & -40 \end{vmatrix} = 400 > 0$$

---

[1] Her aggregate demand curve remains unchanged. Solving the demand equations for q_1 and q_2,

$$q_1 = 16 - 0.2p_1 \qquad q_2 = 9 - 0.05p_2$$

The total demand at any price (p) is the sum of the demands in the two markets:

$$q = q_1 + q_2 = 16 - 0.2p + 9 - 0.05p = 25 - 0.25p$$

Solving for p,

$$p = 100 - 4q$$

which is the demand function (7-10).

The monopolist has increased her profit from 350 to 450 dollars through discrimination. Price is lower in the market with the greater demand elasticity. Further discrimination would be profitable if the monopolist were able to subdivide her consumers into a larger number of groups with different demand elasticities.

Perfect Discrimination

Each point on the demand curve gives the highest single price that consumers are willing to pay for the corresponding quantity of output. Some consumers would be willing to pay more rather than forego consumption of the commodity. They gain a consumers' surplus (see Sec. 3-7) from a single price system. For simplicity assume that income effects are zero so that the ordinary and compensated demand curves coincide (see Sec. 2-5). Consumers' surplus then equals the area under the demand curve less the amount that consumers pay for the commodity.

The *perfectly discriminating monopolist* is able to subdivide her market to such a degree that she sells each successive unit of her commodity for the maximum amount that consumers are willing to pay. The monopolist, thereby, extracts all the consumers' surplus. Her total revenue is the area under her demand curve and her profit is

$$\pi = \int_0^q F(q)\, dq - C(q)$$

Setting the derivative of profit with respect to output equal to zero,

$$\frac{d\pi}{dq} = F(q) - C'(q) = 0$$

and $F(q) = C'(q)$. Profit is maximized by equating marginal price and marginal cost. In diagrammatic terms the perfectly discriminating monopolist operates at a point at which her MC curve intersects her demand curve. The second-order condition for profit maximization:

$$\frac{d^2\pi}{dq^2} = F'(q) - C''(q) < 0$$

requires that the slope of her MC curve be greater than the slope of her demand curve.

Assuming perfect discrimination for the example given by (7-10) and (7-11), profit is

$$\pi = \int_0^q (100 - 4q)\, dq - (50 + 20q)$$

and setting marginal price equal to MC,

$$100 - 4q = 20 \qquad q = 20 \qquad \pi = 750$$

The perfectly discriminating monopolist produces more than the 10 units produced by the simple monopolist and earns a higher profit than the 350 earned by the simple monopolist. Her marginal price is 20, and her average revenue per unit sold is 60, contrasted with a uniform price of 60 for the simple monopolist.

7-3 MONOPOLY: APPLICATIONS

The basic theory of monopoly may be modified to cover a wide variety of situations. Four applications are considered in this section.

The Multiple-Plant Monopolist

Consider a monopolist selling in a single market, who can produce her output in two separate plants. Her profit is the difference between her total revenue and her total production costs for both plants:

$$\pi = R(q_1 + q_2) - C_1(q_1) - C_2(q_2) \tag{7-16}$$

where q_1 and q_2 are the quantities which she produces in the two plants, $R(q_1 + q_2)$ is her revenue function, and $C_1(q_1)$ and $C_2(q_2)$ are her cost functions. Setting the partial derivatives of (7-16) equal to zero,

$$\frac{\partial \pi}{\partial q_1} = R'(q_1 + q_2) - C_1'(q_1) = 0$$

$$\frac{\partial \pi}{\partial q_2} = R'(q_1 + q_2) - C_2'(q_2) = 0$$

or
$$R'(q_1 + q_2) = C_1'(q_1) = C_2'(q_2)$$

The MC in each plant must equal the MR of the output as a whole. Second-order conditions require that the principal minors of the relevant Hessian determinant

$$\begin{vmatrix} R'' - C_1'' & R'' \\ R'' & R'' - C_2'' \end{vmatrix} \tag{7-17}$$

alternate in sign beginning with the negative sign. The reader can verify that (7-17) requires that the MC in each plant must be increasing more rapidly than the MR of the output as a whole.

The Multiple-Product Monopolist

Consider a producer who acts as a monopolist for two distinct but interrelated products with the demand functions

$$q_1 = f_1(p_1, p_2) \qquad q_2 = f_2(p_1, p_2)$$

If the cross derivatives, the $\partial q_i/\partial p_j$ $(i \neq j)$, are positive, the goods are gross substitutes. If they are negative, the goods are gross complements. Assume that single-valued inverse demand functions exist

$$p_1 = F_1(q_1, q_2) \qquad p_2 = F_2(q_1, q_2)$$

Here positive cross derivatives denote complements, and negative derivatives denote substitutes.[1] Finally define revenue functions

$$R_1 = p_1 q_1 = R_1(q_1, q_2) \qquad R_2 = p_2 q_2 = R_2(q_1, q_2)$$

Here $\partial R_i/\partial q_j$ $(i \neq j)$ is positive for complements and negative for substitutes.

The monopolist's profit is

$$\pi = R_1(q_1, q_2) + R_2(q_1, q_2) - C_1(q_1) - C_2(q_2)$$

Setting the partial derivatives equal to zero

$$\frac{\partial \pi}{\partial q_1} = \frac{\partial R_1}{\partial q_1} + \frac{\partial R_2}{\partial q_1} - C_1'(q_1) = 0$$

$$\frac{\partial \pi}{\partial q_2} = \frac{\partial R_1}{\partial q_2} + \frac{\partial R_2}{\partial q_2} - C_2'(q_2) = 0$$

and
$$\frac{\partial R_1}{\partial q_1} + \frac{\partial R_2}{\partial q_1} = C_1'(q_1) \qquad \frac{\partial R_1}{\partial q_2} + \frac{\partial R_2}{\partial q_2} = C_2'(q_2) \qquad (7\text{-}18)$$

The monopolist again equates MC and MR. In (7-18) MR explicitly accounts for the demand interrelation.[2]

Consider a case in which the goods are substitutes with $\partial R_i/\partial q_j < 0$ $(i \neq j)$. An example is a local brewer who produces both premium and ordinary beer. The MC for a beer will be lower than the MR for that beer considered apart from the other beer. An increase in the output of the premium beer is achieved through a reduction of its price which causes a reduction in the sales of the ordinary beer. The first-order conditions (7-18) dictate an optimal price differential for the two beers.

If the goods are complements with $\partial R_i/\partial q_j > 0$ $(i \neq j)$, the MC for each good will be higher than the MR for that good considered alone. Let one good be razor blades and the other razors. An expansion in the output of razors through a reduction in their price will cause an expansion in the revenue from the sale of blades at a given price. An optimal solution might require the sale of razors at a loss because of the favorable effects of their sale on razor-blade profits.

Taxation and Monopoly Output

A lump-sum or a profit tax (with a marginal rate less than 100 percent) will reduce the profit after taxes of a profit-maximizing monopolist, but will not

---

[1] This follows from the assumption that the $\partial q_i/\partial p_i < 0$.

[2] Second-order conditions are henceforth assumed to be satisfied unless otherwise stated.

affect her optimum price-quantity combination. A sales tax, whether based upon quantity sold or value of sales, will reduce her profit and output level and increase her price.

The monopolist cannot avoid a lump-sum tax. It must be paid regardless of the physical quantity or value of her sales or the amount of her profit. Her profit becomes

$$\pi = R(q) - C(q) - T \qquad (7\text{-}19)$$

where T is the amount of the lump-sum tax and π is her profit after the tax payment. Setting the derivative of (7-19) equal to zero,

$$\frac{d\pi}{dq} = R'(q) - C'(q) = 0 \qquad R'(q) = C'(q)$$

Since T is a constant, it vanishes upon differentiation, and the monopolist's output level and price are determined by the equality of MR and MC as would be the case if no tax were imposed.

A profit tax requires that the monopolist pay the government a specified proportion of the difference between her total revenue and total cost. If the tax is a flat rate (constant proportion), her profit after tax payment is

$$\pi = R(q) - C(q) - t[R(q) - C(q)] = (1 - t)[R(q) - C(q)] \qquad (7\text{-}20)$$

where $0 < t < 1$. Setting the derivative of (7-20) equal to zero,

$$\frac{d\pi}{dq} = (1 - t)[R'(q) - C'(q)] = 0$$

Since $1 - t \neq 0$,

$$R'(q) - C'(q) = 0 \qquad R'(q) = C'(q)$$

Since the first-order condition is the same as (7-8), output level and price are unaffected. The only way a monopolist can avoid a profit tax is to reduce her profit before taxes. If she is able to keep a fraction of an increase of profit before taxes, she will maximize her profit after taxes by equating MR and MC.

If a specific sales tax of α dollars per unit of output is imposed,

$$\pi = R(q) - C(q) - \alpha q$$

and
$$\frac{d\pi}{dq} = R'(q) - C'(q) - \alpha = 0 \qquad R'(q) = C'(q) + \alpha \qquad (7\text{-}21)$$

The monopolist maximizes profit after tax payment by equating MR with MC plus the unit tax. Taking the total differential of (7-21),

$$R''(q)\,dq = C''(q)\,dq + d\alpha$$

and
$$\frac{dq}{d\alpha} = \frac{1}{R''(q) - C''(q)}$$

Since $R''(q) - C''(q) < 0$ by the assumption that the second-order condition is fulfilled, $dq/d\alpha < 0$, and the optimum output level declines as the tax rate increases. The imposition of a specific sales tax results in a smaller quantity sold and a higher price.

Return to the example given by (7-10) and (7-11) and assume that the government imposes a tax of 8 dollars per unit upon the monopolist's output:

$$\pi = (100q - 4q^2) - (50 + 20q) - 8q$$

$$\frac{d\pi}{dq} = 72 - 8q = 0 \qquad q = 9 \qquad p = 64 \qquad \pi = 274$$

Sales diminish by 1 unit, price increases by 4 dollars, and the monopolist's profit diminishes by 76 dollars as a result of the imposition of the tax. Price increases by less than the unit tax, but the monopolist's profit decreases by more than the 72 dollar tax revenue. If the government imposed a 72 dollar lump-sum tax upon the monopolist, it would receive the same revenue, the monopolist's profit would be decreased by 4 dollars less, and the consumers would not have to pay a higher price for the product. As a result it is frequently argued that a lump-sum tax is preferable to a sales tax.

The results are similar if the sales tax is a proportion of the value of sales (total revenue),

$$\pi = R(q) - C(q) - sR(q) = (1 - s)R(q) - C(q)$$

$$\frac{d\pi}{dq} = (1 - s)R'(q) - C'(q) = 0 \qquad (1 - s)R'(q) = C'(q) \qquad (7\text{-}22)$$

where $0 < s < 1$. Profits are maximized by equating MC to the portion of the MR that the monopolist is allowed to retain. Taking the total differential of (7-22),

$$(1 - s)R''(q)\,dq - R'(q)\,ds = C''(q)\,dq$$

and

$$\frac{dq}{ds} = \frac{R'(q)}{(1 - s)R''(q) - C''(q)} \qquad (7\text{-}23)$$

Since the first-order condition requires that MR be positive and the second-order condition implies that the denominator of (7-23) is negative, $dq/ds < 0$. The imposition of an ad valorem sales tax also results in a reduced output level and an increased price.

The Revenue-Maximizing Monopolist

It has been suggested that many large firms do not maximize profit, but rather maximize sales revenue subject to the constraint that profit equal or exceed some minimum acceptable level.[1] The monopolist desires to maximize $R(q)$

---

[1] See William J. Baumol, *Business Behavior, Value and Growth* (rev. ed., New York: Harcourt, Brace & World, 1967), chap. 6.

subject to
$$\pi = R(q) - C(q) \geqq \pi^0 \qquad\qquad (7\text{-}24)$$

where π^0 is the minimum acceptable profit.

The revenue function is concave. If the cost function is convex, the profit function is concave, and the Kuhn-Tucker analysis is applicable for the monopolist's maximization problem. The appropriate Lagrange function is

$$L = R(q) + \lambda[R(q) - C(q) - \pi^0]$$

and the Kuhn-Tucker conditions are

$$\frac{\partial L}{\partial q} = R'(q) + \lambda[R'(q) - C'(q)] \leqq 0 \qquad q \geqq 0 \qquad q\,\frac{\partial L}{\partial q} = 0$$

$$\qquad\qquad\qquad\qquad\qquad\qquad\qquad\qquad\qquad (7\text{-}25)$$

$$\frac{\partial L}{\partial \lambda} = R(q) - C(q) - \pi^0 \geqq 0 \qquad\qquad \lambda \geqq 0 \qquad \lambda\,\frac{\partial L}{\partial \lambda} = 0$$

Assume that a unique unrestricted maximum profit, π^*, exists at the output q^* with $R'(q^*) > 0$, $C''(q) > 0$ for $q \geqq q^*$, and $R''(q) < 0$ for $q > 0$. If $\pi^0 > \pi^*$, (7-24) cannot be satisfied and the maximum-revenue problem has no solution. A solution will exist if $\pi^0 \leqq \pi^*$. If $\pi^0 = \pi^*$, q^* is the maximum-revenue solution since it is the only output that satisfies (7-24). If $\pi^0 < \pi^*$, revenue will increase and profit decrease as q is increased beyond q^*. Thus, the monopolist will continue to increase q until either (1) she reaches the unrestricted maximum of $R(q)$, or (2) (7-24) is satisfied as an equality, whichever occurs at the lower output. If (1), (7-25) states that $R'(q) = 0$ and $\lambda = 0$. If (2) happens short of the output for (1), $C'(q) > R'(q) > 0$ and $\lambda > 0$. The multiplier λ gives the rate at which revenue can be expanded per dollar of profit sacrificed.

Consider again the example given by (7-10) and (7-11). Assume that $334 = \pi^0 < \pi^* = 350$. The unrestricted maximum for $R(q)$ is 625 which occurs at $q = 12.5$ with $\pi = 325$. This option may be excluded because it yields too low a profit. The equality of (7-24) is

$$(100q - 4q^2) - (50 + 20q) = 334$$

which may also be written as

$$q^2 - 20q + 96 = 0$$

This quadratic equation has the roots 8 and 12 with respective total revenues of 544 and 624. Thus, the revenue-maximizing monopolist produces 12 units which she sells at a price of 52 to gain a total revenue of 624 and a profit of 334. By contrast, the simple monopolist produces 10 units which she sells at a price of 60 to gain a total revenue of 600 and a profit of 350. From (7-25), $\lambda = 0.25$. The entrepreneur sacrifices at the marginal rate of 4 dollars of profit per dollar of revenue.

The revenue-maximizing monopolist, unlike the simple monopolist, may alter her output if a profit tax is introduced. Consider a case in which her output is determined by the equality of (7-24) both before and after a tax is imposed. Assume that the tax, $0 < t < 1$, is a constant fraction of profit. The equality of (7-24) becomes

$$(1 - t)[R(q) - C(q)] = \pi^0 \tag{7-26}$$

Taking the total differential of (7-26),

$$\frac{dq}{dt} = \frac{R(q) - C(q)}{(1 - t)[R'(q) - C'(q)]}$$

Since the value of q that satisfies (7-26) is greater than q^*, $R'(q) - C'(q)$ is negative. Since $R(q) - C(q)$ and $1 - t$ are positive, $dq/dt < 0$; that is, an increase in the profit-tax rate reduces the maximum-revenue output. If the output for an unrestricted maximum revenue yielded a profit at least as great as the minimum acceptable level both before and after the imposition of a tax, the monopolist would not alter this output.

7-4 MONOPSONY

Monopsony is similar to monopoly in many regards. A monopolistic market has one seller and many competitive buyers. A monopsonistic market has one buyer and many competitive sellers.

A monopsonist cannot purchase an unlimited amount of an input at a uniform price; the price which she must pay for each quantity purchased is given by the market supply curve for the input. Since the supply curves for most inputs are positively sloped, the price which the monopsonist must pay is generally an increasing function of the quantity she purchases.

First consider the case of a monopsonist who uses a single input, which we shall call labor, for the production of a commodity which she sells in a perfectly competitive market. An example might be provided by a producer who is the sole purchaser in a local labor market and sells her output in a competitive national or international market. Her production function states output as a function of the quantity of labor (x) employed:

$$q = h(x) \tag{7-27}$$

The revenue function and cost equation are, as before:

$$R = pq \qquad C = rx$$

where r is the price of labor. However, the price of labor is now an increasing function of the amount employed:

$$r = g(x) \tag{7-28}$$

where $dr/dx > 0$. The *marginal cost of labor* is the rate of change of its cost with respect to the quantity employed:[1]

$$\frac{dC}{dx} = r + xg'(x) \qquad (7\text{-}29)$$

Since $g'(x) > 0$, the marginal cost of labor exceeds its price for $x > 0$.

The monopsonist's profit can be expressed as a function of the amount of labor which she employs:

$$\pi = R - C = ph(x) - rx \qquad (7\text{-}30)$$

Setting the derivative of (7-30) with respect to x equal to zero,

$$\frac{d\pi}{dx} = ph'(x) - r - xg'(x) = 0$$

$$ph'(x) = r + xg'(x) \qquad (7\text{-}31)$$

The first-order condition for profit maximization requires that labor be employed up to a point at which the value of its marginal product equals its marginal cost. The second-order condition requires that the rate of change of the value of the marginal product of labor be less than the rate of change of its marginal cost:

$$\frac{d^2\pi}{dx^2} = ph''(x) - 2g'(x) - xg''(x) < 0$$

$$ph''(x) < 2g'(x) + xg''(x) \qquad (7\text{-}32)$$

The monopsonist's optimum output and the price of labor are determined by solving (7-31) for x and substituting a value for which the second-order conditions is satisfied into (7-27) and (7-28).

The profit-maximizing monopsonist (see Fig. 7-4) will employ x^0 units of labor at a wage rate of r^0 dollars. The equality of the price of labor with the value of its marginal product, the equilibrium point for an entrepreneur who purchases labor in a perfectly competitive market, would result in the employment of $x^{(1)}$ units of labor at a wage rate of $r^{(1)}$. The monopsonist employs a smaller quantity of labor at a lower wage rate.

If the monopsonist's production and labor supply functions are

$$q = 15x^2 - 0.2x^3 \qquad r = 144 + 23.4x$$

and she sells her output in a perfectly competitive market at a price of 3 dollars, her total revenue function and cost equation are

$$R = 45x^2 - 0.6x^3 \qquad C = 144x + 23.4x^2$$

Setting the value of the marginal product of labor equal to its marginal cost,

$$90x - 1.8x^2 = 144 + 46.8x$$

---

[1] The reader should note that marginal cost is here defined with respect to the quantity of labor employed rather than the quantity of output produced. The abbreviated form (MC) is reversed for marginal cost with respect to output level.

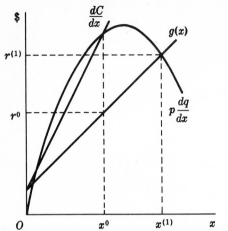

Figure 7-4

which yields the quadratic equation:

$$1.8x^2 - 43.2x + 144 = 0$$

with the roots $x = 4$ and $x = 20$. The second-order condition

$$90 - 3.6x < 46.8$$

is satisfied for $x = 20$. The solution $x = 4$ is a minimum-profit position. Substituting $x = 20$ into the appropriate functions,

$$q = 4400 \qquad r = 612 \qquad \pi = 960$$

If a monopsonist is also a monopolist in the market for her output, the price she receives is a function of the quantity which she sells:

$$p = F(q)$$

Her profit may again be expressed as a function of the quantity of labor which she employs:

$$\pi = pq - rx = F[h(x)]h(x) - rx$$

or more simply,

$$\pi = R(x) - C(x) \tag{7-33}$$

where total revenue and total cost are expressed as functions of the quantity of labor employed. Setting the derivative of (7-33) equal to zero yields the first-order condition that the rate of increase of total revenue from the employment of another unit of labor (the *marginal-revenue product* of labor) must equal its marginal cost. The second-order condition requires that the marginal-revenue product of labor increase less rapidly than its marginal cost.

7-5 MONOPOLISTIC COMPETITION

Monopolistic competition contains elements of both monopoly and perfect competition.[1] It is akin to perfect competition in that the number of sellers is sufficiently large so that the actions of an individual seller have no perceptible influence upon her competitors. It is akin to monopoly in that each seller possesses a negatively sloped demand curve for her distinct product.

Assuming linear demand curves, the price received by each seller is a function of the quantities sold by each of the n firms within the industry:

$$p_k = A_k - a_k q_k - \sum_{\substack{i=1 \\ i \neq k}}^{n} b_{ki} q_i \qquad k = 1, \ldots, n \tag{7-34}$$

where $\partial p_k / \partial q_i = -b_{ki}$ is negative, but numerically small. To facilitate exposition, assume that all firms have identical demand and cost functions; that is, $b_{ki} = b$ for all k and i except $k = i$, $a_k = a$, $A_k = A$, and $C_k(q_k) = C(q_k)$ for all k. Assuming initial price-quantity combinations which are the same for all firms, the industry can be described in terms of the actions of a "representative" firm. The revenue and cost functions of all firms and their maximizing behavior are identical, though their products are differentiated in the eyes of consumers. The demand curve facing the representative firm is

$$p_k = A - a q_k - b \sum_{\substack{i=1 \\ i \neq k}}^{n} q_i \tag{7-35}$$

The profit of the representative firm is

$$\pi_k = q_k \left(A - a q_k - b \sum_{\substack{i=1 \\ i \neq k}}^{n} q_i \right) - C(q_k) \tag{7-36}$$

Since b is numerically small and a quantity change on the part of the representative firm affects each of its $(n - 1)$ competitors to the same degree, the effects of her movements upon the price of any particular competitor are negligible. Therefore, the entrepreneur of the representative firm acts as if her actions had no effects upon her competitors. Equating her MR and MC on the assumption that the output levels of her competitors remain unchanged:

$$A - 2a q_k - b \sum_{\substack{i=1 \\ i \neq k}}^{n} q_i = C'(q_k) \tag{7-37}$$

The second-order condition requires that her MC be increasing more rapidly than her MR. The optimum output level for the kth firm depends upon the aggregate output level of its competitors.

---

[1] See Edward H. Chamberlin, *The Theory of Monopolistic Competition* (8th ed., Cambridge, Mass.: Harvard University Press, 1962).

The symmetry assumption ensures that if it is profitable for the representative firm to make a particular move, it is profitable for all other firms to make the same move. All firms will attempt to maximize profit simultaneously, and quantity variations by the kth firm will be accompanied by identical variations on the part of all the other firms within the industry. The representative firm will not move along the demand curve (7-35) which is constructed upon the assumption that the output levels of the other firms remain unchanged. Its effective demand curve is constructed by substituting $q_k = q_i$ into (7-35):

$$p_k = A - [a + (n-1)b]q_k \qquad (7\text{-}38)$$

The number $(n-1)$ is not of a negligible order of magnitude. A 1 percent increase in the output level of one competitor may cause p_k to decrease by 0.02 percent, but a simultaneous 1 percent increase on the part of 1000 firms may decrease p_k by 20 percent or more. The effective demand curve (7-38) which accounts for simultaneous and identical movements on the part of all sellers has a steeper slope than (7-35). The entrepreneur of the representative firm may realize that she is unable to move along her individual demand curve, but this information is of no use to her, since she has no control over the output levels of her competitors. The other firms change their output levels because they can increase their profits. Their actions are not governed by the actions of the representative firm. The representative firm must take advantage of its opportunity to increase profit and act in the same manner as the other firms.

The representative firm starting from some arbitrary initial price-quantity combination faces two separate demand curves. In Fig. 7-5a, DD is its

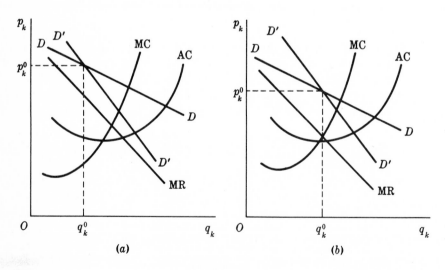

(a)   (b)

Figure 7-5

demand curve for variations of its output level alone, and $D'D'$ is its effective demand curve for identical variations of the output levels of all firms within the industry. The two intersect at the initial price-quantity combination. As all firms increase their output levels, the shape and position of $D'D'$, which is a function of q_k alone [see (7-36)], remain unchanged, and DD, the position of which is dependent upon the outputs of all firms [see (7-35)], "slides" along $D'D'$, always intersecting it at the current output level of the representative firm.

The industry reaches an equilibrium when MR equals MC for all firms. The n simultaneous equations of (7-37) must be solved for the n unknown quantities. It can be proved that the symmetry assumption guarantees that (7-37) will result in equal output levels for all n firms. Therefore, the solution can be obtained by substituting $q_k = q_i$ in (7-37) and solving

$$A - [2a + (n-1)b]q_k = C'(q_k) \tag{7-39}$$

for q_k.† The latter formulation involves only one equation and one variable. The maximum profit and optimum price-quantity combination are the same for all firms. A graphic description of short-run equilibrium is presented in Fig. 7-5b. MR equals MC, and DD intersects $D'D'$ at the equilibrium price-quantity combination.

Free entry and exit drive pure profit to zero in a perfectly competitive industry and can have the same effect in monopolistic competition. The profit of the representative firm can be expressed as a function of its output and the number of firms within the industry if $q_k = q_i$ is substituted in (7-36):

$$\pi_k = Aq_k - [a + (n-1)b]q_k^2 - C(q_k) \tag{7-40}$$

Setting π_k equal to zero, (7-39) and (7-40) are a system of two equations in the two variables q_k and n. The solution of these equations gives the long-run equilibrium values for the output level of the representative firm and the number of firms.

The long-run equilibrium position of the representative firm is pictured in Fig. 7-6. New firms will be induced to enter the industry if the pure profit of the representative firm is greater than zero. As the number of firms increases, the representative firm can sell a smaller output at any given price; i.e., both DD and $D'D'$ are shifted to the left. Long-run equilibrium is attained when MR equals MC, DD is tangent to the average cost curve (indicating that total revenue equals total cost and therefore profit equals zero), and the tangency point is intersected by $D'D'$.

The long-run equilibrium point for the representative firm is to the left of

---

† This solution is not the same as that for an oligopolistic market in which one of the entrepreneurs knows that (7-38) is her effective demand curve. MR is $A - [2a + 2(n-1)b]q_k$ in this case, or $(n-1)bq_k$ dollars less for every output level. The output level at which MR and MC are equated is smaller than that obtained from a solution of (7-39).

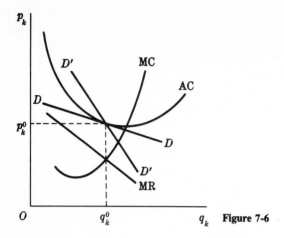

Figure 7-6

the minimum point on its average total cost curve. Price equals average cost, as is true for the representative firm in perfect competition, but price does not equal MC. Contrasted with the results of perfect competition, the representative firm produces a smaller output at a greater average total cost.

7-6 SUMMARY

A monopolistic firm constitutes an industry and is unfettered by the competition of close rivals. A monopolist is free to select any price-quantity combination which lies on her negatively sloped demand curve. Since an expansion of her output results in a reduction of her price, her MR is less than her price. The first-order condition for profit maximization requires the equality of MR and MC. The second-order condition requires that MC be increasing more rapidly than MR. When the production function is introduced explicitly, the monopolist maximizes profit by equating the marginal-revenue product of each input to its price.

If second-order conditions are satisfied, a discriminating monopolist maximizes her profit by equating the MR in each of her markets to the MC for her output as a whole. A perfectly discriminating monopolist captures all the consumers' surplus for her output by equating her marginal price to her MC. A multiple-plant monopolist maximizes her profit by equating the MC in each of her plants to the MR for her output as a whole. A multiple-product monopolist equates MCs to multiple-product MRs.

Neither a lump-sum nor a profit tax will affect the optimum price-quantity combination for a profit-maximizing monopolist. The imposition of either a specific or an ad valorem sales tax will result in a reduction of output and an increase of price. A revenue-maximizing monopolist maximizes sales revenue subject to the condition that profit does not fall below a minimum acceptable level. A profit tax may result in a reduction of output and an increase of price.

A monopsonist faces a rising supply curve for an input. She may be the sole purchaser of a particular type of labor. The monopsonist's marginal cost of labor exceeds the wage rate, since she must increase the wage rate for all her employees in order to expand employment. The first-order condition for profit maximization requires that she employ labor up to the point at which the value of its marginal product equals its marginal cost. If the monopsonist is also a monopolist in her product market, the first-order condition requires that she equate the marginal-revenue product of labor to its marginal cost.

In monopolistic competition an individual seller possesses a negatively sloped demand curve for her distinct product, but her output constitutes such a small part of the total market that her actions do not have perceptible effects upon her rivals. However, simultaneous movements on the part of all sellers cause shifts of the individual demand curves. Short-run equilibrium is achieved when each seller has equated MR and MC. The number of firms within the industry increases or decreases sufficiently to drive the pure profit of the representative firm to zero in the long run.

EXERCISES

7-1 Determine the maximum profit and the corresponding price and quantity for a monopolist whose demand and cost functions are $p = 20 - 0.5q$ and $C = 0.04q^3 - 1.94q^2 + 32.96q$ respectively.

7-2 A monopolist uses one input, X, which she purchases at the fixed price $r = 5$ to produce her output, Q. Her demand and production functions are $p = 85 - 3q$ and $q = 2\sqrt{x}$ respectively. Determine the values of p, q, and x at which the monopolist maximizes her profit.

7-3 Determine the maximum profit and the corresponding marginal price and quantity for a perfectly discriminating monopolist whose demand and cost functions are $p = 2200 - 60q$ and $C = 0.5q^3 - 61.5q^2 + 2740q$ respectively.

7-4 Let the demand and cost functions of a multiplant monopolist be $p = a - b(q_1 + q_2)$, $C_1 = \alpha_1 q_1 + \beta_1 q_1^2$, and $C_2 = \alpha_2 q_2 + \beta_2 q_2^2$ where all parameters are positive. Assume that an autonomous increase of demand increases the value of a, leaving the other parameters unchanged. Show that output will increase in both plants with a greater increase for the plant in which marginal cost is increasing less fast.

7-5 A revenue-maximizing monopolist requires a profit of at least 1500. Her demand and cost functions are $p = 304 - 2q$ and $C = 500 + 4q + 8q^2$. Determine her output level and price. Contrast these values with those that would be achieved under profit maximization.

7-6 Let the demand and cost functions of a monopolist be $p = 100 - 3q + 4\sqrt{A}$ and $C = 4q^2 + 10q + A$ where A is the level of her advertising expenditure. Find the values of A, q, and p that maximize profit.

7-7 A monopsonist uses only labor, X, to produce her output, Q, which she sells in a competitive market at the fixed price $p = 2$. Her production and labor supply functions are $q = 6x + 3x^2 - 0.02x^3$ and $r = 60 + 3x$ respectively. Determine the values of x, q, and r at which she maximizes her profit. Is the monopsonist's production function strictly concave in the neighborhood of her equilibrium production point?

7-8 Consider a market characterized by monopolistic competition. There are 101 firms with identical demand and cost functions:

$$p_k = 150 - q_k - 0.02 \sum_{\substack{i=1 \\ i \neq k}}^{101} q_i \qquad C_k = 0.5q_k^3 - 20q_k^2 + 270q_k \qquad k = 1, \ldots, 101$$

Determine the maximum profit and the corresponding price and quantity for a representative firm. Assume that the number of firms in the industry does not change.

7-9 A monopolist will construct a single plant to serve two spatially separated markets in which she can charge different prices without fear of competition or resale between markets. The markets are 40 miles apart and are connected by a highway. The monopolist may locate her plant at either of the markets or at some point along the highway. Let z and $(40 - z)$ be the distances of her plant from markets 1 and 2 respectively. The monopolist's demand and production cost functions are not affected by her location:

$$p_1 = 100 - 2q_1 \qquad p_2 = 120 - 3q_2 \qquad C = 80(q_1 + q_2) - (q_1 + q_2)^2$$

Determine optimal values for $q_1, q_2, p_1, p_2,$ and z if the monopolist's transport costs are $T = 0.4zq_1 + 0.5(40 - z)q_2$.

SELECTED REFERENCES

Chamberlin, E. H.: *The Theory of Monopolistic Competition* (8th ed., Cambridge, Mass: Harvard University Press, 1962). The first statement of the problems of monopolistic competition and product differentiation. Geometry is used.

Hadar, Josef: *Mathematical Theory of Economic Behavior* (Reading, Mass.: Addison-Wesley, 1971). The theories of monopoly, monopsony, and monopolistic competition are covered in chaps. 6–8. Intermediate mathematics and geometry are used.

Kuenne, Robert E. (ed.): *Monopolistic Competition Theory* (New York: Wiley, 1967). These essays in honor of E. H. Chamberlin cover many aspects of his theory. Most of the essays use little mathematics beyond geometry.

Robinson, Joan: *The Economics of Imperfect Competition* (London: Macmillan, 1933). A pioneer study of monopoly, price discrimination, and monopsony in which many modern concepts were developed. The analysis is generally limited to geometry.

EIGHT

DUOPOLY, OLIGOPOLY, AND BILATERAL MONOPOLY

The market forms considered thus far are characterized by the existence of either a single seller (*monopoly*) or a very large number of sellers (*perfect competition* and *monopolistic competition*). In the former case the seller has no rivals and thus need not be concerned with the effect that his actions may have on rivals. In the latter cases sellers are sufficiently numerous so that the actions of any one seller have only negligible effect on its competitors.

Markets in which the number of sellers is small but greater than one present new problems. A market with two sellers is a *duopoly*, and a market with a small number greater than two is an *oligopoly*. Consider the market for a homogeneous product. Competition among buyers will result in a single price for all sellers, but each seller is sufficiently large in relation to the market so that his actions will have noticeable effects upon his rivals. An output change on the part of one seller will affect the price received by all. The consequences of attempted price variations on the part of an individual seller are uncertain. His rivals may follow his change, or they may not, but he can no longer assume that they will not notice it. The results of any move on the part of a duopolist or oligopolist depend upon the reactions of his rivals. General price-sales relationships cannot be defined for an individual firm, since, in general, reaction patterns are unknown. Unqualified profit maximization is not possible, since an individual firm does not have control over all variables that affect its profit. There is a very large number of possible reaction patterns for duopolistic and oligopolistic markets, and as a result there is a very large number of theories of duopoly and oligopoly. Only a few of the many possible reaction patterns can be discussed in the present chapter.

199

Several specific theories of duopoly and oligopoly with a homogeneous product are discussed in Sec. 8-1. Duopoly and oligopoly with differentiated products are the subject of Sec. 8-2. Duopsony and oligopsony are briefly outlined in Sec. 8-3. The theory of games and its applications for markets with small numbers of participants are the subject of Sec. 8-4. Some of the concepts developed in this chapter are applied to a bilateral monopoly situation in Sec. 8-5.

8-1 DUOPOLY AND OLIGOPOLY: HOMOGENEOUS PRODUCT

A duopolistic industry contains two sellers. An oligopolistic industry contains a number sufficiently small so that the actions of any individual seller have a perceptible influence upon his rivals. It is not sufficient to distinguish oligopoly from perfect competition for a homogeneous product or from the many-sellers case of monopolistic competition for a differentiated product on the basis of the number of sellers alone. The essential distinguishing feature is the interdependence of the various sellers' actions. If the influence of one seller's quantity decision upon the profit of another, $\partial \pi_i / \partial q_j$, is imperceptible, the industry satisfies the basic requirement for either perfect competition or the many-sellers case of monopolistic competition. If $\partial \pi_i / \partial q_j$ is of a noticeable order of magnitude, it is duopolistic or oligopolistic.

The price-quantity combination and profit of a duopolist or oligopolist depend upon the actions of all members of his market. He can control his own output level (or price, if his product is differentiated), but he has no direct control over the other variables which affect his profit. The profit of each seller is the result of the interaction of the decisions of all market members. There are no generally accepted behavior assumptions for oligopolists and duopolists as there are for perfect competitors amd monopolists. There are many different solutions for duopolistic and oligopolistic markets. Each solution is based upon a different set of behavior assumptions.

In this section a solution corresponding to the price-equals-MC condition of perfect competition is established, and then contrasted with comparable results for three solutions based upon specific behavior assumptions. Each is developed for a duopolistic market, but each may be generalized for an oligopolistic market.

The Quasi-competitive Solution

Consider a market in which two firms produce a homogeneous product. The inverse demand function states price as a function of the aggregate quantity sold:

$$p = F(q_1 + q_2) \tag{8-1}$$

where q_1 and q_2 are the levels of the duopolists' outputs. The total revenue of each duopolist depends upon his own output level and that of his rival:

$$R_1 = q_1 F(q_1 + q_2) = R_1(q_1, q_2)$$
$$R_2 = q_2 F(q_1 + q_2) = R_2(q_1, q_2)$$

The profit of each equals his total revenue less his cost, which depends upon his output level alone:

$$\pi_1 = R_1(q_1, q_2) - C_1(q_1)$$
$$\pi_2 = R_2(q_1, q_2) - C_2(q_2)$$

(8-2)

The perfectly competitive solution is characterized by the equality of price and MC. The quasi-competitive solution for a market with a small number of sellers is defined as the solution that would be achieved if each seller followed the competitive rule; it is determined by solving the equations

$$p = F(q_1 + q_2) = C_1'(q_1)$$
$$p = F(q_1 + q_2) = C_2'(q_2)$$

(8-3)

for p, q_1, and q_2. The quasi-competitive solution may or may not be achieved in any particular market. In either event it provides a standard with which various small-number solutions may be compared. Such comparisons are particularly important in welfare economics (see Chap. 11).

For illustration, let the demand and cost functions be given by

$$p = 100 - 0.5(q_1 + q_2) \qquad C_1 = 5q_1 \qquad C_2 = 0.5q_2^2 \qquad (8\text{-}4)$$

Solving (8-3) for the example and substituting in (8-2) gives the quasi-competitive solution as

$$q_1 = 185 \qquad q_2 = 5 \qquad p = 5 \qquad \pi_1 = 0 \qquad \pi_2 = 12.5 \qquad (8\text{-}5)$$

This solution is compared with the solutions that follow.

The Collusion Solution

Duopolists (or oligopolists) may recognize their mutual interdependence and agree to act in unison in order to maximize the total profit of the industry. Both output levels are then under a single control, and the industry is, in effect, a monopoly. Let

$$R(q_1 + q_2) = R_1(q_1, q_2) + R_2(q_1, q_2) = (q_1 + q_2)F(q_1 + q_2)$$

Aggregate profit is

$$\pi = \pi_1 + \pi_2 = R(q_1 + q_2) - C_1(q_1) - C_2(q_2)$$

which is the same as (7-16), the profit function for the two-plant monopolist. Thus, the first-order conditions require that the MC of each producer be equated to MR for output as a whole.

Consider the example given by (8-4). Industry profit is

$$\pi = \pi_1 + \pi_2 = 100(q_1 + q_2) - 0.5(q_1 + q_2)^2 - 5q_1 - 0.5q_2^2$$

Setting the partial derivatives of π equal to zero,

$$\frac{\partial \pi}{\partial q_1} = 95 - q_1 - q_2 = 0 \qquad \frac{\partial \pi}{\partial q_2} = 100 - q_1 - 2q_2 = 0$$

Solving for q_1 and q_2 and substituting in the profit and demand equations,

$$q_1 = 90 \qquad q_2 = 5 \qquad p = 52.5 \qquad \pi_1 = 4275 \qquad \pi_2 = 250 \qquad (8\text{-}6)$$

By contrast to the quasi-competitive solution given by (8-5) total output is much lower, price much higher, and profits much higher. The MCs of the two firms are equal in both solutions, but these now equal industry MR rather than price. The profit levels for (8-6) are those given by the individual profit functions. The final distribution of the aggregate profit may be a matter for negotiation between the duopolists.

The Cournot Solution

The classical solution of the duopoly (and oligopoly) problem is associated with the name of Augustin Cournot, an early-nineteenth-century French economist. As before, the two firms are assumed to produce a homogeneous product. The basic behavior assumption of the Cournot solution is that each duopolist maximizes his profit on the assumption that the quantity produced by his rival is invariant with respect to his own quantity decision. The first duopolist (I for short) maximizes π_1 with respect to q_1, treating q_2 as a parameter, and the second (II for short) maximizes π_2 with respect to q_2 treating q_1 as a parameter.

Setting the appropriate partial derivatives of (8-2) equal to zero,

$$\frac{\partial \pi_1}{\partial q_1} = \frac{\partial R_1}{\partial q_1} - \frac{dC_1}{dq_1} = 0 \qquad \frac{\partial R_1}{\partial q_1} = \frac{dC_1}{dq_1}$$

$$\frac{\partial \pi_2}{\partial q_2} = \frac{\partial R_2}{\partial q_2} - \frac{dC_2}{dq_2} = 0 \qquad \frac{\partial R_2}{\partial q_2} = \frac{dC_2}{dq_2} \qquad (8\text{-}7)$$

First-order conditions require that each duopolist equate his MC to his MR. The second-order condition for each duopolist requires that

$$\frac{\partial^2 \pi_i}{\partial q_i^2} = \frac{\partial^2 R_i}{\partial q_i^2} - \frac{d^2 C_i}{dq_i^2} < 0 \qquad i = 1, 2$$

or

$$\frac{\partial^2 R_i}{\partial q_i^2} < \frac{d^2 C_i}{dq_i^2} \qquad i = 1, 2 \qquad (8\text{-}8)$$

Each duopolist's MR must be increasing less rapidly than his MC.

The maximization process for the Cournot solution is not the same as in the case of the two-plant monopolist, where a single individual controls the values of both output levels. Here each duopolist maximizes his profit with respect to the single variable under his control. It follows that the MRs of the duopolists are not necessarily equal. Let $q = q_1 + q_2$ and $\partial q/\partial q_1 = \partial q/\partial q_2 = 1$. The MRs of the duopolists are

$$\frac{\partial R_i}{\partial q} = p + q_i \frac{dp}{dq} \qquad i = 1, 2$$

The duopolist with the greater output will have the smaller MR.

The duopolistic market is in equilibrium if the values of q_1 and q_2 are such that each duopolist maximizes his profit, given the output of the other, and neither desires to alter his output. The equilibrium solution can be obtained by solving (8-7) for q_1 and q_2 if (8-8) is satisfied. The market process can be described more fully by introducing an additional step before solving for the equilibrium output levels. Reaction functions which express the output of each duopolist as a function of his rival's output are determined by solving the first equation of (8-7) for q_1 and the second for q_2:

$$q_1 = \Psi_1(q_2)$$
$$q_2 = \Psi_2(q_1)$$
$$(8-9)$$

I's reaction function gives a relationship between q_1 and q_2 with the property that for any specified value of q_2 the corresponding value of q_1 maximizes π_1. II's reaction function gives the value of q_2 which maximizes π_2 for any specified value of q_1. An equilibrium solution is a pair of values for q_1 and q_2 which satisfy both reaction functions.

If the demand and cost functions are

$$p = A - B(q_1 + q_2) \qquad C_1 = a_1 q_1 + b_1 q_1^2 \qquad C_2 = a_2 q_2 + b_2 q_2^2$$

with all parameters positive, the profits of the duopolists are

$$\pi_1 = Aq_1 - B(q_1 + q_2)q_1 - a_1 q_1 - b_1 q_1^2$$
$$\pi_2 = Aq_2 - B(q_1 + q_2)q_2 - a_2 q_2 - b_2 q_2^2$$

Setting the appropriate partial derivatives equal to zero,

$$\frac{\partial \pi_1}{\partial q_1} = A - B(2q_1 + q_2) - a_1 - 2b_1 q_1 = 0$$

$$\frac{\partial \pi_2}{\partial q_2} = A - B(q_1 + 2q_2) - a_2 - 2b_2 q_2 = 0$$

The corresponding reaction functions are

$$q_1 = \frac{A - a_1}{2(B + b_1)} - \frac{B}{2(B + b_1)} q_2 \qquad q_2 = \frac{A - a_2}{2(B + b_2)} - \frac{B}{2(B + b_2)} q_1 \qquad (8-10)$$

Since B, b_1, and b_2 are all positive, a rise of either duopolist's output will cause a reduction of the other's optimum output. The reaction functions are

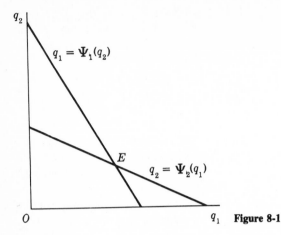

$q_1 = \Psi_1(q_2)$

E

$q_2 = \Psi_2(q_1)$

O q_1 **Figure 8-1**

linear as pictured in Fig. 8-1. An equilibrium is provided by a solution of (8-10), or equivalently, by an intersection point for the reaction curves, such as E in Fig. 8-1. The solution of (8-10) is

$$q_1 = \frac{2(B + b_2)(A - a_1) - B(A - a_2)}{4(B + b_1)(B + b_2) - B^2}$$

$$q_2 = \frac{2(B + b_1)(A - a_2) - B(A - a_1)}{4(B + b_1)(B + b_2) - B^2}$$

The second-order conditions are satisfied by the linear demand and quadratic cost functions:

$$\frac{\partial^2 \pi_1}{\partial q_1^2} = -2(B + b_1) < 0 \qquad \frac{\partial^2 \pi_2}{\partial q_2^2} = -2(B + b_2) < 0$$

Returning to the example of (8-4), the reader may verify that the reaction functions are

$$q_1 = 95 - 0.5q_2 \qquad q_2 = 50 - 0.25q_1 \qquad \qquad (8\text{-}11)$$

and that the equilibrium solution is

$$q_1 = 80 \qquad q_2 = 30 \qquad p = 45 \qquad \pi_1 = 3200 \qquad \pi_2 = 900$$

Comparison with the quasi-competitive solution (8-5) shows that the Cournot duopolists produce a smaller total output, at a higher price and for larger profits. Comparison with the collusion solution (8-6) shows a larger total output at a lower price for a smaller total profit. It follows that with an appropriate agreement on how to distribute industry profit, both duopolists would be better off with the collusion solution than with the Cournot solution. It is easy to show, however, that the collusion solution is not the only one that dominates the Cournot solution. If, for example, I produced 79 units of q_1 and II produced 29 units of q_2 (each 1 unit less than in the Cournot solution), their respective profits would be $\pi_1 = 3239$ and $\pi_2 = 913.5$. Thus, although the Cournot solution is optimal for each duopolist on the assumption that the other produces his Cournot equilibrium output, the Cournot solution is not optimal with respect to joint and coordinated changes in output levels.

The basic behavior assumption of the Cournot solution is rather artificial and weak. Each duopolist acts as if his rival's output were fixed. However, this is not the case. If equilibrium is thought to be reached through a sequence of finite adjustments (see Exercise 8-9), one duopolist sets an output; this induces the other to adjust his output, which in turn induces the first to adjust his, and so on. It is rather unlikely that each will assume that his quantity decisions do not affect his rival's quantity decision if each of his adjustments is immediately followed by a reaction on the part of his rival. If equilibrium is thought to be reached simultaneously, the optimal quantity of duopolist I is not given by $q_1 = \Psi_1(q_2)$, but by $q_1 = \Psi_1[\Psi_2(q_1)]$, and similarly for II, since each knows the behavior pattern of the other. Alternatively, it has been assumed that each maximizes his profit on the assumption that his rival's price remains unchanged, but this is a very unrealistic assumption for a homogeneous product. Duopolists and oligopolists generally recognize their mutual interdependence.

In some cases the Cournot solution coincides with the quasi-competitive solution in the limit as the number of firms increases. As an illustration, assume that there are n firms with output levels $(q_1, q_2, \ldots, q_n)$ and let the inverse demand function be $p = aq^b$ where $q = q_1 + q_2 + \cdots + q_n$, $a > 0$, and $-1 < b < 0$. Let all firms be identical and have total cost given by $C_i = cq_i$ $(i = 1, \ldots, n)$. If there is a homogeneous product and the firms have identical costs, each will produce the output level $q_i = q/n$. To obtain the Cournot solution differentiate

$$\pi_i = aq^b q_i - cq_i \qquad i = 1, 2, \ldots, n$$

with respect to q_i:

$$\frac{\partial \pi_i}{\partial q_i} = aq^b + baq^{b-1}q_i - c = 0$$

Substituting $q = nq_i$,

$$q_i = \frac{c^{1/b}}{n^{(b-1)/b}(an + ab)^{1/b}} \qquad \text{and} \qquad q = \frac{c^{1/b}}{(a + ab/n)^{1/b}}$$

As $n \to \infty$, $q \to (c/a)^{1/b}$. This is the quasi-competitive solution as can be confirmed by solving $aq^b = c$ ($p = MC$ in this case) for q.

The Stackelberg Solution

Generally, the profit of each duopolist is a function of the output levels of both:

$$\pi_1 = h_1(q_1, q_2) \qquad \pi_2 = h_2(q_1, q_2) \tag{8-12}$$

The Cournot solution is obtained by maximizing π_1 with respect to q_1, assuming q_2 to be constant, and π_2 with respect to q_2, assuming q_1 to be constant. More generally, each firm might make some other assumption about its rival's response. Profit maximization by the two duopolists then requires

$$\frac{\partial \pi_1}{\partial q_1} = \frac{\partial h_1}{\partial q_1} + \frac{\partial h_1}{\partial q_2} \frac{\partial q_2}{\partial q_1} = 0$$

$$\frac{\partial \pi_2}{\partial q_2} = \frac{\partial h_2}{\partial q_2} + \frac{\partial h_2}{\partial q_1} \frac{\partial q_1}{\partial q_2} = 0$$

(8-13)

The terms $\partial q_2/\partial q_1$ and $\partial q_1/\partial q_2$ represent the *conjectural variation*, i.e., the assumed response of each firm to its rival's output. To the extent that firms make erroneous assumptions about each other's responses (8-13) will not represent an improvement over the Cournot model.

One of the more interesting sets of assumptions about conjectural variation is contained in the analysis of leadership and followership formulated by the German economist Heinrich von Stackelberg. A *follower* obeys his reaction function (8-9) and adjusts his output level to maximize his profit, given the quantity decision of his rival, whom he assumes to be a leader. A *leader* does not obey his reaction function. He assumes that his rival acts as a follower, and maximizes his profit, given his rival's reaction function. If I desires to play the role of a leader, he assumes that II's reaction function is valid and substitutes this relation into his profit function:

$$\pi_1 = h_1[q_1, \Psi(q_1)]$$

I's profit is now a function of q_1 alone and can be maximized with respect to this single variable. II can also determine his maximum profit from leadership on the assumption that I obeys his reaction function and acts as a follower. I's maximum profit from followership is determined by substituting II's optimum leadership output level in I's reaction function, and II's maximum profit from followership is determined by substituting I's optimum leadership output level in II's reaction function.

Each duopolist determines his maximum profit levels from both leadership and followership and desires to play the role which yields the larger maximum. Four outcomes are possible: (1) I desires to be a leader, and II a follower; (2) II desires to be a leader, and I a follower; (3) both desire to be leaders; or (4) both desire to be followers. Outcome (1) results in consistent behavior patterns and therefore a determinate equilibrium.[1] I assumes that II will act as a follower, and he does; II assumes that I will act as a leader, and he does. Likewise (2) results in a determinate equilibrium. If both desire to be followers, their expectations are not realized, since each assumes that the other will act as a leader. The duopolists must revise their expectations. Under the Stackelberg assumptions, the Cournot solution is achieved if each

---

[1] The first- and second-order conditions for maxima are assumed to be fulfilled in all cases.

desires to act as a follower, knowing that the other will also act as a follower. Otherwise, one must change his behavior pattern and act as a leader before equilibrium can be achieved.

If both desire to be leaders, each assumes that the other's behavior is governed by his reaction function, but, in fact, neither of the reaction functions is obeyed, and a *Stackelberg disequilibrium* is encountered. Stackelberg believed that this disequilibrium is the most frequent outcome. The final result of a Stackelberg disequilibrium cannot be predicted a priori. If Stackelberg was correct, this situation will result in economic warfare, and equilibrium will not be achieved until one has succumbed to the leadership of the other or a collusive agreement has been reached.

Return again to the example given by (8-4). The maximum leadership profit of I is obtained by substituting II's reaction function (8-11) into I's profit equation:

$$\pi_1 = 100q_1 - 0.5q_1^2 - 0.5q_1(50 - 0.25q_1) - 5q_1$$
$$= 70q_1 - 0.375q_1^2$$

Maximizing with respect to q_1,

$$\frac{d\pi_1}{dq_1} = 70 - 0.75q_1 = 0 \qquad q_1 = 93\tfrac{1}{3} \qquad \pi_1 = 3266\tfrac{2}{3}$$

Likewise for II,

$$\pi_2 = 100q_2 - 0.5q_2^2 - 0.5q_2(95 - 0.5q_2) - 0.5q_2^2$$
$$= 52.5q_2 - 0.75q_2^2$$
$$\frac{d\pi_2}{dq_2} = 52.5 - 1.5q_2 = 0 \qquad q_2 = 35 \qquad \pi_2 = 918.75$$

To determine I's maximum followership profit, first determine his output by substituting the leadership output of II (35 units) into his reaction function (8-11), and then compute his profit:

$$q_1 = 95 - 0.5q_2 = 77.5 \qquad \pi_1 = 3003.125$$

Likewise substitute $93\tfrac{1}{3}$ into II's reaction function and then compute his profit:

$$q_2 = 50 - 0.25q_1 = 26\tfrac{2}{3} \qquad \pi_2 = 711\tfrac{1}{9}$$

Each duopolist receives a greater profit from leadership, and both desire to act as leaders. An example in which the Cournot solution is easily determined has become a Stackelberg disequilibrium as the result of an alteration of the basic behavior assumptions.

8-2 DUOPOLY AND OLIGOPOLY: DIFFERENTIATED PRODUCTS

Product differentiation may occur with duopoly and oligopoly as well as with monopolistic competition.

Product Differentiation

The individual producer of a differentiated product in an oligopolistic market faces his own distinct demand curve. The quantity which he can sell depends upon the price decisions of all members of the industry:

$$q_i = f_i(p_1, p_2, \ldots, p_n) \qquad i = 1, \ldots, n \qquad (8\text{-}14)$$

where $\partial q_i / \partial p_i < 0$ and $\partial q_i / \partial p_j > 0$ for all $i \neq j$. An increase of price on the part of the ith seller with all other prices remaining unchanged results in a reduction of his output level. Some of his customers will turn to his competitors. If some other seller should increase his price, the ith seller can sell a larger quantity at a fixed price. Some of his competitor's customers will turn to him. Under monopolistic competition the effects of one producer's actions are spread imperceptibly among a large number of competitors. Under duopoly and oligopoly they are spread perceptibly among a small number.

Individual producers can set either price or quantity. Demand functions may be expressed in inverse form with output levels as independent variables:[1]

$$p_i = F_i(q_1, q_2, \ldots, q_n) \qquad i = 1, \ldots, n \qquad (8\text{-}15)$$

All partial derivatives of (8-15) are negative. If the ith seller increases his output level, with all other output levels constant, p_i will decline, since a larger quantity brings a lower price. If some other seller increases his output level, his price will decline, and the price of the ith firm must also decline in order to maintain q_1 at a constant level. Otherwise some of his customers would turn to the firm with the lowered price.

The Cournot, collusion, and Stackelberg solutions are easily modified for product differentiation by replacing $p = F(q_1 + q_2)$ with individual demand functions:

$$p_1 = F_1(q_1, q_2) \qquad p_2 = F_2(q_1, q_2)$$

The analysis can also be extended to cases in which prices are the independent variables:

$$q_1 = f_1(p_1, p_2) \qquad q_2 = f_2(p_1, p_2)$$

Profits were expressed as functions of quantities:

$$\pi_1 = h_1(q_1, q_2) \qquad \pi_2 = h_2(q_1, q_2)$$

By substitution,

$$\pi_1 = h_1[f_1(p_1, p_2), f_2(p_1, p_2)] = H_1(p_1, p_2)$$

$$\pi_2 = h_2[f_1(p_1, p_2), f_2(p_1, p_2)] = H_2(p_1, p_2)$$

---

[1] The demand functions may be constructed to describe a situation in which price is the independent variable for some sellers and quantity for others. The dependent variable of each seller is then expressed as a function of the independent variables of all sellers.

The profit of each duopolist is a function of both prices, and maximization may proceed with respect to prices.

In the case of differentiated products the duopolists' profits may also depend upon the amounts of their advertising expenditures. If advertising is effective, it allows a firm to sell a larger quantity at a given price or a given quantity at a higher price. The demand curves are

$$p_1 = F_1(q_1, q_2, A_1, A_2) \qquad p_2 = F_2(q_1, q_2, A_1, A_2)$$

where A_1 and A_2 are the amounts of advertising expenditure by I and II respectively. The profit functions become

$$\pi_1 = q_1 F_1(q_1, q_2, A_1, A_2) - C_1(q_1) - A_1$$

$$\pi_2 = q_2 F_2(q_1, q_2, A_1, A_2) - C_2(q_2) - A_2$$

Each duopolist must now maximize his profit with respect to his advertising expenditure as well as his output level.

The Market-Shares Solution

Another form of conjectural variation assumes that II desires to maintain a fixed share of the total sales of a differentiated product, regardless of the effects of his actions on his short-run profits. His major concern is with the long-run advantages that are derived from maintaining a given market share. A quantity change on the part of I will be immediately followed by a proportionate change on the part of II. The relation

$$\frac{q_2}{q_1 + q_2} = k \qquad q_2 = \frac{kq_1}{1-k} \tag{8-16}$$

where k is II's desired market share, will always hold. I is a market leader in the sense that his actions will always be followed by II in a predetermined manner.

I's inverse demand function is $p_1 = F_1(q_1, q_2)$, and his profit function is

$$\pi_1 = q_1 F_1(q_1, q_2) - C_1(q_1)$$

Substituting from (8-16) for q_2,

$$\pi_1 = q_1 F_1\left(q_1, \frac{kq_1}{1-k}\right) - C_1(q_1)$$

I's profit is a function of q_1 alone and may be maximized with respect to this single variable as long as II reacts to maintain his market share.

Let I's demand and cost functions be

$$p_1 = 100 - 2q_1 - q_2 \qquad C_1 = 2.5q_1^2$$

Let $k = \frac{1}{3}$, and therefore $q_2 = 0.5q_1$. I's profit is

$$\pi_1 = q_1(100 - 2q_1 - 0.5q_1) - 2.5q_1^2 = 100q_1 - 5q_1^2$$

Setting the first derivative of π_1 equal to zero, solving for q_1, and substituting in the above relations,

$$\frac{d\pi_1}{dq_1} = 100 - 10q_1 = 0$$

$$q_1 = 10 \qquad q_2 = 5 \qquad p_1 = 75 \qquad \pi_1 = 500$$

I maximizes his profit at an output of 10 units, and II reacts by producing 5 units.

The Kinked-Demand-Curve Solution

Some duopolistic and oligopolistic markets are characterized by infrequent price changes. Firms in such markets usually do not change their price-quantity combinations in response to small shifts of their cost curves as the foregoing market analyses would suggest. The kinked-demand-curve solution presents a theoretical analysis which is consistent with this observed behavior. Starting from predetermined price-quantity combinations, if one of the duopolists lowers his price (increases his quantity), the other is assumed to react by lowering his price (increasing his quantity) in order to maintain his market share. If one of the duopolists raises his price, his rival is assumed to leave his own price unchanged and thereby increase his market share. Price decreases will be followed, but price increases will not.

Assume that the demand and cost functions of the duopolists are

$$p_1 = 100 - 2q_1 - q_2 \qquad C_1 = 2.5q_1^2$$
$$p_2 = 95 - q_1 - 3q_2 \qquad C_2 = 25q_2 \tag{8-17}$$

and that the currently established prices and quantities are $p_1 = 70$, $q_1 = 10$, $p_2 = 55$, and $q_2 = 10$.† If I increased his price, II would leave his own price unchanged at 55 dollars. Substituting $p_2 = 55$ into II's demand function (8-17) and solving for q_2,

$$q_2 = \frac{40 - q_1}{3} \tag{8-18}$$

II's output level and market share will increase as I increases his price and thereby decreases his output level. Substituting the value for q_2 given by (8-18) into I's demand function (8-17),

$$p_1 = \frac{260 - 5q_1}{3} \tag{8-19}$$

---

† The reader can verify that these price-quantity combinations represent a Cournot solution. MC equals MR for each duopolist, on the assumption that his rival's output level remains unchanged. The method by which initial price-quantity combinations are achieved is of little concern for the kinked-demand-curve analysis.

I's price is a function of q_1 alone given the assumption that II maintains his price at 55 dollars. Starting from the initial position, (8-19) is only valid for $p_1 > 70$ and $q_1 < 10$. I's MR function for price increases can be derived by forming his total revenue function from (8-19):

$$R_1 = q_1 \left(\frac{260 - 5q_1}{3} \right)$$

and
$$\frac{dR_1}{dq_1} = \frac{260 - 10q_1}{3} \qquad (8\text{-}20)$$

At $q_1 = 10$, I's MR for a price increase is $53\frac{1}{3}$ dollars.

The demand and MR functions given by (8-19) and (8-20) are not valid if I reduces his price. In this case, II will follow by lowering his price by an amount sufficient to allow him to retain half the total volume of sales. II must increase his output level by the same amount as I in order to maintain his market share: $q_2 = q_1$. Substituting $q_2 = q_1$ into I's demand function (8-17),

$$p_1 = 100 - 3q_1 \qquad (8\text{-}21)$$

I's price is a function of q_1 alone given the fact that II maintains his market share. The demand function given by (8-21) is valid for $p_1 < 70$ and $q_1 > 10$. I's MR function for price decreases can be derived by forming a total revenue function from (8-21):

$$R_1 = q_1(100 - 3q_1)$$

and
$$\frac{dR_1}{dq_1} = 100 - 6q_1$$

At $q_1 = 10$, I's MR for a price decrease is 40 dollars.

The initial position represents a maximum-profit point for I. His MC for an output of 10 units is 50 dollars. He cannot increase his profit by increasing his price (reducing his output level), since MR exceeds MC ($53\frac{1}{3} > 50$) and this difference would be increased by a price increase. He cannot increase his profit by reducing his price (increasing his output level), since MR is less than MC ($40 < 50$) and this difference would be increased by a price reduction. His initial price-quantity combination is optimal for any value of MC from $53\frac{1}{3}$ to 40 dollars. A reduction of his MC by an amount not greater than 10 dollars would not induce him to lower his price and expand his sales. Likewise, an increase of MC by an amount not greater than $3\frac{1}{3}$ dollars would not induce him to increase his price and contract his sales.

Graphically, I's effective demand curve is "kinked" and his effective MR curve discontinuous at his initial output level. His demand curve is $D'D'$ (see Fig. 8-2) if II reacts by maintaining his market share and DD if II reacts by maintaining his price. DD is valid for price increases, and $D'D'$ for price decreases. His effective MR curve follows the MR curve corresponding to DD to the left of his initial output level and the MR curve corresponding to $D'D'$ to the right of his initial output level. I is unable to equate MR and MC.

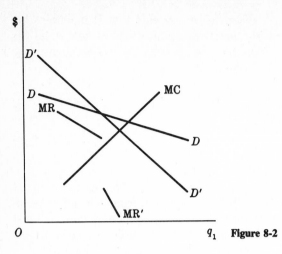

Figure 8-2

8-3 DUOPSONY AND OLIGOPSONY

The case of a monopsonist is considered in Sec. 7-4. In some input markets the number of buyers is greater than one, but still small enough so that the assumption of competitive buying at constant prices cannot be maintained. Such markets are considered in this section. A market with two buyers is a *duopsony*, and a market with a small number greater than two is an *oligopsony*.

A market situation with a small number of buyers is similar to one with a small number of sellers. There are no generally accepted behavior assumptions. Each buyer can control the level of his purchases, but each is noticeably affected by the actions of the other buyers. Most theories of duopoly and oligopoly covering undifferentiated products can be modified to cover duopsony and oligopsony. For illustration, a modified version of the Cournot solution is considered here.

Consider a local labor market in which two firms buy from many competitive sellers. As before, the price of labor is an increasing function of quantity:

$$r = g(x_1 + x_2)$$

where x_1 and x_2 are the amounts purchased by the two firms. Each buyer is assumed to use labor alone to produce a commodity which he sells in a competitive national market at a fixed price. Their production functions are

$$q_1 = h_1(x_1) \qquad q_2 = h_2(x_2)$$

and their profits are

$$\pi_1 = p_1 h_1(x_1) - g(x_1 + x_2)x_1$$
$$\pi_2 = p_2 h_2(x_2) - g(x_1 + x_2)x_2$$

$$(8\text{-}22)$$

The basic Cournot behavior assumption is invoked. Each duopsonist maximizes his profit on the assumption that the other is unaffected by his actions. Setting the appropriate partial derivatives of (8-22) equal to zero,

$$\frac{\partial \pi_1}{\partial x_1} = p_1 h_1'(x_1) - r - x_1 g'(x_1 + x_2) = 0$$

$$\frac{\partial \pi_2}{\partial x_2} = p_2 h_2'(x_2) - r - x_2 g'(x_1 + x_2) = 0$$

and
$$\begin{align} p_1 h_1'(x_1) &= r + x_1 g'(x_1 + x_2) \\ p_2 h_2'(x_2) &= r + x_2 g'(x_1 + x_2) \end{align} \tag{8-23}$$

Each duopsonist equates the value of his marginal product to his marginal cost for the input. The duopsonists will not have the same marginal cost in equilibrium unless $x_1 = x_2$. The duopsonist with the higher purchase level will have the higher marginal cost. The second-order conditions are a straightforward generalization of (7-32): the value of the marginal product of each duopsonist must increase less rapidly than his marginal cost.

Input reaction functions which express the purchases of each duopsonist as a function of the other's purchases are determined by solving the first equation of (8-23) for x_1 and the second for x_2:

$$x_1 = \Phi_1(x_2)$$

$$x_2 = \Phi_2(x_1)$$

The range of possible solutions is similar to that in the duopoly case and can accommodate conjectural variation and Stackelberg-type leadership or followership.

8-4 THEORY OF GAMES

The theories of duopoly and oligopoly discussed in Secs. 8-1 and 8-2 lead to compact mathematical solutions with the differential calculus employed. However, they are subject to question for having arbitrary assumptions about each firm's beliefs about rivals' reactions to its actions. The mathematical theory of games is an alternative approach that has been applied to small-numbers market situations with interdependent outcomes. Noncooperative, or competitive, games, as illustrated by two-person, zero-sum games, are discussed in the first three parts of this section. Cooperative games, in which participants have an interest in joint behavior, are discussed in the last two parts.

Two-Person, Zero-Sum Games

A game may consist of a sequence of moves as in chess, or it may consist of a single move on the part of each of its participants. The present analysis is limited to single-move games. In this context, a *strategy* is the specification of a particular move for one of the participants. A duopolist's strategy consists of selecting a particular value for each of the variables under his control. If price is his only variable, a strategy consists of selecting a particular price. If price and advertising expenditure are both variables, a strategy consists of selecting particular values for both price and advertising expenditure. Each participant is assumed to possess a finite number of strategies though the number may be very large. This assumption rules out the possibility of continuous variation of the action variables. The outcome of the duopolistic game, i.e., the profit earned by each of the participants, is determined from the relevant cost and demand relations once each of the duopolists has selected a strategy.

Games are classified on the basis of two criteria: (1) the number of participants and (2) the net outcome. The first merely involves a counting of the number of participants with conflicting interests. There are one-person, two-person, three-person, and in the general case, n-person games. The second criterion allows a distinction between zero-sum and non-zero-sum games. A zero-sum game is one in which the algebraic sum of the outcomes, e.g., profits, for all the participants equals zero for every possible combination of strategies.[1] Two-person, zero-sum games must be strictly competitive (noncooperative), since if one player always loses what the other wins, there can be no room for cooperation.

A one-person, zero-sum game is uninteresting, since the player gains nothing, regardless of his strategy choice. A monopolist or a monopsonist might be considered as the sole participant in a one-person, non-zero-sum game. A two-person, zero-sum game can be applied to a duopolistic market in which one participant's gain always equals the absolute value of the other's loss. In general, if I has m and II has n strategies, the possible outcomes of the game are given by the profit matrix

$$\begin{bmatrix} a_{11} & a_{12} & \cdots & q_{1n} \\ a_{21} & a_{22} & \cdots & a_{2n} \\ \cdots & \cdots & \cdots & \cdots \\ a_{m1} & a_{m2} & \cdots & a_{mn} \end{bmatrix} \tag{8-24}$$

where a_{ij} is I's profit if I employs his ith strategy and II employs his jth. Since the game is zero-sum, the corresponding profit earned by II is $-a_{ij}$.

For a specific example consider the profit matrix

$$\begin{bmatrix} 8 & 40 & 20 & 5 \\ 10 & 30 & -10 & -8 \end{bmatrix} \tag{8-25}$$

If I employs his first strategy and II employs his second, I's profit is 40, and

---

[1] A zero-sum game is a special case of a constant-sum game, i.e., one in which the sum of the payoffs to the two players is a constant for every combination of strategies. Every constant-sum game may be trivially transformed into a zero-sum game and conversely.

II's is -40. If I employs his second strategy and II employs his third, I's profit is -10, and II's is 10.

The duopolist's decision problem consists of choosing an optimal strategy. I desires the outcome (40) in the first row and second column of (8-25), and II desires the outcome (-10) in the second row and third column. The final outcome depends upon the strategies of both duopolists, and neither has the power to enforce his desires. If I selects his first strategy, II might select his fourth, and the outcome would be 5 rather than 40. If II selects his third strategy, I might select his first, and the outcome would be 20 rather than -10. The theory of games postulates behavior patterns which allow the determination of equilibrium in these situations. I fears that II might discover his choice of strategy and desires to "play it safe." If I selects his ith strategy, his minimum profit, and hence II's maximum, is given by the smallest element in the ith row of the profit matrix: $\min_{j} a_{ij}$. This is I's expected profit from the employment of his ith strategy if his fears regarding II's knowledge and behavior are realized. I's profit will be greater than this amount if II fails to select his appropriate strategy. I desires to maximize his minimum expected profit. Therefore, I selects the strategy i for which $\min_{j} a_{ij}$ is the largest. His anticipated outcome is $\max_{i} \min_{j} a_{ij}$. He cannot earn a smaller profit and may earn a larger one.

II possesses the same fears regarding I's information and behavior. If II employs his jth strategy, he fears that I may employ the strategy corresponding to the largest element in the jth column of the profit matrix: $\max_{i} a_{ij}$. Therefore, II selects the strategy j for which $\max_{i} a_{ij}$ is the smallest, and his expected profit is $-\min_{j} \max_{i} a_{ij}$. The decisions of the duopolists are consistent and equilibrium is achieved if

$$\max_{i} \min_{j} a_{ij} = \min_{j} \max_{i} a_{ij} \qquad (8\text{-}26)$$

Let k be the index for which $\min_{j} a_{kj} = \max_{i} \min_{j} a_{ij}$ and let h be the index for which $\max_{i} a_{ih} = \min_{j} \max_{i} a_{ij}$. If (8-26) holds, the kth and hth strategies of I and II respectively are called an equilibrium pair of strategies.

Returning to the example given by (8-25), I will employ his first strategy. If II anticipates his choice, I's profit will be 5. If I employed his second strategy, and II anticipated his choice, his profit would be -10. II will employ his fourth strategy and limit his loss to 5. Every other column of (8.25) has a maximum greater than 5. In this case

$$\max_{i} \min_{j} a_{ij} = \min_{j} \max_{i} a_{ij} = a_{14} = 5$$

The duopolists' decisions are consistent, and an equilibrium is established. Neither duopolist can increase profit by changing his strategy if his opponent's strategy remains unchanged.

Assume that the profit matrix is

$$\begin{bmatrix} -2 & 4 & -1 & 6 \\ 3 & -1 & 5 & 10 \end{bmatrix} \tag{8-27}$$

where I has two strategies and II has four. This profit matrix and its corresponding game problem can be simplified by introducing the concept of dominance. An inspection of (8-27) reveals that II will never employ his third strategy since he can always do better by employing his first, regardless of I's strategy choice. Each element in the third column is larger, and therefore represents a greater loss for II, than the corresponding element in the first. In general, the jth column dominates the kth if $a_{ij} \leq a_{ik}$ for all i and $a_{ij} < a_{ik}$ for at least one i. The fourth column of (8-27) is dominated by both the first and second columns. Dominance can also be defined with regard to I's strategies. In general, the ith row dominates the hth if $a_{ij} \geq a_{hj}$ for all j and $a_{ij} > a_{hj}$ for at least one j. Neither row of (8-27) dominates the other. A rational player will never employ a dominated strategy. Therefore, the profit matrix can be simplified by the removal of all dominated strategies.

Eliminating the third and fourth columns of (8-27), the profit matrix becomes

$$\begin{bmatrix} -2 & 4 \\ 3 & -1 \end{bmatrix} \tag{8-28}$$

Following the rules established above, I will desire to employ his second strategy, and II will desire to employ his first. These decisions are not consistent:

$$\max_i \min_j a_{ij} = a_{22} = -1 \neq 3 = a_{21} = \min_j \max_i a_{ij}$$

If the duopolists employ these strategies, the initial outcome would be $a_{21} = 3$. If II employs his first strategy, I cannot increase his profit by changing strategies. However, if I employs his second strategy, II can decrease his loss from 3 to -1 by switching to his second strategy. I can then increase his profit from -1 to 4 by switching to his first. II can then decrease his loss from 4 to -2 by switching to his first. The assumptions that lead to an equilibrium position for (8-25) result in endless fluctuations for (8-28), and no equilibrium pair exists.

Mixed Strategies

A particular game may or may not have a solution if the duopolists select their strategies in the manner described above. The impasse presented by games such as (8-28) can be resolved by allowing the duopolists to select their strategies on a probabilistic basis. Let $r_1, r_2, \ldots, r_m$ be the probabilities with which I will employ each of his m strategies, where $0 \leq r_i \leq 1$ ($i = 1, \ldots, m$) and $\sum_{i=1}^m r_i = 1$. Assume that he utilizes some random process to select a particular strategy. For example, if $m = 3$ with $r_1 = 0.3$, $r_2 = 0.1$, and $r_3 = 0.6$, he may assign the numbers 0 through 2 to the first strategy, 3 to the second, and 4 through 9 to the third; select a one-digit number by a random process; and employ the strategy that corresponds to the selected number. A random selection will not allow II to anticipate I's choice even if he knows I's probabilities.

II can randomize his strategy selection by assigning the probabilities $s_1, s_2, \ldots, s_n$ to his strategies, where $0 \leq s_j \leq 1$ $(j = 1, \ldots, n)$ and $\Sigma_{j=1}^n s_j = 1$. The duopolists are now concerned with expected, rather than actual, profits. A duopolist's expected profit equals the sum of the possible outcomes, each multiplied by the probability of its occurrence. For example, if II employs his jth strategy with a probability of one and I selects the probabilities $r_1, \ldots, r_m$, I's expected profit is $\Sigma_{i=1}^m a_{ij} r_i$.

The decision problem of each duopolist is to select an optimal set of probabilities. I fears that II will discover his strategy and that II will select a strategy of his own that will maximize his expected outcome, i.e., minimize the expected outcome for I. II has similar fears about I. The probabilities which the duopolists employ are defined as optimal if

$$\sum_{i=1}^m a_{ij} r_i \geq V \qquad j = 1, \ldots, n \qquad (8\text{-}29)$$

and

$$\sum_{j=1}^n a_{ij} s_j \leq V \qquad i = 1, \ldots, m \qquad (8\text{-}30)$$

where V is defined as the *value of the game*. The relations (8-29) state that I's expected profit is at least as great as V if II employs any of his pure strategies with a probability of one, and the relations (8-30) state that II's expected loss is at least as small as V if I employs any of his pure strategies with a probability of one. A fundamental theory-of-games theorem states that a solution [i.e., values for the rs and ss that satisfy (8-29) and (8-30)] always exists, and that V is unique.

If both duopolists select their strategies on a probabilistic basis, I's expected profit, E_1, can be determined from (8–29):

$$E_1 = \sum_{j=1}^n s_j \left(\sum_{i=1}^m a_{ij} r_i \right) \geq \sum_{j=1}^n s_j V$$

or

$$E_1 = \sum_{j=1}^n \sum_{i=1}^m a_{ij} r_i s_j \geq V \qquad (8\text{-}31)$$

II's expected loss, E_2, can be determined from (8-30):

$$E_2 = \sum_{i=1}^m r_i \left(\sum_{j=1}^n a_{ij} s_j \right) \leq \sum_{i=1}^m r_i V$$

or

$$E_2 = \sum_{j=1}^n \sum_{i=1}^m a_{ij} r_i s_j \leq V \qquad (8\text{-}32)$$

The middle terms in (8-31) and (8-32) are identical: I's expected profit equals

II's expected loss. Combining (8-31) and (8-32):

$$V \leqq E_1 = E_2 \leqq V$$

which proves that

$$E_1 = E_2 = V$$

The expected outcome is the same for each of the duopolists and equals the value of the game if both employ their optimal probabilities. If I employs his optimal probabilities, his expected profit cannot be less than V, regardless of II's strategy choice. It will be greater than V if II employs a nonoptimal set of probabilities. Likewise, if II employs his optimal probabilities, his expected loss cannot be greater than V, regardless of I's strategy choice. It will be less if I employs a nonoptimal set of probabilities.

Linear-Programming Equivalence

Optimal strategies for the duopolists and the value of the game can be determined by converting their game problems into a linear-programming format (see Sec. 5-7). First, consider cases in which $V > 0$. Define the variables

$$z_j = \frac{s_j}{V} \qquad j = 1, \ldots, n \qquad (8\text{-}33)$$

for duopolist II. By this definition

$$\frac{1}{V} = z_1 + z_2 + \cdots + z_n \qquad (8\text{-}34)$$

II desires to make his maximum expected loss as small as possible, or equivalently, he desires to make $1/V$ as large as possible. His linear-programming equivalent is to find values for $z_j \geqq 0$ ($j = 1, \ldots, n$) which maximize (8-34) subject to

$$a_{i1}z_1 + a_{i2}z_2 + \cdots + a_{in}z_n \leqq 1 \qquad i = 1, \ldots, m \qquad (8\text{-}35)$$

The relations of (8-35) are derived by dividing those of (8-30) by V and substituting from (8-33).

Define the variables

$$w_i = \frac{r_i}{V} \qquad i = 1, \ldots, m \qquad (8\text{-}36)$$

for duopolist I. By this definition

$$\frac{1}{V} = w_1 + w_2 + \cdots + w_m \qquad (8\text{-}37)$$

I desires to make his minimum expected profit as large as possible, or equivalently, he desires to make $1/V$ as small as possible. His linear-programming equivalent is to find values for $w_i \geqq 0$ $(i = 1, \ldots, m)$ which minimize (8-37) subject to

$$a_{1j}w_1 + a_{2j}w_2 + \cdots + a_{mj}w_m \geqq 1 \qquad j = 1, \ldots, n \qquad (8\text{-}38)$$

The relations of (8-38) are derived by dividing those of (8-29) by V and substituting from (8-36).

The programming system for I given by (8-37) and (8-38) is the dual of the programming system for II given by (8-34) and (8-35). The reciprocal of the value of the game is given by the maximum value for (8-34) which equals the minimum value of (8-37). Using (8-33) and (8-36), the optimal probabilities for the duopolists are easily determined from the optimal values for the z_j and the w_i.

The linear-programming formulation facilitates a proof that solutions always exist for two-person, zero-sum games. The proof proceeds by first establishing that finite optimal solutions always exist for the equivalent programming systems, and by then demonstrating that the optimal programming solutions provide a solution for the underlying game. Initially assume that all $a_{ij} > 0$. A feasible, but not optimal, solution for the programming system given by (8-34) and (8-35) is provided by $z_j = 0$ $(j = 1, \ldots, n)$. Let $a^0 = \min_{i,j} a_{ij}$. A feasible solution for the programming system given by (8-37) and (8-38) is provided by $w_i = 1/a^0$ $(i = 1, \ldots, m)$. The existence of finite optimal solutions for the programming systems follows from a duality theorem stated in Sec. 5-7: If feasible solutions exist for a programming system and its dual, finite optimal solutions exist for both systems.

Let the optimum values of the programming variables be given by $z_1^*, \ldots, z_n^*$ and $w_1^*, \ldots, w_m^*$. At least one w_i^* must be positive since $w_i^* = 0$ $(i = 1, \ldots, m)$ is not feasible for (8-38). At least one z_j^* must be positive, for if all z_j^* were zero, all the constraints of (8-35) would be satisfied as strict inequalities. But then, as shown by the duality theorem expressed in (5-40), all w_i^* would equal zero, which has already been shown to be impossible. Since at least one w^* and at least one z^* must be positive, it is possible to equate the reciprocals of the optimal values of the objective functions (8-34) and (8-37):

$$V = \frac{1}{\displaystyle\sum_{j=1}^{n} z_j^*} = \frac{1}{\displaystyle\sum_{i=1}^{m} w_i^*}$$

and

$$V \sum_{j=1}^{n} z_j^* = V \sum_{i=1}^{m} w_i^* = 1$$

Substituting from (8-33) and (8-36),

$$\sum_{j=1}^{n} s_j = 1 \qquad s_j \geqq 0 \qquad \sum_{i=1}^{m} r_i = 1 \qquad r_i \geqq 0$$

which are the game probabilities. By substitution from (8-33) and (8-36) into

(8-35) and (8-38), it is easily verified that these probabilities form a game solution as defined by (8-29) and (8-30).

Equations (8-31) and (8-32) define the value of the game as a weighted average of the elements of the profit matrix. It is necessary that V be positive in order to satisfy the nonnegativity requirements for the programming variables. However, in general, one cannot conclude that V is positive unless all the a_{ij} are positive. This difficulty is easily resolved by defining a modified game with a positive value. If one or more $a_{ij} \leq 0$, select a number k with the property that $a_{ij} + k > 0$ for all i and j, and add k to every element of the profit matrix. The value of the modified game exceeds the value of the initial game by k:

$$V' = \sum_{j=1}^{n} \sum_{i=1}^{m} (a_{ij} + k)r_i s_j = \sum_{j=1}^{n} \sum_{i=1}^{m} a_{ij}r_i s_j + k \sum_{j=1}^{n} \sum_{i=1}^{m} r_i s_j = V + k \qquad (8\text{-}39)$$

and is positive by construction. The optimal probabilities for the initial and modified games are the same.[1] Therefore, a solution for the initial game can be obtained from a linear-programming solution for the modified game.

Return to the game given by (8-28). Let $k = 4$. The profit matrix for the modified game is

$$\begin{bmatrix} 2 & 8 \\ 7 & 3 \end{bmatrix}$$

II's linear-programming system is to find values for $z_1, z_2 \geq 0$ that maximize

$$\frac{1}{V'} = z_1 + z_2$$

subject to
$$2z_1 + 8z_2 \leq 1$$
$$7z_1 + 3z_2 \leq 1$$

The reader may verify diagrammatically that the unique optimal solution is $z_1 = 0.1$, $z_2 = 0.1$, $1/V' = 0.2$. Utilizing (8-33) and (8-39), II's optimal probabilities are $s_1 = 0.5$ and $s_2 = 0.5$ with $V = 1$. The reader may verify that the optimal solution for the dual programming system is $w_1 = 0.08$, $w_2 = 0.12$, which gives I's optimal probabilities as $r_1 = 0.4$ and $r_2 = 0.6$.

Cooperative Games

The theory of strictly competitive games is not fully satisfactory as an explanation of oligopoly behavior. The oligopolists' interests are not always diametrically opposed, and their behavior may be characterized by a combination of competitive and cooperative elements. The possibility of coopera-

---

[1] See J. G. Kemeny, J. L. Snell, and G. L. Thompson, *Introduction to Finite Mathematics* (Englewood Cliffs, N.J.: Prentice-Hall, 1957), p. 291.

tion arises in non-zero (nonconstant) sum games. Such games do not necessarily lead to cooperation, although preferred outcomes may be achieved through cooperation. For illustration consider a simple duopolistic market for which the collusive solution is prohibited by law. Assume that bribes and profit redistribution are also illegal. Each duopolist has two strategies: (1) he can declare himself a leader and produce a relatively large output, or (2) he can declare himself a follower and produce a relatively small output. Once each declares himself he must produce his declared output regardless of what his competitor has declared. Assume that the profit matrix is

		Duopolist II		
		Leader	Follower	
Duopolist I	Leader	(200, 250)	(1000, 200)	(8-40)
	Follower	(150, 950)	(800, 800)	

where the first and second numbers in each set of parentheses are I's and II's profit levels respectively.

The best outcome for each duopolist is obtained if he is a leader and the competitor a follower, and the worst is obtained if their roles are reversed. One might argue that a sensible strategy for each would be to declare himself a follower since each would receive a moderately satisfactory profit. However, if I believes that II will be a follower, I should be a leader *a fortiori*. A similar argument applies to II. Since each has an incentive to be a leader, their "uncooperative" behavior leads each to attain his lowest profit level. In fact, the leader strategies of the duopolists constitute an equilibrium pair, whereas the relatively favorable follower strategies do not. It is clear that both could gain from cooperative behavior. However, it is not clear that cooperation can be achieved successfully. Even if each agreed to be a follower, each would have an incentive to break the agreement and declare himself a leader. The possibility of finding cooperative solutions depends upon the possibility of mutually undertaking unbreakable commitments and guarantees.

The Nash Bargaining Solution

Consider a case in which the duopolists attempt to negotiate a cooperative solution for the example (8-40). Assume that each desires to maximize the expected utility of his profits, and that each obeys the von Neumann–Morgenstern axioms. Assume that A, B, C, and D in Fig. 8-3 are the four profit outcomes of (8-40) mapped into utility-space. Let the duopolists employ mixed strategies. The reader may verify that the feasible utility region then is given by the quadrilateral $ABCD$ (see Exercise 8-7). Negotiation involves the selection of a point from this set.

Assume that if the duopolists fail to reach an agreement, either duopolist could threaten to sell his output to a discount house for a guaranteed profit.

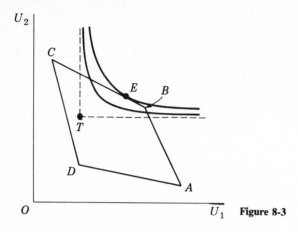

Figure 8-3

Let $\bar{U}_1$ and $\bar{U}_2$ denote the utilities of these profits. The point T in Fig. 8-3 has the coordinates $(\bar{U}_1, \bar{U}_2)$. Neither duopolist need agree to accept a lower profit than that provided by his threat strategy. The aim of a cooperative solution is for the duopolist to select a point northeast of T on the boundary of the feasible utility regions. Obviously, infinitely many such solutions are possible.

According to the Nash bargaining solution the duopolists should agree upon strategies so that the function

$$W = (U_1 - \bar{U}_1)(U_2 - \bar{U}_2) \tag{8-41}$$

is maximized subject to the constraint that only points in the feasible utility region are eligible. An iso-W curve is defined as the locus of utility points that provide a particular value for W. These curves are rectangular hyperbolas with the fixed value of W increasing with distance from T. Two such curves are shown in Fig. 8-3. Point E provides the Nash solution. It lies on the highest iso-W curve that has at least one point in common with the feasible utility region. It is on the line segment connecting points B (both followers) and C (I follower, II leader). I will employ a pure strategy, namely, be a follower. II will employ a mixed strategy. His leadership probability is given by the ratio of BE to BC, and his followership probability by the ratio of EC to BC. The reader should note that this solution entails an interpersonal comparison of von Neumann–Morgenstern utilities.

8-5 BILATERAL MONOPOLY

A monopolist does not have an output supply function relating price and quantity. He selects a point on his buyers' demand function that maximizes his profit. Similarly, a monopsonist does not have an input demand function. He selects a point on his sellers' supply function that maximizes his profit. Bilateral monopoly is a market situation with a single buyer and a single seller. It is not possible for the seller to behave as a monopolist and the buyer to behave as a monopsonist at the same time. The seller cannot exploit a demand function that does not exist, and the buyer cannot exploit a demand function that does not exist. Something must give. Three general outcomes are possible: (1) one of the participants may dominate and force the other to accept his price and/or quantity decisions, (2) the buyer and seller may cooperate and achieve a solution such as the Nash solution, or (3) the market mechanism may break down in the sense that no trade takes place at all. The theories of monopoly, monopsony, and game theory help one understand the various possible outcomes.

Reference Solutions

Consider a case of bilateral monopoly in the market for a produced good, Q_2. The buyer uses Q_2 as an input to produce Q_1 according to his production function: $q_1 = h(q_2)$. He sells Q_1 in a competitive market at the fixed price p_1. The seller uses a single input X for the production of Q_2. He buys X in a competitive market at the fixed price r. Assume that his production function can be expressed in inverse form as $x = H(q_2)$. The solutions that would be achieved by monopoly, monopsony, and quasi-competition provide useful reference points for an analysis of this market.

A monopoly solution would be achieved if the seller dominated and forced the buyer to accept whatever price he set. The buyer's profit is

$$\pi_B = p_1 h(q_2) - p_2 q_2$$

He sets $d\pi_B/dq_2$ equal to zero to maximize profit:

$$\frac{d\pi_B}{dq_2} = p_1 h'(q_2) - p_2 = 0$$

and

$$p_2 = p_1 h'(q_2) \tag{8-42}$$

which is the buyer's inverse demand function for Q_2. The buyer purchases Q_2 up to a point at which the value of his marginal product equals the price set by the seller. The monopolistic seller substitutes from (8-42) for p_2 and maximizes his profit:

$$\pi_S = p_1 h'(q_2) q_2 - r H(q_2)$$

$$\frac{d\pi_S}{dq_2} = p_1 [h'(q_2) + h''(q_2) q_2] - r H'(q_2) = 0$$

$$p_1 [h'(q_2) + h''(q_2) q_2] = r H'(q_2) \tag{8-43}$$

The equilibrium condition (8-43) states that the seller equates his MR and MC. Solve (8-43) for the monopoly output, q_{2S}^*, and substitute this value into (8-42) to obtain the monopoly price, p_{2S}^*. An example of a monopoly solution is given by point S in Fig. 8-4.

A monopsony solution would be achieved if the buyer dominated and forced the seller to accept whatever price he set. The seller's profit is

$$\pi_S = p_2 q_2 - rH(q_2)$$

He sets $d\pi_S/dq_2$ equal to zero to maximize profit:

$$\frac{d\pi_S}{dq_2} = p_2 - rH'(q_2) = 0$$

and

$$p_2 = rH'(q_2) \tag{8-44}$$

which is the inverse supply function for Q_2. The seller produces and sells Q_2 up to a point at which his marginal cost equals the price set by the buyer. The monopsonistic buyer substitutes from (8-44) for p_2 and maximizes his profit:

$$\pi_B = p_1 h(q_2) - rH'(q_2)q_2$$

$$\frac{d\pi_B}{dq_2} = p_1 h'(q_2) - r[H'(q_2) + H''(q_2)q_2] = 0$$

$$p_1 h'(q_2) = r[H'(q_2) + H''(q_2)q_2] \tag{8-45}$$

The equilibrium condition (8-45) states that the buyer equates the value of his marginal product to the marginal cost of the input (MCI). Solve (8-45) for the monopsony output, q_{2B}^*, and substitute this value into (8-44) to obtain the monopsony price, p_{2B}^*. An example of a monopsony solution is given by point B in Fig. 8-4.

Finally, consider the price and quantity that would be achieved if both seller and buyer were price takers. The inverse demand (8-42) and supply (8-44) functions would both be effective. The quasi-competitive quantity, q_{2C}^*, is determined by equating demand and supply price:

$$p_{2C}^* = p_1 h'(q_{2C}^*) = rH'(q_{2C}^*) \tag{8-46}$$

The quasi-competitive price, p_{2C}^*, equals both the value of the marginal product of the buyer and the marginal cost of the seller. This quasi-competitive result

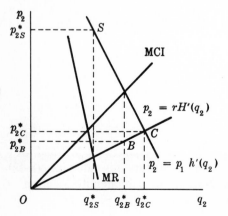

Figure 8-4

may not be a likely outcome for a market characterized by bilateral mono-poly, but it provides another useful reference point. An example of a quasi-competitive solution is given by point C in Fig. 8-4.

Some of the results of a comparison of the monopoly (B), monopsony (S), and quasi-competitive (C) solutions in Fig. 8-4 may be generalized to cover all cases in which the demand curve $[p_1h'(q_2)]$ has negative slope and the supply curve $[rH'(q_2)]$ has positive slope, i.e., cases in which $h''(q_2) < 0$ and $H''(q_2) > 0$. The monopoly and monopsony equilibrium points will always lie to the left of the demand and supply curve intersection. Thus, q_{2C}^* is always greater than q_{2B}^* and q_{2S}^*. In Fig. 8-4, $q_{2B}^* > q_{2S}^*$. This result does not always hold. The monopoly and monopsony outputs depend upon the slopes of the demand and supply curves. The reader may construct a case in which $q_{2B}^* < q_{2S}^*$. The competitive price will always lie between the monopoly and monopsony prices. Since the monopoly equilibrium lies on the demand curve to the left of the quasi-competitive solution, $p_{2S}^* > p_{2C}^*$, and since the monop-sony equilibrium lies on the supply curve to the left of the quasi-competitive solution, $p_{2C}^* > p_{2B}^*$. Let π_{SS}^*, π_{SC}^*, and π_{SB}^* denote the seller's profit levels in the three cases. In general,

$$\pi_{SS}^* > \pi_{SC}^* > \pi_{SB}^*$$

Let π_{BS}^*, π_{BC}^*, and π_{BB}^* denote the buyer's profit levels. In general,

$$\pi_{BS}^* < \pi_{BC}^* < \pi_{BB}^*$$

The proof of these propositions is left as an exercise for the reader.

Collusion and Bargaining

It is often assumed that the market participants will recognize their mutual interdependence and reach a mutually satisfactory agreement as to price and quantity. The bargaining process can be separated into two steps. First, the participants determine a quantity that maximizes their joint profit, and then determine a price that distributes the joint profit among them. Their joint profit is

$$\pi = \pi_B + \pi_S = [p_1h(q_2) - p_2q_2] + [p_2q_2 - rH(q_2)]$$
$$= p_1h(q_2) - rH(q_2)$$

Setting $d\pi/dq_2$ equal to zero,

$$\frac{d\pi}{dq_2} = p_1h'(q_2) - rH'(q_2) = 0$$

and
$$p_1h'(q_2) = rH'(q_2)$$

Joint profit is maximized at an output at which the value of the buyer's marginal product equals the seller's marginal cost. This is the same as the quasi-competitive solution given by (8-39). The optimal collusive output level is the same as the quasi-competitive output level, q_{2C}^*. A collusive bilateral monopoly will behave in the same way as a competitive industry insofar as the outside world is concerned.

The quasi-competitive price does not necessarily follow from a collusive solution. For the prescribed quantity the seller desires as high a price as possible, and the buyer desires as low a price as possible. Let the upper limit be the price that would force the buyer's profit to zero, and the lower limit be the price that would force the seller's profit to zero:

$$\frac{p_1 h(q_{2C}^*)}{q_{2C}^*} \geqq p_2 \geqq \frac{rH(q_{2C}^*)}{q_{2C}^*} \tag{8-47}$$

Since a negative profit would force one of the firms to discontinue operations, price cannot be set beyond these limits.

An alternative is to assume that the buyer can do no worse than the monopoly solution, and that the seller can do no worse than the monopsony solution:

$$p_1 h(q_{2C}^*) - p_2 q_{2C}^* \geqq \pi_{BS}^*$$

$$p_2 q_{2C}^* - rH(q_{2C}^*) \geqq \pi_{SB}^*$$

Solving each inequality for p_2,

$$\frac{p_1 h(q_{2C}^*) - \pi_{BS}^*}{q_{2C}^*} \geqq p_2 \geqq \frac{rH(q_{2C}^*) + \pi_{SB}^*}{q_{2C}^*} \tag{8-48}$$

These limits can be determined from the reference solutions. If π_{BS}^* and π_{SB}^* are positive, (8-48) provides a narrower range for bargaining than (8-47). In either case the determination of a specific price within the bargaining limits will depend upon the relative bargaining power of the buyer and seller.

8-6 SUMMARY

The profit of a duopolist or oligopolist depends upon the actions and reactions of his rivals. Different theories are based upon different assumptions regarding market behavior. One approach is to make assumptions about specific and deterministic responses that firms make to the actions of their rivals. The quasi-competitive solution is based on the assumption that firms equate price and marginal cost. The collusion solution is realized if the market participants join together to maximize total industry profit. The Cournot solution is attained if each participant maximizes his profit on the assumption that the rivals' output levels are unaffected by his actions. The Stackelberg solution rests on the assumption that duopolists explicitly recognize the interdependence of their actions. Each may wish to assume the role of either a leader or a follower, and market equilibrium is achieved if their desires are consistent. These solutions are applicable for both homogeneous and differentiated products. The producers of differentiated products may find advertising profitable.

The market-shares solution is realized if a market participant follows the moves of his rivals in such a way as to maintain his historical share of total industry sales. The kinked-demand-curve solution is realized if a seller assumes that his rivals will follow price reductions, but leave their prices unchanged in response to price increases.

Duopsony and oligopsony are similar to duopoly and oligopoly in that there are no generally accepted behavior assumptions. Most theories of duopoly and oligopoly for undifferentiated products can be modified to cover duopsony and oligopsony. According to the Cournot behavior assumption each buyer selects a purchase level on the assumption that the other buyers are unaffected by his actions.

Noncooperative as well as cooperative game theory may be applied to markets with a small number of participants. Applying the former, a duopolistic market is sometimes treated as a two-person, zero-sum game. Each duopolist selects probabilities for a finite number of strategies that maximize the expected value of his profit, given the most unfavorable strategy choice on the part of the rival. The expected profit of one duopolist (which equals the expected loss of the other) equals the value of the game if both assign optimal probabilities to their strategies. Linear-programming methods can be used to obtain numerical solutions for two-person, zero-sum games.

The application of cooperative game theory requires that market participants be able to make binding agreements with one another. The Nash solution provides a "reasonable" and "fair" division of the aggregate profits from joint action by two participants.

A single seller confronts a single buyer in bilateral monopoly. Price and quantity are determined either through the dominance of one participant, or through bargaining and cooperation. The prices, quantities, and profits that would be achieved under monopoly, monopsony, and quasi-competition provide reference points for an analysis of bilateral monopoly. The quasi-competitive output level maximizes the joint profit of the buyer and seller, and bargaining may be restricted to a price for this quantity. Limits for price bargaining are constructed from assumptions about minimum acceptable profit levels.

EXERCISES

8-1 Consider a duopoly with product differentiation in which the demand and cost functions are $q_1 = 88 - 4p_1 + 2p_2$, $C_1 = 10q_1$, and $q_2 = 56 + 2p_1 - 4p_2$, $C_2 = 8q_2$ for firms I and II respectively. Derive a *price reaction function* for each firm on the assumption that each maximizes its profit with respect to its own price. Determine equilibrium values of price, quantity, and profit for each firm.

8-2 Let duopolist I, producing a differentiated product, face an inverse demand function given by $p_1 = 100 - 2q_1 - q_2$ and have the cost function $C_1 = 2.5q_1^2$. Assume that duopolist II wishes to maintain a market share of $\frac{1}{3}$. Find the optimal price, output, and profit for duopolist I. Find the output of duopolist II.

8-3 Let n duopolists face the inverse demand function $p = a - b(q_1 + \cdots + q_n)$ and let each have identical cost function $C_i = cq_i$. (a) Determine the Cournot solution. (b) Determine the quasi-competitive solution. (c) As $n \to \infty$, does the Cournot solution converge to the quasi-competitive solution?

8-4 Let two duopsonists have production functions $q_1 = 13x_1 - 0.2x_1^2$ and $q_2 = 12x_2 - 0.1x_2^2$ where x_1, x_2 are the input levels employed by the duopsonists. Assume that the input supply function is $r = 2 + 0.1(x_1 + x_2)$ where r is the supply price of the input, and that q_1 and q_2 are sold in competitive markets for prices $p_1 = 2$ and $p_2 = 3$. (a) Find the input reaction functions. (b) Determine the Cournot equilibrium values for $x_1, x_2, q_1, q_2, \pi_1, \pi_2$.

8-5 Let the profit matrix of a two-person, zero-sum game have elements a_{ij} ($i = 1, \ldots, m; j = 1, \ldots, n$), and let r_i ($i = 1, \ldots, m$) and s_j ($j = 1, \ldots, n$) be the optimal probabilities for participants I and II respectively. Prove that these probabilities are also optimal for a game with profit elements $a_{ij} + k$ where k is a constant.

8-6 Consumers distributed uniformly along a straight-line road are the potential market for two duopolists whose decision problem is where to locate their sales offices. Demand is completely inelastic, and consumers will purchase from whichever sales office is nearer. Assume that the road is 4 miles long and that, for simplicity, each firm has exactly five possible strategies: it may locate itself at either end or at the 1-mile, 2-mile, or 3-mile markers. Let the payoffs to the duopolists be their respective market shares. (a) Is this a zero-sum (or constant-sum) game? (b) What is the payoff matrix? (c) What are optimal strategies for the duopolists?

8-7 Show that the feasible utility region for mixed strategies in Fig. 8-3 is $ABCD$ if the duopolists have two pure strategies each as stated in the discussion of Fig. 8-3.

8-8 Let the buyer and seller for the bilateral monopoly discussed in Sec. 8-5 have the production functions $q_1 = 270q_2 - 2q_2^2$ and $x = 0.25q_2^2$ respectively. Assume that the price of q_1 is 3 and the price of x is 6. (a) Determine the values of q_2, p_2 and the profits of the buyer and seller for the monopoly, monopsony, and quasi-competitive solutions. (b) Determine the bargaining limits for p_2 under the assumption that the buyer can do no worse than the monopoly solution and the seller can do no worse than the monopsony solution. (c) Compare your results with Fig. 8-4.

8-9 Assume that the adjustment of each of the two Cournot duopolists to his rival's output level takes a finite length of time. Specifically, let a change in output level from period $t - 1$ to period t be the fixed proportion k of the difference between desired and actual output levels in period $t - 1$. Under what circumstances will this dynamic adjustment process converge to the Cournot equilibrium if the demand function is $p = 100 - (q_1 + q_2)$ and the cost functions are $C_1 = 3q_1$, $C_2 = 2q_2$?

SELECTED REFERENCES

Andrews, P. W. S.: *On Competition in Economic Theory* (New York: St. Martin's, 1964). A nonmathematical review and critique of imperfect-competition theories.

Baumol, William J.: *Business Behavior, Value and Growth* (rev. ed., New York: Harcourt, Brace & World, 1967). Part I covers oligopoly theory. Calculus and geometry are used.

Buchanan, Norman S.: "Advertising Expenditures: A Suggested Treatment," *Journal of Political Economy*, vol. 50 (August, 1942), pp. 537-557. Also reprinted in R. V. Clemence (ed.), *Readings in Economic Analysis*, (Cambridge, Mass.: Addison-Wesley, 1950), vol. 2, pp. 230-250. A geometric determination of the optimum advertising expenditure for a firm.

Cohen, Kalman J., and Richard M. Cyert: *Theory of the Firm* (Englewood Cliffs, N.J.: Prentice-Hall, 1965). Imperfect competition is covered in chaps. 10-13. Calculus and geometry are used.

Cournot, Augustin: *Researches into the Mathematical Principles of the Theory of Wealth*, trans. by Nathaniel T. Bacon (New York: Macmillan, 1897). The original statement of the Cournot solution. Also one of the first applications of mathematics to economics.

Efroymson, Clarence W.: "A Note on Kinked Demand Curves," *American Economic Review,* vol. 33 (March, 1943), pp. 98–109. Also reprinted in Clemence, *Readings in Economic Analysis,* vol. 2, pp. 218–229. A nonmathematical discussion of kinked demand curves and full-cost pricing.

Fellner, William: *Competition Among the Few* (New York: Knopf, 1949). A nonmathematical discussion of oligopoly and bilateral monopoly. Contains an exposition of the Stackelberg solution.

Friedman, J. W.: *Oligopoly and the Theory of Games* (Amsterdam: North-Holland, 1977). A comprehensive survey of the subject with some advanced mathematical treatment.

Luce, R. Duncan, and Howard Raiffa: *Games and Decisions* (New York: Wiley, 1957). A comprehensive treatise with only simple mathematics in the text. More difficult proofs are in appendixes.

Malinvaud, E.: *Lectures on Microeconomic Theory* (Amsterdam: North-Holland, 1972). Duopoly and bilateral monopoly are covered in chap. 6.

NINE

MULTIMARKET EQUILIBRIUM

The analysis of price determination and allocation can be performed on three levels of increasing generality: (1) the equilibrium of an individual consumer or producer, (2) the equilibrium of a single market, and (3) the simultaneous equilibrium of all markets. The first type of analysis is the subject of Chaps. 2 through 5, and the second is the subject of Chaps. 6 through 8. The present chapter is devoted to the third.

A theoretical analysis contains data, variables, and behavior assumptions that allow the determination of specific values for the variables once the data are known. Consider the analysis of an individual consumer. The data are her utility function, her income, and commodity prices. The variables are the quantities of the commodities purchased and consumed, and the basic behavior assumption is her desire to maximize utility. The analysis of an individual producer is similar. The data are her production function and the prices of all outputs and inputs. The variables are the quantities of the inputs she purchases and the quantity of the output she produces and sells. The behavior assumption is her desire to maximize profit. However, the analysis of an individual unit sheds no light upon the determination of prices, since all prices are considered as parameters.

The analysis of equilibrium in a single market is somewhat more general. A single price is determined as the result of optimizing behavior on the part of a large number of consumers and a large number of producers. The data for the analysis of equilibrium in a commodity market are the utility and production functions of all consumers and producers, the incomes of all consumers, the prices of all factors, and the prices of all commodities other than the one under consideration. The explicit variables are the price of the commodity and the purchases and sales of the commodity by each consumer and producer. The condition that the market must be cleared, i.e., aggregate demand must equal aggregate supply, is added to the assumptions of utility and profit maximization. The analysis of a single factor market is similar except that the consumers' incomes are determined by their factor sales.

Every factor and commodity price is a variable for the analysis of its own market and a parameter for the analysis of all other markets. There is no assurance that a consistent set of prices will result from a piecemeal solution, taking one market at a time. It is only by chance that the price assumed for Q_j in the analysis of the market for Q_k will be the same as the price determined in the analysis of the market for Q_j in isolation.

All markets are interrelated. Consumers spend their incomes for all commodities, and the demand for each commodity depends upon all prices. If the goods Q_1 and Q_2 are gross substitutes, an increase in the price of Q_1 will induce consumers as a whole to substitute Q_2 for Q_1. If two goods are complements, an increase in the price of one may induce consumers to restrict their consumption of both (see Sec. 2-5). Pairs of inputs may also be defined as substitutes or complements. Furthermore, production and consumption are not independent. Consumers earn their incomes from the sale of labor services and other productive factors to producers. As a result of these interrelationships, equilibria for all product and factor markets must be determined simultaneously in order to secure a consistent set of prices.

The data for the determination of a general multimarket equilibrium are the utility and production functions of all producers and consumers and their initial endowments of factors and/or commodities. The variables are the prices of all factors and commodities and the quantities purchased and sold by each consumer and producer. The behavior assumptions require utility and profit maximization together with the condition that every market be cleared.

A multimarket equilibrium analysis is developed for a pure-exchange system in Sec. 9-1, and illustrated for two-commodity systems in Sec. 9-2. The analysis is extended to cover production and exchange in Sec. 9-3. The problems of absolute price determination and the choice of a standard of value are considered in Sec. 9-4.

9-1 PURE EXCHANGE

Pure exchange deals with the pricing and allocation problems of a society in which n individuals exchange and consume fixed quantities of m commodities. Each individual possesses an initial endowment of one or more of the commodities and is free to buy and sell at the prevailing market prices. Purchases and sales may be interpreted as barter transactions. Imagine a consumer whose initial endowment consists of twenty pears and three apples and assume that there are no other commodities. The prevailing market prices determine the terms on which the consumer can barter pears for apples or apples for pears. If the prices are 5 cents for pears and 10 cents for apples, she can obtain one apple by selling two pears or two pears by selling one apple. Given market prices and initial endowments, each consumer's trading will be determined by her ordinal utility function. It would be a rare case if none of the consumers was able to increase her satisfaction level through exchange. A consumer will sell a portion of her initial endowment of some commodities and add to her stocks of others as long as she is able to increase her utility index.

Equilibrium of the *i*th Consumer

The excess demand of the *i*th consumer for the *j*th commodity (E_{ij}) is defined as the difference between the quantity she consumes (q_{ij}) and her initial endowment (q_{ij}^0):

$$E_{ij} = q_{ij} - q_{ij}^0 \qquad j = 1, \ldots, m \qquad (9\text{-}1)$$

If her consumption of Q_j exceeds her initial endowment, her excess demand is positive; she purchases Q_j in the market. If her consumption is less than her initial endowment, her excess demand is negative; she sells Q_j in the market. It is not possible to determine the signs of her excess demands a priori. She may either sell or buy Q_j. The sharp distinction between buyers and sellers used throughout Chap. 6 is no longer possible.

The consumer's income equals the value of her initial endowment:

$$y_i = \sum_{j=1}^{m} p_j q_{ij}^0 \qquad (9\text{-}2)$$

This is the amount of purchasing power that she would obtain if she sold her entire endowment. In order to relate the present analysis to that of Chap. 2, assume for the moment that she sells her entire endowment and uses the proceeds to purchase commodities at the prevailing market prices. The value of the commodities that she purchases and consumes must equal her income as given by (9-2):

$$y_i = \sum_{j=1}^{m} p_j q_{ij} \qquad (9\text{-}3)$$

Her purchases will most likely include some of the commodities that she sold, but this does not matter since the acts of buying and selling are assumed costless. The self-canceling transactions can be omitted without affecting the analysis. Therefore, it is henceforth assumed that the consumer does not both buy and sell the same commodity. Her budget constraint can be expressed in terms of her excess demands. Subtracting (9-2) from (9-3) and substituting from (9-1),

$$\sum_{j=1}^{m} p_j(q_{ij} - q_{ij}^0) = \sum_{j=1}^{m} p_j E_{ij} = 0 \qquad (9\text{-}4)$$

The net value of the consumer's excess demands must equal zero. Her budget constraint in this form states that the value of the commodities she buys must equal the value of the commodities she sells.

The equilibrium analysis of the consumer as developed in Chap. 2 needs slight modification to be applicable to a consumer in a pure-exchange economy. The consumer's utility index is a function of the quantities of the commodities she consumes, but can be stated as a function of her excess demands and initial endowments by substituting $q_{ij} = E_{ij} + q_{ij}^0$ from (9-1):

$$U_i = U_i(q_{i1}, \ldots, q_{im}) = U_i(E_{i1} + q_{i1}^0, \ldots, E_{im} + q_{im}^0) \qquad (9\text{-}5)$$

The consumer desires to maximize the value of her utility index subject to a budget constraint. Using the form of the utility function given by (9-5) and the budget constraint (9-4), form the function

$$V_i = U_i(E_{i1} + q_{i1}^0, \ldots, E_{im} + q_{im}^0) - \lambda \left(\sum_{j=1}^{m} p_j E_{ij} \right) \qquad (9\text{-}6)$$

and set the partial derivatives of V_i with respect to the excess demands and λ equal to zero:

$$\frac{\partial V_i}{\partial E_{ij}} = \frac{\partial U_i}{\partial E_{ij}} - \lambda p_j = 0 \qquad j = 1, \ldots, m$$

$$\frac{\partial V_i}{\partial \lambda} = - \sum_{j=1}^{m} p_j E_{ij} = 0 \qquad\qquad (9\text{-}7)$$

Since $dE_{ij}/dq_{ij} = 1$, the first set of equations of (9-7) can be expressed in terms of the utility-index increments:

$$\frac{\partial U_i}{\partial E_{ij}} \frac{dE_{ij}}{dq_{ij}} - \lambda p_j = \frac{\partial U_i}{\partial q_{ij}} - \lambda p_j = 0 \qquad j = 1, \ldots, m$$

The first-order conditions for the individual consumer are the familiar ones developed in Chap. 2. She buys and sells commodities until the rate of commodity substitution for every pair of commodities (the ratio of their utility-index increments) equals their price ratio. Second-order conditions again are ensured by an assumption of regular strict quasi-concavity (see Sec. 2-6).

If the second-order conditions are satisfied, the ith consumer's excess demand functions can be derived from the first-order conditions. Eliminate λ from (9-7) and solve for the m excess demands as functions of commodity prices:

$$E_{ij} = E_{ij}(p_1, \ldots, p_m) \qquad j = 1, \ldots, m \qquad (9\text{-}8)$$

The consumer's excess demands depend upon the prices of all commodities. If her endowment of Q_j is not zero, her excess demand for Q_j may be positive for some sets of prices and negative for others.

It was proved in Sec. 2-3 that consumer demand functions are homogeneous of degree zero in income and prices. A similar theorem can be proved for the pure-exchange barter economy: The consumer's excess demand functions are homogeneous of degree zero in prices; i.e., the excess demands will remain unchanged if all prices are increased or decreased by the same proportion.[1] A doubling of all prices would double both the value of the consumer's initial endowment and the cost of the commodities she purchases. If the consumer's endowment consisted of pears and apples and their prices increased from 5 and 10 cents to 10 and 20 respectively, she could still obtain one apple for two pears or two pears for one apple. In a barter economy of this type the consumer is interested in market exchange ratios rather than absolute price levels.

A graphic description of an individual consumer's equilibrium is contained in Fig. 9-1. Her initial endowment is given by the coordinates of R. Her income line is the locus of all quantity combinations with the same market value as her initial endowment. If $y_i^{(1)}$ is her income line, she will maximize utility by moving to T. She will sell RS units of Q_2 and purchase ST units of Q_1 in moving from R to T. Her excess demand for Q_1 is positive, and her excess demand for Q_2 negative.

Assume that the price of Q_1 increases relative to the price of Q_2 and that the consumer's new income line is $y_i^{(2)}$. Point L is the position of maximum utility on this income line. The consumer will sell MR units of Q_1 and purchase ML units of Q_2 in moving from R to L. A price change has resulted in a change of the signs of her excess demands. Her excess demand for Q_1 is now negative, and her excess demand for Q_2 positive.

The irrelevance of absolute price levels is obvious in the graphic analysis. The consumer's initial endowment is given by a point representing physical quantities. Her income line is drawn through this point with a slope equal to the negative of the ratio of commodity prices. A proportionate change of both

---

[1] The proof is similar to that used in Sec. 2-3. Substitute kp_j into the budget constraint in (9-6), set its partial derivatives equal to zero to obtain a system similar to (9-7), divide the first $(m - 1)$ equations by the mth to eliminate λ and k, and factor k out of the $(m + 1)$th.

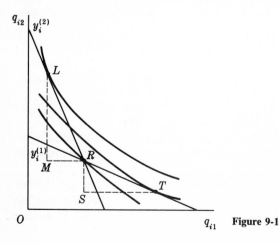

Figure 9-1

prices will leave their ratio unaffected, and neither the slope nor the position of the income line will change.

Market Equilibrium

An aggregate excess demand function for Q_j is constructed by summing the individual excess demand functions of the n consumers:

$$E_j = \sum_{i=1}^{n} E_{ij}(p_1, \ldots, p_j, \ldots, p_m) = E_j(p_1, \ldots, p_j, \ldots, p_m)$$

Aggregate excess demand is also a function of the m commodity prices. Partial equilibrium is attained in the jth market if the excess demand for Q_j equals zero when the remaining $(m - 1)$ prices are assigned fixed values:

$$E_j(p_1^0, \ldots, p_j, \ldots, p_m^0) = 0 \qquad (9\text{-}9)$$

Condition (9-9) is equivalent to the condition that supply equal demand. The equilibrium price for Q_j is obtained by solving (9-9) for p_j and depends upon the prices assigned to the other $(m - 1)$ commodities. The purchases and sales of the individual consumers are determined by substituting the equilibrium price into the individual excess demand functions.

Multimarket Equilibrium

Now treat all prices as variables and consider the simultaneous equilibrium of all m markets. Aggregate excess demand must equal zero in every market:

$$E_j(p_1, \ldots, p_m) = 0 \qquad j = 1, \ldots, m \qquad (9\text{-}10)$$

The equilibrium conditions form a system of m equations in m variables. However, (9-10) contains no more than $(m - 1)$ independent equations.

The budget constraints for the n consumers are not equilibrium conditions, but are identities satisfied for any set of prices. Summing the budget constraints given by (9-4) for all consumers:

$$\sum_{i=1}^{n} \sum_{j=1}^{m} p_j E_{ij} = \sum_{j=1}^{m} p_j E_j = 0 \qquad (9\text{-}11)$$

since $E_j = \sum_{i=1}^{n} E_{ij}$. The aggregate form of the budget constraint is also an identity satisfied for any set of prices. This identity is called *Walras' law*. The equilibrium conditions require that every aggregate excess demand equal zero if all prices are positive. Clearly if $E_j = 0$, the value of the excess demand for Q_j $(p_j E_j)$ must also equal zero. If the first $(m - 1)$ markets are in equilibrium, the aggregate value of their excess demands equals zero:

$$\sum_{j=1}^{m-1} p_j E_j = 0 \qquad (9\text{-}12)$$

Subtracting (9-12) from (9-11),

$$\sum_{j=1}^{m} p_j E_j - \sum_{j=1}^{m-1} p_j E_j = p_m E_m = 0$$

It follows that $E_m = 0$ if $p_m \neq 0$. If equilibrium is attained in $(m-1)$ markets, it is automatically attained in the mth.

Multimarket equilibrium is completely described by any $(m-1)$ equations of (9-10). The addition of an mth equation which is dependent upon the other $(m-1)$ adds no new information. Since the equations (9-10) are functionally dependent, their Jacobian is identically zero, and a locally unique solution does not exist for the p_j (see Sec. A-2). The inability to determine absolute price levels should not be a surprising result if it is remembered that consumers are interested only in exchange ratios in a barter-type economy.

Since the excess demand functions are homogeneous of degree zero in prices, the number of variables can be reduced to $(m-1)$ by dividing the m absolute prices by the price of an arbitrarily selected commodity. If Q_1 is selected, (9-10) may be rewritten as

$$E_j = E_j\left(1, \frac{p_2}{p_1}, \ldots, \frac{p_m}{p_1}\right) \qquad j = 1, \ldots, m \qquad (9\text{-}13)$$

The variables of (9-13) are the prices of the Q_j ($j \neq 1$) relative to the price of Q_1, i.e., the exchange ratios relative to Q_1. Omit any one of the equations in (9-13) to obtain a system of $(m-1)$ equations. This system of differentiable equations has a unique mathematical solution for the $(m-1)$ price ratios if its Jacobian does not vanish in a small neighborhood. The mathematical solution is a multimarket equilibrium if it contains real, nonnegative price ratios and quantities. It is possible to construct specific multimarket systems that have equilibrium solutions, and it is possible to construct specific systems that do not. In this chapter attention is limited to systems for which equilibria exist. The conditions under which equilibrium solutions do and do not exist are considered in Chap. 10.

Once the equilibrium exchange ratios are determined from (9-13), the purchases and sales of each individual can be determined by substituting into the individual excess demand functions. However, a multimarket equilibrium can be determined directly without recourse to aggregate excess demand functions. The individual excess demand functions are homogeneous of degree zero in prices and can be written in the same form as (9-13):

$$E_{ij} = E_{ij}\left(1, \frac{p_2}{p_1}, \ldots, \frac{p_m}{p_1}\right) \qquad \begin{array}{l} i = 1, \ldots, n \\ j = 1, \ldots, m \end{array} \qquad (9\text{-}14)$$

Now add the condition that every market must be cleared:

$$\sum_{i=1}^{n} E_{ij} = 0 \qquad j = 1, \ldots, m \qquad (9\text{-}15)$$

The system formed by (9-14) and (9-15) contains $(mn + m)$ equations with the

mn individual excess demands and the $(m-1)$ exchange ratios as variables. As before, the system is functionally dependent and cannot be solved for absolute price levels.

9-2 TWO-COMMODITY EXCHANGE

Many important aspects of multimarket equilibrium can be illustrated through examples in which two commodities are exchanged by two individuals. Both calculus and geometric examples are presented here.

A Calculus Example

Assume that individual I is endowed with 78 units of Q_1 and no Q_2, and that her utility function is

$$U_1 = q_{11}q_{12} + 2q_{11} + 5q_{12}$$

Substitute $q_{11} = E_{11} + 78$ and $q_{12} = E_{12}$ into her utility function and form the function

$$V_1 = (E_{11} + 78)E_{12} + 2(E_{11} + 78) + 5E_{12} - \lambda(p_1 E_{11} + p_2 E_{12})$$

Set the partial derivatives of V_1 equal to zero:

$$\frac{\partial V_1}{\partial E_{11}} = E_{12} + 2 - \lambda p_1 = 0$$

$$\frac{\partial V_1}{\partial E_{12}} = E_{11} + 83 - \lambda p_2 = 0$$

$$\frac{\partial V_1}{\partial \lambda} = -(p_1 E_{11} + p_2 E_{12}) = 0$$

The reader can verify that the second-order condition presented in Sec. 2-2 is satisfied.

Eliminating λ and solving the first-order conditions for E_{11} and E_{12}, I's excess demand functions are

$$E_{11} = \frac{p_2}{p_1} - 41.5 \qquad E_{12} = 41.5\frac{p_1}{p_2} - 1$$

Her excess demands are functions of the commodity price ratio and are homogeneous of degree zero in prices. I's budget constraint is satisfied for any set of prices:

$$p_1\left(\frac{p_2}{p_1} - 41.5\right) + p_2\left(41.5\frac{p_1}{p_2} - 1\right) = 0$$

The excess demand functions possess the usual properties. An increase of p_1 relative to p_2 will decrease E_{11} and increase E_{12}. An increase of p_2 relative to p_1 will increase E_{11} and decrease E_{12}.

Assume that II's utility function is

$$U_2 = q_{21}q_{22} + 4q_{21} + 2q_{22}$$

and that her endowment consists of 164 units of Q_2 and no Q_1. A derivation similar to that employed for I yields the excess demand functions

$$E_{21} = 84\frac{p_2}{p_1} - 1 \qquad E_{22} = \frac{p_1}{p_2} - 84$$

II's budget constraint is always fulfilled, and her excess demands are homogeneous of degree zero in prices.

Invoking the condition that each market must be cleared

$$E_1 = E_{11} + E_{21} = 85\frac{p_2}{p_1} - 42.5 = 0$$

$$E_2 = E_{12} + E_{22} = 42.5\frac{p_1}{p_2} - 85 = 0$$

Either equation is sufficient for the determination of the equilibrium exchange ratio. Solving the first equation, $p_2/p_1 = 0.5$. Solving the second, $p_1/p_2 = 2$. The solutions are identical. In equilibrium 1 unit of Q_1 can be exchanged for 2 units of Q_2.

Substituting the equilibrium price ratio into the individual excess demand functions,

$$E_{11} = -41 \qquad E_{12} = 82 \qquad E_{21} = 41 \qquad E_{22} = -82$$

I gives 41 units of Q_1 to II in exchange for 82 units of Q_2.

The Edgeworth Box

A geometric picture of a two-person, two-commodity, pure-exchange economy is provided by the *Edgeworth box diagram*. Individual I's indifference map is pictured in the usual way with the origin, O_1, in the southwest corner. Three of her indifference curves are shown in Fig. 9-2a with $U_1^{(1)} < U_1^{(2)} < U_1^{(3)}$. Individual II's indifference-curve diagram is rotated 180 degrees so that its origin, O_2, is in the northeast corner. The quantities q_{21} and q_{22} are measured from right to left and from top to bottom respectively as II moves away from her origin. Utility increases as she moves downward: $U_2^{(1)} < U_2^{(2)} < U_2^{(3)}$. The two indifference-curve diagrams are joined to form a "box" with a width equal to the sum of the two consumers' endowments of Q_1 and a height equal to the sum of their endowments of Q_2. Every point within the box and on its boundary describes a particular distribution of the fixed quantities of the two commodities. For example, O_2 describes the case in which I has all of both commodities.

Consider the initial endowments of q_{11}^0 and q_{12}^0 for I and q_{21}^0 and q_{22}^0 for II described by point A in Fig. 9-2a. The budget constraint for each consumer is

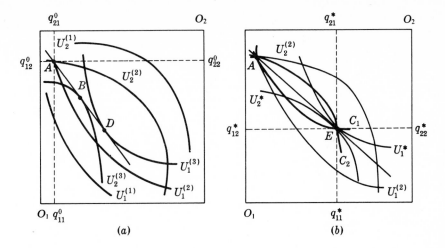

Figure 9-2

represented by a line through A with a slope equal to the negative of the price ratio. Consider the budget line that passes through points B and D. Individual I would maximize her utility by exchanging Q_2 for Q_1 to move from A to D where her RCS equals the price ratio. Similarly, II would maximize her utility by exchanging Q_1 for Q_2 to move from A to B. This price ratio does not provide a multimarket equilibrium. The RCSs of the two consumers are equal, but I desires to buy more Q_1 than II desires to sell and desires to sell more Q_2 than II desires to buy.

An *offer curve* for I is the locus of the utility maximization points, such as D, that are obtained as the budget line is rotated about A to represent different price ratios. I's offer curve is labeled C_1 in Fig. 9-2b. It passes through A since A would be her utility maximization point if the price ratio equaled the slope of her indifference curve at A. If the budget line were more steeply sloped, she would sell Q_1 and buy Q_2. If the budget line were less steeply sloped, she would buy Q_1 and sell Q_2. Her offer curve lies above her initial indifference curve, $U_1^{(2)}$, except at A where the two coincide. Individual II's offer curve, labeled C_2, is constructed in an analogous manner. Point E in Fig. 9-2b where C_1 and C_2 intersect is a multimarket equilibrium. The equilibrium price ratio is given by the negative of the slope of the budget line passing through A and E. The equilibrium utility levels for I and II are U_1^* and U_2^* respectively. Consumer I trades $(q_{12}^0 - q_{12}^*)$ units of Q_2 to II in exchange for $(q_{21}^0 - q_{21}^*)$ units of Q_1.

The Edgeworth box in Fig. 9-3a illustrates a troublesome case that may occur even though the assumption of strict quasi-concavity is satisfied. The initial endowment is A, I's offer curve is C_1, and II's offer curve is C_2. A well-defined unique multimarket equilibrium does not exist. I's endowment of Q_2 is exhausted before the consumers' RCSs can be equated. It is clearly to

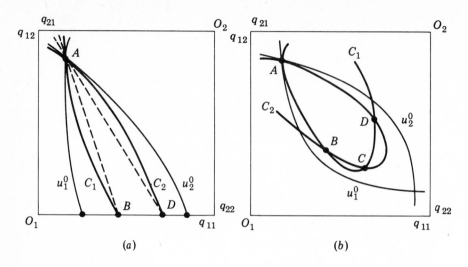

Figure 9-3

the advantage of both consumers to trade. A "reasonable" conjecture is that a final position will lie somewhere on the line segment BD with a price bounded by the slopes of the straight lines AD and AB. Additional assumptions must be introduced before a particular equilibrium point can be selected. Figure 9-3b illustrates a case in which the assumption of strict quasi-concavity is satisfied and three distinct equilibrium points B, C, and D exist. The reader may verify that for some price ratios Q_2 is a Giffen good (see Sec. 2-5) for I and Q_1 is a Giffen good for II.

9-3 PRODUCTION AND EXCHANGE

The multimarket equilibrium analysis is now extended to an economy in which goods are both produced and exchanged. The consumers' initial endowments consist of primary factors such as land and labor power. In addition all profits earned by firms are distributed to consumers. A consumer generally sells factors and uses the proceeds together with her profit income to purchase commodities. She may withhold a portion of her factor endowment for direct consumption. Labor power provides an example. The consumer will seldom supply the full amount of her labor power, but will generally reserve a portion for final consumption in the form of leisure. If a consumer possesses a factor from which she derives no utility, she will supply her entire endowment of that factor regardless of commodity and factor prices. Some consumers may sell one factor and purchase another. An example is provided by a land owner who employs domestic servants. Entrepreneurs use both factors and produced goods for the production of commodities. The produced commodities are useful both as inputs and final consumption goods.[1]

Equilibrium of the ith Consumer

Each of the n consumers is endowed with initial stocks of one or more of s primary goods. The initial endowment of the ith consumer is denoted by $q_{i1}^0, q_{i2}^0, \ldots, q_{is}^0$. She may sell (and buy) at the prevailing market prices $(p_1, p_2, \ldots, p_s)$. The consumer derives utility from the quantities of the primary factors she retains and the quantities of the $(m - s)$ produced commodities she purchases:

$$U_i = U_i(q_{i1}, q_{i2}, \ldots, q_{im}) \tag{9-16}$$

where the produced commodities are numbered from $(s + 1)$ through m.

The consumer's excess demand for a factor equals the quantity she consumes less her initial stock, and her excess demand for a commodity equals the quantity she consumes:

$$\begin{aligned} E_{ij} &= q_{ij} - q_{ij}^0 & j &= 1, \ldots, s \\ E_{ij} &= q_{ij} & j &= s + 1, \ldots, m \end{aligned} \tag{9-17}$$

The excess demand for a factor may be positive, negative, or zero, but will most often be negative, since the consumer generally sells factors in order to buy commodities. Her excess demands for commodities must be positive or zero. The consumer's income equals the value of her factor endowment plus her profit earnings:

$$y_i = \sum_{j=1}^{s} p_j q_{ij}^0 + \sum_{k=s+1}^{m} \sum_{h=1}^{N_k} \theta_{ihk} \pi_{hk} \tag{9-18}$$

where N_k is the number of firms producing the kth commodity, π_{hk} are the profits of the hth firm which produces the kth commodity, and $\theta_{ihk} \geq 0$ is the ith consumer's proportionate share of these profits.[2]

The value of the factors and commodities that an individual consumes must also equal her income:

$$y_i = \sum_{j=1}^{m} p_j q_{ij} \tag{9-19}$$

The consumer's budget constraint is obtained by subtracting (9-18) from (9-19) and substituting from (9-17):

$$\sum_{j=1}^{m} p_j E_{ij} - \sum_{h=s+1}^{m} \sum_{k=1}^{N_k} \theta_{ihk} \pi_{hk} = 0 \tag{9-20}$$

---

[1] It is sometimes necessary to distinguish pure intermediate goods which are not desired by consumers. They are produced by entrepreneurs and used as inputs.

[2] It is assumed that each firm produces a single product. The indices of summation in (9-18) would have to be revised if firms produced joint products.

The net value of her excess demands equals her profit earnings, or losses if negative.

The consumer again desires to maximize her utility level subject to her budget constraint. Form the function

$$Z_i = U_i(E_{i1} + q_{i1}^0, \ldots, E_{is} + q_{is}^0, E_{i,s+1}, \ldots, E_{im})$$
$$- \mu \left(\sum_{j=1}^{m} p_j E_{ij} - \sum_{h=s+1}^{m} \sum_{k=1}^{N_k} \theta_{ihk} \pi_{hk} \right)$$

and set the partial derivatives of Z_i equal to zero:

$$\frac{\partial Z_i}{\partial E_{ij}} = \frac{\partial U_i}{\partial E_{ij}} - \mu p_j = 0 \qquad j = 1, \ldots, m$$

$$\frac{\partial Z_i}{\partial \mu} = - \left(\sum_{j=1}^{m} p_j E_{ij} - \sum_{h=s+1}^{m} \sum_{k=1}^{N_k} \theta_{ihk} \pi_{hk} \right) = 0$$

(9-21)

First-order conditions require that the consumer equate the RCS for every pair of goods to their price ratio. It is shown in Sec. 2-6 that an assumption of regular strict quasi-concavity over a region will ensure satisfaction of the second-order conditions. Consequently, the consumer's excess demand functions can be obtained by solving (9-21) for the m excess demands, as functions of the profit levels in which she has an interest, and the m prices. It is shown below that profits may be expressed as functions of commodity and factor prices. Therefore, the ith consumer's excess demands may be expressed as functions of the prices alone:

$$E_{ij} = E_{ij}(p_1, \ldots, p_m) \qquad j = 1, \ldots, m \qquad (9\text{-}22)$$

Profits are homogeneous of degree one with respect to prices. It is easily verified that the consumer's excess demands are homogeneous of degree zero with respect to the prices of all commodities and factors.

Equilibrium of the hth Firm in the jth Industry

Each firm combines inputs for the production of a single commodity according to the technical rules specified in its production function:[1]

$$\bar{q}_{hj} = f_{hj}(q_{hj1}^*, \ldots, q_{hjm}^*)$$

where $\bar{q}_{hj}$ is the output level of the hth firm in the jth industry and q_{hjk}^* is the quantity of the kth good which the entrepreneur uses as an input. Both the s factors and $(m - s)$ commodities serve as inputs.

The entrepreneur's profit is her competitive revenue less the cost of her inputs:

$$\pi_{hj} = p_j f_{hj}(q_{hj1}^*, \ldots, q_{hjm}^*) - \sum_{k=1}^{m} p_k q_{hjk}^*$$

---

[1] Production is sometimes introduced with the alternative assumption that each firm jointly produces all commodities.

Setting the partial derivatives of profit with respect to each of the inputs equal to zero,

$$\frac{\partial \pi_{hj}}{\partial q^*_{hjk}} = p_j \frac{\partial \bar{q}_{hj}}{\partial q^*_{hjk}} - p_k = 0 \qquad k = 1, \ldots, m \tag{9-23}$$

The entrepreneur will utilize each input up to a point at which the value of its marginal physical product equals its price. If the production function is strictly concave over a region, the second-order conditions will be satisfied over that region, except possibly at isolated points (see Sec. A-3).

Conditions (9-23) imply that $\partial \bar{q}_{hj} / \partial q^*_{hjj} = 1$. If the entrepreneur utilizes her own output as an input—as a wheat farmer utilizes wheat for seed—she will utilize it up to a point at which its marginal physical product equals unity.

The entrepreneur's excess demand functions for her inputs for a strictly concave region of her production function are obtained by solving the m equations of (9-23) for $q^*_{hjk} = E^*_{hjk}$:

$$E^*_{hjk} = E^*_{hjk}(p_1, \ldots, p_m) \qquad k = 1, \ldots, m \tag{9-24}$$

The quantity of each input she purchases is a function of all prices. Since the entrepreneur never supplies (sells) inputs, her excess demands are always nonnegative.

If the jth industry contains N_j identical firms, its aggregate excess demand for the kth input equals the excess demand of a representative firm multiplied by the number of firms within the industry:

$$E^*_{jk} = N_j E^*_{hjk}(p_1, \ldots, p_m) = E^*_{jk}(p_1, \ldots, p_m, N_j) \tag{9-25}$$

An industry's excess demand for an input is a function of all prices and the number of firms within the industry.

The entrepreneur's excess demand for (supply of) her own output is determined by substituting the excess demand functions for her inputs (9-24) into her production function and letting $\bar{E}_{hj} = -\bar{q}_{hj}$:[†]

$$\bar{E}_{hj} = -f_{hj}[E^*_{hj1}(p_1, \ldots, p_m), \ldots, E^*_{hjm}(p_1, \ldots, p_m)]$$

or more simply

$$\bar{E}_{hj} = \bar{E}_{hj}(p_1, \ldots, p_m)$$

The excess demand for the industry as a whole equals the excess demand of a representative firm multiplied by the number of firms:

$$\bar{E}_j = N_j \bar{E}_{hj}(p_1, \ldots, p_m) = \bar{E}_j(p_1, \ldots, p_m, N_j) \tag{9-26}$$

The industry's excess demand depends upon the prices of all goods and the number of firms within the industry.

The entrepreneur's excess demand functions for her output and inputs are homogeneous of degree zero in all prices. If all prices are changed by the

---

[†] Separate excess demand functions are defined for Q_j as an output and as an input. The two could be combined into a single net excess demand without affecting the analysis.

factor $t > 0$, profit becomes

$$\pi_{hj} = tp_j f_{hj}(q^*_{hj1}, \ldots, q^*_{hjm}) - \sum_{k=1}^{m} tp_k q^*_{hjk}$$

Setting the partial derivatives equal to zero,

$$\frac{\partial \pi_{hj}}{\partial q^*_{hjk}} = tp_j \frac{\partial \bar{q}_{hj}}{\partial q^*_{hjk}} - tp_k = 0 \qquad k = 1, \ldots, m$$

or

$$t \left(p_j \frac{\partial \bar{q}_{hj}}{\partial q^*_{hjk}} - p_k \right) = 0 \qquad k = 1, \ldots, m$$

Since $t \neq 0$,

$$p_j \frac{\partial \bar{q}_{hj}}{\partial q^*_{hjk}} - p_k = 0 \qquad k = 1, \ldots, m$$

The first-order conditions from which the excess demands are obtained can be stated in a form identical with (9-23). Since the second-order conditions also remain unchanged, the excess demands are unaffected by a proportionate change of all prices.

Market Equilibrium

The excess demand functions of the consumers and entrepreneurs can be aggregated for both types of goods. The aggregate excess demand for a factor is the sum of the excess demands of the n consumers (9-22) and the $(m - s)$ industries on input account (9-25):

$$E_j = \sum_{i=1}^{n} E_{ij}(p_1, \ldots, p_m) + \sum_{k=s+1}^{m} E^*_{kj}(p_1, \ldots, p_m, N_k) \qquad j = 1, \ldots, s \qquad (9\text{-}27)$$

The aggregate excess demand for a commodity is the sum of the excess demands by the n consumers (9-22), the $(m - s)$ industries on input account (9-25), and its producers (9-26):

$$E_j = \sum_{i=1}^{n} E_{ij}(p_1, \ldots, p_m) + \sum_{k=s+1}^{m} E^*_{kj}(p_1, \ldots, p_m, N_k)$$
$$+ \bar{E}_j(p_1, \ldots, p_m, N_j) \qquad j = s + 1, \ldots, m \qquad (9\text{-}28)$$

The aggregate excess demands given by (9-27) and (9-28) can be stated simply as

$$E_j = E_j(p_1, \ldots, p_m, N_{s+1}, \ldots, N_m) \qquad j = 1, \ldots, m$$

The excess demand for each good is a function of the m prices and the numbers of firms within the $(m - s)$ producing industries.

It is assumed that a short-run equilibrium price can be determined for any of the m markets considered in isolation from the other $(m - 1)$ markets by setting the aggregate excess demand for the good under consideration equal to zero. In the short run the number of firms in the industry as well as the prices of the other $(m-1)$ goods and the numbers of firms within the other $(m-s-1)$ industries are treated as parameters. Utility, production, and excess demand functions are defined for a longer period of time in a long-run analysis. In addition, the number of firms within the industry is a variable in the determination of a long-run equilibrium for a commodity market. Excess demand and profit are both set equal to zero, and the resultant two equations are solved for profit and the number of firms. Short- and long-run equilibrium prices are nonnegative and generate consumption and production quantities within the region for which the excess demand functions are defined.

Walras' Law

Expressing the profit of the hth firm in the jth industry in terms of excess demands and rearranging terms,

$$p_j \bar{E}_{hj} + \sum_{k=1}^{m} p_k E_{hjk}^* + \pi_{hj} = 0 \qquad (9\text{-}29)$$

The net value of a firm's excess demands equals the negative of its profit. Summing (9-20) over all consumers and (9-29) over all producers yields the result

$$\sum_{j=1}^{m} p_j E_j = 0$$

Thus, Walras' law holds as an identity for any set of prices in the production and exchange system. The existence of positive profits does not affect this result. Total profits appear as a negative term in the aggregation of (9-20) and as a positive term in the aggregation of (9-29).

Multimarket Equilibrium

A long-run multimarket equilibrium requires that every market be cleared and that profit equal zero in every industry:[1]

$$\begin{aligned} E_j(p_1, \ldots, p_m, N_{s+1}, \ldots, N_m) &= 0 \qquad j = 1, \ldots, m \\ \pi_j(p_1, \ldots, p_m) &= 0 \qquad j = s+1, \ldots, m \end{aligned} \qquad (9\text{-}30)$$

where π_j is the profit of a representative firm in the jth industry. Again Walras' law results in a functional dependence among the excess demands, and it is not possible to solve (9-30) for absolute price levels.

Equilibrium again is defined in terms of relative, rather than absolute, prices. Since the excess demands of every consumer and producer are homogeneous of degree zero in prices, the aggregate excess demands are homogeneous of degree zero in prices. The profits of each entrepreneur are

---

[1] The profit equations are omitted and the numbers of firms are assumed predetermined for a short-run multimarket equilibrium analysis.

homogeneous of degree one in prices. If all prices are doubled, the entrepreneur's input and output levels will remain unchanged, but her total revenue and total cost, and hence her profit, will be doubled. However, if a long-run equilibrium is established for one set of prices, the system will remain in equilibrium if all prices are changed by the same proportion. A doubling of all prices will leave the excess demands equal to zero. The representative firms' revenues and costs will be doubled, but profit levels will remain equal to zero, and no new firms will be induced to enter any industry.

The number of variables in (9-30) can be reduced by one by dividing the m absolute prices by the price of an arbitrarily selected commodity. If Q_1 is selected, (9-30) can be rewritten as

$$E_j\left(1, \frac{p_2}{p_1}, \cdots, \frac{p_m}{p_1}, N_{s+1}, \ldots, N_m\right) = 0 \qquad j = 1, \ldots, m$$

$$\pi_j\left(1, \frac{p_2}{p_1}, \cdots, \frac{p_m}{p_1}\right) = 0 \qquad j = s+1, \ldots, m$$

(9-31)

It is assumed that this system contains $(2m - s - 1)$ independent equations that can be solved for the equilibrium values of the $(m - 1)$ exchange ratios relative to Q_1 and the $(m - s)$ firm numbers. The equilibrium values of the variables are all nonnegative.

Once the equilibrium exchange ratios and firm numbers are determined, the excess demands of every consumer and entrepreneur can be computed by substituting their values into the individual excess demand functions. A long-run equilibrium solution satisfies the following conditions: (1) every consumer maximizes utility, (2) every entrepreneur maximizes profit, (3) every market is cleared, and (4) every entrepreneur earns a zero profit. The equilibrium values of the individual consumption and production levels are within the regions for which the individual excess demand functions are defined.

9-4 THE NUMÉRAIRE AND MONEY

Multimarket equilibrium has been established for barter-type economies in which circulating money is nonexistent. Commodities and factors are exchanged for other commodities and factors, and the conditions of exchange are completely described by exchange ratios. These systems have been solved for the $(m - 1)$ exchange ratios relative to an arbitrarily selected good, generally called the numéraire. Any set of absolute prices that yields the equilibrium exchange ratios is an equilibrium solution. If there is one such solution, there is an infinite number.

A number of different kinds of money can be introduced into a general equilibrium system. One good may be selected as a standard of value and serve as money in the sense that all prices are expressed in terms of its units.

Money can be established as an abstract unit of account which serves as a standard of value but does not circulate. Under some circumstances circulating paper money can be introduced.

The Numéraire

For m goods there are m^2 exchange ratios taking two commodities at a time: p_j/p_k ($j, k = 1, \ldots, m$). Of these m are identities which state that the exchange ratio of a good for itself equals unity: $p_j/p_k = 1$ for $j = k$. The m^2 exchange ratios are not independent. Consider the identity and the $(m - 1)$ exchange ratios with Q_1 as numéraire. The other $m(m - 1)$ exchange ratios and identities can be derived from these:

$$\frac{p_j}{p_k} = \frac{p_j}{p_1} \cdot \frac{p_k}{p_1} \qquad j, k = 1, \ldots, m \qquad (9\text{-}32)$$

Imagine that Q_1 is pears, Q_2 oranges, and Q_3 apples, and that two oranges exchange for one pear ($p_2/p_1 = 0.5$) and one apple for two pears ($p_3/p_1 = 2$). Utilizing (9-32) four oranges will exchange for one apple: $p_3/p_2 = 4$. The complete set of exchange ratios is given either directly or indirectly by the $(m - 1)$ exchange ratios and the identity for the numéraire.

The numéraire can be changed from Q_1 to Q_k by dividing the exchange ratios and identity for Q_1 by p_k/p_1:

$$\frac{1}{p_k/p_1}\left(1, \frac{p_2}{p_1}, \ldots, \frac{p_k}{p_1}, \ldots, \frac{p_m}{p_1}\right) = \left(\frac{p_1}{p_k}, \frac{p_2}{p_k}, \ldots, 1, \ldots, \frac{p_m}{p_k}\right)$$

The exchange ratios are unaffected by this transformation, and the selection of the numéraire is truly arbitrary.

The numéraire can also serve as a standard of value. Setting its price identically equal to unity, the exchange ratios become $p_j/p_1 = p_j$. The equilibrium exchange ratios are unaffected by this transformation. The equilibrium price of each good is expressed as the number of units of the numéraire which must be exchanged to obtain 1 unit of that good. The price of oranges becomes 0.5 pears per orange, and the price of apples 2 pears per apple. The price of apples is four times as great as the price of oranges, and one apple still exchanges for four oranges in equilibrium. The numéraire has become money in the sense that its units serve as a standard of value. However, it does not serve as a store of value, since it is desired only as a productive factor or consumable commodity on the same basis as all other goods. Any good may serve as a standard of value in this sense.

The expression of prices in terms of a good such as pears is not common practice. Prices are generally expressed in terms of a monetary unit such as dollars. An accounting money is easily introduced into the framework of a general equilibrium system. There is no reason why the price of the numéraire should equal unity. It could be set equal to 2, $\sqrt{2}$, 25, or 200 million. The equilibrium exchange ratios would be unaffected. Accounting money can be introduced by setting the price of the numéraire (or any other good) equal to a specified number of monetary units. Money prices can then be derived for all other goods. If Q_1 is numéraire and p_1 is set equal to β dollars, the dollar price of Q_k (ρ_k) is

$$\rho_k = \beta \frac{p_k}{p_1} \qquad k = 2, \ldots, m$$

If the price of a pear is set equal to 2 dollars, the price of an orange is 1 dollar and the price of an apple 4 dollars. In this case money only serves as an abstract unit of account. It does not exist in a physical sense. Goods still exchange for goods. No one holds money, and no one desires to hold money. Accounting money serves as a standard, but not a store, of value.[1]

It is sometimes convenient to normalize prices by defining a unit of account such that $\sum_{i=1}^{m} p_i = 1$. In this case a composite of all factors and commodities, rather than a single good, serves as a valuation base. The composite definition avoids the difficulties that would arise if a preselected numéraire factor or commodity were a free good in equilibrium (see Sec. 10-1).

Monetary Equilibrium

Commodity money and accounting money are quite different from circulating money which serves as a store of value. The classical economists of the nineteenth century frequently divided the economy into two sectors with regard to equilibrium price determination: the real sector in which exchange ratios are determined, and the monetary sector in which absolute money prices are determined by the quantity of money in existence. The real sector is described in Secs. 9-1 through 9-3. The present task is to add the monetary sector to this analysis. For simplicity the analysis is developed for the case of pure exchange though it is easily extended to cover production and exchange.

Assume that the n consumers also possess initial stocks of paper money denoted by the subscript $(m + 1)$: $(q_{1,m+1}^0, \ldots, q_{n,m+1}^0)$. Paper money serves as a store of value, but does not enter the consumers' utility functions. The ith consumer's excess demand for paper money is defined as the stock she desires to hold less her initial stock:

$$E_{i,m+1} = q_{i,m+1} - q_{i,m+1}^0 \qquad (9\text{-}33)$$

Her excess demand is positive if she adds to her initial stock of money and negative if she reduces it. The consumer's budget constraint (9-4) must be

---

[1] The assumption that money is only a unit of account is implicit throughout the analyses of the consumer and entrepreneur. The consumer's income may be expressed in monetary units, but she spends her entire income and does not desire to hold money. The entrepreneur maximizes her money profit, but she also has no desire to hold money. If she earns a positive profit, she will spend it in her role as a consumer.

redefined to include money:

$$\sum_{j=1}^{m+1} p_j E_{ij} = 0 \tag{9-34}$$

where p_j is the price of the jth commodity. The price of money p_{m+1} equals unity by definition. The consumer may exchange money for commodities or commodities for money. If her excess demand for money is positive, the value of the commodities she sells is greater than the value of those she buys, and she is exchanging commodities for money.

Since money does not enter the consumer's utility function, her excess demand for money cannot be determined by the principles of utility maximization. It is usually assumed that the consumer finds it convenient to hold money in order to facilitate commodity transactions. Assume that the ith consumer desires to hold a quantity of money which is a fixed proportion of the monetary value of her initial endowment of commodities:

$$q_{i,m+1} = \alpha_i \sum_{j=1}^{m} p_j q_{ij}^0 \tag{9-35}$$

where α_i is a constant. Substituting (9-35) into (9-33),

$$E_{i,m+1} = \alpha_i \sum_{j=1}^{m} p_j q_{ij}^0 - q_{i,m+1}^0 \tag{9-36}$$

The aggregate excess demand for money is obtained by summing (9-36) for all n consumers:

$$E_{m+1} = \alpha \sum_{i=1}^{n} \sum_{j=1}^{m} p_j q_{ij}^0 - \sum_{i=1}^{n} q_{i,m+1}^0 = E_{m+1}(p_1, \ldots, p_m) \tag{9-37}$$

No essentials are lost by assuming that $\alpha_i = \alpha$ for $i = 1, \ldots, n$. If the initial endowments of commodities and money are fixed, the excess demand for money is a function of the m commodity prices.

The excess demand functions for the m commodities are determined by maximizing utility for each consumer subject to her budget constraint, including money, solving the first-order conditions in order to obtain individual excess demand functions, and then summing for all consumers. A general equilibrium is established if the excess demand for each commodity and money equals zero:

$$E_j(p_1, \ldots, p_m) = 0 \qquad j = 1, \ldots, m+1 \tag{9-38}$$

This gives a system of $(m + 1)$ equations in the m variable commodity prices. By Walras' law functional dependence exists among the $(m + 1)$ excess demand functions. If the m commodity markets were in equilibrium, the money market would also be in equilibrium; i.e., consumers as a whole would not desire to exchange commodities for money or money for commodities. The quantity of money that consumers desired to hold would equal the quantity in existence. It is assumed that (9-38) contains m independent equations that can be solved for the equilibrium money prices of the m commodities.

The excess demands for commodities and money are not homogeneous of degree zero in commodity prices. If all commodity prices are increased by the factor $t > 0$, the excess demand for money (9-37) becomes

$$E_{m+1} = \alpha \sum_{i=1}^{n} \sum_{j=1}^{m} t p_j q_{ij}^0 - \sum_{i=1}^{n} q_{i,m+1}^0 \tag{9-39}$$

The partial derivative of (9-39) with respect to t is

$$\frac{\partial E_{m+1}}{\partial t} = \alpha \sum_{i=1}^{n} \sum_{j=1}^{m} p_j q_{ij}^0 > 0$$

A proportionate increase of all commodity prices will increase the excess demand for money. If the system is in equilibrium before the price increase, consumers will desire to exchange commodities for money in order to bring their monetary stocks into the desired relation with the monetary values of their initial endowments of commodities. However, there will not be a corresponding negative excess demand for commodities. Any proportionate change of the equilibrium commodity prices will throw the system out of equilibrium.

The excess demands for commodities and money are homogeneous of degree zero in commodity prices and initial money stocks. The excess demand for money becomes

$$E_{m+1} = \alpha \sum_{i=1}^{n} \sum_{j=1}^{m} t p_j q_{ij}^0 - \sum_{i=1}^{n} t q_{i,m+1}^0$$

and

$$\frac{\partial E_{m+1}}{\partial t} = \alpha \sum_{i=1}^{n} \sum_{j=1}^{m} p_j q_{ij}^0 - \sum_{i=1}^{n} q_{i,m+1}^0$$

which equals zero if the money market was in equilibrium before the price change. Each consumer's money stock retains the desired relation to the value of her commodity endowment, and she will not desire to exchange commodities for money or money for commodities.

It can also be demonstrated that a change of the money stock of each consumer by the factor t will result in a change of the money price of each commodity by the same factor, but will leave the real sector unaffected. If equilibrium has been established and then each money stock is increased by the factor t, each consumer will desire to exchange money for commodities, but no one will desire to exchange commodities for money. As a result commodity prices will increase until the existing stocks of money no longer exceed the stocks that consumers desire to hold.

Monetary equilibrium will be reestablished when the values of all commodity stocks are increased by the factor t

$$\sum_{i=1}^{n} \sum_{j=1}^{m} p_j q_{ij}^0 = t \sum_{i=1}^{n} \sum_{j=1}^{m} p_j q_{ij}^0 \tag{9-40}$$

where p_j is the price of the jth commodity after equilibrium has been reestablished. Proportionate increases of all commodity prices: $p_j = t p_j$ $(j = 1, \ldots, m)$ will satisify (9-40), but so will many other price constellations. Consider a nonproportionate set of price changes which satisfies (9-40). It follows that $p_h = u p_h$ and $p_k = v p_k$ where $u > t > v$ for some h and k. The exchange ratio between Q_h and Q_k is now $u p_h / v p_k > p_h / p_k$. The price of Q_h has increased relative to the price of Q_k, and consumers will desire to exchange Q_h for Q_k. If the system was in equilibrium at the initial exchange ratio, the new exchange ratio will result in a positive aggregate excess demand for Q_k and a negative aggregate excess demand for Q_h. The aggregate excess demands for all commodities will equal zero if and only if $p_h / p_k = p_h / p_k$ for $h, k = 1, \ldots, m$. This is consistent with monetary equilibrium if and only if $p_j = t p_j$ $(j = 1, \ldots, m)$. The dichotomization of equilibrium price determination is complete. Equilibrium exchange ratios are determined by the consumers' utility functions and the real values of their initial endowments. Money prices are determined by the quantity of money.

The introduction of circulating paper money into a static general equilibrium system is possible, but rather artificial. Equation (9-39) postulates a mode of behavior that is logically, though not mathematically, inconsistent with utility maximization: the consumer desires to hold a stock of money from which she derives no utility rather than spend it on commodities from which she does. It is difficult to find motives for holding money in a static system that is in no way connected with preceding or succeeding points in time. The interesting problems of money only arise in a dynamic analysis in which behavior is considered over time.

Money in the Utility Function

Putting money directly in the utility function provides an alternative to (9-35). The rationale is that money stocks yield utility by facilitating exchange. The first-order conditions for the ith consumer may be written

$$\frac{U_{ij}}{U_{i,m+1}} = p_j \qquad j = 1, \ldots, m$$

$$\sum_{i=1}^{m} p_j(q_{ij} - q_{ij}^0) + (q_{i,m+1} - q_{i,m+1}^0) = 0$$

(9-41)

where Q_{m+1} is money with unit price. Again, the increase of a price with money endowment constant will result in a substitution of goods for money.

Let the money endowment and all commodity prices change by the proportion $t > 0$. The first-order conditions become

$$\frac{U_{ij}}{U_{i,m+1}} = t p_j \qquad j = 1, \ldots, m$$

$$\sum_{i=1}^{m} t p_j(q_{ij} - q_{ij}^0) + (q_{i,m+1} - t q_{i,m+1}^0) = 0$$

(9-42)

The economy can be separated into real and monetary sectors if the values for q_{ij} ($j = 1, \ldots, m$) that satisfy (9-41) and t times the value for $q_{i,m+1}$ that satisfies (9-41) satisfy (9-42). Equivalently, separation is possible if the excess demand functions for commodities and money are homogeneous of degrees zero and one respectively in commodity prices and money endowment. A change of money endowments by the same proportion for all consumers would result in changes of desired money stocks and commodity prices by the same proportion, and leave desired-commodity consumption levels unchanged.

In general, separation is not possible. However there are cases in which it is. If the RCSs of (9-41) and (9-42) all change proportionately with money holdings, separation is possible. In this case the commodity quantities that satisfy (9-41) will also satisfy (9-42) with money holdings changed by the proportion t. An example is provided by the frequently used utility function

$$U_i = q_{i1}^{\alpha_1} q_{i2}^{\alpha_2} \cdots q_{im}^{\alpha_m} q_{i,m+1}$$

Its RCSs are proportional to money holdings

$$\frac{U_{ij}}{U_{i,m+1}} = \frac{\alpha_j q_{i,m+1}}{q_{ij}} \qquad j = 1, \ldots, m$$

The reader may verify that the excess demand functions exhibit the appropriate homogeneity. The conclusions for the typical consumer will hold for aggregate excess demands if each consumer's RCSs are proportional to his or her money holdings, and the money endowment of each is changed by the same proportion.

9-5 SUMMARY

A multimarket equilibrium analysis allows the determination of a consistent set of prices for all goods. In a pure-exchange system individuals are endowed with commodity stocks. Each is free to buy and sell commodities at prevailing prices subject to her budget constraint, which states that the value of her sales must equal the value of her purchases. Individual excess demand functions are derived from the first-order conditions for utility maximization. Aggregate functions are obtained by summing the individual functions for each commodity. The sum of the aggregate excess demands multiplied by prices identically equal to zero. This follows from the individual budget constraints and is known as *Walras' law*. All the individual, and therefore the aggregate, functions are homogeneous of degree zero in prices. Consumer behavior is determined by exchange ratios rather than absolute prices. Multimarket equilibrium requires that the excess demand for every commodity equal zero. The m excess demands are functionally dependent as a result of Walras' law, and an equilibrium solution for the system is expressed in terms of the $(m - 1)$ exchange ratios for the commodities relative to an arbitrarily selected numéraire.

Production is introduced in the second stage of the analysis. The consumers' endowments are assumed to consist of primary factors which they generally sell to entrepreneurs in order to be able to purchase produced commodities. The consumer receives predetermined proportions of the profits and losses earned by firms. The consumer's excess demand functions for factors and commodities are derived from her first-order conditions for utility maximization. Each entrepreneur used both factors and commodities as inputs for the production of a single commodity. An entrepreneur's excess demand functions for her inputs are derived from her first-order conditions for profit maximization. The excess demand for her output is obtained by substituting the input values into her production function. The entrepreneur's excess demands are also homogeneous of degree zero in prices. Aggregate excess demand functions for each factor and commodity are obtained by summing the functions of the individual consumers and entrepreneurs. Walras' law again holds for the aggregate functions. A symmetry assumption is introduced, and the aggregate excess demands become functions of prices and the number of firms in each industry. Long-run equilibrium requires that every market be cleared and that the profit of the representative firm in each industry equal zero. Again, the excess demands are functionally dependent. A long-run equilibrium solution is expressed in terms of $(m - 1)$ exchange ratios and the number of firms in each industry.

The exchange ratios between every pair of commodities can be determined from the exchange ratios relative to the numéraire. The numéraire can serve as money in the standard-of-value sense. Its price can be set equal to unity and all other prices expressed in terms of its units. Alternatively, prices can be normalized by setting their sum equal to unity. Abstract accounting money can serve as a standard of value. Circulating paper money can be introduced, and its quantity will determine absolute, but not relative, prices in a pure-exchange system if consumers are assumed to hold a money stock equal to a fixed proportion of the value of their commodity endowments. This result does not hold in general if money is introduced directly into the utility function. It does hold for the special case in which the RCS of money per unit of each commodity changes proportionately with each consumer's money holdings.

EXERCISES

9-1 Consider a two-person, two-commodity, pure-exchange, competitive economy. The consumers' utility functions are $U_1 = q_{11}q_{12} + 12q_{11} + 3q_{12}$ and $U_2 = q_{21}q_{22} + 8q_{21} + 9q_{22}$. Consumer I has initial endowments of 8 and 30 units of Q_1 and Q_2 respectively; II has endowments of 10 units of each commodity. Determine excess demand functions for the two consumers. Determine an equilibrium price ratio for this economy.

9-2 Construct offer curves as mathematical functions from the first-order conditions for the two consumers described in Exercise 9-1. Show that the equilibrium derived in Exercise 9-1 satisfies both offer curves.

9-3 Derive excess demand functions for the inputs and output of a representative firm with the production function $\bar{q}_{hj} = (q^*_{hj1})^\alpha (q^*_{hj2})^\beta$ where $\alpha, \beta > 0$ and $\alpha + \beta < 1$.

9-4 Consider a two-person, two-commodity, pure-exchange economy with paper money. The utility functions are $U_1 = q_{11}q_{12}^{0.5}$ and $U_2 = q_{21}q_{22}^{0.5}$. Consumer I has initial endowments of 30 units of Q_1, 5 units of Q_2, and 43 units of money; II has respective endowments of 20, 10, and 2. Each of the consumers desires to hold a money stock equal to one-fifth of the value of her initial commodity endowment. Determine equilibrium money prices for Q_1 and Q_2. Show that the equilibrium prices would triple if the initial money stocks of I and II were increased to 129 and 6 respectively.

9-5 Reformulate the monetary analysis centering upon (9-35) in terms of a composite commodity and money.

SELECTED REFERENCES

Allen, R. G. D.: *Mathematical Economics* (London: Macmillan, 1956). Multimarket equilibrium is covered in chap. 10. The necessary mathematical concepts beyond the calculus are developed in the text.

Arrow, K. J., and F. H. Hahn: *General Competitive Analysis* (San Francisco: Holden-Day, 1971). Advanced mathematics is used to provide a comprehensive account of multimarket equilibrium.

Kuenne, Robert E.: *The Theory of General Economic Equilibrium* (Princeton, N.J.: Princeton University Press, 1963). A detailed treatise using fairly simple mathematics.

Quirk, James, and Rubin Saposnik: *Introduction to General Equilibrium Theory and Welfare Economics* (New York: McGraw-Hill, 1968). Basic concepts are covered in the first two chapters. Simplified set-theoretic mathematics is used.

Varian, Hal P.: *Microeconomics* (New York: Norton, 1978). Chap. 6 covers general equilibrium theory. Simplified modern mathematics is used.

Walras, Léon: *Elements of Pure Economics*, trans. by William Jaffé (Homewood, Ill.: Irwin, 1954). The original statement of multimarket equilibrium theory.

TOPICS IN MULTIMARKET EQUILIBRIUM

Appropriate multimarket equilibrium solutions are assumed to exist in Chap. 9. This assumption is convenient, but the mere formulation of a multimarket system gives no assurance of the existence of an equilibrium solution. Some systems have no mathematical solution; others have many. The existence of a mathematical solution may not be adequate. Economics places bounds upon the admissible values for the variables. Prices must be given by nonnegative,[1] real numbers. Furthermore, the consumption levels of each consumer and the input and output levels of each firm must be nonnegative. A mathematical solution which contains, for example, negative consumption levels is meaningless.

Section 10-1 contains a discussion of the existence of multimarket equilibria. Static and dynamic stability conditions are extended to multimarket systems in Sec. 10-2, and the uniqueness of equilibrium is considered in Sec. 10-3. The multimarket input-output system and its linear production functions are the subject of Sec. 10-4.

---

[1] If the price of a commodity were negative, purchasing power would be transferred from sellers to buyers rather than from buyers to sellers. Negative prices are not always nonsensical. The possession of discommodities such as garbage will reduce a consumer's utility level, and he will generally be willing to pay for their removal. The possibility of meaningful negative prices is eliminated by centering attention upon the commodity counterparts of discommodities. The consumer may be considered to buy garbage-removal service rather than sell garbage, and the garbage collector may be considered to sell garbage-removal service rather than buy garbage. The price of garbage-removal service is positive and equal in absolute value to the negative price of garbage.

10-1 EXISTENCE OF EQUILIBRIUM

The question of the existence of an admissible solution may be considered on two different levels. One may desire to determine whether or not a particular numerically implemented multimarket system possesses an equilibrium solution. On a more general level one may desire to prove an existence theorem which states that equilibrium solutions exist for all multimarket systems that satisfy a number of general assumptions.

This section begins with a discussion of existence for particular sets of excess demand functions. Attention is then turned to the general problem of existence for a short-run version of the production and exchange system presented in Sec. 9-3. First, restrictions are placed upon individual utility and production functions that ensure the existence of appropriate individual and aggregate excess demand functions. Next, the mathematical techniques underlying Brouwer's fixed-point theorem are introduced. This theorem is then used to prove that multimarket equilibria exist for all systems with utility and production functions that conform to the stated restrictions. Finally, more advanced existence theorems based upon more general restrictions are outlined.

Solutions for Particular Systems

A locally univalent solution of N differentiable equations in N variables exists if its Jacobian does not vanish in a small neighborhood (see Sec. A-2). The system of m equations obtained by setting the excess demands equal to zero cannot be solved for the absolute values of the m prices. Since the aggregate budget constraint is always satisfied, the excess demands are functionally dependent, and their Jacobian vanishes identically. The nonexistence of a locally unique solution for absolute prices is meaningful from the economic viewpoint, since the excess demands are homogeneous of degree zero in all prices.

By letting $p_1 = 1$ and omitting the excess demand equation for Q_1 the system is reduced to $(m - 1)$ equations in $(m - 1)$ variable prices. Thus far, it has been assumed that these equations are independent and a univalent solution exists for the reduced system. This assumption is not necessarily true. Consider the three-commodity reduced system given by

$$E_2 = -2p_2 - 4p_3 + 10 = 0$$
$$E_3 = -3p_2 - 6p_3 + 15 = 0$$

The Jacobian of this system vanishes identically, and it cannot be solved for unique values of p_2 and p_3. The excess demand functions for Q_2 and Q_3 are not independent. The functional dependence in this case is $E_3 = 1.5E_2$. Society as a whole always demands and supplies Q_2 and Q_3 in a fixed proportion. Any set of values for p_2 and p_3 which satisfies $p_2 = 5 - 2p_3$ will result in multimarket equilibrium. Examples are $p_2 = 1$, $p_3 = 2$, and $p_2 = 3$, $p_3 = 1$. In this case the Jacobian test states that a locally univalent solution does not exist, but it provides no aid in determining that other solutions do exist.

A system that passes the Jacobian test has unique local mathematical solutions but a solution might contain negative prices or imply negative consumption and production levels for some market participants, and not be admissible as a multimarket equilibrium. Each numerical multimarket system may be treated individually. First apply the nonvanishing Jacobian condition to determine whether a locally unique mathematical solution exists. If one does, attempt to solve the system and examine its solution(s) from the viewpoint of admissibility. If the Jacobian of the system vanishes, one must apply whatever methods appear appropriate in the particular circumstances to determine whether or not equilibrium solutions exist.

Brouwer's Fixed-Point Theorem

The solution method proposed for particular systems is not helpful for a consideration of existence for abstract multimarket systems that are not numerically implemented, nor for systems in which the excess demand functions contain "kinks" at which derivatives are not defined. In these cases it is necessary to prove an existence theorem which states that all multimarket systems satisfying stated assumptions possess equilibrium solutions. Most existence proofs rest on one or another of a class of mathematical theorems called fixed-point theorems. Brouwer's fixed-point theorem is one of the least difficult of those used in economics. The mathematical techniques upon which it is based are discussed now.

A *point-to-point mapping* in n-dimensional space is a rule or set of rules which associates a point in n-dimensional space with some other point in this space. Let (x_1, x_2) denote a point in two-dimensional space, and let (x'_1, x'_2) denote its associated point. The rules $x'_1 = x_1 + x_2$ and $x'_2 = x_1^2 x_2$ provide an example of a mapping in two-dimensional space. Both x'_1 and x'_2 may be expressed as functions of x_1 and x_2. In general, a mapping in n-dimensional space may be written as

$$x'_i = f_i(x_1, \ldots, x_n) \qquad i = 1, \ldots, n$$

or in more compact notation it may be written as $x' = F(x)$ where $x = (x_1, \ldots, x_n)$ and $x' = (x'_1, \ldots, x'_n)$. This is analogous to the way in which functions are denoted, except that x and x' represent points with n coordinates rather than single numbers. The point x' is called the *image* of point x. A mapping is *continuous* if each of the functions $f_i(x)$ $(i = 1, \ldots, n)$ composing it is continuous.

A mapping may be defined for some subset of points in its coordinate space. For example, the mapping $F(x)$ may be defined only for points lying on a circle with center at the origin and radius equal to unity, i.e., for points the coordinates of which satisfy $x_1^2 + x_2^2 = 1$. A mapping is *into itself* if the associated points also lie in the point set for which the mapping is defined.

The following functions provide an example of a mapping of the set of points lying on the unit circle into itself:[1]

$$x_1' = \frac{x_1}{\sqrt{x_1^2 + x_2^2}} \qquad x_2' = \frac{x_2}{\sqrt{x_1^2 + x_2^2}}$$

A point set is *convex* if every point on a straight-line segment connecting any two points in the set is also in the set. The point set formed by the circumference of a circle is not convex since a line segment joining two distinct points in the set contains points inside the circle which are not in the set. The point set formed by the circumference and interior of a circle is convex.

A point set in *n*-dimensional space is *bounded from above* if there exists a vector of *n* finite numbers $x^* = (x_1^*, \ldots, x_n^*)$ such that $x_i^* \geqq x_i$ for all $x = (x_1, \ldots, x_n)$ in the set. It is *bounded from below* if there exists a set of *n* finite numbers x^0 such that $x_i^0 \leqq x_i$ for all x in the set. A *bounded* set is bounded from both above and below. The point set formed by the circumference of a circle is bounded, but the point set formed by the positive quadrant of the coordinate space is not.

A point set is *closed* if, whenever every point of a convergent infinite sequence is in the set, the limit point of that sequence is also in the set.[2] The point set defined by $0 < x < 1$ is not closed because every point in the infinite sequence $\frac{1}{2}, \frac{1}{3}, \frac{1}{4}, \ldots, 1/n, \ldots$ is in the set, but the limit of the sequence, zero, is not. The point set defined by $0 \leqq x \leqq 1$ is closed.

Brouwer's fixed-point theorem states that *a continuous mapping of a closed, bounded, convex set into itself has a fixed point*; i.e., if $F(x)$ is the mapping, there exists a point x^* in the set on which the mapping is defined such that $x^* = F(x^*)$. At least one point gets mapped into itself. Consider as an example the mapping $F(x)$ shown in Fig. 10-1. The mapping is defined in the interval $0 \leqq x \leqq 1$ which is a closed, bounded, and convex set of points on the real line. The mapping is also continuous. Hence, there must be at least one point where the graph of $F(x)$ intersects a 45-degree line through the origin. Point A in Fig. 10-1 is such an intersection with the property that $x^* = F(x^*)$.

An illustrative existence proof using Brouwer's fixed-point theorem is now formulated for a short-run version of the multimarket system developed in Sec. 9-3. In this context short run means that the number of firms in each industry is predetermined, and the profits of individual firms need not equal zero. The proof proceeds in two stages. First, the existence of aggregate excess demand functions with suitable properties is proved. Second, the existence of equilibrium prices satisfying these functions is proved.

---

[1] If $F(x)$ were defined for all points in two-dimensional space, the mapping would carry two-dimensional space into the unit circle and would not be into itself.

[2] A different, but equivalent, definition of a closed point set is given in Sec. 5-7.

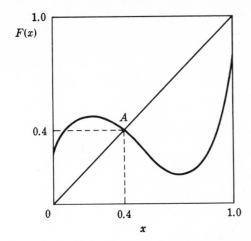

Figure 10-1

Existence of Excess Demand Functions

The typical ith consumer is assumed to be endowed with stocks of each of s primary goods. He may sell portions of these stocks and buy the s primary and $(m - s)$ produced goods in competitive markets at nonnegative prices. He selects a consumption bundle that maximizes his utility subject to his budget constraint, which requires that the value of his consumption bundle equal the value of his initial primary-goods stocks plus his share of profits from production. For simplicity it is assumed that he receives profits from at least one firm in each industry. His utility function is defined for nonnegative consumption levels, and is assumed to be regular strictly quasi-concave with strictly positive marginal utilities. As before, the utility of the ith consumer is denoted by U_i, and his consumption of the jth good by q_{ij}. The following *interior assumption* is also invoked: $U_i = U_i^0$, where U_i^0 is a constant, if $q_{ij} = 0$ for some j, and $U_i > U_i^0$ if $q_{ij} > 0$ for all j. This rules out the possibility of corner solutions similar to the one shown in Fig. 2-4b, and ensures that the first-order conditions will be satisfied at a point with all quantities positive if all prices are positive. Weaker assumptions are used in more advanced analyses.

A global univalence theorem (see Sec. A-3) states that single-valued excess demand functions will exist for the ith consumer if the principal minors of the Jacobian ($\mathcal{J}$) of (9-21):

$$\mathcal{J} = \begin{vmatrix} U_{11} & \cdots & U_{1m} & -p_1 \\ \cdot\cdot\cdot\cdot\cdot\cdot\cdot\cdot\cdot\cdot\cdot\cdot\cdot\cdot\cdot \\ U_{m1} & \cdots & U_{mm} & -p_m \\ -p_1 & \cdots & -p_m & 0 \end{vmatrix}$$

alternate in sign. The assumption of regular strict quasi-concavity guarantees that the minors will have the desired signs.

Positive marginal utilities and the interior assumption assure that the first-order conditions will be fulfilled with all consumption levels positive if all prices are positive.[1] Thus, single-valued excess demand functions of the form

$$E_{ij} = E_{ij}(p_1, \ldots, p_m) \qquad j = 1, \ldots, m \qquad (10\text{-}1)$$

exist for the ith consumer. These functions are continuous and homogeneous of degree zero in prices.

It is convenient to limit attention to price combinations that lie within the normalized price set, i.e., numbers $(p_1, \ldots, p_m)$ which satisfy

$$\sum_{j=1}^{m} p_j = 1 \qquad p_j \geqq 0 \qquad (10\text{-}2)$$

Since the excess demand functions considered here are homogeneous of degree zero in prices, no generality is lost by limiting attention to the normalized price set (see Sec. 9-4).[2]

The excess demand functions (10-1) have the domain $p_k > 0$ ($k = 1, \ldots, m$). They do not directly accommodate zero prices. The restrictions placed upon the utility functions imply that $E_{ij} \to \infty$ as $p_j \to 0$. The application of Brouwer's fixed-point theorem that will be used to prove the existence of equilibrium prices requires that finite excess demands be generated by zero prices. This requirement can be met by the use of an artifice. Define the numbers k_j ($j = 1, \ldots, m$) such that for a primary good ($j = 1, \ldots, s$), k_j exceeds the total endowment of all consumers, and for a produced good ($j = s + 1, \ldots, m$), k_j exceeds the maximum output of Q_j that could be secured if the economy's entire endowment of primary goods were devoted to the production of Q_j.

Now, construct a set of *pseudo excess demand functions* on the assumption that the ith consumer maximizes utility subject to his budget constraint and the additional requirements that $E_{ij} \leqq k_j$ ($j = 1, \ldots, m$). These functions have the normalized price set (10-2) as their domain. The pseudo functions are the same as the conventional functions (10-1) for all price points for which

$$E_{ij}(p_1, \ldots, p_m) \leqq k_j \qquad j = 1, \ldots, m$$

However, these inequalities are not satisfied for all points in the normalized price set. One or more of the inequalities are violated if one or more prices are either zero or sufficiently small to generate excess demands larger than the corresponding upper bounds.

---

[1] This result would not hold in general if it were possible for the consumer to receive a negative profit income sufficiently large to make his total income zero or negative. For the system considered here the possibility of a negative profit income is excluded by assumptions covering production.

[2] The normalized price set does not cover the situation in which all prices are zero. This is no loss, however, since such a situation cannot be a multimarket equilibrium.

Assume that u of the upper bounds are effective as strict equalities, and renumber the goods so that $E_{ij} = k_j$ ($j = 1, \ldots, u$). Substitute these equalities and form the Lagrange function

$$Z_i = U_i(k_1, \ldots, k_u, E_{i,u+1}, \ldots, E_{im}) - \mu\left(\sum_{j=1}^{u} p_j k_j + \sum_{j=u+1}^{m} p_j E_{ij} - \sum_{k=s+1}^{m} \sum_{h=1}^{N_k} \theta_{ihk} \pi_{hk}\right)$$

Set the $(m - u + 1)$ partial derivatives of this function equal to zero:

$$\frac{\partial Z_i}{\partial E_{ij}} = U_j - \mu p_j = 0 \qquad j = u + 1, \ldots, m$$

$$\frac{\partial Z_i}{\partial \mu} = -\left(\sum_{j=1}^{u} p_j k_j + \sum_{j=u+1}^{m} p_j E_{ij} - \sum_{k=s+1}^{m} \sum_{h=1}^{N_k} \theta_{ihk} \pi_{hk}\right) = 0$$

where $U_j = \partial U_i / \partial E_{ij}$. The Jacobian of this system is

$$\mathcal{H} = \begin{vmatrix} U_{u+1,u+1} & \cdots & U_{u+1,m} & -p_{u+1} \\ \cdots & \cdots & \cdots & \cdots \\ U_{m,u+1} & \cdots & U_{mm} & -p_m \\ -p_{u+1} & \cdots & -p_m & 0 \end{vmatrix}$$

where $U_{jh} = \partial^2 U_i / \partial E_{ij} \partial E_{ih}$. By construction $p_j > 0$ ($j = u + 1, \ldots, m$). The regular strict quasi-concavity of the utility function ensures that the principal minors of $\mathcal{H}$, a subset of those of $\mathcal{J}$, will alternate in sign. Thus, limited excess demand functions exist on the assumption that u of the excess demands equal their upper bounds. These limited functions are the pseudo excess demand functions for all price points for which the values they generate for the $(m - u)$ unconstrained excess demands do not exceed their upper bounds.

The conventional excess demand functions (10-1) cover the case $u = 0$. The index u may assume values from 0 through $(m - 1)$. The assumptions underlying the utility function and the construction of the k_j's exclude the case in which all upper bounds are effective; that is, $u = m$. There are $m!/(m - u)!\,u!$ combinations[1] of the m possible upper bounds in which u upper bounds are effective. The total number of sets of limited excess demand functions (L) for all possible combinations is

$$L = \sum_{u=1}^{m-1} \frac{m!}{(m-u)!\,u!} = 2^m - 1$$

The number L may be very large, but is finite. Pseudo excess demand functions for the ith consumer, denoted by

$$E_{ij} = \hat{E}_{ij}(p_1, \ldots, p_m) \qquad j = 1, \ldots, m \tag{10-3}$$

are formed from the L sets of limited excess demand functions. The pseudo functions are not given by a single set of m individual equations as has been

---

[1] The number $n!$ (read n factorial) is the product of the integers 1 through n: $n! = 1 \cdot 2 \cdot 3 \cdots (n - 1)n$. By definition $0! = 1$.

the practice in most cases heretofore. They are given by L sets of m individual equations each and rules that specify which set is appropriate for each price point. By advanced methods it can be proved that the pseudo excess demand functions (1) have the normalized price set (10-2) as their domain, (2) are single-valued; i.e., if more than one set of limited excess demand functions is valid for a price point, each valid set will give identical values for the E_{ij} at that point, and (3) are continuous but in general do not have continuous first- and second-order partial derivatives. Since the underlying L sets of limited excess demand functions satisfy the consumer's budget constraint, the pseudo functions also satisfy it. The construction of pseudo functions would be a formidable task for even relatively small numbers of commodities. Fortunately, their construction is not necessary. It is only necessary to know that they exist and to know their properties.

A partition of the price simplex for pseudo excess demand functions is illustrated in Fig. 10-2. The price simplex is represented by a triangle in $p_1 p_2$-space. The value of p_3 is given implicitly by the identity $p_3 = 1 - p_1 - p_2$. The origin represents $(0, 0, 1)$. The hypotenuse is the locus of points for which $p_3 = 0$. All three prices are positive for points in the interior of the triangle.

For three goods there are seven $(2^3 - 1)$ sets of limited excess demand functions. The lines near the axes and the hypotenuse divide the simplex into seven areas corresponding to the seven sets. The effective limits for the seven areas are as follows:

Area	Effective limits
I	k_2
II	k_1
III	k_3
IV	k_1, k_2
V	k_2, k_3
VI	k_1, k_3
VII	None

The continuity of the pseudo functions is reflected by the boundaries for which one or more sets provide identical excess demands. An extreme case is given by point A for which the sets corresponding to I, III, V, and VII each provide the same excess demand levels. The boundaries need not be linear as illustrated in Fig. 10-2 (see Exercise 10-6).

The procedures for constructing excess demand functions for the firm are similar to those employed for the consumer. The entrepreneur of the hth firm in the jth industry uses the m goods as inputs for the production of the jth. He sells his output and buys his inputs in competitive markets at nonnegative prices. His production function is defined for nonnegative input and output levels, and is assumed to be strictly concave with strictly positive marginal

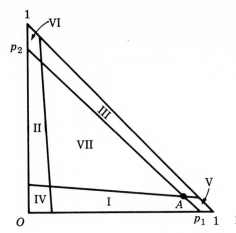

Figure 10-2

products. As before, the output level for the hth firm in the jth industry is denoted by $\bar{q}_{hj}$, and the quantity of the kth good that it uses as an input by q_{hjk}^*.

The following interior assumption is also invoked: $\bar{q}_{hj} = 0$ if $q_{hjk}^* = 0$ for some k, and $\bar{q}_{hj} > 0$ if $q_{hjk}^* > 0$ for all k with $\lim \bar{q}_{hj}/q_{hjk}^* = +\infty$ as $q_{hjk}^* \to 0$ and $\lim \bar{q}_{hj}/q_{hjk}^* = 0$ as $q_{hjk}^* \to +\infty$.

The restrictions placed upon the production function ensure satisfaction of the first- and second-order conditions for all points within the interior of the simplex, i.e., for all prices positive, and ensure the existence of conventional excess demand functions for this domain of the form

$$E_{hjk}^* = E_{hjk}^*(p_1, \ldots, p_m) \qquad k = 1, \ldots, m$$

$$\bar{E}_{hj} = \bar{E}_{hj}(p_1, \ldots, p_m)$$

(10-4)

The restrictions also imply ranges of $E_{hjk}^* > 0$ $(k = 1, \ldots, m)$ and $\bar{E}_{hj} < 0$.

The conventional functions (10-4) do not directly accommodate zero prices. Pseudo excess demand functions are defined for the producer on the assumption that he maximizes profit subject to the additional requirements that $E_{hju}^* = q_{hju}^* \leq k_u$ $(u = 1, \ldots, m)$. No direct limit is placed upon his output level. Output and input levels are assumed to equal zero if output price equals zero: $\bar{q}_{hj} = q_{hj1}^* = \cdots = q_{hjm}^* = 0$ if $p_j = 0$. Limited excess demand functions are defined for each possible combination of effective upper bounds by substituting the appropriate $q_{hju}^* = k_u$ into the firm's profit equation and determining optimal values as functions of prices for the remaining input levels and the output level. Pseudo excess demand functions for the jth firm in the hth industry, denoted by

$$E_{hjk}^* = \hat{E}_{hjk}^*(p_1, \ldots, p_m) \qquad k = 1, \ldots, m$$

$$\bar{E}_{hj} = \hat{E}_{hj}(p_1, \ldots, p_m)$$

(10-5)

are formed from the limited functions. As in the case of the consumer, it can be proved that (1) the pseudo functions have the normalized price set as their domain, (2) they are single-valued, and (3) they are continuous.

By advanced methods it can be proved that each firm's maximum profit is positive if its output price is positive and zero if its output price is zero. The significance of this is twofold. First, it means that no firm will produce at a negative profit. Second, it means that each consumer will have a positive income if any price is positive. Each consumer has a positive stock of each primary good, and will have a positive income if the price of any primary good is positive. If the prices of all primary goods are zero, he will still have a positive profit income if any output price is positive. This is a consequence of the assumption that each consumer has a share of profits from at least one firm in every industry.

Conventional aggregate excess demand functions for the domain $p_k > 0$ $(k = 1, \ldots, m)$,

$$E_j = E_j(p_1, \ldots, p_m) \qquad j = 1, \ldots, m \qquad (10\text{-}6)$$

are obtained by summing the conventional functions for the individual consumers and producers given by (10-1) and (10-4) respectively. Aggregate pseudo excess demand functions with the normalized price set as their domain, denoted by

$$E_j = \hat{E}_j(p_1, \ldots, p_m) \qquad j = 1, \ldots, m \qquad (10\text{-}7)$$

are formed from the pseudo functions for the individual consumers and producers given by (10-3) and (10-5) respectively. For each price point the aggregate pseudo functions give the sums of the excess demands dictated by the appropriate limited functions for each individual consumer and producer. The continuity of both sets of aggregate functions follows from the continuity of the corresponding individual functions. Each set of aggregate functions satisfies Walras' law. An important property of the aggregate pseudo functions from the viewpoint of an existence proof is that E_j is positive and finite if $p_j = 0$.

Existence of Equilibrium Prices[1]

In general, a multimarket equilibrium exists if there is at least one normalized price point such that

$$E_j = 0 \quad \text{if } p_j > 0 \quad \text{and} \quad E_j \leq 0 \quad \text{if } p_j = 0 \quad j = 1, \ldots, m$$

For notational convenience let a point in the normalized price set be denoted by $\mathbf{p} = (p_1, \ldots, p_m)$. The normalized price set is closed, bounded, and convex. For $m = 2$ it is a line from $(1,0)$ to $(0,1)$. For $m = 3$ it is a triangle. The

---

[1] The general form of the existence proof used here was suggested by J. G. Kemeny and J. L. Snell, *Mathematical Methods in the Social Sciences* (Boston: Ginn, 1962), pp. 38–39.

existence proof proceeds by devising a suitable mapping of the normalized price set into itself, showing that it has a fixed point, and demonstrating that the fixed point defines a multimarket equilibrium.

Define m functions by

$$g_j(\mathbf{p}) = \max\,[p_j + \hat{E}_j(\mathbf{p}), 0.5p_j] > 0 \qquad j = 1, \ldots, m \tag{10-8}$$

Since by (10-2) prices cannot be negative and since a zero price implies a positive excess demand, it follows that all the functions of (10-8) always have positive values. Let

$$h(\mathbf{p}) = \sum_{j=1}^{m} g_j(\mathbf{p}) > 0 \tag{10-9}$$

Since $h(\mathbf{p})$ is always positive, division by it is a legitimate operation. Define m new functions by

$$f_j(\mathbf{p}) = \frac{g_j(\mathbf{p})}{h(\mathbf{p})} > 0 \qquad j = 1, \ldots, m \tag{10-10}$$

These functions define a continuous mapping of prices. The continuity of the mapping follows from the continuity of (10-8) and (10-9). Since

$$\sum_{j=1}^{m} f_j(\mathbf{p}) = \frac{\sum_{j=1}^{m} g_j(\mathbf{p})}{h(\mathbf{p})} = 1$$

by (10-9), the image points satisfy the definitions of the normalized price set, and (10-10) maps this set into itself. It follows from Brouwer's fixed-point theorem that the normalized price set contains at least one point $\mathbf{p}^*$ such that

$$p_j^* = f_j(\mathbf{p}^*) = \frac{g_j(\mathbf{p}^*)}{h(\mathbf{p}^*)} > 0 \qquad j = 1, \ldots, m \tag{10-11}$$

All components of $\mathbf{p}^*$ are positive since (10-11) is a special case of (10-10). It remains to be shown that all excess demands equal zero at a point defined by (10-11) before it can be concluded that such a point constitutes a multimarket equilibrium.

Each $g_j(\mathbf{p}^*)$ is at least as great as $0.5p_j^*$. If each $g_j(\mathbf{p}^*)$ were equal to $0.5p_j^*$, the sum $h(\mathbf{p}^*)$ would equal 0.5 as established by (10-8) and (10-2). If any $g_j(\mathbf{p}^*)$ exceeds $0.5p_j^*$, $h(\mathbf{p}^*)$ will exceed 0.5. If all $g_j(\mathbf{p}^*) = 0.5p_j^*$, it follows from (10-8) that all $\hat{E}_j(\mathbf{p}^*) < 0$. This implies that $\sum_{j=1}^{m} p_j^* \hat{E}_j(\mathbf{p}^*) < 0$, which contradicts Walras' law. Thus, it cannot be true that $g_j(\mathbf{p}^*) = 0.5p_j^*$ for all j. Assume that it is true for some j. Then from (10-11)

$$p_j^* = \frac{g_j(\mathbf{p}^*)}{h(\mathbf{p}^*)} = \frac{0.5p_j^*}{h(\mathbf{p}^*)} < p_j^*$$

since $h(\mathbf{p}^*) > 0.5$, but this is also a contradiction. It then follows from (10-8) and (10-11) that

$$p_j^* = \frac{p_j^* + \hat{E}_j(\mathbf{p}^*)}{h(\mathbf{p}^*)} \qquad j = 1, \ldots, m \tag{10-12}$$

Multiplying both sides of the jth equation of (10-12) by $\hat{E}_j(\mathbf{p}^*)$ and adding the resultant m equations,

$$\sum_{j=1}^{m} p_j^* \hat{E}_j(\mathbf{p}^*) = \frac{\sum_{i=1}^{m} p_i^* \hat{E}_i(\mathbf{p}^*) + \sum_{j=1}^{m} [\hat{E}_j(\mathbf{p}^*)]^2}{h(\mathbf{p}^*)}$$

It follows from Walras' law that the left-hand side and the first term in the numerator on the right-hand side are zero. Thus,

$$\sum_{j=1}^{m} [\hat{E}_j(\mathbf{p}^*)]^2 = 0$$

A sum of squares can equal zero only if each term equals zero; hence $\hat{E}_j(\mathbf{p}^*) = 0$ for all j, and the fixed point $\mathbf{p}^*$ is a multimarket equilibrium set of prices. Since all equilibrium prices are positive, (10-6) gives the aggregate excess demands, and (10-1) and (10-4) give the individual excess demands.[1] The consumption level for each good by each consumer is positive and finite. The output and input levels for each producer are positive and finite.

A great deal of effort was expended in defining pseudo excess demands for zero prices only to discover that the restrictions placed upon the individual utility and production functions always generate positive equilibrium prices. However, if the zero-price case had not been accommodated, it would not have been possible to define a mapping of the *closed* normalized price set (10-2), and Brouwer's fixed-point theorem would not have been applicable.

Advanced Existence Proofs

Existence was proved for a competitive economy for which individual utility and production functions are continuous with continuous first- and second-order partial derivatives and obey stated restrictions. This, as all other existence proofs, is based upon a sufficiency rather than a necessity argument. All systems that satisfy the restrictions possess equilibrium points, but there are systems with equilibrium points that do not satisfy them. A number of authors have employed advanced mathematics to formulate existence proofs that are based upon generally weaker restrictions.[2]

One of the most complete and least restrictive existence proofs was formulated by Gerard Debreu.[3] It is summarized in approximate form here. Analysis is in terms of point sets rather than functions. To prove existence, Debreu utilizes the Kakutani fixed-point theorem, which generalizes the

---

[1] The k_j are defined to be too large to be consistent with the economy's endowments. Consequently, none of the excess demand limits is effective in equilibrium. Equilibrium prices lie in areas comparable to area VII in Fig. 10-2.

[2] An excellent summary of the assumptions employed by different authors is given by James Quirk and Rubin Saposnik, *Introduction to General Equilibrium Theory and Welfare Economics* (New York: McGraw-Hill, 1968), chap. 3.

[3] *Theory of Value* (New York: Wiley, 1959).

Brouwer theorem from point-to-point to point-to-set mappings. A consumption set for the ith consumer is defined as the collection of all possible points representing commodity consumption levels (nonnegative numbers) and endowments (nonpositive numbers). It is assumed that each consumer's consumption set (1) is closed, convex, and bounded from below, (2) contains no saturation point, and (3) contains a bundle strictly smaller than the consumer's initial endowment. Assumptions about consumer preferences are based upon rankings. A consumer's optimum consumption bundle for a given set of prices need not be unique.

A firm is allowed to produce more than one good. Outputs are described by positive and inputs by negative numbers. It is assumed that each firm may remain idle using no inputs. Debreu's remaining assumptions about production cover the economy as a whole rather than individual firms. An aggregate production set is defined as all possible input and output combinations for the economy as a whole. The aggregate production set is assumed to be closed and convex. Thus, increasing returns are not possible for the economy, but they are possible for individual firms. Free disposal of inputs is allowed. Production is assumed to be irreversible; i.e., inputs cannot be produced with outputs. All competitive economies that fulfill Debreu's assumptions have one or more equilibrium points. However, there are systems that violate one or more of his assumptions that possess equilibrium points.

10-2 STABILITY OF EQUILIBRIUM

Once existence has been proved, one may ask under what conditions a system will return to an equilibrium point following a disturbance, and under what conditions a system will have only one equilibrium point. Meaningful statements can be made about stability and uniqueness for systems that conform to the general assumptions considered in the preceding section. As yet, little can be said about systems that adhere to the relatively weak assumptions of the Debreu existence proof. Since the analysis of stability provides guidelines for the analysis of uniqueness, stability is considered first.

The effects of a disturbance in one market upon the equilibria in other markets are ignored in Sec. 6-8 in accordance with the assumptions of partial equilibrium analysis. A general equilibrium analysis involves an explicit recognition of the interrelated nature of all markets. The excess demand for each good is a function of the prices of all goods. A disturbance in one market normally will upset equilibrium in other markets. The stability of a single market depends upon the adjustments following the induced disturbances in other markets. Both the static and dynamic conditions for stability in a single market are extended to a multimarket system in the present section. The static conditions are often called the *Hicksian* conditions in honor of their formulator, J. R. Hicks. The Walrasian behavior assumptions (see Sec. 6-8) are employed throughout the present section.

Static Stability

Let Q_1 serve as numéraire and set its price identically equal to unity. The stability condition for a two-market system is the same as the condition for a single market. There is only one independent equation and only one variable price: $E_1 = E_1(p_2)$ and $E_2 = E_2(p_2)$. The aggregate budget constraint, Walras' law, $E_1 + p_2 E_2 = 0$, is always satisfied. A relaxation of the equilibrium condition for Q_2 so that $E_2 \neq 0$ necessarily implies a relaxation of the equilibrium condition for Q_1 such that $dE_1 + p_2\, dE_2 = 0$. The differentials dE_1 and dE_2 and therefore the derivatives dE_1/dp_2 and dE_2/dp_2 must be of opposite sign except for the trivial case in which both equal zero. Equilibrium is stable according to the static Walrasian assumption if $dE_2/dp_2 < 0$ (or equivalently if $dE_1/dp_2 > 0$). If equilibrium is restored in the market for Q_2, equilibrium is automatically restored in the market for the numéraire; i.e., if E_2 equals zero, E_1 must also equal zero. The unique problems of multimarket stability arise only for systems with three or more interrelated markets.

If $\partial E_k/\partial p_j \neq 0$, a displacement of equilibrium in the market for Q_j will cause a displacement of equilibrium in the market for Q_k. Walrasian stability for an isolated market requires that $\partial E_j/\partial p_j < 0$ where $\partial E_j/\partial p_j$ is a partial derivative and all other prices are assumed to remain unchanged. The total derivative dE_j/dp_j must be utilized for a multimarket analysis. Its value may be computed under a number of alternative assumptions regarding the adjustment of other markets. One possibility is to assume that equilibrium is restored in all markets other than those for Q_j and the numéraire.[1] There are many possible price-adjustment patterns other than the case of complete inflexibility, in which none of the other $(m-2)$ markets adjusts, and the case of complete flexibility, in which they all adjust. In general, one can imagine a system with M "rigid prices" which will not change from their initial equilibrium values during the period under consideration where M may be any number from one through $(m-1)$. The price of the numéraire is always rigid as a result of its definition.

The most stringent stability conditions for the market for Q_j $(j \neq 1)$ require that the total derivative dE_j/dp_j be negative for all possible combinations of rigid and flexible prices. The market for Q_j is perfectly stable by the Hicksian definition if $dE_j/dp_j < 0$ under the following conditions: (1) if all the $(m-1)$ prices other than p_j are rigid, (2) if $(m-2)$ of the prices are rigid but p_h is flexible and adjusts so that $E_h = 0$, (3) if $(m-3)$ of the prices are rigid but p_h and p_k are flexible and adjust so that $E_h = 0$ and $E_k = 0$, and so on up to the final case in which the prices of all goods other than the numéraire are flexible. The system as a whole is perfectly stable if the $(m-1)$ markets for the goods other than the numéraire are perfectly stable.

---

[1] Since the aggregate budget constraint is always satisfied, $p_j E_j + E_1 = 0$ if Q_1 is numéraire. The violation of the equilibrium condition for the numéraire provides the slack necessary to allow the excess demand for Q_j to take on a nonzero value.

The excess demand functions for a system with m goods are

$$E_j = E_j(p_2, \ldots, p_m) \qquad j = 2, \ldots, m \qquad (10\text{-}13)$$

The excess demand function for the numéraire is omitted, since it can be derived from the other $(m - 1)$. The effects of price changes upon the excess demands are computed by total differentiation of (10-13),

$$
\begin{aligned}
dE_2 &= b_{22}\, dp_2 + b_{23}\, dp_3 + \cdots + b_{2m}\, dp_m \\
dE_3 &= b_{32}\, dp_2 + b_{33}\, dp_3 + \cdots + b_{3m}\, dp_m \\
&\cdots\cdots\cdots\cdots\cdots\cdots\cdots\cdots\cdots\cdots \\
dE_m &= b_{m2}\, dp_2 + b_{m3}\, dp_3 + \cdots + b_{mm}\, dp_m
\end{aligned}
\qquad (10\text{-}14)
$$

where $b_{jk} = \partial E_j / \partial p_k$. Since b_{jk} may be assumed constant in a small neighborhood about an equilibrium point, (10-14) forms a system of $(m - 1)$ simultaneous linear equations in the $(m - 1)$ variables $(dp_2, \ldots, dp_m)$. The coefficients of (10-14) form the Jacobian of $E_2, \ldots, E_m$ with respect to $p_2, \ldots, p_m$.

Consider the case in which equilibrium is displaced in the market for Q_j and all other prices are rigid. Substituting $dp_k = 0$ for $k = 2, \ldots, m$ and $j \neq k$ into (10-14) the $(j-1)$st equation becomes[1]

$$dE_j = b_{jj}\, dp_j$$

Dividing through by dp_j, the first condition for the perfect stability of the market for Q_j is

$$\frac{dE_j}{dp_j} = b_{jj} < 0 \qquad (10\text{-}15)$$

Condition (10-15) is identical with the stability requirement for an isolated market. Perfect stability for the system as a whole requires that (10-15) hold for $j = 2, \ldots, m$, and thus the first condition for perfect stability requires the isolated stability of every market in the system.

Now consider the case in which equilibrium is displaced in the market for Q_j, p_h adjusts, and all other prices are rigid. Substituting $d\dot{E}_h = 0$ and $dp_k = 0$ for $k \neq j, h$ into (10-14), the equations for Q_j and Q_h become

$$dE_j = b_{jj}\, dp_j + b_{jh}\, dp_h$$

$$0 = b_{hj}\, dp_j + b_{hh}\, dp_h$$

---

[1] A displacement of equilibrium in the market for Q_j will cause displacements of the equilibria in the other markets. The other equations of (10-14) become

$$dE_k = b_{kj}\, dp_j$$

Since the other prices are assumed rigid, these displacements will not react back upon the excess demand for Q_j, and nonzero excess demands will continue to exist in the other markets.

Using Cramer's rule to solve for dp_j,

$$dp_j = \frac{\begin{vmatrix} dE_j & b_{jh} \\ 0 & b_{hh} \end{vmatrix}}{\begin{vmatrix} b_{jj} & b_{jh} \\ b_{hj} & b_{hh} \end{vmatrix}} = dE_j \frac{b_{hh}}{\begin{vmatrix} b_{jj} & b_{jh} \\ b_{hj} & b_{hh} \end{vmatrix}}$$

Dividing through by the constant term on the right and by dp_j, the second condition for the perfect stability of the market for Q_j is

$$\frac{dE_j}{dp_j} = \frac{\begin{vmatrix} b_{jj} & b_{jh} \\ b_{hj} & b_{hh} \end{vmatrix}}{b_{hh}} < 0 \qquad (10\text{-}16)$$

Perfect stability of the market for Q_h requires that the denominator of (10-16) be negative. Therefore, perfect stability for the system as a whole requires that the numerator of (10-16) be positive.

Finally, consider the case in which equilibrium is displaced in the market for Q_j, p_h and p_i adjust, and the other $(m-4)$ prices are rigid. Substituting $dE_h = dE_i = 0$ and $dp_k = 0$ for the other $(m-4)$ prices into (5-58), the relevant equations become

$$dE_j = b_{jj}\, dp_j + b_{jh}\, dp_h + b_{ji}\, dp_i$$
$$0 = b_{hj}\, dp_j + b_{hh}\, dp_h + b_{hi}\, dp_i$$
$$0 = b_{ij}\, dp_j + b_{ih}\, dp_h + b_{ii}\, dp_i$$

Using Cramer's rule to solve for dp_j,

$$dp_j = \begin{vmatrix} dE_j & b_{jh} & b_{ji} \\ 0 & b_{hh} & b_{hi} \\ 0 & b_{ih} & b_{ii} \end{vmatrix} : \begin{vmatrix} b_{jj} & b_{jh} & b_{ji} \\ b_{hj} & b_{hh} & b_{hi} \\ b_{ij} & b_{ih} & b_{ii} \end{vmatrix}$$

Expanding the numerator by its first column and solving for dE_j/dp_j, the third condition for the perfect stability of the market for Q_j is

$$\frac{dE_j}{dp_j} = \begin{vmatrix} b_{jj} & b_{jh} & b_{ji} \\ b_{hj} & b_{hh} & b_{hi} \\ b_{ij} & b_{ih} & b_{ii} \end{vmatrix} : \begin{vmatrix} b_{hh} & b_{hi} \\ b_{ih} & b_{ii} \end{vmatrix} < 0 \qquad (10\text{-}17)$$

Letting $j = h$ and $h = i$ in requirement (10-16), perfect stability of the market for Q_h requires that the denominator of (10-17) be positive. Therefore, perfect stability for the system as a whole requires that the numerator of (10-17) be negative.

Perfect stability for the system as a whole requires that the Jacobian determinants of order $[1, 2, 3, \ldots, (m-1)]$:

$$b_{jj}, \begin{vmatrix} b_{jj} & b_{jh} \\ b_{hj} & b_{hh} \end{vmatrix}, \begin{vmatrix} b_{jj} & b_{jh} & b_{ji} \\ b_{hj} & b_{hh} & b_{hi} \\ b_{ij} & b_{ih} & b_{ii} \end{vmatrix}, \ldots$$

be alternatively negative and positive for all values of $j, h, i, \ldots$.

The conditions for perfect stability are stronger than necessary for the consideration of many multimarket systems. If the system contains no rigid prices, the only relevant value for dE_j/dp_j is the one computed on the assumption that the other $(m-2)$ markets adjust. Following the computational procedure outlined above, the market for Q_2 is stable if

$$\frac{dE_2}{dp_2} = \frac{\mathscr{B}}{\mathscr{B}_{22}} < 0 \tag{10-18}$$

where $\mathscr{B}$ is the Jacobian determinant of the complete system given by (10-14) and $\mathscr{B}_{22}$ is the cofactor of b_{22}. In the Hicksian terminology the system as a whole is *imperfectly stable* if a condition similar to (10-18) holds for all goods other than the numéraire. It is interesting to note that imperfect stability does not necessarily imply the isolated stability of each market.

Consider the following excess demand functions for three-commodity systems:

(1) $E_2 = -2p_2 + 3p_3 - 5$ $E_3 = 4p_2 - 8p_3 + 16$
(2) $E_2 = 2p_2 - 3p_3 + 5$ $E_3 = -4p_2 + 4p_3 - 4$
(3) $E_2 = 2p_2 + 3p_3 - 13$ $E_3 = 4p_2 - 8p_3 + 16$

The equilibrium prices are $p_2 = 2$ and $p_3 = 3$ for all three examples. System (1) satisfies all the conditions for perfect stability:

$$\frac{dE_2}{dp_2} = \frac{\partial E_2}{\partial p_2} = -2 < 0 \qquad \frac{dE_2}{dp_2} = \frac{\begin{vmatrix} -2 & 3 \\ 4 & -8 \end{vmatrix}}{-8} = -0.5 < 0$$

$$\frac{dE_3}{dp_3} = \frac{\partial E_3}{\partial p_3} = -8 < 0 \qquad \frac{dE_3}{dp_3} = \frac{\begin{vmatrix} -2 & 3 \\ 4 & -8 \end{vmatrix}}{-2} = -2 < 0$$

System (2) fails to satisfy the conditions for perfect stability, but satisfies the conditions for imperfect stability:

$$\frac{dE_2}{dp_2} = \frac{\begin{vmatrix} 2 & -3 \\ -4 & 4 \end{vmatrix}}{4} = -1 < 0 \qquad \frac{dE_3}{dp_3} = \frac{\begin{vmatrix} 2 & -3 \\ -4 & 4 \end{vmatrix}}{2} = -2 < 0$$

The markets for both Q_2 and Q_3 are unstable when considered in isolation, but the system as a whole is stable if both prices adjust. System (3) fails to satisfy the conditions for either perfect or imperfect stability.

Dynamic Stability

The conditions for the dynamic stability of a multimarket system with continuous adjustment represent a generalization of the conditions for the dynamic stability of a single market with continuous adjustment as presented in Sec. 6-8. An explicit statement of the laws of price change is introduced, and the time paths of the prices following a disturbance are investigated. Many different types of dynamic adjustment processes may be introduced to describe the behavior of the participants in particular systems. In general, a multimarket equilibrium is dynamically stable if every price approaches an equilibrium level over time following a slight displacement from equilibrium, i.e., if

$$\lim_{t \to \infty} p_{jt} = p_{je} \qquad j = 2, \ldots, m$$

where p_{jt} is the price of Q_j at time t and p_{je} is an equilibrium price of Q_j.

Assume that the first of the m goods is again numéraire. The dynamic adjustment equations are

$$\frac{dp_j}{dt} = k_j E_j(p_2, \ldots, p_m) \qquad j = 2, \ldots, m \qquad (10\text{-}19)$$

where the $k_j > 0$ are speed of adjustment coefficients. Assume that units are defined so that all k_j equal one.

The total differential of the jth excess demand function is

$$dE_j = \sum_{k=2}^{m} \frac{\partial E_j}{\partial p_k} dp_k \qquad j = 2, \ldots, m$$

An analog to the approximation (6-23) for a single market is obtained by replacing the differentials dE_j and dp_k with deviations from equilibrium values, $E_j - E_{je}$ and $p_k - p_{ke}$:

$$E_j \approx \sum_{k=2}^{m} \frac{\partial E_j}{\partial p_k} (p_k - p_{ke}) \qquad j = 2, \ldots, m \qquad (10\text{-}20)$$

since $E_{je} = 0$. Substituting from (10-20) into (10-19),

$$\frac{dp_j}{dt} = b_{j2}p_2 + \cdots + b_{jm}p_m + c_j \qquad j = 2, \ldots, m \qquad (10\text{-}21)$$

where the c_j are constants that depend upon the equilibrium values of the prices. The local stability properties of (10-19) are ascertained from an examination of the solution of this system of simultaneous linear differential equations. A solution of (10-21) (see Sec. A-6) is of the form[1]

$$p_j = a_{j2}e^{\lambda_2 t} + \cdots + a_{jm}e^{\lambda_m t} + p_{je} \qquad j = 2, \ldots, m \qquad (10\text{-}22)$$

where the a_{jk} are coefficients depending on the initial conditions and the λ_k are the $(m - 1)$ roots of the polynomial given by

$$\begin{vmatrix} b_{22} - \lambda & \cdots & b_{2m} \\ \cdots\cdots\cdots\cdots\cdots\cdots \\ b_{m2} & \cdots & b_{mm} - \lambda \end{vmatrix} = \beta_{m-1}\lambda^{m-1} + \cdots + \beta_1\lambda + \beta_0 = 0 \qquad (10\text{-}23)$$

The time paths of the p_j will converge to their equilibrium values p_{je} if each of the $(m - 1)$ roots of (10-23) is negative or has a negative real part.

---

[1] The form of (10-22) requires slight modification if two or more of the roots are identical. The local stability condition, however, remains unchanged.

In general, Hicksian stability is neither necessary nor sufficient for dynamic stability in the case of continuous adjustment. Advanced mathematics has been used to prove theorems about the conditions under which (10-19) is stable and the conditions under which Hicksian and dynamic stability are synonymous.[1] An important theorem states that *the dynamic system is locally stable and also has Hicksian stability if all commodities are strict gross substitutes*; that is, $b_{ii} < 0$ for all i, and $b_{ij} > 0$ for all $j \neq i$.

This theorem is now proved for the three-good case. Hicksian stability requires that

$$b_{22} < 0 \qquad b_{33} < 0 \qquad b_{22}b_{33} - b_{23}b_{32} > 0 \qquad (10\text{-}24)$$

The first two inequalities of (10-24) follow immediately from gross substitutability. Differentiating the aggregate budget constraint totally,

$$dE_1 + p_2\, dE_2 + E_2\, dp_2 + p_3\, dE_3 + E_3\, dp_3 = 0$$

Let $dp_3 = 0$, and alternately let $dp_2 = 0$:

$$b_{12} + p_2 b_{22} + E_2 + p_3 b_{32} = 0$$
$$b_{13} + p_2 b_{23} + p_3 b_{33} + E_3 = 0$$

At equilibrium $E_2 = E_3 = 0$:

$$p_2 b_{22} + p_3 b_{32} = -b_{12} < 0$$
$$p_2 b_{23} + p_3 b_{33} = -b_{13} < 0$$

and

$$-p_2 b_{22} > p_3 b_{32} \qquad -p_3 b_{33} > p_2 b_{23}$$

Since the right-hand sides in these inequalities are positive by assumption, all four terms are positive, and their product is

$$p_2 p_3 b_{22} b_{33} > p_2 p_3 b_{23} b_{32}$$

which establishes the third inequality of (10-24). Therefore, gross substitutability implies Hicksian stability.

For the three-good case the polynomial of (10-23) is

$$\lambda^2 + \beta_1 \lambda + \beta_0 = \lambda^2 - (b_{22} + b_{33})\lambda + (b_{22}b_{33} - b_{23}b_{32}) = 0$$

Since β_1 and β_0 are both positive, both roots are negative if real, or have negative real parts if complex. Therefore, gross substitutability implies that the dynamic system is locally stable.

A system is *globally stable* if it will return to equilibrium following a disturbance of any magnitude. The analysis of global stability for a unique

---

[1] The major source of stability theorems is K. J. Arrow and L. Hurwicz, "On the Stability of Competitive Equilibrium, I," *Econometrica*, vol. 26 (October, 1958), pp. 522–552; and K. J. Arrow, H. D. Block, and L. Hurwicz, "On the Stability of Competitive Equilibrium, II," *ibid.*, vol. 27 (January, 1959), pp. 82–109. Advanced mathematics is employed in these articles. Simplified discussions of these and other stability theorems are given by J. Quirk and R. Saposnik, *op. cit.*, chap. 5.

equilibrium using a Liapunov function (see Sec. 6-8) is easily extended to multimarket systems. Define a Liapunov function, $V(t)$, as the squared distance of the prices from their equilibrium values:

$$V(t) = \sum_{j=1}^{m} [p_j - p_{je}]^2 \qquad (10\text{-}25)$$

This function has the necessary properties: it equals zero if all prices are at their equilibrium values and is positive if one or more prices are not. A system is globally stable if $dV(t)/dt < 0$ whenever $p_j \neq p_{je}$ for some j.

The analysis is illustrated by proving the following theorem: *A system that possesses a unique equilibrium and satisfies the Weak axiom of revealed preference (see Sec. 3-5) in the aggregate is globally stable.* Differentiating (10-25), substituting $dp_j/dt = E_j$ from (10-19), and invoking Walras' law,

$$\frac{dV(t)}{dt} = 2 \sum_{j=1}^{m} (p_j - p_{je}) \frac{dp_j}{dt} = 2 \sum_{j=1}^{m} (p_j - p_{je}) E_j = -2 \sum_{j=1}^{m} p_{je} E_j \qquad (10\text{-}26)$$

In terms of excess demands the Weak axiom states that

$$\sum_{j=1}^{m} p_j E_{je} \leq \sum_{j=1}^{m} p_j E_j \qquad \text{implies} \qquad \sum_{j=1}^{m} p_{je} E_{je} < \sum_{j=1}^{m} p_{je} E_j \qquad (10\text{-}27)$$

where the p_j are prices such that $p_j \neq p_{je}$ for one or more j, and the E_j are the excess demands that correspond to these prices. The left side of the first expression in (10-27) equals zero because $E_{je} = 0$ for all j, and the right side equals zero by Walras' law. Thus, the strict equality holds for the first expression, and the second expression is valid. The left side of the second expression in (10-27) also equals zero. Therefore, $\sum_{j=1}^{m} p_{je} E_j > 0$, the derivative (10-26) is negative, and the system is globally stable.

10-3 UNIQUENESS OF EQUILIBRIUM

Most existence proofs state that classes of multimarket systems have one or more equilibrium points. Uniqueness proofs state that subclasses of systems satisfying existence proofs have unique equilibrium points. Most of the observations about uniqueness for a single market in Sec. 6-7 can be extended to multimarket systems. In general, if the total derivatives dE_j/dp_j $(j = 2, \ldots, m)$ do not change sign and do not equal zero for any values of the p_j, there cannot be more than one equilibrium point. This is a sufficient, but not necessary, condition for uniqueness.

A variety of cases is illustrated for two-commodity systems in Fig. 10-3. In Fig. 10-3a, $dE_2/dp_2 < 0$ throughout, but there is no equilibrium point, and a consideration of uniqueness is meaningless. This case emphasizes that an existence proof must precede a uniqueness proof. In Fig. 10-3b, $dE_2/dp_2 < 0$ throughout, there is a unique equilibrium point, and it is globally stable. In Fig. 10-3c, $dE_2/dp_2 > 0$ throughout, there is a unique equilibrium point, but it

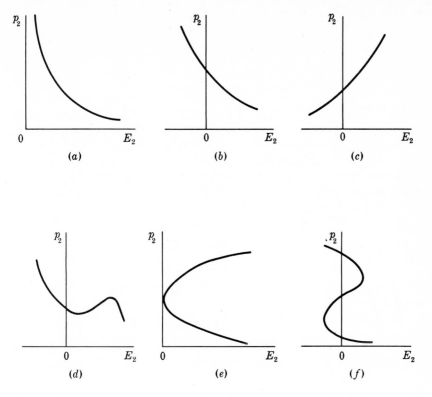

Figure 10-3

is unstable. Cases of this type are of limited interest because of their instability. The systems illustrated in Fig. 10-3d and 10-3e have unique equilibrium points, but do not satisfy the condition for dE_2/dp_2. In Fig. 10-3f the condition is violated, and there are multiple equilibrium points.

Hicksian stability [see Eqs. (10-15) to (10-18)] requires that $dE_j/dp_j < 0$ for all j in a neighborhood of equilibrium. A system that satisfies the Hicksian stability conditions throughout has a unique equilibrium. Thus, a uniqueness proof can proceed by proving Hicksian stability throughout. In the last subsection it was proved that gross substitutability for a three-good system implies Hicksian stability throughout. Thereby, gross substitutability for a three-good system implies a unique equilibrium point. This theorem may be generalized to m goods.

If the Weak axiom (10-27) holds for the aggregate excess demands, uniqueness follows trivially. Proof is by contradiction. Assume that there are two equilibrium points, and evaluate (10-27) for these points. The first relation of (10-27) is satisfied because $E_{je} = E_j = 0$. For the same reason both terms in the second relation of (10-27) are zero, and it becomes $0 < 0$, which is a contradiction.

10-4 THE INPUT-OUTPUT MODEL

The input-output model, sometimes called the Leontief model for its originator W. W. Leontief, provides a multimarket analysis with empirical orientation. Its basic assumptions are rather different from those of the models thus far considered. Utility functions are omitted, and consumer demands are usually treated as exogenous without explicit regard to the equilibrium of individual consumers.[1] The industry, rather than the firm, is the unit of production. Each industry uses a single linear production activity to produce a single output. Both produced outputs and nonproduced factors serve as inputs. These assumptions allow equilibria to be determined from the solutions of simultaneous linear equations. The parameters for such equations are often determined empirically.

Output Determination

Assume that an economy has m produced goods and n nonproduced factors. A linear production activity (see Sec. 5-6) for the jth industry $(j = 1, \ldots, m)$ gives the minimum quantities of the two types of inputs necessary to secure one unit of the jth good: $a_{ij} \geq 0$ $(i = 1, \ldots, m)$ for the produced inputs and $b_{ij} \geq 0$ $(i = 1, \ldots, n)$ for the factors. The output of the ith industry, q_i, is absorbed by interindustry input uses and final consumption uses, y_i:

$$q_i = a_{i1}q_1 + a_{i2}q_2 + \cdots + a_{im}q_m + y_i \qquad i = 1, \ldots, m$$

Moving the output variables to the left-hand side, the input-output balance equations may be written as

$$
\begin{aligned}
(1 - a_{11})q_1 - \quad a_{12}q_2 \ -\cdots- \quad a_{1m}q_m &= y_1 \\
- a_{21}q_1 \ +(1 - a_{22})q_2 -\cdots- \quad a_{2m}q_m &= y_2 \\
\cdots \cdots \cdots \cdots \cdots \cdots \cdots \cdots \cdots \\
- a_{m1}q_1 \ - \quad a_{m2}q_2 \ -\cdots+(1 - a_{mm})q_m &= y_m
\end{aligned}
\qquad (10\text{-}28)
$$

The quantity of each good available for final consumption equals total output less interindustry input requirements.

Cramer's rule may be applied to express output levels as functions of final consumption levels if the determinant of the coefficient array of (10-28), $\mathscr{A}$, is not zero:

$$
\begin{aligned}
q_1 &= \beta_{11}y_1 + \beta_{12}y_2 + \cdots + \beta_{1m}y_m \\
q_2 &= \beta_{21}y_1 + \beta_{22}y_2 + \cdots + \beta_{2m}y_m \\
\cdots \cdots \cdots \cdots \cdots \cdots \cdots \cdots \\
q_m &= \beta_{m1}y_1 + \beta_{m2}y_2 + \cdots + \beta_{mm}y_m
\end{aligned}
\qquad (10\text{-}29)
$$

---

[1] An "open" input-output system contains one or more exogenous sectors. All sectors are endogenous in a "closed" system. Nearly all current analysis is for "open" systems, and the description in the text is limited to these. The reader interested in the properties of a closed system is referred to Wassily W. Leontief, *The Structure of American Economy, 1919–1939* (2d ed., New York: Oxford, 1951).

where $\beta_{ij} = \mathcal{A}_{ji}/\mathcal{A}$ is the cofactor of the element in the jth row and ith column of the array (10-28), $\mathcal{A}_{ji}$, divided by the determinant of the array. Equations (10-29) provide a general solution for the input-output system (10-28) if $q_i \geqq 0$ $(i = 1, \ldots, m)$ whenever $y_i \geqq 0$ $(i = 1, \ldots, m)$. A necessary and sufficient condition for (10-29) to be a general solution is that $\beta_{ij} \geqq 0$ $(i,j = 1, \ldots, m)$. Existence conditions in terms of the a_{ij} are considered below. In the meantime limit attention to systems for which (10-29) is a general solution.

The coefficient β_{ij} for $i \neq j$ gives the direct and indirect input requirements for the ith good necessary to support one unit of final consumption of the jth. The direct requirement is a_{ij}. The indirect requirements are the inputs of i necessary to produce the inputs of the m goods necessary for j, the inputs necessary to produce those inputs, and so on. It follows that $\beta_{ij} \geqq a_{ij}$. The coefficient β_{jj} gives the direct and indirect input requirements of j for j to cover the unit of final consumption. It follows that $\beta_{jj} \geqq 1 + a_{jj}$. Factor requirements are easily determined from output requirements:

$$x_i = b_{i1}q_1 + b_{i2}q_2 + \cdots + b_{im}q_m \qquad i = 1, \ldots, n$$

where x_i is the quantity of the ith nonproduced factor used as an input. Substituting for the q_j from (10-29),

$$x_i = \gamma_{i1}y_1 + \gamma_{i2}y_2 + \cdots + \gamma_{im}y_m \qquad i = 1, \ldots, n \qquad (10\text{-}30)$$

where
$$\gamma_{ij} = \sum_{h=1}^{m} b_{ih}\beta_{hj} = 0 \qquad \begin{matrix} i = 1, \ldots, n \\ j = 1, \ldots, m \end{matrix} \qquad (10\text{-}31)$$

The nonnegativity of the γ_{ij} follows from the nonnegativity of the b_{ih} and the β_{hj}. The coefficient γ_{ij} gives the quantity of the ith factor necessary to produce the quantities of the m goods which directly and indirectly support a final consumption unit of the jth good.

Decomposability

An input-output system is *decomposable* if it contains one or more self-sufficient groups of less than m industries each. Industries within a self-sufficient group do not require inputs from industries outside the group. The output levels of industries outside a self-sufficient group are independent of the output and final consumption levels of the industries within the group. The following five-industry system contains two self-sufficient groups:

$$\begin{bmatrix} a_{11} & a_{12} & a_{13} & a_{14} & 0 \\ a_{21} & a_{22} & a_{23} & a_{24} & a_{25} \\ 0 & 0 & a_{33} & a_{34} & a_{35} \\ 0 & 0 & a_{43} & a_{44} & a_{45} \\ 0 & 0 & 0 & 0 & a_{55} \end{bmatrix} \qquad (10\text{-}32)$$

where the listed coefficients are positive. Industries 1 and 2 form a self-sufficient group. They secure inputs from each other, but not from the remaining three industries. The output levels of industries 3, 4, and 5 are unaffected by the output and final consumption levels of 1 and 2. Industries 1, 2, 3, and 4 form another self-sufficient group. They do not require inputs from 5, and 5's output level is independent of the output and final consumption levels of 3 and 4 as well as 1 and 2.

A decomposable input-output system can be solved by parts. If the coefficients of (10-32) are inserted in the balance equations (10-28), the fifth equation may be solved for q_5. Given q_5, the third and fourth equations may be solved for q_3 and q_4; and given q_3, q_4, and q_5, the first two equations may be solved for q_1 and q_2.

In general, the coefficient β_{ij} in (10-29) will equal zero if and only if the ith industry is outside a self-sufficient group which contains the jth. The direct and indirect requirements matrix that corresponds to (10-32) is

$$\begin{bmatrix} \beta_{11} & \beta_{12} & \beta_{13} & \beta_{14} & \beta_{15} \\ \beta_{21} & \beta_{22} & \beta_{23} & \beta_{24} & \beta_{25} \\ 0 & 0 & \beta_{33} & \beta_{34} & \beta_{35} \\ 0 & 0 & \beta_{43} & \beta_{44} & \beta_{45} \\ 0 & 0 & 0 & 0 & \beta_{55} \end{bmatrix}$$

where the listed coefficients are positive. An *indecomposable* system contains no self-sufficient groups, and thereby, all the β_{ij} are positive.

An input-output system is *completely decomposable* if each industry is contained in a self-sufficient group of less than m industries. For example,

$$\begin{bmatrix} a_{11} & a_{12} & 0 & 0 \\ a_{21} & a_{22} & 0 & 0 \\ 0 & 0 & a_{33} & a_{34} \\ 0 & 0 & a_{43} & a_{44} \end{bmatrix}$$

Industries 1 and 2 only secure inputs from each other, and industries 3 and 4 only secure inputs from each other. Output levels for each group may be determined without regard to the output and final consumption levels of the other. If a system is completely decomposable, $\beta_{ij} > 0$ for i and j in the same self-sufficient group, and $\beta_{ij} = 0$ for i and j in different groups.

Existence

The mere formulation of an input-output system does not guarantee that it has a general solution with $q_i \geq 0$ $(i = 1, \ldots, m)$ for all $y_i \geq 0$ $(i = 1, \ldots, m)$. Two equivalent, but rather different, sets of necessary and sufficient conditions for the existence of a general solution are presented here. The *Hawkins-Simon conditions*[1] require that all the principal minors of the coefficient array of

---

[1] See David Hawkins and Herbert A. Simon, "Note: Some Conditions of Macroeconomic Stability," *Econometrica*, vol. 17 (July–October, 1949), pp. 245–248.

(10-28) be positive:

$$1 - a_{11} > 0, \begin{vmatrix} 1 - a_{11} & -a_{12} \\ -a_{21} & 1 - a_{22} \end{vmatrix} > 0, \dots, \begin{vmatrix} 1 - a_{11} & \cdots & a_{1m} \\ \dots\dots\dots\dots\dots\dots \\ -a_{m1} & \cdots & 1 - a_{mm} \end{vmatrix} > 0 \quad (10\text{-}33)$$

The first and subsequent inequalities of (10-33) require that $a_{ii} < 1$ ($i = 1, \dots, m$). If $a_{ii} \geq 1$ for some i, one or more units of i would be required to produce one unit of i. No net output can be secured under such circumstances. The last condition of (10-33) requires that the determinant of (10-28) be positive.

An equivalent set of necessary and sufficient conditions for the existence of a general solution concerns the column sums of the input coefficients. These conditions require that there exist a set of numbers $d_j > 0$ ($j = 1, \dots, m$) such that

$$\sum_{i=1}^{m} d_i a_{ij} \leq d_j \qquad j = 1, \dots, m \qquad (10\text{-}34)$$

with the strict inequality holding for at least one j in each self-sufficient group of industries.[1] If a system is indecomposable, the strict inequality need hold for only one industry.

Price and Income Determination

Applying the competitive condition that price equals unit cost for each industry,

$$p_j = a_{1j}p_1 + \cdots + a_{mj}p_m + b_{1j}r_1 + \cdots + b_{nj}r_n \qquad j = 1, \dots, m$$

where p_i ($i = 1, \dots, m$) and r_i ($i = 1, \dots, n$) are the prices of goods and factors respectively. By rearranging terms,

$$
\begin{aligned}
(1 - a_{11})p_1 - \quad a_{21}p_2 \quad - \cdots - \quad a_{m1}p_m \quad &= v_1 \\
- a_{12}p_1 + (1 - a_{22})p_2 - \cdots - \quad a_{m2}p_m \quad &= v_2 \\
\cdots\cdots\cdots\cdots\cdots\cdots\cdots\cdots\cdots\cdots & \\
- a_{1m}p_1 - \quad a_{2m}p_2 \quad - \cdots + (1 - a_{mm})p_m &= v_m
\end{aligned}
\qquad (10\text{-}35)
$$

where $v_j = b_{1j}r_1 + b_{2j}r_2 + \cdots + b_{nj}r_n \qquad j = 1, \dots, m \qquad (10\text{-}36)$

is the *value added* per unit of the jth output.

The coefficient array on the left of (10-35) is the same as the array on the left of (10-28) except that the rows and columns are interchanged. The determinant values of the two arrays are equal, and the cofactor of the element in the ith row and jth column of one array equals the cofactor of the element in the jth row and ith column of the other. The solution of (10-35) for

---

[1] A proof is given by Lionel McKenzie, "Matrices with Dominant Diagonals and Economic Theory," in K. J. Arrow, S. Karlin, and P. Suppes (eds.), *Mathematical Methods in the Social Sciences, 1959* (Stanford, Calif.: Stanford University Press, 1960), p. 50.

the p_js is

$$
\begin{aligned}
p_1 &= \beta_{11}v_1 + \beta_{21}v_2 + \cdots + \beta_{m1}v_m \\
p_2 &= \beta_{12}v_1 + \beta_{22}v_2 + \cdots + \beta_{m2}v_m \\
&\;\;\cdots\cdots\cdots\cdots\cdots\cdots\cdots\cdots \\
p_m &= \beta_{1m}v_1 + \beta_{2m}v_2 + \cdots + \beta_{mm}v_m
\end{aligned}
\tag{10-37}
$$

where the β_{ij} are the same as the coefficients in (10-29) with rows and columns
of the arrays interchanged. If (10-29) is a general solution for (10-28) with
$\beta_{ij} \geqq 0$ $(i, j = 1, \ldots, m)$, it follows that (10-37) is a general solution for (10-35),
that is, $p_j \geqq 0$ $(j = 1, \ldots, m)$ for all $r_i \geqq 0$ $(i = 1, \ldots, n)$.

Substituting from (10-36) and (10-31), (10-37) may be written

$$
p_j = \gamma_{1j}r_1 + \gamma_{2j}r_2 + \cdots + \gamma_{nj}r_n \qquad j = 1, \ldots, m \tag{10-38}
$$

The price of each good equals the value of the factors which are directly and
indirectly required for its production. If (10-37) is a general solution, a
necessary and sufficient condition that the prices of all goods be positive is
that at least one factor with positive price be required for the production of at
least one good in each self-sufficient group. An indecomposable system has
the minimum requirement that at least one factor with positive price be required
for the production of at least one good.

If an input-output system has only one nonproduced factor, its price may
be set at unity, and (10-38) may be solved for the prices of produced goods in
factor units. If a system has more than one factor, additional information is
required for a determination of the r_i, consequently, the p_j.

Income at market price equals the value of the final consumption levels.
Substituting first from (10-38) and then from (10-30),

$$
\sum_{j=1}^{m} p_j y_j = \sum_{i=1}^{n} \sum_{j=1}^{m} r_i \gamma_{ij} y_j = \sum_{i=1}^{n} r_i x_i
$$

Income at market price equals income at factor cost, or put in another way,
factor payments just exhaust the value of net output.

The Substitution Theorem

If an input-output system has a general solution, produced and factor input
levels are uniquely determined for any specified set of final consumption
requirements. There is no opportunity for substitution among inputs. In Sec.
5-6 it is shown that a degree of input substitution is possible in the production
of a good if more than one linear activity is available. The input-output model
is easily extended to allow multiple production activities for each good. No
essentials are lost by assuming that each industry has the same number, u, of
linear production activities. Let a_{ij}^k denote the quantity of the ith good
required to produce a unit of the jth using the kth activity for the jth, and let
q_j^k denote the output level of the kth activity for the jth good. The existence
of multiple activities suggests that a prescribed set of final demands may be
met by alternative sets of produced and factor input levels.

If an economy has only one scarce factor, it desires to minimize the quantity of that factor, x, necessary to meet its final consumption requirements. This optimization problem may be placed within the linear-programming format (see Sec. 5-7): select nonnegative output levels, $q_j^k \geqq 0$ $(k = 1, \ldots, u; j = 1, \ldots, m)$, that minimize

$$x = \sum_{k=1}^{u} \sum_{j=1}^{m} b_j^k q_j^k \tag{10-39}$$

where b_j^k is the unit factor requirement of the kth activity for the jth good, subject to the conditions that the net output of each good be sufficient to meet its final consumption requirement:

$$\sum_{k=1}^{u} [(1 - a_{11}^k)q_1^k - a_{12}^k q_2^k \quad - \cdots - \quad a_{1m}^k q_m^k] \quad \geqq y_1$$

$$\sum_{k=1}^{u} [-a_{21}^k q_1^k + (1 - a_{22}^k)q_2^k - \cdots - \quad a_{2m}^k q_m^k] \quad \geqq y_2 \tag{10-40}$$

$$\cdots \cdots \cdots \cdots$$

$$\sum_{k=1}^{u} [-a_{m1}^k q_1^k \quad - \quad a_{m2}^k q_2^k \quad - \cdots + \quad (1 - a_{mm}^k)q_m^k] \geqq y_m$$

Assume for convenience that $y_i > 0$ $(i = 1, \ldots, m)$.

Each combination of m activities, one for each good, drawn from the um available activities constitutes an input-output system. There are u^m such systems. Each system which has a general solution (assume that there is at least one) provides a feasible solution for (10-40). Every feasible solution for (10-40) must have at least one activity for each good since a positive net output is specified for each. An important linear-programming theorem (see Sec. 5-7) states that an optimal solution for a system with m constraints need contain no more than m activities at positive levels. It may be concluded that one or more of the input-output systems will be optimal.

The dual programming system[1] for (10-39) and (10-40) is to find values for $p_i \geqq 0$ $(i = 1, \ldots, m)$ that maximize

$$I = \sum_{i=1}^{m} p_i y_i \tag{10-41}$$

subject to

$$
\begin{aligned}
(1 - a_{11}^1)p_1 - \quad & a_{21}^1 p_2 - \cdots - \quad a_{m1}^1 p_m \quad \leqq b_1^1 \\
- a_{21}^1 p_1 + \quad & (1 - a_{22}^1)p_2 - \cdots - \quad a_{m2}^1 p_m \quad \leqq b_2^1
\end{aligned}
$$

$$\cdots \cdots \cdots \cdots \cdots \cdots$$

$$
\begin{aligned}
- a_{1m}^1 p_1 - \quad & a_{2m}^1 p_2 - \cdots + (1 - a_{mm}^1)p_m \leqq b_m^1 \\
(1 - a_{11}^2)p_1 - \quad & a_{21}^2 p_2 - \cdots - \quad a_{m1}^2 p_m \quad \leqq b_1^2
\end{aligned} \tag{10-42}
$$

$$\cdots \cdots \cdots \cdots \cdots \cdots$$

$$- a_{1m}^u p_1 - \quad a_{2m}^u p_2 - \cdots + (1 - a_{mm}^u)p_m \leqq b_m^u$$

---

[1] The initial system (10-39) and (10-40) is in the same format as the general dual system given by (5-37) and (5-38), and the dual system (10-41) and (10-42) is in the same format as the general initial system given by (5-31) and (5-32). The duality theorems of linear programming are symmetric and hold regardless of the classification of the two systems as initial and dual.

The dual variables are the prices of the m goods measured in factor units. By rearranging terms, the constraints (10-42) may be written

$$p_j \leqq \sum_{i=1}^{m} a_{ij}^k p_i + b_j^k \qquad k = 1, \ldots, u \qquad j = 1, \ldots, m$$

This is the familiar condition that unit revenue (in factor units) is less than or equal to unit cost (in factor units) for each of the linear production activities. The duality theorem stated by (5-42) ensures the competitive condition that price equals cost for each activity operated at a positive level in the optimal input-output system, and (5-46) ensures the equality of the optimal values of income at factor cost (10-39) and income at market value (10-41).

The introduction of the possibility of substitution leads to questions about the constancy of empirical input-output coefficients. Will the coefficients remain at their observed base-year values as final consumption requirements change from their base-year values? The substitution theorem for input-output models answers yes. Specifically, it states that an input-output system is optimal for all $y_i \geqq 0$ $(i = 1, \ldots, m)$ if it is optimal for any particular set of values for the y_i's. This theorem follows easily from a parametric property of linear-programming systems: a change in the requirements for a system will leave the set of activities contained in its optimal solution unchanged if they remain feasible.[1] Since the optimal input-output system has a general solution, its output levels will be nonnegative for all nonnegative final consumption requirements, and the substitution theorem is established. Output levels will be changed by changes in final consumption requirements, but the prices of goods are unaffected. The substitution theorem might be called the nonsubstitution theorem. Substitution is possible, but it is never observed in a one-factor economy. The substitution theorem is not valid for economies with more than one factor.

10-5 SUMMARY

The mere formulation of a multimarket system gives no assurance that an equilibrium solution exists. Particular numerical systems may be examined individually to determine existence. An existence proof states that systems which satisfy a number of general restrictions possess equilibrium solutions. The existence of excess demand functions is proved for an illustrative system. Then Brouwer's fixed-point theorem is used to prove that one or more equilibrium price sets exist for the system. The Debreu existence proof, which is based upon much weaker assumptions, is outlined.

The static and dynamic conditions for multimarket stability represent a generalization of the Walrasian condition for a single market. Perfect stability

---

[1] A proof of the substitution theorem is given by David Gale, *Theory of Linear Economic Models* (New York: McGraw-Hill, 1960), pp. 303–305.

in the static Hicksian sense requires that the total derivatives dE_j/dp_j $(j = 2, \ldots, m)$ be negative for all possible combinations of rigid and flexible prices. Imperfect stability requires that the total derivatives be negative, given the assumption that all prices are flexible. An analysis of dynamic stability requires an explicit statement of the laws of price adjustment over time. A multimarket system is dynamically stable if all prices approach their equilibrium values over time following a disturbance. Dynamic stability and Hicksian stability are synonymous for a system with continuous adjustment if all commodities are strict gross substitutes. A system with a unique equilibrium is globally stable if its excess demand functions satisfy the Weak axiom of revealed preference. If a solution exists for a system that satisfies the Hicksian conditions for perfect stability throughout, the solution is unique. The Weak axiom also implies uniqueness.

A single linear production activity is used for each of m goods in the input-output model. Produced outputs and nonproduced factors serve as inputs. A general solution for an input-output system gives outputs as linear functions of final consumption levels. A system is decomposable if it contains one or more self-sufficient groups of less than m industries. Competitive (zero-profit) prices for the produced goods can be derived from factor prices. The input-output model can be generalized to allow more than one activity per good. The substitution theorem states that input substitution will not take place in an economy with multiple production activities if there is only one nonproduced factor.

EXERCISES

10-1 Use a Jacobian test to determine whether solutions exist for the following three-commodity systems:

(a) $E_2 = -8p_2 + 24p_3 + 6 = 0$; $E_3 = 10p_2 - 30p_3 + 8 = 0$

(b) $E_2 = -3p_2 - p_2p_3 + p_3 = 0$; $E_3 = p_2 - p_2p_3 - 3p_3 = 0$

(c) $E_2 = -4p_2 + 8p_3 + 4 = 0$; $E_3 = p_2^2 - 2p_2 - 4p_2p_3 + 4p_3 + 4p_3^2 + 1 = 0$

10-2 Find equilibrium prices for the three-commodity system given by

$$E_2 = 2p_2^2 + 22p_2 - 13p_2p_3 - 64p_3 + 20p_3^2 + 48 = 0$$
$$E_3 = p_2 - 2p_3 + 2 = 0$$

10-3 Consider the system (10-14) with $b_{ii} < 0$ $(i = 2, \ldots, m)$ and $b_{ij} = 0$ for $i > j$. Show that the system possesses perfect Hicksian stability in this case.

10-4 Assuming continuous adjustment, do the solutions for Exercise 10-2 satisfy the conditions for dynamic local stability?

10-5 Consider a system with one primary good, Q_1, and one produced good, Q_2. Assume that each consumer has a positive initial endowment of the primary good, and a positive share of the profits of at least one firm. Assume that all individual utility functions are of the form $U_i = q_{i1}q_{iw}$ $(i = 1, \ldots, n)$, and that the production function for a representative firm is of the form $\bar{q}_{h2} = (q_{h21}^*)^\alpha (q_{h22}^*)^\beta$ with α, $\beta > 0$ and $\alpha + \beta < 1$. Show that this system meets the assumptions underlying the existence proof of Sec. 10-1.

10-6 Consider pseudo excess demand functions for a consumer in pure exchange with the utility function $U_i = q_{i1}q_{i2}^\alpha q_{i3}^\beta$ with α, $\beta > 0$. Show that the boundaries similar to those shown in Fig. 10-2 are straight lines.

10-7 The a_{ij} coefficients for a three-industry, input-output system are

$$\begin{bmatrix} 0.2 & 0.1 & 0.6 \\ 0.5 & 0.4 & 0.4 \\ 0.1 & 0.4 & 0.2 \end{bmatrix}$$

Use the Hawkins-Simon conditions to determine whether this system has a general solution.

10-8 Use the column-sum conditions given by (10-34) to determine whether the input-output system of Exercise 10-7 has a general solution.

SELECTED REFERENCES

Arrow, K. J., and F. H. Hahn: *General Competitive Analysis* (San Francisco: Holden-Day, 1971). Advanced mathematics is used. Existence, stability, and uniqueness are covered in chaps. 5, 11–12, and 9 respectively.

Debreu, Gerard: *Theory of Value* (New York: Wiley, 1959). Advanced mathematics is used to prove the existence of competitive equilibrium.

Hicks, J. R.: *Value and Capital* (2d ed., Oxford: Clarendon Press, 1946). Multimarket equilibrium is covered in chaps. IV–VIII. The mathematical development is contained in an appendix.

Leontief, W. W.: *The Structure of American Economy*, 1919–1939 (2d ed., New York: Oxford, 1951). A description of the input-output model by its originator.

Metzler, Lloyd A.: "Stability of Multiple Markets: The Hicks Conditions," *Econometrica*, vol. 13 (October, 1945), pp. 277–292. An advanced mathematical discussion of the Hicksian and dynamic multimarket stability conditions.

Miernyk, W. H.: *The Elements of Input-Output Analysis* (New York: Random House, 1965). An elementary nonmathematical description of empirical input-output systems.

Nikaido, Hukukane: *Convex Structures and Economic Theory* (New York: Academic, 1968). Existence, stability, and uniqueness are covered in this volume for the mathematically sophisticated reader.

Quirk, James, and Rubin Saposnik: *Introduction to General Equilibrium Theory and Welfare Economics* (New York: McGraw-Hill, 1968). Existence and stability are treated in chaps. 3 and 5 respectively. Mathematical concepts are simplified and developed in the text.

Samuelson, Paul A.: *Foundations of Economic Analysis* (Cambridge, Mass.: Harvard University Press, 1948). Dynamic multimarket stability is discussed in chap. IX.

ELEVEN

WELFARE ECONOMICS

The objective of welfare economics is the evaluation of the social desirability of alternative economic states. An economic state is a particular arrangement of economic activities and of the resources of the economy. Each state is characterized by a different allocation of resources and a different distribution of the rewards for economic activity. Although the economist may not always be able to prescribe a method by which one state of the economy can be transformed into another, policy measures frequently will be available for changing an existing situation. It is important to know in such cases whether the contemplated change is desirable. Imagine, for example, that the economy can attain multimarket equilibrium at two different sets of commodity and factor prices. Since the desires of consumers and entrepreneurs are consistent at both equilibria, society can choose between them, if at all, only on welfare grounds. The principles by which such problems might be solved fall within the domain of welfare economics.

The welfare of a society depends, in the broadest sense, upon the satisfaction levels of all its consumers.[1] But almost every alternative to be judged by welfare economists will have favorable effects on some people and unfavorable effects on others. In light of this, the economist has two choices. She may decline to deal with cases in which a proposed social change

---

[1] Statements of this kind are based on ethical beliefs or value judgments and cannot be proved. It is reasonable to postulate that the concept of social welfare transcends the more restricted notion of economic welfare. For example, social welfare may depend on, in addition to what goods are produced and how they are distributed among people, the manner in which society is organized politically, the extent to which social decisions are reached by a democratic process, etc. The present analysis places primary emphasis on analyzing economic welfare.

improves the lot of some and deteriorates the lot of others and content herself with analyzing situations in which unambiguous welfare improvements are possible. Alternatively, she may decide to make interpersonal comparisons of utility and analyze a broader class of situations. In the former case she is primarily concerned with efficient allocation of resources. In the latter, she must make explicit value judgments. In principle one would hope that these will rest on a social consensus, since the economist has no more competence than anyone else to say that a particular move is desirable if it has unfavorable effects upon some members of society.

The Pareto conditions for economic efficiency are derived in Sec. 11-1. The possible fulfillment of these conditions under perfect and imperfect competition is discussed in Secs. 11-2 and 11-3. External effects in consumption and production, and the theory of public goods are the subjects of Sec. 11-4, and the attainment of the Pareto conditions through taxes and subsidies is described in Sec. 11-5. Social welfare conditions are considered in Sec. 11-6, and the theory of second best is presented in Sec. 11-7.

11-1 PARETO OPTIMALITY

An allocation is described by specific consumption levels for each consumer and specific input and output levels for each producer. Pareto optimality provides a definition of the economic efficiency of allocations that serves as the basis for much of welfare economics. An allocation is *Pareto-optimal* or *Pareto-efficient* if production and distribution cannot be reorganized to increase the utility of one or more individuals without decreasing the utility of others. Conversely, an allocation is *Pareto-nonoptimal* if someone's utility can be increased without harming anyone else. One allocation is said to be *Pareto-superior* to another if the utility of at least one individual is higher and the utility of none is lower, even though the allocation may not be Pareto-optimal.

Analyses of Pareto optimality usually stop short of value judgments and interpersonal comparisons of utility levels. Consequently, changes which improve the positions of some individuals but cause a deterioration in those of others cannot be evaluated in terms of efficiency; the net effects of the moves may or may not be beneficial. However, welfare can be said to increase (diminish) if at least one person's position improves (deteriorates) with no change in the positions of other. Clearly no situation can be optimal unless all possible improvements of this variety have been made.[1] The abstraction from distributional considerations limits the number of questions that may be answered with the Pareto apparatus. For example, a society

---

[1] The present discussion is limited to static efficiency. No attention is paid to the welfare aspects of resource allocation over time, the time path of welfare, or the welfare aspects of alternative time paths for the economy.

might have a Pareto-optimal allocation in which one consumer had 99 percent of all goods, but most people would not consider this to be a satisfactory allocation.

Pareto Optimality for Consumption

A distribution of consumer goods (including leisure and other withheld primary factors) is Pareto-optimal if every possible reallocation of goods that increases the utility of one or more consumers would result in a utility reduction for at least one other consumer. Pareto optimality will be achieved if each consumer's utility is a maximum given the utility levels of all other consumers. For illustration assume that there are only two consumers denoted by the first subscripts 1 and 2 and only two goods Q_1 and Q_2. The utility functions of the consumers are $U_1(q_{11}, q_{12})$ and $U_2(q_{21}, q_{22})$ where $q_{11} + q_{21} = q_1^0$ and $q_{12} + q_{22} = q_2^0$. Now assume that consumer II enjoys the level of satisfaction $U_2^0 = $ constant. In order to maximize the utility of consumer I subject to this constraint, form the function

$$U_1^* = U_1(q_{11}, q_{12}) + \lambda [U_2(q_1^0 - q_{11}, q_2^0 - q_{12}) - U_2^0]$$

where λ is a Lagrange multiplier, and set its partial derivatives equal to zero:

$$\frac{\partial U_1^*}{\partial q_{11}} = \frac{\partial U_1}{\partial q_{11}} - \lambda \frac{\partial U_2}{\partial q_{21}} = 0$$

$$\frac{\partial U_1^*}{\partial q_{12}} = \frac{\partial U_1}{\partial q_{12}} - \lambda \frac{\partial U_2}{\partial q_{22}} = 0$$

$$\frac{\partial U_1^*}{\partial \lambda} = U_2(q_1^0 - q_{11}, q_2^0 - q_{12}) - U_2^0 = 0$$

and
$$\frac{\partial U_1 / \partial q_{11}}{\partial U_1 / \partial q_{12}} = \frac{\partial U_2 / \partial q_{21}}{\partial U_2 / \partial q_{22}} \tag{11-1}$$

The left-hand side of (11-1) is consumer I's RCS, and the right-hand side is II's. The RCSs of the consumers must be equal to achieve Pareto optimality in consumption.[1] If (11-1) were not satisfied, it would be possible to redistribute the goods in such a way as to increase I's utility without reducing II's. The argument is symmetric. Condition (11-1) also results from maximization of II's utility given a fixed level for I's. Thus, if (11-1) were not satisfied, it would also be possible to increase II's utility without reducing I's. The mathematical analysis for the two-consumer case is easily generalized for any number of consumers.

The argument can be presented in terms of an Edgeworth box diagram (see Sec. 9-2). The dimensions of the rectangle in Fig. 11-1 represent the total available quantities of Q_1 and Q_2 in a pure-exchange economy. Any point in

---

[1] Of course, the second-order conditions must also be fulfilled. It is postulated throughout the remainder of this section that the second-order conditions are fulfilled.

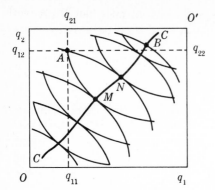

Figure 11-1

the box represents a particular distribution of the commodities between the two consumers. For example, if the distribution of commodities is given by point A, the quantities of Q_1 and Q_2 consumed by I are measured by the coordinates of A, using the southwest corner O as the origin; the quantities consumed by II are measured by the coordinates of point A, using the northeast corner O' as the origin. The indifference map of I is drawn, using O as the origin, and the indifference map of II, using O' as the origin. The RCSs of the two consumers are equal where an indifference curve of I is tangent to an indifference curve of II. The locus of all such points is the *contract curve* CC. The mathematical form of the contract curve is given by (11-1), which is a function of q_{11} and q_{12}.

The rates of commodity substitution are unequal at point A, and it is possible to increase the utility levels of both consumers by altering the existing distribution. If the final position (after a redistribution of Q_1 and Q_2) is between M and N, both consumers will have gained, since both will be on higher indifference curves than at A. If the final point is at M or N, one consumer will have gained without any deterioration in the other's position. If a point on the contract curve is reached, it is not possible to improve further the position of either consumer without a deterioration in the position of the other. According to the conditions of Pareto optimality any point from M to N is unambiguously superior to A. However, the evaluation of alternative points on the contract curve would involve an interpersonal comparison of utilities and is therefore not possible within the present framework.

Pareto Optimality for Production

Assuming that consumers are not satiated and that each individual's utility level is independent of the quantities consumed by others, an increment in the quantity of any consumer good without a decrement in the quantity of any other consumer good can lead to a utility increment for at least one consumer without utility decrements for others. Therefore, Pareto optimality among producers requires that the output level of each consumer good be at a maximum given the output levels of all other consumer goods.

Assume that there are two producers using two inputs to produce two goods with the production functions

$$q_1 = f_1(x_{11}, x_{12})$$

and
$$q_2 = f_2(x_{21}, x_{22})$$

where $x_{11} + x_{21} = x_1^0$ and $x_{12} + x_{22} = x_2^0$ are the available input quantities and q_1 and q_2 are the output levels. Maximize the output of good I subject to the constraint that the output of II is at the predetermined level q_2^0. Form the function

$$L = f_1(x_{11}, x_{12}) + \lambda[f_2(x_1^0 - x_{11}, x_2^0 - x_{12}) - q_2^0]$$

and set its partial derivatives equal to zero:

$$\frac{\partial L}{\partial x_{11}} = \frac{\partial f_1}{\partial x_{11}} - \lambda \frac{\partial f_2}{\partial x_{21}} = 0$$

$$\frac{\partial L}{\partial x_{12}} = \frac{\partial f_1}{\partial x_{12}} - \lambda \frac{\partial f_2}{\partial x_{22}} = 0$$

$$\frac{\partial L}{\partial \lambda} = f_2(x_1^0 - x_{11}, x_2^0 - x_{12}) - q_2^0 = 0$$

and
$$\frac{\partial f_1/\partial x_{11}}{\partial f_1/\partial x_{12}} = \frac{\partial f_2/\partial x_{21}}{\partial f_2/\partial x_{22}} \qquad (11\text{-}2)$$

The left-hand side of (11-2) is I's RTS for X_1 and X_2, and the right-hand side is II's. The RTSs of producers must be equal to achieve Pareto optimality in production. If (11-2) were not satisfied, it would be possible to increase the output of one good without decreasing the output of the other. In fact, as the reader may verify, it would be possible to increase the outputs of both goods.

Pareto Optimality in General

The Pareto conditions derived for consumers and producers are generalized and extended in a consideration of the economy as a whole. Consider an economy with m consumers, N producers, n primary factors, and s produced goods. For simplicity assume that each consumer consumes all produced goods, and each producer uses all primary factors and produces all goods. The consumers' utility functions are

$$U_i = U_i(q_{i1}^*, \ldots, q_{is}^*, x_{i1}^0 - x_{i1}^*, \ldots, x_{in}^0 - x_{in}^*) \qquad i = 1, \ldots, m \qquad (11\text{-}3)$$

where q_{ik}^* is the quantity of Q_k consumed by the ith consumer, x_{ij}^0 is her fixed endowment of the jth primary factor, x_{ij}^* is the amount that she supplies to producers, and $x_{ij}^0 - x_{ij}^*$ is the amount that she consumes. Production functions are given in implicit form:

$$F_h(q_{h1}, \ldots, q_{hs}, x_{h1}, \ldots, x_{hn}) = 0 \qquad h = 1, \ldots, N \qquad (11\text{-}4)$$

where q_{hk} is the output of Q_k by the hth firm and x_{hj} is the amount of X_j which it uses. The aggregate amounts of primary factors supplied by consumers equal the aggregate amounts used by producers:

$$\sum_{i=1}^{m} x_{ij}^* = \sum_{h=1}^{N} x_{hj} \qquad j = 1, \ldots, n \tag{11-5}$$

and the aggregate consumption levels of produced goods equal their aggregate output levels:

$$\sum_{i=1}^{m} q_{ik}^* = \sum_{h=1}^{N} q_{hk} \qquad k = 1, \ldots, s \tag{11-6}$$

Pareto optimality will be achieved if the utility of each consumer is a maximum given the utility levels of all other consumers subject to the constraints (11-4), (11-5), and (11-6). Consider the maximization of consumer I's utility subject to these constraints. Form the Lagrange function

$$Z = U_1(q_{11}^*, \ldots, x_{1n}^0 - x_{1n}^*) + \sum_{i=2}^{m} \lambda_i [U_i(q_{i1}^*, \ldots, x_{in}^0 - x_{in}^*) - U_i^0]$$

$$+ \sum_{h=1}^{N} \theta_h F_h(q_{h1}, \ldots, x_{hn}) + \sum_{j=1}^{n} \delta_j \left(\sum_{i=1}^{m} x_{ij}^* - \sum_{h=1}^{N} x_{hj} \right) + \sum_{k=1}^{s} \sigma_k \left(\sum_{h=1}^{N} q_{hk} - \sum_{i=1}^{m} q_{ik}^* \right)$$

where the λ_i, θ_h, δ_j, and σ_k are Lagrange multipliers. Setting the partial derivatives of Z equal to zero,

$$\frac{\partial Z}{\partial q_{1k}^*} = \frac{\partial U_1}{\partial q_{1k}^*} - \sigma_k = 0 \qquad\qquad \frac{\partial Z}{\partial x_{1j}^*} = -\frac{\partial U_1}{\partial (x_{1j}^0 - x_{1j}^*)} + \delta_j = 0$$

$$\frac{\partial Z}{\partial q_{ik}^*} = \lambda_i \frac{\partial U_i}{\partial q_{ik}^*} - \sigma_k = 0 \qquad\qquad \frac{\partial Z}{\partial x_{ij}^*} = -\lambda_i \frac{\partial U_i}{\partial (x_{ij}^0 - x_{ij}^*)} + \delta_j = 0 \tag{11-7}$$

$$\frac{\partial Z}{\partial q_{hk}} = \theta_h \frac{\partial F_h}{\partial q_{hk}} + \sigma_k = 0 \qquad\qquad \frac{\partial Z}{\partial x_{hj}} = \theta_h \frac{\partial F_h}{\partial x_{hj}} - \delta_j = 0$$

where $i = 2, \ldots, m$; $h = 1, \ldots, N$; $k = 1, \ldots, s$; and $j = 1, \ldots, n$. The partials with regard to the multipliers must also be set equal to zero; i.e., the constraints must be satisfied.

The conditions for Pareto optimality may be written in more familiar form. Solving (11-7) for σ_j / σ_k,

$$\frac{\sigma_j}{\sigma_k} = \frac{\partial U_1 / \partial q_{1j}^*}{\partial U_1 / \partial q_{1k}^*} = \cdots = \frac{\partial U_m / \partial q_{mj}^*}{\partial U_m / \partial q_{mk}^*} = \frac{\partial F_1 / \partial q_{1j}}{\partial F_1 / \partial q_{1k}} = \cdots = \frac{\partial F_N / \partial q_{Nj}}{\partial F_N / \partial q_{Nk}}$$

$$j, k = 1, \ldots, s \tag{11-8}$$

Conditions (11-8) state that the RCSs for all consumers and the RPTs for all producers must be equal for every pair of produced goods. Imagine that (11-8) were violated for Q_j and Q_k so that RCS $= \frac{1}{3}$ for some consumer and RPT $= \frac{2}{3}$ for some producer. Three units of Q_j could be transformed into two units of Q_k by moving along the producer's transformation curve. If the consumer surrendered three units of Q_j (the position of all other consumers remaining unchanged), she would require only one unit of Q_k in exchange in order to remain on the same indifference curve and avoid a diminution of utility. The satisfaction level of this consumer could therefore actually be increased by performing the technological transformation of three units of Q_k into two of Q_j. Such an improvement is not possible if the RCSs and RPTs are equal.

Solving (11-7) for δ_j/δ_k,

$$\frac{\delta_j}{\delta_k} = \frac{\partial U_1/\partial(x_{1j}^0 - x_{1j}^*)}{\partial U_1/\partial(x_{1k}^0 - x_{1k}^*)} = \cdots = \frac{\partial U_m/\partial(x_{mj}^0 - x_{mj}^*)}{\partial U_m/\partial(x_{mk}^0 - x_{mk}^*)} = \frac{\partial F_1/\partial x_{1j}}{\partial F_1/\partial x_{1k}} = \cdots = \frac{\partial F_N/\partial x_{Nj}}{\partial F_N/\partial x_{Nk}}$$

$$j, k = 1, \ldots, n \qquad (11\text{-}9)$$

Conditions (11-9) state that the RCSs for all consumers and the RTSs for all producers must be equal for every pair of primary goods. If this condition were violated for some consumer and some producer, it would be possible to increase the consumer's utility by an exchange between the consumer and producer.

Finally, solving (11-7) for δ_j/σ_k,

$$\frac{\delta_j}{\sigma_k} = \frac{\partial U_1/\partial(x_{1j}^0 - x_{1j}^*)}{\partial U_1/\partial q_{1k}^*} = \cdots = \frac{\partial U_m/\partial(x_{mj}^0 - x_{mj}^*)}{\partial U_m/\partial q_{mk}^*} = -\frac{\partial F_1/\partial x_{1j}}{\partial F_1/\partial q_{1k}} = \cdots = -\frac{\partial F_N/\partial x_{Nj}}{\partial F_N/\partial q_{Nk}}$$

$$\begin{array}{l} j = 1, \ldots, n \\ k = 1, \ldots, s \end{array} \qquad (11\text{-}10)$$

Conditions (11-10) state that the consumers' RCSs between factors and commodities must equal the corresponding producers' rates of transforming factors into commodities, i.e., their MPs.[1] If (11-10) were violated for some consumer and producer, the consumer's utility could be increased by surrendering some of the factor for more of the commodity, or some of the commodity for more of the factor.

A Pareto-optimal state is described by the marginal conditions (11-8), (11-9), and (11-10) plus the additional condition that it is not possible to increase the utility of one or more consumers without diminishing the utility of others by discontinuing the production of one or more goods. It is assumed here that the latter condition is always fulfilled. Pareto optimality is defined in terms of physical rates of substitution between factors and commodities without reference to market prices. The Lagrange multipliers δ_j $(j = 1, \ldots, n)$ and σ_k $(k = 1, \ldots, s)$ are efficiency prices; Pareto optimality would be achieved if all consumers and producers adjusted their rates of substitution to efficiency price ratios. Any set of market prices for factors and commodities such that $r_j = \alpha\delta_j$ $(j = 1, \ldots, n)$ and $p_k = \alpha\sigma_k$ $(k = 1, \ldots, s)$, where $\alpha > 0$, will serve as efficiency prices and lead to a Pareto-optimal state. It is of interest for welfare economics to ask whether particular market prices are efficiency prices, or equivalently, to ask whether particular forms of market organization will lead to Pareto optimality.

[1] The reader unfamiliar with the MP definition used in (11-10) should consult Sec. 4-6.

11-2 THE EFFICIENCY OF PERFECT COMPETITION

Consumers buy commodities and sell primary factors. Firms sell commodities and buy primary factors. In perfect competition all consumers and firms face the same set of prices for commodities and factors, and no consumer or firm has an effect on these through its actions. If consumers are utility maximizers, each will equate her RCS for any pair of goods to the corresponding price ratio:

$$RCS_{kj} = \frac{p_j}{p_k} \tag{11-11}$$

where j and k can each refer to either commodities or primary factors. If firms are profit maximizers, they will equate their RPTs, RTSs, and MPs to the corresponding price ratios:

$$RPT_{kj} = \frac{p_j}{p_k} \tag{11-12}$$

if j and k both refer to commodities,

$$RTS_{kj} = \frac{p_j}{p_k} \tag{11-13}$$

if j and k both refer to factors, and

$$MP_{jk} = \frac{p_j}{p_k} \tag{11-14}$$

if j refers to a commodity and k to a factor. Comparison of (11-11) through (11-14) with (11-8), (11-9), and (11-10) shows that the conditions for Pareto optimality are fulfilled in perfect competition.

The foregoing argument establishes that perfect competition is sufficient for Pareto optimality. The following indicates that it is normally necessary as well. Assume conditions (11-8) through (11-10) hold. Equations (11-11), (11-12) and (11-14) can be written combined as

$$RPT_{kj} = \frac{\text{marginal cost of } Q_j \text{ in terms of } X_i}{\text{marginal cost of } Q_k \text{ in terms of } X_i} = \frac{p_i/MP_{ij}}{p_i/MP_{ik}} = \frac{p_j}{p_k} = RCS_{kj} \tag{11-15}$$

where j and k refer to commodities and i to a factor. If prices were not equal to marginal costs, (11-15) could hold only if prices were proportional to marginal costs, i.e., if

$$p_j = \theta \, \frac{p_i}{MP_{ij}} \qquad p_k = \theta \, \frac{p_i}{MP_{ik}} \tag{11-16}$$

But rearranging (11-16),

$$\frac{p_i}{p_j} = \frac{1}{\theta} \, MP_{ij} \qquad \frac{p_i}{p_{k\cdot}} = \frac{1}{\theta} \, MP_{ik} \tag{11-17}$$

The left-hand sides of (11-17) equal the consumers' rate of substitution between Q_j (or Q_k) and X_i; the right-hand side is $1/\theta$ times the producers' rate of transformation between Q_j (or Q_k) and X_i. Conditions (11-10) are violated; the consumers' and producers' corresponding rates of substitution and transformation are not equal. Consumers do not provide the optimal amount of X_i (labor), and allocation cannot be Pareto-optimal.

Perfect competition represents a welfare optimum in the sense of fulfilling the requirements of Pareto optimality unless one or more of the assumptions mentioned earlier in this section are violated. Second-order conditions must be fulfilled for all consumers and producers. If they were violated for one or more producers or consumers, the equality of the relevant rates of substitution or transformation would not ensure optimality. In fact, the point at which the rates of substitution and transformation are equal may be a "pessimum" rather than an optimum. The optimum is then represented by a corner solution (see Fig. 2-4a). Pareto optimality may not be achieved under perfect competition if one or more consumers are satiated. The marginal utility increments of a satiated consumer equal zero for each good, and her rates of substitution are not defined. Goods may be diverted from her to other consumers with no reduction of her utility and increases of theirs. Illustrations of Pareto nonoptimality under perfect competition if external effects exist for consumption or production are given in Sec. 11-4.

There are cases in which perfect competition is Pareto-optimal, but some of the marginal equalities are not satisfied. Corner solutions may result even if all utility and production functions are of appropriate shape, provided that the consumers' RCSs are always greater (or smaller) than the corresponding producers' RPTs. One of the goods will not be produced, and Pareto optimality for the goods in question must be described in terms of marginal inequalities.

11-3 THE EFFICIENCY OF IMPERFECT COMPETITION

With few exceptions monopoly, oligopoly, monopsony, and other forms of imperfect competition will lead to Pareto-nonoptimal resource allocations. The marginal conditions realized under imperfect competition will normally violate the Pareto-optimal conditions given by (11-8), (11-9), and (11-10).

A partial-equilibrium approach is used here to judge the efficiency of particular sectors of an economy. It is assumed that conditions (11-11) through (11-14) are satisfied by all sectors other than the one under consideration. Consequently, that sector is judged by whether or not it satisfies these conditions. In the multimarket approach used in Sec. 11-1 conditions for Pareto optimality are derived without reference to market prices. Here, external prices are assumed to allocate efficiently. Situations for which this assumption is violated are considered in Sec. 11-7 below.

Imperfect Competition in Consumption

Imperfect competition will exist if one or more consumers are unable to buy as much of a commodity or sell as much of a factor as they desire without noticeably affecting its price. For illustration assume that there are two consumers, one factor, and two commodities. The utility functions are

$$U_1 = U_1(q_{11}, q_{12}, x_1^0 - x_1) \qquad U_2 = U_2(q_{21}, q_{22}, x_2^0 - x_2)$$

where x_i^0 is the factor endowment of the ith consumer, x_i is the quantity of factor that she supplies, and q_{ik} is her consumption of Q_k. Let the supply price of Q_1 depend upon the aggregate amount demanded: $p_1 = g(q_1)$ where $q_1 = q_{11} + q_{21}$ and $g'(q_1) > 0$. The budget constraints of the consumers are

$$rx_1 - g(q_1)q_{11} - p_2q_{12} = 0$$
$$rx_2 - g(q_1)q_{21} - p_2q_{22} = 0$$

Each maximizes her utility index subject to her budget constraint. Form the functions

$$L_1 = U_1(q_{11}, q_{12}, x_1^0 - x_1) + \lambda_1[rx_1 - g(q_1)q_{11} - p_2q_{12}]$$
$$L_2 = U_2(q_{21}, q_{22}, x_2^0 - x_2) + \lambda_2[rx_2 - g(q_1)q_{21} - p_2q_{22}]$$

and set the appropriate partial derivatives equal to zero:

$$\frac{\partial U_i}{\partial q_{i1}} - \lambda_i[p_1 + q_{i1}g'(q_1)] = 0$$

$$\frac{\partial U_i}{\partial q_{i2}} - \lambda_i p_2 = 0 \qquad -\frac{\partial U_i}{\partial(x_i^0 - x_i)} + \lambda_i r = 0 \qquad i = 1, 2 \qquad (11\text{-}18)$$

$$rx_i - g(q_1)q_{i1} - p_2q_{i2} = 0$$

and $\quad \dfrac{\partial U_i/\partial q_{i1}}{\partial U_i/\partial q_{i2}} = \dfrac{p_1 + q_{i1}g'(q_1)}{p_2} \qquad \dfrac{\partial U_i/\partial q_{i1}}{\partial U_i/\partial(x_i^0 - x_i)} = \dfrac{p_1 + q_{i1}g'(q_1)}{r} \qquad i = 1, 2$

The consumers behave as duopsonists (see Sec. 8-3). Their equilibrium RCSs given by (11-18) reflect the marginal costs of acquiring additional quantities of Q_1 rather than p_1.†

If $q_{11} \neq q_{21}$, the marginal costs of Q_1 differ for the consumers, their RCSs differ, and the allocation of Q_1, Q_2, and X between them is Pareto-nonoptimal. If $q_{11} = q_{21}$, their RCSs are equal, but differ from the RPTs and MPs of producers which are equated to price ratios.

Imperfect Competition in Commodity Markets

For convenience limit attention to a single commodity, Q, with price p, and a single factor, X, with price r. Conditions (11-10) for Pareto optimality will be satisfied if producers equate their MPs and consumers equate their RCSs to

---

† Again it is assumed that the second-order conditions are fulfilled.

the factor-commodity price ratio:

$$MP = \frac{r}{p} = RCS \tag{11-19}$$

If it is assumed that consumers always satisfy (11-19), Pareto optimality will be achieved if producers equate price and MC (marginal cost):

$$p = \frac{r}{MP} = MC \tag{11-20}$$

If one or more producers fail to satisfy (11-20) the resultant allocation will be Pareto-nonoptimal. The equality of price and MC is a normal result under perfect competition, but it is an unusual result under imperfect competition.

The simple monopolist (see Sec. 7-1) equates MR (marginal revenue), which is less than price, to MC and thereby creates a Pareto-nonoptimal allocation. The perfectly discriminating monopolist (see Sec. 7-2) is an exception to the rule that imperfect competition is Pareto-nonoptimal. She equates marginal price to MC. Conditions (11-19) and (11-20) are satisfied if p is appropriately interpreted as marginal price for both consumers and producer. In perfect competition both buyer and seller gain from trade; in perfectly discriminating monopoly all gains are absorbed by the seller. The income distributions which result from these two forms of market organization are quite different, but both are Pareto-optimal.

The revenue-maximizing monopolist (see Sec. 7-3) maximizes her sales revenue subject to the condition that her profit equal or exceed a minimum acceptable level. Her minimum acceptable profit is generally less than her maximum monopoly profit, and her output level is generally higher than the level that would be achieved under simple monopoly. The revenue-maximizing monopolist would satisfy condition (11-20) if (1) her minimum acceptable profit equaled the profit that is earned at an output for which price equals MC and MC is increasing, and (2) her MR were nonnegative at this point. Since she has no particular motive to select such a point, the occurence of both (1) and (2) would be a remarkable coincidence. In general, one cannot expect the revenue-maximizing monopolist to satisfy the conditions necessary for Pareto optimality.

Duopoly and oligopoly also will normally result in Pareto-nonoptimal allocations. Condition (11-20) is violated in all the cases considered in Sec. 8-1. In each case one or more of the market participants equate some form of MR to MC. The same comment applies for the analysis of monopolistic competition presented in Sec. 7-5.

Imperfect Competition in Factor Markets

Consider a factor market in which the sellers behave as perfect competitors. Conditions (11-10) for Pareto optimality will be fulfilled if each buyer of the input equates the value of her MP to the factor price:

$$p\,MP = r \tag{11-21}$$

If one or more buyers fail to satisfy (11-21), the resultant allocation will be Pareto-nonoptimal. Condition (11-21) is normally satisfied under perfect competition, and normally violated under imperfect competition among buyers.

The monopsonist (see Sec. 7-4) equates the value of her MP to her marginal cost for the factor, which is greater than its price, and thereby creates a Pareto-nonoptimal allocation. It is left as an exercise for the reader to formulate an analysis for a perfectly discriminating monopsonist parallel to the analysis for a perfectly discriminating monopolist, and to demonstrate that the resultant allocation is Pareto-optimal. Nearly all theories of duopsony and oligopsony involve equating the value of MP to some form of marginal input cost, and thereby violate (11-21).

The Efficiency of Bilateral Monopoly

The markets thus far considered have imperfect competition on the seller's side and perfect competition on the buyers', or perfect competition on the sellers' side and imperfect competition on the buyers'. The term bilateral monopoly in its broadest sense covers markets in which there is imperfect competition on the part of both buyers and sellers.

The case of a monopsonistic buyer and a monopolistic seller is covered in Sec. 8-5. The specific outcome for such markets depends upon the relative bargaining strength of the participants. In Sec. 8-5 it was shown that input and output levels will be identical with those that would be achieved by perfect competition if the monopsonist and monopolist maximize their joint profit. The resultant allocation is Pareto-optimal. The distribution of their joint profit is immaterial from the viewpoint of Pareto optimality, although it may be rather important to them. This result is easily generalized to cover markets in which the aggregate number of buyers and sellers is greater than two, provided that they maximize their joint profit.

11-4 EXTERNAL EFFECTS IN CONSUMPTION AND PRODUCTION

The conclusion that perfect competition leads to Pareto-optimal allocations is contingent upon the assumption that there are no external effects in consumption and production, i.e., that the utility level of a consumer does not depend upon the consumption levels of others and that the total cost of an entrepreneur does not depend upon the output levels of others. Pareto optimality may not be realized under conditions of perfect competition if there are external effects in consumption and production.

Interdependent Utility Functions

Assume that the utility level of one consumer depends upon the consumption of another. Extreme altruism may increase the satisfaction of the ith consumer if the consumption level of the jth consumer is raised. The desire to "keep up with the Joneses" may have the opposite effect.

Assume that there are two consumers with the utility functions

$$U_1 = U_1(q_{11}, q_{12}, q_{21}, q_{22})$$
$$U_2 = U_2(q_{11}, q_{12}, q_{21}, q_{22})$$

where $q_{11} + q_{21} = q_1^0$, $q_{12} + q_{22} = q_2^0$. In order to maximize the utility of I subject to the constraint that the utility of II is at the predetermined level $U_2^0 = $ constant, form the function

$$U_1^* = U_1(q_{11}, q_{12}, q_1^0 - q_{11}, q_2^0 - q_{12}) + \lambda[U_2(q_{11}, q_{12}, q_1^0 - q_{11}, q_2^0 - q_{12}) - U_2^0]$$

and set the partial derivatives equal to zero:

$$\frac{\partial U_1^*}{\partial q_{11}} = \frac{\partial U_1}{\partial q_{11}} - \frac{\partial U_1}{\partial q_{21}} + \lambda\left[\frac{\partial U_2}{\partial q_{11}} - \frac{\partial U_2}{\partial q_{21}}\right] = 0$$

$$\frac{\partial U_1^*}{\partial q_{12}} = \frac{\partial U_1}{\partial q_{12}} - \frac{\partial U_1}{\partial q_{22}} + \lambda\left[\frac{\partial U_2}{\partial q_{12}} - \frac{\partial U_2}{\partial q_{22}}\right] = 0$$

$$\frac{\partial U_1^*}{\partial \lambda} = U_2(q_{11}, q_{12}, q_1^0 - q_{11}, q_2^0 - q_{12}) - U_2^0 = 0$$

and
$$\frac{\partial U_1/\partial q_{11} - \partial U_1/\partial q_{21}}{\partial U_1/\partial q_{12} - \partial U_1/\partial q_{22}} = \frac{\partial U_2/\partial q_{11} - \partial U_2/\partial q_{21}}{\partial U_2/\partial q_{12} - \partial U_2/\partial q_{22}} \qquad (11\text{-}22)$$

Equation (11-22) is a condition for Pareto optimality. It generally differs from (11-8) which states that I's RCS must equal II's. Perfect competition results in the attainment of (11-8), but not of (11-22). Since the partial derivatives of the utility functions are functions of all variables, the optimum position of each consumer depends upon the consumption level of the other. For example, assume that the only external effect present in the two-consumer system is $\partial U_2/\partial q_{11} < 0$. Equation (11-22) becomes

$$\frac{\partial U_1/\partial q_{11}}{\partial U_1/\partial q_{12}} = \frac{\partial U_2/\partial q_{11} - \partial U_2/\partial q_{21}}{-\partial U_2/\partial q_{22}}$$

The RCS of consumer II must be greater for an optimal distribution than it would be in the absence of external effects.

It can be shown diagrammatically that condition (11-8) does not necessarily ensure Pareto optimality in the presence of external effects. Figure 11-2a and 11-2b give the indifference maps of consumers I and II respectively. Assume that in the initial situation I consumes the commodity batch represented by A and II consumes the batch represented by F. These points—at which their RCSs are equal—are reached by individual utility maximization with no regard for possible external effects. Assume that I is

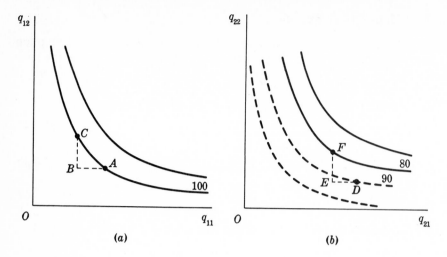

Figure 11-2

not affected by II's consumption, and II's utility level is reduced by I's consumption of Q_1 (but not of Q_2). II's indifference map (solid curves) is drawn on the assumption that I's consumption is given by A. In their individual equilibrium situations I's utility index is 100, and II's, 80. Let the distribution of commodities be altered such that the aggregate quantities consumed remain unchanged and I moves to C and II to D. The utility level of consumer I has not been changed by this reallocation. However, the diminution of her consumption of Q_1 changes II's utility level for every commodity combination consumed by the latter: II's relevant indifference curves after the change in I's consumption are given by the dotted curves in Fig. 11-2b. Consumer II's utility level is increased to 90 since her new position is at D. One can conclude that II's utility level can be increased without diminishing I's utility level; hence the equality of the RCSs does not ensure Pareto optimality.

Public Goods

A different type of externality in consumption occurs when goods are consumed collectively. Each member of society gains satisfaction from the total output of a *public good*. No one's satisfaction is diminished by the satisfaction gained by others, and it is not possible for anyone to appropriate a public good for her own personal use, as is the case with ordinary goods.

The conditions for Pareto optimality given by (11-8) and (11-10) are not valid for public goods. New conditions must be formulated. No essentials are lost by the simplifying assumptions that there are two consumers, one producer, one ordinary good, one public good, and one primary factor. The consumers' utility functions are

$$U_i = U_i(q_{i1}, q_2, x_i^0 - x_i) \qquad i = 1, 2$$

where q_{i1} is the consumption of the ordinary good Q_1 by the ith consumer, q_2 is the total output of the public good Q_2, x_i^0 is the ith consumer's endowment of the primary factor X, and x_i is the amount that she supplies for production. The implicit production function is

$$F(q_1, q_2, x) = 0$$

where $q_1 = q_{11} + q_{21}$ is the output of Q_1 and $x = x_1 + x_2$ is the amount of X used in production.

Conditions for Pareto optimality are obtained by maximizing I's utility assuming that II's utility is at a predetermined level and that the production function is satisfied. Form the Lagrange function

$$Z = U_1(q_{11}, q_2, x_1^0 - x_1) + \lambda [U_2(q_{21}, q_2, x_2^0 - x_2) - U_2^0]$$
$$+ \theta F(q_1, q_2, x) + \delta(x_1 + x_2 - x) + \sigma(q_1 - q_{11} - q_{21})$$

where λ, θ, δ, and σ are undetermined multipliers. Setting the partial derivatives of Z equal to zero,

$$\frac{\partial Z}{\partial q_{11}} = \frac{\partial U_1}{\partial q_{11}} - \sigma = 0 \qquad \frac{\partial Z}{\partial x_1} = -\frac{\partial U_1}{\partial(x_1^0 - x_1)} + \delta = 0$$

$$\frac{\partial Z}{\partial q_{21}} = \lambda \frac{\partial U_2}{\partial q_{21}} - \sigma = 0 \qquad \frac{\partial Z}{\partial x_2} = -\lambda \frac{\partial U_2}{\partial(x_2^0 - x_2)} + \delta = 0$$

$$\frac{\partial Z}{\partial q_2} = \frac{\partial U_1}{\partial q_2} + \lambda \frac{\partial U_2}{\partial q_2} + \theta \frac{\partial F}{\partial q_2} = 0 \qquad (11\text{-}23)$$

$$\frac{\partial Z}{\partial q_1} = \theta \frac{\partial F}{\partial q_1} + \sigma = 0 \qquad \frac{\partial Z}{\partial x} = \theta \frac{\partial F}{\partial x} - \delta = 0$$

It is assumed that the partial derivatives with respect to the Lagrange multipliers are also set equal to zero.

For ordinary goods (11-8) states that the RCS for every consumer must equal the corresponding RPT for every producer. Equations (11-23) imply that[1]

$$\frac{\partial U_1/\partial q_2}{\partial U_1/\partial q_{11}} + \frac{\partial U_2/\partial q_2}{\partial U_2/\partial q_{21}} = \frac{\partial F/\partial q_2}{\partial F/\partial q_1} \qquad (11\text{-}24)$$

The sum of the RCSs of Q_1 for Q_2 for the consumers must equal the RPT of Q_1 for Q_2 in production. The RCSs of the individual consumers need not be equal. Imagine that I and II have respective RCSs of 3 and 2 units of Q_1 per unit of Q_2, but that the producer's RPT is 4 units of Q_1 per unit of Q_2.

---

[1] Substitute $\lambda = \sigma/(\partial U_2/\partial q_{21})$ and $\theta = -\sigma/(\partial F/\partial q_1)$ in the equation for $\partial Z/\partial q_2$, divide through by $\sigma = \partial U_1/\partial q_{11}$, and rearrange terms.

Condition (11-24) is violated and the allocation of Q_2 and Q_1 is Pareto-nonoptimal. If I and II surrendered 3 and 2 units of Q_1 respectively, the producer could increase the output of Q_2 by more than 1 unit and thereby increase the utility levels of both consumers.

Equations (11-23) also imply that

$$\frac{\partial U_1/\partial q_2}{\partial U_1/\partial (x_1^0 - x_1)} + \frac{\partial U_2/\partial q_2}{\partial U_2/\partial (x_2^0 - x_2)} = -\frac{\partial F/\partial q_2}{\partial F/\partial x} \tag{11-25}$$

The sum of the RCSs of X for Q_2 must equal the reciprocal of the MP of X in the production of Q_2. Finally, solving (11-23) for δ/σ,

$$\frac{\delta}{\sigma} = \frac{\partial U_1/\partial (x_1^0 - x_1)}{\partial U_1/\partial q_{11}} = \frac{\partial U_2/\partial (x_2^0 - x_2)}{\partial U_2/\partial q_{21}} = -\frac{\partial F/\partial x}{\partial F/\partial q_1} \tag{11-26}$$

The RCS of X for Q_1 for each consumer should equal the MP of X in the production of Q_1. Condition (11-26) is the same as (11-10).

The analysis of public goods is easily generalized. If there is more than one primary factor, (11-9) is in force: the RCSs of all consumers and the RTSs of all producers must be equal for every pair of primary factors. If there is more than one ordinary good, (11-8) is in force: the RCSs of the consumers must equal the RPTs of the producers. If there are two public goods, their aggregate RCS, which may be expressed as the ratio of their aggregate RCSs for an arbitrarily selected ordinary good, must equal their RPT (see Exercise 11-4).

Lindahl Equilibrium

Public goods cannot be purchased and sold in the market in the same way as ordinary goods. No consumer can acquire a quantity of a public good that is exclusively hers. However, it is possible to design a scheme that results in equilibrium in a "pseudo market" for a public good.

Consider an economy with two consumers, one producer, one ordinary good, one public good, and a primary factor which is available in a fixed amount and yields no utility to the consumers. The utility functions are

$$U_1 = U_1(q_{11}, q_2) \qquad U_2 = U_2(q_{21}, q_2) \tag{11-27}$$

where Q_1 is the ordinary and Q_2 the public good. The production function is

$$F(q_1, q_2) - x^0 = 0 \tag{11-28}$$

with

$$q_1 = q_{11} + q_{21} \tag{11-29}$$

where $x^0 = x_1^0 + x_2^0$ is the fixed amount of the primary factor, and x_1^0 and x_2^0 are the amounts held by the two consumers. Let p_1 be the market price for Q_1, and p_2 the price received by the producer per unit of the public good. Assume that I and II are charged αp_2 and $(1 - \alpha)p_2$ respectively per unit of the public good produced where $0 < \alpha < 1$. Let the price of the primary factor equal one.

The consumers maximize their utility functions (11-27) subject to the budget constraints

$$p_1 q_{11} + \alpha p_2 q_2 = x_1^0 \qquad p_1 q_{21} + (1 - \alpha) p_2 q_2 = x_2^0 \qquad (11\text{-}30)$$

They equate their perceived price ratios to their RCSs

$$\frac{\alpha p_2}{p_1} = \frac{\partial U_1 / \partial q_2}{\partial U_1 / \partial q_{11}} \qquad \frac{(1 - \alpha) p_2}{p_1} = \frac{\partial U_2 / \partial q_2}{\partial U_2 / \partial q_{21}} \qquad (11\text{-}31)$$

Adding Eqs. (11-31),

$$\frac{p_2}{p_1} = \frac{\partial U_1 / \partial q_2}{\partial U_1 / \partial q_{11}} + \frac{\partial U_2 / \partial q_2}{\partial U_2 / \partial q_{21}} \qquad (11\text{-}32)$$

The producer maximizes profit (with x^0 considered fixed) subject to the constraint given by (11-28). She thus equates the price ratio and her RPT:

$$\frac{p_2}{p_1} = \frac{\partial F / \partial q_2}{\partial F / \partial q_1} \qquad (11\text{-}33)$$

It follows from (11-32) and (11-33) that (11-8) is satisfied and a Pareto-optimal allocation is achieved. The system formed by (11-28) through (11-33) has seven independent equations in seven variables: q_1, q_2, q_{11}, q_{21}, p_1, p_2, and α.† The solution values represent Lindahl equilibrium.

An alternative way of visualizing the process is as follows. Utility maximization is used to derive demand functions for goods $f_{11}(p_1, \alpha p_2)$, $f_{12}(p_1, \alpha p_2)$, $f_{21}[p_1, (1 - \alpha) p_2]$, $f_{22}[p_1, (1 - \alpha) p_2]$ where f_{ij} is the ith consumer's demand for the jth good. The producer's supply functions are derived from profit maximization and are $g_1(p_1, p_2)$, $g_2(p_1, p_2)$. Equilibrium in the market for the ordinary good requires

$$f_{11}(p_1, \alpha p_2) + f_{21}[p_1, (1 - \alpha) p_2] = g_1(p_1, p_2) \qquad (11\text{-}34)$$

Equilibrium in the pseudo market for the public good requires

$$f_{12}(p_1, \alpha p_2) = f_{22}[p_1, (1 - \alpha) p_2] = g_2(p_1, p_2) \qquad (11\text{-}35)$$

where the first equality expresses the requirement that each consumer consume the same amount of the public good, and the second that the amount demanded equal the amount supplied. The three equations in (11-34) and (11-35) determine p_1, p_2, and α; the quantities are then determined from the f_{ij}.

For illustration assume that the utility and production functions are

$$U_1 = q_{11}^{0.5} q_2 \qquad U_2 = q_{21}^2 q_2 \qquad q_1^2 + q_2^2 - x^0 = 0$$

---

† Equation (11-32), which is the sum of two of the other equations, is not independent.

and assume that $x^0 = 1600$ with $x_1^0 = 128$ and $x_2^0 = 1472$. The independent equations of (11-28) through (11-33) are

$$q_1^2 + q_2^2 = 1600 \qquad q_1 = q_{11} + q_{21}$$

$$\frac{p_2}{p_1} = \frac{q_2}{q_1} \qquad \frac{\alpha p_2}{p_1} = \frac{2q_{11}}{q_2} \qquad \frac{(1-\alpha)p_2}{p_1} = \frac{q_{21}}{2q_2}$$

$$p_1 q_{11} + \alpha p_2 q_2 = 128 \qquad p_1 q_{21} + (1-\alpha)p_2 q_2 = 1472$$

The reader may verify that this system has the following solution:

$$q_1 = 32 \qquad q_{11} = 1\tfrac{1}{3} \qquad q_{21} = 30\tfrac{2}{3}$$

$$q_2 = 24 \qquad p_1 = 32 \qquad p_2 = 24 \qquad \alpha = \tfrac{4}{27}$$

External Economies and Diseconomies

It was shown that the $p = MC$ criterion is necessary for Pareto optimality in the producing sector. The equality of price and marginal cost for all commodities and firms implies that the corresponding RPTs of different firms are the same. The RPT (the slope of the transformation curve) measures the opportunity cost or the real sacrifice, in terms of opportunities foregone, of producing an additional unit of a commodity. Until now this opportunity cost has been considered internal to the firm: in order to produce an additional unit of Q_j it has to sacrifice the production of a certain number of units of Q_k. The relevant measure of the sacrifice from society's point of view is the number of units of Q_k that society has to give up in order to produce an additional unit of Q_j. The opportunity cost is the same from the private and social points of view in the absence of external economies and diseconomies. If such external effects are present in the productive sphere, one must take into account the interdependence between the costs of the ith firm and the output of the hth (see Sec. 6-3).

Assume for simplicity's sake that there are only two firms with the cost functions

$$C_1 = C_1(q_1, q_2) \qquad C_2 = C_2(q_1, q_2) \tag{11-36}$$

where q_1 and q_2 are the output levels. The cost functions (11-36) express the existence of external effects. If each firm maximizes its profit individually, price will equal MC or

$$p = \frac{\partial C_1}{\partial q_1} \qquad p = \frac{\partial C_2}{\partial q_2}$$

The profit of each firm depends upon the output level of the other, but neither can affect the output of the other, and thus each firm maximizes its profit with respect to the variable under its control.

The welfare associated with production can be measured by the difference between the social benefit created and the social cost incurred. The social benefit derived from $q_1 + q_2$ units of the commodity can be measured by the total revenue $p(q_1 + q_2)$, i.e., by the amount that consumers are willing to pay for the output. The social costs are measured by the sum of the costs incurred by both entrepreneurs producing the commodity, $C_1(q_1, q_2) + C_2(q_1, q_2)$. In order to attain Pareto optimality, one must maximize the entrepreneurs' joint profits on the assumption that neither can influence price:

$$\pi = \pi_1 + \pi_2 = p(q_1 + q_2) - C_1(q_1, q_2) - C_2(q_1, q_2)$$

Setting the partial derivatives equal to zero,

$$\frac{\partial \pi}{\partial q_1} = p - \frac{\partial C_1}{\partial q_1} - \frac{\partial C_2}{\partial q_1} = 0$$

$$\frac{\partial \pi}{\partial q_2} = p - \frac{\partial C_1}{\partial q_2} - \frac{\partial C_2}{\partial q_2} = 0$$

(11-37)

The second-order conditions require that the principal minors of the relevant Hessian

$$\begin{vmatrix} -\dfrac{\partial^2 C_1}{\partial q_1^2} - \dfrac{\partial^2 C_2}{\partial q_1^2} & -\dfrac{\partial^2 C_1}{\partial q_1\, \partial q_2} - \dfrac{\partial^2 C_2}{\partial q_1\, \partial q_2} \\[3mm] -\dfrac{\partial^2 C_1}{\partial q_1\, \partial q_2} - \dfrac{\partial^2 C_2}{\partial q_1\, \partial q_2} & -\dfrac{\partial^2 C_1}{\partial q_2^2} - \dfrac{\partial^2 C_2}{\partial q_2^2} \end{vmatrix}$$

alternate in sign. These conditions imply that

$$\frac{\partial^2 C_1}{\partial q_1^2} + \frac{\partial^2 C_2}{\partial q_1^2} > 0 \qquad \frac{\partial^2 C_1}{\partial q_2^2} + \frac{\partial^2 C_2}{\partial q_2^2} > 0$$

The partial derivatives $\partial C_1 / \partial q_1$ and $\partial C_2 / \partial q_2$ are the *private* marginal costs because they measure the rate of increase of an individual entrepreneur's total cost as her output level rises. Individual maximization requires that price equal private marginal cost and that private marginal cost be increasing. The sums $\partial C_1 / \partial q_1 + \partial C_2 / \partial q_1$ and $\partial C_1 / \partial q_2 + \partial C_2 / \partial q_2$ are *social* marginal costs because they measure the rate of increase of the industry's costs as the output level of a particular firm increases. Pareto optimality requires that price equal the *social marginal cost* of each entrepreneur and that *social marginal cost be increasing*. The equality of price and social marginal cost guarantees that the consumers' RCS will equal not the individual firms' RPTs but society's RPT, since the ratio of the social marginal costs measures, from society's point of view, the alternatives foregone by producing an additional unit of a commodity.

Assume that firm I experiences external economies and firm II experiences external diseconomies. Then $\partial C_1 / \partial q_2 < 0$ and $\partial C_2 / \partial q_1 > 0$. As a result, $\partial C_1 / \partial q_1 + \partial C_2 / \partial q_1$ in (11-37) can be made to equal price only if $\partial C_1 / \partial q_1$ is smaller than under individual profit maximization. With increasing MC this means that the firm which is the cause of external diseconomies should produce a lower level of output for welfare maximization than in the case of individual maximization. By analogous reasoning the firm which is the cause of external economies should increase its output. These output changes can generally be accomplished by appropriate taxation and subsidization of the output levels of the firms concerned.

Assume that the cost functions of the two firms are

$$C_1 = 0.1q_1^2 + 5q_1 - 0.1q_2^2 \qquad C_2 = 0.2q_2^2 + 7q_2 + 0.025q_1^2$$

Firm I experiences external economies and is the cause of external diseconomies; the converse holds for firm II. Assuming that the price is 15 dollars and setting it equal to MC for both firms,

$$15 = 0.2q_1 + 5 \qquad q_1 = 50 \qquad \pi_1 = 290$$
$$15 = 0.4q_2 + 7 \qquad q_2 = 20 \qquad \pi_2 = 17.5$$

For Pareto optimality form the joint profit function

$$\pi = 15(q_1 + q_2) - 0.125q_1^2 - 5q_1 - 0.1q_2^2 - 7q_2$$

and set the partial derivatives equal to zero:

$$\frac{\partial \pi}{\partial q_1} = 15 - 0.25q_1 - 5 = 0$$

$$\frac{\partial \pi}{\partial q_2} = 15 - 0.20q_2 - 7 = 0$$

Here $q_1 = 40$, $q_2 = 40$, and $\pi = 360$. The reader may verify that the second-order conditions are satisfied. Total profits are greater in this case than under individual maximization

$$290 + 17.5 = 307.5 < 360$$

Individual maximization does not ensure Pareto optimality. Pareto optimality requires that the RCS equal the rate at which society can transform one commodity into another. In the absence of external effects, the private and social rates of product transformation are identical. In the presence of external economies or diseconomies individual maximization results in the fulfillment of socially "wrong" or irrelevant marginal conditions. Of course, aggregate profits *have* to be redistributed among the individual firms. Without such redistribution, some firms would experience a diminution in their profits, and the resulting position could not be said to be socially preferable. In the present example, 400 dollars accrue to firm I and −40 dollars to firm II as a result of joint maximization. A redistribution of any amount greater than 57.5, but less than 110, dollars from firm I to firm II will leave each better off than under individual maximization.

11-5 TAXES AND SUBSIDIES

Sections (11-3) and (11-4) contain many examples in which market economies deviate from the marginal conditions necessary for Pareto optimality. Such economies usually can be led to Pareto optimality through the imposition of appropriate taxes and subsidies. Per unit taxes (subsidies) will decrease (increase) the levels of consumption and production activities by increasing (decreasing) their marginal costs if marginal costs are increasing. Accompanying lump-sum taxes and subsidies, which do not affect activity levels, may be used to distribute the gains from a movement to a Pareto-optimal allocation.

The achievement of Pareto optimality through taxation is illustrated for two specific cases: external effects in production, and monopoly. Unit taxes and subsidies are designed to lead market participants to observe the desired marginal conditions, and lump-sum taxes and subsidies are designed to leave consumers and producers at initial utility and profit levels. It is then demonstrated that positive net tax revenues provide social dividends that can be used to increase the utility of one or more members of society.

External Effects in Production

If external effects are present, Pareto optimality normally can be achieved by imposing unit subsidies to increase the outputs of firms that generate external economies, and unit taxes to decrease the outputs of firms that generate external diseconomies. Return to the two-firm example presented in Sec. 11-4. A Pareto-optimal allocation is determined by equating the social MC of each firm to the competitive price:

$$0.25q_1^* + 5 = 15 \qquad q_1^* = 40 \qquad \pi_1^* = 400$$
$$0.20q_2^* + 7 = 15 \qquad q_2^* = 40 \qquad \pi_2^* = -40$$

Let a tax of t dollars per unit be imposed on the output of firm I, and a subsidy of s dollars per unit be imposed on the output of firm II. Assume that each firm continues to equate its private MC to the competitive price:

$$0.2q_1 + 5 + t = 15 \qquad 0.4q_2 + 7 - s = 15 \tag{11-38}$$

The tax and subsidy are designed to achieve the Pareto-optimal outputs. Substituting $q_1 = 40$ and $q_2 = 40$ in (11-38), the appropriate values for the tax and subsidy are $t = 2$ and $s = 8$. Lump-sum taxes, L_1 and L_2, are imposed to leave the profits of the firms at their initial levels:

$$L_1 = \pi_1^* - \pi_1^0 - tq_1^* = 30$$
$$L_2 = \pi_2^* - \pi_2^0 + sq_2^* = 262.5$$

Since profits remain unchanged, the utility levels of those who receive the profits are unchanged by this move to Pareto optimality. A *social dividend, S,* is defined as the net tax proceeds:

$$S = tq_1^* - sq_2^* + L_1 + L_2 = 52.5$$

The social dividend may be used to increase the utility levels of one or more members of society.

Monopoly

Consider an economy in which a monopolist producing good Q is the only cause for deviation from Pareto optimality. The monopolist's demand and cost functions are $p = f(q)$ and $C = C(q)$. Her profit-maximizing output and price, q^0 and p^0, are determined by equating MR and MC:

$$p^0 + q^0 f'(q^0) = C'(q^0) \qquad (11\text{-}39)$$

Her equilibrium is pictured as point E in Fig. 11-3. The monopolist's price is too high and her quantity too low for Pareto optimality. Pareto-optimal quantity and price, q^* and p^*, are determined by equating price and MC:

$$p^* = C'(q^*) \qquad (11\text{-}40)$$

which occurs at point A in Fig. 11-3.

A unit subsidy will increase the monopolist's MR and may be used to induce her to expand her output to the Pareto-optimal level. The relevant equilibrium condition is

$$p^* + q^* f'(q^*) + s = C'(q^*) \qquad (11\text{-}41)$$

Solve (11-41) for s utilizing (11-40) and the definition of MR:

$$s = -q^* f'(q^*) = p^* - \text{MR}^*$$

The desired unit subsidy equals the difference between price and MR at the Pareto-optimal output, the distance CA in Fig. 11-3. The monopolist's effective MR curve is shifted upward until it intersects the original demand curve at A.

The total subsidy is given by the area of the rectangle $FCAp^*$ in Fig. 11-3. The monopolist's cost increment for the move from q^0 to q^* is given by the area lying under her MC curve between these outputs, and her revenue increment from sales is given by the corresponding area lying under her MR

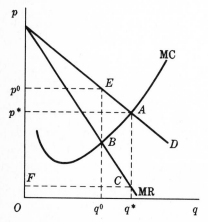

Figure 11-3

curve. Her profit reduction is the area CAB which lies between her MC and MR curves. In general,

$$\pi^0 - \pi^* = \int_{q^0}^{q^*} [f(q) + qf'(q) - C'(q)] \, dq$$

It is obvious from Fig. 11-3 that the subsidy exceeds the profit reduction. The imposition of a lump-sum tax equal to the area $FCBAp^*$ will leave the monopolist's profit at its initial level. In general, the lump-sum tax, L_M, is

$$L_M = \pi^* - \pi^0 + sq^*$$

The net cost of the movement to the Pareto-optimal output equals the monopolist's profit differential. A social dividend will remain if consumers may be taxed by a larger amount without utility reductions.

Assume that the income elasticity of demand for the commodity under consideration is zero for every consumer. In this case, the ordinary demand curve coincides with the compensated demand curve that passes through the monopoly equilibrium point (see Sec. 2-3). The area under the demand curve from q^0 to q^* gives the amount that consumers can pay while retaining the utility levels that they achieved under monopoly (see Sec. 3-7). The corresponding area under the MR curve gives the amount that they actually pay for a move from q^0 to q^*. The area that lies between the demand and MR curves is the total of lump-sum taxes, L_C, that can be collected from consumers leaving them at their initial utility levels:

$$L_C = \int_{q^0}^{q^*} [-qf'(q)] \, dq$$

and the corresponding social dividend is the net tax collected from consumers and the producer:

$$S = L_C + L_M - sq^*$$

Figure 11-3 shows that the social dividend is always positive under monopoly. The lump-sum taxes for consumers are given by the area $BCAE$, the net payment to the monopolist by the area BCA, and the social dividend by the area BAE which is sometimes called the *dead-weight loss* due to monopoly.

The assumption of zero income elasticities is not necessary to secure a positive social dividend. Assume that each consumer has a positive income elasticity. The price reduction for Q will have positive income effects, consumers can pay the lump-sum taxes given by the area $BCAE$, the social dividend BAE can be achieved, and in addition each consumer can have a utility higher than her initial level.

Let the monopolist's demand and cost functions be

$$p = 240 - 8q \qquad C = 2q^2$$

Equating MR and MC,

$$240 - 16q^0 = 4q^0 \qquad q^0 = 12 \qquad p^0 = 144$$
$$MR^0 = MC^0 = 48 \qquad \pi^0 = 1440$$

The Pareto-optimal quantity and price are obtained by letting price equal MC:

$$240 - 8q^* = 4q^* \qquad q^* = 20 \qquad p^* = MC = 80$$
$$MR^* = -80 \qquad \pi^* = 800$$

It is of interest to note that MR is negative for the Pareto-optimal solution in this case. The optimal unit subsidy and lump-sum tax are

$$s = p^* - MR^* = 160 \qquad L_M = \pi^* - \pi^0 + sq^* = 2560$$

Assume that all consumers have zero income elasticities for Q. The consumers' lump-sum taxes and the social dividend are

$$L_C = \int_{12}^{20} 8q \, dq = (4)(20)^2 - (4)(12)^2 = 1024$$

$$S = L_C + L_M - sq^* = 384$$

11-6 SOCIAL WELFARE FUNCTIONS

The determination of socially optimal allocations of resources requires explicit comparisons of the utility levels of the various members of society. It is necessary to know whether a change from which some individuals gain and some lose is desirable. Pareto optimality is not sufficient for this purpose, but such decisions can be made after the explicit introduction of a social welfare function. A common procedure is to express social welfare as a function of the utility levels of all members. Social welfare might be an ordinal index, but individual utilities must be cardinal, at least in the sense that they are unique except for origin and units of measure. The form for a social welfare function is not unique. It depends upon the value judgments of its formulators. It might be derived from a common consensus, or it might be imposed in a dictatorial fashion.

In this section, first, the properties of social optima are considered on the assumption that a social welfare function exists. Second, the determination of social welfare functions is discussed in the light of the Arrow impossibility theorem. Third, interpersonal utility analysis is illustrated for a particular form of social welfare function.

Determination of a Welfare Optimum

Assume that there exists a social welfare function of the general form

$$W = W(U_1, U_2, \ldots, U_n) \tag{11-42}$$

where U_i is the level of the utility index of the ith individual. Assume that society consists of two individuals whose utility functions are

$$U_1 = U_1(q_{11}, q_{12}, x_1^0 - x_1) \qquad U_2 = U_2(q_{21}, q_{22}, x_2^0 - x_2)$$

where q_{ij} is the amount of the jth commodity consumed by the ith individual and x_i the amount of work performed by the ith individual. Assume that society's production function is

$$F(q_{11} + q_{21}, q_{12} + q_{22}, x_1 + x_2) = 0 \qquad (11\text{-}43)$$

Assume finally that the social welfare function is

$$W = W(U_1, U_2) \qquad (11\text{-}44)$$

The goal of society is to maximize (11-44) subject to the constraint given by (11-43). Form the function

$$W^* = W[U_1(q_{11}, q_{12}, x_1^0 - x_1), U_2(q_{21}, q_{22}, x_2^0 - x_2)]$$
$$+ \lambda F(q_{11} + q_{21}, q_{12} + q_{22}, x_1 + x_2)$$

and set its partial derivatives equal to zero:

$$\frac{\partial W^*}{\partial q_{11}} = W_1 \frac{\partial U_1}{\partial q_{11}} + \lambda F_1 = 0$$

$$\frac{\partial W^*}{\partial q_{12}} = W_1 \frac{\partial U_1}{\partial q_{12}} + \lambda F_2 = 0$$

$$\frac{\partial W^*}{\partial x_1} = - W_1 \frac{\partial U_1}{\partial (x_1^0 - x_1)} + \lambda F_3 = 0$$

$$\frac{\partial W^*}{\partial q_{21}} = W_2 \frac{\partial U_2}{\partial q_{21}} + \lambda F_1 = 0 \qquad (11\text{-}45)$$

$$\frac{\partial W^*}{\partial q_{22}} = W_2 \frac{\partial U_2}{\partial q_{22}} + \lambda F_2 = 0$$

$$\frac{\partial W^*}{\partial x_2} = - W_2 \frac{\partial U_2}{\partial (x_2^0 - x_2)} + \lambda F_3 = 0$$

$$\frac{\partial W^*}{\partial \lambda} = F(q_{11} + q_{21}, q_{12} + q_{22}, x_1 + x_2) = 0$$

It is assumed that the system of seven equations given by (11-45) can be solved for its seven variables. A welfare optimum is completely determined as a result of the introduction of distributional value judgments in the form of the social welfare function.[1] It can easily be verified that the resulting

---

[1] In terms of the Edgeworth box diagram discussed in Sec. 9-2, the introduction of the social welfare function is equivalent to ranking all points on the contract curve from the point of view of social preferability.

allocation is Pareto-optimal. Move the second terms of the first six equations in (11-45) to the right and then divide the first equation by the second and the third and fourth equations by the fifth and sixth respectively:

$$\frac{\partial U_1/\partial q_{11}}{\partial U_1/\partial q_{12}} = \frac{F_1}{F_2} = \frac{\partial U_2/\partial q_{21}}{\partial U_2/\partial q_{22}} \qquad \frac{\partial U_1/\partial q_{11}}{\partial U_1/\partial (x_1^0 - x_1)} = \frac{F_1}{F_3} = \frac{\partial U_2/\partial q_{21}}{\partial U_2/\partial (x_2^0 - x_2)}$$

The RCSs are the same for both consumers and equal the corresponding RPT. The rate at which consumers substitute leisure (the counterpart of work) for commodities equals the MP of labor. This proves Pareto optimality if the second-order conditions are also satisfied.

Social Preference and Indifference

In an effort to create a social analog to individual indifference curves, economists have tried to derive contour lines in the commodity space which represent alternative combinations of aggregate quantities of commodities among which society as a whole is indifferent. *Scitovsky contours* are derived in the following fashion. Assume that all individuals enjoy specified levels of utility and that the outputs of all commodities but one are at specified levels. Then determine the smallest quantity of the remaining commodity necessary to meet the above specifications. The problem is expressed mathematically for a two-person, two-commodity economy as follows. Minimize

$$q_{11} + q_{21}$$

subject to
$$U_1(q_{11}, q_{12}) - U_1^0 = 0$$
$$U_2(q_{21}, q_{22}) - U_2^0 = 0$$
$$q_{12} + q_{22} = q_2^0$$

This problem can be solved by forming the function

$$V = q_{11} + q_{21} + \lambda_1[U_1(q_{11}, q_{12}) - U_1^0] + \lambda_2[U_2(q_{21}, q_2^0 - q_{12}) - U_2^0] \qquad (11\text{-}46)$$

where λ_1 and λ_2 are Lagrange multipliers, and setting the partial derivatives with respect to q_{11}, q_{12}, q_{21}, λ_1, and λ_2 equal to zero. The minimum total quantity of Q_1 necessary to satisfy the conditions of the problem is generally determinate. For each possible value of q_2^0 a different optimal value of q_1^0 ($= q_{11} + q_{21}$) can be determined. The locus of all (q_1^0, q_2^0) points for given values of U_1 and U_2 forms a Scitovsky contour.[1]

If the individual indifference curves are convex, the Scitovsky contours will be convex. However, these contours are not "social" indifference curves, as it might appear from their shapes alone. A completely different Scitovsky contour is obtained if the specified values of U_1 and U_2 are changed. Take for example point A on the Scitovsky contour S_1 in Fig. 11-4. For any point on S_1

---

[1] The reader may verify that points on a Scitovsky contour represent a Pareto-optimal distribution of commodities by finding the partial derivatives of (11-46).

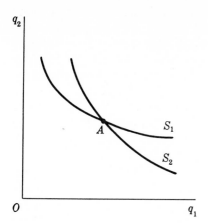

Figure 11-4

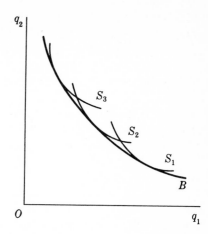

Figure 11-5

the total quantities of Q_1 and Q_2 must be distributed between the two consumers in such a manner that I enjoys the utility level U_1^0 and II the level U_2^0. But the quantities corresponding to A could also be distributed in a different manner, one that results in a utility level $U_1^{(1)}$ for I and $U_2^{(1)}$ for II. By carrying out the maximization process as indicated in (11-46) for these new values of U_1 and U_2, an entirely new set of points is determined, which describe a new Scitovsky contour corresponding to the different utility levels assigned to individuals. This new contour S_2 must have a common point with S_1 at A, but there is clearly no reason to expect that the two contours will coincide throughout their lengths. S_1 and S_2 may therefore either intersect at A (as in Fig. 11-4) or be tangent to each other. Neither case is consistent with the usual properties of indifference curves.

Intersecting social indifference curves can be eliminated through the introduction of optimization. Let the social welfare function be $W = W(U_1, U_2)$ in a two-person society. Find the Scitovsky contours corresponding to all distributions of utility (U_1, U_2) for which $W(U_1, U_2) = W^0$. These contours are shown in Fig. 11-5. The least ordinate corresponding to any value of q_1 represents the minimum amount of Q_2 necessary to ensure society the welfare level W^0. Therefore the envelope B of the Scitovsky contours in Fig. 11-5 is the locus of minimal combinations of Q_1 and Q_2 necessary to ensure society the welfare level W^0 and is called a *Bergson contour*.[1]

The problem of finding the point of maximum welfare can thus be solved in two equivalent ways.

---

[1] See J. de V. Graaff, *Theoretical Welfare Economics* (London: Cambridge University Press, 1957), chap. III. The felicitous terms *Scitovsky contour* and *Bergson contour* are due to Graaff. Bergson contours are nonintersecting in the absence of external effects but do not necessarily possess the "right" convexity.

1. Each point on the aggregate transformation function defines a commodity combination that can be attained with the available resources. Even if only Pareto-optimal distributions of commodities are considered, a contract curve and thus an infinite number of ways in which utility can be distributed among consumers correspond to each point on the aggregate transformation function.[1] Find all possible ways of distributing utility among consumers corresponding to all points satisfying the transformation function. Of all these utility distributions choose the one for which $W(U_1, U_2, \ldots, U_n)$ is a maximum. The solution is obtained by examining points in the utility space.

2. Determine all Bergson contours. Each of these contours corresponds to a different welfare level. Choose that point on the aggregate transformation function which lies on the highest attainable Bergson contour. A solution is thus also obtained by examining points in the commodity space. The equivalence of the two procedures is obvious from the fact that both are equivalent to maximizing $W(U_1, \ldots, U_n)$ subject to the constraint given by the aggregate production function.

The Arrow Impossibility Theorem

K. J. Arrow has investigated the formulation of social preferences. He describes individual and social preferences in terms of the rankings of alternative states formed by the relation "is at least as well liked as" (see Sec. 2-1). Individual utility and social welfare functions are special cases of this more general relation.

There are many ways in which social preferences may be formed from individual preferences. Social preferences might be determined by a dictator, or they might be determined by a majority vote of the individual members of society. Social preferences could be determined by vote, with the number of votes an individual casts depending upon the letter of the alphabet with which her surname begins. For example, people whose names begin with A cast one vote, those whose names begin with B cast two votes, and so on. It is obvious that not all conceivable ways of translating individual preferences into social preferences are equally desirable, acceptable, or sensible. Arrow has stated five axioms which he believes that social preference structures must satisfy to be minimally acceptable. The axioms are approximately as follows:

Complete ordering As in the case of the individual, social preferences must be completely ordered by the relation "is at least as well liked socially as" and therefore must satisfy the conditions of completeness, reflexivity, and transitivity (see Sec. 2-1). The Pareto ranking, which states that allocation A is socially preferred to allocation B if at least one person's utility is higher in A

---

[1] The geometric representation of the possible ways of distributing utility among two consumers corresponding to a given point on the aggregate transformation curve is called a *utility possibility curve*.

and no one's utility is lower, is not complete and therefore does not satisfy this axiom.

Responsiveness to individual preferences Assume that A is socially preferred to B for a given set of individual preferences. If individual rankings change so that one or more individuals raise A to a higher rank and no one lowers *A* in rank, A must remain socially preferred to B. This axiom would be violated if there were some individuals against whom society discriminates in the sense that, when their desire for some alternative increases relative to other alternatives, the social desirability of that alternative is reduced.

Nonimposition Social preferences must not be imposed independently of individual preferences. If no individual prefers B to A and at least one individual prefers A to B, society must prefer A to B. This axiom ensures that social preferences satisfy the Pareto ranking. Let A be an allocation such that no member of society has a lower utility than at B and one or more members have higher levels. The nonimposition axiom requires that society prefer A to B.

Nondictatorship Social preferences must not totally reflect the preferences of any single individual; i.e., it must not be true that society prefers A to B if and only if the *i*th individual prefers A to B. If this axiom were violated, the *i*th individual would be a dictator.

Independence of irrelevant alternatives The most preferred state in a set of alternatives must be independent of the existence of other alternatives. Assume that when alternatives A, B, and C are available, society prefers A to B to C. If C were no longer available, it must not be true that society then prefers B to A.

Arrow's axioms reflect value judgments, but they appear reasonable and intuitively appealing to most economists. Unfortunately, his impossibility theorem states that, in general, it is not possible to construct social preferences that satisfy all five axioms.[1] Some sets of individual preferences will yield social preferences that satisfy the axioms, but there are sets of well-behaved individual preferences that will not. If one of Arrow's axioms other than the complete-ordering axiom is discarded, social preferences that satisfy the remaining four axioms may be constructed from any well-behaved set of individual preferences. If the nonimposition axiom is discarded, social preferences that always give the same ranking to each alternative may be imposed. If the nondictatorship axiom is discarded, social preferences may be

---

[1] The proof of the possibility theorem is based upon advanced mathematics. An intuitive proof is given by James Quirk and Rubin Saposnik, *Introduction to General Equilibrium Theory and Welfare Economics* (New York: McGraw-Hill, 1968), pp. 108–116.

equated with the preferences of some individual. If the independence-of-irrelevant-alternatives axiom is discarded, social preferences may be defined as some weighted average of individual preferences.

Another way around Arrow's dilemma is to limit individual preferences so that social preferences that satisfy all five axioms can always be constructed. One possibility is to assume that all individuals always assign the same ranking to each alternative. Other, more complicated, possibilities also exist.

Income Distribution and Equity

Until recently, most economists have believed that interpersonal utility comparisons were outside the domain of economic analysis. Consequently, they had little or nothing to say about income distribution and equity. Attitudes are changing, however, and these subjects are being introduced explicitly into economic theory. An extreme is provided by Rawls' principle of social justice which states that society is no better off than its worst-off member.[1] The corresponding social welfare function is

$$W = \min(U_1, U_2, \ldots, U_n) \tag{11-47}$$

where cardinal utility indices for society's n members are assumed to be comparable. This function is highly egalitarian. Maximization of (11-47) results in equal utility levels for all members of society in the absence of production. Some inequality would exist in a society with production if the inequality provided adequate production incentives.

Consider the class of strongly additive (see Sec. 3-2) social welfare functions given by

$$W = \sum_{i=1}^{n} U_i^\alpha \tag{11-48}$$

where the cardinal utility indices are strictly positive. A few properties may be derived from (11-48), but a complete analysis requires specification of the individual utility indices. One possibility is to let each individual's utility be a linear and homogeneous function of her income:

$$U_i = \beta_i y_i \qquad (i = 1, \ldots, n) \tag{11-49}$$

where β_i is the constant positive marginal utility of the ith consumer which reflects her capacity to "enjoy" income. Substituting (11-49) into (11-48) allows social welfare to be expressed as a function of individual income levels

$$W = \sum_{i=1}^{n} \beta_i^\alpha y_i^\alpha \tag{11-50}$$

For simplicity, assume that there is an income of given size, y^0, to be

---

[1] J. Rawls, *A Theory of Justice* (Cambridge, Mass.: Harvard University Press, 1971).

distributed. The introduction of production and production incentives is left as an exercise for the reader.

Let income be distributed to maximize social welfare subject to an aggregate budget constraint. Form the Lagrange function

$$L = \sum_{i=1}^{n} \beta_i^\alpha y_i^\alpha + \delta \left(y^0 - \sum_{i=1}^{n} y_i \right)$$

and set its partials equal to zero:

$$\frac{\partial L}{\partial y_i} = \alpha \beta_i^\alpha y_i^{\alpha-1} - \delta = 0 \qquad (i = 1, \ldots, n)$$

$$\frac{\partial L}{\partial \delta} = y^0 - \sum_{i=1}^{n} y_i = 0$$

The marginal social welfare of income for each individual is equated to δ. Evaluating the first principal minor requirement of the second-order conditions,

$$\frac{\partial^2 W}{\partial y_1^2} + \frac{\partial^2 W}{\partial y_2^2} = \alpha(\alpha - 1)(\beta_1^\alpha y_1^{\alpha-2} + \beta_2^\alpha y_2^{\alpha-2}) < 0$$

which is only satisfied for $0 < \alpha < 1$. Thus, the second-order conditions require that (11-50) be a strictly concave function of positive income levels.

Though values for α outside the open unit interval are possible (see Exercise 11-12), attention here is limited to values that lie within this interval. If the β values are the same for all consumers, income equality is achieved for any α value within the interval. If the β values differ, the degree of income equality is inversely related to α. Solve the appropriate first-order conditions for y_i/y_j:

$$\frac{y_i}{y_j} = \left(\frac{\beta_i}{\beta_j} \right)^{\alpha/(1-\alpha)}$$

As $\alpha \to 0$, $(y_i/y_j) \to 1$, the case of complete income equality; as $\alpha \to 1$, $(y_i/y_j) \to 0$ or ∞, depending upon whether β_i is less than or greater than β_j.

Consider a two-person example with $U_1 = 2y_1$ and $U_2 = y_2$. A dollar of income for I yields twice as much utility as a dollar for II. In this case

$$\frac{y_1}{y_2} = 2^{\alpha/(1-\alpha)} \qquad \text{and} \qquad y_1 = \frac{2^{\alpha/(1-\alpha)}}{1 + 2^{\alpha/(1-\alpha)}} y^0$$

I receives 89 percent of total income for $\alpha = 0.75$, 67 percent for $\alpha = 0.5$, 56 percent for $\alpha = 0.25$, and 50.2 percent for $\alpha = 0.01$.

11-7 THE THEORY OF SECOND BEST

A positive social dividend can always be achieved by a move from a Pareto-nonoptimal allocation to a Pareto-optimal allocation. Therefore, the satisfaction of the Pareto conditions is often considered the welfare target toward which society should move. It may well occur, however, that one or more of the Pareto conditions cannot be satisfied because of institutional restrictions. A best welfare position is unattainable in this case, and it is relevant to inquire whether a second-best position can be attained by satisfying the remaining Pareto conditions. The theory of second best says no: if one or more of the necessary conditions for Pareto optimality cannot be satisfied, in general it is neither necessary nor desirable to satisfy the remaining conditions.

The essential characteristics of the theory of second best can be illustrated for a simplified system with one consumer, one implicit production function, n commodities, and a fixed supply of one primary factor not desired by the consumer. The results for this system can be generalized to cover the more complete system presented in Sec. 11-1. The necessary conditions for Pareto optimality are obtained by maximizing the consumer's utility subject to the production function. Form the Lagrange function

$$L = U(q_1, \ldots, q_n) - \lambda F(q_1, \ldots, q_n, x^0)$$

and set its partial derivatives equal to zero:

$$\frac{\partial L}{\partial q_i} = U_i - \lambda F_i = 0 \qquad i = 1, \ldots, n \tag{11-51}$$

where $U_i = \partial U/\partial q_i$ and $F_i = \partial F/\partial q_i$. It follows that

$$\frac{U_i}{U_j} = \frac{F_i}{F_j} \qquad i, j = 1, \ldots, n \tag{11-52}$$

If (11-51) is satisfied, the RCS for every pair of commodities will equal the corresponding RPT.

Assume that institutional conditions prevent the attainment of one of the conditions of (11-51), say the first. The failure to meet this condition can be expressed in various ways. One of the simplest is the assumption that

$$U_1 - kF_1 = 0 \tag{11-53}$$

where k is a positive constant which differs from the optimal value of λ given by a solution of (11-51) and the production function.

The conditions for a second-best welfare optimum are obtained by maximizing utility subject to the aggregate production function *and* (11-53). Form the Lagrange function

$$L = U(q_1, \ldots, q_n) - \lambda F(q_1, \ldots, q_n, x^0) - \mu(U_1 - kF_1)$$

where λ and μ are both undetermined multipliers, and set its partial derivatives equal to zero

$$\frac{\partial L}{\partial q_i} = U_i - \lambda F_i - \mu(U_{1i} - kF_{1i}) = 0 \qquad i = 1, \ldots, n$$

$$\frac{\partial L}{\partial \lambda} = -F(q_1, \ldots, q_n, x^0) = 0 \qquad \frac{\partial L}{\partial \mu} = -(U_1 - kF_1) = 0 \tag{11-54}$$

A solution for this system cannot have $\mu = 0$.† Move the last two terms in each equation of (11-54) to the right-hand side and divide the ith equation by the jth:

$$\frac{U_i}{U_j} = \frac{\lambda F_i + \mu(U_{1i} - kF_{1i})}{\lambda F_j + \mu(U_{1j} - kF_{1j})} \qquad i, j = 1, \ldots, n \qquad (11\text{-}55)$$

In general, nothing is known a priori about the signs of the cross partial derivatives U_{1i}, U_{1j}, F_{1i}, and F_{1j}. Therefore, in general, one may not expect any of the usual Pareto conditions to be required for the attainment of a second-best optimum.

The theory of second best has been used to question the desirability of partial-equilibrium policies that might be used to attain the Pareto conditions on a piecemeal basis for markets considered in isolation. The counter-argument to this is that although piecemeal policy is not valid in general, it is valid for many specific cases. For example, assume that the commodities are numbered so that Paretian violations in consumption are limited to Q_i with $i \le h$, and violations in production are limited to Q_i with $i \le k$. If the utility and production functions are both weakly separable (see Sec. 3-2) so that

$$U = U[U_1(q_1, \ldots, q_h), U_2(q_{h+1}, \ldots, q_n)]$$
$$F[F_1(q_1, \ldots, q_k), F_2(q_{k+1}, \ldots, q_n, x^0)] = 0$$

the Paretian conditions (11-52) hold for all goods with index $i > \max(h, k)$, and piecemeal analysis is valid for these goods.

Proponents of piecemeal policy argue that the Pareto conditions provide reasonable guidelines for policy for Q_i, $i \ne 1$, unless Q_i is closely related to a good for which the Pareto conditions are violated. Consider the derivative for q_i in (11-54). The parenthesized term reflects the influence of the violated Pareto condition. If this term is small relative to the other terms, it is argued that the violated condition may be ignored in the formulation of policy for Q_i. Chewing gum and railway locomotives, for example, are very distantly related in consumption and production. Therefore, policy for the locomotive industry should not be influenced by imperfect competition in the chewing-gum industry.

11-8 SUMMARY

The purpose of welfare economics is to evaluate the social desirability of alternative allocations of resources. In the absence of elaborate value judgments concerning the desirability of alternative income distributions, a simple value judgment is to consider a reallocation to represent an improvement in welfare if it makes at least one person better off without making anybody worse off. If it is not possible to reallocate resources without making at least

---

† If $\mu = 0$, the first equation of (11-54) becomes $U_1 - \lambda F_1 = 0$, which contradicts the assumption contained in (11-53).

one person worse off, the existing allocation is Pareto-optimal. The usual first-order conditions for Pareto optimality require that (1) the RCS of each consumer and the RPT of each producer be equal for each pair of commodities, (2) the RCS of each consumer and the RTS of each producer be equal for each pair of primary factors, and (3) the RCS of each consumer and the MP of each producer be equal for each factor-commodity pair. Second-order conditions must also be fulfilled for Pareto optimality.

Perfect competition normally results in the fulfillment of the first-order conditions for Pareto optimality. It is in this sense that perfect competition represents a welfare optimum. It does not guarantee that the second-order conditions are fulfilled; nor does it ensure that the distribution of income (or of utility) is optimal in any sense. In addition, the definition of optimum welfare in terms of Pareto optimality leaves a certain amount of indeterminacy in the analysis, since every point on a contract curve is Pareto-optimal and one cannot choose between them without additional ethical judgments.

Imperfect competition among consumers or producers will normally lead to violations of the first-order conditions for Pareto optimality. Even if, by accident, consumers' RCSs were equal to producers' RPTs for all commodities, Pareto optimality would still not be attained as a result of divergences between consumers' RCSs for commodities and labor and the producers' corresponding rates of transforming labor into commodities. Perfectly discriminating monopoly and bilateral monopoly are exceptions. These forms of imperfect competition lead to Pareto-optimal allocations.

The first-order conditions for Pareto optimality must be modified in the presence of external effects in consumption or production. In general perfect competition will not lead to Pareto optimality if external effects are present. The equality of RCSs will not lead to Pareto optimality if utility functions are interdependent. Pareto optimality requires that the sum of the consumers' RCSs between a public good and an ordinary good equal the corresponding RPT for each producer. Particular pricing schemes for public goods might be used to achieve Lindahl equilibrium in pseudo markets for such goods. Price must equal social MC rather than private MC if there are external effects in production.

Systems of taxes and subsidies generally can be designed to lead a market economy from a Pareto-nonoptimal allocation to a Pareto-optimal one. Unit taxes and subsidies are used to make market participants observe appropriate marginal conditions, and lump-sum taxes and subsidies are used to secure a desired income distribution.

The indeterminacy which remains in the analysis of Pareto optimality can be removed by explicitly introducing a social welfare function which states society's (or a dictator's) preferences among alternative distributions of utility among individuals. Rather than a single social welfare function there are many, each expressing the evaluations of different groups of people. A welfare optimum is determined by translating the social welfare function into the commodity-space and finding a point on society's transformation function that lies on the highest Bergson contour. Such welfare optima are always Pareto-optimal. The Arrow impossibility theorem states that, in general, it is not possible to construct social preferences from individual preferences without violating one or more of five axioms that most economists believe that social preferences should satisfy. In recent years economists have increasingly made interpersonal utility comparisons, and judged particular social welfare functions in terms of their effects upon income distribution and equity.

The theory of second best states that if one or more of the first-order conditions for Pareto optimality cannot be satisfied because of institutional constraints, in general it is neither necessary nor desirable to satisfy the remaining Pareto conditions. This theory has been used to question the desirability of policies to attain the Pareto conditions on a piecemeal basis.

EXERCISES

11-1 Consider a two-person, two-commodity, pure-exchange economy with $U_1 = q_{11}^\alpha q_{12}$, $U_2 = q_{21}^\beta q_{22}$, $q_{11} + q_{21} = q_1^0$, and $q_{12} + q_{22} = q_2^0$. Derive the contract curve as an implicit function of q_{11} and q_{12}. What condition on the coefficients α and β will ensure that the contract curve is a straight line?

11-2 An economy satisfies all the conditions for Pareto optimality except for one producer who is a monopolist in the market for her output and a monopsonist in the market for the single input that she uses to produce her output. Her production function is $q = 0.5x$, the demand function for her output is $p = 100 - 4q$, and the supply function for her input is $r = 2 + 2x$. Find the values of q, x, p, and r that maximize the producer's profit. Find the values for these variables that would prevail if she satisfied the appropriate Pareto conditions.

11-3 Consider a two-person, two-commodity, pure-exchange economy with $U_1 = q_{11}^\alpha q_{12} q_{21}^\gamma q_{22}^\delta$, $U_2 = q_{21}^\beta q_{22}$, $q_{11} + q_{21} = q_1^0$, and $q_{12} + q_{22} = q_2^0$. Derive the contract curve of Pareto-optimal allocations as an implicit function of q_{11} and q_{12}. How does this differ from the contract curve for Exercise 11-1? Under what conditions will the two curves be identical?

11-4 Consider an economy with two consumers, two public goods, one ordinary good, one implicit production function, and a fixed supply of one primary factor that does not enter the consumers' utility functions. Determine the first-order conditions for a Pareto-optimal allocation. In particular, what combination of RCSs must equal the RPT for the two public goods?

11-5 Construct excess demand functions for the two goods of the Lindahl-equilibrium example given by (11-27) through (11-35), and solve these functions to obtain the equilibrium solution.

11-6 Assume that the cost functions of two firms producing the same commodity are

$$C_1 = 2q_1^2 + 20q_1 - 2q_1q_2 \qquad C_2 = 3q_2^2 + 60q_2$$

Determine the output levels of the firms on the assumption that each equates its private MC to a fixed market price of 240. Determine their output levels on the assumption that each equates its social MC to the market price.

11-7 Determine taxes and subsidies that will lead the producer described in Exercise 11-2 to a Pareto-optimal allocation and leave her profit unchanged.

11-8 Determine taxes and subsidies that will lead the firms described in Exercise 11-4 to their Pareto-optimal output levels but leave their profits unchanged. What is the size of the social dividend secured by this change in allocation?

11-9 Consider an economy with two commodities and fixed factor supplies. Assume that the social welfare function defined in commodity space is $W = (q_1 + 2)q_2$ and that society's implicit production function is $q_1 + 2q_2 - 1 = 0$. Find values for q_1 and q_2 that maximize social welfare.

11-10 Assume that there are two consumers and two commodities. Let the utility functions be $U_1 = q_{11}q_{12}$ and $U_2 = q_{21}q_{22}$ with $q_{11} + q_{21} = q_1$ and $q_{12} + q_{22} = q_2$. Show that Scitovsky contours are given by $q_1q_2 = (\sqrt{U_1} + \sqrt{U_2})^2$.

11-11 Consider a society of n individuals and m alternatives with the following preference structure. Each individual ranks the alternatives from 1 through m in decreasing order of preference. The ranks are summed over individuals, and the alternative with the smallest sum is chosen. Verify that the first four of the Arrow axioms are satisfied by this method of social choice, and that the axiom of the independence of irrelevant alternatives is not.

11-12 Determine the consequences of distributing a given income to maximize the social welfare given by (11-50) in each of the following cases: (a) $\alpha < 0$, (b) $\alpha = 0$, and (c) $\alpha \geq 1$.

11-13 Consider a simplified economy with one consumer, one implicit production function, three commodities, and a fixed supply of one primary factor where

$$U = q_1q_2q_3 \qquad \alpha_1q_1 + \alpha_2q_2 + \alpha_3q_3 - x^0 = 0$$

Find values for q_1, q_2, and q_3 that maximize utility subject to the production function. Assume that institutional constraints result in a violation of one of the Pareto conditions so that

$$\frac{\partial U/\partial q_1}{\partial U/\partial q_3} = k\frac{\alpha_1}{\alpha_3}$$

where $k \neq 1$. Find second-best values for q_1, q_2, and q_3 as functions of k.

SELECTED REFERENCES

Arrow, K. J.: *Social Choice and Individual Values* (New York: Wiley, 1951). A treatise on the problems of constructing a social welfare function. Difficult for those unfamiliar with the mathematics of sets.

Bator, F. M.: "The Simple Analytics of Welfare Maximization," *American Economic Review*, vol. 47 (March, 1957), pp. 22–59. A geometric exposition of some fundamental results of welfare economics.

Baumol, W. J.: *Welfare Economics and the Theory of the State* (2d ed., London: G. Bell, 1965). Contains a discussion of the welfare implications of perfect competition and monopoly and an analysis of some of the nineteenth-century literature on welfare. Mathematics is in appendixes.

Bergson, A.: "A Reformulation of Certain Aspects of Welfare Economics," *Quarterly Journal of Economics*, vol. 52 (February, 1938), pp. 310–334. Also reprinted in R. V. Clemence (ed.), *Readings in Economic Analysis* (Cambridge, Mass.: Addison-Wesley, 1950), vol. 1, pp. 61–85. The first modern mathematical treatment of welfare economics.

Davis, Otto A., and Andrew B. Whinston: "Welfare Economics and the Theory of Second Best," *Review of Economic Studies*, vol. 32 (1965), pp. 1–14. Discusses situations in which the Pareto conditions are valid for second-best optima. Calculus is used.

Graaff, J. de V.: *Theoretical Welfare Economics* (London: Cambridge, 1957). A treatise on welfare incorporating some modern theories. The mathematics is in appendixes.

Harberger, A. C.: "Three Basic Postulates for Applied Welfare Economics: An Interpretive Essay," *Journal of Economic Literature*, vol. 9 (September, 1971), pp. 785–797. A mostly nonmathematical argument for using changes in consumer surplus as measures of welfare change.

Lipsey, R. G., and Kelvin Lancaster: "The General Theory of Second Best," *Review of Economic Studies*, vol. 24 (1956–1957), pp. 11–32. The first formal statement of the theory of second best. Calculus is used.

Quirk, James, and Rubin Saposnik: *Introduction to General Equilibrium Theory and Welfare Economics* (New York: McGraw-Hill, 1968). A modern treatment of welfare economics is presented in chap. 4. Advanced mathematical concepts are simplified and developed in the text.

Roberts, D. J.: "The Lindahl Solution for Economies with Public Goods," *Journal of Public Economics*, vol. 3 (February, 1974), pp. 23-42. An advanced discussion of the existence of Lindahl equilibria.

Samuelson, Paul A.: *Foundations of Economic Analysis* (Cambridge, Mass.: Harvard, 1948). Chap. VIII contains a discussion of the social welfare function and the conditions for maximum welfare. The mathematics is mostly incidental.

Samuelson, Paul A.: *Collected Scientific Papers*, ed. by J. E. Stiglitz (Cambridge, Mass.: M.I.T., 1966), 2 vols. The utility feasibility function is developed in chap. 77, and public goods are covered in chaps. 92–94. Geometry and calculus are used.

Scitovsky, T.: "A Reconsideration of the Theory of Tariffs," *Review of Economic Studies*, vol. 9 (1941–1942), pp. 89–110. Also reprinted in American Economic Association, *Readings in the Theory of International Trade* (New York: McGraw-Hill, 1949), pp. 358–389. The concept of Scitovsky contours was introduced and applied to international trade theory in this article.

Sen, A.: *On Economic Inequality* (Oxford: Clarendon Press, 1973). A modern and sophisticated discussion of welfare theory employing only little mathematics.

TWELVE

OPTIMIZATION OVER TIME

The theories of consumption and production as presented in earlier chapters cover optimization for a single time period. In a short-run analysis entrepreneurs are assumed to possess plants of fixed size, but beyond this, the decisions of optimizing units for successive time periods are assumed to be independent. The consumer spends his entire income during the current period and maximizes the level of a utility index defined only for goods consumed during the current period. Similarly, the entrepreneur's production function relates inputs and outputs during the current period, and he maximizes his profit for the current period.

Time is introduced in both discrete and continuous terms in the present chapter. Multiperiod utility and production functions are defined, and the single-period theories of consumption and production are extended to cover optimization for T-period horizons. This introduction of time is accompanied by a number of simplifying assumptions. Time is divided into periods of equal length, and market transactions are assumed to be limited to the first day of each period. During the remaining days of each period the consumers supply the factors they have sold and consume the commodities they have purchased; entrepreneurs apply the inputs they have purchased and produce commodities for sale on the next marketing date. The consumer's current expenditure is no longer bounded by a single-period budget constraint. He may spend more or less than his current income and borrow or lend the difference. Entrepreneurs also have the option of borrowing and lending.

The introduction of continuous time allows analysis of problems in which time itself is a relevant variable, such as the determination of an optimal life for a piece of durable equipment. It is assumed that market transactions may take place at any point in time in the continuous analysis.

The bond market and the concepts of compounding and discounting are described in Sec. 12-1. Section 12-2 contains an extension of the theory of the consumer to the multiperiod case with a consideration of time preference and the effects of interest rates upon consumption expenditures over time. Section 12-3 contains a discussion of how production theory can be extended to the multiperiod case. Bond-market equilibrium and interest-rate determination are covered in Sec. 12-4. Continuous discounting is introduced and optimization criteria developed in Sec. 12-5. The retirement and replacement of durable equipment is the subject of Sec. 12-6. Exhaustible resources are covered briefly in Sec. 12-7, and investment in human capital is treated in Sec. 12-8.

12-1 BASIC CONCEPTS

Multiperiod analysis requires the introduction of several new concepts to describe the methods and costs of borrowing and lending.

The Bond Market

Borrowing and lending are introduced with the following simplifying assumptions: (1) consumers and entrepreneurs are free to enter into borrowing and lending contracts only on the first day of each period; (2) there is only one type of credit instrument: bonds with a one-period duration; (3) the bond market is perfectly competitive; (4) borrowers sell bonds to lenders in exchange for specified amounts of current purchasing power, expressed in terms of money of account; and (5) loans plus borrowing fees are repaid without default on the following marketing date.

These assumptions represent a considerable simplification of actual credit markets, but they allow the easy derivation of many basic results which can be extended to more complicated markets. Each of the above assumptions can be modified to broaden the coverage of the analysis. Assumption (1) follows from the discrete definition of time utilized in multiperiod analyses. This assumption is modified in Sec. 12-5. Assumption (2) could be altered by assuming the existence of different types of credit instruments, e.g., promissory notes and mortgages, with different maturities. Assumption (3) can be relaxed by drawing on the analysis of imperfect competition. Assumptions (4) and (5) can also be altered in a number of ways.

Let b_t be the bond position of some individual at the end of trading on the tth marketing date. The sign of b_t signifies whether he is a borrower or lender. If $b_t < 0$, he is a borrower with bonds outstanding and must repay b_t dollars plus the appropriate borrowing fee on the $(t + 1)$st marketing date. If $b_t > 0$, he is a lender who holds the bonds of others and will receive b_t dollars plus the appropriate borrowing fee on the $(t + 1)$st marketing date.

Since borrowing fees are also expressed in terms of money of account, they may be quoted as proportions of the amounts borrowed. On the $(t + 1)$st marketing date a borrower must repay $(1 + i_t)$ times the amount borrowed on the tth. The proportion i_t is the market rate of interest connecting the tth and $(t + 1)$st marketing dates. Interest rates are frequently expressed as percentages. If the interest rate is i_t, the borrowing fee is $100i_t$ percent of the amount borrowed. For example, the borrowing fee is 5 percent if $i_t = 0.05$.

Market Rates of Return

Individuals desiring to borrow for a duration of more than one period can sell new bonds on successive marketing dates to pay off the principal and interest on their maturing issues. Similarly, lenders may reinvest their principal and interest income. Consider the case of an individual who invests b_t dollars on the tth marketing date and continues to reinvest both principal and interest until the τth marketing date. The value of his investment at the beginning of the $(t + 1)$st marketing date is $b_t(1 + i_t)$. If he invests the entire amount, the value of his investment at the beginning of the $(t + 2)$nd marketing date is $b_t(1 + i_t)(1 + i_{t+1})$. The value of his investment at the beginning of the τth marketing date is

$$b_t(1 + i_t)(1 + i_{t+1}) \cdots (1 + i_{\tau-1})$$

The total return on this investment is

$$J = b_t(1 + i_t)(1 + i_{t+1}) \cdots (1 + i_{\tau-1}) - b_t$$

The average and marginal rates of return ($\xi_{t\tau}$) for this investment are equal and constant:

$$\xi_{t\tau} = \frac{J}{b_t} = \frac{dJ}{db_t} = (1 + i_t)(1 + i_{t+1}) \cdots (1 + i_{\tau-1}) - 1 \qquad (12\text{-}1a)$$

For example, if $\tau = t + 2$, $i_t = 0.10$, and $i_{t+1} = 0.06$,

$$\xi_{t,t+2} = (1.10)(1.06) - 1 = 0.166$$

Since the investor is earning interest on his previous interest income, the compound market rate of return exceeds the sum of the individual interest rates. It is interesting to note that only the levels of the interest rates, and not the order of their sequence, affect the market rate of return. The market rate of return remains 0.166 for $i_t = 0.06$ and $i_{t+1} = 0.10$.

It is convenient to define

$$\xi_{tt} = 0 \qquad (12\text{-}1b)$$

which states that an investor will earn a zero rate of return if he buys and sells bonds on the same marketing date. A positive return is earned only if bonds are held until a future marketing date. The market rates of return defined by (12-1) are applicable for borrowing as well as lending.

If the investor expects a constant rate of interest,

$$i_t = \cdots = i_{\tau-1} = i$$

Equations (12-1a) and (12-1b) become

$$\xi_{t\tau} = (1 + i)^{\tau - t} - 1$$

which can be evaluated from a compound-interest table for specific values of $(\tau - t)$ and i.

Discount Rates and Present Values

The existence of a bond market implies that a rational individual will not consider 1 dollar payable on the current $(t = 1)$ marketing date equivalent to 1 dollar payable on some future marketing date. If he invests 1 dollar in bonds on the current marketing date, he will receive $(1 + i_1)$ dollars on the second marketing date. One dollar payable on the second marketing date is the market equivalent of $(1 + i_1)^{-1} = 1/(1 + i_1)$ dollars payable on the first. It is possible to lend $(1 + i_1)^{-1}$ dollars on the first marketing date and receive 1 dollar on the second, or borrow $(1 + i_1)^{-1}$ dollars on the first and repay 1 dollar on the second. The ratio $(1 + i_1)^{-1}$ is the *discount rate* for amounts payable on the second marketing date. The *present value*, sometimes called the discounted value, of y_2 dollars payable on the second marketing date is $y_2(1 + i_1)^{-1}$ dollars.

Discount rates can be defined for amounts payable on any marketing date. In general, the discount rate for amounts payable on the tth marketing date is

$$[(1 + i_1)(1 + i_2) \cdots (1 + i_{t-1})]^{-1} = (1 + \xi_{1t})^{-1}$$

It follows from (12-1) that an investment of $(1 + \xi_{1t})^{-1}$ dollars on the first marketing date will have a value of 1 dollar on the tth.

An entire income or outlay stream can be expressed in terms of its present value, a single number. Consider the income stream $y_1, y_2, \ldots, y_\tau$ where y_t is the income payable on the tth marketing date. The present value (y) of this stream is

$$y = y_1 + \frac{y_2}{(1 + \xi_{12})} + \cdots + \frac{y_\tau}{(1 + \xi_{1\tau})}$$

If all interest rates are positive, $(1 + \xi_{1t})$ increases and the present value of any fixed amount decreases as t increases. If all interest rates are 0.10, the present value of a dollar payable on the second marketing date is approximately 0.91 dollars, a dollar payable on the fifth is approximately 0.68, and a dollar payable on the tenth approximately 0.42.

The computation of present values allows an economically meaningful comparison of alternative income and outlay streams. Assume that the interest rate is 0.10 and consider two alternative two-period income streams: $y_1 = 100$, $y_2 = 330$, and $y_1 = 300$, $y_2 = 121$. The first income stream contains 9 dollars more than the second, but the second will be preferred at an interest rate of 0.10, since its present value (410 dollars) exceeds the present value of the first (400 dollars). The preferability of the second stream can be demonstrated by transforming it into a stream directly comparable to the first. The second income stream gives its holder 200 dollars more on the first marketing date than the first income stream. Let him invest these 200 dollars in bonds on the first marketing date. This leaves a spendable income of 100 dollars on the first marketing date and adds 220 dollars to his spendable income on the second. The transformed income stream is $y_1 = 100$, $y_2 = 341$, which is clearly preferable to the first income stream. This result can be generalized: Regardless of how an income stream is transformed through borrowing and lending, an income stream with a greater present value can be transformed into a preferred stream.

12-2 MULTIPERIOD CONSUMPTION

A consumer generally receives income and purchases commodities on each marketing date. His present purchases are influenced by his expectations regarding future price and income levels, and he must tentatively plan purchases for future marketing dates. If his expectations prove correct and his tastes do not differ from the expected pattern, his tentative plans will be carried out on future marketing dates. If his expectations are not realized, he will revise his tentative plans. The present discussion is restricted to a consumer who formulates an integrated plan on the current marketing date for his consumption expenditures on n goods over a horizon containing T periods. His horizon is simply the period of time for which he plans on the current marketing date. It may be of any length, but for simplicity assume that it corresponds to the remainder of his expected lifetime. It is not essential that he actually know how long he will live; it is only necessary that he presently plan as if he did. If his life expectancy should change in the future, he would alter his horizon accordingly and revise his plans.

Multiperiod Utility Functions

In the most general case the consumer's ordinal utility index depends upon his planned consumption of each of the n goods in each of the T time periods:

$$U = U(q_{11}, \ldots, q_{n1}, q_{12}, \ldots, q_{n2}, \ldots, q_{1T}, \ldots, q_{nT}) \tag{12-2}$$

where q_{jt} is the quantity of Q_j that he purchases on the tth marketing date and consumes during the tth period.

The construction of a single utility index does not imply that the consumer expects his tastes to remain unchanged over time. It only implies that he plans as if he knew the manner in which they will change. For example, he may know that a baby carriage will yield a great deal of satisfaction during the years in which he is raising a family and no satisfaction at all during the years of his retirement. The utility index (12-2) is not necessarily valid for the consumer's entire planning horizon. It merely expresses his present expectations. A change in his objective circumstances or subjective desires may cause him to revise his utility index on some future marketing date.

Though much of the analysis of multiperiod consumption is formally identical with the analysis for a single period, the explicit introduction of time and interest rates presents a number of new problems. Attention is centered upon the unique problems of multiperiod consumption by assuming that actual and expected commodity prices are fixed in value and remain unchanged. Consequently, analysis may be simplified by invoking the composite-commodity theorem (see Sec. 3-6). Let c_t be the consumer's total expenditure for commodities on the tth marketing date:

$$c_t = \sum_{j=1}^{n} p_{jt}q_{jt} \qquad t = 1, \ldots, T \tag{12-3}$$

and redefine (12-2) in terms of these composite-commodity consumption expenditures:

$$U = V(c_1, \ldots, c_T) \tag{12-4}$$

which gives the maximum value of the utility index corresponding to each consumption-expenditure pattern.

The consumer's time-substitution rate:

$$-\frac{\partial c_\tau}{\partial c_t} = \frac{V_t}{V_\tau} \qquad t, \tau = 1, \ldots, T$$

is the rate at which consumption expenditure on the τth marketing date must be increased to compensate for a reduction of consumption expenditure on the tth in order to leave the consumer's satisfaction level unchanged. No generality is lost by limiting attention to the cases for which $\tau > t$. If the consumer's time-substitution rate is 1.06, his consumption expenditure on the τth marketing date must be increased at the rate of 1.06 dollars for each dollar of consumption expenditure sacrificed on the tth. In other words he must receive a premium of at least 0.06 dollars before he will postpone a dollar's worth of consumption expenditure from period t to period τ. This minimum premium is defined as the consumer's *rate of time preference* for consumption in period t rather than period τ and is denoted by $\eta_{t\tau}$:

$$\eta_{t\tau} = -\frac{\partial c_\tau}{\partial c_t} - 1 \qquad t, \tau = 1, \ldots, T \qquad \tau > t \tag{12-5}$$

The consumer's rates of time preference may be negative for some consumption time patterns; i.e., he may be willing to sacrifice a dollar's worth of consumption in period t in order to secure less than a dollar's worth in a later period. If expected consumption expenditures are 10,000 dollars on the tth marketing date and only 1 dollar on the τth, $\eta_{t\tau}$ would most likely be negative. The consumer's subjective rates of time preference are derived from his consumption-utility function and depend upon the levels of his consumption expenditures. They are independent of the market rates of interest and his borrowing and lending opportunities.

The Budget Constraint

The consumer expects to receive the earned-income stream $(y_1, y_2, \ldots, y_T)$ on the marketing dates within his planning horizon. Generally, his expected-income stream is not even over time. One possibility is a relatively low earned income during the early years of the consumer's working life, which increases as he gains training and seniority and reaches a peak during the middle years of his working life. The consumer's earned income may then begin to fall and become zero after retirement. Whatever his earned-income stream may be, it will seldom coincide with his desired consumption stream. Through borrowing and lending he is able to reconcile the two streams.

The consumer's total income receipts on the tth marketing date are the sum of his earned income and his interest income from bonds held during the preceding period: $y_t + i_{t-1}b_{t-1}$. His interest income will be positive if his bond holdings are positive and negative if his bond holdings are negative, i.e., if he is in debt. His expected savings on the tth marketing date, denoted by s_t, are defined as the difference between his expected total income and total consumption expenditures on that date:

$$s_t = y_t + i_{t-1}b_{t-1} - c_t \qquad t = 1, \ldots, T \qquad (12\text{-}6)$$

where i_1 is the rate of interest determined on the initial marketing date and i_t $(t = 2, \ldots, T - 1)$ is the rate of interest that the consumer expects to prevail on the tth marketing date. The consumer's savings will be negative if his expenditures exceed his total income.

If the consumer is at the beginning of his earning life, his initial bond holdings (b_0) represent his inherited wealth. If he is revising his plans at a date subsequent to the beginning of his earning life, his bond holdings also reflect the results of his past savings decisions. To simplify the present analysis assume that he is at the beginning of his earning life and that $b_0 = 0$. On each marketing date the consumer will increase or decrease the value of his bond holdings by the amount of his savings on that date:

$$b_t = b_{t-1} + s_t \qquad t = 1, \ldots, T \qquad (12\text{-}7)$$

A "typical" consumer might dissave and go into debt during the early years of his earning life while he is earning a comparatively low income, buying a home, and raising a family; then save to retire his debts and establish a positive bond position during the remainder of his working life; and finally dissave and liquidate his bonds during retirement.

Taking (12-6) and (12-7) together, the consumer's planned bond holdings after trading on the τth marketing date can be expressed as functions of his earned incomes, his consumption levels, and interest rates:

$$b_1 = (y_1 - c_1)$$
$$b_2 = (y_1 - c_1)(1 + i_1) + (y_2 - c_2)$$
$$b_3 = (y_1 - c_1)(1 + i_1)(1 + i_2) + (y_2 - c_2)(1 + i_2) + (y_3 - c_3)$$

and in general, utilizing (12-1*a*),

$$b_\tau = \sum_{t=1}^{\tau} (y_t - c_t)(1 + \xi_{t\tau}) \qquad \tau = 1, \dots, T \tag{12-8}$$

The consumer's bond holdings after trade on the τth marketing date equal the algebraic sum of all his savings, net of interest expense or income, through that date with interest compounded on each.

In the single-period case the optimizing consumer would buy a sufficiently large quantity of each commodity to reach complete satiation if he did not possess a budget constraint. A similar situation would arise in the multiperiod case if there were no limitation upon the amount of debt that he could amass over his lifetime. The budget constraint for a multiperiod analysis can be expressed as a restriction upon the amount of the consumer's terminal bond holdings (b_T). He may plan to leave an estate (or debts) for his heirs, but for simplicity assume that he plans to leave his heirs neither assets nor debts. Evaluating b_T from (12-8), his budget constraint is:

$$b_T = \sum_{t=1}^{T} (y_t - c_t)(1 + \xi_{tT}) = 0$$

Dividing through by the constant $(1 + \xi_{1T})$ and moving the consumption-expenditure terms to the right, the consumer's budget constraint can also be written as

$$\sum_{t=1}^{T} y_t(1 + \xi_{1t})^{-1} = \sum_{t=1}^{T} c_t(1 + \xi_{1t})^{-1} \tag{12-9}$$

since

$$\frac{1 + \xi_{tT}}{1 + \xi_{1T}} = \frac{(1 + i_t) \cdots (1 + i_{T-1})}{(1 + i_1) \cdots (1 + i_{T-1})} = \frac{1}{(1 + i_1) \cdots (1 + i_{t-1})} = (1 + \xi_{1t})^{-1}$$

The Consumption Plan

The consumer desires to maximize the level of his lifetime utility index (12-4) subject to his budget constraint (12-9). Form the function

$$V^* = V(c_1, \dots, c_T) + \mu \sum_{t=1}^{T} (y_t - c_t)(1 + \xi_{1t})^{-1}$$

and set its partial derivatives equal to zero:

$$\frac{\partial V^*}{\partial c_t} = V_t - \mu(1 + \xi_{1t})^{-1} = 0 \qquad t = 1, \dots, T$$

$$\frac{\partial V^*}{\partial \mu} = \sum_{t=1}^{T} (y_t - c_t)(1 + \xi_{1t})^{-1} = 0 \tag{12-10}$$

Then

$$-\frac{\partial c_\tau}{\partial c_t} = \frac{(1 + \xi_{1t})^{-1}}{(1 + \xi_{1\tau})^{-1}} = 1 + \xi_{t\tau} \qquad t, \tau = 1, \dots, T \qquad \tau > t \tag{12-11}$$

and substituting from (12-5),

$$\eta_{t\tau} = \xi_{t\tau} \qquad t, \tau = 1, \ldots, T \qquad \tau > t$$

The consumer in this case adjusts his subjective preferences to his market opportunities by equating his rate of time preference between every pair of periods to the corresponding market rate of return. If $\eta_{t\tau}$ were less than $\xi_{t\tau}$, the consumer could buy bonds and receive a premium greater than necessary to maintain indifference. If $\eta_{t\tau}$ were greater than $\xi_{t\tau}$, he could increase his satisfaction by selling bonds and increasing his consumption in period t at the expense of consumption in period τ. Though $\eta_{t\tau}$ may be negative for some consumption-expenditure patterns, the observed (optimum) values of $\eta_{t\tau}$ will always be positive if the interest rates are positive. The reader may verify that second-order conditions are satisfied if (12-4) is regular strictly quasi-concave, or equivalently, if rates of time preference are decreasing.

For a numerical example consider a hypothetical consumer with a two-period horizon. Assume that his utility function is $U = c_1 c_2$ and that his actual and expected incomes are $y_1 = 10,000$, $y_2 = 5250$. Form the function

$$V^* = c_1 c_2 + \mu[(10,000 - c_1) + (5250 - c_2)(1 + i_1)^{-1}]$$

and set its partial derivatives equal to zero:

$$\frac{\partial V^*}{\partial c_1} = c_2 - \mu = 0$$

$$\frac{\partial V^*}{\partial c_2} = c_1 - \mu(1 + i_1)^{-1} = 0$$

$$\frac{\partial V^*}{\partial \mu} = (10,000 - c_1) + (5250 - c_2)(1 + i_1)^{-1} = 0$$

If the interest rate is 0.05 (5 percent), the optimum consumption expenditures are $c_1 = 7500$ and $c_2 = 7875$. The consumer's rate of time preference for these expenditures equals the interest rate (market rate of return):

$$\eta_{12} = -\frac{dc_2}{dc_1} - 1 = \frac{c_2}{c_1} - 1 = \frac{7875}{7500} - 1 = 0.05$$

The regular strict quasi-concavity of the utility function ensures the second-order condition.

The two-period horizon case can be described graphically by giving a new interpretation to the conventional indifference-curve diagram. The consumer's earned-income stream is given by the coordinates of point A in Fig. 12-1. Let y^0 be the present value of this income stream. The consumer's budget constraint is

$$y^0 - c_1 - c_2(1 + i_1)^{-1} = 0$$

The locus of all consumption points with a present value of y^0 forms a straight line with negative slope equal to the market exchange rate, $(1 + i_1)$, between consumption expenditures on the first and second marketing dates. One dollar

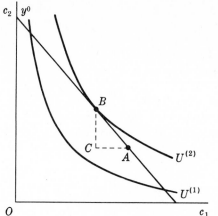

Figure 12-1

of income on the first marketing date can be transformed into $(1 + i_1)$ dollars of consumption expenditure on the second if the consumer lends at the market rate of interest. Likewise, $(1 + i_1)$ dollars of income on the second marketing date can be transformed into 1 dollar of consumption expenditure on the first if the consumer borrows at the market rate of interest. Assume that the consumer's budget constraint is given by the line labeled y^0 in Fig. 12-1. If he borrows on the first marketing date, he will move along his budget line going to the right of point A. If he lends, he will move along his budget line going to the left of point A.

The curves labeled $U^{(1)}$ and $U^{(2)}$ are members of the family of time indifference curves. Each is the locus of consumption expenditures yielding a given level of satisfaction. The slope of a time indifference curve is $-(1 + \eta_{12})$. These curves reflect the assumption that the rate of time preference is decreasing. The coordinates of the tangency point B give the optimal consumption expenditures. The consumer will buy AC dollars worth of bonds on the first marketing date and will spend the principal and interest, CB, for consumption goods on the second.

Substitution and Income Effects

The effects of a change in the rate of interest upon the consumer's optimal consumption levels can be separated into income and substitution effects by methods similar to those employed in Sec. 2-5.

Assume that the consumer's horizon encompasses two marketing dates. In order to determine the effects of changes in the interest rate and earned-income levels, differentiate the first-order conditions (12-10) totally for $T = 2$:

$$
\begin{aligned}
V_{11}\,dc_1 + \quad V_{12}\,dc_2 - \quad\quad d\mu &= 0 \\
V_{21}\,dc_1 + \quad V_{22}\,dc_2 - (1+i_1)^{-1}\,d\mu &= -\mu(1+i_1)^{-2}\,di_1 \\
- dc_1 - (1+i_1)^{-1}\,dc_2 \quad\quad\quad\quad &= -dy_1 - (1+i_1)^{-1}\,dy_2 \\
&\quad + (y_2 - c_2)(1+i_1)^{-2}\,di_1
\end{aligned}
\qquad (12\text{-}12)
$$

The array of coefficients on the left-hand side of (12-12) is the same as the array for the bordered Hessian which is positive by the second-order condition.

Using Cramer's rule to solve (12-12) for dc_1,

$$dc_1 = -\mu(1+i_1)^{-2}\frac{\mathcal{D}_{21}}{\mathcal{D}} di_1 + [-dy_1 - (1+i_1)^{-1} dy_2 + (y_2 - c_2)(1+i_1)^{-2} di_1]\frac{\mathcal{D}_{31}}{\mathcal{D}}$$

$$(12\text{-}13)$$

where $\mathcal{D}$ is the bordered Hessian determinant and $\mathcal{D}_{t\tau}$ is the cofactor of the element in its tth row and τth column. Dividing (12-13) through by di_1 and assuming that $dy_1 = dy_2 = 0$,

$$\frac{\partial c_1}{\partial i_1} = -\mu(1+i_1)^{-2}\frac{\mathcal{D}_{21}}{\mathcal{D}} + (y_2 - c_2)(1+i_1)^{-2}\frac{\mathcal{D}_{31}}{\mathcal{D}} \qquad (12\text{-}14)$$

Let y denote the present value of the consumer's earned-income stream:

$$y = y_1 + y_2(1+i_1)^{-1}$$

An increase of y_1 by 1 dollar or of y_2 by $(1+i_1)$ dollars will each increase y by 1 dollar. The rate of increase of c_1 with respect to a dollar's increase in the present value of the consumer's earned-income stream can be derived from (12-13):

$$\frac{\partial c_1}{\partial y} = \frac{\partial c_1}{\partial y_1} = (1-i_1)\frac{\partial c_1}{\partial y_2} = -\frac{\mathcal{D}_{31}}{\mathcal{D}} \qquad (12\text{-}15)$$

A change of i_1 will alter the present values of the consumer's earned-income and consumption streams. Consider those changes of i_1 which are accompanied by changes in c_1 and c_2 such that the level of the consumer's utility index remains unchanged: $dU = V_1 dc_1 + V_2 dc_2 = 0$. Since (12-11) requires that $V_2/V_1 = (1+i_1)^{-1}$, it follows that

$$-dc_1 - (1+i_1)^{-1} dc_2 = 0$$

and from (12-12) it follows that

$$-dy_1 - (1+i_1)^{-1} dy_2 + (y_2 - c_2)(1+i_1)^{-2} di_1 = 0$$

Substituting into (12-13)

$$\left(\frac{\partial c_1}{\partial i_1}\right)_{U=\text{const}} = -\mu(1+i_1)^{-2}\frac{\mathcal{D}_{21}}{\mathcal{D}} \qquad (12\text{-}16)$$

Substituting $-(y_1 - c_1)(1+i_1)^{-1} = (y_2 - c_2)(1+i_1)^{-2}$, which follows from the budget constraint, and utilizing (12-15) and (12-16), (12-14) may be written as

$$\frac{\partial c_1}{\partial i_1} = \left(\frac{\partial c_1}{\partial i_1}\right)_{U=\text{const}} + (y_1 - c_1)(1+i_1)^{-1}\left(\frac{\partial c_1}{\partial y}\right)_{i_1=\text{const}}$$

The total effect of a change in the rate of interest is the sum of a substitution and an income effect. The income effect equals the rate of change of consumption expenditure with respect to an increase in the present value of the consumer's earned-income stream weighted by his bond holdings multiplied by a discount factor.

The sign of the substitution effect is easily determined. From the first-order conditions $\mu > 0$, and from the second-order condition $\mathcal{D} > 0$. Evaluating $\mathcal{D}_{21}$,

$$\mathcal{D}_{21} = -\begin{vmatrix} V_{12} & -1 \\ -(1+i_1)^{-1} & 0 \end{vmatrix} = (1+i_1)^{-1} > 0$$

Therefore, the substitution effect with respect to c_1 in (12-14) is negative. The substitution effect with respect to c_2 is

$$\left(\frac{\partial c_2}{\partial i_1}\right)_{U=\text{const}} = -\mu(1+i_1)^{-2}\frac{\mathcal{D}_{22}}{\mathcal{D}}$$

Since $\mathcal{D}_{22} = -1 < 0$, the substitution effect with respect to c_2 is positive. An increase of the interest rate will induce the consumer to substitute consumption in period 2 for consumption in period 1 as he moves along a given time indifference curve. This follows from the fact that an increase of the interest rate is equivalent to an increase in the prices of commodities on the first marketing date relative to those on the second. If the consumer reduces consumption in period 1 and purchases bonds, his interest earnings will be greater, and he will be able to purchase a larger quantity of commodities on the second marketing date for each dollar's worth of purchases sacrificed on the first.

Although an increase of income may cause a reduction in the purchases of a particular commodity, it is difficult to imagine a situation in which an increase of income will cause a reduction in the aggregate consumption expenditure on any of the marketing dates. One can assume that $(\partial c_1/\partial y)_{i_1=\text{const}}$ is positive for all except the most extraordinary cases. If this is true, the direction of the income effect is determined by the sign of the consumer's bond position $(y_1 - c_1)$ at the end of trading on the first marketing date. If the consumer's bond holdings are positive, an increase of the interest rate will increase his interest income and is equivalent to an increase of his earned income. If he is in debt, an increase of the interest rate will increase his interest expense and is equivalent to a reduction of his earned income. In this case both effects are negative, and the total effect, $\partial c_1/\partial i_1$, will therefore be negative. If his bond position is positive, the total effect will be positive or negative depending upon whether the value of the income effect is larger or smaller than the absolute value of the substitution effect.

12-3 INVESTMENT THEORY OF THE FIRM

Production is seldom instantaneous. Generally, time must elapse between the application of inputs and the securing of outputs. Assume that (1) the entrepreneur buys inputs and sells outputs only on the marketing dates within his horizon, (2) he performs the technical operations of his production process in the time between marketing dates, (3) during the tth period he applies the inputs he purchased on the tth marketing date, and (4) on the $(t+1)$st marketing date he sells the outputs secured during the tth period. These assumptions serve to define the time sequence of production. The following analysis could be based on many alternative sets of time-sequence assumptions without any major changes of its results.

A many-input–many-output production function is introduced with a time dimension. An assumption of unchanged input and output prices makes it possible to treat the investment expenditures and revenues from sales on each of the marketing dates within the entrepreneur's horizon as the only variables and confine the analysis to an investigation of their interrelationships and the effects of the interest rates.

Special cases have played an important role in the development of microeconomic investment theory. Cases are frequently distinguished on the basis of input and output time structures. The simplest case is *point-input–point-output*, which covers investment in working capital: all inputs are purchased on one marketing date, and all outputs are sold on a subsequent marketing date. Tree growing and wine aging often serve as examples. The *multipoint-input–point-output* case covers the production of an output which requires the application of inputs during a number of successive periods. Shipbuilding might fall into this category. The *point-input–multipoint-output* case covers an investment in a durable good which is purchased on one marketing date and is used for the production of outputs during a number of successive periods. Finally, there is the general *multipoint-input–multipoint-output* case. The first three cases are, of course, embraced by the fourth. In the present section attention is limited to the general and *point-input–point-output* cases.

The Multiperiod Production Function

Consider an entrepreneur who desires to formulate an optimal production plan for a horizon encompassing L complete periods and $(L+1)$ marketing dates. Following the notation of Sec. 4-6, the entrepreneur's production function can be written in implicit form as

$$F(q_{12}, \ldots, q_{s,L+1}, x_{11}, \ldots, x_{nL}) = 0 \qquad (12\text{-}17)$$

where q_{jt} $(j = 1, \ldots, s; \ t = 2, \ldots, L+1)$ is the quantity of the jth output secured during the $(t-1)$st period and sold on the tth marketing date and x_{it} $(i = 1, \ldots, n; t = 1, \ldots, L)$ is the quantity of the ith input purchased on the tth marketing date and applied to the production process during the tth period. Any outputs which the entrepreneur may sell on the initial marketing date are the result of past production decisions, and their levels enter (12-17) as constants rather than variables. On the $(L+1)$st marketing date the entrepreneur plans to sell the outputs secured during the Lth period, but does not plan to purchase inputs, since he does not anticipate production in any period beyond the Lth. The multiperiod production function relates the input and output levels for all periods within the entrepreneur's planning horizon. The inputs applied during each period contribute to the production of outputs during all periods, and it is usually impossible to attribute a particular output to inputs applied during a specific period. However, it is possible to ascertain the effects of marginal variations and compute the marginal product for each input applied during each period with respect to each output secured during each period.

The Investment-Opportunities Function

The producer can maximize his profit from multiperiod production subject to (12-17) in a manner similar to that described in Sec. 4-6. The reader need only use present values of prices rather than simple prices. To focus attention upon the time aspects of production it is assumed here that present and future prices have known and unchanging values. Input expenditures and output revenues on each date are treated as composite variables which are related by an implicit investment-opportunities function:

$$H(I_1, \ldots, I_L, R_2, \ldots, R_{L+1}) = 0 \qquad (12\text{-}18)$$

where
$$I_t = \sum_{i=1}^{n} r_{it} x_{it} \quad \text{and} \quad R_t = \sum_{j=1}^{s} p_{jt} q_{jt}$$

are composite commodities representing investments and revenues respectively. The function (12-18) is derived from (12-17) and the assumption that the appropriate marginal conditions are satisfied for all pairs of input and output variables corresponding to the same date. Given all the revenues and all but one of the investment expenditures, (12-18) gives the minimum value for the remaining investment expenditure. Similarly, given all but one of the revenues and all the investment expenditures, (12-18) gives the maximum value for the remaining revenue.

The entrepreneur possesses both external and internal investment opportunities: he can purchase bonds and he can invest in his own firm. His external rates of return are the same as those for consumers, as given by (12-1). In the general case, average internal rates of return cannot be defined in a manner parallel to average market rates of return, since it is not possible to attribute the entire revenue on the τth marketing date to the investment on any particular marketing date. Each revenue depends upon all the investment expenditures. However, marginal internal rates of return can be defined for any investment-revenue pair, assuming that all other investments and revenues remain unchanged. The *marginal internal rate of return*[1] from investment on the tth marketing date with respect to revenue on the τth, denoted by $\rho_{t\tau}$, is

$$\rho_{t\tau} = \frac{\partial R_\tau}{\partial I_t} - 1 = -\frac{\partial H/\partial I_t}{\partial H/\partial R_\tau} - 1 \qquad \begin{array}{l} t = 1, \ldots, L \\ \tau = 2, \ldots, L+1 \end{array} \qquad (12\text{-}19)$$

Each of the marginal internal rates of return depends upon the levels of all the planned revenues and investment expenditures.

The marginal internal rate of return functions given above by (12-19) are independent of the market rates of interest and the entrepreneur's borrowing and lending opportunities. For given input and output prices (12-19) provides a description in marginal terms of the objective technical framework within which the entrepreneur operates. For some investment and revenue combinations $\rho_{t\tau}$ may be negative.

The Investment Plan

From the set of investment and revenue streams that satisfy (12-18) the entrepreneur desires to select one that maximizes the present value of his profit stream. Form the function

$$\pi^* = \sum_{t=2}^{L+1} R_t(1 + \xi_{1t})^{-1} - \sum_{t=1}^{L} I_t(1 + \xi_{1t})^{-1} + \mu H(I, \ldots, R_{L+1})$$

and set its partial derivatives equal to zero:

$$\frac{\partial \pi^*}{\partial R_t} = (1 + \xi_{1t})^{-1} + \mu \frac{\partial H}{\partial R_t} = 0 \qquad t = 2, \ldots, L+1$$

$$\frac{\partial \pi^*}{\partial I_t} = -(1 + \xi_{1t})^{-1} + \mu \frac{\partial H}{\partial I_t} = 0 \qquad t = 1, \ldots, L$$

$$\frac{\partial \pi^*}{\partial \mu} = H(I_1, \ldots, R_{L+1}) = 0$$

where $\mu < 0$.† Substituting from (12-19), the first-order conditions require that

$$\rho_{t\tau} = \xi_{t\tau} \qquad \begin{array}{l} t = 1, \ldots, L \\ \tau = 2, \ldots, L+1 \end{array} \qquad (12\text{-}20)$$

---

[1] There is no generally accepted name for this concept. Friedrich Lutz and Vera Lutz, *The Theory of Investment of the Firm* (Princeton, N.J.: Princeton University Press, 1951), use "marginal internal rate of return." Irving Fisher, *The Theory of Interest*, (New York: Kelley and Millman, 1954), uses "marginal rate of return over cost." Other names for this or closely allied concepts include "marginal productivity of investment," "marginal efficiency of investment," and "marginal efficiency of capital."

† The first-order conditions require that $\partial H/\partial R_t$ and $\partial H/\partial I_t$ be of opposite sign. The investment-opportunities function is assumed to be constructed so that $\partial H/\partial R_t > 0$ and $\partial H/\partial I_t < 0$ for the optimum production plan. If a solution were obtained with the signs reversed, it would only be necessary to redefine (12-18) as $-H$ to obtain the desired form.

The entrepreneur must equate each of his marginal internal rates of return to the corresponding market rate of return.

The second-order conditions require that

$$\begin{vmatrix} H_{11} & H_{12} & H_1 \\ H_{21} & H_{22} & H_2 \\ H_1 & H_2 & 0 \end{vmatrix} < 0, \quad \begin{vmatrix} H_{11} & H_{12} & H_{13} & H_1 \\ H_{21} & H_{22} & H_{23} & H_2 \\ H_{31} & H_{32} & H_{33} & H_3 \\ H_1 & H_2 & H_3 & 0 \end{vmatrix} < 0, \dots \tag{12-21}$$

where H_j is the first-order partial derivative of the implicit function (12-18) with respect to the jth variable and H_{jk} is the second-order partial derivative with respect to the jth and kth variables. All the above determinants must be negative.[1] These conditions must hold regardless of the order in which the $2L$ investments and revenues are listed.

Expanding the first determinant of (12-21),

$$2H_1 H_2 H_{12} - H_{22} H_1^2 - H_{11} H_2^2 < 0 \tag{12-22}$$

The rate of change of the marginal internal rate of return for investment on the tth marketing date with respect to revenue on the τth is

$$\frac{\partial \rho_{t\tau}}{\partial I_t} = \frac{\partial^2 R_\tau}{\partial I_t^2} = -\frac{1}{H_2^3}(H_{11} H_2^2 - 2H_{12} H_1 H_2 + H_{22} H_1^2)$$

where $H_1 = \partial H / \partial I_t$ and $H_2 = \partial H / \partial R_\tau$. Since (12-22) must hold for the variables listed in this order and since $H_2 > 0$, (12-22) implies that

$$\frac{\partial \rho_{t\tau}}{\partial I_t} < 0 \qquad \begin{aligned} t &= 1, \dots, L \\ \tau &= 2, \dots, L+1 \end{aligned} \tag{12-23}$$

Thus, the second-order conditions imply that all the marginal internal rates of return be decreasing.

If conditions (12-20) and (12-23) were not satisfied, the entrepreneur could increase the present value of his profit by either selling bonds and expanding internal investment or buying bonds and contracting internal investment.

Point-Input–Point-Output

In the simplest case the entrepreneur invests on one marketing date and receives the resultant revenue on the next. He may repeat the production process over time, but his production on the first marketing date only affects his revenue on the second, and his effective planning horizon includes one full period and two marketing dates.

---

[1] Second-order conditions require that the principal minors of the Hessian determinant of the second-order derivatives of π^* bordered by the first-order derivatives of $H(I_1, \dots, R_{L+1})$ be alternately positive and negative. Conditions (12-21) are obtained by factoring out $\mu < 0$.

The entrepreneur's revenue can generally be stated as an explicit function of his investment expenditure:

$$R_2 = h(I_1) \tag{12-24}$$

In this special case all revenues on the second marketing date can be attributed to investment on the first, and it is possible to define an average internal rate of return:

$$\frac{R_2 - I_1}{I_1} = \frac{h(I_1)}{I_1} - 1$$

The average internal rate of return can be compared with the corresponding market rate of return i_1.

The entrepreneur desires to maximize the present value of his profit from operation:

$$\pi = R_2(1 + i_1)^{-1} - I_1$$

Substituting from (12-24), π can be stated as a function of I_1 alone:

$$\pi = h(I_1)(1 + i_1)^{-1} - I_1$$

Differentiating, $\qquad \dfrac{d\pi}{dI_1} = h'(I_1)(1 + i_1)^{-1} - 1 = 0 \tag{12-25}$

Rearranging terms and substituting from (12-1) and (12-19), the first-order condition becomes

$$\rho_{12} = i_1 = \xi_{12}$$

The entrepreneur equates his marginal internal rate of return to the corresponding market rate of return—in this case the market rate of interest.

The second-order condition requires that

$$\frac{d^2\pi}{dI_1^2} = h''(I_1)(1 + i_1)^{-1} < 0$$

and if $i_1 > -1$, $\qquad\qquad h''(I_1) < 0 \tag{12-26}$

The marginal internal rate of return must be decreasing.

Imagine that (12-26) is satisfied, but $\rho_{12} > \xi_{12}$. The marginal return from borrowing funds for internal use exceeds their interest cost, and the entrepreneur can increase his profit by expanding investment. Conversely, if $\rho_{12} < \xi_{12}$, he is earning less on the marginal dollar of internal investment than he must pay for it, and he can increase his profit by contracting investment to buy bonds.

By total differentiation of (12-25),

$$h''(I_1)\, dI_1 = di_1$$

and $\qquad\qquad \dfrac{dI_1}{di_1} = \dfrac{1}{h''(I_1)} < 0 \tag{12-27}$

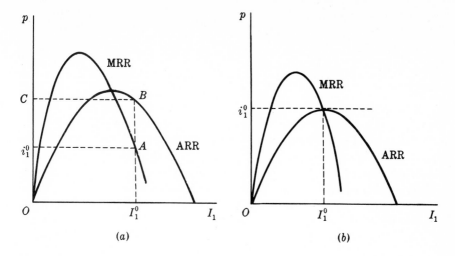

Figure 12-2

If the second-order condition is satisfied, (12-27) is negative: an increase in the rate of interest will cause the entrepreneur to reduce his investment expenditure.

Possible shapes for the average and marginal internal return functions, labeled ARR and MRR respectively, are pictured in Fig. 12-2a. Both the average and marginal rates increase, reach a peak, and then decline as investment is increased. If the interest rate is i_1^0, the entrepreneur will invest I_1^0 dollars. For this level of investment the marginal internal and market rates of return are equal (first-order condition), and the marginal internal rate is decreasing (second-order condition). The entrepreneur's total interest cost is given by the area $OI_1^0 A i_1^0$, his total return by $OI_1^0 BC$, and his net return by $i_1^0 ABC$.

In a perfectly competitive system the net return of the representative firm in each industry will be driven down (or increased) to zero by the entry (or exit) of firms. A long-run competitive equilibrium is pictured in Fig. 12-2b. The optimal investment of the representative firm is I_1^0. The average and marginal internal rates of return are equal, and the average internal rate of return now equals the rate of interest.

12-4 INTEREST-RATE DETERMINATION

The methods of partial and multimarket equilibrium analyses can be utilized for bond markets, and interest-rate determination can be included within the general pricing process. A closer analogy with the earlier analyses of market equilibrium is obtained if the use of loanable funds rather than bonds is treated as the commodity for sale.[1] A demand for (supply of) bonds is equivalent to a supply of (demand for) loanable funds. An interest rate is the price of using loanable funds for a specified period of time. By convention, interest rates are expressed as proportions of the amounts borrowed, but they can be expressed in terms of money of account, as are all other prices. Let 100 dollars serve as a unit of purchasing power. An interest rate of i_t is then the equivalent of a price of $100i_t$ dollars per unit of purchasing power.

First, consider a partial-equilibrium analysis of the loanable-funds market. From the individual equilibrium conditions derived in Secs. 12-2 and 12-3 the current excess demand for loanable funds by each consumer and entrepreneur can be expressed as a function of the current and expected interest rates. It is convenient to use excess demand functions rather than demand and supply functions, since individual consumers and entrepreneurs may demand loanable funds at one interest rate and supply them at another.

A theory of interest-rate expectations must be formulated before market equilibrium can be determined. Many different expectation theories might be utilized. One possibility is to assume that individuals expect future interest rates to be at fixed levels regardless of the current interest rate; future interest rates then enter the current excess demand functions as constants rather than variables. Another possibility is the expectation that future interest rates will equal the current interest rate: $i_1 = i_2 = i_3 \ldots$. Still another possibility is the expectation that the current absolute change of the interest rate will be realized in the future: $i_1 - i_0 = i_2 - i_1 = i_3 - i_2 = \ldots$, or in general, $i_t = i_0 + t(i_1 - i_0)$. Each of these expectation assumptions allows the individual excess demands to be stated as functions of the current interest rate alone. An aggregate excess demand function is constructed by summing the individual functions. Since the individual excess demands are transformed into functions of the current interest rate before aggregation, it is not necessary that all individuals plan for horizons of the same length. An equilibrium current interest rate is one for which the excess demand for current loanable funds equals zero. It reflects time preference and the productivity of investment. In equilibrium the rate of time preference for each consumer and the marginal internal rate of return for each producer equal the interest rate.

Multimarket equilibrium theory can also be extended to include the interest rate and multiperiod expectations. Theories of price and interest-rate expectations must be introduced to allow the individual excess demands for each commodity and loanable funds to be expressed as functions of only current prices and the current interest rate.[2] Multimarket equilibrium is then determined by the requirement that the excess demand for every commodity and for loanable funds simultaneously equal zero.

---

[1] In the present analysis there is assumed to be no circulating money. Loanable funds represent general purchasing power expressed in terms of a money of account.

[2] See J. R. Hicks, *Value and Capital* (2d ed., Oxford: Clarendon Press, 1946), chap. XVI, for a specific theory of price expectations.

The formulation of the mathematical requirements for specific cases of single-market and multimarket equilibrium is left as an exercise for the reader.

12-5 INVESTMENT THEORY AND THE ROLE OF TIME

Investment theory is characterized by the fact that time elapses between the application of inputs and the attainment of the resultant outputs. The multi-period approach tends to obscure some of the time aspects of production. The variables are dated, but investment and revenue variations are limited to integral units of time. The discrete definition of time makes it difficult to deal with problems in which the elapsed time for which inputs are invested is of importance. The tools necessary for a continuous treatment of time are developed and applied in this section. The applications provide examples for the point-input–point-output, continuous-input–point-output, and point-input–continuous-output cases. The analysis of durable equipment in Sec. 12-6 provides examples for the continuous-input–continuous-output case.

Continuous Compounding and Discounting

It is assumed that time is continuous and that transactions may take place at any point in time. A time period, such as a year, is necessary to provide a unit with which to measure time, but it has no other significance. Since elapsed time is now a variable, let $t = 0$ represent the present. The value $t = \tau$ now represents a point in time τ periods hence, where τ no longer need be an integer.

The procedures of Sec. 12-1 do not allow the determination of compound and present values for sums due on dates for which t is not an integer. Since time is assumed to be a continuous variable, interest is assumed to be compounded continuously. If interest were compounded once a year, an initial amount of w would increase to $w(1 + i)^t$ in t years. If interest were compounded twice a year, one-half of the annual interest rate would be applied every six months, and w would increase to $w(1 + i/2)^{2t}$ in t years. In general, if interest were compounded n times per year, w would increase to $w(1 + i/n)^{nt}$ in t years.

The effect of continuous compounding is obtained by letting $n \to \infty$. Let $z = (1 + i/n)^{nt}$. Instead of finding $\lim (z)$ as $n \to \infty$, it is convenient to take the natural logarithm and find $\lim [\ln (z)]$ as $n \to \infty$. The natural logarithm may be written as the quotient of two functions of n:

$$\ln (z) = nt \ln (1 + i/n) = \frac{\ln (1 + i/n)}{1/nt} = \frac{h(n)}{g(n)} \qquad (12\text{-}28)$$

The numerator and denominator of (12-28) both approach zero as $n \to \infty$.

L'Hôpital's rule[1] is employed to find the limit:

$$\lim_{n \to \infty} [\ln (z)] = \lim_{n \to \infty} \frac{h'(n)}{g'(n)} = \lim_{n \to \infty} \frac{-(i/n^2)/(1 + i/n)}{-(1/n^2 t)} = \lim_{n \to \infty} \frac{it}{1 + i/n} = it$$

and since the natural logarithm is a continuous function,

$$\lim_{n \to \infty} \left(1 + \frac{i}{n}\right)^{nt} = e^{it}$$

where the irrational number $e \approx 2.71828$ is the base of the system of natural logarithms.

If interest is compounded continuously, the value of principal and compound interest after t years of a present investment of w is we^{it} where i is the interest rate per year which is assumed to remain unchanged and where t may take any nonnegative value. The present value of the amount u payable at time t is ue^{-it} since a present investment of ue^{-it} in bonds will have a value of u at time t.

Point and Flow Values

Production and consumption are assumed to take place continuously over time in the multiperiod framework. However, inputs are purchased, costs incurred, outputs sold, and revenues realized only on discrete marketing dates. These point values are easily generalized for the continuous framework. Transactions may take place at any point in time, and their values may be functions of the time at which they occur. For illustration, let R_T be a dollar revenue realized at time T, and let R_T be given by the continuous function $R(T)$. The present value of the revenue is $R(T)e^{-iT}$ with the time derivative

$$\frac{d[R(T)e^{-iT}]}{dT} = [R'(T) - iR(T)]e^{-iT}$$

which is discounted marginal revenue with respect to time.

Inputs, outputs, costs, and revenues also may be realized as flows over time in a continuous analysis. Flows may occur at constant rates over time, or their rates may be functions of time. Consider a variable continuous revenue flow. Let $R = R(t)$ be the rate of the flow at instant t measured in dollars per year. No revenue is realized in an instant. However, a finite revenue is realized over a finite time interval. The present value of the revenue stream $R(t)$ from $t = 0$ through $t = T$, denoted by R_{0T}, is given by a definite integral:

$$R_{0T} = \int_0^T R(t)e^{-it}\, dt$$

[1] See the statement and application of L'Hôpital's rule given in Sec. 5-2.

The time derivative of the discounted revenue stream:

$$\frac{dR_{0T}}{dT} = R(T)e^{-iT}$$

is simply the present value of the rate of flow at $t = T$.

The notation $R(T)$ is used to denote both a point value and a rate of flow at a particular point in time. Their distinction, however, should be clear from the specific contexts in which they are used.

Consider the income stream $R(t)$ from 0 through T, and a point value at T with equal present value:

$$\int_0^T R(t)e^{-it} \, dt = R_T e^{-iT}$$

Solving for R_T,

$$R_T = \int_0^T R(t)e^{-i(T-t)} \, dt \tag{12-29}$$

which provides a means for converting a flow into an equivalent point value.

Now consider a constant income flow, a, with present value equal to that of a point value T periods hence:

$$R_T e^{-iT} = \int_0^T ae^{-it} \, dt = a \int_0^T e^{-it} \, dt = a\delta$$

where

$$\delta = \frac{1 - e^{-iT}}{i} = \int_0^T e^{-it} \, dt \tag{12-30}$$

is the present value of a 1-dollar income stream for T years. Finally, solving for a,

$$a = \frac{i}{(e^{iT} - 1)} R_T$$

which provides a means for converting a point value into an equivalent constant flow.

Point-Input–Point-Output

The simplest investment problem in which time is a variable occurs if all inputs are applied at one point in time and all outputs are sold at a later point in time. Imagine an entrepreneur engaged in the process of wine aging. He purchases a cask of grape juice for I_0 dollars and waits while it ferments and ages. Assume that fermentation and aging are costless processes so that his only other cost is foregone interest on his initial investment. Further assume that the sales value of the wine, a point value, is a function of the length of its aging period, $R(T)$.

The entrepreneur's optimization problem is to select an aging period, i.e., a value for T, that maximizes the present value of his profit:

$$\pi = R(T)e^{-iT} - I_0$$

Setting the derivative of π with respect to T equal to zero,

$$\frac{d\pi}{dT} = [R'(T) - iR(T)]e^{-iT} = 0$$

Dividing by $e^{-iT} \neq 0$ and rearranging terms,

$$\frac{R'(T)}{R(T)} = i \tag{12-31}$$

The entrepreneur must equate his proportionate marginal rate of return with respect to time $[R'(T)/R(T)]$ to his proportionate marginal rate of cost with respect to time (i).

The second-order condition requires that

$$\frac{d^2\pi}{dT^2} = [R''(T) - 2iR'(T) + i^2R(T)]e^{-iT} < 0$$

Substituting from (12-31) for i and multiplying through by $e^{iT}/R(T) > 0$,

$$\frac{R''(T)R(T) - [R'(T)]^2}{[R(T)]^2} < 0 \tag{12-32}$$

which is the derivative of $R'(T)/R(T)$. The proportionate marginal rate of return with respect to time must be decreasing; i.e., its derivative must be negative. If (12-31) and (12-32) are satisfied for $T = T^0$, the entrepreneur's marginal earnings from wine aging would exceed his earnings from investing $R(T)$ in the bond market if his investment period were slightly shorter than T^0, and would be less than bond earnings if it were slightly longer than T^0.

The effect of a change of the rate of interest upon the aging period can be determined by total differentiation of (12-31):

$$R''(T) \, dT - iR'(T) \, dT - R(T) \, di = 0$$

and
$$\frac{dT}{di} = \frac{R(T)}{R''(T) - iR'(T)} < 0 \tag{12-33}$$

The numerator of (12-33) is positive, and (12-32) together with (12-31) requires that its denominator be negative. An increase in the rate of interest will lead the entrepreneur to shorten his aging period, and a decrease will lead him to lengthen it.

Continuous-Input–Point-Output

Consider an investment process in which an entrepreneur incurs a cost flow over time, but sells his entire output at a single point in time. An example is provided by an entrepreneur engaged in tree growing. He purchases a seedling for I_0 dollars at $t = 0$, incurs a cultivation cost flow of $G(t)$ dollars per year while the tree is growing, and sells the tree for $R(T)$ dollars at $t = T$. The present value of the entrepreneur's profit is

$$\pi = R(T)e^{-iT} - I_0 - \int_0^T G(t)e^{-it}\, dt$$

Setting the derivative of π with respect to T equal to zero,

$$\frac{d\pi}{dT} = [R'(T) - iR(T) - G(T)]e^{-iT} = 0$$

Multiplying by e^{iT} and rearranging terms,

$$\frac{R'(T) - G(T)}{R(T)} = i$$

The entrepreneur sells the tree when his proportionate marginal rate of return with respect to time net of cultivation cost equals the rate of interest. The second-order condition requires that the proportionate net marginal rate of return be decreasing with respect to time. Again, an increase in the interest rate will shorten the growing period.

Point-Input–Continuous-Output

Consider now a case in which a single investment, say in durable equipment, yields a revenue stream over time. For simplicity assume that the equipment earns revenue at a constant rate of R dollars per year during its life, and assume that the investment cost of the equipment is a continuous function of its life: $I_0 = I(T)$ where $I'(T) > 0$. The present value of the profit from operating the equipment is

$$\pi = \int_0^T Re^{-it}\, dt - I(T)$$

Setting the derivative of π with respect to T equal to zero,

$$\frac{d\pi}{dT} = Re^{-iT} - I'(T) = 0$$

and

$$Re^{-iT} = I'(T) \tag{12-34}$$

The optimal life for the equipment occurs at a point at which the present value of the additional revenue from increased durability equals the marginal cost of durability.

The second-order condition for a maximum requires that

$$\frac{d^2\pi}{dT^2} = -iRe^{-iT} - I''(T) < 0 \tag{12-35}$$

and is necessarily satisfied if the marginal cost of durability is increasing, i.e., if $I''(T) > 0$. Differentiating (12-34) totally and solving for dT/di,

$$\frac{dT}{di} = \frac{TRe^{-iT}}{-iRe^{-iT} - I''(T)} < 0$$

since the denominator is negative by (12-35). An increase in the interest rate will decrease durability, and a decrease will increase it.

12-6 RETIREMENT AND REPLACEMENT OF DURABLE EQUIPMENT

Further consideration of durable equipment based on another set of assumptions provides examples of continuous-input–continuous-output processes.

Assumptions

Consider a machine used for the production of a single output, Q, which is sold for a competitive price, p, that is invariant over time. Let q_t denote the flow of output at instant t. The corresponding revenue flow is pq_t. The machine is purchased at $t = 0$ at the fixed cost I_0. The input cost flow, C_t, is a function of q_t, and the maintenance cost flow for the machine, M_t, is a function of both output flow and machine age:

$$C_t = C(q_t) \qquad M_t = M(q_t, t)$$

The machine can be sold for scrap when the entrepreneur no longer desires to use it for production. The scrap value of the machine at time T, S_T, is a decreasing function of the age of the machine: $S_T = S(T)$ where $S'(T) < 0$. The derivative $S'(T)$ gives the rate of loss of market value from continuing to use the machine, and is called *depreciation*.

The entrepreneur's optimization problem can be separated into two parts: (1) the determination of optimum input and output levels for each point in time while machines are in operation, and (2) the determination of optimal lives for one or more machines. Optimal input and output levels are considered first. Then criteria for an optimal lifetime are determined for a single machine and for an infinite chain of machines.

The Quasi-Rent Function

Assume that the entrepreneur has decided to operate a machine from $t = 0$ through $t = T$. Given this decision the initial cost and scrap value of the machine may be ignored. The entrepreneur's problem is to maximize the present value of the *quasi-rent* flow from the operation of the machine, i.e., the difference between the present value of his sales revenue flow and the present value of his variable cost flow. Since revenues and costs at different points in time are independent in the cases considered here, the entrepreneur can maximize the present value of his quasi-rent flow over the life of the machine by maximizing his rate of discounted quasi-rent flow at each point in time. Furthermore, since the discount factor, e^{-it}, is a constant for any fixed value of t, the entrepreneur can achieve the desired result by maximizing his rate of quasi-rent flow at each point in time without discounting.

The entrepreneur's rate of quasi-rent flow at instant t, Z_t, is

$$Z_t = pq_t - C(q_t) - M(q_t, t) \tag{12-36}$$

Setting the derivative of Z_t with respect to q_t equal to zero,

$$\frac{\partial Z_t}{\partial q_t} = p - \frac{dC_t}{dq_t} - \frac{\partial M_t}{\partial q_t} = 0$$

and

$$p = \frac{dC_t}{dq_t} + \frac{\partial M_t}{\partial q_t} \tag{12-37}$$

The entrepreneur equates his rate of marginal cost flow, which in this case is a sum of input and maintenance costs, to his fixed rate of marginal revenue flow, p. The reader may verify that the second-order condition requires that the sum of the marginal costs increase with output.

Assume that (12-37) may be solved for the optimum value of q_t as a function of t. Substituting this function into (12-36), an optimal quasi-rent stream may be expressed as a function of t:

$$Z_t = Z(t)$$

The quasi-rent function gives the maximum quasi-rent obtainable at each point in time from the operation of the machine. It is based upon the underlying optimal combinations of inputs and output. The quasi-rent function holds for all values of t, and its form is unaffected by the selection of a particular value for machine life. Thus, the quasi-rent function may be used for analyses of machine life without the explicit introduction of outputs, revenues, and costs.

Retirement of a Single Machine

Consider an entrepreneur who desires to purchase one machine, invest his quasi-rent stream in the bond market at the going rate of interest, invest his scrap value in the bond market at the end of the machine's life, and then retire. The present value of his profit from the operation of the machine is the present value of his quasi-rent stream, minus the cost of the machine, plus the present value of the scrap receipts:

$$\pi_1 = \int_0^T Z(t)e^{-it}\, dt - I_0 + S(T)e^{-iT} \tag{12-38}$$

Differentiating,
$$\frac{d\pi_1}{dT} = [Z(T) - iS(T) + S'(T)]e^{-iT} = 0$$

and
$$Z(T) + S'(T) = iS(T) \qquad (12\text{-}39)$$

The entrepreneur will retire the machine when his marginal quasi-rent less depreciation flow equals the interest return from investing the scrap value in the bond market. The reader may verify that the second-order condition requires that the quasi-rent less depreciation flow decrease more rapidly than the alternative bond-market return and that an increase in the interest rate will hasten the machine's retirement.

Replacement for a Chain of Machines

Consider an entrepreneur who plans for an infinite horizon and an infinite chain of machines succeeding each other. Assume that his quasi-rent function, initial cost, and scrap value function are the same for each machine except for dates, and assume that the planned lives of the machines are identical. The present value of the profit from the operation of the first machine is given by (12-38). The present values of the profits from the operation of the second and third machines are

$$\pi_2 = \int_T^{2T} Z(t-T)e^{-it}\,dt - I_0 e^{-iT} + S(T)e^{-i2T} = \pi_1 e^{-iT}$$

$$\pi_3 = \int_{2T}^{3T} Z(t-2T)e^{-it}\,dt - I_0 e^{-i2T} + S(T)e^{-i3T} = \pi_1 e^{-i2T}$$

and in general,

$$\pi_k = \left[\int_0^T Z(t)e^{-it}\,dt - I_0 + S(T)e^{-iT} \right] e^{-i(k-1)T}$$

The present values of the profits from successive machines are identical except for discount factors that reflect the times over which their profits are earned.

The present value of the aggregate profit from an infinite chain of machines is

$$\pi = \sum_{k=1}^{\infty} \pi_k = \frac{\displaystyle\int_0^T Z(t)e^{-it}\,dt - I_0 + S(T)e^{-iT}}{1 - e^{-iT}}$$

where $1/(1 - e^{-iT})$ is the sum to infinity of the geometric progression $(1 + e^{-iT} + e^{-i2T} + e^{-i3T} + \cdots)$.† Setting the derivative of π with respect to T equal to zero,

$$\frac{d\pi}{dT} = \frac{[Z(T) - iS(T) + S'(T)]e^{-iT}(1 - e^{-iT}) - ie^{-iT}\left[\int_0^T Z(t)e^{-it}\,dt - I_0 + S(T)e^{-iT}\right]}{(1 - e^{-iT})^2}$$
$$= 0$$

---

† In general, consider the geometric progression $a,\ ar,\ ar^2,\ ar^3, \ldots$ in which the nth term is ar^{n-1}. If $r < 1$, the progression is convergent, and its sum to infinity is $a/(1 - r)$. In the present case $a = 1$ and $r = e^{-iT} < 1$.

Multiplying by $e^{iT}(1 - e^{-iT})$ and rearranging terms,

$$Z(T) + S'(T) = \frac{1}{\delta}\left[\int_0^T Z(t)e^{-it}\,dt - I_0 + S(T)\right] \qquad (12\text{-}40)$$

where δ, as defined by (12-30), is the present value of a 1-dollar income stream for T years. A machine is replaced when its marginal rate of quasi-rent flow per year net of depreciation equals the present value of the average return per year of a new machine net of its investment cost less the scrap value of the old machine. The bracketed term on the right-hand side of (12-40) gives a return for T years. Division by δ converts it to an annual basis. The second-order condition requires that the marginal return on the old machine be decreasing more rapidly than the average return on the new machine.

The first-order condition for the infinite-machine case (12-40) is quite different from the first-order condition for the one-machine case (12-39). Their difference reflects the difference in the options available to the entrepreneur. In the one-machine case he has a choice between continuing to operate the machine and investing its scrap value in the bond market. In the infinite-machine case he has a choice between operating an existing machine and operating a new machine.

12-7 EXHAUSTIBLE RESOURCES

Consider an entrepreneur who extracts output from an exhaustible resource such as a coal mine or an oil well. Let his horizon extend over n discrete time periods. "Exhaustible" in the present context means that extraction is limited to a fixed aggregate. The entrepreneur is assumed to know present and future prices for his output, and have access to a competitive bond market with an unchanging interest rate. For simplicity assume that the extraction cost for each period depends on the quantity extracted during that period according to the cost function $C = C(q_t)$ where $C''(q_t) > 0$. The essential results derived below hold for more complicated cost functions.

The entrepreneur desires to formulate a plan that maximizes the present value of his profit from extraction. Form the function

$$Z = \sum_{t=1}^n [p_t q_t - C(q_t)](1 + i)^{-t} + \lambda\left(q^0 - \sum_{t=1}^n q_t\right)$$

where q^0 is the aggregate extractable quantity. Setting partials to zero,

$$\frac{\partial V}{\partial q_t} = [p_t - C'(q_t)](1 + i)^{-t} - \lambda = 0 \qquad (t = 1, \ldots, n)$$

$$\frac{\partial V}{\partial \lambda} = q^0 - \sum_{t=1}^n q_t = 0$$

and $\qquad [p_t - C'(q_t)](1 + i)^{-t} = \lambda \qquad (t = 1, \ldots, n) \qquad (12\text{-}41)$

Second-order conditions are satisfied by the assumption of increasing MC.

The first-order conditions (12-41) require that the present value of the difference between price and MC be the same for each period. The magnitude of the multiplier λ provides a measure of the scarcity of the resource. If price is constant over time, output must decline over time in order to satisfy (12-41). The entrepreneur will push output toward the present because of his opportunity to invest in the bond market. In order to maintain an even output for "future generations," i.e., $q_t = q$ $(t = 1, \ldots, n)$, price must increase over time at a rate sufficient to allow the gap between price and marginal cost to increase at the interest rate. Specifically, $p_{t+1} = p_t(1 + i) - iC'(q)$. The rate of increase for price approaches the interest rate as t increases. Price must increase even more rapidly if output is to increase over time.

12-8 HUMAN CAPITAL

Labor inputs are not necessarily of uniform and unchanging productive capacity. In many cases it is possible to invest in human, as well as physical, capital. The return from such investment is derived from the value of increased labor productivity. The costs for investment in human capital are of two types: (1) direct costs such as teachers' salaries and textbooks, and (2) the opportunity cost of foregone earnings. If a student were not studying or being trained, he would be producing output and earning an income.

The analysis of human capital investment is illustrated here with three problems. The first requires a yes-or-no decision as to whether an individual should continue his education or enter the labor force on a full-time basis. The calculation of rates of return for investment in human capital are introduced in this context. Second, the costs of training workers to meet specified job requirements are calculated and discussed. Third, a model is developed which allows the determination of optimal investment in human capital over an entire earnings cycle.

Investment in Education

Consider an individual who must decide whether to enter the labor force or continue his education. He, in effect, selects one of two alternative income streams. A hypothetical example is given in Fig. 12-3. The decision is made upon graduation from high school at $t = 0$. Income streams terminate with retirement at $t = T$. If the individual enters the labor force immediately, his income stream is $g(t)$. If he goes to college, it is $f(t)$. College entails an investment in human capital. The income difference

$$\int_0^\tau [g(t) - f(t)] \, dt$$

is its cost, and the difference

$$\int_\tau^T [f(t) - g(t)] \, dt$$

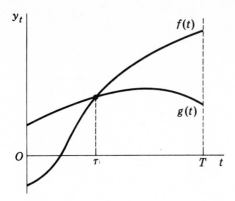

Figure 12-3

is its return. Investment cost involves both direct costs and the cost of foregone earnings.

The rate of return for investment in a college education, denoted by r, is determined by equating the present values of its costs and returns:

$$\int_0^T [f(t) - g(t)]e^{-rt}\, dt = 0$$

This equation may be solved for its single variable, r. A decision is made by comparing r to the market rate of interest, i. If $r > i$, college is a desirable investment. If $r < i$, it is not.

Consider a simple example with $T = 50$, $f(t) = 800e^{0.12t}$, and $g(t) = 2400e^{0.08t}$, which is somewhat different from the example pictured in Fig. 12-3. Here, $\tau \approx 27.5$, and the above integral is

$$\int_0^{50} [800e^{0.12t} - 2400e^{0.08t}]e^{-rt}\, dt = 800\left[\frac{(e^{(6-50r)} - 1)}{0.12 - r} - \frac{3(e^{(4-50r)} - 1)}{0.08 - r}\right] = 0$$

which has the solution $r \approx 0.088$. A college education is a favorable investment for rates of interest lower than 8.8 percent.

Investment in Training

Consider a competitive firm that employs homogeneous labor that is paid a wage equal to the value of its marginal product. For an illustration of investment in training, assume that the government requests that the firm hire some members of a disadvantaged group whose initial marginal product values are substantially below the wage rate. Specifically, let output price equal one, and assume that for the disadvantaged $MP = f(t)$ where $f(t) < w$ for $t < T$ and $f(t) = w$ for $t \geq T$. The cost of training, V, is the present value of the difference between the wage rate and $f(t)$:

$$V = \int_0^T [w - f(t)]e^{-it}\, dt$$

The distribution of these costs among the firm, the disadvantaged, and the government depends upon the institutional setting.

The entire cost would be borne by the disadvantaged in a competitive society without government intervention. The firm would be indifferent between hiring a trained worker at a wage of w, and a disadvantaged worker at a wage of $f(t)$. Another possibility is to let the government pay the training costs to the firm, and let the firm in turn pay the disadvantaged worker a wage of w.

Consider an example for which $f(t) = w(1 - e^{-t})$, where t is measured in years. Clearly, $f(t) \to w$ as $t \to \infty$. In fact $f(t)$ converges rather quickly; $f(5) = 0.99326w$. The present value of the cost of training for a twenty-year employment period with an interest rate of 8 percent is

$$\int_0^{20} [w - w(1 - e^{-t})e^{-it}] \, dt = w \int_0^{20} e^{-1.08t} \, dt = \frac{w(1 - e^{-21.6})}{1.08} \approx 0.926w$$

The present value of the training cost equals slightly less than one year's wage.

Earnings-Cycle Investment

Human capital, as well as physical capital, is subject to depreciation over time. Yesterday's knowledge may have less value than today's. Often it is possible to offset depreciation and increase one's stock of human capital through further learning. The determination of optimal rates of investment in human capital over the earnings cycle provides an important problem for economic analysis.[1]

Consider a person whose earnings cycle extends from $t = 0$ through $t = T$. His stock of human capital at a point in this cycle is denoted by K_t with

$$K_t = K_{1t} + K_{2t} \tag{12-42}$$

where the subscripts 1 and 2 denote the quantities of human capital used to generate income and to generate more human capital respectively. Income at t, denoted by y_t, is

$$y_t = aK_{1t} \tag{12-43}$$

where $a > 0$. New human capital is produced from current human capital according to the strictly concave production function

$$q_t = \alpha K_{2t}^\beta \tag{12-44}$$

where $\alpha > 0$ and $0 < \beta < 1$. The rate of change of the human capital stock is

[1] See Y. Ben-Porath, "The Production of Human Capital and the Life Cycle of Earnings," *Journal of Political Economy*, vol. 75 (August, 1967), pp. 352–365.

given by the differential equation

$$\frac{dK_t}{dt} = q_t - \delta K_t \qquad (12\text{-}45)$$

where δ is the human-capital depreciation rate.

The investment cost for the production of human capital, C_t, is foregone earnings:

$$C_t = aK_{2t} \qquad (12\text{-}46)$$

An optimal investment program is one which maximizes the present value of the individual's income stream

$$V = \int_0^T y_t e^{-it} \, dt \qquad (12\text{-}47)$$

subject to (12-42) through (12-46).

Obtaining a complete solution for the maximization of (12-47) requires mathematical tools beyond those utilized here. However, a number of aspects of an optimal solution can be inferred and analyzed. The marginal cost of producing a unit of human capital at t is obtained by differentiating (12-46) subject to (12-44):

$$\frac{dC_t}{dq_t} = \frac{a}{\alpha^{1/\beta}\beta} q_t^{(1-\beta)/\beta} \qquad (12\text{-}48)$$

Further differentiation of (12-48) shows that MC is increasing with respect to q_t but is constant with respect to t. An additional unit of human capital at t generates an income stream of a less depreciation. The present value of this marginal revenue is

$$\frac{dR_t}{dq_t} = a \int_t^T e^{-(i+\delta)\tau} \, d\tau = \frac{a}{(i+\delta)} (e^{-(i+\delta)t} - e^{-(i+\delta)T}) \qquad (12\text{-}49)$$

Further differentiation of (12-49) shows that this MR is constant with respect to q_t, but is decreasing with respect to t.

Observation suggests phases for investment in human capital. During the early years of the horizon MR $>$ MC for $K_{2t} = K_t$. The entire stock of human capital is used to produce more human capital and income is zero. During the middle years as MR declines, the stock is used both to produce more and to generate income. In this phase MR $=$ MC. Equating (12-48) and (12-49),

$$q_t = \left\{ \frac{\alpha^{1/(1-\beta)}\beta}{(i+\delta)} [e^{-(i+\delta)t} - e^{-(i+\delta)\tau}] \right\}^{\beta/(1-\beta)} \qquad (12\text{-}50)$$

The reader may verify that $dq_t/dt < 0$. The production of human capital declines continuously with the decline in MR during the second phase. Eventually, a point is reached at which additions are not adequate to offset depreciation, i.e., $q_t < \delta K_t$, and the human-capital stock declines thereafter.

12-9 SUMMARY

Consumers and entrepreneurs are assumed to have free access to a perfectly competitive bond market and may adjust their income and outlay streams over time through borrowing (selling bonds) and lending (buying bonds). An interest rate expresses the cost of borrowing, or income from lending, for a duration of one period, as a proportion of the amount borrowed or lent. Market rates of return for durations longer than one period are defined as compounds of the interest rates connecting pairs of successive periods. Discount rates are defined as the reciprocals of the corresponding market rates of return. An entire income or cost stream can be reduced to a single number, its present value, by multiplying each of its elements by the appropriate discount rate and summing.

The consumer's utility index is defined as a function of the quantities of n goods that he consumes during each of the T periods within his planning horizon. He desires to maximize the level of this index subject to a lifetime budget constraint, which requires the equality of the present values of his consumption and earned-income streams. If prices are assumed to remain unchanged, his utility index can be expressed as a function of his consumption expenditures. The consumer's rate of time preference for consumption during period t rather than period $\tau(> t)$ is defined as the smallest premium which he will accept as compensation for postponing a marginal dollar's worth of a consumption expenditure. The first-order conditions for constrained utility maximization require that the consumer equate his rates of time preference to the corresponding market rates of return. Substitution and income effects with respect to changes in the rate of interest can be defined analogously to the single-period case.

An entrepreneur is assumed to formulate a production plan for a planning horizon encompassing L periods and $(L + 1)$ marketing dates. On the tth marketing date he sells the outputs produced during the $(t - 1)$st period and purchases inputs for application to the production process during the tth period. He desires to maximize the present value of his net operating revenues subject to the technical rules specified in his multiperiod production function.

The analysis of the entrepreneur's investment problems can also be simplified by assuming that actual and expected prices remain unchanged and that he always combines inputs and produces outputs so that intraperiod RTSs and RPTs are equated to the appropriate price ratios. The entrepreneur's investment-opportunities function relates his investment expenditures and revenues on the assumption that he performs this preliminary optimization. Marginal internal rates of return are defined for each of the revenues with respect to each of the investments. First-order conditions require that each marginal internal rate of return be equated with the corresponding market rate of return. Second-order conditions imply that each of the marginal internal rates be decreasing. The general analysis is applied to the special case of point-input–point-output.

Single-market and multimarket equilibrium analyses can be extended to include the current interest rate and multiperiod expectations. In equilibrium the rate of time preference for each consumer and the marginal internal rate of return for each producer equal the interest rate.

A continuous framework is developed in which interest is compounded continuously, transactions may take place at any point in time, and time itself may be treated as a variable. This framework is used for three applications with the following results:

1. Point-input–point-output with input fixed and output variable; the marginal internal rate of return with respect to time equals the interest rate at the end of an optimal investment period.
2. Continuous-input–point-output with both input and output variable; the investment-period criterion is the same as (1) except that the marginal rate of return is calculated net of variable cost.
3. Point-input–continuous-output with input variable and output fixed; at the end of an optimal investment period the present value of the marginal revenue from lengthening the period equals the marginal cost of lengthening it.

The operation of durable equipment provides examples for the continuous-input–continuous-output case. A quasi-rent function gives the maximum difference between revenue and variable cost flows at each instant of time. It is obtained by equating the sum of marginal input and maintenance cost flows to price. An entrepreneur will retire a single machine when his marginal quasi-rent less depreciation return equals the alternative interest return on scrap value. A machine within an infinite chain will be replaced when its marginal quasi-rent less depreciation return equals the average return net of investment cost for a new machine.

Profit from the extraction of an output from an exhaustible resource over a T-period horizon is maximized if the present value of the difference between price and MC is the same for each period. If price is constant, this implies a declining output level over time.

Direct expenditures and foregone earnings are the costs of investment in human capital, and the values of increased labor productivity are the return. The rate of return from an investment in education is determined by equating the present values of the income streams that would be earned with and without the education. The investment is undertaken if its return exceeds the market rate of interest. The cost of job training is given by the present value of the difference between the value of the marginal product of a trained worker and that of the trainee during the training period. In a simple model of a person's earnings cycle it is assumed that his income is proportional to his human-capital stock. His stock is increased through investment with a cost of foregone earnings, and is decreased through depreciation over time. The entire stock of human capital may be used to produce more human capital during the early part of the earnings cycle. However, after such a phase the rate of investment in human capital decreases with time, and eventually investment is less than depreciation.

EXERCISES

12-1 Consider two alternative income streams: $y_1 = 300$, $y_2 = 321$, and $y_1 = 100$, $y_2 = 535$. For what rate of interest would the consumer be indifferent between the two streams?

12-2 A consumer's consumption-utility function for a two-period horizon is $U = c_1 c_2^{0.6}$; his income stream is $y_1 = 1000$, $y_2 = 648$; and the market rate of interest is 0.08. Determine values for c_1 and c_2 that maximize his utility. Is he a borrower or lender?

12-3 An entrepreneur invests on one marketing date and receives the resultant revenue on the next. The explicit form of his investment-opportunities function is $R_2 = 24\sqrt{I_1}$, and the market rate of interest is 0.20. Find his optimum investment level.

12-4 Consider a bond market in which only consumers borrow and lend. Assume that all 150 consumers have the same two-period consumption-utility function: $U = c_1 c_2$. Let each of 100 consumers have the expected-income stream $y_1 = 10,000$, $y_2 = 8400$, and let each of the remaining 50 consumers have the expected-income stream $y_1 = 8000$, $y_2 = 14,000$. At what rate of interest will the bond market be in equilibrium?

12-5 An entrepreneur will receive 1000 dollars at $t = 5$. Determine an equivalent constant continuous-income stream from $t = 0$ to $t = 5$ if the interest rate is 10 percent. Note: $e^{0.5} = 1.64872$.

12-6 Consider an entrepreneur engaged in a point-input–point-output wine-aging process. His initial cost is 20, the sales value of the wine is $R(T) = 100\sqrt{T}$, and the rate of interest is 0.05. How long is his optimal investment period?

12-7 An entrepreneur is engaged in a repeated point-input–point-output process. He invests I_0 dollars and receives a revenue of $R(T)$ dollars T years later. At T he will again invest I_0 dollars and receive another revenue of $R(T)$ dollars at $2T$. Assume that he repeats this cycle indefinitely. Interest is compounded continuously at the constant rate i. What is the present value of the entrepreneur's profit from such an infinite chain? Formulate his first-order condition for profit maximization. Compare this result with the first-order condition for the unrepeated case.

12-8 An entrepreneur is engaged in tree growing. He purchases a seedling for 4 dollars, incurs a cultivation cost flow at a rate of $G(t) = 0.4t$ dollars per year during the life of the tree, and sells the tree at $t = T$ for $R(T) = 4 + 8T - T^2$ dollars. The market rate of interest is 0.20. Determine an optimal length for his cultivation period, T. Apply the appropriate second-order condition to verify that your solution is a maximum.

12-9 An entrepreneur is considering the variable revenues and costs from the operation of a machine to produce the output Q which sells at the fixed price $p = 52$. His input cost flow would be at the rate $C_t = 5q_t^2$ dollars per year, and his maintenance cost flow would be at the rate $M_t = 2q_t + 3t$ dollars per year. Construct a quasi-rent function for the machine.

12-10 An entrepreneur plans for a one-machine horizon. He purchases the machine for 500 dollars. Its scrap value at time T is $S(T) = 500 - 40T$. The rate of interest is 0.05. The machine yields a quasi-rent flow at the rate $Z_t = 85 - 4t$ dollars per year. When should the entrepreneur retire this machine?

12-11 An entrepreneur with a two-year horizon desires to extract 100 units of output from an exhaustible resource. His extraction costs are $C_t = 0.5q_t^2$, the interest rate is 10 percent, and the constant selling price for the output is 100 dollars. How much output should he extract in each year?

SELECTED REFERENCES

Allen, R. G. D.: *Macro-economic Theory* (New York: St Martin's, 1967). Chap. 3 contains a discussion of investment theory using differential and integral calculus.

Fisher, Irving: *The Theory of Interest* (New York: Kelley and Millman, 1954). A classic statement of many of the concepts of this chapter which contains verbal, geometric, and mathematical descriptions.

Friedman, Milton: *A Theory of the Consumption Function* (Princeton, N.J.: Princeton, 1957). Chap. II contains a theory of multiperiod consumption. The remainder of the volume is devoted to its statistical verification.

Hicks, J. R.: *Value and Capital* (2d ed., Oxford: Clarendon Press, 1946). Parts III and IV and the mathematical appendix contain multiperiod analyses.

Lutz, Friedrich, and Vera Lutz: *The Theory of Investment of the Firm* (Princeton, N.J.: Princeton, 1951). A detailed study of many different investment problems in which time is treated as a continuous variable. A knowledge of differential and integral calculus is helpful, but not absolutely necessary.

Modigliani, Franco, and Richard Brumberg: "Utility Analysis and the Consumption Function," in Kenneth K. Kurihara (ed.), *Post Keynesian Economics* (New Brunswick, N.J.: Rutgers, 1954), pp. 388–436. A theoretical and empirical study of lifetime consumption patterns. Some knowledge of calculus and mathematical statistics is required.

Nickell, S. J.: *The Investment Decisions of Firms* (Cambridge: Cambridge University Press, 1978). An exposition of modern theory using the calculus.

Smith, Vernon L.: *Investment and Production* (Cambridge, Mass.: Harvard, 1961). A detailed treatment of investment theory. Geometry and calculus are used.

APPENDIX

MATHEMATICAL REVIEW

This appendix contains a brief review of some of the mathematical concepts that are used in the text. Rigorous proofs are generally omitted; in fact, many statements are not proved at all.

The major tools of analysis are algebra and differential and integral calculus. The solution of simultaneous equations and the use of determinants are outlined in Sec. A-1. The fundamentals of differential calculus are discussed in Sec. A-2. The analysis of maxima and minima is discussed in Sec. A-3. The basic properties of integrals are reviewed in Sec. A-4, and the appendix ends with discussions of difference and differential equations in Secs. A-5 and A-6 respectively.

A-1 SIMULTANEOUS EQUATIONS, MATRICES, AND DETERMINANTS

A system of n equations in n variables can be written as

$$
\begin{aligned}
a_{11}x_1 + a_{12}x_2 + \cdots + a_{1n}x_n &= b_1 \\
a_{21}x_1 + a_{22}x_2 + \cdots + a_{2n}x_n &= b_2 \\
&\cdots \cdots \cdots \cdots \cdots \cdots \cdots \cdots \cdots \\
a_{n1}x_1 + a_{n2}x_2 + \cdots + a_{nn}x_n &= b_n
\end{aligned}
\tag{A-1}
$$

where the a's are coefficients and the b's constant terms. Any set of n numbers that preserves all n of the equalities in (A-1) when substituted for the x's is a solution for this system. A simple example of a system of simultaneous equations is

$$
\begin{aligned}
3x_1 - 5x_2 &= 11 \\
x_1 + 2x_2 &= 11
\end{aligned}
$$

Its only solution is $x_1 = 7$, $x_2 = 2$.

The a's, x's and b's of (A-1) may be collected into rectangular arrays called matrices and denoted by boldface letters:

$$
\mathbf{A} = \begin{bmatrix} a_{11} & a_{12} & \cdots & a_{1n} \\ a_{21} & a_{22} & \cdots & a_{2n} \\ \multicolumn{4}{c}{\cdots\cdots\cdots\cdots\cdots} \\ a_{n1} & a_{n2} & \cdots & a_{nn} \end{bmatrix}, \quad \mathbf{x} = \begin{bmatrix} x_1 \\ x_2 \\ \vdots \\ x_n \end{bmatrix}, \quad \mathbf{b} = \begin{bmatrix} b_1 \\ b_2 \\ \vdots \\ b_n \end{bmatrix}
$$

A matrix with m rows and n columns is of order $(m \times n)$. An $(m \times 1)$ matrix is a column vector and a $(1 \times n)$ matrix is a row vector; each may be simply called a vector. The typical element of the matrix $\mathbf{A}$ is a_{ij} where the first subscript denotes a row and the second denotes a column. For example, a_{57} is the element in the fifth row and seventh column of $\mathbf{A}$. Addition and subtraction are defined for matrices of the same order. In this case the typical element of $\mathbf{C} = \mathbf{A} + \mathbf{B}$ is $c_{ij} = a_{ij} + b_{ij}$. Subtraction is defined by replacing the plus signs with minuses. Addition and subtraction are not defined for matrices of different order. The multiplicative product $\mathbf{C} = \mathbf{AB}$ is defined if and only if the number of columns in $\mathbf{A}$ is the same as the number of rows in $\mathbf{B}$. If $\mathbf{A}$ is of order $(m \times n)$ and $\mathbf{B}$ is of order $(n \times p)$, $\mathbf{C}$ is of order $(m \times p)$, and the typical element is $c_{ij} = \sum_{k=1}^{n} a_{ik} b_{kj}$. A special case of interest is one in which $\mathbf{A}$ is a row vector and $\mathbf{B}$ is a column vector with the same number of components. The vector product $\mathbf{AB}$ is the sum of the products of like-numbered elements. A square matrix has the same number of columns as rows. If $\mathbf{A}$ and $\mathbf{B}$ are square and of the same order, the product $\mathbf{BA}$ is defined as well as $\mathbf{AB}$. In general, matrix multiplication is not commutative, and $\mathbf{BA} \neq \mathbf{AB}$. The typical element of the scalar product $k\mathbf{A}$, where k is a number and $\mathbf{A}$ is a matrix, is ka_{ij}.

The system of linear equations in (A-1) may be written compactly in matrix notation as

$$\mathbf{Ax} = \mathbf{b} \tag{A-2}$$

where $\mathbf{A}$, $\mathbf{x}$, and $\mathbf{b}$ are as defined above.

A determinant is a number derived from a square array of numbers according to rules to be specified. It is denoted either by vertical lines on both sides of the array from which it is calculated or by a letter. If $\mathbf{A}$ denotes the matrix, $\mathscr{A}$ denotes the determinant:

$$
\mathscr{A} = \begin{vmatrix} a_{11} & a_{12} & \cdots & a_{1n} \\ a_{21} & a_{22} & \cdots & a_{2n} \\ \multicolumn{4}{c}{\cdots\cdots\cdots\cdots\cdots} \\ a_{n1} & a_{n2} & \cdots & a_{nn} \end{vmatrix}
$$

The rule by which a determinant is calculated from an array is merely stated here.[1] Products of numbers (or elements) are formed from $\mathbf{A}$ such that each

---

[1] For more extensive discussion see A. C. Aitken, *Determinants and Matrices* (New York: Interscience, 1951), chap. II; S. Perlis, *Theory of Matrices* (Cambridge, Mass.: Addison-Wesley, 1952), chap. IV; or G. Birkhoff and S. MacLane, *A Survey of Modern Algebra* (rev. ed., New York: Macmillan, 1953), chap. X.

product contains one and only one element from each row and one and only one element from each column. Thus a determinant is defined only for square arrays. All such products can be written with the row indices in natural order $(1, 2, 3, \ldots, n)$. Examples are the products $a_{11}a_{22} \ldots a_{nn}$ and $a_{12}a_{21}a_{33} \ldots a_{nn}$. If the number of *inversions*[1] among the column indices is even, the sign of the product is left unchanged. If the number of inversions among the column indices is odd, it is changed from minus to plus or from plus to minus. The value of the determinant is the algebraic sum of all such products. Consider the determinant

$$\mathscr{A} = \begin{vmatrix} a_{11} & a_{12} \\ a_{21} & a_{22} \end{vmatrix} = a_{11}a_{22} - a_{12}a_{21}$$

Only two products can be formed from the matrix **A** according to the rule stated above. A negative sign precedes the second term, since it contains one inversion (an odd number) of the column subscripts when the row subscripts are written in natural order.[2]

If the matrix is[3]

$$\begin{bmatrix} 3 & 2 \\ -1 & 4 \end{bmatrix}$$

the determinant is $12 + 2 = 14$.

The above rule is very cumbersome if the matrix contains a large number of rows and columns. Generally, a determinant is more easily evaluated by an expansion in terms of *cofactors*. For any element a_{ij} of the matrix **A** form an array by striking out the ith row and the jth column of the original matrix. The determinant of the remaining array, which contains $(n - 1)$ rows and $(n - 1)$ columns, is the *minor* of the element a_{ij}.† The cofactor of this element is its minor multiplied by $+1$ if $(i + j)$ is even and by -1 if $(i + j)$ is odd. The determinant $\mathscr{A}$ can be written as

$$\mathscr{A} = a_{i1}\mathscr{C}_{i1} + a_{i2}\mathscr{C}_{i2} + \cdots + a_{in}\mathscr{C}_{in}$$

for any given row index i where $\mathscr{C}_{ij}$ is the cofactor of the element in the ith

---

[1] An inversion is an instance in which a lower index follows a higher one. For example, the indices 1, 2 are in natural order; the sequence 2, 1 contains one inversion. The sequence 1, 3, 2, 5, 4 contains two inversions, since it contains two instances in which a lower index follows a higher one: 3 comes before 2, and 5 before 4. The sequence 4, 3, 2, 1, 5 contains six inversions.

[2] The same result is obtained by counting the number of inversions among row subscripts when the column subscripts are written in natural order. The reader may check that if a matrix has n rows and n columns, the number of terms in the expression for its determinant is $n!$ (read "n factorial"), that is, $n \cdot (n - 1) \cdots 3 \cdot 2 \cdot 1$. See Aitken, *op. cit.*, pp. 26–36.

[3] The matrix or the array itself is written with square or round brackets. The operation of forming the determinant, however, is indicated by vertical bars instead of brackets.

† The diagonal of the array running in northwest-southeast direction is the principal diagonal. Minors of elements on the principal diagonal (i.e., of a_{11}, a_{22}, etc.) are called principal minors. The principal minor of a_{11} in the original determinant $\mathscr{A}$ is a determinant of the order $(n - 1) \times (n - 1)$ and is denoted by $\mathscr{A}_{11}$. The principal minor of a_{22} in the minor $\mathscr{A}_{11}$ is a determinant of order $(n - 2) \times (n - 2)$ and is denoted by $\mathscr{A}_{11,22}$. This $(n - 2) \times (n - 2)$ determinant is itself a principal minor of the original determinant.

row and jth column. Similarly,

$$\mathscr{A} = a_{1j}\mathscr{C}_{1j} + a_{2j}\mathscr{C}_{2j} + \cdots + a_{nj}\mathscr{C}_{nj}$$

for any column index j. Since a determinant can be expanded in terms of any single row or column, the multiplication of any row or column of the array **A** by a number k changes the value of the determinant by the same multiple.

Imagine that the ith row of the matrix is multiplied by k. Then expanding the new determinant in terms of the ith row and denoting it by $\mathscr{A}^*$,

$$\mathscr{A}^* = ka_{i1}\mathscr{C}_{i1} + ka_{i2}\mathscr{C}_{i2} + \cdots + ka_{in}\mathscr{C}_{in} = k\mathscr{A}$$

The expansion

$$a_{i1}\mathscr{C}_{j1} + a_{i2}\mathscr{C}_{j2} + \cdots + a_{in}\mathscr{C}_{jn} \qquad \text{for } i \neq j$$

is an expansion by *alien cofactors* and equals zero.[1] Using this theorem it can be proved that adding a multiple of any row (or column) to any other row (or column) leaves the value of the determinant unchanged. For example, multiply the jth row by k, add it to the ith row, and denote the new determinant by $\mathscr{A}^{**}$. Expanding $\mathscr{A}^{**}$ in terms of its ith row:

$$\begin{aligned}
\mathscr{A}^{**} &= (a_{i1} + ka_{j1})\mathscr{C}_{i1} + (a_{i2} + ka_{j2})\mathscr{C}_{i2} + \cdots + (a_{in} + ka_{jn})\mathscr{C}_{in} \\
&= a_{i1}\mathscr{C}_{i1} + a_{i2}\mathscr{C}_{i2} + \cdots + a_{in}\mathscr{C}_{in} + k(a_{j1}\mathscr{C}_{i1} + a_{j2}\mathscr{C}_{i2} + \cdots + a_{jn}\mathscr{C}_{in}) \\
&= \mathscr{A}
\end{aligned}$$

since the term in parentheses in the second equation is an expansion by alien cofactors and therefore equals zero.

The system of simultaneous equations in (A-1) can be solved by *Cramer's rule*, which states that the solution for x_j is given by the ratio of two determinants, the denominator being the determinant of the coefficients of the system of equations and the numerator being the determinant of the coefficients with the jth column replaced by the column of constant terms, provided that the determinant in the denominator does not vanish. First applying the rule that multiplying a column of the array multiplies the value of the determinant by the same number and then applying the rule that adding multiples of one column to some other column does not alter the value of the determinant, the solution for x_1 is derived as follows:

$$x_1\mathscr{A} = \begin{vmatrix} a_{11}x_1 & a_{12} & \cdots & a_{1n} \\ a_{21}x_1 & a_{22} & \cdots & a_{2n} \\ \multicolumn{4}{c}{\dotfill} \\ a_{n1}x_1 & a_{n2} & \cdots & a_{nn} \end{vmatrix} = \begin{vmatrix} a_{11}x_1 + a_{12}x_2 & a_{12} & \cdots & a_{1n} \\ a_{21}x_1 + a_{22}x_2 & a_{22} & \cdots & a_{2n} \\ \multicolumn{4}{c}{\dotfill} \\ a_{n1}x_1 + a_{n2}x_2 & a_{n2} & \cdots & a_{nn} \end{vmatrix} = \cdots$$

$$= \begin{vmatrix} a_{11}x_1 + a_{12}x_2 + \cdots + a_{1n}x_n & a_{12} & \cdots & a_{1n} \\ a_{21}x_1 + a_{22}x_2 + \cdots + a_{2n}x_n & a_{22} & \cdots & a_{2n} \\ \multicolumn{4}{c}{\dotfill} \\ a_{n1}x_1 + a_{n2}x_2 + \cdots + a_{nn}x_n & a_{n2} & \cdots & a_{nn} \end{vmatrix} = \begin{vmatrix} b_1 & a_{12} & \cdots & a_{1n} \\ b_2 & a_{22} & \cdots & a_{2n} \\ \multicolumn{4}{c}{\dotfill} \\ b_n & a_{n2} & \cdots & a_{nn} \end{vmatrix}$$

---

[1] See Birkhoff and MacLane, *op. cit.*, p. 286.

by substituting the column of constants from (A-1) for the sums in the first column. Denoting the determinant on the right-hand side by $\mathscr{A}_1$, the solution for x_1 is

$$x_1 = \frac{\mathscr{A}_1}{\mathscr{A}} \qquad\qquad (A\text{-}3)$$

as stated. The expression (A-3) is meaningless if $\mathscr{A} = 0$. In this case no unique solution exists, and the rows of the array are *linearly dependent* or, equivalently, the matrix is *singular*.[1]

If the value of a determinant is zero, any of the n equations can be expressed as a linear combination of the remaining $(n-1)$. For example, the nth equation might then be obtained by multiplying the first equation by 6 and adding 3 times the second to the first. The nth equation contains no new information and can be omitted, because it depends linearly on the first $(n-1)$ equations. For example, assume that the nth equation is a linear combination of the first $(n-1)$ equations. The ith equation is

$$\sum_{j=1}^{n} a_{ij}x_j = b_i$$

and the nth is

$$\sum_{i=1}^{n-1} c_i \sum_{j=1}^{n} a_{ij}x_j = \sum_{i=1}^{n-1} c_i b_i$$

where the c's are constants not all equal to zero. Any set of x's which satisfies the first $(n-1)$ equations necessarily satisfies the nth. The last equation adds no new information. The system is reduced to $(n-1)$ equations in n variables. If no $(n-1)$-rowed minor vanishes, it is possible to solve for any $(n-1)$ variables in terms of the constant terms and the remaining variable.

If the original system of n equations is *homogeneous* (all constant terms equal zero), all the x's are zero if the determinant of the system is nonvanishing. According to Cramer's rule each x is expressed as a fraction. The denominator is nonzero by hypothesis. The numerator vanishes for every x, because all b's equal zero, and the determinant of any array with a column of zeros is itself zero. If the determinant vanishes, it is possible to solve only for the relative values of the variables, and the solution is unique except for a factor of proportionality. For example, if the system of simultaneous equations is

$$3x_1 - 4x_2 = 0$$
$$6x_1 - 8x_2 = 0$$

---

[1] The rows of the matrix **A** are defined to be linearly dependent if it is possible to find a set of numbers $c_1, c_2, \ldots, c_n$ such that $\sum_{i=1}^{n} c_i a_{ij} = 0$ for all values of the index j, provided that the c's are not all equal to zero. It can be proved that the value of the determinant of the array is zero if and only if the rows (or the columns) of the matrix are linearly dependent. See Aitken, *op. cit.*, pp. 62 and 64.

the determinant is $(3)(-8) - (6)(-4) = 0$. Hence the two equations are not independent, and the second equation can be omitted.[1] Then

$$3x_1 - 4x_2 = 0$$

or
$$\frac{x_1}{x_2} = \frac{4}{3}$$

Any set of values satisfies the system as long as the relation between x_1 and x_2 is as $4:3$. Numerical values for the variables can only be obtained by choosing an arbitrary value for one of them.

    The rank of a matrix is the order of the largest nonzero determinant that can be formed from its rows and columns. Since a determinant is defined only for square arrays, if the matrix **A** is of order $(m \times n)$, $m < n$, its rank cannot exceed m. The rank is also equal to the number of linearly independent rows (or, what is the same thing, columns) in the matrix. Necessary and sufficient conditions for solving a system of simultaneous equations can be stated in terms of the rank of certain matrices. These conditions hold irrespective of whether the number of equations is greater than, equal to, or less than the number of variables. Given the system of equations $\mathbf{Ax} = \mathbf{b}$ where **A** is $(m \times n)$, there may be no solution, exactly one solution, or many solutions. Define **C** as an $m \times (n + 1)$ matrix the first n columns of which are **A** and the $(n + 1)$th is **b**. A necessary and sufficient condition for the existence of a (not necessarily unique) solution is that the rank of **A** equal the rank of **C**. If **C** has greater rank than **A**, the system is inconsistent and no solution exists. An example is

$$5x_1 + 2x_2 = 10$$
$$10x_1 + 4x_2 = 11$$

The rank of **A** is 1 and the rank of **C** is 2. Subtracting 2 times the first equation from the second yields the impossible result $0 = -9$.

A-2 CALCULUS

Functions, Limits, Continuity

The relation $y = f(x)$ (read "y is a function of x") means that a rule exists by which it is possible to associate values of the variable y with values of the variable x. Examples are $y = 1/x$, $y = 3x^2$, $y = \ln \sin x$, and $y = 1$ when x is an odd integer and $y = 0$ for any other value of x. In each case values of y correspond to given values of x according to the rule of association specified in the form of the function.

    A function may not be defined for all possible values of x: $y = 1/x$ cannot

---

[1] It does not matter which equation is omitted. Discarding the first leads to the same answer.

be evaluated for $x = 0$, and $y = \ln \sin x$ cannot be evaluated for values of x for which $\sin x$ is negative. The subset of all real numbers for which a function is defined is a region called the *domain* of the function. Thus the function $y = x^2$ has all the real numbers as its domain. The function values corresponding to the x values in the domain may themselves constitute a subset of the real numbers. This region is called the *range* of the function. The above function has the nonnegative real numbers as its range.

The relation $y = f(x)$ is an *explicit* function, since y is expressed in terms of x. If the functional relation between y and x is denoted by $g(y, x) = 0$, y is an *implicit* function of x. Specifying a value of x implicitly defines a value of y such that the expression on the left-hand side reduces to zero when the appropriate values of x and y are substituted in it. The relations $y = x^2$, $y = ax + b$, and $y = \sqrt[3]{x}$ provide examples of explicit functions; the expressions $ax + b - y = 0$, $x^2 - y^2 = 0$, and $e^y + y - x + \ln x = 0$ are examples of implicit functions. In order to rewrite an implicit function in explicit form it is necessary to solve the equation $g(y, x) = 0$ for y. This is not always possible. The implicit function $e^y + y - x + \ln x = 0$ cannot be written in explicit form because the equation cannot be solved analytically for x or y. An explicit function can always be rewritten in implicit-function form. For example, the explicit function $y = 3x^4 + 2 \sin x - 1$ becomes $y - 3x^4 - 2 \sin x + 1 = 0$ in implicit form.

A function may have more than one argument. It is then a function of several variables and may be denoted by $f(x_1, x_2, \ldots, x_n)$ or, letting $\mathbf{x}$ be the vector $(x_1, x_2, \ldots, x_n)$, by $f(\mathbf{x})$. The concepts discussed above are equally valid for functions of several variables.

A function $f(x)$ is *convex* over the interval (a, b) if

$$f[\lambda x_1 + (1 - \lambda)x_2] \leqq \lambda f(x_1) + (1 - \lambda)f(x_2) \qquad \text{(A-4)}$$

for all $a \leqq x_1, x_2 \leqq b$, and all $0 \leqq \lambda \leqq 1$. It is *strictly convex* over the interval if the strict inequality holds in (A-4) for all $0 < \lambda < 1$. A function is *concave* over the interval (a, b) if

$$f[\lambda x_1 + (1 - \lambda)x_2] \geqq \lambda f(x_1) + (1 - \lambda)f(x_2) \qquad \text{(A-5)}$$

for all $0 \leqq \lambda \leqq 1$, and *strictly concave* if the strict inequality holds for all $0 < \lambda < 1$.

The left-hand sides of (A-4) and (A-5) give function values at points which are interpolations between the values x_1 and x_2. The right-hand sides give interpolations of the function values corresponding to x_1 and x_2. Strict convexity (strict concavity) over an interval means that for any pair of x values in the interval, x_1 and x_2 with $x_1 < x_2$, the function values $f(x)$ for $x_1 < x < x_2$ lie below (above) the line segment connecting $f(x_1)$ and $f(x_2)$. The function pictured in Fig. A-1a is concave over the interval (a, b). The function in Fig. A-1b is convex over the interval (a, b). In fact, it is convex over a wider interval. A linear function satisfies the equalities in (A-4) and (A-5), and the two interpolations give identical values. Thus, a linear function

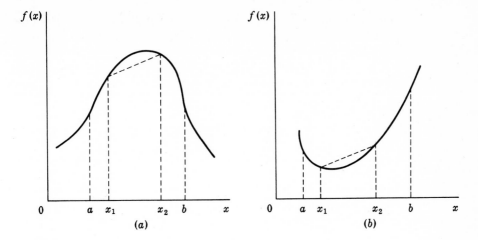

Figure A-1

is both convex (but not strictly convex) and concave (but not strictly concave).

These definitions and concepts are adapted in straightforward fashion to functions of several variables. Thus, the function $f(x_1, x_2, \ldots, x_n)$ is convex over a region if

$$f[\lambda x_1^{(1)} + (1 - \lambda)x_1^{(2)}, \lambda x_2^{(1)} + (1 - \lambda)x_2^{(2)}, \ldots, \lambda x_n^{(1)} + (1 - \lambda)x_n^{(2)}]$$
$$\leq \lambda f(x_1^{(1)}, x_2^{(1)}, \ldots, x_n^{(1)}) + (1 - \lambda)f(x_1^{(2)}, x_2^{(2)}, \ldots, x_n^{(2)}) \qquad \text{(A-6)}$$

for all pairs of points $(x_1^{(1)}, x_2^{(1)}, \ldots, x_n^{(1)})$ and $(x_1^{(2)}, x_2^{(2)}, \ldots, x_n^{(2)})$ in the region and all $0 \leq \lambda \leq 1$. The function is strictly convex if the strict inequality holds for all $0 < \lambda < 1$. The function is concave over the region if

$$f[\lambda x_1^{(1)} + (1 - \lambda)x_1^{(2)}, \lambda x_2^{(1)} + (1 - \lambda)x_2^{(2)}, \ldots, \lambda x_n^{(1)} + (1 - \lambda)x_n^{(2)}]$$
$$\geq \lambda f(x_1^{(1)}, x_2^{(1)}, \ldots, x_n^{(1)}) + (1 - \lambda)f(x_1^{(2)}, x_2^{(2)}, \ldots, x_n^{(2)}) \qquad \text{(A-7)}$$

and strictly concave if the strict inequality holds for $0 < \lambda < 1$.

A related but different concept is that of quasi-concavity. Consider the above function of n variables at two points $\mathbf{x}^{(1)} = (x_1^{(1)}, x_2^{(1)}, \ldots, x_n^{(1)})$ and $\mathbf{x}^{(2)} = (x_1^{(2)}, x_2^{(2)}, \ldots, x_n^{(2)})$. The function is quasi-concave over a region if

$$f[\lambda \mathbf{x}^{(1)} + (1 - \lambda)\mathbf{x}^{(2)}] \geq \min[f(\mathbf{x}^{(1)}), f(\mathbf{x}^{(2)})] \qquad \text{(A-8)}$$

for all $\mathbf{x}^{(1)}$ and $\mathbf{x}^{(2)}$ in the region and all $0 \leq \lambda \leq 1$. The function is strictly quasi-concave if the strict inequality holds for $0 < \lambda < 1$. Quasi-convexity and strict quasi-convexity are defined by reversing the inequality in (A-8).

It is easy to show that a concave function is quasi-concave. No generality is lost by assuming that $f(\mathbf{x}^{(1)}) \geq f(\mathbf{x}^{(2)})$. Putting the concavity definition of (A-7) in vector terms

$$f[\lambda \mathbf{x}^{(1)} + (1 - \lambda)\mathbf{x}^{(2)}] \geq \lambda f(\mathbf{x}^{(1)}) + (1 - \lambda)f(\mathbf{x}^{(2)}) \geq f(\mathbf{x}^{(2)})$$

proving quasi-concavity. Quasi-concavity does not imply concavity. If $f(\mathbf{x}^{(1)}) = f(\mathbf{x}^{(2)}) = y$, (A-8) becomes

$$f[\lambda \mathbf{x}^{(1)} + (1 - \lambda)\mathbf{x}^{(2)}] \geqq y$$

This special case is of particular interest in the theory of consumer behavior and in the theory of the firm.

A sequence of numbers is a list or enumeration of numbers such as 1, 2, 3, 4, 5, ...; or 1, $\frac{1}{2}$, $\frac{1}{3}$, $\frac{1}{4}$, $\frac{1}{5}$, ...; or 2, 1, $\frac{1}{2}$, $\frac{1}{4}$, $\frac{1}{8}$, ...; or 1, 0, -1, 0, 1, ... Each number in a sequence can be assigned an index indicating how "far out" the number is in the sequence. Thus in the third sequence above, $x_2 = 1$. The sequence converges to a limit K if there exists a number K with the property that the numerical magnitude of the difference between K and an item in the sequence is arbitrarily small (can be made as small as one desires) if one takes an item in the sequence sufficiently "far out," i.e., an item with sufficiently high index, and if the difference remains at least as small for every item in the sequence with even higher index. The first and fourth of the above sequences have no limit. The second and third have the limit zero.

The explicit function $f(x)$ (or, what is the same thing, the variable y) approaches the limit L as x approaches the number a, if the value of the function can be made to be as near the number L as is desired by taking x values which are sufficiently close to a, and if the value of the function remains at least as near L for all x values even closer to a. The process of finding the limit of $f(x)$ at $x = a$ may be visualized in the following manner. Take successive values $x_1, x_2, \ldots$, etc., of x that form a sequence converging to a. Substitute these values of x in $f(x)$. This results in a sequence of values $f(x_1), f(x_2), \ldots$, etc. If this sequence converges to a number L, $f(x)$ has the limit L at $x = a$. A limit exists if L is finite. The operation of taking the limit of $f(x)$ is denoted by $\lim_{x \to a} f(x) = L$.

The function $f(x) = 1 + 1/x$ approaches the limit 1 as $x \to \infty$ (x approaches infinity). However, this result cannot be obtained by substituting ∞ for x in $1 + 1/x$ because $1/\infty$ does not equal zero. $A/B = C$ implies that $A = BC$. If $1/\infty = 0$, then $1 = (\infty)(0)$. Since this is untrue, the problem must be resolved by a different reasoning, namely by an application of the definition of the limit. In fact, ∞ is not a number, but rather a direction. Its appearance in a formula is equivalent to the command to list the positive integers in increasing order and go as far as possible, i.e., to take the limit. The value of y can be made to differ from 1 by less than 0.1 by selecting a value for x greater than 10. If $x = 20$, $1 + 1/x = 1.05$, which differs from 1 by only 0.05. Likewise, y can be made to differ from 1 by less than $1/1,000,000$ by selecting a value for x greater than 1,000,000. The difference between the value of y and the number 1 can be made smaller than any prespecified number by taking an x that is sufficiently large.

The function $f(x)$ is continuous at the point $x = a$ if the following

conditions are fulfilled: (1) $\lim_{x \to a} f(x)$ exists, (2) $f(a)$ exists, (3) $f(a) = \lim_{x \to a} f(x)$.†
The function is continuous in the interval $a < x < b$ if it is continuous at every point in the interval. This definition of continuity implies that the function must be "continuous" in the everyday sense of the word: one must be able to draw the graph of the function without lifting the pencil from the paper.[1] Analogous definitions for the limit of a function and for continuity exist for functions of several variables.

Derivatives for Functions of One Variable

Assume that the function $y = f(x)$ is continuous in some interval. If the independent variable x changes by a small quantity Δx, the value of the function will change by the quantity Δy. Hence $y + \Delta y = f(x + \Delta x)$. The change in the value of the function can be expressed as

$$\Delta y = f(x + \Delta x) - f(x) \tag{A-9}$$

Dividing both sides of (A-5) by Δx:

$$\frac{\Delta y}{\Delta x} = \frac{f(x + \Delta x) - f(x)}{\Delta x} \tag{A-10}$$

The average rate of change of y per unit change of x for the interval x to $x + \Delta x$ is given by (A-10). For example, imagine that if one walks another half-hour, one covers an additional distance of 2 miles. The independent variable time is changed from x to $x + \frac{1}{2}$ hours; $\Delta y = 2$ miles, $\Delta x = \frac{1}{2}$ hour, and $\Delta y / \Delta x = $ average speed = 4 miles per hour. The derivative of $f(x)$, denoted by dy/dx, $f'(x)$, or $\dot{y}$, is defined as the rate of change of $f(x)$ as Δx approaches zero:

$$\frac{dy}{dx} = f'(x) = \lim_{\Delta x \to 0} \frac{f(x + \Delta x) - f(x)}{\Delta x}$$

The derivative is the rate of change or the speed in terms of the above example, or, to put it differently, the limit of the average rate of change (average speed) as Δx (the time interval) approaches zero. If the graph of $f(x)$

---

† At this point $x = a$ the value of the function must be finite, and this value must equal the limit of the function as x approaches a. The function $y = 1$ when x is an odd integer and $y = 0$ for any other value of x is not continuous when x is an odd integer. If $f(x)$ and $g(x)$ are two functions which are both continuous at $x = a$, then $f(x) + g(x)$, $f(x)g(x)$, and $f(x)/g(x)$ [provided that $g(x) \neq 0$] are also continuous.

[1] Note that a function that has "corners" or "kinks" but no gaps is continuous. The absolute value of a number x (denoted by $|x|$) is defined as follows:

$$|x| = x \qquad \text{if } x \geq 0$$
$$|x| = -x \qquad \text{if } x < 0$$

The function $y = |x|$ has a kink at $x = 0$, but is continuous.

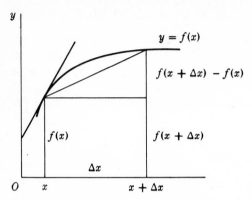

Figure A-2

is plotted, the derivative calculated at the point $x = a$ is the slope of the curve representing $f(x)$ at the point $x = a$. The average rate of change is the slope of the secant between two points on the curve, and the derivative is the slope of the tangent to the curve at a given point. These concepts are illustrated in Fig. A-2. Continuity of $f(x)$ is a necessary but not sufficient condition for the existence of a derivative. The function $y = |x|$ is continuous everywhere, but $\lim_{\Delta x \to 0} (\Delta y / \Delta x)$ does not exist at the origin.

The derivative of a derivative is a second derivative, denoted by d^2y/dx^2, and is defined as

$$\frac{d^2y}{dx^2} = \lim_{\Delta x \to 0} \frac{f'(x + \Delta x) - f'(x)}{\Delta x}$$

The second derivative is the rate of change of the first derivative, i.e., the rate at which the slope of the function is changing. In terms of the previous example it is the acceleration or the rate of change of speed. Higher-order derivatives are defined similarly.

Techniques of Differentiation

To differentiate a function is to find its derivative. Some of the more important techniques of differentiation are stated below without proof:[1]

1. $f(x) = c$ (constant), $f'(x) = 0$
2. $f(x) = x^n$, $f'(x) = nx^{n-1}$
3. $f(x) = g(x)h(x)$, $f'(x) = g'(x)h(x) + g(x)h'(x)$
4. $f(x) = g(x)/h(x)$, $h(x) \neq 0$, $f'(x) = [g'(x)h(x) - g(x)h'(x)]/[h(x)]^2$
5. $f(x) = g[h(x)]$, $f'(x) = g'[h(x)]h'(x)$ (function of a function rule)

---

[1] Proofs can be found in any standard elementary text on calculus. See R. Courant, *Differential and Integral Calculus* (2d ed., New York: Interscience, 1936), vol. I, pp. 136–140, 173, 175; or A. C. Chiang, *Fundamental Methods of Mathematical Economics* (2d ed., New York: McGraw-Hill, 1974), pp. 164–184.

6. $f(x) = \ln x$, $f'(x) = 1/x$
7. $f(x) = \ln [g(x)]$, $f'(x) = g'(x)/g(x)$
8. $f(x) = e^{g(x)}$, $f'(x) = g'(x)e^{g(x)}$
9. $f(x) = a^x$, $f'(x) = a^x \ln a$
10. If $y = f(x)$ is single-valued and continuous, and can be written in inverse form as $x = g(y)$ such that $f'(x)$ is continuous and $\neq 0$, $f'(x) = 1/g'(y)$ or $dy/dx = 1/(dx/dy)$ (inverse-function rule).

Partial Derivatives for Functions of Many Variables

The definitions of a limit and continuity are easily generalized to a function of n independent variables

$$y = f(x_1, x_2, \ldots, x_n)$$

The partial derivative of y with respect to x_i is

$$f_i = \frac{\partial y}{\partial x_i} = \lim_{\Delta x_i \to 0} \frac{f(x_1, x_2, \ldots, x_i + \Delta x_i, \ldots, x_n) - f(x_1, x_2, \ldots, x_n)}{\Delta x_i}$$

which is the rate of change of the function with respect to x_i, all other variables remaining constant. The techniques of differentiation are the same as those for a function of a single variable; all variables other than x_i are treated as constants. For example, if

$$y = 3x_1 x_2^2 + x_2 \ln x_1$$

then $\qquad \dfrac{\partial y}{\partial x_1} = 3x_2^2 + \dfrac{x_2}{x_1} \qquad$ and $\qquad \dfrac{\partial y}{\partial x_2} = 6x_1 x_2 + \ln x_1$

Higher-order derivatives are determined by successive partial differentiation; $\partial^2 y/\partial x_i^2$ is the partial derivative of f_i with respect to x_i, also denoted by f_{ii}; $\partial^2 y/\partial x_i \, \partial x_j$ is the partial derivative of f_i with respect to x_j (one of the second cross partial derivatives) and is denoted by f_{ij}. For the previous example

$$\frac{\partial^2 y}{\partial x_2 \, \partial x_1} = 6x_2 + \frac{1}{x_1}$$

If the first and second cross partial derivatives are continuous, $f_{ij} = f_{ji}$. The partial derivatives of the implicit function $f(x_1, x_2, \ldots, x_n) = 0$ are obtained by assuming that $y = f(x_1, x_2, \ldots, x_n)$ and calculating $\partial y/\partial x_1$, $\partial y/\partial x_2$, etc.

The Total Differential

For a function of a single variable

$$\frac{dy}{dx} = f'(x)$$

The symbol dy/dx denotes the derivative and was not interpreted as a fraction composed of the quantities dy and dx. Defining dx as an increment or change in the independent variable, dy can be defined as

$$dy = f'(x)\, dx \tag{A-11}$$

This is the *differential* of $f(x)$. At a given point x^0 the value of the function is $y^0 = f(x^0)$, and (A-11) can be rewritten in terms of deviations from this point as

$$y - y^0 = f'(x^0)(x - x^0) \tag{A-12}$$

which is the equation of the tangent to $y = f(x)$ at the point (x^0, y^0). Hence, (A-11) is the general form of the equation of the tangent to the function. For small changes of x (A-12) gives the approximate value of the corresponding change of $f(x)$.

The *total differential* of a function of n variables is defined as

$$dy = f_1\, dx_1 + f_2\, dx_2 + \cdots + f_n\, dx_n \tag{A-13}$$

which is the general form of the equation of the tangent plane (or hyperplane) to the surface (or hypersurface) defined by $y = f(x_1, x_2, \ldots, x_n)$. It also provides an approximate value of the change in the function when all variables are permitted to vary, provided that the variation in the independent variables is small. The *total derivative* of the function with respect to x_i is

$$\frac{dy}{dx_i} = f_1 \frac{dx_1}{dx_i} + \cdots + f_i + \cdots + f_n \frac{dx_n}{dx_i}$$

or the rate of change of y with respect to x_i when all other variables are permitted to vary and where all x_j are specified functions of x_i.

Let the first-order partial derivatives be denoted by the vector $\nabla f = (f_1, f_2, \ldots, f_3)$ which is called the gradient of f. Now consider values for the dx's such that the value of the function remains unchanged with $dy = 0$. This special case of (A-13) can be written as the vector product

$$\nabla f\, \mathbf{dx} = 0 \tag{A-14}$$

where $\mathbf{dx} = (dx_1, dx_2, \ldots, dx_n)$. Contour or level curves of f are defined by (A-14), and $\mathbf{dx}$ is a displacement vector tangent to the contour. The gradient is perpendicular to the tangent and points in the direction in which the function is increasing (locally) fastest.

The second differential of $y = f(x_1, x_2, \ldots, x_n)$ is obtained by taking the total differential of (A-13):

$$d^2 y = \sum_{i=1}^{n} \sum_{j=1}^{n} f_{ij}\, dx_i\, dx_j$$

which provides an approximate value of the change in the value of the function when all variables are permitted to vary within a small neighborhood.

Assume that $y = f(x_1, x_2)$, $x_1 = g(w_1, w_2)$, and $x_2 = h(w_1, w_2)$. The partial derivatives of y with respect to w_1 and w_2 are determined by the *composite-function rule* derived below. Taking total differentials

$$dy = \frac{\partial y}{\partial x_1} dx_1 + \frac{\partial y}{\partial x_2} dx_2 \qquad (A\text{-}15)$$

$$dx_1 = \frac{\partial x_1}{\partial w_1} dw_1 + \frac{\partial x_1}{\partial w_2} dw_2 \qquad (A\text{-}16)$$

$$dx_2 = \frac{\partial x_2}{\partial w_1} dw_1 + \frac{\partial x_2}{\partial w_2} dw_2 \qquad (A\text{-}17)$$

and substituting (A-16) and (A-17) into (A-15) and collecting terms on dw_1 and dw_2.

$$dy = \left(\frac{\partial y}{\partial x_1} \frac{\partial x_1}{\partial w_1} + \frac{\partial y}{\partial x_2} \frac{\partial x_2}{\partial w_1} \right) dw_1 + \left(\frac{\partial y}{\partial x_1} \frac{\partial x_1}{\partial w_2} + \frac{\partial y}{\partial x_2} \frac{\partial x_2}{\partial w_2} \right) dw_2 \qquad (A\text{-}18)$$

The expression (A-18) is itself a total differential in which the first term in parentheses equals $\partial y/\partial w_1$ and the second one equals $\partial y/\partial w_2$. Hence

$$\frac{\partial y}{\partial w_1} = \frac{\partial y}{\partial x_1} \frac{\partial x_1}{\partial w_1} + \frac{\partial y}{\partial x_2} \frac{\partial x_2}{\partial w_1} = f_1 g_1 + f_2 h_1$$

$$\frac{\partial y}{\partial w_2} = \frac{\partial y}{\partial x_1} \frac{\partial x_1}{\partial w_2} + \frac{\partial y}{\partial x_2} \frac{\partial x_2}{\partial w_2} = f_1 g_2 + f_2 h_2 \qquad (A\text{-}19)$$

If the independent variables of a function $f(x_1, x_2)$ are themselves functions of some other variables w_1 and w_2, $f(x_1, x_2)$ is differentiated partially with respect to w_1 and w_2 according to (A-19). This is the *composite-function rule.* By further differentiation of the first equation of (A-19),

$$\frac{\partial^2 y}{\partial w_1 \, \partial w_2} = f_{11} g_1 g_2 + f_{12}(g_1 h_2 + g_2 h_1) + f_{22} h_1 h_2 + f_1 g_{12} + f_2 h_{12}$$

Given the implicit function $f(x_1, x_2, \dots, x_n) = 0$, the partial derivative $\partial x_j/\partial x_i$ is obtained by first finding the total differential

$$f_1 \, dx_1 + f_2 \, dx_2 + \cdots + f_n \, dx_n = 0$$

dividing by dx_i

$$f_1 \frac{dx_1}{dx_i} + f_2 \frac{dx_2}{dx_i} + \cdots + f_j \frac{dx_j}{dx_i} + \cdots + f_i + \cdots + f_n \frac{dx_n}{dx_i} = 0$$

and setting all differentials other than dx_j and dx_i equal to zero. Then

$$f_j \frac{\partial x_j}{\partial x_i} + f_i = 0$$

and

$$\frac{\partial x_j}{\partial x_i} = -\frac{f_i}{f_j} \qquad (A\text{-}20)$$

Equation (A-20) is the *implicit-function rule*. By further differentiation of (A-20),

$$\frac{\partial^2 x_j}{\partial x_i^2} = -\frac{f_j[f_{ii} + f_{ji}(\partial x_j/\partial x_i)] - f_i[f_{ij} + f_{jj}(\partial x_j/\partial x_i)]}{f_j^2} = -\frac{f_{ii}f_j^2 - 2f_{ij}f_if_j + f_{jj}f_i^2}{f_j^3}$$

Envelopes

Let $f(x, y, k) = 0$ be an implicit function of the variables x and y. The form of this function is assumed to depend on the magnitude of the parameter k. In general, $f(x, y, k) = 0$ describes a curve in the xy plane. A different curve corresponds to each possible value of k. The envelope of this family of curves is itself a curve with the property that it is tangent to each member of the family. The equation of the envelope is obtained by taking the partial derivative of $f(x, y, k)$ with respect to k and eliminating k from the two equations

$$f(x, y, k) = 0$$
$$f_k(x, y, k) = 0$$

This method of obtaining the envelope is generally applicable, provided that $f_{kk} \neq 0$ and $f_x f_{yk} - f_y f_{xk} \neq 0$.†

Implicit-Function Theorem and Jacobians

Assume that the implicit function $f(x, y) = 0$ is continuous and has continuous first partial derivatives. Consider a point (x^0, y^0) for which $f(x^0, y^0) = 0$ and assume that $f_y(x^0, y^0) \neq 0$. The *implicit-function theorem* states that there exists a neighborhood of points about (x^0, y^0) such that for any x value in the neighborhood there corresponds a *unique* y value in the neighborhood with the property that $f(x, y) = 0$. The implicit-function theorem thus asserts the existence, under the stated conditions, of a unique solution, $y = \phi(x)$.‡ It gives a sufficient condition for the *local univalence* of solutions. Solutions may exist if $f_y(x^0, y^0) = 0$, but if f_y vanishes throughout an entire neighborhood, then no unique solution exists in that neighborhood. This is true *a fortiori* if f_y vanishes identically.

An example where $f_y(x^0, y^0) = 0$, but where a unique solution exists nevertheless, is given by $f(x, y) = (x - y)^2$. The equation $(x - y)^2 = 0$ possesses the unique solution $y = x$; yet $f_y = -2(x - y) = 0$ at any point satisfying the original equation. An example where $f_y(x, y) = 0$ throughout a neighborhood is given by $f(x, y) = x - 1$. It is clear that $f(x, y) = 0$ is satisfied by $x = 1$ and any value of y; hence no unique solution exists.[1]

The question of the existence of a locally unique solution for n simul-

---

† For proof see W. F. Osgood, *Advanced Calculus* (New York: Macmillan, 1925), pp. 186–193.
‡ Moreover, the solution is differentiable under the stated conditions.
[1] For rigorous proofs and geometric arguments see Courant, *op. cit.*, vol. II, pp. 111–122.

taneous equations in n unknowns requires a generalization of the implicit-function theorem and the concept of the *Jacobian*. Consider the system of simultaneous equations

$$
\begin{aligned}
f^1(x_1, x_2, \ldots, x_n) &= y_1 \\
f^2(x_1, x_2, \ldots, x_n) &= y_2 \\
&\cdots\cdots\cdots\cdots \\
f^n(x_1, x_2, \ldots, x_n) &= y_n
\end{aligned}
\tag{A-21}
$$

The Jacobian of (A-21) is the determinant of the first partial derivatives of the functions f^i and is denoted by

$$
\mathcal{J} = \frac{\partial(y_1, y_2, \ldots, y_n)}{\partial(x_1, x_2, \ldots, x_n)} =
\begin{vmatrix}
\dfrac{\partial y_1}{\partial x_1} & \dfrac{\partial y_1}{\partial x_2} & \cdots & \dfrac{\partial y_1}{\partial x_n} \\
\multicolumn{4}{c}{\cdots\cdots\cdots\cdots\cdots} \\
\dfrac{\partial y_n}{\partial x_1} & \dfrac{\partial y_n}{\partial x_2} & \cdots & \dfrac{\partial y_n}{\partial x_n}
\end{vmatrix}
\tag{A-22}
$$

The appropriate generalization of the implicit-function theorem is the following: If the functions $f^i(x_1, x_2, \ldots, x_n)$, $(i = 1, 2, \ldots, n)$ are continuous and possess continuous first partial derivatives and if the Jacobian (A-22) is nonvanishing at the point $(x_1^0, x_2^0, \ldots, x_n^0)$ satisfying (A-21), then, in some neighborhood about the point $(y_1^0, y_2^0, \ldots, y_n^0)$ there exist unique inverse functions $x_i = \phi^i(y_1, y_2, \ldots, y_n)$, $(i = 1, 2, \ldots, n)$. As in the case of the simple implicit-function theorem, no general assertion may be made if the Jacobian vanishes at $(x_1^0, x_2^0, \ldots, x_n^0)$. However, if $\mathcal{J} = 0$ in an entire neighborhood about $(x_1^0, x_2^0, \ldots, x_n^0)$, local univalence does not hold. The proof of this theorem is suggested by the following argument for the two-variable case. Consider the equations

$$
f(x_1, x_2) = y_1 \tag{A-23}
$$

$$
g(x_1, x_2) = y_2 \tag{A-24}
$$

If the Jacobian does not vanish, not all partial derivatives may equal zero. Assume that $f_1 \neq 0$. Then by the implicit-function theorem

$$
x_1 = \phi(x_2, y_1) \tag{A-25}
$$

Substituting in (A-24),

$$
F = g[\phi(x_2, y_1), x_2] - y_2 = 0 \tag{A-26}
$$

Then

$$
\frac{\partial F}{\partial x_2} = g_1\phi_1 + g_2 \tag{A-27}
$$

Substituting (A-25) in (A-23),

$$
G = f[\phi(x_2, y_1), x_2] - y_1 = 0
$$

Since G is identically equal to zero, its partial derivative with respect to x_2

also equals zero:

$$\frac{\partial G}{\partial x_2} = f_1 \phi_1 + f_2 = 0 \tag{A-28}$$

Solving (A-28) for ϕ_1 and substituting its value in (A-27),

$$\frac{\partial F}{\partial x_2} = g_1 \left(-\frac{f_2}{f_1} \right) + g_2 = \frac{f_1 g_2 - f_2 g_1}{f_1} \tag{A-29}$$

Since by hypothesis the Jacobian (the numerator) and f_1 do not vanish, $\partial F / \partial x_2 \neq 0$ and (A-26) can be solved for x_2. Therefore

$$x_2 = h(y_1, y_2) \tag{A-30}$$

Substituting (A-30) into (A-25) gives the solution for x_1.

A second relevant theorem states that the existence of a function $H(y_1, y_2, \ldots, y_n) = 0$, that is, functional dependence among the equations of (A-21), is necessary and sufficient for the Jacobian of (A-21) to vanish throughout a neighborhood of the point $(x_1^0, x_2^0, \ldots, x_n^0)$. The proof of sufficiency can be suggested as follows. Assume that there exists a functional dependence $H(y_1, y_2) = 0$. Taking the total differential,

$$H_1 \, dy_1 + H_2 \, dy_2 = 0$$

Substituting for dy_1 and dy_2 their values obtained by differentiating (A-23) and (A-24) and collecting terms,

$$(H_1 f_1 + H_2 g_1) \, dx_1 + (H_1 f_2 + H_2 g_2) \, dx_2 = 0$$

Since this must hold for all values of dx_1 and dx_2, the bracketed terms must each equal zero:

$$H_1 f_1 + H_2 g_1 = 0 \qquad H_1 f_2 + H_2 g_2 = 0$$

Moving the second terms to the right-hand side and dividing the first equation by the second,

$$\frac{H_1 f_1}{H_1 f_2} = \frac{-H_2 g_1}{-H_2 g_2}$$

or

$$f_1 g_2 - f_2 g_1 = 0 \tag{A-31}$$

The left-hand side of (A-31) is the Jacobian which equals zero.

As an example, consider the functions

$$x_1^2 - 2x_2 - 2 = y_1$$
$$x_1^4 - 4x_1^2 x_2 + 4x_2^2 = y_2$$

The functional dependence between them is given by $(y_1 + 2)^2 - y_2 = 0$. The Jacobian

$$\frac{\partial(y_1, y_2)}{\partial(x_1, x_2)} = \begin{vmatrix} 2x_1 & -2 \\ 4x_1^3 - 8x_1 x_2 & -4x_1^2 + 8x_2 \end{vmatrix} = (-8x_1^3 + 16x_1 x_2) - (-8x_1^3 + 16x_1 x_2) = 0$$

vanishes identically.

If the functions (A-23) and (A-24) are linear, the first theorem reduces to the familiar proposition that the determinant of the array of coefficients must be nonvanishing. This condition is fulfilled if the number of equations equals the number of variables and if the equations are not functionally dependent. If the Jacobian of a system of linear equations vanishes, the equations are linearly dependent (see Sec. A-1).

Local univalence means that a unique solution exists in a particular neighborhood. Global univalence means that a unique solution exists over an entire region. Global univalence obviously implies local univalence. However, a nonvanishing Jacobian will not ensure the global univalence that is often desired in economic theory. Global univalence theorems are normally based upon the properties of underlying functions, e.g., strict concavity.[1] Global univalence is discussed briefly in Sec. A-3, and two theorems are described in Sec. 10-1.

A-3 MAXIMA AND MINIMA

A (relative) maximum (minimum) of a function of one or more variables is an extreme point within the domain of the function such that all other valid points within a small neighborhood have function values that are no larger (smaller). All extreme points are stationary points, i.e., points at which the value of the function does not change. However, not all stationary points are extreme points. A strict maximum (minimum) is strictly larger (smaller) than neighboring points. A global maximum (minimum) is the largest (smallest) value over all valid points within the domain of the function. An unconstrained maximum (minimum) might be anywhere within the domain of the function. A constrained maximum (minimum) can only occur at points within the domain that satisfy one or more specific constraints.

Unconstrained Maxima and Minima

Let $y = f(x_1, x_2, \ldots, x_n)$ be denoted by $y = f(\mathbf{x})$ where $\mathbf{x}$ is an n-component vector. A Taylor series expansion is used to provide a proof of necessary conditions for an unconstrained maximum.[2] Assume that the point $\mathbf{x}^0$ provides a maximum,† let $\Delta \mathbf{x} = (\Delta x_1, \ldots, \Delta x_n)$ be an arbitrary displacement in the space of the x variables, and let θ_1 and θ_2 be two numbers with θ_1 restricted to be positive and θ_2 restricted to $0 < \theta_2 < 1$. Then, if $f(\mathbf{x})$ is continuous with

---

[1] See H. Nikaido, *Convex Structures and Economic Theory* (New York: Academic, 1968), chap. 13.

[2] A. C. Chiang, *op. cit.*, pp. 268–270.

† Attention is limited to maxima that occur at points within the interior of the domain of the function. Maxima that occur at the boundary of the domain are covered in the discussion of maxima and minima with inequality constraints.

continuous first and second partial derivatives, the value of the function at the point $x^0 + \theta_1\Delta x$ (i.e., at a point displaced from the location of the maximum by the vector $\theta_1\Delta x$) is

$$f(x^0 + \theta_1\Delta x) = f(x^0) + \theta_1 \sum_{i=1}^{n} f_i(x^0)\Delta x_i + \frac{\theta_1^2}{2} \sum_{i=1}^{n} \sum_{j=1}^{n} f_{ij}(x^0 + \theta_1\theta_2\Delta x)\Delta x_i\Delta x_j \quad \text{(A-32)}$$

Since $f(x^0)$ is a maximum, $f(x^0) \geq f(x^0 + \theta_1\Delta x)$ for all sufficiently small values of θ_1, and (A-32) therefore implies

$$\theta_1 \sum_{i=1}^{n} f_i(x^0)\Delta x_i + \frac{\theta_1^2}{2} \sum_{i=1}^{n} \sum_{j=1}^{n} f_{ij}(x^0 + \theta_1\theta_2\Delta x)\Delta x_i\Delta x_j \leq 0 \quad \text{(A-33)}$$

Dividing both sides of (A-33) by θ_1 and taking the limit as θ_1 approaches zero,

$$\sum_{i=1}^{n} f_i(x^0)\Delta x_i \leq 0 \quad \text{(A-34)}$$

Since Δx is an arbitrary vector, this result also holds for the vector $\Delta z = (-\Delta x_1, \ldots, -\Delta x_n)$, in which case (A-33) becomes

$$-\sum_{i=1}^{n} f_i(x^0)\Delta x_i \leq 0 \quad \text{(A-35)}$$

The only way in which (A-34) and (A-35) can both hold is if $f_i(x^0) = \partial f(x^0)/\partial x_i = 0$ for all $i = 1, \ldots, n$. Consequently, a necessary condition for a maximum (and for a minimum) is that all first-order partial derivatives equal zero. Otherwise, it would not be possible to satisfy both (A-34) and (A-35). These equalities are called the first-order conditions.

Substituting 0 for $f_i(x^0)$ in (A-33), dividing by $\theta_1^2/2$ and letting θ_1 approach zero,

$$\sum_{i=1}^{n} \sum_{j=1}^{n} f_{ij}(x^0)\Delta x_i\Delta x_j \leq 0 \quad \text{(A-36)}$$

The left-hand side of (A-36) is a quadratic form with the Δx_i as variables and the second-order partial derivatives as coefficients. The inequality (A-36) requires that the quadratic form be negative semidefinite, i.e., negative or zero for all possible Δx. The implied conditions on the second-order partial derivatives are called the second-order conditions. First-order conditions are the same for maxima and minima. The quadratic form on the left of (A-36) must be positive semidefinite for a minimum, i.e., positive or zero for all possible Δx.

It can be shown that (A-36) is negative definite (negative for all possible Δx except $x = 0$) if and only if the principal minors obtained from the Hessian determinant of second-order partial derivatives

$$\begin{vmatrix} f_{11} & f_{12} & \cdots & f_{1n} \\ f_{21} & f_{22} & \cdots & f_{2n} \\ \cdots & \cdots & \cdots & \cdots \\ f_{n1} & f_{n2} & \cdots & f_{nn} \end{vmatrix}$$

by deleting the last $(n - i)$ rows and columns $(i = n - 1, n - 2, \ldots, 0)$ alternate in sign:

$$f_{11} < 0, \begin{vmatrix} f_{11} & f_{12} \\ f_{21} & f_{22} \end{vmatrix} > 0, \ldots, (-1)^n \begin{vmatrix} f_{11} & f_{12} & \cdots & f_{1n} \\ f_{21} & f_{22} & \cdots & f_{2n} \\ \cdots\cdots\cdots\cdots\cdots\cdots \\ f_{n1} & f_{n2} & \cdots & f_{nn} \end{vmatrix} > 0 \qquad \text{(A-37)}$$

The quadratic form is positive definite if and only if the principal minors are all positive.[1] Extreme values are determined by solving the n equations $f_1(\mathbf{x}^0) = 0, f_2(\mathbf{x}^0) = 0, \ldots, f_n(\mathbf{x}^0) = 0$ for the n variables $x_1^0, x_2^0, \ldots, x_n^0$, calculating the signs of the principal minors of the Hessian, and determining whether they are appropriate for a maximum or minimum.

Let $f(x)$ be a function of one variable. Necessary conditions for a maximum at $x = x^0$ are

$$\text{(A)} \quad f'(x^0) = 0 \qquad \text{and} \qquad f''(x^0) \leqq 0$$

and sufficient conditions are

$$\text{(B)} \quad f'(x^0) = 0 \qquad \text{and} \qquad f''(x^0) < 0$$

The inequalities are reversed for a minimum. Conditions (A) are not sufficient and conditions (B) are not necessary. The former assertion is illustrated by the function $f(x) = x^3$. Then $f'(x) = 3x^2$ and $f''(x) = 6x$. At $x = 0$ conditions (A) are satisfied, but the function does not possess an extreme point at 0 (although it does have a stationary point). The latter assertion is illustrated by $f(x) = -x^4$ which has a maximum at the origin even though the second derivative (as well as the first) vanishes at that point. If the second derivative of $y = f(x)$ is zero, there are three possibilities: (1) $d^3y/dx^3 \neq 0$, (2) $d^3y/dx^3 = 0$ and $d^4y/dx^4 \neq 0$, or (3) $d^3y/dx^3 = 0$ and $d^4y/dx^4 = 0$. If (1) holds, the function has an inflection point (i.e., the first derivative has an extreme value) rather than a maximum or minimum. If (2) holds, the function has a maximum or minimum according to whether the fourth derivative is negative or positive. If (3) holds, the signs of the fifth and sixth derivatives must be examined and (1) and (2) applied with d^5y/dx^5 replacing d^3y/dx^3 and d^6y/dx^6 replacing d^4y/dx^4. Not all cases are covered by this criterion, however, as is illustrated by the function $y = e^{-1/x^2}$ for $x \neq 0$ and $y = 0$ for $x = 0$.[†] The function has a minimum at the origin and has infinitely many derivatives with a zero value at that point. Similar considerations hold for functions of several variables.

The satisfaction of the first-order condition at a point in an interval in which a twice-differentiable function is strictly concave (strictly convex) is

[1] The numbering of the variables is arbitrary. The sign conditions on the principal minors imply that all minors of given order are of the same sign. For example, in the two-variable maximum case the conditions $f_{11} < 0$ and $f_{11}f_{22} - f_{12}^2 > 0$ imply that f_{22} is negative.

[†] See K. Sydsaeter, "Letter to the Editor on Some Frequently Occurring Errors in the Economic Literature Concerning Problems of Maxima and Minima," *Journal of Economic Theory*, vol. 9 (December, 1974), pp. 464–466.

necessary and sufficient for the existence of a unique global maximum (minimum) at that point. If the case of the vanishing second derivative mentioned in the last paragraph is ignored, the proof is easy.[1] Consider the case of a strictly concave function. Select two distinct x values, x_1 and x_2, in the interval. Rewrite (A-5) as a function of λ,

$$g(\lambda) = f[\lambda x_1 + (1 - \lambda)x_2] - \lambda f(x_1) - (1 - \lambda)f(x_2) > 0$$

for $0 < \lambda < 1$, with the limiting values $g(0) = 0$ and $g(1) = 0$. It follows from the continuity of $f(x)$, and hence the continuity of $g(\lambda)$, that $g(\lambda)$ has a maximum in the closed interval $0 \leq \lambda \leq 1$. The first-order condition for this maximum is

$$g'(\lambda) = f'(x)(x_1 - x_2) - f(x_1) + f(x_2) = 0$$

where x represents $\lambda x_1 + (1 - \lambda)x_2$. The second-order condition is[2]

$$\frac{d^2 g(\lambda)}{d\lambda^2} = f''(x)(x_1 - x_2)^2 < 0$$

which implies that $f''(x) < 0$. A similar derivation implies that $f''(x) > 0$ for a strictly convex function. Thus, strict concavity (strict convexity) ensures satisfaction of the second-order condition for a maximum (minimum). Let x^0 provide a maximum with $f'(x^0) = 0$. Since $f''(x) < 0$, $f'(x) < 0$ for all $x > x^0$, and $f'(x) > 0$ for all $x < x^0$. There cannot be a second value of x for which the first derivative equals zero; x^0 is a globally unique maximum. Similarly, minima for strictly convex functions are globally unique. Analogous arguments hold for functions of n variables. Assume strict concavity and let x denote a vector. In this case

$$g'(\lambda) = \sum_{i=1}^{n} f_i(\mathbf{x})(x_{1i} - x_{2i}) - f(\mathbf{x_1}) + f(\mathbf{x_2}) = 0$$

and

$$g''(\lambda) = \sum_{i=1}^{n} \sum_{j=1}^{n} f_{ij}(\mathbf{x})(x_{1i} - x_{2i})(x_{1j} - x_{2j}) < 0$$

which implies that the Hessian matrix is the matrix of a negative definite quadratic form which is (together with the first-order conditions) sufficient for a maximum which can be shown to be globally unique.

Allied theorems state that if $f''(x) > 0$ over an interval, $f(x)$ is strictly convex over the interval, and if $f''(x) < 0$ over an interval, $f(x)$ is strictly concave over the interval. These theorems provide an easy means of testing the convexity or concavity of particular functions. For example, consider the function $f(x) = x^3 - 3x^2 + 3x$. Its second derivative is $f''(x) = 6x - 6$ which is negative for $x < 1$ and positive for $x > 1$. Hence, $f(x)$ is strictly concave for $x < 1$, and strictly convex for $x > 1$. In the n-variable case, the determinants

---

[1] The second derivative of a strictly convex or strictly concave function can only vanish at isolated points. It cannot vanish in a neighborhood.

[2] The function of a function rule for second derivatives is used. In general, if $\phi(x) = \psi[h(x)]$, $\phi''(x) = \psi''[h(x)]h'(x)^2 + \psi'[h(x)]h''(x)$.

given by (A-37) provide a means for testing for the convexity or concavity of particular functions. If the determinants alternate in sign as shown for (A-37) over an interval, the corresponding function is strictly concave over the interval. If the determinants of (A-37) are all positive over an interval, the function is strictly convex over the interval. For example, consider $f(x_1, x_2) = 2x_1^{0.5}x_2^{0.4}$. Evaluating the first two determinants of (A-37),

$$f_{11} = -0.5x_1^{-1.5}x_2^{0.4} \qquad f_{11}f_{22} - (f_{12})^2 = 0.08x_1^{-1}x_2^{-1.2}$$

If follows that $f(x_1, x_2)$ is strictly concave for $x_1 > 0$, $x_2 > 0$.

A function of several variables may have stationary points that are neither maxima nor minima. Such stationary points may be points of inflection (as in the one-variable case), or they may be saddle points. The latter are stationary points of the function for which there is no counterpart in the one-variable case, and are characterized by the fact that the function reaches a maximum along some directions but a minimum along some others. A simple example is provided by $f(x, y) = x^2 - y^2$ which has a saddle point at the origin.

Maxima and Minima with Equality Constraints

Many maximum and minimum problems in economics are such that the independent variables are not permitted to take on all possible values; the variables are "constrained" to satisfy some side relation. The constrained-maximum problem is to maximize the function $f(x_1, x_2, \ldots, x_n)$ subject to the constraint that only those values of $x_1, x_2, \ldots, x_n$ that satisfy the equation

$$g(x_1, x_2, \ldots, x_n) = 0$$

are admissible. For example, the function

$$f(x_1, x_2) = (x_1 - 1)^2 + (x_2 - 2)^2$$

has an unconstrained minimum at the point $x_1 = 1$, $x_2 = 2$. However, if this function is subject to the requirement that $x_1 - x_2 - 2 = 0$, its minimum value is achieved at the point $x_1 = \frac{5}{2}$, $x_2 = \frac{1}{2}$. The function $f(x_1, x_2)$ defines a surface in three-dimensional space. The equation $x_1 - x_2 - 2 = 0$ defines a straight line in the horizontal x_1x_2 plane. The constrained-minimum problem is one of finding the lowest point of the surface defined by $f(x_1, x_2)$ such that this point is above the straight line defined by the constraint. These concepts are illustrated with reference to a maximum problem in Fig. A-3. The unconstrained maximum occurs at the point M. The constraint is given by the line AB. All points on the surface other than those lying above the line AB, namely the points along the curved line PNQ, are irrelevant. The constrained maximum occurs at the point N. The result will generally differ from the unconstrained case, and the constrained maximum will generally be lower than the unconstrained maximum. It, of course, cannot be higher.

Sufficient conditions for a maximum are derived for a two-variable

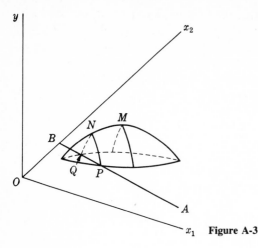

Figure A-3

constrained example with reference to the unconstrained case. Sufficient conditions for the n-variable case are stated, but not derived.

Let $f(x_1, x_2)$ be maximized subject to the constraint $g(x_1, x_2) = 0$. Assume that at least one of the partial derivatives of $g(x_1, x_2)$, say $\partial g/\partial x_2$, does not vanish in some region. Then, by the implicit-function theorem, one can find a unique solution $x_2 = h(x_1)$, and substituting in the function to be maximized one obtains $f[x_1, h(x_1)]$. This is a function of one variable, and its un-constrained maximum with respect to x_1 satisfies the constraint. As stated above, sufficient conditions for a maximum are $df[x_1, h(x_1)]/dx_1 = 0$, $d^2f[x_1, h(x_1)]/dx_1^2 < 0$. Differentiating to obtain the first-order condition

$$\frac{df}{dx_1} = f_1 + f_2 \frac{dh}{dx_1} = 0 \tag{A-38}$$

But $dh/dx_1 = dx_2/dx_1 = -g_1/g_2$, since the constraint must be satisfied for all eligible (x_1, x_2) values, and hence $g_1 dx_1 + g_2 dx_2 = 0$. Substituting in (A-38),

$$f_1 + f_2\left(-\frac{g_1}{g_2}\right) = 0 \tag{A-39}$$

Now define $-f_2/g_2 = \lambda$. Then (A-39) becomes

$$f_2 + \lambda g_2 = 0 \tag{A-40}$$

It is also true that

$$f_1 + \lambda g_1 = 0 \tag{A-41}$$

Equations (A-40) and (A-41) and the constraint are the first-order conditions for a maximum.

The first-order conditions can also be obtained by forming the Lagrange function

$$F(x_1, x_2, \lambda) = f(x_1, x_2) + \lambda g(x_1, x_2) \tag{A-42}$$

where λ is called a Lagrange multiplier, and setting its partial derivatives with respect to x_1, x_2, and λ equal to zero. This yields three equations in the three variables x_1, x_2, and λ, and the solution to this system gives the point or points at which $f(x_1, x_2)$ achieves a maximum (provided that the second-order condition to be discussed below is also satisfied) subject to $g(x_1, x_2) = 0$.[†]

The second-order condition requires the second derivative of $f[x_1, h(x_1)]$ to be negative. Differentiating (A-38) with respect to x_1,

$$\frac{d^2f}{dx_1^2} = f_{11} + f_{12}\frac{dh}{dx_1} + f_{21}\frac{dh}{dx_1} + f_{22}\left(\frac{dh}{dx_1}\right)^2 + f_2\frac{d^2h}{dx_1^2} < 0 \qquad \text{(A-43)}$$

Noting that $f_{12} = f_{21}$ for functions with continuous second partial derivatives and that $dh/dx_1 = -g_1/g_2$, (A-43) becomes

$$\frac{d^2f}{dx_1^2} = f_{11} - 2f_{12}\left(\frac{g_1}{g_2}\right) + f_{22}\left(\frac{g_1}{g_2}\right)^2 - f_2\left[\frac{[g_{11} + g_{12}(-g_1/g_2)]g_2 - [g_{21} + g_{22}(-g_1/g_2)]g_1}{g_2^2}\right]$$

$$= \frac{1}{g_2^2}\left[f_{11}g_2^2 + f_{22}g_1^2 + 2f_{12}g_1g_2 - \left(\frac{f_2}{g_2}\right)(g_{11}g_2^2 + g_{22}g_1^2 - 2g_{12}g_1g_2)\right] < 0$$

Further noting that $-f_2/g_2$ was defined as λ, this becomes

$$\frac{d^2f}{dx_1^2} = \frac{1}{g_2^2}[(f_{11} + \lambda g_{11})g_2^2 + (f_{22} + \lambda g_{22})g_1^2 - 2(f_{12} + \lambda g_{12})g_1g_2] < 0 \qquad \text{(A-44)}$$

Since $g_2^2 > 0$ (note that to be able to invoke the implicit-function theorem g_2 has to be assumed nonzero), condition (A-44) is easily verified to be equivalent to the following condition on the *bordered Hessian* determinant:

$$\begin{vmatrix} f_{11} + \lambda g_{11} & f_{12} + \lambda g_{12} & g_1 \\ f_{12} + \lambda g_{12} & f_{22} + \lambda g_{22} & g_2 \\ g_1 & g_2 & 0 \end{vmatrix} > 0$$

The terms in the upper-left-hand 2×2 portion are the second partial derivatives of $F(x_1, x_2, \lambda)$ with respect to x_1 and x_2; the rightmost column and bottom row contain the first partial derivatives of the constraint, and the element in the southeast corner is zero. The second-order condition (A-45) is equivalent to the requirement that the quadratic form $\Sigma_{i=1}^2 \Sigma_{j=1}^2 f_{ij}\, dx_i\, dx_j$ be negative for all values of the dx's that satisfy $g_1\, dx_1 + g_2\, dx_2 = 0$ except $dx_1 = dx_2 = 0$.

The first-order conditions for a constrained minimum in the two-variable case are also given by (A-40) and (A-41). The second-order condition requires that the bordered Hessian be negative. In this case the quadratic form must be positive for values of the dx's that satisfy $g_1\, dx_1 + g_2\, dx_2 = 0$ except $dx_1 = dx_2 = 0$.

First- and second-order sufficient conditions for maxima and minima for functions of n variables with $m < n$ constraints can be derived in analogous fashion. The one-constraint problem is to maximize $f(x_1, \ldots, x_n)$ subject to

---

[†] If the function F were formed by writing $g - \lambda g$ rather than $f + \lambda g$, the only difference would be a change in the sign of λ.

$g(x_1, \ldots, x_n) = 0$. Form the Lagrange function

$$F(x_1, \ldots, x_n, \lambda) = f(x_1, \ldots, x_n) + \lambda g(x_1, \ldots, x_n)$$

First-order conditions require that the first partial derivatives of F must vanish for both maxima and minima. This condition gives $(n + 1)$ equations in $(n + 1)$ variables

$$\frac{\partial F}{\partial x_1} = f_1 + \lambda g_1 = 0$$

$$\cdots\cdots\cdots\cdots$$

$$\frac{\partial F}{\partial x_n} = f_n + \lambda g_n = 0 \qquad\qquad \text{(A-45)}$$

$$\frac{\partial F}{\partial \lambda} = g(x_1, x_2, \ldots, x_n) = 0$$

The last equation ensures that the constraint is satisfied. The solution of this system of simultaneous equations gives the point or points at which $f(x_1, x_2, \ldots, x_n)$ achieves a maximum (or minimum) subject to $g(x_1, x_2, \ldots, x_n) = 0$.

Second-order conditions require that the quadratic form

$$\sum_{i=1}^{n} \sum_{j=1}^{n} f_{ij} \, dx_i \, dx_j$$

be negative for a maximum (positive for a minimum) for all values of the dx's that satisfy

$$g_1 \, dx_1 + g_2 \, dx_2 + \cdots + g_n \, dx_n = 0$$

other than $dx_i = 0$ for all i. Form the determinants

$$\begin{vmatrix} F_{11} & F_{12} & g_1 \\ F_{21} & F_{22} & g_2 \\ g_1 & g_2 & 0 \end{vmatrix}, \begin{vmatrix} F_{11} & F_{12} & F_{13} & g_1 \\ F_{21} & F_{22} & F_{23} & g_2 \\ F_{31} & F_{32} & F_{33} & g_3 \\ g_1 & g_2 & g_3 & 0 \end{vmatrix}, \ldots, \begin{vmatrix} F_{11} & F_{12} & \cdots & F_{1n} & g_1 \\ F_{12} & F_{22} & \cdots & F_{2n} & g_2 \\ \cdots & \cdots & \cdots & \cdots & \cdots \\ F_{n1} & F_{n2} & \cdots & F_{nn} & g_n \\ g_1 & g_2 & \cdots & g_n & 0 \end{vmatrix}$$

which are obtained by bordering the principal minors of the Hessian determinant of second partial derivatives of F by a row and a column containing the first partial derivatives of the constraint. The element in the southeast corner of each of these arrays is zero.

The second-order conditions for a constrained maximum will be satisfied if these bordered determinants alternate in sign, starting with plus; i.e., the signs of the determinants from left to right must be $+$, $-$, $+$, etc. The second-order conditions for a constrained minimum will be satisfied if they are all negative. These conditions together with (A-45) are sufficient for constrained maxima and minima.[1]

---

[1] See Samuelson, *op cit.*, appendix A; Allen, *op. cit.*, chap. XIX; and for a rigorous treatment of some aspects of this problem, G. Debreu, "Definite and Semi-definite Quadratic Forms," *Econometrica*, vol. 20 (April, 1952), pp. 295–300.

The Lagrange function for the two-constraint case is

$$F(x_1, \ldots, x_n, \lambda_1, \lambda_2) = f(x_1, x_2, \ldots, x_n) + \lambda_1 g^1(x_1, x_2, \ldots, x_n) + \lambda_2 g^2(x_1, x_2, \ldots, x_n)$$

where λ_1 and λ_2 are both undetermined Lagrange multipliers. First-order conditions for extreme points require that

$$\frac{\partial F}{\partial x_1} = f_1 + \lambda_1 g_1^1 + \lambda_2 g_1^2 = 0$$

$$\cdots\cdots\cdots\cdots\cdots\cdots\cdots$$

$$\frac{\partial F}{\partial x_n} = f_n + \lambda_1 g_n^1 + \lambda_2 g_n^2 = 0$$

$$\frac{\partial F}{\partial \lambda_1} = g^1(x_1, x_2, \ldots, x_n) = 0$$

$$\frac{\partial F}{\partial \lambda_2} = g^2(x_1, x_2, \ldots, x_n) = 0$$

Second-order conditions require that the quadratic form of second-order partials be negative for a maximum (positive for a minimum) for all nontrivial sets of values of the dx's that satisfy

$$g_1^1 \, dx_1 + g_2^1 \, dx_2 + \cdots + g_n^1 \, dx_n = 0$$

$$g_1^2 \, dx_1 + g_2^2 \, dx_2 + \cdots + g_n^2 \, dx_n = 0$$

Border the following principal minors of the Hessian of F with the first partials of the two constraints

$$\begin{vmatrix} F_{11} & F_{12} & F_{13} & g_1^1 & g_1^2 \\ F_{21} & F_{22} & F_{23} & g_2^1 & g_2^2 \\ F_{31} & F_{32} & F_{33} & g_3^1 & g_3^2 \\ g_1^1 & g_2^1 & g_3^1 & 0 & 0 \\ g_1^2 & g_2^2 & g_3^2 & 0 & 0 \end{vmatrix}, \ldots, \begin{vmatrix} F_{11} & \cdots & F_{1n} & g_1^1 & g_1^2 \\ \cdots\cdots\cdots\cdots\cdots\cdots\cdots \\ F_{n1} & \cdots & F_{nn} & g_n^1 & g_n^2 \\ g_1^1 & \cdots & g_n^1 & 0 & 0 \\ g_1^2 & \cdots & g_n^2 & 0 & 0 \end{vmatrix}$$

In the two-constraint case, the second-order conditions for a maximum will be satisfied if the above determinants alternate in sign, starting with minus, and those for a minimum will be satisfied if they are all positive. If there are $m < n$ constraints, border the principal minors of order $(m + 1)$ through n with the partial derivatives of the m constraints. The second-order conditions for a maximum will be satisfied if the determinants alternate in sign, starting with the sign of $(-1)^{m+1}$, and those for a minimum will be satisfied if all the specified determinants have the sign of $(-1)^m$.

Constrained Optima and Quasi-Concavity (Quasi-Convexity)

By advanced methods it has been proved that $f(x_1, x_2, \ldots, x_n)$ cannot have more than one constrained maximum (minimum) in an interval if the determinantal conditions for a constrained maximum (minimum) hold over the interval. In this case the satisfaction of conditions (A-45) is sufficient for the existence of a unique global maximum (minimum) within the interval.

Form a determinant by bordering the Hessian of f with its first-order partial derivatives:

$$\begin{vmatrix} f_{11} & \cdots & f_{1n} & f_1 \\ \cdots\cdots\cdots\cdots\cdots\cdots \\ f_{n1} & \cdots & f_{nn} & f_n \\ f_1 & \cdots & f_n & 0 \end{vmatrix} \qquad\qquad \text{(A-46)}$$

If f is quasi-concave, the principal minors of orders 2 through n of (A-46) are alternately nonnegative and nonpositive.[1] If f is strictly quasi-concave, they are alternately positive and negative almost everywhere. The only possible exclusions are subsets of points which have no interiors, i.e., isolated points, lines or curves.[2] If f is *regular strictly quasi-concave* within a domain, such subsets of points do not exist within that domain, and the principal minors of (A-46) are strictly positive and negative.

In the one-constraint case if f is regular strictly quasi-concave and g is linear, the second-order conditions for a constrained maximum are satisfied whenever the first-order conditions are. Substitute $f_i = \lambda g_i$ from (A-45) into (A-46), and divide the last row and last column of the resultant determinant by $1/\lambda$ so that (A-46) becomes

$$\lambda^2 \begin{vmatrix} f_{11} & \cdots & f_{1n} & g_1 \\ \cdots\cdots\cdots\cdots\cdots\cdots \\ f_{n1} & \cdots & f_{nn} & g_n \\ g_1 & \cdots & g_n & 0 \end{vmatrix}$$

the principal minors of which have the signs required for satisfaction of the second-order conditions. Similarly, if f is regular strictly quasi-convex and minimized subject to a linear constraint, the second-order conditions follow from the first-order conditions.

If there is more than one constraint and/or g is nonlinear, the connections between the second-order conditions and quasi-concavity (quasi-convexity) become more complex. If g is nonlinear in the one-constraint case, $f_{ij} \neq F$, and regular strict quasi-concavity is no longer sufficient to ensure the second-order conditions for constrained maximization. This case is covered by Exercise A-11.

Maxima and Minima with Inequality Constraints

One sometimes desires to maximize $f(x_1, \ldots, x_n)$ subject to two sets of inequality constraints

$$g^i(x_1, \ldots, x_n) \geqq 0 \qquad i = 1, \ldots, m \qquad\qquad \text{(A-47)}$$

$$x_1, \ldots, x_n \geqq 0 \qquad\qquad \text{(A-48)}$$

---

[1] See K. J. Arrow and A. C. Enthoven, "Quasi-Concave Programming," *Econometrica*, vol. 29 (October, 1961), pp. 779–800.

[2] For examples of such functions see D. W. Katzner, *Static Demand Theory* (New York: Macmillan, 1970), pp. 54, 211.

The first set restricts relationships among the x's, and the second requires the variables to be nonnegative. This is a nonlinear-programming problem. Necessary and sufficient conditions for a maximum may be stated in terms of a function similar to the Lagrange function used for the equality case. Form the function

$$F(x_1, \ldots, x_n, \lambda_1, \ldots, \lambda_m) = f(x_1, \ldots, x_n) + \sum_{i=1}^{m} \lambda_i g^i(x_1, \ldots, x_n) \quad \text{(A-49)}$$

The *Kuhn-Tucker conditions* for (A-49) are as follows

$$\frac{\partial F}{\partial x_j} = f_j + \sum_{i=1}^{m} \lambda_i g_j^i \leqq 0 \qquad j = 1, \ldots, n \quad \text{(A-50)}$$

$$\frac{\partial F}{\partial \lambda_i} = g^i \geqq 0 \qquad i = 1, \ldots, m \quad \text{(A-51)}$$

$$x_j \geqq 0 \qquad j = 1, \ldots, n \quad \text{(A-52)}$$

$$\lambda_i \geqq 0 \qquad i = 1, \ldots, m \quad \text{(A-53)}$$

$$\left(f_j + \sum_{i=1}^{m} \lambda_i g_j^i \right) x_j = 0 \qquad j = 1, \ldots, n \quad \text{(A-54)}$$

$$\lambda_i g^i = 0 \qquad i = 1, \ldots, m \quad \text{(A-55)}$$

The first two sets of conditions, (A-50) and (A-51), are similar to the first-order conditions in the case of equality constraints; the difference is that these partial derivatives are not required to be zero, but nonpositive and nonnegative respectively. The second pair of conditions ensures that all variables, including the Lagrange multipliers, are nonnegative. The last set of conditions are the complementarity conditions.

The reason for the presence of inequalities in (A-50) and (A-51) can be given intuitively in terms of a one-variable case subject to a nonnegativity requirement. Imagine that one wishes to maximize $f(x)$ subject to $x \geqq 0$. There are two possibilities, if a maximum exists: (1) An unconstrained maximum occurs at some point where x is positive or zero, in which case the appropriate first-order condition is $f'(x) = 0$. (2) An unconstrained maximum exists at a point at which $x < 0$. Since negative values of x are not admissible by the statement of the problem, the largest admissible function value must occur at $x = 0$. But at this point the function must be declining in value, i.e., $f'(x)$ must be negative, for if this were not true, an unconstrained maximum would occur at some positive x value, contradicting the assumption that it does not. Hence $f'(x) \leqq 0$ covers all possible cases when the restriction $x \geqq 0$ is imposed. Moreover, and this gives an intuitive underpinning to the complementarity condition (A-54), $f'(x)x$ must equal zero at the maximum: if $x > 0$, then $f'(x)$ must equal zero as argued above; if $f'(x)$ is nonzero (i.e., negative), then x must equal zero and the maximum occurs at the origin.

If $f(x_1, \ldots, x_n)$ and the $g^i(x_1, \ldots, x_n)$ $i = 1, \ldots m$ are all concave, the Kuhn-Tucker conditions are *sufficient conditions* for a maximum. In other words, if concavity holds, x^0 and λ^0 vectors that solve (A-50) through (A-55) have the property that the x^0 vector solves the maximum problem. The Kuhn-Tucker conditions are *necessary conditions* for a maximum if the so-called *constraint-qualification* condition is met. This condition basically ensures that the region of points in x-space not ruled out by the constraints, called the feasible region, has a shape that is well-behaved. Feasible regions are not well-behaved in this sense if the constraints become tangent to one another (see Exercise A-15). Such regions are not often encountered in economics. In the text it is assumed that the constraint qualification is met so that given concave functions, the Kuhn-Tucker conditions are necessary and sufficient.

The above framework is easily modified to accommodate minimization subject to inequality constraints. Reverse the inequalities in (A-47), (A-50), and (A-51). The modified Kuhn-Tucker conditions are necessary and sufficient for a minimum if the underlying functions are all convex and the constraint qualification is met. An alternative is to maximize the negative of the function for which a minimum is desired with the conditions unaltered.

The Lagrange multipliers for the inequality constraints have similar interpretations to the multipliers for equality constraints and the dual variables of linear programming (see Sec. 5-7). They give the rate at which the optimal value of the objective function increases per unit increment in the constraints if the appropriate partial derivatives are defined. If the optimal values of the variables satisfy a constraint as a strict inequality, the corresponding dual variable equals zero.

A-4 INTEGRALS

The integral of a function $f(x)$ is another function $F(x)$ which has the property that its derivative equals $f(x)$; $F'(x) = f(x)$. An integral is unique except for an arbitrary additive constant c, since a constant vanishes on differentiation. Thus if $F(x)$ is an integral of $f(x)$, so is $F(x) + c$. Integration is the process of finding the integral and is in a sense differentiation in reverse. The integral $F(x) + c$ is known as the indefinite integral and is denoted by

$$\int f(x)\, dx = F(x) + c$$

The techniques for finding the indefinite integrals of various kinds of functions can be difficult. Some of the simple rules of integration are stated below without proof:[1]

1. $f(x) = g'(x)$, $\int f(x)\, dx = g(x)$
2. $f(x) = g(x) + h(x)$, $\int f(x)\, dx = \int g(x)\, dx + \int h(x)\, dx$
3. $f(x) = cg(x)$ (c a constant), $\int f(x)\, dx = c \int g(x)\, dx$

[1] See Courant, *op. cit.*, vol. I, pp. 141–143, 207–210.

4. $f(x) = x^k \; (k \neq -1), \; \int f(x) \, dx = x^{k+1}/(k+1)$

5. $f(x) = 1/x, \; \int f(x) \, dx = \log x$

6. $f(x) = e^{ax}, \; \int f(x) \, dx = \dfrac{1}{a} e^{ax}$

7. If $x = g(u)$, then $\int f(x) \, dx = \int f[g(u)]g'(u) \, du$

8. If $u = u(x), \; v = v(x),$ then $\int u'(x)v(x) \, dx = u(x)v(x) - \int u(x)v'(x) \, dx$ (integration by parts)

Integration can be used to calculate the area under a curve. The function $f(x)$ is plotted in Fig. A-4. To calculate the area between the x axis and the curve between points a and b, subdivide the distance $(b - a)$ into segments of width Δx_i, and then erect rectangles of height $f(x_i)$ over each segment. The height of each rectangle is the value of the function evaluated at the left-hand boundary of each segment. The required area A is approximately $\Sigma f(x_i) \, \Delta x_i$.† As the width of the rectangles becomes smaller, the expression $\Sigma f(x_i) \, \Delta x_i$ comes closer to the true area A. In fact,

$$A = \lim_{\Delta x_i \to 0} \Sigma f(x_i) \, \Delta x_i$$

provided that this limit exists.[1] Now change the right-hand-side boundary b of the area under consideration to a variable boundary x. The area from a to a variable right-hand-side boundary x is a function of x and will be denoted by $A(a, x)$. A somewhat larger area would result if the right-hand-side boundary were somewhat farther to the right, i.e., if this boundary were $x + \Delta x$. The

---

† The sum of these rectangles underestimates the area under the curve. If the height of the rectangles were given by the value of the function corresponding to the right-hand boundary of each segment, the approximation would overestimate the correct area. Either method is permissible for the analysis.

[1] The limit exists if the function $f(x)$ is continuous.

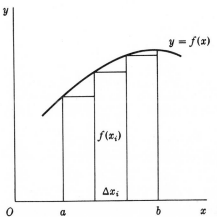

Figure A-4

resulting area will be denoted by $A(a, x + \Delta x)$. The difference between these two areas is

$$A(a, x + \Delta x) - A(a, x) = A(x, x + \Delta x)$$

The area between the points x and $x + \Delta x$ is also given by the width of the interval Δx multiplied by the value of the function $f(x)$ at some point between x and $x + \Delta x$. Denote this value of x by x_0:

$$A(a, x + \Delta x) - A(a, x) = f(x_0)\, \Delta x$$

or

$$\frac{A(a, x + \Delta x) - A(a, x)}{\Delta x} = f(x_0)$$

When Δx approaches zero, $x + \Delta x$ approaches x, and hence x_0 approaches x, since x_0 is between x and $x + \Delta x$. Taking limits

$$\frac{dA}{dx} = \lim_{\Delta x \to 0} \frac{A(a, x + \Delta x) - A(a, x)}{\Delta x} = f(x)$$

This proves that the derivative of the area under a function is the function itself or that the integral of a function is the area under it. The area $A(a, b)$ is the *definite* integral of $f(x)$ between the points a and b. If $F(x)$ is an indefinite integral of $f(x)$, the definite integral between a and b is

$$\int_a^b f(x)\, dx = F(b) - F(a)$$

An example of definite integration is provided by

$$\int_0^b \alpha e^{-rx}\, dx = -\frac{\alpha e^{-rb}}{r} + \frac{\alpha}{r} = \frac{\alpha(1 - e^{-rb})}{r}$$

The mean value theorem for integrals states that if $f(x)$ is continuous over the interval from a to b, then $\int_a^b f(x)\, dx = f[a\theta + b(1-\theta)](b-a)$ for some $0 \le \theta \le 1$. This means that the definite integral equals the width of the interval times the integrand evaluated at some appropriate point in the interval.

The limits of integration may be functions of a variable x as in $g(x) = \int_{\psi_1(x)}^{\psi_2(x)} f(x, y)\, dy$. In this case the integral's derivative is

$$g'(x) = \int_{\psi_1(x)}^{\psi_2(x)} \frac{\partial f(x, y)}{\partial x}\, dy - \psi_1'(x) f[x, \psi_1(x)] + \psi_2'(x) f[x, \psi_2(x)]\dagger$$

A-5 DIFFERENCE EQUATIONS

Consider the sequence of numbers $1, 4, 9, 16, 25$, etc., and denote them by $y_1, y_2, \ldots, y_t, \ldots$. The first differences of this sequence are $\Delta y_1 = y_2 - y_1 = 3$, $\Delta y_2 = y_3 - y_2 = 5$, $\Delta y_3 = y_4 - y_3 = 7$, etc. The second differences are the

† Courant, *op. cit.*, vol. II, pp. 219–220.

differences between the first differences or $\Delta^2 y_1 = \Delta y_2 - \Delta y_1 = 2$, $\Delta^2 y_2 = \Delta y_3 - \Delta y_2 = 2$, etc. In this particular sequence of numbers the second differences are constant and equal 2. This can be written as

$$\Delta^2 y_t = 2 \tag{A-56}$$

Equation (A-56) can also be written as the difference between two first differences, or

$$\Delta y_{t+1} - \Delta y_t = 2 \tag{A-57}$$

Each of the first differences in (A-57) can be written as the difference between two members of the sequence, or

$$(y_{t+2} - y_{t+1}) - (y_{t+1} - y_t) = y_{t+2} - 2y_{t+1} + y_t = 2 \tag{A-58}$$

Equation (A-58) is a difference equation; it is expressed in terms of the differences of a sequence of numbers. It relates the $(t + 2)$nd member of the sequence to the $(t + 1)$st and the tth members. In general, difference equations relate the tth member of a sequence to some previous members. The general linear difference equation of nth order with constant coefficients is

$$a_0 y_t + a_1 y_{t-1} + a_2 y_{t-2} + \cdots + a_n y_{t-n} + b = 0 \tag{A-59}$$

Equation (A-59) is linear because no y is raised to any power but the first and because it contains no products or other functions of the y's. It is an nth-order equation because the most distant value of y upon which y_t depends is y_{t-n}. Thus (A-58) is a linear difference equation of second order with constant coefficients. A difference equation is homogeneous if $b = 0$. Equation (A-58) is non-homogeneous.

The Nature of the Solution

The homogeneous first-order equation is

$$y_t = a y_{t-1} \tag{A-60}$$

Given the information that $y_0 = 2$, $y_1 = 2a$ can be determined from (A-60) by substituting the value of y_0 on the right-hand side. Then $y_2 = a(2a) = 2a^2$. In this fashion it is possible to calculate the value of y for any value of t. This procedure is cumbersome and can be avoided by finding a general solution for the difference equation. A general solution is an expression, usually a function of t, which gives the value of y_t immediately upon substitution of the desired value of t. A function of t must be found such that $y_t = f(t)$. Any such function is a solution if it satisfies the difference equation. In the first-order case the solution $f(t)$ must satisfy[1]

$$f(t) = af(t - 1) \tag{A-61}$$

---

[1] A difference equation can also be regarded as defining y as a function of t. To every value of t there corresponds a value of y with the proviso that the independent variable t can take on only integral values, i.e., 0, 1, 2, 3, etc.

In addition the solution must also be consistent with the *initial conditions*. The initial conditions are a statement about the value of y at one or more specified points in the sequence. The number of initial conditions must be the same as the order of the equation in order to obtain a complete solution. Only one initial condition is necessary in the first-order case. This was given by $y_0 = 2$ in the previous example. The problem is to find the solution or solutions that satisfy the difference equation and then to select the solution that also satisfies the initial conditions.[1] Subsequent discussion is confined to linear difference equations of first order with constant coefficients.

Homogeneous Equations

Equation (A-60) can be written as

$$\frac{y_t}{y_{t-1}} = a \qquad \text{for all } t$$

Therefore,
$$y_t = \frac{y_t}{y_{t-1}} \frac{y_{t-1}}{y_{t-2}} \cdots \frac{y_2}{y_1} \frac{y_1}{y_0} y_0 = a^t y_0$$

The term a^t is itself a solution since it satisfies (A-60):

$$a^t = a(a^{t-1})$$

If $f(t)$ is a solution, so is $cf(t)$ where c is a constant. Thus assume that the general solution is $y_t = ca^t$. This satisfies the difference equation because

$$ca^t = a(ca^{t-1})$$

The parameter a is given by the difference equation and c is determined on the basis of the initial condition such that the general solution ca^t is consistent with it. In the previous example the initial condition was given by $y_0 = 2$. $y_0 = ca^0 = c = 2$, and the general solution is $y_t = 2a^t$.

Nonhomogeneous Equations

Two steps are required to find the solution of a nonhomogeneous difference equation. The first one is to find the solution $f(t)$ of the corresponding homogeneous equation. The second one is to find the *particular solution* denoted by $g(t)$. The final general solution is $f(t) + g(t)$. The nonhomogeneous equation is

$$ay_t + by_{t-1} + c = 0 \qquad \text{(A-62)}$$

The solution of the homogeneous part of (A-62) is $k(-b/a)^t$. To find a

---

[1] For details see W. J. Baumol, *Economic Dynamics* (2d ed., New York: Macmillan, 1959), chaps. 9–13; and S. Goldberg, *Introduction to Difference Equations* (New York: Wiley, 1958), chaps. II–III.

particular solution substitute in (A-62) $y_t = K$ (constant) and solve for K:

$$aK + bK + c = 0$$

and
$$K = \frac{-c}{a+b}$$

provided that $a + b \neq 0$. Then the general solution is

$$y = k\left(-\frac{b}{a}\right)^t - \frac{c}{a+b}$$

where k is determined in accordance with the initial conditions. If $a + b = 0$, assume that the particular solution is $y_t = Kt$, substitute this in (A-62), and solve for K. Then the general solution is $y = k(-b/a)^t + Kt$, where $K = c/b$.

A-6 DIFFERENTIAL EQUATIONS

An equation in which the variables are derivatives is called a *differential equation*. Examples are given by (1) $dy/dt = 17$, (2) $d^2y/dt^2 + b\, dy/dt + cy = 0$, and (3) $dy/dt + by^2 = c$. Equations (1) and (2) are linear differential equations because they are linear in y and its derivatives. Equations such as (3) are nonlinear and are not considered here.[1] The general nth-order linear differential equation with constant coefficients is

$$a_0 \frac{d^n y}{dt^n} + a_1 \frac{d^{n-1} y}{dt^{n-1}} + \cdots + a_n y + b = 0 \tag{A-63}$$

This equation is homogeneous if $b = 0$. The homogeneous first-order equation is

$$\frac{dy}{dt} = by \tag{A-64}$$

A general solution is a function $y = f(t)$ that satisfies the equation and yields the value of y upon substitution of a value of the independent variable t. As in the case of difference equations, solutions must also satisfy initial conditions.

The solution of (A-64) can be obtained by integration. Treating dy and dt as differentials, (A-64) may be written as

$$\frac{dy}{y} = b\, dt$$

Integrating both sides,
$$\int \frac{1}{y}\, dy = \int b\, dt$$

[1] These equations are also called ordinary differential equations since the derivatives occurring in them are total derivatives. Equations containing partial derivatives are called partial differential equations. These latter are encountered less frequently in economic applications than are ordinary differential equations.

It follows that

$$\log y = bt + c \tag{A-65}$$

where c stands for the constant of integration which is determined from initial conditions. From (A-65) the solution for (A-64) is

$$y = e^{bt+c} = ke^{bt}$$

where $k = e^c$. Given the initial condition $y = y_0$ when $t = 0$, it follows that $k = y_0$, and the solution is

$$y = y_0 e^{bt}$$

The derivation of solutions to higher-order equations has many similarities to the corresponding derivations for difference equations. For any differential equation of the form of (A-64) a solution is provided by $e^{\lambda t}$ where λ is an as yet undetermined number. In the second-order case, $a\,d^2y/dt^2 + b\,dy/dt + cy = 0$, the substitution of $e^{\lambda t}$ yields

$$a\lambda^2 e^{\lambda t} + b\lambda e^{\lambda t} + ce^{\lambda t} = 0$$

Dividing by $e^{\lambda t}$,

$$a\lambda^2 + b\lambda + c = 0$$

Since the quadratic yields, in general, two roots λ_1 and λ_2, the general solution will be of the form $y = k_1 e^{\lambda_1 t} + k_2 e^{\lambda_2 t}$. Given the initial conditions $y = y_0$ and $dy/dt = y_0'$ when $t = 0$,

$$y_0 = k_1 + k_2 \qquad y_0' = k_1\lambda_1 + k_2\lambda_2$$

and the constants are

$$k_1 = \frac{y_0' - \lambda_1 y_0}{\lambda_1 - \lambda_2} \qquad k_2 = -\frac{y_0' - \lambda_2 y_0}{\lambda_1 - \lambda_2}$$

if $\lambda_1 \neq \lambda_2$. If the solution to the characteristic equation is a pair of complex numbers $\lambda = \theta_1 \pm \theta_2 i$, the solution of the second-order differential equation becomes

$$y = e^{\theta_1 t}(k_1 \cos \theta_2 t + k_2 \sin \theta_2 t)$$

where k_1 and k_2 are determined, as before, from the initial conditions.

The particular solution for a nonhomogeneous differential equation is found in the same way as for difference equations: assume that $y = K$ (constant) provides a solution. Substitute this trial solution in

$$a\frac{d^2y}{dt^2} + b\frac{dy}{dt} + cy + d = 0$$

and solve for K, provided that $c \neq 0$.† The general solution is, as before, the sum of the particular solution and the solution to the homogeneous equation.

---

† If $c = 0$, one assumes $y = Kt$; if b is also equal to zero, the trial particular solution becomes Kt^2. See also Sec. A-5.

EXERCISES

A-1 Use Cramer's rule to solve the following system of simultaneous equations:

$$\begin{aligned} 2x_1 + 3x_2 &= 13 \\ x_1 + x_2 + x_3 &= 0 \\ 5x_1 - 6x_2 + x_3 &= -13 \end{aligned}$$

A-2 Differentiate the following functions:

(a) $f(x) = 6x^3 + 2x^2 - x + 12$.

(b) $f(x) = 4\sqrt{x}$.

(c) $f(x) = e^{-x}(x - 2)$.

(d) $f(x) = 4x^3/(2x^2 - x)$.

(e) $f(x) = \ln(x^{-3})$.

A-3 Determine the values of x at which the following functions possess maximum and minimum values:

(a) $f(x) = x^2 - 2x + 5$.

(b) $f(x) = x^3 - 27x^2 + 195x + 3$.

(c) $f(x) = \ln(x^2 - x + 1)$.

A-4 Determine whether the following functions are strictly convex, strictly concave, or neither over the specified intervals:

(a) $f(x) = x^2 - 3x + 4$, for $x = $ any real number.

(b) $f(x) = \ln x$, for $x > 0$.

(c) $f(x) = e^{ax}$, for $x \leq 0$.

(d) $f(x) = x^3 - 2x^2 + x$, for $x \geq 0$.

A-5 Determine f_{11} and f_{12} for the following functions of two variables:

(a) $f(x_1, x_2) = x_1^2 x_2^2 - x_1 x_2 + 3x_1 - 2x_2$.

(b) $f(x_1, x_2) = \ln(2x_1 + 3x_2)$.

(c) $f(x_1, x_2) = x_2^{x_1}$.

A-6 Take the total differential of $y = 2x_1 x_2^2 + x_2 e^{x_3} + \ln x_1$.

A-7 Construct the envelope of the family of curves in the xy plane given by $y - 2x^2 - xk + k^2 = 0$.

A-8 Find values for x_1 and x_2 which maximize

$$f(x_1, x_2) = 5x_1 + 10x_2 + x_1 x_2 - 0.5x_1^2 - 3x_2^2$$

A-9 Let $f(x_1, x_2) = e^{-x_1^2 - x_2^2}(2x_1^2 + 3x_2^2)$. Verify that this function has maxima at $(1, 0)$ and $(-1, 0)$, saddle points at $(0, 1)$ and $(0, -1)$, and a minimum at $(0, 0)$. Draw the (approximate) contours or level curves of the function.

A-10 Let $f(x_1, x_2) = Ax_1^\alpha x_2^\beta$, where A, α, $\beta > 0$, be defined for the domain x_1, $x_2 > 0$. Demonstrate that the function is strictly concave within its domain if and only if $\alpha + \beta < 1$.

A-11 Let $f(x_1, x_2)$ be maximized subject to $g(x_1, x_2) = 0$. Assume that optimal values for the appropriate Lagrange multiplier are strictly positive. Show that strict quasi-concavity for both f and g and regular strict quasi-concavity for one of the two functions is sufficient to ensure the second-order conditions whenever the first-order conditions are satisfied.

A-12 Find values for x_1 and x_2 that maximize $f(x_1, x_2) = x_1^2 x_2$ subject to the requirement that $5x_1 + 2x_2 = 300$. Demonstrate that the appropriate second-order condition is satisfied.

A-13 Find values of x_1 and x_2 that maximize $f(x_1, x_2) = (x_1 + 25)^{1/4} x_2^{1/4}$ subject to the requirements that $5x_1 + 10x_2 \leq 100$ and $x_1, x_2 \geq 0$.

A-14 Find functions of two variables with the domains $x_1, x_2 > 0$ that are

(a) Quasi-concave, but not strictly quasi-concave and not concave.

(b) Strictly quasi-concave, but not concave.

(c) Quasi-concave, but not strictly quasi-concave and not strictly concave.

(d) Strictly quasi-concave and concave, but not strictly concave.

A-15 Find the optimal solution to the nonlinear-programming problem: maximize x_1 subject to $(1 - x_1)^3 - x_2 \geq 0$ and $x_1, x_2 \geq 0$. Show that the Kuhn-Tucker conditions are not satisfied at the maximum. Explain why they are not.

A-16 Demonstrate that the simultaneous equations

$$x_1^2 + 4x_1x_2 + 4x_2^2 = y_1$$
$$x_1 + 2x_2 = y_2$$

do not possess solutions of the form $x_i = \phi^i(y_1, y_2)$, $i = 1, 2$.

A-17 Find $\int f(x)\, dx$ if
(a) $f(x) = x^2 - 2x$.
(b) $f(x) = (2x + 1)/(x^2 + x)$.
(c) $f(x) = ae^{-bx}$.

A-18 Evaluate the following definite integrals:
(a) $\int_6^{10} (2x + 3)\, dx$.
(b) $\int_1^e (1/x)\, dx$.

A-19 Solve the following nonhomogeneous difference equation:

$$2y_t - y_{t-1} - 6 = 0 \quad \text{and} \quad y_0 = 10$$

A-20 Solve the homogeneous second-order differential equation:

$$\frac{d^2y}{dt^2} + 5\frac{dy}{dt} + 6y = 0$$

where $y_0 = 6$ and $y_0' = 3$.

SELECTED REFERENCES

Aitken, A. C.: *Determinants and Matrices* (New York: Interscience, 1951). A concise reference work that is too difficult for the beginner.

Allen, R. G. D.: *Basic Mathematics* (New York: St. Martin's, 1964). A modern text of particular interest to economists.

———: *Mathematical Analysis for Economists* (London: Macmillan, 1938). A survey of the calculus with many economic illustrations.

Apostol, T. M.: *Calculus*, vols. I and II (2d ed., New York: Wiley, 1967). A comprehensive and definitive treatise.

Baumol, W. J.: *Economic Dynamics* (2d ed., New York: Macmillan, 1959). Chaps. 9–13 contain an introduction to linear difference equations and chap. 14 contains an introduction to differential equations.

Chiang, A. C.: *Fundamental Methods of Mathematical Economics* (2d ed., New York: McGraw-Hill, 1974). A detailed treatment of algebra, calculus, linear and nonlinear programming, and other topics of interest to economists. The level of the work makes it accessible for readers without advanced preparation.

Goldberg, S.: *Introduction to Difference Equations* (New York: Wiley, 1958). A beginning text with many examples drawn from economics.

Goursat, E.: *A Course in Mathematical Analysis*, vol. I, trans. by E. R. Hedrick (Boston: Ginn, 1904). A classic treatise. Recommended for intermediate and advanced students.

Hadley, G.: *Linear Algebra* (Reading, Mass.: Addison-Wesley, 1961). Determinants are covered in chap. 3.

Intriligator, Michael D.: *Mathematical Optimization and Economic Theory* (Englewood Cliffs, N.J.: Prentice-Hall, 1971). A text covering the theory of maximization and applications to many subjects in economics.

Klein, E.: *Mathematical Methods in Theoretical Economics* (New York: Academic, 1973). A comprehensive and fairly advanced coverage of the parts of algebra and topology most frequently employed in economics. Calculus is not covered.

Nikaido, H.: *Convex Structures and Economic Theory* (New York: Academic, 1968). Global univalence is covered in chap. 7. Advanced mathematics is used.

Perlis, S.: *Theory of Matrices* (Cambridge, Mass.: Addison-Wesley, 1952). A specialized treatment of determinants and matrices.

Roberts, B., and D. L. Schulze: *Modern Mathematics and Economic Analysis* (New York: W. W. Norton, 1973). An intermediate-level exposition of most mathematical tools encountered in economics.

Samuelson, Paul A.: *Foundations of Economic Analysis* (Cambridge, Mass.: Harvard University Press, 1948). A mathematical approach to economic theory. An appendix contains a survey of some of the mathematical tools employed in the text. The treatment will prove difficult for all but advanced students.

ANSWERS FOR EVEN-NUMBERED EXERCISES

Chapter 2

2-2 For a strictly concave function $f[\lambda q_1^0 + (1-\lambda)q_1^{(1)}, \lambda q_2^0 + (1-\lambda)q_2^{(1)}] > \lambda f(q_1^0, q_2^0) + (1-\lambda)f(q_1^{(1)}, q_2^{(1)})$. Let $\lambda = 0.5$, multiply through by 2, and rearrange terms to obtain the desired result.

2-4 Form the function $V = q_1^\gamma q_2 + \lambda(y - p_1 q_1 - p_2 q_2)$, and set its partial derivatives equal to zero:

$$\gamma q_1^{\gamma-1} q_2 - \lambda p_1 = 0 \qquad q_1^\gamma - \lambda p_2 = 0 \qquad y - p_1 q_1 - p_2 q_2 = 0$$

which yields $p_1 q_1 = \gamma p_2 q_2$, a positively sloped straight line through the origin.

2-6 V is a monotonic transformation of the utility function given in Exercise 2-3. Specifically, $V = U^4 + \ln U$.

2-8 $\dfrac{r}{W}\dfrac{dW}{dr} = \dfrac{(48-T)r}{(r+1)[T(r+2)-48]}$

2-10 Here, $S_{11} = -p_2^2\lambda/\mathcal{D}$, $S_{12} = p_1 p_2 \lambda/\mathcal{D}$, and $p_1(-p_2^2\lambda/\mathcal{D}) + p_2(p_1 p_2 \lambda/\mathcal{D}) = 0$.

2-12 Form the Lagrange function

$$V = f(q_1, q_2, q_3) + \lambda(y - p_1 q_1 - p_2 q_2 - p_3 q_3) + \mu(z - c_1 q_1 - c_2 q_2 - c_3 q_3)$$

where the p's and c's are dollar prices and ration-coupon prices respectively. The Kuhn-Tucker conditions are

$$\frac{\partial V}{\partial q_i} = f_i - \lambda p_i - \mu c_i \leqq 0 \qquad q_i \geqq 0 \qquad q_i \frac{\partial V}{\partial q_i} = 0 \qquad i = 1, 2, 3$$

$$\frac{\partial V}{\partial \lambda} = y - p_1 q_1 - p_2 q_2 - p_3 q_3 \geqq 0 \qquad \lambda \geqq 0 \qquad \lambda \frac{\partial V}{\partial \lambda} = 0$$

$$\frac{\partial V}{\partial \mu} = z - c_1 q_1 - c_2 q_2 - c_3 q_3 \geqq 0 \qquad \mu \geqq 0 \qquad \mu \frac{\partial V}{\partial \mu} = 0$$

There are three possible outcomes: (1) the budget constraint is binding, but the coupon constraint is not; (2) the coupon constraint is binding, but the budget constraint is not; and (3) both constraints are binding. The imposition of rationing would not alter the consumer's purchases if his coupon allotment were sufficiently generous so that z is not less than the coupon requirements for his former purchases; i.e., case (1) above provides the optimal solution.

Assume that (3) prevails, and that all outputs are positive. The Kuhn-Tucker conditions yield

$$\frac{f_i}{f_j} = \frac{\lambda p_i + \mu c_i}{\lambda p_j + \mu c_j} \qquad i, j = 1, 2, 3$$

RCSs (the f_i/f_j) equal generalized price ratios where the generalized prices are the dollar and ration-coupon prices weighted by the corresponding marginal utilities, i.e., the Lagrange multipliers.

Chapter 3

3-2 Using vector notation let $g(\mathbf{q})$ be a homogeneous function and let $f(\mathbf{q})$ be a monotonic increasing function of g. Since the two functions provide the same ordering, $g(\mathbf{q}^0) = g(\mathbf{q}^{(1)})$. From homogeneity

$$g(t\mathbf{q}^0) = t^k g(\mathbf{q}^0) = t^k g(\mathbf{q}^{(1)}) = g(t\mathbf{q}^{(1)})$$

and finally, it follows that $f(t\mathbf{q}^0) = f(t\mathbf{q}^{(1)})$.

3-4 Maximization of utility subject to the budget constraint $v_1 q_1 + v_2 q_2 = 1$ yields the demand functions

$$q_1 = \frac{\alpha v_2}{v_1} \qquad q = \frac{1}{v_2} - \alpha$$

and the indirect utility function

$$U = \alpha \ln\left(\frac{\alpha v_2}{v_1}\right) + \frac{1}{v_2} - \alpha$$

with the derivatives

$$\frac{\partial U}{\partial v_1} = -\frac{\alpha}{v_1} \qquad \frac{\partial U}{\partial v_2} = -\frac{1 - \alpha v_2}{v_2^2}$$

Finally, by Roy's identity

$$q_1 = \frac{-\alpha/v_1}{[-\alpha v_1/v_1 - v_2(1 - \alpha v_2)/v_2^2]} = \frac{\alpha v_2}{v_1}$$

$$q_2 = \frac{-(1 - \alpha v_2)/v_2^2}{[-\alpha v_1/v_1 - v_2(1 - \alpha v_2)/v_2^2]} = \frac{1}{v_2} - \alpha$$

which are the same as the demand functions derived above.

3-6 The consumer maximizes $q_1 q_2 q_3$ subject to $y = p_1 q_1 + p_2 q_2 + p_3 q_3 = p_1 q_c + p_3 q_3$. Substituting $q_c = q_1 + p_2 q_2/p_1$ in her utility function, write the Lagrange function as

$$V = \left(q_c - \frac{p_2}{p_1} q_2\right) q_2 q_3 + \lambda(y - p_1 q_c - p_3 q_3)$$

and set the partial derivatives equal to zero:

$$q_2 q_3 - \lambda p_1 = 0 \qquad \left(-\frac{p_2}{p_1}\right) q_2 q_3 + \left(q_c - \frac{p_2}{p_1} q_2\right) q_3 = 0$$

$$\left(q_c - \frac{p_2}{p_1} q_2\right) q_2 - \lambda p_3 = 0 \qquad y - p_1 q_c - p_3 q_3 = 0$$

Solving for q_c yields $q_c = (2y)/(3p_1)$.

3-8 Choose two points on the utility scale arbitrarily; for example, $U(A) = 200$ and $U(D) = 100$. Then

$$U(B) = (0.4)(200) + (0.6)(100) = 140$$

$$U(C) = (0.2)(140) + (0.8)(100) = 108$$

3-10 The consumer can only reduce the dispersion of outcomes in this case. She cannot eliminate uncertainty. Equate the expected utilities from insurance and no insurance:

$$(0.10)(152,380 - R)^{0.5} + (0.90)(160,000 - R)^{0.5}$$
$$= (0.05)(90,000)^{0.5} + (0.05)(40,000)^{0.5} + (0.90)(160,000)^{0.5} = 385$$

The value $R = 11,004$ provides a·solution for this equation.

Chapter 4

4-2 The MPs, $f_1 = 100 + 20x_2 - 25x_1$ and $f_2 = 100 + 20x_1 - 25x_2$, are positive over the domain $0.8x_1 + 4 > x_2 > 1.2x_1 - 5$, and $f_{11} = f_{22} = -25 < 0$, $f_{11}f_{22} - f_{12}^2 = 225 > 0$ throughout two-dimensional space. It is also necessary to impose the condition that the input values be nonnegative.

4-4 Equating MC to price:

$$3q^2 - 20q + 17 = 5 \quad \text{and} \quad 3q^2 - 20q + 12 = 0$$

which has the roots $q = 6$ and $q = \frac{2}{3}$. At $q = 6$, $d^2C/dq^2 = 6q - 20 = 16 > 0$, hence this is the maximum profit solution; MC is decreasing at $q = \frac{2}{3}$.

The output elasticity of cost at $q = 6$ is

$$\frac{C}{q}\frac{dq}{dC} = \frac{q^3 - 10q^2 + 17q + 66}{q} \frac{1}{3q^2 - 20q + 17} = \left(\frac{24}{6}\right)\left(\frac{1}{5}\right) = 0.8$$

since $dq/dC = 1/(dC/dq)$.

4-6 Total profit is

$$\pi = p_1q_1 + p_2q_2 - rx = p_1q_1 + p_2q_2 - rA(q_1^\alpha + q_2^\beta)$$

Setting the partial derivatives equal to zero,

$$\frac{\partial \pi}{\partial q_1} = p_1 - r\alpha Aq_1^{\alpha-1} = 0 \qquad \frac{\partial \pi}{\partial q_2} = p_2 - r\beta Aq_2^{\beta-1} = 0$$

Whence

$$q_1 = \left(\frac{p_1}{r\alpha A}\right)^{1/(\alpha-1)} \qquad q_2 = \left(\frac{p_2}{r\beta A}\right)^{1/(\beta-1)}$$

The production relation is strictly convex for $q_1, q_2 > 0$ if the principal minors of the relevant Hessian are positive within this domain. The second direct partials are the first-order minors:

$$\frac{\partial^2 x}{\partial q_1^2} = \alpha(\alpha - 1)Aq_1^{\alpha-2} \qquad \frac{\partial^2 x}{\partial q_2^2} = \beta(\beta - 1)Aq_2^{\beta-2}$$

These are both positive for $q_1, q_2 > 0$ since $\alpha, \beta > 1$ by hypothesis. Finally,

$$\frac{\partial^2 x}{\partial q_1 \partial q_2} = 0 \quad \text{and} \quad \frac{\partial^2 x}{\partial q_1^2}\frac{\partial^2 x}{\partial q_2^2} - \left(\frac{\partial^2 x}{\partial q_1 \partial q_2}\right)^2 > 0$$

Chapter 5

5-2 Let k_1 and k_2 denote the input use ratios for Q_1 and Q_2 respectively, and let r denote the input price ratio. The equilibrium conditions are

$$k_1 = a_1 r^{\sigma_1} \quad \text{and} \quad k_2 = a_2 r^{\sigma_2}$$

By hypothesis, $\sigma_1 > \sigma_2$ and $a_1 < a_2$. The input use ratios would be the same if $k_1 = k_2$: $a_1 r^{\sigma_1} = a_2 r^{\sigma_2}$ which implies that $r = (a_2/a_1)^{1/(\sigma_1-\sigma_2)}$. Dividing the expression for k_1 by that for k_2,

$$\frac{k_1}{k_2} = \frac{a_1}{a_2} r^{(\sigma_1-\sigma_2)}$$

Since $\sigma_1 - \sigma_2 > 0$ by hypothesis, a price ratio greater than $(a_1/a_2)^{1/(\sigma_1-\sigma_2)}$ would make $k_1 > k_2$ and conversely.

5-4 By Shephard's lemma

$$\frac{\partial C}{\partial r_1} = (1 + r^{-1/2})q = x_1 \qquad \frac{\partial C}{\partial r_2} = (1 + r^{1/2})q = x_2$$

where $r = r_1/r_2$. Solving for $r^{1/2}$,

$$r^{1/2} = \frac{q}{x_1 - q} = \frac{x_2 - q}{q}$$

which yields the production function

$$q = \frac{x_1 x_2}{x_1 + x_2} = \frac{1}{1/x_1 + 1/x_2} = 0.5[0.5x_1^{-1} + 0.5x_2^{-1}]^{-1}$$

which by (5-7) is CES with $\sigma = 0.5$ ($\rho = 1$), $A = 0.5$, and $\alpha = 0.5$.

5-6 The input requirements for a unit of output producing half with the first activity and half with the third are

$$(0.5)(1, 6) + (0.5)(3, 3) = (2, 4.5)$$

The second activity requires $(2, 5)$, and consequently is inefficient.

5-8 The appropriate Lagrange function for (5-31) and (5-32) is

$$L = \sum_{j=1}^{n} p_j q_j + \sum_{i=1}^{m} r_i \left(x_i^0 - \sum_{j=1}^{n} a_{ij} x_j \right)$$

Since all functions are concave (linear), the Kuhn-Tucker conditions are applicable.

(1) $\dfrac{\partial L}{\partial q_j} = p_j - \sum_{i=1}^{m} r_i a_{ij} \leq 0$ \qquad (2) $\dfrac{\partial L}{\partial q_j} q_j = 0$ \qquad (3) $q_j \geq 0 \quad j = 1, \ldots, n$

(4) $\dfrac{\partial L}{\partial r_i} = x_i^0 - \sum_{j=1}^{n} a_{ij} q_j \geq 0$ \qquad (5) $\dfrac{\partial L}{\partial r_i} r_i = 0$ \qquad (6) $r_i \geq 0 \quad i = 1, \ldots, m$

Conditions (1) are the same as dual constraints (5-39). Conditions (2) ensure the satisfaction of (5-41) and (5-43), and conditions (5) ensure (5-40) and (5-42).

Chapter 6

6-2 $AVC = 0.04q^2 - 0.8q + 10$ and its minimum is found by setting its derivative equal to zero:

$$\frac{d(AVC)}{dq} = 0.08q - 0.8 = 0$$

Hence $q = 10$, at which point $AVC = 6$ and $MC = 0.12q^2 - 1.6q + 10$. Substitute $p = MC$, multiply through by 12.5, and solve for $q = (20 \pm 5\sqrt{3p - 14})/3$. The positive branch gives outputs at which MC is increasing. Hence

$$S = 0 \quad \text{if} \quad p < 6 \quad \text{and} \quad S = \frac{20 + 5\sqrt{3p - 14}}{3} \quad \text{if} \quad p \geq 6$$

6-4 Firms will have a profit maximum of zero if $p = MC = AC$, which occurs at the minimum of the AC curve. $AC = q^2 - 4q + 8$ and reaches a minimum at $q = 2$, at which point $p = 4$. The long-run supply curve is horizontal and the amount supplied is $2n$ where n is the number of firms. At $p = 4$ the quantity demanded is 1600. Hence $1600 = 2n$, and $n = 800$.

6-6 The entire supply will come from domestic sources as long as price is less than 20. When price reaches 20, domestic supply is 180. Thereafter, the supply curve is horizontal. Domestic supply remains at 180, price remains at 20, and imports are $q - 180$.

6-8 The cost functions including cost of transportation are $c_1 = 0.5q_1^2 + 6q_1$ for firms in location I and $C_2 = 0.5q_2^2 + 10q_2$ for firms in location II. The first-order conditions for profit maximization are $(q_1 + 6) = p = (q_2 + 10)$, and the two types of supply functions for the firms are

$$S_1 = 0 \quad \text{if} \quad 0 \leq p < 6 \quad \text{and} \quad S_1 = p - 6 \quad \text{if} \quad 6 \leq p$$

$$S_2 = 0 \quad \text{if} \quad 0 \leq p < 10 \quad \text{and} \quad S_2 = p - 10 \quad \text{if} \quad 10 \leq p$$

The aggregate supply function is

$$S = 0 \quad \text{if} \quad 0 \leq p < 6, \quad S = 50p - 300 \quad \text{if} \quad 6 \leq p < 10$$

and

$$S = 100p - 800 \quad \text{if} \quad 10 \leq p$$

6-10 By (6-21), $dp/dt = kE(p)$ and local stability in the neighborhood of the equilibrium price p_e requires that $dp/dt = kE'(p_e)(p - p_e)$ have a negative real root. In the present case $E(p) = 25p - \sqrt{5p}$, and $E(p) = 0$ yields $p_e = 5$. $E'(p) = -25/p^2 - 0.5\sqrt{5/p}$ and $E'(5) = -1.5 < 0$ which ensures local stability.

6-12 If $p_0 = 0.8p_e$ and applying (6-27), the time path is $p_t = [1 - 0.2(A/a)^t]p_e$ and $0.99p_e \leq p_t \leq 1.01p_e$ when $-0.05 \leq (A/a)^t \leq 0.05$.

(a) Substituting for A and a gives $-0.05 \leq (-0.9)^t \leq 0.05$. Taking the logarithm of $0.9^t = 0.05$ gives $t \approx 28.4$.

(b) Substituting gives $0.2^t = 0.05$ for the right limit which is attained for $t \approx 1.8$.

Chapter 7

7-2 The monopolist's profit is

$$\pi = (85 - 3q)q - 5x = (85 - 6\sqrt{x})(2\sqrt{x}) - 5x = 170\sqrt{x} - 17x$$

Maximizing,

$$\frac{d\pi}{dx} = \frac{85}{\sqrt{x}} - 17 = 0$$

which has the solution $\sqrt{x} = 5$, $x = 25$. Since $d^2\pi/dx^2 = -42.5x^{-3/2} < 0$, this is a maximum. When $x = 25$,

$$q = 2\sqrt{x} = 2\sqrt{25} = 10 \quad \text{and} \quad p = 85 - 3q = 55$$

7-4 The monopolist's profit is

$$\pi = a(q_1 + q_2) - b(q_1 + q_2)^2 - \alpha_1 q_1 - \beta_1 q_1^2 - \alpha_2 q_2 - \beta_2 q_2^2$$

Set the partial derivatives equal to zero:

$$\frac{\partial \pi}{\partial q_1} = a - 2b(q_1 + q_2) - \alpha_1 - 2\beta_1 q_1 = 0$$

$$\frac{\partial \pi}{\partial q_2} = a - 2b(q_1 + q_2) - \alpha_2 - 2\beta_2 q_2 = 0$$

Take total differentials with respect to q_1, q_2, and a, rearrange terms,

$$2(b + \beta_1) \, dq_1 + 2b \, dq_2 = da$$

$$2b \, dq_1 + 2(b + \beta_2) \, dq_2 = da$$

and solve for dq_1 and dq_2:

$$dq_1 = \frac{2\beta_2}{\mathcal{D}} da \qquad dq_2 = \frac{2\beta_1}{\mathcal{D}} da$$

where $\mathcal{D} = 4[b(\beta_1 + \beta_2) + \beta_1\beta_2] > 0$. Hence, $dq_1/da > 0$ and $dq_2/da > 0$. Furthermore, since the rate of change of MC in the ith plant is $dMC_i/dq_i = 2\beta_i$, output will increase more in the first plant if MC is increasing faster in the second ($\beta_2 > \beta_1$). It will increase more in the second if $\beta_1 > \beta_2$.

7-6 Profit is

$$\pi = (100 - 3q + 4\sqrt{A})q - (4q^2 + 10q + A)$$

Setting the partials equal to zero,

$$\frac{\partial \pi}{\partial q} = (100 - 6q + 4\sqrt{A}) - (8q + 10) = 0$$

$$\frac{\partial \pi}{\partial A} = \frac{2q}{\sqrt{A}} - 1 = 0$$

From the second equation $q = \sqrt{A}/2$. Substituting in the first equation and solving for $\sqrt{A} = 30$ and $A = 900$, the corresponding output and price are $q = 15$, $p = 175$. It can be verified that the second-order conditions are satisfied.

7-8 The kth firm equates its MR and MC:

$$MR_k = 150 - 2q_k - 0.02 \sum_{\substack{i=1 \\ i \neq k}}^{101} q_i = 1.5q_k^2 - 40q_k + 270 = MC_k$$

Since all firms produce identical outputs under the present circumstances,

$$\sum_{\substack{i=1 \\ i \neq k}}^{101} q_i = 100q_k$$

The equality of MR and MC may be expressed by

$$150 - 4q_k = 1.5q_k^2 - 40q_k + 270$$

and

$$q_k^2 - 24q_k + 80 = (q_k - 4)(q_k - 20) = 0$$

with the roots $q_k = (4, 20)$. It is easily verified that only the larger of these outputs is relevant. For $q_k = 20$, $p_k = 90$, and $\pi_k = 400$.

Chapter 8

8-2 I's profit is

$$\pi_1 = q_1(100 - 2q_1 - 0.5q_1) - 2.5q_1^2 = 100q_1 - 5q_1^2$$

Setting the first derivative equal to zero, and solving for q_1 yields

$$\frac{d\pi_1}{dq_1} = 100 - 10q_1 = 0$$

$$q_1 = 10 \qquad q_2 = 5 \qquad p_1 = 75 \qquad \pi_1 = 500$$

8-4 The profit functions are

$$\pi_1 = 2(13x_1 - 0.2x_1^2) - [2 + 0.1(x_1 + x_2)]x_1$$

$$\pi_2 = 3(12x_2 - 0.1x_2^2) - [2 + 0.1(x_1 + x_2)]x_2$$

Setting the appropriate partial derivatives equal to zero yields the input reaction functions

$$x_1 = 24 - 0.1x_2 \qquad x_2 = 42.5 - 0.125x_1$$

Solving the reaction functions for x_1 and x_2, and substituting in the production and profit functions yields

$$x_1 = 20 \qquad q_1 = 180 \qquad \pi_1 = 200$$

$$x_2 = 40 \qquad q_2 = 320 \qquad \pi_2 = 640$$

8-6 The sum of the market shares equals one. Consequently, this is a constant-sum game. The payoff matrix in terms of I's shares is

I/II	0-mile	1-mile	2-mile	3-mile	4-mile
0-mile	0.500	0.125	0.250	0.375	0.500
1-mile	0.875	0.500	0.375	0.500	0.625
2-mile	0.750	0.625	0.500	0.675	0.750
3-mile	0.625	0.500	0.375	0.500	0.875
4-mile	0.500	0.375	0.250	0.125	0.500

Each duopolist will locate at the midpoint (the 2-mile marker) with equal shares

$$\max_i \min_j a_{ij} = \min_j \max_i a_{ij} = 0.500$$

8-8 For the monopoly case the buyer's profit maximum is derived from

$$\pi_B = 3(270q_2 - 2q_2^2) - p_2 q_2 \qquad \frac{d\pi_B}{dq_2} = 810 - 12q_2 - p_2 = 0$$

and the demand function is $p_2 = 810 - 12q_2$. The monopolistic seller's profit maximum is derived from

$$\pi_S = (810 - 12q_2)q_2 - 1.5q_2^2 \qquad \frac{d\pi_S}{dq_2} = 810 - 27q_2 = 0$$

The monopoly solution is

$$q_{2S}^* = 30 \qquad p_{2S}^* = 450 \qquad \pi_{BS}^* = 5400 \qquad \pi_{SS}^* = 12{,}150$$

For the monopsony case the seller's profit maximum is derived from

$$\pi_S = p_2 q_2 - 1.5q_2^2 \qquad \frac{d\pi_S}{dq_2} = p_2 - 3q_2 = 0$$

and the supply function is $p_2 = 3q_2$. The monopsonistic buyer's profit maximum is derived from

$$\pi_B = 3(270q_2 - 2q_2^2) - (3q_2)q_2 \qquad \frac{d\pi_B}{dq_2} = 810 - 18q_2 = 0$$

The monopsony solution is

$$q_{2B}^* = 45 \qquad p_{2B}^* = 135 \qquad \pi_{SB}^* = 3037.50 \qquad \pi_{BB}^* = 18{,}225$$

The quasi-competitive solution is obtained by equating price and MC

$$q_{2C}^* = 54 \qquad p_{2C}^* = 162 \qquad \pi_{SC}^* = 4374 \qquad \pi_{BC}^* = 17{,}496$$

with a total profit of 21,870. The bargaining limits are $135 \leq p_2 \leq 450$.

Chapter 9

9-2 The equilibrium conditions for the consumers are

$$\frac{p_1}{p_2} = \frac{E_{12} + 42}{E_{11} + 11} = \frac{q_{12} + 12}{q_{11} + 3} \qquad \frac{p_1}{p_2} = \frac{E_{22} + 8}{E_{21} + 19} = \frac{q_{22} + 8}{q_{21} + 9}$$

where the rightmost terms are obtained by substituting $E_{ij} = q_{ij} - q_{ij}^0$. Substituting for p_1/p_2 into the budget constraints gives the offer curves

$$2q_{11}q_{12} - 18q_{11} - 5q_{12} = 186 \qquad 2q_{22}q_{21} - 2q_{21} - q_{22} = 170$$

Substituting the equilibrium price ratio, $p_2/p_1 = 0.5$, in the individual excess demand functions derived in Exercise 9-1: $q_{11} = 13$, $q_{12} = 20$, $q_{21} = 5$, $q_{22} = 20$. Substituting these quantities in the offer curves shows that they are satisfied.

9-4 The budget constraint for the ith consumer includes her excess demand for money:

$$p_1 E_{i1} + p_2 E_{i2} + 0.2(p_1 q_{i1}^0 + p_2 q_{i2}^0) - q_{i3}^0 = 0 \qquad i = 1, 2$$

where q_{i3}^0 is i's initial money stock. Individual excess demand functions are obtained from the consumers' first-order conditions.

Setting aggregate excess demand equal to zero for each of the commodities,

$$E_{11} + E_{21} = 10 - \frac{12p_2}{p_1} + \frac{2q_3^0}{3p_1} = 0$$

$$E_{12} + E_{22} = \frac{9 - 20p_1}{p_2} + \frac{q_3^0}{p_2} = 0$$

where $q_3^0 = q_{13}^0 + q_{23}^0$ is the aggregate money stock. Multiplying the first equation by p_1 and the second by p_2, and rearranging terms,

$$-10p_1 + 12p_2 = \frac{2q_3^0}{3} \qquad 20p_1 - 9p_2 = \frac{q_3^0}{3}$$

These linear equations have the solution

$$p_1 = \frac{q_3^0}{15} \qquad p_2 = \frac{q_3^0}{9}$$

It is obvious that commodity prices vary in proportion to the aggregate money stock.

If money endowments are $43 + 2 = 45$, prices are $p_1 = 3$, $p_2 = 5$. If money endowments are tripled to $129 + 6 = 135$, prices are tripled to $p_1 = 9$, $p_2 = 15$.

Chapter 10

10-2 Substitution for p_2 from the second equation into the first gives the quadratic equation $p_3^2 - 5p_3 + 6 = 0$ with the roots 3 and 2. The second equation gives 4 and 2 as the corresponding values for p_2. Thus, there are two equilibrium solutions: $(p_2 = 4, p_3 = 3)$ and $(p_2 = 2, p_3 = 2)$.

10-4 For a three-commodity system (10-23) is

$$\lambda^2 - (b_{22} + b_{33})\lambda + (b_{22}b_{33} - b_{23}b_{32}) = 0$$

For the system of Exercise 10-2

$$b_{22} = 4p_2 + 22 - 13p_3 \qquad b_{23} = -13p_2 - 64 + 40p_3$$

$$b_{32} = 1 \qquad b_{33} = -2$$

For the equilibrium $(4, 3)$, the quadratic is $\lambda^2 + 3\lambda - 2 = 0$ with the roots $\lambda = -1.5 \pm \sqrt{4.25}$. The equilibrium is unstable since one of the roots is positive. For the equilibrium $(2, 2)$ the quadratic is $\lambda^2 - 2\lambda + 2 = 0$ with the roots $\lambda = 1 \pm i$. This equilibrium is also unstable since the real part of the roots is positive.

10-6 The consumer's excess demand function for Q_2, derived from the constrained utility maximization, multiplied by p_2 is

$$p_2 E_{i2} = \frac{\alpha[p_1 q_{i1}^0 + p_2 q_{i2}^0 + (1 - p_1 - p_2)q_{i3}^0]}{(1 + \alpha + \beta)} - p_2 q_{i2}^0$$

This is a linear equation in prices when k_{i2} is substituted for E_{i2} to form a boundary. Similar derivations can be made for the other boundaries.

10-8 Let $d_1 = 0.7$, $d_2 = 0.8$, and $d_3 = 1.0$. Then

$$(0.7)(0.2) + (0.8)(0.5) + (1.0)(0.1) = 0.64 < 0.7$$
$$(0.7)(0.1) + (0.8)(0.4) + (1.0)(0.4) = 0.79 < 0.8$$
$$(0.7)(0.6) + (0.8)(0.4) + (1.0)(0.2) = 0.94 < 1.0$$

and the conditions are satisfied. Many other values for the d's will also satisfy the conditions.

Chapter 11

11-2 The producer's profit is $96q - 12q^2$, and its maximization yields $q = 4$, $x = 8$, $r = 18$, and $p = 84$. Total cost with r as a parameter is

$$C = rx = 2rq$$

The Pareto condition is that price equal the appropriate MC:

$$100 - 4q = 2r = 2[2 + 2(2q)] = 4 + 8q$$

with the solution $q = 8$, $x = 16$, $r = 34$, $p = 68$.

11-4 Let q_{11} and q_{21} be the quantities of the ordinary good, q_2 and q_3 the quantities of the public goods, and x^0 the fixed quantity of the primary factor. A Pareto-optimal allocation is found by maximizing the utility of the first consumer subject to the condition that the second enjoy a fixed level of utility and subject to the requirement that the production function be satisfied. Maximize

$$V = U_1(q_{11}, q_2, q_3) + \lambda[U_2^0 - U_2(q_{21}, q_2, q_3)] + \theta F(q_{11} + q_{21}, q_2, q_3, x^0)$$

where F denotes the production function. The first-order conditions are

$$\frac{\partial V}{\partial q_{11}} = \frac{\partial U_1}{\partial q_{11}} + \theta F_1 = 0 \qquad \frac{\partial V}{\partial q_2} = \frac{\partial U_1}{\partial q_2} - \lambda \frac{\partial U_2}{\partial q_2} + \theta F_2 = 0$$

$$\frac{\partial V}{\partial q_{21}} = -\lambda \frac{\partial U_2}{\partial q_{21}} + \theta F_1 = 0 \qquad \frac{\partial V}{\partial q_3} = \frac{\partial U_1}{\partial q_3} - \lambda \frac{\partial U_3}{\partial q_3} + \theta F_3 = 0$$

and the requirements that the constraints be satisfied.

The RPT between the public goods is F_2/F_3. Moving the last terms in the equations on the right to their right-hand sides and dividing one by the other, and then substituting for λ its solution from the equations on the left,

$$\frac{F_2}{F_3} = \frac{\dfrac{\partial U_1}{\partial q_2} - \lambda \dfrac{\partial U_2}{\partial q_2}}{\dfrac{\partial U_1}{\partial q_3} - \lambda \dfrac{\partial U_3}{\partial q_3}} = \frac{\dfrac{\partial U_1/\partial q_2}{\partial U_1/\partial q_{11}} + \dfrac{\partial U_2/\partial q_2}{\partial U_2/\partial q_{21}}}{\dfrac{\partial U_1/\partial q_3}{\partial U_1/\partial q_{11}} + \dfrac{\partial U_2/\partial q_3}{\partial U_2/\partial q_{21}}}$$

which requires that the RPT equal the ratio of the sums of the RCSs of the consumers between the ordinary good and the public goods.

11-6 Equating private MCs to price,

$$\frac{\partial C_1}{\partial q_1} = 4q_1 + 20 - 2q_2 = 240 \qquad \frac{\partial C_2}{\partial q_2} = 6q_2 + 60 = 240$$

which have the solution $q_1^c = 70$, $q_2^c = 30$.

The social cost function is the sum of the individual cost functions:

$$C = 2q_1^2 + 20q_1 - 2q_1q_2 + 3q_2^2 + 60q_2$$

The social MCs of the firms are now equated to the market price:

$$\frac{\partial C}{\partial q_1} = 4q_1 + 20 - 2q_2 = 240 \qquad \frac{\partial C}{\partial q_2} = -2q_1 + 6q_2 + 60 = 240$$

which have the solution $q_1^* = 84$, $q_2^* = 58$.

11-8 If unit subsidies of s_1 and s_2 are paid to producers, their cost functions become

$$C_1 = 2q_1^2 + 20q_1 - 2q_1q_2 - s_1q_1 \qquad C_2 = 3q_2^2 + 60q_2 - s_2q_2$$

Letting private MC equal price for each producer,

$$4q_1 + 20 - 2q_2 - s_1 = 240 \qquad 6q_2 + 60 - s_2 = 240$$

which for $q_1^* = 84$, $q_2^* = 58$ yields $s_1 = 0$, $s_2 = 168$.

While the producers were maximizing profits without subsidies, their maximum profits were $\pi_1^0 = 9800$, $\pi_2^0 = 2700$. After subsidization their profits are $\pi_1^* = 14{,}112$, $\pi_2^* = 348$. The appropriate lump-sum taxes and social dividend are

$$L_1 = \pi_1^* - \pi_1^0 + s_1q_1^* = 4312 \qquad L_2 = \pi_2^* - \pi_2^0 + s_2q_2^* = 7392$$
$$S = L_1 + L_2 - s_1q_1^* - s_2q_2^* = 1960$$

11-10 A Scitovsky contour is found by minimizing the total quantity of Q_1, given the quantity of Q_2 and the utility levels of the consumers. Using the first-order conditions and the constraints, λ_1 and λ_2 can be eliminated with the result

$$U_1^0 - U_2^0 - q_1q_2 + 2\sqrt{U_2^0 q_1 q_2} = 0$$

Letting $q_1q_2 = Z^2$, this is a quadratic equation:

$$Z^2 - (2\sqrt{U_2^0})Z + (U_2^0 - U_1^0) = 0$$

which has the solution

$$Z = \frac{2\sqrt{U_2^0} \pm \sqrt{4U_1^0}}{2} = \sqrt{U_2^0} \pm \sqrt{U_1^0}$$

Since the solution $\sqrt{U_2^0} - \sqrt{U_1^0}$ might make Z negative, which makes no sense in the present context, the final solution is

$$q_1q_2 = Z^2 = (\sqrt{U_1^0} + \sqrt{U_2^0})^2$$

as required.

11-12 If $\alpha \geq 1$, welfare is maximized by allocating all income to the individual for whom β_i is largest. If two or more individuals tie for the largest β_i, all income is allocated to one of those tying. If $\alpha = 0$, all income distributions give $W = n$. If $\alpha < 0$, no finite welfare maximum exists since welfare can be made infinitely large by depriving any individual of all income.

Chapter 12

12-2 The function to be maximized is

$$V = c_1 c_2^{0.6} + \lambda[(1000 - c_1) + (1/1.08)(648 - c_2)]$$

The first-order conditions are

$$\frac{\partial V}{\partial c_1} = c_2^{0.6} - \lambda = 0 \qquad \frac{\partial V}{\partial c_2} = 0.6c_1c_2^{-0.4} - \frac{\lambda}{1.08} = 0$$

$$\frac{\partial V}{\partial \lambda} = 1000 - c_1 + \frac{1}{1.08}(648 - c_2) = 0$$

with the solution $c_1 = 1000$, $c_2 = 648$. The consumer is neither borrower nor lender.

12-4 The Lagrange function for each consumer is

$$V^* = c_1 c_2 + \mu[(y_1 - c_1) + (y_2 - c_2)(1 + i)^{-1}]$$

See the partials equal to zero,

$$\frac{\partial V^*}{\partial c_1} = c_2 - \mu = 0 \qquad \frac{\partial V^*}{\partial c_2} = c_1 - \mu(1 + i)^{-1} = 0$$

$$\frac{\partial V^*}{\partial \mu} = (y_1 - c_1) + (y_2 - c_2)(1 + i)^{-1} = 0$$

and solve for

$$c_1 = \frac{y_1 + y_2(1+i)^{-1}}{2}$$

The consumer's excess demand for bonds is

$$y_1 - c_1 = \frac{y_1 - y_2(1+i)^{-1}}{2}$$

Bond-market equilibrium requires that aggregate excess demand by the two groups of consumers equal zero:

$$100[5000 - 4200(1+i)^{-1}] + 50[4000 - 7000(1+i)^{-1}] = 700{,}000 - 770{,}000(1+i)^{-1}$$

with the solution $i = 0.10$.

12-6 The present value of the entrepreneur's profit is

$$\pi = 100\sqrt{T}\, e^{-0.05T} - 20$$

which is maximized when $d\pi/dT = 0$:

$$\frac{d\pi}{dT} = \left(\frac{50}{\sqrt{T}} - 5\sqrt{T}\right) e^{-0.05T} = 0$$

which has the solution $T = 10$.

12-8 The present value of the entrepreneur's profit is

$$\pi = (4 + 8T - T^2)e^{-0.2T} - 4 - \int_0^T 0.4te^{-0.2t}\, dt$$

Setting the derivative with respect to T equal to zero,

$$\frac{d\pi}{dT} = (8 - 2T)e^{-0.2T} - 0.2(4 + 8T - T^2)e^{-0.2T} - 0.4Te^{-0.2T} = 0$$

with the roots $T = (2, 18)$. The second-order condition requires that

$$\frac{d^2\pi}{dT^2} = e^{-0.2T}(-0.04T^2 + 1.2T - 5.44) < 0$$

and is satisfied for $T = 2$, but not for $T = 18$.

12-10 The present value of the entrepreneur's profit is the present value of the quasi-rent stream, minus the original cost, plus the present value of the scrap value:

$$\pi = \int_0^T (85 - 4t)e^{-0.05t}\, dt - 500 + (500 - 40T)e^{-0.05T}$$

Letting $d\pi/dT = 0$ gives the solution $T = 10$.

Appendix

A-2 The derivatives are:
  (a) $f'(x) = 18x^2 + 4x - 1$.
  (b) $f'(x) = 2/\sqrt{x}$.
  (c) $f'(x) = -e^{-x}(x - 2) + e^{-x} = e^{-x}(3 - x)$.
  (d) $f'(x) = [12x^2(2x^2 - x) - (4x - 1)4x^3]/(2x^2 - x)^2$.
  (e) $f'(x) = [1/x^{-3}][-3x^{-4}] = -3/x$.

A-4 The answers are determined by the signs of the second derivatives:
  (a) $f''(x) = 2 > 0$, and $f(x)$ is strictly convex.
  (b) $f''(x) = -1/x^2 < 0$, and $f(x)$ is strictly concave.
  (c) $f''(x) = a^2 e^{ax} > 0$, and $f(x)$ is strictly convex.
  (d) $f''(x) = 6x - 4$ which does not have a unique sign for $x \geq 0$, and $f(x)$ is neither strictly convex nor strictly concave over the entire interval.

A-6 The total differential is

$$dy = \left(2x_2^2 + \frac{1}{x_1}\right) dx_1 + (4x_1x_2 + e^{x_3}) dx_2 + x_2e^{x_3} dx_3$$

A-8 Setting the partial derivatives equal to zero,

$$f_1 = 5 + x_2 - x_1 = 0 \qquad f_2 = 10 - 6x_2 + x_1 = 0$$

These equations have the solution $x_1 = 8$, $x_2 = 3$. The second-order conditions for a maximum are satisfied by this solution:

$$f_{11} = -1 < 0 \qquad \begin{vmatrix} f_{11} & f_{12} \\ f_{21} & f_{22} \end{vmatrix} = \begin{vmatrix} -1 & 1 \\ 1 & -6 \end{vmatrix} = 5 > 0$$

A-10 If $\alpha + \beta < 1$, the principal minors of the Hessian will alternate in sign, beginning with minus, as required for strict concavity:

$$f_{11} = \alpha(\alpha - 1)Ax_1^{\alpha-2}x_2^{\beta} < 0$$

$$\begin{vmatrix} f_{11} & f_{12} \\ f_{21} & f_{22} \end{vmatrix} = \begin{vmatrix} \alpha(\alpha - 1)Ax_1^{\alpha-2}x_2^{\beta} & \alpha\beta Ax_1^{\alpha-1}x_2^{\beta-1} \\ \alpha\beta Ax_1^{\alpha-1}x_2^{\beta-1} & \beta(\beta - 1)Ax_1^{\alpha}x_2^{\beta-2} \end{vmatrix}$$

$$= \alpha\beta(1 - \alpha - \beta)A^2x_1^{2(\alpha-1)}x_2^{2(\beta-1)} > 0$$

Conversely, $\alpha + \beta \geq 1$ will violate the requirement that the Hessian be positive, and concavity cannot hold.

A-12 Form the Lagrange function

$$V = x_1^2x_2 + \lambda(5x_1 + 2x_2 - 300)$$

where λ is an undetermined multiplier, and set its partial derivatives equal to zero:

$$\frac{\partial V}{\partial x_1} = 2x_1x_2 + 5\lambda = 0 \qquad \frac{\partial V}{\partial x_2} = x_1^2 + 2\lambda = 0$$

$$\frac{\partial V}{\partial \lambda} = 5x_1 + 2x_2 - 300 = 0$$

Substitute $2x_2 = 5x_1/2$ from the first two equations into the third:

$$5x_1 + \frac{5x_1}{2} - 300 = 0$$

which gives the solution $x_1 = 40$, $x_2 = 50$.

The second-order condition, which requires that the bordered Hessian be positive, is satisfied:

$$\begin{vmatrix} 2x_2 & 2x_1 & 5 \\ 2x_1 & 0 & 2 \\ 5 & 2 & 0 \end{vmatrix} = 40x_1 - 8x_2 = 1200 > 0$$

A-14 A function is concave if $f_{11} \leq 0$ and $\mathcal{H} = f_{11}f_{22} - f_{12}^2 \geq 0$, and strictly concave if the strict inequalities hold. A function is quasi-concave if $\mathcal{D} = f_{12}^2 f_1 f_2 - f_{11}f_2^2 - f_{22}f_1^2 \geq 0$, and strictly quasi-concave if the strict inequality holds. The reader may verify that the following functions have the desired properties by evaluating the appropriate determinants:

    (a) $f(x_1, x_2) = -(\ln x_1 - \ln x_2)$.
    (b) $f(x_1, x_2) = x_1x_2$.
    (c) $f(x_1, x_2) = x_1 + x_2$.
    (d) $f(x_1, x_2) = x_1^{0.5}x_2^{0.5}$.

A-16 The Jacobian is

$$\mathcal{J} = \begin{vmatrix} 2x_1 + 4x_2 & 4x_1 + 8x_2 \\ 1 & 2 \end{vmatrix} = 0$$

and vanishes identically. Since the left-hand side of the first equation is the square of the left-hand side of the second, any solution satisfying one will satisfy the other if $y_1 = y_2^2$. If $y_1 \neq y_2^2$ there is no solution at all.

A-18 (a) $\displaystyle\int_6^{10} (2x + 3)\, dx = (x^2 + 3x)_{10} - (x^2 + 3x)_6 = 130 - 54 = 76.$

(b) $\displaystyle\int_1^e \frac{1}{x}\, dx = (\ln x)_e - (\ln x)_1 = 1 - 0 = 1.$

A-20 The appropriate quadratic is $x^2 + 5x + 6 = 0$ with the roots $(-2, -3)$. The solution has the form

$$y = k_1 e^{-2t} + k_2 e^{-3t}$$

Using the initial conditions, $y_0 = k_1 + k_2 = 6$, $y_0' = -2k_1 - 3k_2 = 3$ gives $k_1 = 21$, $k_2 = -15$.

INDEX

INDEX